A Right to Offend

A Right to Offend

Brian Winston

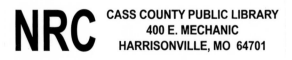
BLOOMSBURY

LONDON · NEW DELHI · NEW YORK · SYDNEY

Bloomsbury Academic

An imprint of Bloomsbury Publishing Plc

50 Bedford Square   175 Fifth Avenue
London   New York
WC1B 3DP   NY 10010
UK   USA

www.bloomsbury.com

First published 2012

British Library Cataloguing-in-Publication Data

A catalogue record for this book is available from the British Library.

ISBN: HB: 978-1-84966-015-0
PB: 978-1-84966-003-7

Printed and bound in Great Britain by the
MPG Books Group, Bodmin, Cornwall.

In memory of
Tim Hewat and Alex Valentine
Executive Producers, *World in Action*

Preface and Acknowledgements

On 5 August 1971, Richard Neville, Jim Anderson and Felix Denis were fined and given custodial sentences under the Obscene Publications Act (1964), as the publishers and editors of a magazine, *Oz*, issue number 28, dated May 1971. As part of the response, an emergency edition of *Oz*'s sister publication, *Ink*, a weekly newspaper and admittedly a minor player in the then flourishing underground press, appeared in defiance. The 'Repression in Britain' issue of *Ink: The Other Newspaper*, dated 1 September 1971, was, in my opinion, a pretty good effort. Gerald Scarfe kindly donated to it a cartoon of Mrs Mary Whitehouse CBE, a noisy campaigner for 'cleaned up' media, fornicating with Rupert Bear, a cartoon character, under the eyes of the Pope. 'Mrs Mary Righteous explains her position to the Pope' was the caption. I edited this issue of *Ink* and was honoured to run the Scarfe cartoon as our front page; but so marginal to my career have I considered the episode that I have never included it in my CV. Not that I was ashamed of having been involved, nor of the paper we produced; but my contribution to *Ink* was otherwise pretty peripheral – the odd piece on the media – and I was only asked to edit this one issue as the result of a vote at a meeting which I did not attend. (Indeed, I did not even know the meeting was being held.) I omitted *Ink* from my CV because I considered the *Oz* affair to be but a last skirmish in the war for free expression which was, as far as my understanding then went, over. The trial was nothing more than a late futile sally by the defeated armies of repression. The defendants were soon released on appeal and the gaiety of the nation was thereby much enhanced. A joy of life has been watching Denis, the defendant the judge dismissed as being 'very much less intelligent' than the other two, become a very, very rich magazine mogul.

A letter was received from Mary Whitehouse's lawyers:

> The drawing and caption on the front cover of the issue to which we have referred are, as you no doubt intended, extremely unpleasant and offensive to her personally, and undoubtedly hold her up to ridicule and contempt ... We shall ... be glad to hear what offer you are prepared to make to compensate our client for the embarrassment and annoyance and injury caused to her.

In those halcyon, long-lost days, despite the glib reference to 'ridicule and contempt' by the lawyers, the common law's long-established position was that no cartoon would likely be taken seriously enough to bring its subject materially into ridicule or contempt (or, for that matter, to complete the ancient triad, 'hatred' either). As for embarrassment, immaterial annoyance and offence, the common law then tended to take the robust view that these were not matters for the courts and certainly no basis for compensation. In the event, after this letter, the rest was silence and whoever compensated the lawyers for their trouble, it was not us.

Four decades later, I have come to realize that, in 1971, the war was far from won and the mission of securing the basic right of free expression, even insofar as we had got by that date – which (not least because of the regulation of broadcasting) was by no means that far – has not been accomplished, not remotely. The recognition of that error of opinion fuels this book and expands on its preceding, more celebratory account, *Messages: Free Expression, Media and the West from Gutenberg to Google*.

I owe a tremendous debt of gratitude to many who have been of crucial help in the preparation of this book. I am indebted to the editorial board of the *British Journalism Review* for providing a forum for discussion and to colleagues there, especially Steve Barnett and Julian Petley. (I know that much of what follows does not accord with their opinions which makes their generosity to me in the course of the preparation for this book all the more valued.) I must thank Anita Abram, Roger Laughton, Annabel Leventon and, in North America, Robert Richards and Gail Vanstone. Tony Garnett's thoughtfulness has been deeply invaluable. To the University of Lincoln's academic faculty, beyond a general gratitude for creating from scratch a real scholarly environment, I owe specific thanks to Ian Baguley, Jane Chapman, Barnie Choudhury, Scott Davidson, Richard Keeble, Geoff Thompson, John Tulloch, and, most of all, to Frances Mannsåker for endless help. I must also thank Emily Drewe, Lee Ann Tutton and Chloë Shuttlewood at Bloomsbury Academic. What began as an intervention in the time-honoured debate about free expression became evermore entangled in current events. I am grateful that they, and the press, had the patience to let me attempt to deal with this. Finally, a deep debt of gratitude to Howard Watson, a veritable knight when it comes to slaying the dragons of error. Needless to say, any such beasts still roaming this text are not his responsibility. Indeed, more even than usual, blunders in what follows are most assuredly not the fault of any of these generous folk. They are mine alone.

Contents

Assumptions

Imagine that it might be possible to assemble the sum total of our knowledge
of European history from the fifth century to the present ... in an electronic
memory. Imagine that the computer was then asked to indicate the one
problem which recurred most frequently, in time and space, throughout this
lengthy history. Without a doubt, that 'problem is liberty or rather liberties.
The word liberty is the operative word.

Fernand Braudel (Braudel, 1995: 315)

In the twenty-first century, this is still the case. Herein discussion of the
foundational problem of liberty is focused on the liberty of free speech and the
current condition of the principle that protects it: the right of free expression.
The following assumptions are made:

- Of all the legacies of the eighteenth-century European Enlightenment,
  the concept of a right of free expression is here taken to be central and
  paramount. Reason is fed by information, freely communicated. To
  abridge that freedom is to strike at reason.
- Moreover, without a right of free expression no other essential right
  can be guaranteed. The other human rights might all have a more direct
  bearing on an individual's well-being than does the right of free speech;
  however, on its exercise depends the right to life, liberty and security
  of person; the right to marry, to own property (including intellectual
  property), to a free conscience, to peaceful assembly, to take part in
  government, to equality before the law; the right to work and to leisure,
  to health and shelter, to education; the right to freedom of movement, to
  privacy (from government intrusion).
- This does not mean that free expression is to be an unfettered right.
  It must be constrained. Unfettered, it can be destructive, damaging to
  the privacy, reputation or even the safety of individuals; undermining
  the authority of Christian religious orthodoxy; attacking local secular
  power and, at times, threatening the very security of the Western state.
  Unfettered free expression has therefore never been a civilized option
  because it can have such negative effects, the avoidance of which
  is, exactly, a (if not the) crucial foundation of society. It cannot be
  above the general law. Therefore, as the proto-liberal Whig MP John
  Trenchard and the journalist Thomas Gordon (using the collective *nom
  de plume* 'Cato') wrote in 1721: 'Freedom of Speech ... is the Right

of every Man, as far as by it he does not hurt and controul the Right of another; and this is the only Check which it ought to suffer, the only Bounds which it ought to know' ('Cato', 1721). This is the 'harm principle'.

- Rising Western sensitivities, utterly worthy in themselves, expand the 'harm principle' from damage to persons that can be externally verified to hurts that can only be self-attested. Crucially among these, being offended or taking offence, a state which cannot be confirmed by others, chillingly falls within the compass of the harm principle.
- This is dangerously chilling as freedom of expression can only be said to exist if it encompasses a right to offend. The right to offend is the right of expression's touchstone, just as the right of expression is the touchstone to human rights in general.
- Free expression should be media-blind, unregulated as to content beyond the general provision of the law, suitably defined, applied and rendered accessible. As John Locke put it of the press, special laws (these days including those establishing regulatory bodies) are 'very needless' (King, 1829: 208).
- The privilege of free speech is so great that ownership of multiple cross-media platforms should be constrained in the name of democratic diversity. This allocative function – which is distinct from the regulation of content – properly belongs to the state.

Although we are in a time of considerable liberty of expression, the right is under attack from without and within the West. The *fatwa* issued against the author Salman Rushdie by Imam Khomeini in 1989, for writing a novel, *The Satanic Verses*, has cast a long shadow over the exercise of free speech, directly challenging its validity. The shadow has fallen on to a Western intellectual landscape where, with sensitivities growing, the privileges of speech were being evermore seriously questioned. In fact, a veritable *trahison des clercs* – a betrayal of principles by writers and academics – was underway in many quarters, treasonously undermining the fundamentals of the Enlightenment. And then, in 2010, abuses of the privileges of expression in the central forum of the press reached a crescendo in the UK, causing outrage and adding yet more force to the external demands post-*fatwa* for direct censorship and the internal treasonous doubts of the *clercs* requiring, in effect, much the same. The press abuses uncovered in the 'Hackgate' scandal, being in essence illegalities, were thus straightforwardly breeches of the harm principle and as such irrelevant to the question of free expression. But, in the event, proposals to constrain the abuses, beyond the application of the general law, further chilled the right of free speech. The shadow of the *fatwa*, the *trahison des clercs* and the abuses of Hackgate all mount a comprehensive **Prosecution** of the right. This is outlined in this book's first part.

Part Two essays a **Defence** of free expression – in effect, of Western values. It takes three approaches. The 'Histories' of the West's long battle to establish freedom of expression, struggles that caused 'Cato' to describe it as a 'sacred' right, are deployed to dispel the shadow of the *fatwa*. To frustrate the treasonous intellectual *clercs* a brief rebuttal of their attacks on the 'Enlightenment' is mounted. To correct the abuses of privilege highlighted by Hackgate, a consideration of the 'Law', and how it might be reformed better to contain harms, is offered.

When the writing of this book began two years ago, a central premise was that the measure of freedom given to print, settled by centuries of conflict, now needed to be extended to all other media. However, as the book goes to press, it is the case, at least in Britain, that the matter of journalistic freedom looks nowhere as settled as it did until recently. The current damage to the principle, admittedly, has been largely self-inflicted by those who should guard it most; but the broader uncertain commitment to free expression, glaringly revealed in the Western response to the *fatwa* and its aftermath, undercuts the right just as much. It is still the central premise of this book that this liberty should be media-blind, unregulated except directly by law and constrained only by the harm principle and limitation on ownership. Now, though, the argument is also that the established media-specific right of a free press needs be defended as well, after all.

John Milton, Thomas Paine and William Cobbett stir in their graves.

If all printers were determined not to print anything till they were sure it would offend nobody, there would be very little printed.

Benjamin Franklin (Franklin, 1731)

Rights must not be confused with morality, neither should those who make statements that displease us be dragged into court ...

Tzvetan Todorov (Todorov, 2009: 123)

PART ONE

Prosecution

1

The Shadow of the *Fatwa*

On 12 February 1989, the mob irrupted in Pakistan. In London the previous September, Salman Rushdie had published in English his novel, *The Satanic Verses*. A section of this, some 70 of the book's 500-plus pages, satirized Islam, the Qur'an and the Prophet Muhammad. It had been translated into Urdu, apparently badly, and its insults were being cried through the streets of Pakistan. In Islamabad, a crowd of 10,000 attacked the American Cultural Center. They managed to burn an American flag but not much else. The police opened fire and five protesters were dead. A sixth fatality was one of the Center's Pakistani guards, also shot dead (Pipes, 2003: 25). The following day, in a further commotion occasioned by the book in Srinagar, Kashmir, another man died and sixty were injured. *The Satanic Verses* affair, which was to mark a new stage in the complex and vexatious history of the West's struggle for liberty – specifically liberty of speech – had claimed its first blood.

Outrage about *The Satanic Verses* had been simmering among British Muslims for months and large demonstrations had occurred in northern English cities at which copies of it had been publicly burned. A high-level campaign, fronted by Sunni interests funded by the Saudis, had mounted a sophisticated but futile effort to convince the Thatcher government to ban the book. In India, Khushwant Singh, a celebrated Indian Sikh writer who was Penguin of India's editorial advisor, warned against releasing it because of its 'derogatory' references to Islam (K. Malik, 2009: 1). He was convinced it was going to 'cause a whole lot of trouble' and, by sharing this opinion with the Indian press, he ensured that it would. The Hindu Congress Party government promptly banned its publication in India at the behest of alerted Muslim politicians, whose votes were important to it.

From Western perspectives, such opinions and mayhem were somewhat incomprehensible, a complete over-reaction. Blasphemy – rude words about the deity – after long being in decline in the West was, in effect no longer any sort of offence. As for obscenity, the book was a dense fiction whose rudest word was 'fart'.

Any believer in freedom of expression and in the function and validity of literature can appreciate why a Western reader, educated in a presumably secular, liberal-humanist culture, may be bedevilled by all the fuss and furore about a mere book, a work of fiction containing a troubling dream sequence. However, in order to understand the enormity of what has been done (by Rushdie), a circumspect, tolerant reader needs to appreciate what the Prophet Muhammad means to a Muslim across the Muslim world and throughout their immigrant communities in the West. (A. Malik, 2005: 100)

Banning and burning books, though, strains such appreciation. Circumspection needs also to acknowledge the strength of the West's long liberal commitment to human rights, born of its own internal and often bloodstained struggles for freedom. This history centrally embraces the capstone of the right of free expression without which none other can be guaranteed. Moreover, despite the ever-increasing need in integrated Western societies to maintain social cohesion, the circumspect Westerner can also note that the 'enormity' of the book's harm was entirely self-attested. It had provoked not the attacks of Western bigots but the violent reaction of outraged Muslims.

Despite their reaction, and without prejudice to its authenticity or the depths of its religious roots, there was nothing inevitable about the Rushdie uproar. Fictions by other Muslim authors had appeared in something of the same critical spirit. In 1959, for example, the greatest Egyptian writer of the Christian twentieth century, Naguib Mahfouz, produced *Children of Gebalawi* in which he rewrote the histories of the Abrahamic monotheisms as a modernist fairy-story. It was, some thought, 'a humanist fable that questions the existence of god' (Ruthven, 2006: 385); but, although it had caused controversy, its publication did not prevent him writing thirty-four more novels. In 1986, two years before *The Satanic Verses*, the highly regarded Somali novelist, Nuruddin Farah, published his novel *Maps* in English without uproar. This was despite the fact that he had 'clearly taken the path of a cultural apostate' (Mazrui, 1992).[1] Such equanimity, though, was to be no more. The British Muslim reaction and the Indian ban had rendered *The Satanic Verses'* publication extraordinary.

These, though, were mere embers to be blown into a conflagration in Iran. Images of incensed Muslims crying 'God is Great' and being shot dead for their trouble in the Indian subcontinent had been widely broadcast across the Muslim world, the *Umma*, and beyond. In Tehran, they apparently shocked the Shi'a Republic's supreme leader, the Imam Ruhollah al-Musavi al-Khomeini (Pipes, 2003: 26). It is possible that Khomeini knew nothing of Rushdie's book before 13 February although it had been reviewed in Iran – in completely measured albeit negative tones, and extracts read on the Farsi services of foreign radio stations (K. Malik, 2009: 6; Moin, 1999: 283).[2] Be that as it may, following news of the riots, the Imam called in a secretary and dictated:

In the name of Him, the Highest. There is only one God to whom we shall all return. I inform all zealous Muslims of the world that the author of the book entitled *The Satanic Verses* – which has been compiled, printed and published in opposition to Islam, the Prophet and the Qur'an – and all those involved in its publication who were aware of its contents, are sentenced to death (K. Malik, 2009: 8)

The *fatwa*'s impact was to be immense, but only indirectly so. Despite the seriousness of Khomeini's challenge to the fundamentals of Western liberalism, the licence he hereby gave for repeated outrages, the poison he injected into inter-communal relations, the deaths he aided and abetted, in immediate terms he failed, almost completely, to alter the situation. As far as the *fatwa*'s stated objectives went, the results were, basically, a fiasco. Rushdie, the author, yet lives; so do most of those 'involved' in publication of *The Satanic Verses*, although, disgracefully and outrageously, some of those peripherally concerned with the book were despicably murdered or grievously assaulted. It is only because Khomeini did not call for the book to be eradicated that its continued existence in the world (a copy, one of millions, lies on the desk as this is being typed) cannot also be claimed as part of his failure.

Nevertheless, the effect was to be electric – as electric as the seizure of the hostages at the American embassy in Tehran had been a decade earlier when Khomeini had been first consolidating his power. Internally in Iran and internationally, the *fatwa* was the act of a veritable caliph exercising global reach. It impacted on the inter-communal politics of states and Muslim communities worldwide.

The text of the *fatwa* led the Islamic Republic of Iran Broadcasting (IRIB aka Tehran Radio) news bulletin at 2 p.m. on 14 February. The following day was declared a day of national mourning because of the perfidy of the book. The nation was mobilized for a cause which, whatever its status as an outrage to Iranian public opinion, assuredly had nothing to do with the country's manifold immediate problems. An Islamic charitable foundation posted a reward for Rushdie's head: $1 million for a non-Muslim, 200 million rials ($3 million at the official rate of exchange, actually $170,000 on the market) for an Iranian. Assassins across the *Umma* promptly declared their intentions of obeying the Imam's injunction.

The Tehran Radio broadcast had been picked by the BBC's monitoring operation and it was the BBC World Service, seeking his reaction, who informed Rushdie that he had been condemned to death. Rushdie was hustled into hiding under British police protection. The massive disruption to his life was to persist for more than a decade. Immediately, though, he apologized for any offence he might have caused.

Khomeini responded that it was not enough.

That there were clear and obvious immediate political advantages to Khomeini in no way precludes the reality of the religious affront he, and millions of others, felt. Whatever the strength of self-attested feeling involved, however, the politics of the *fatwa* were immediately self-evident. As had happened with the hostages affair, Khomeini, at a stroke, silenced internal opposition, abandoned a decision on his successor which he had come to regret and stifled emerging moves seeking better relations with the West. Internationally, he consolidated his position as a defiant Muslim voice. Before February, it had been the Sunni, historically dominate within the *Umma*, who had led such protests against Rushdie as had happened. With the *fatwa*, defence of the Prophet's reputation came to rest with the leader of their traditional rivals, the Shi'a. Khomeini spurred on the four quasi-Apocalyptic horses of censorship and fire, riot and blood. Previously, the censorship had been erratic, the riots few and fire had been manifested only in the minor form of symbolic burnings of the book. Spilt blood now appeared not as the collateral outcome of inchoate riot but as the cold-blooded result of planned murder and assault. What had been a canter became a gallop for all four horses.

Censorship: following a meeting of Muslim foreign ministers a month after the *fatwa* in Riyadh, a ban – but not, significantly, Rushdie's head – was called for. Within the *Umma*, only in Turkey was the book to remain legal and in a number of states – Zanzibar, Malaysia, Indonesia – possession of it was made a crime. Papua New Guinea, Thailand, Sri Lanka, Kenya, Tanzania, Liberia and Sierra Leone also joined the ban.

Fire spread. After the book was published in the United States, which had gone ahead as planned on 22 February 1989, arson became the weapon of choice for those obeying the Imam's writ in the West. The *Riverdale Press*, a 12,000 circulation suburban New York weekly newspaper, was firebombed on 28 February following the publication of an editorial in Rushdie's defence. Eleven days after the book appeared, the *Modesto Bee* reported two explosions in a bookstore in Berkeley, ironically the 'birthplace of "The Free Speech Movement"', as the story highlighted (Maclay, 1989: B4). Two major American bookstore chains withdrew the book. In April, May and September no less than ten British bookstores, half of them run by Rushdie's publisher Penguin, were firebombed. One blast injured a passer-by (Hansard, 1994). None of this had an appreciable effect on sales. The two chains of US bookstores, their commitment to profit reversing their early failure to defend free expression, stocked the book but did not display it. With or without their efforts, within a month *The Satanic Verses* was top of the *New York Times* bestseller list where it remained for two months more. It was on the list for a total of six months, a more than respectable outcome for a dense, thick literary fiction.

Riot: Indians took to the streets again in Mumbai. Forty people were wounded and twelve died within days of the *fatwa*. On 27 May, 15–20,000 gathered in Parliament Square in London and, under rumoured Shi'a auspices, burnt the book and Rushdie in effigy, peacefully (as it were). Worse, though, was yet to come. Years after the *fatwa*, on 2 July 1993, a hotel at which a conference celebrating a Turkish poet of the sixteenth century was being held was fired by a mob demanding the head of the book's Turkish translator, Aziv Nesin. They held back the firefighters and thirty-seven people were incinerated, confirming an observation made long ago by the poet Heinrich Heine: '*Dort wo man Bücher verbrennt, verbrennt man auch am Ende Menschen*' ('Where they burn books, at the end they also burn people') (Heine, 1823). Nesin had been smuggled out and survived.[3]

Blood: the rampaging mob is one thing but cold-blooded murder is of a different order. Deaths, as in Turkey, arising from the mob's mayhem are a species of collateral damage; conspiracy to kill is not. Just as inchoate thoughts of suicide become infinitely more dangerous to the person having them when considered planning begins, so here the danger to the West of mass anger becomes the more chilling when the killing becomes so considered. It took more than two years for the assassins to strike. When they did so, it was against a very peripheral actor in the publishing process, a practitioner of 'the most anonymous of professions': translation (Weinberger, 2000). Rushdie's Japanese translator, Hitoshi Igarashi, forty-four, an associate professor at the University of Tsukuba, north of Tokyo, was an Islamic scholar, educated in part in Iran prior to Khomeini's revolution. He was stabbed to death in his office at his university by an unknown assailant on 11 July 1991. The Japanese police have never apprehended the killer. Others escaped death but were seriously wounded. Just before Igarashi's murder, Ettore Capriolo, the book's Italian translator, was stabbed many times at his flat in Milan. He survived, as did William Nygaard, the Norwegian publisher who was shot on 11 October 1993. These assailants were never caught either.

To defend, in any way, the censorship, riot, arson and murder that marked *The Satanic Verses* affair in the name of a faith is surely to offer a slur on that faith far, far worse than any mere novelist's words could. It is to go beyond the madness of crowds. There can be no moral fudge here. From the Western standpoint, legal causality does not accept that the cause of death is – as it were – birth; and it cannot be stretched to argue the justifiable cause of these deaths and assaults was *The Satanic Verses*. On the contrary, Khomeini, quite unambiguously, was in Western eyes an accessory to repeated criminal acts. It is not a matter of claiming a dubious cultural universality to suggest that, if other legal or faith systems are deemed to hold a different view, they thereby exhibit a jurisprudential or moral deficiency. If, in this instance, universality is denied as being nothing more than Western particularism, then so be it.

Khomeini died on 3 June 1989, barely four months after the *fatwa*. Two million people came to the funeral, an uncontrollable mass. His body had to be airlifted to the cemetery since it could not progress by land. The eulogy claimed him as 'the most divine personality in the history of Islam' after the Prophet and the Twelve Imams and the saints (Coughlin, 2009: 247, 249). The Rushdie *fatwa* was emphatically stated to be still in force despite the Imam's death; nevertheless, as the decade turned, Iranian intransigence slowly fractured. By 1995 Rushdie had started to appear in public and, in 1998, although Iranian radical Islamicists increased the bounty on his head, the Tehran government more or less formally announced that the matter was closed. Hardliners insisted that it was not, and at the tenth anniversary of the *fatwa* in 1999 they were still offering a bounty of millions of rials; but, outside Iran, attention was no longer being paid. No hitmen appeared. In effect, the matter was indeed closed. It had become overtly what it had been, at least in part, covertly from the outset: a proxy for strains within Iranian politics.

As for Rushdie, in June 2007, he was knighted by the Queen. For many Muslims, who could of course see no possible basis for this honour in the man's achievement as a major, late twentieth-century writer in English, the knighthood was nothing but a slap at Islam. A more balanced view can acknowledge it as both. Protesting crowds gathered once more in Pakistan and Malaysia, whose minister for religious affairs, Mohammed Ijaz ul-Haq, revived the *fatwa*, at least virtually, by saying that, unless the British withdrew the title, it would be right to blow up Rushdie (Campbell, 2007: 7). In the UK, the thousands were now reduced to just hundreds at a single demonstration protesting the honour at the mosque in Regent's Park. Possibly they had learned a small lesson in public relations, though. Two decades on, the demonstrators were perhaps also now sensitized to the counterproductive impact of book burning. They just burned the flag of St George and screamed, with albeit overstated but nevertheless impeccable republican fervour, that the Queen should go to hell. In the north, where the British reaction to the book had started, Tasaddiq Rehman, spokesperson for the Muslim Council of Europe (actually, it would seem, a local group in Blackburn) announced a similar demonstration would be held, but nobody turned up. 'Mr Rehman was unavailable for comment,' reported a Bolton newspaper (Anon, 2007a). Two years after that, twenty years on from the *fatwa*, Rushdie was interviewed by a journalist in Columbia: 'You write a lot about the clash of religions in your literature. Have you ever suffered as a result of this?' he was asked. 'Just the once,' he replied (Muir, 2009: 37).

Hyperbole suffuses *The Satanic Verses* affair but it is not to overstate the case to claim it as 'a portent of a new kind of conflict' (K. Malik, 2009: ix). It is the mode of censorship – the extra-territorial, quasi-judicial sanctioning of mob rule and murder to suppress expression – which is new. Repression of the expression of political dissent or social deviance in jurisdictions both liberal and authoritarian, whether by due process or by state terror, long preceded Khomeini and continues apace.[4] The *fatwa* marked an anarchic extension of this sorry but normal state of affairs. That it failed in its overt objectives is not the point; much less that, outside of Iran, it also largely failed in its covert ones too.

The victory of the West – the book was published, sold millions and the author lives – was, at least up to the present, pyrrhic and not only because of those who gave their lives or, as is the case of Rushdie himself, were terrorized into spending years on the run. The victory was pyrrhic because, since 1989, the outcome has been a heightened sense of anguish about free expression. Creativity has been – is – threatened and the publication, performance or exhibition of works, destined almost always for limited distribution and circulation, now run the danger of being transformed, by the actions of the mob or lone assassins, into occasions of mayhem and terror.

What is new here for the central Western problem of liberty is that these conflicts are not disputes entirely within the culture, expressions of a time-honoured tension between Western liberality and Western authoritarianism. That quarrel, as will be explored below, has been contained by the Whiggish assumption that the struggle for free expression had been, more or less, won over the past few centuries. True, the reality of this 'victory' was questioned; but only by those who, with varying degrees of cynicism, queried overall the actual extent of liberalism's liberalism. The *fatwa* created a new template for anybody affronted by a specific act of free expression to respond with an aggression previously unseen.

Without Khomeini's *fatwa*, no *fatwa* would have been issued calling for Naguib Mahfouz's murder in 1989 so long after *Children of Gebalawi's* publication. But, prompted by the award of the Noble prize in the year Rushdie published *The Satanic Verses*, it was. Eventually Mahfouz was knifed in the throat by an assassin acting in obedience to it in Cairo in 2004. He survived the attack and died, aged ninety-four, in 2006. During Ramadan, on the night of 26 September 2008, exactly twenty years after the appearance of *The Satanic Verses*, a London publisher who had announced in his list a romantic novel about one of Muhammad's wives, *The Jewel of Medina* by Sherry Jones, had his house firebombed. The incompetent local amateur *jihadis*, who had been under police surveillance, were immediately arrested. But, more significantly, beyond such direct imitation, the contagion has spread widely and in reaction to all forms of expression, not just fiction.

American Christians, in effect learning from their Muslim neighbours, besieged a Manhattan theatre where a play suggesting Christ's homosexuality was being staged (Sterngold, 1998). And as with American Christians, so with British Sikhs. In 2004, the Birmingham Sikh community managed to get a play, set in a *gurdwara* (a Sikh place of worship), taken off following a riot during which considerable damage was caused. The author was threatened with death. In London, in May 2006, the Hindu Forum of Britain managed to close an art exhibition because it was offended by nude representations of Hindu deities (Anon, 2006a). The artist was a Muslim.

Without question, though, a case for the systematic media misrepresentation of Muslims can be easily made. Of course, it can also be made of most other groups from, say, women athletes through to the disabled to human rights activists, to every ethnicity, all religions; but post-*fatwa*, the willingness to take offence also knows no limits. Outrage has greeted even the most careful works of fiction, the most painstaking reporting, the most obtuse artistic expression. By now in the West, all agitators could announce themselves as offended community officials, on behalf of some high-sounding organization or other, and call for repression. Short of demanding murder, which might still attract the attention of the secular authorities, there seemed little downside to such a course. In the aftermath of *The Satanic Verses*, negative responses, aggressively expressed by ethnic or religious minorities living in the West, to cultural activities became an intermittent but regular occurrence. A new genre of news story has appeared: 'Art/Media Provokes Ethnic/Religious Outrage/ Disorder/Crime'.

Examples of suppression abound. The Tate has removed a sculpture featuring the holy texts of the Abrahamic faiths; theatres have cut references to Islam from Marlowe's *Tamburlaine the Great* and eschewed Muslim settings (Anthony, 2009: 8). (Marlowe, who famously thought religion was a 'toy', would likely have expected no better.) The Deutsche Oper cancelled Mozart's *Idomeneo* because its set featured representations of Muhammad, Jesus and the Buddha (Anon, 2006b).[5]

When Marlowe and Mozart cannot be staged in the West without considering the consequences of so doing in terms of religious sensibilities, it is not too far-fetched to claim that 'a crisis for free expression' is at hand (Glanville, 2008: 34). 'Who would dare to write a book like *The Satanic Verses* nowadays? And if some brave or reckless author did dare, who would publish it?' (Anthony, 2009: 7). The extent of the chilling effect on creativity cannot be known. 'Respect for religion has now become acceptable grounds for censorship' (Glanville, 2008: 34). Nothing is more affected by this than the right to offend, a particularly ancient Western tradition. As Quintilian put it: '*Saturam quidem tota nostra est*' – 'satire [in essence, offensive rude comment] is at least totally our thing'– just as the Mediterranean is our sea, *mare nostrum*. And just as that idea has caused trouble from the Punic Wars to Benito Mussolini, so has the Western tolerance for *satura*, from the Greeks on, similarly disturbed our neighbours – as *The Satanic Verses* and subsequent uproars show.

Take cartoons: in November 2011, the French satiric magazine, *Charlie Hebdo*, published a special edition ('*rédacteur en chef* Mohamet') with a cartoon of the Prophet on the cover saying: '100 lashes if you don't die laughing.' In consequence its headquarters suffered a serious arson attack (Anon, 2011c). The long-running prime-time US cartoon series 'South Park' regularly mocks Mormons, Scientologists, Jews, the Queen – everybody. The show even got away with Muhammad as a superman who became a beaver in 2001 (prior to 9/11). The chill caught up with it, though, in 2006. It was censored from depicting him in an episode made in support of another cartoon that had caused an uproar – in fact, it had caused mayhem as great as *The Satanic Verses*.

In September 2005, a small right-wing Danish newspaper, the *Jellands-Posten*, had run twelve cartoons on a thin news day under the headline '*Muhammeds ansigt*' – 'Muhammad's Face' (Klausen, 2009: 13–18). One was a realistically sketched portrait of a bearded Muslim – which because of the headline could be read as the Prophet. A brooch was pinned to his turban with the legend in Arabic: 'There is no God but God. Muhammad is the Messenger of God.' Also sticking in the turban was a fizzing stick of dynamite.

The template established by *The Satanic Verses* affair furnished the underlying pattern of the events that followed: attacks on the cartoonist, demonstrations by local Muslims and attacks on Danish websites by computer-literate Islamist hackers. There were disturbances and demonstrations in Syria, Lebanon, Indonesia, Afghanistan, Somalia, Iran, Egypt, Bosnia-Herzegovina, Finland, France, Great Britain, Iraq, India (Kashmir), the Philippines, Palestine, Turkey and, of course, Pakistan. Between February and May 2006, some 250 people are estimated to have died in riots and at least 800 were injured. In response to a call for a boycott of Danish goods, sales fell across the Middle East. Overall, the uproar cost Denmark an estimated $180 million in lost revenue in that first year, the main victim being the dairy company, Arla (Klausen, 2009: 150).

So regular had protests become, and, increasingly, so much did they erode public support for tolerance, that those intolerant of minorities and hostile to social liberalism could exploit such reactions. The editors of *Jellands-Posten* were in just such a business. Like a bear-master prodding the creature to dance, the provocateur produces work guaranteeing that the hostility of the minority would take forms that would earn it general opprobrium – the object of the exercise. This is as new a problem as the censorship *fatwa*s. So, Denmark, a country previously noted for its tolerance, with only a 2 per cent immigrant population, nevertheless has come to legislate Europe's most draconian anti-immigration laws. It harbours an increasingly powerful Islamophobic political party in its parliament, the Folketing.

For the provocateurs concerned, however, this could be a dangerous game. Theo van Gogh was an independent Dutch filmmaker who had made a career out of cheap outrage (Baruma, 2006). With Ali Hirst, an anti-Muslim Somalian refugee who had become a right-wing Dutch MP, he made the short film *Submission*. It was a deliberate provocation with Qur'anic quotes, a naked woman in a see-through burka and a narration itemizing instances of abuse by Muslim men. Three months after the film was transmitted, on 2 November 2004, on a quiet street in Amsterdam, Mohammed Bouyeri, a twenty-six year-old unemployed Moroccan Berber, ambushed van Gogh, repeatedly shooting him. When he was dead, Bouyeri slit his throat and pinned a note on his body with a second knife. He is now in a Dutch prison; but it can be noted that in the previously tolerant Netherlands, as in Denmark, a right-wing Islamophobic political party holds the third largest block of seats in the parliament. It has only thus far been kept out of the country's coalition government with difficulty.

In Britain, publicity-seeking, self-appointed anti-immigrant groups arguably had learned too well the techniques of the political stunt. The extremist right-wing English Defence League (EDL) was born in the spring of 2009 in direct response to a small self-publicizing, supposedly Islamist cell that chose to disrupt a British Army regimental homecoming parade marking the end of a tour of duty in Afghanistan, in Luton. Onlookers turned on the Muslim demonstrators. The EDL, which coalesced in the aftermath of this event, is the most violent fascistic movement to have been seen in Britain since the National Front in 1970s. As the liberal Muslim commentator Ziauddin Sardar[6] put it: 'Why worry about Islamophobia and those who paint Islam in all the colours of darkness? Some Muslims do a good enough job of making a mockery of Islam themselves, thank you!' (Sardar, 2008: 21).

His is not the only voice reflecting what could be a changed understanding within the community of how to deal with provocations. No *fatwa*, for example, had been issued against the Danish cartoonists and, indeed, some Sunni authorities, albeit for the most part in India and the Western diaspora outside the *Umma's* heartland, had issued *fatwa*s condemning violence on that and other occasions (Sjølie, 2010: 13; McVeigh, 2010: 27). Following the *Charlie Hebdo* arson, France's main Muslim organization, Le Conseil Français du Culte Musulman was unambiguous. While of course deploring the issue, it also reaffirmed 'with force' ('*fermement*') its total opposition to any act or form of violence' (Anon, 2011c). Other cartoons and feature films poking fun at Islam have appeared without reaction from the offended. Perhaps there is no more hopeful sign that a change might be underway than the appearance in popular culture of comedians with Muslim backgrounds. Shazia Mirza made her mark by doing her act in a hijab. Her breakthrough routine famously started: 'My name is Shazia Mirza. At least, that's what it says on my pilot's license' (Gilliat-Ray, 2010: 243). Azhar Usman, an American attorney who has made a second career as a Muslim stand-up comic, claims that the concept of a 'Muslim comedian' is far from oxymoronic: 'There was a guy who was a companion of the Prophet who was given the title of "jester of the Prophet"' (Manzoor, 2007: 10).

Inayat Bunglawala, who was involved in the first Rushdie book burnings, also reflects a growing understanding in certain quarters of Muslim opinion: 'Looking back now, I readily acknowledge we were wrong to have called for [*The Satanic Verses*] to be banned. Today I can better appreciate the concerns and fears generated by the images of the book-burnings in Bradford and calls for Rushdie to be killed ... Our detractors were right. The freedom to offend is a necessary freedom' (Bunglawala, 2007: 33).

Yet one must remain cautious. We are still in a sorry situation and not all people understand that the seemingly simple, holy instruction always to slaughter the disrespectful is far from simple, being neither incontrovertibly holy nor inevitably unchanging. 'South Park' got a joke about Muhammad on the air in 2010 only to be warned by an American convert to Islam that Theo van Gogh's fate awaits the show's makers (Hassaballa, 2010). The shadow lingers.

2

The Treason of the Clerks

Egregious intimidation of expression remains a fact of contemporary life – if not directly encouraged, then certainly countenanced by a weak, confused, merely rhetorical Western intellectual commitment to the right of free speech. Western politicians' pusillanimity, though, is sometimes a justifiable consequence of *raisons d'état*. Rushdie was treated like a pariah by the Thatcher government as the crisis deepened in early 1989. Some of this reflected a 'Little England' hostility to Rushdie's own ethnicity as 'an outstanding villain ... a record of despicable acts of betrayal of his upbringing, religion, adopted home and nationality' (in the words of Lord Tebbit) (K. Malik, 2009: 33). More, though, it reflected a hidden situation that required support for Rushdie be muted. A group closely attached to Hezbollah, Khomeini's main allies in Lebanon, had been holding the Archbishop of Canterbury's emissary to the Middle East, Terry Waite, hostage since February 1987. The hope was that rhetoric condemning the book would keep the negotiations for his release alive. In the event, though, the failure to defend the right encouraged the Muslim campaign in Britain calling for censorship but did not secure Waite's freedom. He languished in Lebanon for nearly two further years (BBC, 1991).

Basically, though, governments speak with a forked tongue. On the one hand, there might be a genuine commitment to tolerance of minority sensitivities, not least in the name of social cohesion; but on the other, certainly post 9/11 and the Madrid and London bombings, the 'war on terror' brought in evermore draconian abridgements of freedom. The former anyway gave ground on Western principle to no advantage, not even its ostensible objective of social cohesion. For instance, the Labour minister in charge of racial equality at the time of the Sikh uproar in Birmingham said: 'When people are moved by theatre to protest ... it is a great thing ... that is a sign of the free speech, which is so much part of the British tradition'. This rhetoric has been judged as 'foolish' but stronger epithets suggest themselves (Robertson and Nicol, 2008: 234; quoted in Tripathi, 2009: 163). Such tolerance of the intolerant ultimately encourages it and consequential counter-bigotries.

It is a political given not to expect principled behaviour from politicians so these failures to stand by the right are perhaps unsurprising. Far more grievous is the unexpected deepening of the shadow across free speech occasioned by sections of Western intellectual opinion. For example, the Khushwant Singh role in *The Jewel of Medina* incident was played by Denise Spellberg.

She read the manuscript for Random House in New York and found it 'offensive', 'ugly'. 'I don't have a problem with historical fiction,' she claimed. As an historian, she reasonably stated that she did have 'a problem with the deliberate misinterpretation of history'. But, with the concept of the fictional seemingly eluding her, she concluded, 'You can't play with a sacred history and turn it into soft-core pornography' (Doward and Townsend, 2008: 9). An email from her to a Muslim activist was all it took for Random House to abandon the book.

Stanley Fish, very much a public intellectual and a voice previously raised against Rushdie, argued that, as the Random House decision was not governmentally mandated, it did not amount to censorship: it was merely 'a judgement call' – a matter of applying not fundamental principles but Weberian 'learned general rules' for the conduct of business (Swedberg, 2005: 19). This is what publishers do all the time as they either accept or reject manuscripts. One can note, though, that Fish's intervention against Rushdie, in the course of making this point, smacked of something rather more unpleasant than just taking a Jesuitical position on censorship. He took the opportunity to pronounce Rushdie 'a self-appointed poster boy for the First Amendment', a charge of such cheapness as to demean its maker (Fish, 2008).

Such opinion gives comfort to such as Khomeini and treasonously undermines a crucial Western principle. That principle is objected to by other intellectual opinion-formers in less ad hominem terms. Consider Tom Stoppard. In 2006, he wrote, somewhat startlingly in *Index on Censorship* (motto: 'for free expression'): 'The "human right" of free speech is a non-starter … It seems to have no foundation' (Stoppard, 2006: 134–6). 'Is the right of free expression self-evident?' he asked. Were this direct question in Latin, it would carry the particle '*num*' to indicate the expected answer is a negative: 'no, it is not self-evident'. It can be disputed. Despite citing what he described as 'the Voltairean credo' ('*Je ne suis pas d'accord avec un mot de ce que vous dites, mais je me battrai jusqu'à la mort pour votre droit de le dire*')[1] being at 'the foundation of [his] anglophilia', Stoppard talks of the liberty of speech as a 'shibboleth'. Of course, not least since he has prayed in Voltaire, one defends *jusqu'à la mort* Stoppard's right to hold this view, but as with Fish's opinion of Rushdie, it gives comfort to the enemies of free expression.

Stoppard deploys a range of objections to the right: 'That I have the right to express myself freely at all times in all circumstances entails the idea that free speech is a "basic human right" possessed by each individual, and, as such, trumps the interests of the society or group, including my neighbour.' But it should not be able to do this. He sees no reason to give it such primacy.

'A "human right" is, by definition, timeless,' he says. Whence this definition of timelessness? Apparently, it is from Thomas Jefferson whose 'inalienable rights' in the American Declaration of Independence were 'self-evident' because they had been 'endowed by God'. But, although rights cannot have a history, Stoppard claims that Jefferson's intervention demonstrates that this one does and that, in fact, this also displays a lack of divine origin.

Moreover, that the idea is a comparatively new one is obvious:

> To St Augustine, religious tolerance would have been an oxymoron. The concept of pluralism as a virtue is a thousand years more modern than St Augustine. To say, therefore, that the right of free speech was always a human right which in unenlightened societies was suspended from the year dot until our enlightened times is surely beyond even our capacity for condescension.

Ergo, it cannot be an all-powerful, 'trumping' right.

Additionally, as free speech is not found in all places and at all times, it cannot be a right, Stoppard claims. It is not universal, because it is culturally specific; and universality, he says, is essential to a right. Moreover, what, he asks, is to stop a democratic society from agreeing to impose censorship?

None of this reduces free speech rhetoric to a 'shibboleth', however. The harm principle denies speech a 'trumping' power. So what that rights are a human construct with a history? Universality is not essential. Not all democratic decisions are morally well-founded. That is no reason to abandon democracy; and these are no reason to make free speech a 'non-starter' either (see Chapter 10.1).

Such attacks as this have been heard for as long as the right has been claimed. 'What signifies a declaration, for example, that "the liberty of the press shall be inviolably preserved"?' asked Alexander Hamilton in 1788, arguing against just such a declaration – a text that was to become enshrined as the First Amendment to the American Constitution. 'What is the liberty of the press? ... I hold it to be impracticable and from this I infer, that its security, whatever fine declarations may be inserted in any Constitution respecting it must altogether depend on public opinion, and on the general spirit of the people and of the Government' (Hamilton, 1981 [1788]: 632).

On its face, it was not unreasonable to suggest that free speech is undeserving of a privileged position because it is, in a utilitarian sense, the least important of all human rights in terms of achieving a just society and quiet enjoyment of material sufficiencies. Hamilton was right to refer to public opinion and the 'general spirit of the people' as free expression's crucial guardians. Free speech is today protected by charters of rights and specific legislation. Expression in the West, especially in matters of sexual representations but also, largely, in political thought as well has never been more liberal. Nevertheless, a paradox arises. External rejections of Western values, the convolutions of Western realpolitik, reactions to the misfeasances of Western media and Western intellectual uncertainty are expressions of public opinion, indicating a weakening of the 'general spirit of the people'. With authority ever-ready to abridge freedoms in the name of, at best, public order (or, at worst, self-interest), these documents cannot be relied on to protect the right – as Hamilton suggested would always be the case. It needs the 'spirit of the people' and, arguably, the spirit of the people needs a clear intellectual and political focus.

But decline of public support meshes with a more general, and more measured, slowly developing critique of Enlightenment values after these were last seriously defended, in arms, in the Second World War. Western cultural voices, those of the 'treasonous clerks', had long been undercutting the Enlightenment concept of human rights, including a right of free expression. The downsides of the enshrinement of reason, the dangers to society of undercutting authority in its name, were being pointed up. It can be argued that such hostile public intellectual opinions were, and are, more damaging than any political backsliding. After all, the intellectuals lack the justifications and legitimacy of state power – the cover of realpolitik. The response of the West to the challenge of the Khomeini *fatwa* was thus bedevilled by the erosion of Western certainties about Enlightenment rights in general and confusions about free speech in particular.

There had always been fissures in Western thinking. The intellectual descendants of those who opposed the Enlightenment at its eighteenth-century outset – the philosophical and political 'right', as it may be – were increasingly ready to dilute human rights into 'entitlements' dependent on reciprocal 'responsibilities' on the part of those claiming them. By the twenty-first century, it was 'respectable' to make this connection and in so doing – in terms of human rights, at least – make a nonsense of them. These rights exist by virtue of the humanity of those claiming them, exactly independent of their behaviour. To assert otherwise is to open a very dangerous box indeed as the bloody history of the twentieth century so dramatically illustrates. Nevertheless, it is to be expected within terms of the illiberal authoritarian tradition.

More worrying was that some on the left were, for a variety of reasons, as hostile to free expression as any right-wing authoritarian (Wolff, Moore and Marcuse, 1969).

Whereas formerly it could be more or less safely assumed that liberal-minded people regarded freedom of expression as an intrinsic good, now many of them regard it as a problem that can harm and offend and thus needs to be curtailed. This is particularly the case, as Julian Petley points out, in an ethnically diverse society (Petley, 2009: 173).

As a result:

> The strong conviction that freedom of speech is a universal value is challenged today not only by freedom's oldest opponents (the despots and ruling thieves who fear it), but also by new enemies, who claim to speak for justice not tyranny. These new enemies point to other values we respect, including self determination, equality and freedom from racial hatred and prejudice, as reasons why the

right of free speech should now be demoted to a much lower grade of urgency. (Dworkin, 2010: v)

The growing suspicion of Enlightenment values constitutes a *trahison des clercs* – a treason against the West by its own intellectual opinion-formers.

3

The Abuses of 'Hackgate'

Milly Dowler, a thirteen-year-old schoolgirl, was abducted in Walton-on-Thames, Surrey, UK, on 21 March 2002. Her body was discovered the following September: she had been murdered. On 23 June 2011, Levi Bellfield, a serial killer already in prison for two other murders, was convicted in the Dowler case. Two weeks later, the *Guardian* revealed that voice-messages on the girl's mobile phone had been tampered with in the days following her disappearance nine years before.[1] This had suggested to the police and her family that she might still have been alive.

Suspicion for the 'hacking', an unauthorized breaking of security to listen to or read live or recorded conversations and texts, fell on a private investigator working for the *News of the World*. The details of this are unimportant here (Leigh, 2012b: 3). They did, however, lead directly to a situation threatening to the exercise of press freedom as that has been understood in democracies. It is this – the possibility of greater state control of the press in Britain than has been seen since the 1860s – that makes 'Hackgate', as it was quickly christened, of a piece with the Rushdie *fatwa* and the *trahison des clercs*. Outraged public opinion mounted what was, in effect, nothing less than an internal challenge to the principle of free expression. This easily matched the external challenge of Khomeini and those who emulate him. And it confirmed the uncertainties and hostilities of those who would deny the privileges of speech altogether.

The *News of the World* affair further exposed the Western fault lines that had so confused and bedevilled the Western responses to the *fatwa* and its legacy. The one medium of mass communications which can be said to have exercised a measure of freedom, the press, was now to be threatened with controls as great as those which had been placed on other newer media, such as broadcasting. Instead of arguing that, in a mature democracy, press freedoms need to be logically extended to other media, it has become necessary to defend the ground already won. Abuse of power by the British press had grown, seemingly neutering political power and muzzling the police. Where once press freedom was grounded in the principle of 'publish and be damned' (that is, speak and run the risk of legal reprimand), now the rule appeared to be 'publish with no fear of consequences from any quarter'. Defending the right to offend – the perimeter, as it were, of the general right of free expression – becomes mired in a need to condemn any sense that expression is, somehow, above the law.

The *News of the World* was now owned by Rupert Murdoch's News International. It had, from the moment of its founding in 1843, specialized in crime and titillation. It was merely keeping up with its traditions and, indeed, the traditions of the popular press that go back to the seventeenth century. Despite the press's crucial role as a guardian of freedom, the seeds of such a scandal had been planted long, long ago. The free press, as we understand it, was born in the confusions of the English Civil War. Its pioneers were in the pockets of King and Parliament, its function PR as much as news. In fact, integrity was something of a luxury and truthfulness was as much a matter of branding – a way of making seventeenth century news publications 'vendible' – as it was any guarantor of veracity. The press, always in the business of entertainment as well as information-provision, sells itself on truth but, at least in its more populist modes, provides it somewhat parsimoniously. In words attributed to the great early nineteenth-century innovator of the cheap newspaper, James Gordon Bennett of the *New York Herald*: 'Many a good newspaper story has been ruined by over verification.'

That sex and entertainment as well as politics were also of first importance to the press's agenda is confirmed at the outset of this history by seventeenth-century titles such as the *Mecurius Fumigosus*. The scatological model for the *News of the World* is thus this time-honoured. And as for celebrity, of Nell Gwynn, the Earl of Rochester could confidently write at that time: 'Who does not know her name? She is a killer dame.'

The deepest source of the problem, however, is neither the press's economical approach to the truth nor its addiction to scandal and celebrity. It is its willingness not merely to observe and report on the world but to intervene to obtain material for its pages. This is, of course, crucial to its ability to 'guard the guardians'[2] – a foundation upon which the right to retail information 'necessary to a democratic society' (as the European Convention on Human Rights has it) rests. However, it is also the root of the internal threat to the right: intervention easily leads to abuse, abuse to protest and protest to censorship. Controlling abuse legitimates internal Western calls for control as loud as any external cries demanding censorship.

News reports originally came to publishers from their readers but, before the end of the seventeenth century, furnishing news became a paying job, albeit not a particularly honourable one. Reporters, 'intelligencers', were seen as morally suspect as soon as they started to appear. They were considered too consanguineous with spies to be well received by public opinion. Indeed, Daniel Defoe, a prolific publisher of news, was actually a political spy on the side. By the early nineteenth century, the spy began to ask questions. James Gordon Bennett's innovation was to talk, in 1836, to a witness in sensational murder trial. He interviewed the madam of a fancy Manhattan bordello where a prostitute had been killed. He wrote in justification: 'let us not suppose but courts and juries and justices have a right alone to examine a matter affecting our morals' (Gordon Bennett, 1836b: 1).

Gordon Bennett made interviews a regular feature. He conducted the first ever with a president, Martin Van Buren, in 1839, producing a type of exclusive that was to become prized. One of the century's biggest 'stunts' was an interview engineered for the *Herald* by James Gordon Bennett Jr, his son, in partnership with the London *Daily Telegraph*'s Joseph Levy. Henry Stanley was sent to Africa to look for the supposedly lost David Livingstone by the two papers. It was decades before the interview was entirely trusted as a technique, though. In Britain, it was seen as being always ripe for corruption and it was not until the late 1880s that it became 'acclimatized', as W.T. Stead, editor of the *Pall Mall Gazette* and a man much taken with American journalistic practices, put it (Lasky, 2000: 164). Interviews encouraged journalism to cross a crucial line by filling the pages of the papers with something more than mere reports, accurate or not, on what was happening anyway.

In September 1887, a young female reporter from Pittsburgh, born Elizabeth Cochran but given the byline 'Nellie Bly' by her first editor, was sent to expose the evils of the New York Woman's Lunatic Asylum. She was to do this neither by mere observation, nor with interviews but by pretending to be an amnesiac madwoman and being admitted to the institution. This marked a new level of intervention – the exposé – using a technique which, when adopted by twentieth-century social scientists, would be termed 'participant observation'. Her report, though, was suffused with subterfuge; but that it was 'true' justified the means. 'Inside the Madhouse' was perceived as journalism clearly acting as the guardians' guardian. It served the public interest in an obviously straightforward way. Any moral ambiguities in obtaining the information were thus implicitly taken care of. Such 'muckraking' soon became the cutting edge of journalism's essential legitimacy as a protector of basic rights. It was the essence of the 'New Journalism'. This was exemplified by the furious circulation war fought out between the *New York World* owned by Joseph Pulitzer and his great rival, William Randolph Hearst's *New York Journal*. Together they were at the heart of the so-called 'Yellow Press'.[3]

In 1897, Hearst sent a reporter, the dashing Richard Harding Davies, and, as a great coup, the best-known American painter of his generation, Frederick Remington, to cover the suppression of a two-year-old revolt in the Spanish colony of Cuba. He was eager to exacerbate tensions between the United States and Spain by sensationalizing Spain's ruthless suppression of its colony. However, when his men got to the island, Remington cabled from Havana that all was quiet. Hearst famously cabled back (although he always denied it): 'PLEASE REMAIN. YOU FURNISH THE PICTURES AND I'LL FURNISH THE WAR' (Nasaw, 2000: 127).

Gordon Bennett Jr's boast after Stanley's triumphant expedition, 'I make the news', had become an evermore important goal for proprietors. Hearst got his Spanish-American war and although it was certainly not his doing alone (or even at all), he was not loath to claim credit as its instigator (despite denying the telegram). The New Journalism sanctioned newspaper proprietors in such achieved, attempted or claimed exercises of power and influence. Hearst's *Journal*'s tagline was 'While Other's Talk, *The Journal* Acts' – solving crimes, taking public utility companies and construction firms to court, and conducting campaigns. New Journalism was filling the columns of the papers with, essentially, 'scoops' (an Americanism new in this context in the 1880s) furnished by the consequences of their own actions.

Journalism's most enduring intervention into reality, however, was engineered not by Hearst but by Pulitzer. France, prompted by the upcoming centenary of the Declaration of Independence, determined to honour the American republic by presenting it with a large statue but, in the United States, a public appeal for funds to build a pedestal for the gift faltered. As the 110th anniversary approached, Pulitzer decided to solve a somewhat embarrassing problem. An editorial declared: '*The World* is the people's paper and it now appeals to the people to come forward and raise this money' (Anon, 1885: 4). Around 120,000 did, the pedestal was built and the Statue of Liberty was unveiled in 1886. The press was not only making the news, it was moulding the landscape.

And, of course, it could all go wrong.

In Britain, Stead, who was using the *Pall Mall Gazette* as a channel for the importation of these new American ideas in journalism, was in the process of becoming 'The Man with the Muck-rake' (Smith, 1979: 144). He decided to expose then widespread sexual exploitation of children (T. Fisher, 1995). As the son of a non-conformist minister and himself a teetotal lay-preacher, he was publically identified with the 'Purity Lobby'. His instincts, though, remained that of the populist New Journalist, titillating his readership. Thus, he did not simply report on the trade in children. He set 'a Special and Secret Commission of Inquiry' which, in the course of its investigations in the summer of 1885, actually bought a young girl to demonstrate how easy a thing this was to do. The Commission's report was published in the *Pall Mall Gazette* as 'The Maiden Tribute of Modern Babylon' (Stead, 1885b). On the Saturday prior to publication, Stead wrote 'A Frank Warning' about the upcoming exposé: 'All those who are squeamish ... will do well not to read the Pall Mall Gazette of Monday and the following days' (Stead, 1885a).

With such self-serving rhetoric, it is perhaps no wonder that his actions were viewed as less than morally pure, especially when the girl in question said she thought she was being hired for a respectable maid's job. His rivals were not kind: 'the vilest parcel of obscenity that has ever yet issued from the public press', one paper called it. Nor was the judge any more sympathetic when the case for 'Unlawfully taking Eliza Armstrong, aged 13, out of the possession and against the will of her father' came before him. Stead was found guilty of abduction and indecent assault and given three months without hard labour.

Such incidents, however, were of sufficient rarity not to provoke general reaction and the press's hard-won freedom, to which we shall return, remained unquestioned (see Chapter 4). The emergence of the press barons by the turn of the twentieth century and the concomitant concentration of ownership was more a worry. Over time, though, some journalists, notably the National Union of Journalists (NUJ), suggested a measure of oversight might be appropriate to maintain ethical standards. However, having itself adopted a code of practice in 1936 and being concerned with the power of the employers, the Union also began to argue for a Royal Commission to investigate ownership in the industry. It was established in 1947 by the reformist Labour government, which agreed that concentration of ownership was the problem. Given the preponderance of right-wing titles, this was scarcely surprising.

The Commission was not a success, although it did establish the National Archives to facilitate access to official documentation. Otherwise it failed to contain the press barons. A measure of this is that they controlled 42 per cent of circulation at the time of the inquiry and they held 57 per cent, in just three groupings, forty years later (Curran and Seaton, 2009: 98). However, the Commission did recommend the establishment of a press council. The proprietors were inclined to ignore this but, four years later, foot-dragging brought the threat of the statutory imposition of such a body, so a feeble General or Press Council was established by the industry. It consisted entirely of professionals – editors – which quickly destroyed any credibility to which it might have aspired as a self-controlling regulator.

The politicians, though, were constrained – properly by the fundamentals of the right of free expression, but also, perhaps less legitimately, by a certain reluctance to tackle the proprietors whose power to harm their interests was well established. Anyway, the number of incidents occurring over the years, in the context of thousands of stories and millions of readers, remains miniscule. Of course, the ineffectiveness of the sort of self-regulation first proposed in the late 1940s has inhibited the number of complainants coming forward, but nevertheless only a few thousand are involved. The complaints are predominantly about accuracy, not privacy, harassment or intrusions into grief. And some 90 per cent of them are likely to be frivolous. Given the limited scope, thus revealed, of the problem, why would politicians risk offending the press and why would the press anyway be concerned?[4]

Despite nothing being done about concentration after 1949 and the General Council doing little either about the admittedly still comparatively rare lapses of conduct that came before it, a second Royal Commission was established in 1961. The barons again survived this, their baronies intact, as did the Council, though not in the later instance without a severe mauling: 'We hope that in future the Press Council will be more vigilant in demonstrating the independence and impartiality to which it lays claim' (Curran and Seaton, 2009: 334).

The hope was in vain, although it did reform its membership to include 20 per cent lay figures; and it became a little more active, formally ruling on press misconduct as well as defending against any perceived threats to press freedom. The toxic mix of evermore liberal social standards and shrinking circulations, however, in general lowered the already limited willingness of the press to be constrained in its pursuit of sensation and economic survival. The two were now so inextricably intertwined that even its collective understanding that there might be a problem was becoming increasingly attenuated. After all, was there not a free press – an inalienable right of freeborn Englishmen, etc? And had not Parliament shown itself to be unwilling or incapable or both of dealing with journalism – especially over the issue of invasion of privacy? The right to invade came to be seen as the touchstone of press liberty. Governments were leery of pursuing it, although there was, increasingly, awareness that the issue was important. A draft privacy bill in 1970 was thus opposed by the government, but a committee of inquiry was set up instead. In its report of 1973, it did not recommend legislation but the Press Council was again castigated. Equal membership of lay and professional councillors was called for as well as prominent displays of corrections and apologies in the press.

In emulation of the inquiries into broadcasting, which had been occurring regularly every decade, more or less, since the 1920s, the government returned to the fray the following year and a third Royal Commission was appointed, with, yet again, ownership as its first focus. It reported in 1977 and, yet again, the Press Council was lambasted: 'It is unhappily certain that the council has so far failed to persuade the knowledgeable public that it deals satisfactorily with complaints against newspapers'. Its proposal, however, that a written Code of Conduct for journalists be produced was dismissed, after four years of deliberation by the press and the Press Council. The NUJ had already withdrawn from the Council in 1980, have determined that it was 'incapable of reform'.

History was now replaying itself like a jumping vinyl record. Two MPs proposed private privacy bills and, in 1989, the government responded with a further inquiry, the fifth since the Second World War. Unlike the parallel series of broadcasting reports that had established the BBC and television, these press investigations had produced little or nothing. Concentration of ownership continued; unethical behaviour was, at best, unchanged. In the face of this new investigation under Sir David Calcutt, despite strident headlines about the 'Establishment' censoring 'your paper' and the like, the press was forced into a measure of response. The then Heritage Minister, David Mellor, who had a responsibility for culture (including the press), while being interviewed for *Hard News*, a Channel Four programme about the press itself, said: 'I do believe the press – the popular press – is drinking in the last chance saloon'

(Greenslade, 2004: 539). Curbs on the 'sacred cow of press freedom' were in order, he thought.

A further incident occurred when a reporter and photographer entered the hospital room of a popular actor who had been involved in a very serious car accident, even trying to interview the man. The *Sunday Sport* successfully resisted an injunction, trumpeting its triumph over 'censorship'. Lord Justice Glidewell, quietly exhorting Parliament to act, said: 'It is well known in English Law there is no right of privacy.' 'Bollocks to the Press Council', screamed the *Sport*'s headline (Greenslade, 2004: 549–50).[5] The minister and the actor, though, did take (or at least slacken) the wind out of the press's sails and the Council moved a little. In 1991, it was rebranded as the Press Complaints Commission (PCC) and, most notably, finally produced a Code of Practice. Otherwise little changed. In fact, the PCC was even more limited in one regard than was the Press Council. As its remit was solely to deal with complaints, it lacked its predecessor's authority to pronounce on general press issues.

Sir David Calcutt was not impressed with the PCC and, in a second report in 1993, he said: 'I therefore regret that I have reached the conclusion that the Press Complaints Commission, as set up by the press, has not proved itself to be an effective regulator, and have had to recommend that the Government should now introduce a statutory regime' (Calcutt, 1993: section 8.2).

But the power of the press thwarted any such move. Not unnaturally, the PCC takes a different view of the effectiveness of self-regulation and its own performance:

> After overcoming the teething problems associated with most new organizations, the PCC has continued to grow in stature – building on the accomplishments of its early years ... A further inquiry into self-regulation of the press by the Select Committee in 2007 concluded that the system of self regulation should be maintained for the press, and that there was no case for a statutory regulator. It further concluded that a privacy law was undesirable. (Press Complaints Commission, 2009)

It is not entirely possible to resolve this difference of view but perhaps the fate of David Mellor gives a clue. In July 1992, his adulterous affair with an 'actress' was exposed by the *Sunday Mirror* in a classic 'kiss-and-tell' exclusive. Phones had been hacked, not by the paper, but by the landlord of what one must in this context presumably call Mellor's 'love nest'. Details of Mellor's curious erotic behaviour, primarily involving a soccer jersey, made him, in any case a somewhat unprepossessing figure of a man, a laughing stock and after two months he was forced to resign. The case, though, is not a clear example of the bullying persecution of a figure on the outdated grounds of sexual prurience. Mellor's resignation was because of a direct breech of the ministerial code, not his adulterous sexual cavorting. He had accepted hospitality – a month-long holiday in a luxury villa in Spain – from the wealthy daughter of a prominent

Palestine Liberation Organization (PLO) figure and he had failed to declare this. Clearly, an exposé of this politically sensitive connection was obviously justified on 'public interest' grounds in ways that his private sexual activities were not. It is such tangled webs that bedevil the issue – although it can be noted that the connection with the PLO was initially published without any repercussions or follow-up. It took the soccer shirt to gain the press's serious attention.

The press continued to drink, undisturbed, in Mellor's Last Chance Saloon. Sections of it have behaved for the last sixty-odd years like the fictional *bravi* – dandified heavies – Alessandro Manzoni described at the beginning of his classic novel 1827 historical novel, *I Promessi Sposi* (*The Betrothed*), set in seventeenth-century Lombardy. These *bravi* were banned, Manzoni tells us, in 1588 and in 1593, in 1598 and again in 1600, and in 1612, 1618, 1627, which was 'a year, a month, and two days' before we encounter the two specimens in the novel's opening scene. In 1947, 1961, 1970, 1977, 1989, 1991 and 1993, the *bravi* of the English press were similarly cautioned and threatened and with as little effect – until the new century and 'Hackgate'.

Within the context of untrammelled power, the current fall from grace turns upon the outsourcing, as it were, of the central journalistic function of reporting to private investigators. This is a consequence of allowing money to dominate the news-gathering process, especially when the bought information is deemed to be crucial to survival in a sharply declining, viciously competitive market. This combination, although easily accommodated by the popular press's traditions, is of recent appearance. Yet not all journalists – certainly not those of an older generation – are purblind defenders of contemporary practice:

> If you sit in the office duplicating the agencies or putting your name on PR handouts, you are not a reporter at all ... A reporter is somebody who turns up a piece of information ... and enquires into it further. When I was a child we called it 'digging'. A reporter doesn't accept any information at face value ... What a reporter doesn't do – or didn't – was employ a so-called 'private eye' to do the job for him. For God's sake ... how did that habit ever take off? What sort of editor or news editor originally told a hapless hack: 'What? You can't find the facts? Why not employ a private detective?' (Barker, 2012)

The money was there, in the desperate search for sensation to staunch the decline of readers, to obey any instruction to buy in such help. This is not seen as a fault but, for professionals, is a source of admiration: 'I respected the *News of the World*... I admired its chutzpah and envied the proprietorial indulgence when it needed to spend many thousands of pounds on a solid story' (Young, 2011: 47). Proprietors, of course, had long since become extremely powerful multimedia barons with the money to spend in defence of their interests.

Rumblings continued about Hackgate, but were more or less confined to the reporting of Nick Davies in the *Guardian*. It was the epitome of the boring news story – in the spirit of 'Small Earthquake in Peru. Not Many Dead';[6] in effect, it was an annoying distraction only being scratched at by a bastion of currently somewhat despised liberal opinion. In the United States, the matter was seen slightly differently. As it is now the headquarters of Murdoch's international operation, coverage of the scandal was a gift to his rivals. Moreover, any proven criminal conspiracy in his British company resulting in convictions would raise the possibility of parallel legal attacks in the States. It might be a much desired fantasy on the part of many but, perhaps, New Corporation could be put out of business.

Anyway, in the United States, journalism ethics are taken more seriously than in Britain. The history of the relationship between society (including government) and the press is conditioned not by spokespersons for both sides in a seventeenth-century civil war but by the oppositional speaking of truth to power which played so central a role in the eighteenth-century struggle for independence from Britain (see Chapter 5.1). The professional norms of American journalism, although as self-imposed as are the British, are far stricter. The Society of Professional Journalists' Code of Ethics contains, for example, guidance for keeping a proper distance:

> Journalists should be free of obligation to any interest other than the public's right to know.
>
> Journalists should:
>
> - Avoid conflicts of interest, real or perceived.
> - Remain free of associations and activities that may compromise integrity or damage credibility.
> - Refuse gifts, favors, fees, free travel and special treatment, and shun secondary employment, political involvement, public office and service in community organizations if they compromise journalistic integrity.
> - Disclose unavoidable conflicts.
> - Be vigilant and courageous about holding those with power accountable.
> - Deny favored treatment to advertisers and special interests and resist their pressure to influence news coverage.
> - Be wary of sources offering information for favors or money; avoid bidding for news. (Society of Professional Journalists, 1996–2011)

Apart from killing the development of a similar set of rules in the UK for decades, it is still not unknown for British journalists to treat this sort of thing with a grain of salt. When the Society of Professional Journalists' Code's preamble talks of 'public enlightenment' being 'the forerunner of justice and the foundation of democracy', wonder at pomposity is a not unusual British response. British journalists are quick to point out that plagiarism, fabrication and bias, all specifically highlighted by the American Code as sin, occur nevertheless. This fact then justifies cynicism. That such incidents might be exceptions that prove the rule is not considered when American practice is being so scornfully dismissed.[7] Yet the American situation is nevertheless different. Ever since the *Moser* case in 1908, the distinction that was then drawn between journalism and advertising is seen as implicitly acknowledging the press's social role (*Moser v. Press Pub. Co.*, 1908). On a day-to-day basis, the Society of Professional Journalists' Code remains a bedrock of behaviour. Although this view can be disputed as too trusting, the fact is that American journalism scandals, when they have occurred, have not involved the possibility of criminal misfeasance.

The *Guardian*'s dogged pursuit eventually bore fruit in the revelation of the 2002 Dowler missing-calls mystery in the summer of 2011. Now it was no longer a question of tittle-tattle. How the calls had disappeared from Milly's phone was less significant than the fact that hacking had not been limited to celebrity phones. The phones of the families of the two children murdered in Soham the same year as Milly; of the victims of the terrorist attack on London in July 2005; of the McCanns whose daughter disappeared in Portugal two years later; of war widows whose partners had been killed in Afghanistan: all were suggested as having been targets. In some of these cases, the police appeared to have been, potentially, protecting systematic criminal evidence-tampering so as not to embarrass their friends at the Murdoch papers. Over all, there was a sense of moral revulsion.

The cull of News International's executives now continued as a number resigned and were arrested. The officer investigating 'Hackgate', Assistant Commissioner John Yates 'of the Yard', who had made a name for himself by aggressively pursuing a previous 'cash for honours' scandal under Blair, resigned because of his close association with one of the arrested *News of the World* executives. The Murdochs were forced to appear before a committee of the House of Commons and, in a final attempt to cauterize the damage, on 10 July 2011, they closed the paper. It was just a few months shy of 168 years since that first 'EXTRAORDINARY CHARGE OF DRUGGING AND VIOLATION' story had appeared under the *News of the World* banner. Days later the Dowlers were in Downing Street to meet the Prime Minister and Sir Brian Leveson, a Lord Justice of Appeal, was named as the chair of a very wide-ranging inquiry.

Obviously Hackgate does not speak to the fundamentals of free expression. None claim journalistic privilege for criminality, although professional opinion is perhaps too quick to seek justifications for it. Despite the deliberately created glib confusion between what interests the public and the public interest, some facts are clear: it cannot be in the public interest to commit a crime such as evidence tampering – or even to undertake actions that could result in evidence tampering. It cannot be in the public interest to harass and bully. It cannot be in the public interest to corrupt officials. By this much, at least, the true nature of the 'public interest' is clear. The worse aspect of Hackgate is, rather, the degree to which the press's invulnerability appears to have been acquired by tacit or active collusion on the part of officials and politicians. Had the authorities discharged their duties, press abuse would have been appropriately chilled. This is not to say that it would have been prevented but it would have been contained by the old freedom: 'publish and be damned'. It is not that the law is lacking to control the most egregious aspect of press behaviour but that it was not applied.

To take one telling example, it was revealed in the inquiry that legal opinion had been sought by the Information Commissioner's Office (ICO), which is charged with oversight of the operation of data protection legislation, in 2003. That year a raid on a private investigator had discovered that his clients included the newspapers. The lawyer's opinion was that this was illegal, but such was the atmosphere even his suggested remedy, that the ICO merely advise senior editors they were probably behaving illegally, was not taken (Robinson and Sabbagh, 2011: 17). The Data Commissioner at the time, Richard Thomas, told Lord Justice Leveson that he did nothing not because he was 'wary of the power of the press' but because, he said, his officials were afraid 'it would have been bogged down the office for many years. [The press] would have gone all the way to [the European Court of Human Rights in] Strasbourg and challenged the ICO every step of the way' (Robinson and O'Carroll, 2011: 24). That those with the wealth to pursue a defence through the law can buy themselves protection might be an obvious truth but to have it thus set down is astonishing.

Equally astounding is the failure to contain the activities of door-stepping reporters and bullying paparazzi. One celebrity gave evidence to Leveson that she had even been spat at by a photographer to get a reaction. Sienna Miller told the inquiry that, 'she was followed by around 15[8] men on a daily basis when she first became famous at the age of 21. "It's very intimidating," the actor said, adding: "Because they have cameras, it's legal"' (Robinson, O'Carroll and Halliday, 2011). But, under a variety of statutes, it might well not be. Certainly the law was there, for example, the 1997 Protection from Harassment Act:[9]

> The law creates an offence of pursuing 'a course of conduct which amounts to harassment of another'. Harassment is defined as 'alarming the person or causing the person distress' ... In 2001, the act was used to prosecute protesters outside the US intelligence base at Menwith Hill ... In the same year a protester in Hull was arrested under the act for "staring at a building". In 2004, police in Kent arrested a woman who had sent two polite emails to an executive at a drugs company ... In 2007, the residents of a village in Oxfordshire were injuncted from protesting ... Having discovered what a useful tool it had become, in 2005 the government amended the act in a way that seemed deliberately to target peaceful protesters and smear them as stalkers.[10] (Monbiot, 2009)

But not, it would seem from Ms Miller's experience, if they are carrying cameras.

The reason for inaction, that the public interest affords a crucial defence underpinned by the right of free expression, only persuades if, indeed, it means merely whatever interests the public. Such an argument, though, can be used to justify public hanging; it too would no doubt be 'interesting' to the public. The ineffectual Press Complaints Commission's Code, in effect, enshrines this sophistry as an unexplained truism: 'There is a public interest in freedom of expression itself' (Press Complaints Commission, 2011). Nor are the press's tendentious rhetorical glosses on this – for example, that celebrities need publicity, and are merely objecting to situations that they have not approved – any excuse for the lack of prosecutions. This certainly, anyway, cannot justify harassing those who accidentally, as it were, find themselves in the public eye. Despite the lack of a tort of invasion of privacy, the law has shown itself capable of acting to protect the press's victims, even before the Human Rights Act came into force in 2000 (see Chapter 12.1). It is to stretch credulity to claim nothing could be done to control the excesses of the paparazzi and harassing door-stepping – especially since much, if not most, of the worst behaviour was occasioned opportunistically with no new, specific story to pursue.

The threat of legal action against and even prison for journalists, like the burning of books, is fretted with the baggage of totalitarianism. Some claim any arrest of journalists raises this spectre; but it does not. Journalists cannot be above the law and clear evidence of illegal behaviour must be punished. Such criminal behaviour is quite other from the pursuit of truth by legitimate means. The public interest can be defined, with more precision than the Press Complaints Commission has managed to do, to preserve the press's role (including that of providing entertainment) without the right of free expression being threatened. As it is, there is no question that the British press – and not just that part of it owned by Murdoch – has traduced its privileges. Machismo – 'if it bleeds it leads', etc. – infuses the ambiance of journalism. It has led to a situation where, in Britain, the flow of news, that which – in a democracy – the public has a right to know, is threatened with the (previously unthinkable) possible reimposition of state control.

The scandal began by costing a national title. Murdoch's business expansion plans for satellite television were immediately thwarted. And the parade of executives and journalists helping the police with their inquiries started on a long march. The stench of corruption thickened as subsequent accusations of even more blatant illegality – the bribery of the police and other officials – at the *Sun*, a second Murdoch UK title, were made in February 2012. Again, no claim of privilege can be made but cauterizing the alleged criminality brings a threat to free speech in its wake (Doward, 2012: 1). This time, therefore, the threat was a lot realer than it had been. The drinking in the saloon was over and the lights were now going out. The price of the drinks, though, was so great that basic hard-won freedoms were in danger of being demanded as pay-back in the resultant gloom. Hackgate and its aftermath put regulation and registration – concepts of control not seriously considered for centuries – on the saloon's bar.

And already in the gloom were public intellectuals, *les clercs*, questioning the centrality of the right of expression and the Imam Khomeini with his *fatwa* denying its validity all together and crying for censorship. All three constitute elements in the case for the prosecution. The defence attempted below begins with a rebuttal from history of the demand for censorship.

PART TWO

Defence

Not all the cases included in Part Two are actual court 'cases' but all the parties, patents and laws to which they refer are, or were, in existence.[1]

SECTION ONE

Histories – To Dispel the Shadow of the *Fatwa*

Of the three prongs of attack, the most fundamental is Khomeini's *fatwa* since it rejects the very concept of a right of free expression and, indeed, of human rights in general. However much Western social harmony in a multicultural world demands that such other voices be heard, Khomeini's view must be opposed. After all, the West considers rights central, the right of free speech included. Why this can be held to be 'sacred' is a consequence of the long, and often bloody, history of the struggle to achieve it. That history lies at the heart of any defence against external threats to Western freedom.

4

Actiones: Cases

4.1 *Defence of the Seven Sacraments against Martin Luther* (1521): For a right of conscience and a right to publish

Free expression is linked to religion through conscience: 'Liberty of conscience is the unalienable human right, essential to the autonomy of the individual [and this] underlies freedom of speech' (Richards, 1988: 331). Liberty of conscience demands freedom of speech and the demand is first made, in the West, in connection with religious belief. Free speech was initially, quite literally, a matter of faith.

Like all human institutions, the Christian Church was subject to dispute and strife. It was, after all, itself born of a schismatic break with Judaism and its claim on universality, even within its own aegis, has been constantly undercut. The parade of cases – in law, they would once have been called *actiones* in the West's lingua franca – is unending. In the Christian second century, the row was about the God of the Old Testament; in the fourth, it was over the nature of Christ; by the sixth, it was the authority of bishops; and the Great Schism between the Eastern and Western Churches, still unhealed a millennium later, occurred in the eleventh century.

Stresses in the universal Church also involved the laity's individual relationship with the Almighty, with people insisting on a right of personal address without the intervention of a priestly caste and, often, rejecting (to one degree or another) the material world, especially the Church's pomp and circumstance. Such opposition was worse than the trauma of schism. Successive heresies of this kind, sometimes reflecting ancient Manichaean and Gnostic beliefs, were extirpated, or at least their eradication was attempted: the Bogomils in the Balkans in the tenth century, the Waldensians in twelfth-century France as well as the Cathars and thereafter, in the German lands, the Cult of the Free Spirit. Theology apart, what is consistent in all this persistent dissent and protest is that it arises from the driven need of the unorthodox to speak out according to their understandings and the demands of their consciences. The response of the Church to the critique of its worldliness these belief systems presented was not, however, limited to crusade and the stake.

Within the hierarchy, some were equally prepared to address the laxity and luxury of their fellows, albeit with less heretical proposals for reform; others essayed a direct challenge to heresy but without redress to brutality.

The Dominicans or Blackfriars, for example, were specifically founded by St Dominic to turn the Cathars back to the true Church (Lambert, 1998: 1). There were individuals, too. It is, of course, seriously ahistorical to refer to these reforming medieval ecclesiastics, such as Nicolas of Cusa (Kues), whose background was in canon law, as 'liberal'; but 'schoolmen' with their range of intellectual curiosity and sophistication, scientific as well as theological, could exhibit an attractive, if circumscribed and (in the strict meaning of word) academic, openness. Nicolas, known as Cusenius, was made a cardinal and, at the Pope's behest, sought reconciliation with the Eastern Church. In the process he became one of those gatherers of ancient Greek texts which were soon to fuel the Renaissance. He even contemplated a dialogue with the Muslims, as St Francis had also essayed two centuries earlier.

In the 1430s, at the Council of Basle, Cusenius called for the assembled bishops and abbots to provide their clergy with accurate copies of the Bible and the Missal for everyday use in every parish. He was after more than accuracy. Only the Vulgate was sanctioned; unauthorized biblical texts were otherwise forbidden and any corrupted text, even in the Latin, was de facto unorthodox. Bibles in the vernacular, such as John Wycliffe's English translation of the Vulgate's Latin in the fourteenth century, were tools of heresy, leading all too easily to catastrophic (from the Church's standpoint) opinions. It could have been no surprise to the religious authorities to discover that Wycliffe's followers, the Lollards, were not merely interested in reading the Holy Writ in their mother tongue. They also believed, as other dissenters had done before them, in fundamentally destructive ideas such as a lay clergy or the legitimacy of a refusal to pay tithes.

These dissenting movements were far-flung and long-lived.[1] Lollardy was carried, somehow, in the baggage of Richard II when he travelled with his bride, Anne of Bohemia, daughter of the Holy Roman Emperor, to visit her homeland. A generation later in Bohemia, Wycliffe's thought produced Jan Hus, a protesting priest, who was burned at the stake in 1415. Just over a hundred years after that, on 31 October 1517, Martin Luther, again an alienated churchman enraged by the same abuses of formulaic and corrupt religious practices, pinned an open letter to the Bishop of Mainz on the door of the Schlosskirche, the relic-rich Castle Church of All Saints, in Wittenberg. This was the act which, conventionally, marks the formal starting point of the great Protestant Reformation, another unhealed schism.

The focus of Martin Luther's hostility was the sale of indulgences, a corrupt and much misunderstood business, seemingly involving the literal buying-off of sin. The Bishop challenged by Luther was first among equals in the German clergy. He had encouraged the sale of indulgences because he owed money to Pope Leo X; and the Pope needed yet more money in his turn for the building of St Peter's in Rome. It was this last endeavour that specifically aroused the ire of the Reverend Dr Luther of the University of Wittenberg. The document accompanying his letter, the *Disputatio pro declaratione virtutis indulgentiaru* (*Ninety-five Theses on the Power and Efficacy of Indulgences*), outlined his complaint. Number 86 read: 'Why does not the Pope, whose wealth is to-day greater than the riches of the richest, build just this one church of St Peter with his own money, rather than with the money of poor believers?'

Plain speaking of this order, in an age of deference and protocol, to a figure cloaked in religious majesty is a cogent, dramatic display of the right of free expression's force and strength. 'Speaking truth to power' (as the Quakers were to put it many centuries later) is the essence of that right – the purest expression of it as a 'good'. Luther's epistolary skill, though, demonstrated in the autumn of 1517 something more than the potency of speech. His attack also highlighted that a new mode of amplifying the human voice had appeared, extending the reach of an individual's influence, even beyond what writing could achieve. With Luther, the mass media enters the West's history.

Luther begins with a letter – in Latin, handwritten – but his revolt was to continue in the vernacular and it was to be in print. Some three years after the *Ninety-five Theses*, he wrote an *Address to the Nobility of the German Nation respecting the Reformation of the Christian Estate.* Unlike the *Ninety-Five Theses*, this, *An den christlichen Adel deutscher Nation*, was not in Latin: nor did it begin as handwritten poster. Within three weeks of publication as a pamphlet on 18 August 1520, 4,000 copies had been printed and distributed. Thirteen more editions appeared over the next two years. Print allowed expression not only to become more widely diffused but also, therefore, automatically supposedly more powerful. For authority, the time-honoured difficulties that free expression causes, exemplified by Luther, were exacerbated by the introduction of printing from moveable type in the mid-fifteenth century. Printing marks a significant way station in *la longue durée* (as French historians have it) of the West's 'problem' with liberty.

The rapid spread of printing and the volume of material produced give clear evidence of impact. Before 1500, more than 100 presses had been established, mainly in the Italian and German lands but also in England, France, Spain, Bohemia, Poland and the Balkans. Africa's first press was set up in Ethiopia in 1515; the Americas' first in Mexico in 1539 (Eisenstein, 1983; Febvre and Martin, 1977; Steinberg, 1955). It is estimated that between the 1450s and 1460s, when the brisk diffusion of printing began, and 1500, some 15 to 20 million items flowed from the presses. Not all were books by any means; the majority was as ephemeral as the calendar which, dated 1448, is the oldest surviving product of Johannes Gutenberg's printing house, or the indulgences which so infuriated Luther in the next century.

It is, however, to fall into the trap of technological determinism to overstate how much print technology meant to Luther's effectiveness. Thomas Hobbes' assessment should be kept in mind: 'The invention of *Printing*, though ingenious, compared with the invention of *Letters*, is no great matter'

(Hobbes, 2002 [1651]: 21, italics in original). The press, after all, was as much available to the Church to combat heresy as it was to the heretics to spread their ideas. The war of pamphlets Luther's rebellion instigated produced *Lutheran Maniacs* as well as *The Donkey Pope* and both sides indulged in vicious printed propaganda. Sixteenth-century Protestantism triumphed in the marketplace of ideas, at least in northwestern Europe, because it was selling a more effective message, not merely because its case was made, in part, in print. Luther himself was, moreover, in an unambiguous line of dissent stretching back centuries. Printing had not hitherto been a necessary condition for the spread of heresy. So although print certainly played a role in the efficient spread of Protestantism, the argument cannot be that without printing Luther's success would have been impossible.

As is often the case with technological innovations, the development depended less on the discovery of new knowledge than on the astute application of prior understanding and technique (see Chapters 6.2, 7.1, 8.1, 9.1, 9.2). With print, all the essentials were certainly known and in use – fundamentally the press (to be found in the manufacturing of oil and wine and the increasing production of paper) and metal-casting (punches and stamps). It is social circumstances, not the individual discovery of new science, that produces the 'invention', a term which is therefore something of a misnomer (Winston, 1998). Printing was not 'invented' in the classic 'Eureka' sense, for nothing new was needed or discovered to produce the flatbed press. The goldsmith Gutenberg's only truly original contribution was, perhaps, a hand-held mould for casting sorts.

Printing from moveable type occurs in the West in the mid-fifteenth century because of two distinct prime movers. One was the Church and the other the town. For the Church, print was a blessing and also, as was soon revealed, a curse. It promulgated the Word but it also distributed heresy. Controlling print, though, was straightforward, at least in theory. Any unsanctioned expression was anathema to the Church and was forbidden – a somewhat black-and-white matter. For secular authorities, the challenge was slightly more complicated. The press was of use for official communications but unauthorized printing was not, automatically, seditious. It could, in certain circumstances, also be of value: news, for example. Prior to print, this had been as much as possible a closely guarded state monopoly but now news, some of it, was of value to the markets in which law-abiding burghers and professionals conducted their business. Distinguishing between the useful and the damaging was challenging. Outright prohibition was not necessarily the answer.

The Church, then, was itself initially a prime mover providing part of the supervening social necessity that led Gutenberg and, almost certainly, others into the system engineering that put together the printing press in the mid-fifteenth century.[2] Demands, such as that made by Cusenius, for accurate texts created a market need beyond scribal capacity. Printing was greeted as 'an ascent towards God', 'a divine art' (Febvre and Martin, 1977: 171). Among the first hundred presses were some sited at monasteries – Cluny and Cîteaux, for example – replacing major scriptoria. Ecclesiastical authority was seduced by its own desire to exploit the technology but it quickly realized the dangers. Enthusiasm was soon replaced by fear and suspicion. As Pope Alexander IV, Leo's successor, put it: 'the art of printing can be of great service in so far as it furthers the circulation of useful and tested books; but it can bring about serious evils if it is permitted to widen the influence of pernicious works' (Putnam, 2003 [1906]: 80).

The Church had for centuries exercised a dominant position in the production of texts and direct control of the scriptoria afforded it a ready means of oversight, but it also knew how to deal with the danger of material written and copied outside its walls. Ecclesiastical authorities had first banned a book by edict of the Council of Ephesus in 150 CE. Even before Luther's effective use of the press vividly illuminated the danger, the papacy had acted. As early as 1479, Pope Sixtus V authorized the Rector and Dean of the University of Cologne to impose ecclesiastical penalties on all printing, selling or reading such texts as they determined to be heretical. The printers protested to Rome that censorship was killing their business and left the city. Bishops and rectors were not everywhere.

On the other hand, the Pope (when he put his mind to it as censor) was everywhere – albeit initially in an intermittent and rather haphazard way. Any text might fall foul and be denied an *imprimatur* – a right to be printed. In the same year that Luther was hammering his *Ninety-five Thesis* to the church door in Wittenberg, for example, Pope Leo had banned a printed edition of a work by Tacitus. One way for the printers to avoid difficulties was to seek prior approval for a text on a voluntary basis; or the authorities could establish a licensing system for the granting of such approvals. The award of a licence would then protect a printer's investment in an edition, affording the advantages of a monopoly to balance the negative restrictions of censorship. This form of prior constraint was matched by another idea, which caught on from the middle sixteenth century as the Church sought to extend its control over secular as well as religious printing. Since the flow of unsuitable material was proving to be unstoppable, publishing lists of books – *indices* – for the faithful to avoid was deemed necessary to the Church's spiritual health. The various ad hoc systems of control, licence and *index*, local and papal, which had grown up over the previous century, coalesced in 1559, when the Vatican itself undertook the task of issuing a comprehensive *Index Librorum Prohibitorum* (A List of Banned Books).

There was a problem with this rationalization of previous more local attempts to extend the *imprimatur* to cover all books, including secular works. Just as with the periodic burning of manuscripts, banning a work supplied it with the oxygen of publicity. It was, essentially, counter-productive. Luther was condemned in 1519 by theological faculties in Leuven and Cologne and by the Pope Leo on 15 June 1520; this last was marked with a burning of all his printed works and an effigy of the man himself for good measure. He also, of course, figured in the *Index*: reading the *libri et scripti omnia* of Martinus Lutherus meant excommunication. But: '*notabitur Romae, legetur ergo*' – 'if it is banned in Rome, then it's bound to be read'. Censors, though, have never been deterred by ineffectualness of their activities, much less by the exposure of their purblind lack of comprehension (most famously, perhaps, exemplified by the prohibition of Galileo and Copernicus); and the *Index* survived for four centuries until it was itself banned as inutile in 1966.

Secondly, there was the town: there were urban social forces also pushing the pioneers into engineering the system that produced printing. These arose from the reviving, post-Black Death urban world of the fifteenth century and matched the reformist impulses in the Church (Winston, 2005: 9). Although blessed by the religious demand for uncorrupted sacred texts, print was, in fact, in essence an urban child sired by ever-growing urban demand. Lawyers, doctors and merchants increasingly needed printed materials as much as did priests; and urban life in general increased the requirement for literacy, which itself made use of texts as teaching tools. Much of this urban thirst had been met, outside of the Church's scriptoria, with a sophisticated industry of manuscript production run by the stationers. In fact, the Church's monopoly over copying the word was already being significantly undercut by this urban activity prior to print. The stationers had long since created the edition – multiple copies of the same text. Many hands working simultaneously at different sections sped the production of complete books. Illustrations were commissioned from dedicated studios of limners and the final product was sent to specialized binderies. The trickle of secular, not to say pagan, ancient learning that had been entering Europe in the baggage of men such as Cusenius became as much a mainstay of urban manuscript production as did religious texts. Over 2,000 manuscript copies of Aristotle, for example, have survived from the century before Gutenberg. After the fall of Constantinople to the Turks in 1453, the trickle became a flood as Greek refugees fled Byzantium carrying a hoard of manuscripts with them into Western European exile.

Print well illustrates, at least at the outset of its diffusion, the truth of Marshall McLuhan's 'rearview mirror effect' – 'We see the world through a rear-view mirror. We march backwards into the future' (McLuhan, 1967: 75). Much was left in place. After all, printing from woodblocks – xylography – was already an established part of the stationers' business. The infrastructure of book making, distributing and selling remained the same. The first printed words, using Gutenberg's black-faced *textura* font, aped the manuscript style of the monastic scriptoria to disguise their mechanical origin. But in the course of the next century, the modern book emerged: paper instead of vellum; title pages, instead of the *incipit* – first word identification of manuscripts; through-numbered pages instead of chapter and verse; tables of contents, alphabetized indexing; cross-referencing (Eliot and Rose, 2009). Copperplates, which also came into use at this time, wore out more slowly than did the old woodblocks. Crucial labels on illustrations and diagrams therefore tended to wander less, copy to copy, and the production of uncorrupted scientific texts improved. And writing changed. The technical demands of print itself produce a revolution in fonts. Aldus Manutius (born Teobaldo Mannucci) was reprinting the ancient texts in Venice in the 1490s. He had his designer, Francesco Griffo, create a typeface more appropriate than *textura* black-face. Griffo turned to the lettering on Roman monuments and the result is before you as you read this page: the typeface is but a variation on Griffo's theme.[3]

The printing house was soon a site of modernity in more ways than one. The scribal function was made redundant, replaced by the printer, and with the printers also came the 'chapel' – the trade union shop. Printing houses had rapidly produced specialized job functions. Compositors and press-men often worked twelve-hour days with a day off only every other week. The first strikes for better conditions were recorded in 1539. Johann of Speyer, one of Gutenberg's original employees, took the flatbed press to Venice and, in 1469, was awarded a patent for the press so that 'over the next five years no one at all should have the desire, possibility, strength or daring to practise the said art of printing books in this the renowned state of Venice and its dominions,' except the said Johann (Venice State Archives). Patenting contents – copywriting – took longer to establish as a legal precedent. In the common law, when it was introduced in the early eighteenth century, it reserved the right to the publisher of the physical book rather than to the owner of the intellect that provided its contents; that is, the author.

Royal and noble courts (some of which – being held by princes of the Church – were also ecclesiastical) were as eager as was the Church itself to exploit the technology for their own secular purposes of informing the citizenry and moulding public opinion. The monastic scriptoria had their counterparts, after all, in medieval royal chanceries. Although proclamations and writs of instruction persisted in being handwritten on vellum after the diffusion of the technology, the authorities also began to use the new method of printing for a variety of purposes (Bellanger, 1969; Shaaber, 1966 [1929]; Smith, 1979). The French throne printed up the texts of its treaties and government ordinances began to appear in printed copies but, as the term for these publications indicates, they were *occasionnels*. Before the turn of the sixteenth century one every two months or so was the norm. The practice was not limited to France. For example, at that time, Matthias Corvinus, King of Hungary and Bohemia, was in intermittent and long-standing conflict with his neighbour, the Prince of Wallachia, Vlad III. That the latter is well known to us as Vlad the Impaler – Dracula – speaks to the effectiveness of Matthias' propaganda war against him. Take, for instance, the 1485 printed pamphlet *Dracole Waida* (*The Devil*

Prince), replete with a vivid woodcut of Vlad calmly lunching at an open-air table, uncaring of the forest of impaled corpses behind him.

In 1486, Henry VII of England had printed a broadsheet containing the text of the Papal Bull confirming the legitimacy of his seizure of the throne from Richard III and his marriage to Elizabeth of York. The first commercially printed pamphlet in English devoted to chronicling a recent occurrence, the Battle of Flodden Field between the English and the Scots in 1513, appeared soon after the clash: *Hereafter ensue the trewe encountre of batayle lately don betwene Englade and Scotlande* (Shaaber, 1966 [1929]: 121; Oates, 1951). That same year, a printed digest of reports was published in Poland: *Neue Zeitung auss Litten und von den Muscowitte (News from Lithuania and concerning the Muscovites)* reporting the Russian invasion of Lithuania, a matter of obvious concern to the Polish king, Sigismund the Old (Ingelhart, 1987: 16). In such publications the printers were not emulating the slow pace of the chroniclers but rather following that of the wandering minstrels, albeit on paper and in prose. In the fourteenth century, for instance, one such troubadour, Laurence Minot, had produced a series of ballads 'trewly to tell' of recent English victories over the French in the Hundred Years War and over the Scots (James and Simons, 1989).

Print, clearly, was of use to thrones. Henry VIII of England even joined in the religious pamphlet war then raging. In 1521, his *Assertio septem sacramentorum adversus Martinum Lutherum (Defence of the Seven Sacraments against Martin Luther)* earned him the title '*Fidei Defensor*' ('Defender of the Faith') from a grateful Pope.[4] Like the young Henry, the Holy Roman (i.e. German) Emperor Charles V was also moved that same year to support Rome. Rather than write against Luther, he simply censored him, enacting a *fatwa* (as it were) – an imperial 'edict and mandate': 'Against each and every one of the books and writings under the name of the said Luther already published or to be published, and also against those who henceforth will print, buy, or sell those books and writings' (Jensen, 1973: 75).

By 1536, though, Henry, in consequence of his marital difficulties, had declared himself head of an English Church. He had *The determination of the universities of Italy and Fraunce, that it is so unlawfull for a man to marie his brothers wyfe, that the pope hath no power to dispence therewith* printed as a pamphlet. It was part of his propaganda strategy to justify his dispute with the Pope over the 'Great Matter' of his divorce. He also used the press to tackle resistance to his new Church. One pamphlet that same year addressed the arguments of the northern rebels risen, in a 'Pilgrimage of Grace', to oppose the new dispensation and the dissolution of the monasteries. Continuous opposition to the Henrician religious settlement fuelled 'Kett's Rebellion' in the following reign. It too occasioned a printed response.

More than that: beyond using the press in such disputes, printed publications could also less contentiously re-enforce the majesty of the Crown in happier circumstances. The French fifteenth-century *occasionnels* included reports of Charles VIII's royal progresses. In England, Henry VIII publically chronicled his reign in pamphlets: *Joyfull medytacyon of the coronacyon of Henry the eyght*; *The noble tryumphaunt Coronation of Quene Anne*; and so on. Nevertheless, as with the Church, so with the state: the press was a two-edged sword and states marched with Church in seeking to control it – not only for heresy but also for sedition. They licensed printers, as in Venice in 1469. They used the *imprimatur* on individual texts; the Duke of Milan, for example, issued a five-year licence in 1483 to print the *Convivium* of the early humanist Francesco Filelfo. They issued *indices*: the English Crown did so in 1529 and followed up with the prior constraint of a licensing system the following year. Every work published in France after 1563 needed the Chancellor's seal.

The crucial step in England, however, was taken in 1557 by Mary Tudor. By granting a royal charter to the Company of Stationers (which now also included bookbinders as well as booksellers), in effect she acquired their services as the agents of control over 'the mistery or art of Stationery'. In return the printers obtained, *avant la lettre*, a virtual copyright on their products. Mary's purpose was exactly 'to provide a suitable remedy against the seditious and heretical books which were daily printed and published' (Blagden, 1960: 21). Policing was willingly forthcoming because the Company was as eager to protect its own monopoly over production, distribution and sales as it was to defend the Crown's interests. They delivered the service by requiring that all works be registered with them at Stationers Hall.

The members of the Company were master-printers who had been admitted to this rank after vetting by the Archbishop of Canterbury and the Bishop of London. The churchmen determined how many presses the kingdom needed – initially twenty-five, subsequently falling to twenty – and, therefore, how many masters to allow. Presses outside London, except in the universities of Oxford and Cambridge, were not licensed and most towns and cities did not get one until, with the power of the throne much altered, the early eighteenth century (Blagden, 1960: 71). Although this example of the English genius for devolving governmental functions to front organizations was weakened somewhat when Queen Elizabeth I gave the Court of the Star Chamber oversight of the Company, nevertheless the trade was, in effect, its own censor. The French Crown followed suit in 1618 with a *Chambre des Syndicats* but Louis XIII undercut the elegance of the English arrangement by insisting court officials sat in on the printers' meetings. This made the *Chambre* into an overt organ of state – which the Company, brilliantly, was not.

Control did not work, of course. A flatbed printer broke down into a comparatively light load for a horse and cart. Assembled, it could fit into any room or barn and it was but a day's work to produce a hundred or more sheets. In the reign of Elizabeth, for example, in 1588, the year of the Armada, anonymous Presbyterian pamphlets signed 'Martin Marprelate' appeared attacking the episcopacy of the new Church of England with a satire every bit as ferociously offensive as the Lutherans had ever deployed against the Church of Rome. Here sedition mixed with a new heresy: Presbyterianism was as threatening to the Church of England as the rebels' Catholicism had been in previous reigns.

It was under the umbrella of such controversies that the first professional writers – in the sense of people who tried to live by their pens alone – emerged. Taking the part of the bishops in the Marprelate controversy was one of Thomas Nashe's earliest professional efforts. A master of the colloquial voice, he was to write pamphlets, prefaces, poetry, humour and the first picaresque novel in English. The arrival of such figures bolstered the printer's entrepreneurial capacity. Among their most vendible opportunities, though, was the printing of regular news; but this was to be as fraught as publishing any overtly seditious writing. Controlling the latter through direct censorship was not easy but it was a straightforward task for the authorities. On the other hand, the changing economic system mandated printed news, publicly distributed, and so a far more nuanced response than extirpation was required.

4.2   *The Master & Wardens of the Company of Stationers v. Mr John Milton* (1644): For an unlicensed press

Unlike seditious publications, printed news was not self-evidently noxious; on the contrary, much of it was of overt economic value to the state. Nevertheless, the first instinct of the authorities had been to maintain their monopoly, even in the face of truthful reporting. In 1544, for example, Henry VII had banned the printing of newsbooks because:

> certain light persones not regarding what they reported, wrote, or sett forthe had caused to be imprinted and divulged certaines newes of the prosperous successes of the King's Majesties's army in Scotland, whereas, although the effect of the victory was indeed true, yet the circumstances in divers points were in some parte over slenderly, in some parte untruly and amisse reported (Andrews, 1859: 23–4).

This blanket hostility, even to favourable publications, could not be maintained since the state was committed to economic growth. Mercantilism and then capitalism were the agents of such growth and they each had an insatiable need for information. Trade and industry could not function well without it. News was as much a necessity to the burgher as potentates had long demonstrated it to be for them. The returning ambassador – men famously 'sent to lie abroad for their country' – provided rulers with the accounts of events and insights that the exercise of state power required. Now the merchants required no less.

For urban citizens, this need for information was met in part by gatherings that brought people of affairs together, such as court sessions in London or the great European trade fairs. These functioned as much as marts of news as they did of business. Early German and Italian bankers also established, via their factors, their own information networks. The bankers' factors set up permanent foreign residencies earlier than did the royal ambassadors whose sojourns were still temporary. Factors returned regular reports to headquarters where they were hand-copied to be shared with privileged clients. By the first half of the sixteenth century, these reports had become, in effect, intermittent newsletters and the idea of such a communication had spread. In London, some of the surviving scriveners, or students at the Inns of Court acting as scriveners, became professional news-gatherers for the purpose of copying and selling correspondence of this kind to subscribers scattered across the country (Raymond, 2005: 5). St Paul's became notorious as a clearing-house for news: 'It is the eares Brothell and satisfies their lust, and ytch' as Bishop John Earle noted in the early seventeenth century (Earle, 1811 [1628]: 105).

The Duke of Newcastle suggested to Charles II that such privately circulated documents did the throne much harm and should be banned because 'every man has now become a statesman, both home and abroad merely due to the weekly gazette' (Baron, 2001: 41).[5] The advice was unheeded and, by the 1660s, Henry Muddiman, for instance, was issuing subscribers, for some as often as three-times a week, a private hand-copied newsletter for the hefty fee of £5 per annum. Muddiman was successful because, with excellent Royalist connections, he had established an extensive private network of informers, spies, postmasters, clergy and customs officials. These were also among his readers and he generally encouraged 'citizen journalism' by asking all of them to send him news: 'Sir. In your last you desired me acquaint you what non-conformists, papists and others were indicted at quarter sessions ...' (Sutherland, 2004: 6). By the early eighteenth century, the handwritten copy had finally yielded to print. The newsletters still sometimes used italic fonts and the opening salutation 'S^r' to reflect their epistolary origins. They are with us yet in the extremely high-priced form of subscription publications, now electronically transmitted, produced for particular commercial and industrial sectors.

For the limited number of newsletter recipients, there was then, as now, no reason to make the news public. On the contrary: the power the information bestowed, as with the noble ambassadors reports, was its point, one that was lost without privacy. The very fact of widely publicizing general news was still seen as something improper, encouraging, as a contemporary put it: 'lavish and licentious talking in matters of state, either at home or abroad, which the common people know not how to understand' (Raymond, 2005: 8). In fact, if news was printed and freely sold, could it even still be news? As Ben Jonson has characters explain in his 1625 satire, *The Staple of News*:

– O Sir! it is the printing we oppose.
– We not forbid that any *News* be made,
But that't be printed; for when *News* is printed,
It leaves, Sir, to be *News,* while 'tis but written –
– Though it be ne're so false, it runs *News* still (Jonson, 1625: Act 1, Sc 5)

The advantages to be gained from retailing information of a political or economic nature remained far from self-evident. The letters of the late medieval bankers' factors, and their successors, can therefore be seen not only as a precursor of, and a parallel to, the newspaper but also, paradoxically, a cause for the slow development of the printed, publically sold version. In the sixteenth and seventeenth centuries, the merchants' taste for privileged private information matched the hostility of secular authorities to the broadcasting, as it were, of commercial, diplomatic and political – especially internal political – information.

There were, however, contrary pressures coming from the printers and the public; the former to make money, the latter to be informed and entertained. This standoff between repressive forces and public appetite would take the better part of two centuries after Gutenberg to resolve (but not remove – the tension persists).[6] Despite official publications and private newsletters prior to 1500, nothing appeared in print in the incunabula era prior to 1500 that can be seen as a direct antecedent of the newspapers.

News, nevertheless, offered printers an obvious entrepreneurial opportunity. Even though printing attracted the attention of officialdom, it was clearly worth the risk; and, intermittently, news publications did begin to appear after 1500 in the form of the 'newsbook'. The public had a demonstrable thirst for them. For every merchant wishing to keep information secret, there were rivals wishing to know it. More than that, there was also a human desire for news and gossip – for sensation and excitement – which rendered the printing of such material vendible. Take Vlad having his gruesome lunch in *Dracole Waida*, for example. It might have been political propaganda but it was titillating, memorable. The *trewe encountre* and *Neue Zeitung* publications, whose contents and titles turn them into the earliest surviving sixteenth-century newsbooks, speak to this appetite too. The Polish example precociously introduced the very term by which this type of publication would be known: *Zeitung.* To this day, it is the German for 'newspaper'. In English, this term 'newspaper' was slower to arrive; in fact, it does not enter the language for another 160 some years. On the other hand, that the English newsbook announced itself in 1513 as 'trewe' was of great significance. News publications were to be called many things before the modern terms were settled on; but what they all had in common across Europe was an explicit or implicit claim on the truth – even if truth was not always actually in evidence.

The sensationalist news-agenda – accounts of dreadful crimes, natural disasters and unnatural occurrences, often illustrated with crude woodcuts as in *Dracole Waida* – demanded exploitation, so patent was public appetite for it. However, from the outset, this agenda threatened journalism's claim of truth, with 'truth' more a sales pitch rather than a guarantee of content. Sensation, safer to print than political or economic news, was very vendible; but sensation was ever a threat to veracity. That the material be 'trewe' soon became rather optional. The word '*veritable*' – real, genuine, true – was frequently invoked especially in the titles of the newsbooks devoted to miracles. These publications were, after all, in parallel to the flood of overheated religious pamphleteering appearing both in learned Latin and all the vernacular languages. The point is that the modern tabloid newspaper's contents, and its often cavalier way with fact, are as time-honoured as the broadsheet's more sober and respectable diet of serious coverage. The justification for being economical with the truth was that, despite its use to bolster journalism's saleability, the activity from the outset was, in fact, as much to do with entertainment as with veracity. The excuse for this is equally time-honoured. As Jonson has the hero of *The Staple of News* say of journalism's abuse of truth:

> Why, methinks, Sir, if the honest common People
> Will be abus'd, why should not they ha' their pleasure
> In the believing Lyes, are made for them (Jonson, 1625: Act 1, Sc 5)

The lies of the sensationalist newsbooks, though, were not the problem for authority. It was the serious 'quality' news agenda covering current political and economic affairs that evoked the more repressive response. Nevertheless such was the public's thirst that the printers eventually began to brave official disapproval and were emboldened to begin publications devoted to such self-evidently contentious but saleable material. To create the newspaper (that is: an unbound, regularly issued, sequentially numbered, printed digest of current events and, eventually, opinion), printers had to produce public, not private, newsletters; print combinations of newsletters and reports from their correspondents; print these combinations on a regular basis; and, finally, absorb the agenda of the newsbooks and the pamphlets. In the face of hostility, despite public support, the innovative effort to establish journalism as a new type of legitimate activity took decades and only made progress when the authoritarian political grip was, for one reason or another, weakened.

It was in republican Venice that, from the 1530s, the authorities shared with their fellow citizens regular *Notizie* and *Avisi*. These echoed the ancient public notices of the doings of the Roman Senate, the *Acta Diurna*, which had been posted on white boards, albums. The Venetian single subject newsletters, at first handwritten and subsequently printed, were widely distributed but were also read aloud at certain places in the city. Illiterate citizens of the republic could pay a small coin, a *gazzetta*, to listen. The publications were as much a precursor of twentieth-century broadcast news bulletins as of seventeenth-century newspapers. The term, in English 'gazette', came to denote the newsletter, private or public. By 1570, they were appearing in many cities in the German lands. By the 1590s, enterprising printers were gathering such publications together for reprinting as digests: *News Lately come on the last day of Februarie* (1591); or, *Certen newes written towardes London from Italye Fraunce Hungarie and other places* (1602).

Another option was also being explored. Following the occasional *aviso* which appeared after the great fairs, in 1594, Michael ap Isselt began publishing in Latin in Cologne a periodical digest of recent events on a twice yearly basis. It was a sort of cross between the old idea of the chronicle and the new fashion for newsletters. The *Mercurius Gallobelgicus*, as its name implied, focused on events in France and the Low Countries but he also covered Spain, Italy, England, Germany and Poland. It circulated widely through Europe and only ceased publication in 1635. It was emulated and it gave a further name to news publications: *Mercuries*, with 'mercurists' as a term for those who wrote for them. This was not only a pleasingly classical reference to the messenger of the Gods; it also offered a measure of protection. The mercurist was, after all, only a messenger.

Obviously, though, the newsletter digests were a clearer way forward (Boyce, Curran and Wingate, 1978; Frank, 1961; Black, 2001; Harris and Lee, 1986). Given that developments in journalism required authority to be at least somewhat distracted, it is no accident that the next stage, the printing of such digests on a regular basis, took place in Europe's other republic, the then recently independent United Provinces of the Netherlands. In the midst of a fifty-year war to throw off Spanish rule (the last three decades of which were part of a general European conflagration), printing flourished. Indeed, Dutch printing, not just of news, constituted a major breech in all other countries' attempts to control their own presses. What those authorities banned, the Dutch profitably published in the appropriate vernacular and smuggled back across the borders.

The military setbacks suffered by the Dutch in the first years of the seventeenth century distracted the local licensing authority, the States General. Printers such as Abraham Verhoeven and Caspar van Hilten seized the opportunity. Verhoeven began his *Nieuwe Tijdinghen*, marked by unusually fine engravings rather than the usual crude woodcuts, in Antwerp in 1605. He was publishing weekly by 1617. The following year, in Amsterdam, van Hilten had started a weekly *Courante uyt Italien, Duytslant &c* and that term, 'Coranto' in English, also caught on. Verhoeven was being translated into French from 1615 and both French and English editions of van Hilten appeared. Corantos sprung up all across Europe over the next decade. In 1620, another Amsterdam printer, George Veseler, employed Pieter van der Keere to produce one in English especially for export across the Channel. The continental war, the climactic struggle between Protestants and Catholics, was the big story. The conflict was to last for thirty years.

After some false starts, Dutch-style corantos started to appear in English, printed in London. Domestic news, though, had been clearly forbidden by a decree of the Star Chamber in 1586; and even foreign reports could see the printer thrown into prison. Nevertheless, the printers went on defiantly publishing 'every week (at least) corantos with all manner of newes, and as strange stuffe as any we have from Amsterdam' (Raymond, 2005: 8). By the time of the outbreak of the English Civil War in 1641, two senior freemen of the Company of Stationers, Nathaniel Bourne and Nathaniel Butter,[7] had been publishing a coranto, eventually known as the *Weekly News*, with print runs of between 250 and 600 copies in each edition, for a number of years.

The isomorphism between the stability of governments and the development of journalism – the stronger the former, the slower the latter – was now to be seen in England. Civil commotion was to be the midwife of the journalism of the English-speaking world. It was in English that the preceding century's worth of experiments was to be melded together into the modern newspaper: combative, opinionated, competitive and, of course, titillating and entertaining, as well as threatening to authority by its very nature. During the upheaval of the Civil War in middle decades of the seventeenth century, on the London presses the objectivity of publications from the *gazzetti* to the corantos was bonded with the sensationalism of the newsbooks and, eventually, the opinion of the pamphlets. Innovations took place elsewhere, such as the first daily paper – the *Einkommende Zeitung* (*Incoming News*) – which appeared in Leipzig in 1650; but the tradition of official information held greater sway and accommodated these developments. The changes in English practice were more draconian. The modern newspaper, as the exemplum of what the 'free press' could, indeed should, look like, emerged in England as Stuart absolutism faltered.

When King Charles I was forced by Act of Parliament to abolish the court of the Star Chamber in 1641, and with it the prerogatives of the Company of Stationers, this style of English newspaper was quick to appear. First, the vexed question of reporting on the affairs 'of the three kingdoms' was resolved. Without clear authority, 'now by strange alteration and vicissitude of times we talke of nothing else but what is done in England' (Raymond, 2005: 145). The corantos became weekly journals – 'Diurnals', 'Mercuries' or 'Intelligences' – devoted to the big domestic story, the Civil War. They promised, and often delivered, as one motto (masthead or tagline) had it: 'Truth impartially related from thence [London] to the whole Kingdome, to prevent mis-information.'

The speed of the press had increased in the early seventeenth century with the introduction of a counterweight to raise the platen. Now it was possible to produce some 150 impressions per hour (iph), around a tenfold increase over Gutenberg's rate. Over 2,000 sheets a day were within the capacity of a print shop with, say, two flatbeds. A bestselling title, the scrivener Samuel Pecke's *Diurnall Occurrences* of 1641 and 1642, or his *Perfect Diurnall* thereafter, could sell 3,000 copies an edition. Pecke was also among the pioneers of what was eventually to be another profound development. He sold space in his journals for advertising books and land-sales, an innovation that much enhanced his profit but did not earn him praise: 'Peck [sic] the Perfect Diurnall maker, the last page of which most commonly he lets out to the Stationers for sixpence a piece to place therein the titles of their books' (Keith Williams, 1977: 164). Over the coming centuries, the power of commercial announcements to subvert the integrity of the press would become an increasingly persistent worry.

In the heat of war and upheaval, others were less sober and the English press owes more to Marchmont Nedham, an Oxford graduate, than to ex-scriveners and printers such as Pecke and his fellow diurnalists. They attempted a measure of accuracy and sober reporting. The Parliamentarian Nedham, and Sir John Birkenhead, his Royalist opponent, did not. Nedham became Oliver Cromwell's leading propagandist after being publisher of the main Parliamentary journal, the *Mercurius Britannicus* (which had revived a title sometimes used by Butter and Bourne). This had promised that it would be *Communicating the affaires of great Britaine: For the better Information of the People*, but, in Nedham's hands, its tone was far from sober:

> Where is King Charles? What's become of him? The strange variety of opinions leaves nothing certain: for some say, when he saw the Storm coming after him as far as Bridgewater, he ran away to his dearly beloved in Ireland; yes, they say he ran away out of his own Kingdome very Majestically ... Because there is such a deale of uncertainty; and therefore (for the satisfaction of my Countrymen) it were best to send a Hue and Cry after him. If any man can bring tale or tiding of a wilfull King, which hath gone astray these foure years from his Parliament, with a guilty Conscience, bloody Hands, a Heart full of broken Vowes and Protestations ... Then give notice to Britannicus, and you shall be well paid for your paines: So God save the Parliament. (Nedham, 1645)

Nedham, at age twenty-three, had been deputed to combat the *Mecurius Aulicus* being produced at the King's headquarters in Oxford by Birkenhead. Birkenhead had begun the war in print but Nedham soon caught up. For example, he published Charles I's private letters, captured after the disastrous Royalist defeat at Naseby in 1643. He also contributed to the development of printed advertisements, running a separate journal for that purpose, the *Public Advisor*. Yet for him, the principle business of the mercurist was less such scoops and revenue-raising ventures than it was to write a persuasive propagandistic descant on the affairs of the day. As he was to explain to his readers: 'I tooke up my pen for disabusing his Majesty, and for disbishoping and dispoing his good subjects, and for taking off vizards and vailes and disguises which the Scribes and Pharisees at Oxford had put upon a treasonable and Popish cause' (Frank, 1961: 59).

Such partisanship was not new; it was the stuff of pamphleteering. Indeed, in his colloquial style Nedham was following pamphleteers such as Thomas Nashe; but Nashe was no newsman. Nedham was and that is what was new. The importation of opinion, colloquial address and the possibility of giving offence in a news publication where it had previously not been sanctioned and had not appeared is the essential development of the press during the English Civil War. The mixture was potent, as Anthony à Wood, writing at the time in Royalist Oxford, attested: 'Siding with the rout and scum of the people [Nedham] made them weekly sport by railing at all in his Intelligence called *Mercurius Britannicus*, wherein his endeavours were to sacrifice the fame of some lord, or any person of quality, and of the king himself, to the beast with many heads' (Andrew, 1859: 42).

Cromwell had needed Nedham to counter Birkenhead. Both he and Charles I, though, were unable fully to monitor these vitriolic pens. Not that they did not try. After the abolition of the Star Chamber a 'Committee of Examinations' was appointed by the Parliamentarians to continue to exert control over printing (Jebb, 1918: xvii). In June 1643, they re-empowered the Company of Stationers to register all titles prior to publication (Blagden, 1960: 146). The following August, John Milton, poet, pamphleteer and schoolmaster, addressed an anonymous pamphlet, scandalously arguing for divorce, to the Parliament: *The Doctrine and Discipline of Divorce, Restored to the good of both sexes from the Bondage of Canon Law and other Mistakes to the true meaning of the scripture in the law and gospel compared.*

Milton was thirty-five and had just married Mary Powell who was half his age. This had not been a success and, within a month, Mary had returned to her family. He followed up the *Doctrine and Discipline* pamphlet with a second recalling the arguments propounded a century earlier during the 'Great Matter' of Henry VIII's divorce. Milton took no notice of the recently restored powers of the Company and the publications were unlicensed. However, even among the spate of unsanctioned publications that had appeared after the Star Chamber was abolished, Milton's work was thought to be egregiously offensive. It confirmed the view of the Lords that licensing was urgently needed: 'Ordered, the gentleman-usher attending this house, shall repair to the Lord Mayor of London, and the master and wardens of the Company of Stationers, to them know, that this house expects a speedy account of them, what they have done in finding out the author, printer, or publisher of the scandalous libel' (Ivimey, 1833: 59).

The Company had 'Messengers' for such tasks and soon reported back that: 'they had used their best endeavours to find out the printer and author of the scandalous libel; but they cannot yet make any discovery thereof'.

Milton's response to the Stationers' search was the *Areopagitica, A speech of Mr. John Milton for the Liberty of VNLICENC'D PRINTING, to the*

PARLIAMENT OF ENGLAND, the first great plea for free media in the language, signed and published – but still unlicensed – on 25 November 1644:

> If we think to regulate printing, thereby to rectify manners, we must regulate all recreations and pastimes, all that is delightful to man ... A little generous prudence, a little forbearance of one another, and some grain of charity might win all these diligences to join, and unite in one general and brotherly search after Truth; could we but forego this prelatical tradition of crowding free consciences and Christian liberties into canons and precepts of men ... Believe it, Lord and Commons, they who counsel ye to such suppressing, do as good as bid ye suppress yourselves. (Milton, 1963 [1644]: 53)

Milton might well have set off down this road because of his marital difficulties and he might well have had a limited vision of the freedom for which he was arguing. In the great phrase 'As good almost kill a man as kill a good book' the crucial adjective is 'good'. Milton's sense of the right for which he was arguing might not apply, say, to Catholics, whose books were, to Puritans such as him, far from 'good'. No more did Euripides have slaves in mind when he wrote the tag Milton translated for the title page of the *Areopagitica*: 'This is true liberty when free born men having to advise the public may speak free.' Such caveats aside, the words he wrote so ringingly, nevertheless, encapsulated the right and its importance: 'Give me the liberty to know, to utter, and to argue freely according to conscience, above all liberties.'

In response, the Stationers were quick to petition Parliament. A month after the *Areopagitica* appeared, they were remonstrating against the 'frequent printing of scandalous Books by divers as Hezekiah Woodward and Jo. Milton' (Forsyth, 2009: 92). Parliament ordered the writers to appear before the magistrates but there is no record of Milton doing so. This is but one indication that the reimposition by the Commonwealth of the Tudor censorship apparatus was not going to be straightforward. In general, the Company of Stationers was outmanoeuvred in the conditions of war. A year after their powers were restored, unlicensed printing still continued. Not even the flow of Royalist publications could be interrupted: the *Mecurius Aulicus* was available in Parliamentarian London every week together with eleven other news publications. The *Areopagitica* not only argued for a free press; in the event, its distribution was also a demonstration of it.

Yet Milton had not solved the problems thrown up by the exercise of free expression. He had not been minded, it would seem, to confront them directly at all. In March 1649, he was appointed Secretary of Foreign Tongues, or Latin Secretary, to the Committee of Foreign Affairs, in Cromwell's republican government. It was a post he was to hold for the ten years of the Interregnum of Commonwealth and Protectorate. Startlingly, given his previous rhetoric, the licensing of publications was added to his duties by Cromwell in 1655 in yet another attempt to control the presses (Forsyth, 2009: 109–10). Unlicensed printing, after all, was only a right to be allowed for 'good' books and 'bad' heretical Catholic, seditious Royalist, pornographic and other blasphemous publications kept appearing. They required censoring and Milton was the censor. However, his flexible behaviour cannot, and does not, diminish the force of his argument in the *Areopagitica*. It does, though, illustrate what would be a regular feature in the struggle for free expression: that there is no necessary connection between the moral integrity of those arguing for, or excising, the right and the value of the right itself. In the marketplace of ideas, printing, including journalism, brings in train a sharpening of the contradictions between high-minded fundamentals and low or duplicitous practices. Milton, in this regard, was no better than Nedham.

Marchmont Nedham is very much the model for what would become the stereotypical journalist, a confusing mixture of the exalted and the debased. He fell out with Parliament, fled to Charles, only to upset him and flee back to Cromwell again. He was to gain the reputation of a cat, always landing on his feet. On the one hand, he could be passionate for a cause; on the other, he was a hack with extremely elastic principles – but, above all, he was a vivid and effective communicator. Arguably, it was this mix as much as the developing concept of what the constituent elements of 'news' were, that allowed him and his peers during the Civil War to lay the foundations for the English-speaking press. They delineated what would be thereafter its underlying scope, tone and attitude – especially its willingness to balance entertainment against truth in the former's favour. At its most extreme, the Royalist John Crouch's *Mecurius Democraticus* (later *Fumigosus*) mocked the serious new agenda as a *Perfect Nocturnall* (Crouch 1654–5; Frank, 1961: 229). Deliberatively offensive, satirically pornographic stories and jokes about farts, private parts and witches acquired an implicit oppositional political bite under the rule of the Puritans during the Interregnum. It was publications such as the *Fumigosus* that had moved Cromwell to reinforce the censorship apparatus.

The Restoration of 1660 brought Charles Stuart to the throne but he found it no easier than Cromwell had to control the press. Pressmen were as flexible in their loyalty as ever. Even the smuttiness continued: there is, for example, a 'three-in-a-bed romp' story involving a dissenting parson in the *Loyal Protestant*, a propaganda paper, of 1682 (Harris and Lee, 1986: 35). The producer of newsletters, Henry Muddiman, was an enthusiastic supporter of the Restoration. He was asked by the authorities to undertake the publication of printed news, which he did: the *Parliamentary Intelligencer*, followed by the *Mercurius Publicus* and the *Kingdom's Intelligencer* – all 'Published by Order'. With Birkenhead, he was awarded a monopoly but that did not buy subservience. He told Samuel Pepys he was in the business 'only to get money' and, as for his political masters, he 'did talk very basely of many of them'. Pepys thought him 'a good scholar' but an 'arch rogue' (Pepys, 1659–60). The genie of a free press had been let out of the bottle and would not be easily controlled ever again. As a result, there is nothing in today's newspapers that would strike a seventeenth-century reader as truly novel. Apart from photographs instead of engravings and sport, all other sorts of stories – foreign and domestic, political, economic and social (including crime and scandal) – were covered and little mud remained un-slung.

Partisan squibs, libelling Protestant divines, for example, might have been to the taste of the restored court but, as ever, the output of the press was at least as likely to be hostile to their cause as it was to cause them amusement. Charles II, though, lacked the absolute power of his forbears, and his efforts to force the press to toe the line were not effective. He could not, for example, simply re-establish a Star Chamber, so he had to find new remedies acceptable to Parliament. In 1662, a Licensing Act was brought in: 'for preventing the frequent Abuses in printing seditious, treasonable, and unlicensed Books and Pamphlets, for the regulating of Printing and printing Presses'. The abuses were the 'heretical, schismatical, blasphemous, and treasonable books, pamphlets and papers' that constantly appeared. An Office of the Surveyor of the Press was established with specific, Star Chamber-like, censorship powers but also with the additional monopoly of news publication. Registration was required but, instead of the Company of Stationers pursuing unlicensed presses, the Surveyor was given the right of a general warrant. This, uniquely, named no suspects. To serve them, the Surveyor took over the Company of Stationers' Messengers who now became the King's Messengers to the Press with the power 'to search all houses and shops where they shall know, or upon some probable reason suspect any books and papers to be printed, bound or stitched, especially printing houses, booksellers shops and warehouses, and bookbinders' houses and shops'.[8]

Roger L'Estrange, fervent Royalist and author of *Considerations and Proposals In Order to the Regulation OF THE PRESS TOGETHER WITH Diverse Instances of Treassonous, and Seditious Pamphlets, Proving the Necessity thereof*, was appointed Surveyor. L'Estrange, who believed 'it is the Press that has made 'um Mad, and the Press must set 'um Right again', was not quite the ideal choice his opinions suggested he would be (Goldie, 2008). He might have thought, ideally enough for a censor, that print 'makes the multitude too familiar with the actions and counsels of their superiors, too pragmatical, too censorious'; but, although a prolific pamphleteer, he was no journalist, a flaw even in a news monopolist. He immediately ousted Muddiman and Birkenhead, to produce the *Intelligencer. Published for the Satisfaction of the People*, *The Newes*; and, later, the *Observator*. These might have been issued 'With Privilege' but they were also insufficiently popular, which rendered him vulnerable. During the plague year of 1665, the year when the word 'journalist' entered the language, Muddiman reingratiated himself with the court, which had removed to Oxford. His weekly *Oxford Gazette* was also printed 'By Authority', in two columns on a half folio sheet.

It was effective and L'Estrange was bought off as a news baron, although he remained 'Licensor'. When the court returned to London Muddiman's paper became the *London Gazette* and, after missing one issue because of the Great Fire of 1666, it has been continually published ever since. It has, though, metamorphosed from a journalistic 'newspaper' (a word new in 1670), into an 'Official Newspaper of Record for the UK' recording 'official, regulatory and legal information'.[9]

Although the task was obviously better suited to his tastes, in the long term L'Estrange really did not fare much better as a censor. The old problems of finding illicit presses persisted, of course, but that did not deter him. He was assiduous in seeking them out and seizing publications in his zeal to extirpate non-conformity and sedition. Yet it was no longer only a question of finding a press or copies of offending materials in bookshops. News was increasingly well distributed. Paradoxically, L'Estrange himself contributed to this. He introduced 'book women', who continued the old tradition of hawking broadsheets, to sell his newspapers. Newspapers were also an attraction in the new-fangled coffee-shops that had become a major physical expression of the English social sphere. Yet what was to prove debilitating was not the logistics of suppression, which of itself worked well enough overall, but a faltering political will.

The armed civil clashes of the middle decades of the century had settled into an ongoing conflict between two opposed wings of mainstream political opinion. Everybody was a Royalist now; but while some were happy to have royal power restored to the maximum extent it could be, others wished to preserve the hard-won prerogatives of Parliament against any such encroachments. Charles had not been, in the context of this ongoing struggle, strong enough to make the Licensing Act of 1662 permanent. Parliament had demanded the right to renew it every two years. In 1679, with Charles having prorogued the Commons because they were threatening to remove his Catholic brother James from the succession, the Act, un-renewed, fell by the wayside. As in 1641 following the abolition of the Star Chamber, too many unlicensed publications sprouted up for the King's Messengers to control them effectively. In 1683, Charles acted against these titles by proclamation. Five years later his successor, brother James II, managed to get the Act renewed until 1693 and extended thereafter for another two years.

When it came up for further renewal in 1695, the Whig, Edward Clarke, MP, and good friend of John Locke, argued that, as laws existed for the general control of expression, a specific law further to control the press was 'very needless' (Sutherland, 2004: 25). The phrase is Locke's: 'Every one being answerable for the books he publishes, prints or sells containing anything seditious or against law makes this or any other act for restraint of printing very needless' (King, 1829: 208).

The Act was not renewed and England, quietly through this lapse, became the first Western state to abandon formal censorship. It might be thought that such a momentous development would be celebrated in the liberal narrative of the nation but it is not. Locke's arguments remain buried among his 'minor essays' (Goldie, 1997), and Edward Clarke is no better remembered than any other seventeenth-century representative of the Taunton constituency. No great Miltonic cry for liberty was invoked, after all. Locke's case merely relied on the obvious: that the law already provided for the control of sedition, blasphemy, obscenity and libel. There was no suggestion that the older laws be reformed or liberalized. The lapsing of the Act did not mean that the authorities gave up attempting to control the press. Nevertheless, prior constraint of printing was soon to be thought fundamentally contrary to English law and the Surveyor of the Press, as Licensor, was himself rendered 'very needless'. In fact, the office had collapsed under a weight of corruption the previous year, 1694. These were no small matters. Most importantly, the lapse of the Act provided lift-off for the next stages of the struggle for press freedom.

For the moment (and, some would say, for long thereafter), the principle was to be no more than: publish and be damned. And damned one would most assuredly be. The law, after 1695, still stood ready to deal with any who offended by breaching these restrictions in print. The King's Messengers to the Press with their general warrants, licences to trawl, were not disbanded. As far as the authorities were concerned, special laws or no, as Lord Chief Justice Holt put it in 1704: 'If men should not be called to account for possessing the people with an ill opinion of the government, no government can subsist' (*R. v. Tutchin*, 1704: 527). The search for alternative systems for the control of political speech and other forms of printed expression which would not amount to prior constraint was underway. It was a quest that would not be abandoned in Britain until the 1860s.

4.3   *R. v. Wilkes* (1774): For libel trial by jury

English newspapers nevertheless continued to develop. Pamphleteering also flourished. There were now specialized magazines catering to ladies or learned societies or carrying nothing but literary and other reviews, or political comment, or just advertisements. The newspapers constantly absorbed their contents as additional features adding, for example, regular reviews and, by the end of the eighteenth century, printing opinion in the form of editorials. Their titles had become stable and the earliest corantos' changing lists of places, whence the reports they contained, were transforming into headlines. The first English daily appeared in 1702 but that, as its name – the *Daily Courant* – suggests, was the only innovative thing about it. It was a two-column, single sheet printed on one side and, in the old-fashioned way, it carried foreign news gleaned from continental publications. Other weekly, bi-weekly or tri-weekly newspapers employed, for the gathering of domestic news, the ill-regarded paid correspondents and hired informants: 'intelligencers'.

On the business side, distributing the paper emerged as the separate function of the publisher with yet others, often women, handling sales. London's first news kiosk selling this plethora of unbound publications was opened by Ann Dodd in 1721. Networks of hawkers crying the news through the streets, a necessity given that Britain's slow postal system rendered subscriptions delivered as mail basically unworkable, encouraged sensationalism. 'Read all about it', however, was no prescription for sobriety. The taste for sensation, present from the earliest newsbooks and sustained by the excesses of the newspaper war during the years of civil conflict, continued unabated into the eighteenth century and, indeed, up to the present. By 1750, the system was handling 100,000 copies of the newspapers and magazines a week.

Pre-publication censorship had come to be considered unconstitutional. By the mid-eighteenth century, at least as far as the press was concerned, legal opinion now agreed with the radical view of many political writers and thinkers from Milton, through Locke to John Trenchard, Thomas Gordon and others. The illegitimacy of censorship – 'prior constraint' – was a matter of settled law. It was offensive to the rights of those who the Civil War radical, John Lilburne, had dubbed 'free-born Englishmen'. In the 1760s, the great jurist William Blackstone in his authoritative *Commentaries on the Laws of England* put it thus: 'The liberty of the press is indeed essential to the nature of a free state; but this consists in laying no *previous* restraints on publications, and not in freedom from censure for criminal matter when published' (Blackstone, 1979 [1769]: 151).

In effect, publish and be damned was enshrined as the agreed position. The effect of this doctrine, though, was a long way from establishing a press actually free in practice. The freedom it brought was, at best, more designed to allow the technical possibility of equality of access rather than to enshrine any principle of free expression as a fundamental right. The majority of printers were simply in business and were by no means eager to look for the trouble that printing political news brought in its train. For them, this vision of the press as a freely accessible, neutral – as it were – channel of communication, albeit for a restricted range of information and opinion, was entirely acceptable (Pasley, 2001: 28).

The consequence was that, subsequent to the removal of the licensing system, no universal right was established; certainly none that could be applied to other modes of expression. Consider the different situation of the theatre throughout this period. Any public performance had to be vetted by the Lord Chamberlain, a system imposed by the Prime Minister Robert Walpole who brought in a theatrical Licensing Act in 1737 (see Chapter

6.1). The inconsistency of such blatant prior constraint on the one mode of expression but not on the other, and the dangers this posed as a precedent, was well understood. Arguing, futilely, against the Bill proposing stage censorship in the House of Lords, the Earl of Chesterfield said:

> The Bill now before you I apprehend to be of a very extraordinary, a very dangerous Nature. It seems designed not only as a restraint on the Licentiousness of the Stage; but it will prove a most arbitrary Restraint on the Liberty of the stage; and I fear, it looks yet further, I fear it tends towards a Restraint on the Liberty of the Press, which will be a long Stride towards the destruction of Liberty itself. (Chesterfield, 1737: 401)

The stage was fettered, but Lord Chesterfield's concern was otherwise unfounded. The theatrical Licensing Act of 1737 was not used as a precedent.[10] Matters had gone too far for prior constraint to be reimposed on print. Opinion was too firmly in support of at least a measure of press freedom.

Of course, some expression was clearly generally agreed to be unacceptable even in print and could be dealt with accordingly. The apparatus for the control of published religious opinion, for example, had developed in the sixteenth century and was still in place. As an outcrop of heresy, the offence of blasphemy, 'verbal offence against the sacred', easily embraced offending texts published in print. In 1612, Thomas Helwys, who had established London's first Baptist chapel, wrote a plea for religious liberty, *A Short Declaration of the Mistery of Iniquity*. He had the temerity to send a copy to James I and it earned him a prison sentence (Levy, 1995: 105).

With secular printing, on the other hand, a degree of legitimate censorship over some forms of cultural expression was agreed to be needed. Although some booksellers had been prosecuted for selling obscene material in the seventeenth century, the common law on obscene publications is grounded in a case of disturbing the peace. Legally, printed obscenity turned out to be within the aegis of the laws on vagrancy. It had nothing to do with censorship per se; it was – as with the wandering homeless poor, or strolling players – a matter of keeping the peace. This subtly removed the issue of free speech. Thus, Edmund Curll, publisher of an English translation of the late seventeenth-century French pornographic book, *Venus in the Closter*, in 1727, was found guilty of causing just such a disturbance. It was this case that afforded the precedent. Obscene expression was not protected but the press was still 'free'.

This did not really mean, though, that the press was really 'free'. History and public temper might have made overt prior control impossible, but the authorities continued to restrain the press by other uses of the law. To control political expression, three methods in particular came into play: the crime of seditious libel, usually uncovered by the widespread use of the general warrant; the specific prohibition of parliamentary reporting; and the imposition of taxes (money in) and bribery (money out). Public opinion, though, was not unaware of de facto censorship by these other means. The public was inclined to believe that the entire official effort was, in fact, 'very needless'. This was now a society that thought of itself as 'free', one where the press should be considered an accessible channel of more or less open communication.

For the authorities, it was just too 'free' for comfort. Circulations of individual titles had risen to the many thousands. In 1721, at the height of the South Sea Bubble economic scandal, the publisher of the weekly *London Journal* claimed to have sold 20,000 copies of one edition 'before the evening' of the day of publication (Sutherland, 2004: 229). Given multiple readership, in the coffee-houses for example, and the limited numbers of the elite, the penetration was significant. Moreover, with generally comparative high levels of literacy among the rest of London's teeming 700,000 population and throughout the kingdoms of Great Britain, it is easy to see the basis of official concern.

The forces of repression were everywhere, often exhibiting a scant regard for the niceties of the law. If the King's Messengers were not available, local magistrates might, illegally, usurp and extend their functions. Daniel Defoe, for example, reported that over 200 copies of Nathaniel Mist's *Weekly Journal*, the main Jacobite opposition paper to the Hanoverian king, were seized from the carrier by the magistrates in Rochester, Kent. Their justification was that the paper 'did so much Mischief among the Seaman and Tradesfolks' (Sutherland, 2004: 40).[11] Despite this constant harassment, as well as imprisonment virtually every year, Mist conducted the paper, latterly *Mist's Weekly Journal*, for over a decade. When he was, on one occasion, put in the pillory, he was not attacked by the crowd. He finally fled to France in 1728 to work directly for the deposed James II's son, James Stuart, the Old Pretender.

Between public opinion and official fearfulness there was a standoff. For more than a century, journalists like Mist were never silenced and the government was never placated; but, in the event, the journalists prevailed. The result was that, slowly, the power of the state to coerce the print industry into docile behaviour was rolled back with the help of public pressure of one sort or another.

The first legal instrument of repression was the law on politically vexed publications – the offence of criminal or seditious libel. Defamation in the form of a tort of slander – that is, causing externally measurable harm to an individual's reputation through speech – had been known to the Romans. In England, questions of slander had been initially brought before the ecclesiastical courts. The law dealing with the same problem – injury through words – was more slowly developed if the words were written: libel. Criminal, or seditious, libel was not clearly distinguished until the Star Chamber did so in *The Case de Libellis Famosis* heard in 1605 (Coke, 2003). Seditious libel was moreover a crime that – unlike murder, for instance – did not require proof of a guilty intention, *mens rea*. The very appearance of a libel, once proved, was of itself sufficient for conviction (Holt, 1816: 27). Truth was no defence: 'the greater the truth the greater the libel'. Publication, for whatever reason or by accident in some way, was the *actus reus*, the guilty act: 'The crime consists in publishing a libel; a criminal intention in the writer is no part of the definition of the crime of libel at common law' (Holt, 1816: 48). As a 'court of criminal equity', the Star Chamber had the de facto ability to create new offences in this way, one of the powers that was to make it so hated. It also formulated the civil tort of libel as well, a consequence of its ban on duelling. In civil libel, unlike slander but as with the crime, damage was assumed as a consequence of publication and did not have to be proved (see Chapter 11.7).

While Whig and Tory publications might except a degree of official tolerance since power could, and did, change hands between them, excluded political voices were, as much as possible, silenced – free press or no. Printing Jacobite material in support of the Stuart pretenders to the throne and/or calling for the overthrow of the Hanoverians who had replaced them could, and did, expose the perpetrators to the possibility of fines, pillory, prison or even the noose. Mist was lucky compared with many who shared his opinions; Elizabeth Powell, for instance.

Women were involved with print not only as distributors of newspapers. It was not unknown for a widow to continue her husband's business. Mrs Powell took over the family concern when her spouse went into hiding after publishing seditious Jacobite pamphlets. Equally committed to the cause, she continued not only to print but also to write such material and she went on doing so after his death in October 1716. Powell, who claimed in print to be 'an afflicted Woman struggling for Bread for herself, her children', denied that she had anything to do with the contents of the publications coming from her printing shop. She would not desist and was repeatedly imprisoned. She found an 'old *Italian proverb*', or so she claimed, to use as a 'Cautionary Maxim', or masthead on her publications: 'To speak ill of Grandees is to run ones self into Danger; but whoever will speak well of 'em must tell Many a Lye.' It would regulate her future conduct, she said: it did in that she remained in 'Danger' (McDowell, 1998: 75–6).

The son of another woman printer, teenager John Matthews, published the incendiary anonymous Jacobite pamphlet *Vox Populi Vox Dei* in 1719: 'I hope some patriot will rouze the People to shake off this Arbitrary Government' (Monod, 1993: 95). He did it merely to make, he claimed, some pocket money. He was betrayed by his mother's journeyman and apprentice, themselves otherwise being held liable by the Messengers for the offending pamphlet. Young John was hanged for publishing a seditious criminal libel. Mrs Powell's response was to reissue *Vox Populi Vox Dei*. The London public's response, irrespective of their support for, or hostility to, the Jacobites, was to turn young Matthews into a martyr for liberty (McDowell, 1998: 79). The state's remedy had exactly the opposite effect to the one intended, a not unusual outcome for such draconian repression. Public sympathy was anyway on the side of the persecuted because of the law's obvious unfairness. It was always the more easily identifiable printers, booksellers or news hawkers who were caught and condemned, rather than the much harder to discover actual writers, many of whom were anonymous. The press was afforded a measure of protection by outpourings of outraged public support when it was attacked. The disturbances stood proxy for the deep divisions of the political class, now firmly identifiable as Whig or Tory. The country was well on its way to believing that: 'There is nothing, indeed, upon which Englishmen are justly more sensible, than upon whatever has the appearance of effecting the liberty of the press' (Holt, 1816: 59).

It became increasingly hard to secure convictions. In 1756, for example, the administration was advised that prosecuting the *London Evening Post*, which had suggested the government was behaving unconstitutionally, would be unwise: 'The temper of the times must ... be consulted in prosecutions of this nature, and from all I have heard and been informed it is at present in too inflamed and convulsed a state to advise any prosecution at this time' (Black, 2001: 128). Exceptional affront to authority, personally taken, would be needed for this caution to be overcome.

The libertine and radical, John Wilkes, was, it can be agreed, 'a man of abandoned and profligate character, a buffoon whose common conversation is blasphemy and baudry' and an 'ugly fellow', as a journalist wrote at the time (Garner, 1996: 34); but he was also the Member of Parliament for Aylesbury. The authorities were well aware that this would cause them problems when they determined to prosecute Wilkes for criminal libel, following an article in the forty-fifth issue of his paper, the *North Britain*, attacking King George III. The paper was more of a regular series of partisan pamphlets commenting on the news than a news-gathering enterprise. In *No. Forty-Five*, Wilkes had feigned to worry that the 'odious measures' being proposed by the administration would bring the King into disrepute: 'I wish as much as any man in the Kingdom to see the honour of the Crown maintained in a manner truly becoming royalty: I lament to see it sunk even to prostitution' (Wilkes, 2009 [1763]: 354–5). This had, apparently, deeply offended His Majesty personally. Even the issue number, forty-five, impishly recalled the date of the last Stuart attempt to regain the throne in 1745.

The Scottish Earl of Bute was the North Briton Wilkes had in his sights when named his paper. Bute was a man sensitive to the possibility of being associated with the Jacobite cause and, although he had just relinquished office, Wilkes, who hated him, felt he was still exercising considerable influence. The article, to which George III took considerable personal exception, was in official opinion an 'infamous and seditious libel tending to influence the minds and alienate the affections of the people from His Majesty and to excite them to traitorous insurrections against his Government' (F. Williams, 1957: 42).

It caused a sensation and was reprinted by five other publications. A general warrant was issued and forty-eight people were detained by the Messengers. (The first tranche of printers apprehended were, embarrassingly, entirely unconnected with Wilkes and all eventually received significant damages for wrongful arrest) (Garner, 1996: 34–7). For Wilkes' benefit, the government altered the usual form of the warrant to read 'seditious *and treasonous* libel' in an attempt to meet his inevitable plea of parliamentary privilege. Wilkes was arrested but released by Lord Chief Justice Pratt on exactly this basis – privilege. Another charge was laid against him but he had fled to the Continent.

In the ongoing uproar caused by these events, a London mob of thousands repeatedly appeared crying 'Wilkes and Liberty'. Government supporters could be blasé about this, claiming that 'the mob are as usual for the libeller' (Garner, 1996: 27); but acting against the libeller was exciting them, exactly, 'to traitorous insurrections' more directly than the original article had done. Apart from vividly demonstrating to the ruling class this paradox, the real long-term significance of the affair was not the issue of privilege, which after all only applied to a few members of the political elite, but the legality of the general warrant. Lord Chief Justice Pratt raised doubts as to its legitimacy in common law early on in the sequences of cases the affair occasioned. In a debate, sprung on the Commons late one night by Wilkes' friends, the House determined that 'a general warrant for apprehending and seizing the authors, printers and publishers of a sedition libel, together with their papers, is not warranted by law' (Garner, 1996: 53). As result of these opinions, the general warrant could no longer be used. It would not help with Wilkes, but the answer for the government, of course, was to return to the usual specific warrant naming an individual. There, though, the difficulty of the anonymous writer, which had caused the development of the general warrant in the first place, remained.

Six years after *No. Forty-Five*, an anonymous and highly well-informed correspondent, using the pseudonym 'Junius', began publishing a series of 'letters' in Henry Woodfall's *Public Advertiser*. The Wilkes affair was still by no means resolved. Wilkes upon his return from exile had been both imprisoned by the government and elected as an MP by the voters of Middlesex. The mob, demonstrating before his prison, were fired upon by the militia and seven were killed – the 'Massacre of St George's Fields'; but the magistrate who ordered the shots was himself arraigned and only protected with difficulty by the government (Sherrard, 1971 [1930]: 190).

Wilkes was evermore popular and repeatedly elected by the voters only to be denied his seat by the Tories who, eventually, installed their man (whom he had defeated) in his stead. 'Junius' was among the voices protesting this blatant abuse of democracy. In the *Public Advertiser* of 19 December 1769, he impudently remembered the Bloodless Revolution of 1688, whereby the present royal house had been invited to occupy the throne, to warn the King that he, 'while he plumes himself upon the security of his title to the Crown, should remember that as it was acquired by one revolution, it may be lost by another' ('Junius', 1978: 173). Woodfall doubled his circulation that week and was, inevitably, served with a warrant, a legitimate one which named him. 'Junius' went free; his identity was not uncovered by the Messengers and remains a mystery to this day. Woodfall and three others printers, all named, went to trial. One printer's case was heard in the City of London and he was found guilty. Woodfall and two others were arraigned before Lord Chief Justice Mansfield, in Westminster (*R. v Woodfall*, 1770).

The case backfired and was to lead to the abandonment of the system wherein juries only decided on the issue of publication. Mansfield, as judge, found that the 'Junius' letter was indeed a criminal libel and, as he explained to the jury, for him to do so presented no problem to the principle of a free press: 'As for the liberty of the press, I will tell you what it is; the liberty of press is, that a man may print what he pleases without a licence; as long as it remains so, the liberty of the press is not restrained' (Cranfield, 1978: 67).

The jury, limited to determining proof of publication and nothing more, could not disagree with this. Instead, despite the 5,000 plus copies of the magazine in circulation, they found that the article had not been published and thereby made an ass of the law. Given the potential hostility of juries in all these cases, this meant, in effect, that the usefulness of seditious libel as a tool of repression was seriously blunted. The general view, in the words of the *Gazetteer*, was that: 'The late decisions of the two very spirited London juries have given a mortal blow to the present despotic, feeble, and unprincipled administration' (Black, 2001: 129).

Remedial action took some time to develop but eventually in 1792, a new act was passed. Charles Fox, the Whig politician responsible for the legislation, adopted a pretence: that the determination of libel had been removed from the jury's purview where it really belonged by the autocratic Star Chamber. This was an unacceptable absolutist corruption, and thus Fox's Libel Act was 'generally considered restorative of the common law, and therefore merely declaratory' (Holt, 1816: 57).[12] In fact, for the first time, it made jurors determine the libel and then had the judge, as an automatic consequence of a guilty finding, declare it published. This, though, was still no sure solution as juries repeatedly refused to convict. Prosecutions became rarer and rarer. In the decade from 1816, there were 167; from 1825–34 there were only sixteen (Curran and Seaton, 2003: 7). Over the course of the century, because of public opinion and divisions in the ruling class, the repression of expression had been shown to need more than officialdom's annoyance if it was to be sustained. In a revision of the 1792 Act, the Libel Act of 1843 permitted a defence of truth, and thus planted the seeds of a public interest defence for the press, for the first time.[13] Nevertheless, the law of libel still allowed for criminal rather than civil actions if the libeller published any matter knowing it to be untrue. It was not until 2009 that it was finally removed (Heawood, 2009).[14]

A pattern had been established whereby, not least because of public intransigence at a variety of levels, authority's tenacious insistence on controlling the press was slowly undercut. The struggle for a right to report parliamentary debates was to follow much the same course as the fight to abolish the general warrant; and the same is true of the campaign to remove the taxes on newspapers. As for the general warrant and the function of the jury in criminal libel trials, the mysterious 'Junius' in effect had the last word:

> Let it be impressed upon your mind, let it be instilled into your children, that the liberty of the press is the palladium of all civil, political, and religious rights of an Englishman, and that the right of juries to return a general verdict, in all cases whatsoever, is an essential part of our constitution, not to be controlled or limited by judges, nor in any shape questioned by the legislature. (Cobbett, Howell and Howell, 1811: 1109; 'Junius', 1978: 8–9)

4.4 The Case of Brass Crosby, esq. Lord Mayor of London on a Commitment by the House of Commons (1771): For the reporting of Parliament

Because of the second area of state constraint of the press, the words of Lord Chesterfield spoken in the House of Lords, quoted above, were in fact not his.

Of that speech, J. and E. Kimber, the editors of the *London Magazine* in which they were published, said: 'We cannot pretend that it is exactly in the Words made use of by the noble Speaker; and therefore, if we have in the Copy committed any Mistakes either with respect to the Argument or the Expression, we must forewarn the pert Political Critiks of the present, and of every future Age, not to impute them to the original Author' (Anon [J. and E. Kimber], 1737: 401).

In fact, they wrote the speech and their warning has been often forgotten. They were not alone in this deception for it was common practice at the time. In 1784, Samuel Johnson was at dinner when the decline of standard of debate in the Commons was remarked on and a particular speech of William Pitt the Elder's in 1741 was singled out for praise: 'That speech,' Johnson confessed, 'I wrote it in a garret in Exeter Street' (Martin, 2008: 205).[15] Johnson explained that he was then working for Edward Cave, the proprietor of the *Gentleman's Magazine*. Cave had coined the term 'magazine' for a periodical with miscellaneous contents.[16] Cave employed a reporter, one Guthrie, and he bribed the doorkeepers in Westminster to let Guthrie listen to the debates; but he was not allowed to do anything as conspicuous as taking down notes. Guthrie, who had an excellent memory, had to write up as much as he could recall as soon as he left the chamber; however, he was no stylist. The notes were therefore furnished to writers, such as Johnson, who produced the text of the speeches for the printers (F. Williams, 1957: 36).

That procedure, though, did not make the publication legal. It was not. The licensed reporting of Parliament had been allowed until a decision of the Commons taken after the return of the King in 1660. The House had then determined that its debates were privileged and banned the reporting of them. There was more justification for this than there was for controlling offensive oppositional speech outside Westminster. Both Houses were technically the High Court of Parliament and, just as there was no prima facie right to report what lay behind any other court's judgments, so all that needed be known of Parliament's decisions was recorded in its acts. Revealing the debates that had led to them was dangerous both because it created greater opportunity for interpretation and uncertainty; and, moreover, it furnished potential foreign enemies with insight into the basis of policy. The earlier inhibition on making diplomatic and political news public was still in play. In 1689, the Bill of Rights, which enshrined in statute the terms offered to William and Mary when they came to the throne, specifically allowed that 'the freedom of speech and debates or proceedings in Parliament ought not to be impeached or questioned in any court or place out of Parliament'; but the Parliament saw this 'absolute privilege' as a defence to their own freedom of speech, rather than an enshrinement of a right of third parties to report such speech. Nevertheless, the public increasingly believed it had the right to know what its representatives were up to; and, crucially, it was prepared to pay for newspapers and magazines that furnished such information.

As with the standoffs over the general warrant and the jury determination of libel, this led to a veritable campaign for a right to publish the debates. The campaign was: 'kept alive by guerrilla engagements in which the printers, pitting their ingenuity against a Parliament determined to treat every report as a breach of privilege were repeatedly censured, committed to Newgate or otherwise punished only to start doing it all over again' (F. Williams, 1957: 40).

Cave's use of Guthrie was but one ploy. MPs in the reports were referred to by their initials. Reports were not published in a timely fashion, either, but held for the end of a session. Therefore, they tended to be more a staple of the magazines than the newspapers. That was what the Kimbers were about in the *London Magazine*. Cave produced reports purportedly of deliberations in the 'Senate of Lilliput'. The printers were much aided in these skirmishes by the fact that juries were even less inclined to convict over privilege than they were over sedition. And not only juries.

In 1771, a printer, who had reported the debates, was seized by a Messenger within the city of London for contempt of the privilege of the House of Commons. He complained to the Lord Mayor, Brass Crosby, who, in his capacity as the city's chief magistrate, promptly released him. Crosby, a close supporter and ally of John Wilkes, was then himself arraigned before the Court of Common Pleas for contempt of the House. The same crowds that had gathered when Wilkes was incarcerated gathered again. Eventually, against this background of uproar, the court, which was anyway not eager to hear the case, declared it could not know the basis of the Common's privilege – actually the *lex et consuetudine Parliamenti* (the law and customs of Parliament), which is not quite the same thing as the common law (Howell, 1816: 1137). The court released the Lord Mayor.[17]

As with the removal of licensing and the abandonment of the general warrant, this, rather than any direct legislative action, effected the change in everyday practice. The standoff produced an otherwise unannounced de facto decision of House not to pursue its privilege in the matter of reports any longer. In consequence, it tacitly licensed an extension of its absolute privilege, which was not to be questioned for the next 220 years. Not only could reports be published, it was also assumed that they shared the privileges of the debates themselves.

By the next decade, the parliamentary reports had, in the words of the *Town and Country Magazine*, 'necessarily become matters of the upmost consequence to all our readers' (Black, 2001: 130). Reporters were now allowed to take down notes but had no guaranteed places in the gallery.[18]

By the early nineteenth century, a number of printers were publishing titles devoted solely to reporting Parliament but one, Thomas Hansard, eventually established himself as the most authoritative. He had left his father – the government's official printer – to set-up on his own but, at first, he was merely a jobbing printer. He was contracted by the radical writer and publisher, William Cobbett, to print the *Debates* which Cobbett issued as a supplement to his weekly *Political Register*. The *Debates* was the first attempt at producing a comprehensive account of all the discussions in the House. Cobbett – 'the Contentious Man' – was the most important polemicist of the day and, despite constant harassment, he had been publishing his *Political Register* from 1802. In 1809, he protested in its pages his outrage at the flogging of mutinous local English militiamen by professional Hanoverian – German – troops at the Isle of Ely and was prosecuted for seditious libel: 'What, shall the rascals *mutiny* and that, too, when the German Legion is so near ... Well, done, Lord Castlereigh' (Cobbett, 1809: 993). This was deemed to be a great insult to the Army and Cobbett was found guilty and given two years in Newgate for writing it. Hansard, to the distress of his father, received three months in the King's Bench Prison, in Southwark, for printing it.

In the financial chaos this caused, Cobbett sold the *Debates* to Hansard who, in 1829, decided to put his name on the title page. Thereafter, the right to report Parliament was no longer in contention. *Hansard* became the official record of the house and when, in 1886, Parliament finally employed its own reporters, *Hansard* persisted as the name of the publication (Anon, n.d.). The pubic reporting of Parliament was thus a settled matter – until 2009. Perhaps it still is (see Chapter 11.8).

4.5   *R. v. Hetherington* (1841): For the end of press taxation

Cobbett, too, had persisted. Upon his release in 1812, he was feted at a formal dinner attended by 600 people. Although he had to flee the country in 1817, he returned and continued to publish the *Register* until his death in 1835, campaigning vigorously for parliamentary reform and other radical causes. At the age of seventy, after the passage of the great Parliamentary Reform Act of 1832 for which he had worked so hard, he was returned to Parliament as an MP. It was his fifth attempt and he died within three years of taking his seat. Among the many unachieved causes he supported was a campaign for the removal of the taxes on newspapers. This was not to happen until some thirty years after his death.

Taxes on printed sheets of news and a duty on advertisements had been introduced in 1712 and constituted, after seditious libel and the prohibition against parliamentary reporting, the last basic method developed by the authorities to control the press. It was initially designed to prevent the publication of Whig papers opposed to the Tory administration's attempts to bring the War of the Spanish Succession to a close. It was thus introduced 'for political purposes, as much as for fiscal purposes' and, as such, had to be buried in a general act imposing duties on a variety of goods (Dowell, 1884: 340).[19] From 1 August 1712, a printed sheet (size undefined) was taxed at 1d and half sheets at 1/2d. One shilling was levied for every advertisement printed. Joseph Addison greeted its introduction in the *Spectator*: 'This is the day on which many of our authors will probably publish their last words' (Anon [Joseph Addison], 1712). The Tory, Jonathan Swift, wrote privately to Esther Johnson (his virtual ward) that: 'Do you know Grubb St [where professional writers were concentrated][20] is dead and gone last week? No more ghosts or murders now for love or money' (Swift, 1948 [1712]: 453).

Addison and Swift spoke too soon. Printers were quick to play with folded sheets and other ploys – increasing their size or doubling the columns to save space, for example. A newspaper of a page-and-a-half attracted no tax, so poorly drafted was the Act, and therefore soon appeared. When that loophole was plugged in 1725, farthing newspapers, which also attracted no tax, were cried through the streets. The tax burden, however, was less for government-supporting publications. In 1742, after twenty-one years of cabinet dominance, Sir Robert Walpole resigned, defeated on a vote of no confidence. An MPs' 'Committee on Secrecy', analogous to a modern public inquiry, was set-up to uncover corruption during his time in office. It discovered that over the previous decade Walpole had returned in bribes no less than £50,077/18/0d, some £4.3 million in modern money,[21] to toady editors, publishers and writers. The tax might have come in to benefit the Tories but, throughout Walpole's long tenure as de facto Prime Minster, it was Whig papers that gained from his largesse.

Another source of corruption was the mail system. By the turn of the eighteenth century, the six Post-Office Clerks of the Road had come to frank newspapers for posting and keep the proceeds as part of their emolument. At the same time, Members of Parliament were allowed to use the mail, during sessions and for periods afterwards, to send letters, and soon newspapers, for free. This privilege was easily abused by them, as well as those – some hundreds, including Edward Cave – they appointed as their proxies; and by others who simply forged their signatures. Again, it was sympathetic titles that were allowed free carriage, albeit, because of the MPs' range of affiliations, on a more equitable basis than that in place for distributing government bribes.

The final stage of distribution, the point of sale, remained the most vulnerable to official repression. The news-hawkers, who were especially essential to the distribution of the farthing press, were pursued with a new act of 1743, passed at the behest of the coffee-house proprietors. These were expected to provide newspapers for their clients and they objected to the total cost of proliferating titles and the rivalry of having them sold in the street. The 1743 Act, like its predecessors, only worked for a time and new unstamped farthing papers again began to appear. Despite the tax, the general warrant and seditious libel, circulations of the stamped press rose inexorably from an estimated annual 2.5 million in 1713 to nearly 11 million in 1756. In 1757, yet another act defined the size of a sheet and closed that loophole. This too had no effect on rising circulations – 12.6 million by 1775 – plus significant numbers of unstamped papers and magazines. In the final analysis, the tax's biggest impact was to shrink the size of the print used and make text arranged in narrow columns the usual mark of a news publication (Black, 2001: 73, 78). English newspapers reached the final stage of development as far as written content was concerned towards the end of the century. Then opinion, in the form of editorials and columns, and even fiction (Law, 2000), came to coexist with news of all kinds, including coverage of sport and cultural reviews, in the same publication.

The high cost of newspapers, three times as much as the contemporary price in Paris or New York, had the perverse effect, from the authorities' point of view, of bringing people – literate radical workers, for example – together to obtain and read papers. Such gatherings were an outcome they otherwise were at pains to avoid. Papers were even available for hire – a business made illegal, of course, but to no effect. High cost, caused by the tax, encouraged the production of unstamped publications and these exactly reflected the most vigorous oppositional politics. As the authorities became evermore alarmed in the aftermath of the French Revolution and during the lengthy wars that followed, a plethora of unstamped revolutionary sheets appeared: the *Black Dwarf*, the *Republican*, the *Cap of Liberty*. Many of the titles were short-lived but there were over 200 of them. The government, ignoring the failed experiment of L'Estrange after the Restoration, issued its own papers, the *Anti-Cobbett* and the *White Dwarf*, but there was no taste for them. The demand for the abolition of the tax itself became embedded in the general demand, from a rapidly industrializing society, for political reform. This included extending the franchise, reorganizing Parliament and abolishing the Corn Laws, which had kept the price of bread high in the interest of the landed gentry. It also called for the removal of newspaper taxes.

In the summer 1819, the radical landowner, MP and friend of Cobbett, Henry Hunt, known as 'Orator Hunt', was touring the country campaigning for parliamentary reform. To witness the meeting of 16 August in St Peter's Field in Manchester, which attracted a crowd estimated at anything up to 120,000, a proto-press corps, with reporters from five newspapers, assembled (Anon, 1819: 55). Two were from Manchester, one from Leeds and one from Liverpool. The fifth, John Tyas, was the leading reporter of the London *Times* who had been covering Hunt's meetings. He was a master of shorthand. Although systems had been in existence for a long time, the technique was only being more generally adopted by the press at this time.[22] It was considered rather invasive – stealing a person's words – but Hansard, for example, employed shorthand writers for reporting parliamentary debates. He, though, allowed MPs a sight of what the reporters heard them say so that they could make corrections.

As Hunt began his speech 'all was quiet and orderly' but the Manchester Yeoman Cavalry, called out by the magistrates to keep the peace, without warning attacked the crowd: 'A cry was made by the cavalry, "Have at their flags". In consequence, they immediately dashed not only at the flags which were in the wagon but those which were posted among the crowd, *cutting most indiscriminately to the right and to the left* to get at them … From that moment the Manchester Yeomanry Cavalry lost all command of temper' (Anon, 1819: 41).

The presence of Tyas, who was – ironically – like his paper no friend of Hunt or reform, brought to national attention the events of that day. A constable arrested him, dismissing his explanation that 'we merely attended to report the proceedings of the day'. The policeman was unimpressed: 'Oh! Oh! You then are one of their writers – you must go before the Magistrates.' They, at least, had the good sense to treat him with courtesy, unlike Hunt whom he witnessed being beaten up (Anon, 1819: 42–3).

To the fury of his editor, the long-serving Thomas Barnes, Tyas was held overnight. Within two days of his release, he and his colleagues had made known the outcome: 400 injured and eleven dead, including, most shockingly, two women. John Taylor, *Manchester Gazette*, filed the initial report to the *Times* because of Tyas' incarceration. *The Times* articulated public outrage. It was, though, James Wroe of the *Manchester Observer* who, it can be argued, probably did more than any to secure the memory of the melee by naming it, in an echo of a recent climatic battle, the 'Peterloo Massacre'.

The government, too, in effect lost all control of temper. It hastily passed six repressive Acts, four of which were directed at the possibility of armed mobs, which it had no occasion, beyond its own paranoia, to believe were in prospect. The requirement for prior permission to have public meetings of more than fifty people was one measure. The last two Acts were directed against the press. The first of them increased the maximum penalty for criminal libel to fourteen years transportation,[23] but this did nothing to solve the problem of juries being unwilling to convict in the first place. As noted above, after a flurry in the years following Peterloo, prosecutions continued to tail off. The second Act extended the principle of the Stamp Tax to include the posting of sureties and bonds for 'good behaviour'.[24]

The laws were now absurdly complex in attempting to establish, for example, a distinction between 'public news, intelligences and occurrences'; and 'remarks on the news' (Collet, 1899: 59). One consequence of this was that theatre reviews were the former, and taxed, while book reviews were considered the later and therefore not taxed. This loophole allowed William Cobbett, for one, to publish an unstamped version of his *Political Register* at 2d, which only contained opinion and was therefore a 'pamphlet'. The weekly *Register* was stamped. It cost, including the tax of 4d, 1/1½d – nearly seven times as much. The duty on advertisements had also risen to 3/6d (Black, 2001: 166). If the 'newspaper' exceeded 2,295 square inches ('exclusive of margins') the duty went up a penny; 'a sheet must not be less than 21 inches by 17. The *Times* at this date consisted of four pages, each 15½ inches by 22, a superficies of 682 square inches. The price was sevenpence. It could not, under these circumstances, be published without a stamp' (Collet, 1899: 17–19, 59) unless it appeared on the first day on the month or the two days thereafter at more than a twenty-six-day interval. That time-lapse would make it a pamphlet that attracted no duty – as long, of course, as it carried no 'public news, intelligences and occurrences'. And so on; and so on.

The tax was becoming a nonsense, not least because proceeding against publishers for avoidance inevitably caused riots. Sir Robert Peel, entering the cabinet for the first time in 1822 as Home Secretary, therefore halted prosecutions against the unstamped press. The tax on the adverts newspapers carried remained. The stamp, still being collected as a source of revenue, nevertheless slowly followed the claim of privilege over parliamentary reporting and the general warrant into desuetude as a means of control.

Seditious libel, although equally prone to cause civil disorder, was left on the statute book.

The newspaper legislation in the Six Acts also undercut any loyalty that the Establishment press might be expected to have for the authorities. Thomas Barnes was appalled by the Acts and not readily reassured by the administration's protestations that 'respectable' papers (e.g. *The Times*) were not its object. Although *The Times* remained hostile to reform, in 1821 it broke with the Establishment to take Queen Charlotte's part in her divorce action against the King. This, augmenting a willingness to introduce new technologies such as the steam-driven press, was the basis of the paper's emerging overwhelming dominance of the stamped news market. At first known as 'The Turncoat', it soon became 'The Thunderer'. It was always thereafter, despite its conservative instincts, ready to strike an independent line if it felt so inclined and intuited that its public backed it.

And the unstamped press, despite the constant threat of seditious libel and the surety, was only subdued for a decade. Thereafter, it again flourished. In 1831, the *Poor Man's Guardian*, one of the new-born illegal titles that had started to appear, carried the blatant masthead that it was: 'FOR THE PEOPLE. PUBLISHED IN DEFIANCE "LAW" TO TRY THE POWERS OF "RIGHT" AGAINST THAT OF "MIGHT"' (Collet, 1899: 33). Arthur Hetherington, its publisher, was persistently prosecuted but he and others were not deterred. Soon it was estimated that more than two million readers a year saw these papers, more than read the stamped press. This readership thirsted for political change. Unrest was not reduced by the measure of reform achieved in the great Reform Act of 1832 nor, in 1846, by the abolition of the Corn Laws. During these years, protest coalesced around a draft parliamentary Bill which was, in effect, a comprehensive set of political demands, including universal male franchise – the 'People's Charter'. Chartism spread its message at mass meetings and with petitions with more than a million signatures, but it also made good use of the media. Plays dramatizing the issue of liberty were mounted – one, for example, on the trial of Robert Emmet, the Irish radical who was, in 1803, the last person to be hanged, drawn and quartered; but most central to the campaign was 'unstamped press agitation' (Thompson, 1986: 118). 'Every great town had its Chartist press' (McCarthy, 1901: 98).

Not all of these titles were unstamped, though. For example, an ex-MP and Chartist leader in Leeds, Fergus O'Connor, was publisher of the most successful northern Chartist weekly, the stamped *Northern Star*. At its peak in 1839, it was selling 30,000 an edition. In his first issue, O'Connor, who was to make a good living out of the venture, had to apologize for stamping the paper: 'Reader – Behold that little red spot, in the corner of my newspaper. That is the Stamp; the Whig *beauty* spot; your *plague* spot' (Thompson, 1986: 49). The stamp, however, not only threatened the radical credibility of the publication; it did not protect O'Connor from the authorities either. He was sentenced in 1840 for seditious libel and served eighteen months. The paper, though, continued to appear and continued to earn him money. O'Connor had revealed the entrepreneurial possibilities of a cheap press, even as he, Hetherington and others had illuminated its destabilizing potential.

John Cleave took the matter a stage further. A printer, Cleave was a political protégée of Hetherington but his *Cleave's Weekly Police Gazette*, which he started in 1834, brought together the political news of the *Poor Man's Guardian* or the *Northern Star* with the substance of official police crime reports, augmented with additional titillations. The formula was massively successful, soon achieving and sustaining regular sales figures that matched the *Northern Star*'s circulation at the height of Chartist activity in 1836. Notices of Chartist meetings coupled with reports of murders and robberies proved very vendible and this was soon noticed by less politically engaged entrepreneurs, such as Edward Lloyd. For Lloyd the possibility of a sensationalist publication *without* the Chartism was obvious. After all, Cleave was actually exploiting a taste that Lloyd and his peers had established for sensational fiction among the burgeoning urban classes, including a literate proletariat. He had a thriving business, undisturbed by the authorities, publishing part-works on highwaymen and footpads or, another example, a history of piracy 'of all nations' and the like. The gothic tradition yielded 'penny bloods', which were to become 'penny dreadfuls': e.g. *Vice and its Victims; or, Phoebe the Peasant's Daughter*; and, most famously, *Sweeney Todd, The Demon Barber of Fleet Street*. In 1842, he started a cheap Sunday news digest, *Lloyd's Penny Weekly Miscellany*.[25] His journalistic instinct, justified by Cleave's formula as well the original newsbook sensationalist tradition, was closer to the penny dreadfuls that had made him successful than to, say, Thomas Barnes or even Fergus O'Connor. *Lloyd's Weekly* was to become one of the most popular of all nineteenth-century titles widely read by exactly the classes who scared the Establishment: but the paper fed them no agitational politics.

The point was made even more clearly the following year when John Browne Bell, backed by some £15,000 of venture capital (as it might be), founded the *News of the World*. In the first issue, 1 October 1843 there was indeed a lead column, 'The Politician: The State of the Nation', but its contents were essentially an advertisement for the new paper's apolitical (that is, essentially conservative) editorial position:

> The general utility of all classes is the idea with which this paper originated. To give to the poorer classes of society a paper that would suit their means, and to the middle, as well as the rich, a journal, which from its immense circulation, should command their attention, have been the influencing motives that have caused the appearance of 'The News of the World'.

What suited their means and commanded their attention was: 'EXTRAORDINARY CHARGE OF DRUGGING AND VIOLATION' and

'JOKES (From Punch of Yesterday)', which shared the rest of the front page. Echoing the early newsbooks and the seventeenth-century nocturnals, readers were given a weather forecast: 'October. This month will record fearful storms and earthquakes, especially in the middle of the month from the 11th to the 17th.' The earthquakes did not disrupt the 60,000 sales a week Bell was soon claiming.

To produce this volume of copies required the new labour-intensive, extremely expensive steam-driven rotary presses. Although an engine of modernity, the technology of the press itself had actually developed little in the centuries since Gutenberg. The counter-weighted platen was the only major advance until a metal flatbed appeared in 1800. This doubled the print area and increased the possible iph to 400 plus sheets. Going faster than this, though, required moving beyond the flatbed altogether to the cylinder and then applying steam power. In 1813, John Walter II, son of *The Times'* founder and Barnes' proprietor, had installed vertical German Koenig steam presses secretly and, overnight, produced a paper with a new work force (Aitchison, 2007: 75).[26] The paper's masthead became 'Printed by Steam', causing William Hazlitt mockingly to suggest that *The Times* 'seems to be written as well as printed by a steam-engine' (Hazlitt, 2009 [1821]: 69). These presses increased the iph to 1,100 an hour. *The Times* remained in the forefront acquiring new machinery with ever-increasing capacity.

Bigger newspapers required ever larger numbers of reporters and sub-editors as well as highly skilled, and organized, printers. All these developments worked to enhance the newspaper's appearance and content – and production costs. The arrival of the telegraph, essentially developed as a signalling system for the new railways, also impacted costs – at least, it did so after the publishers overcame their initial reluctance to meet telegraphy's tariffs. Carrier-pigeons, after all, were cheaper and could be dedicated to flying to specific scattered newspaper offices; but the emerging business of wholesaling news – especially commercial information such as stock prices – to the press encouraged the use of the telegraph from the 1850s onwards (see Chapter 7.1). The technology helped make news a perishable commodity – useless if delayed – which it had never been before. The centuries of artisanal production came to an end. A Cobbett, for instance, with a couple of printers, could no longer in effect conduct a running battle with the authorities while meeting his readers thirst for timely information.

The net result of these developments was to render the taxes 'very needless'. In fact, they were increasingly seen as a barrier to the entrepreneurialism of the conservative businessmen who could command the financial resources now being required to run a successful publication. Sensationalist content without the political messages attached could wean the public away from the radical press with papers so 'safe' that they would not need to be taxed. Increasingly, as Chartism faltered in the 1840s and the prosperity of mid-Victorian Britain grew, the public bought into the new publications. Even the law of libel was, in the face of juries unwilling to convict, amended to allow the papers a defence of truth – 'public interest' – a concept previously unknown to the common law. It was becoming ever clearer that all the repressive efforts of officialdom since the Civil War had failed to bring the press into line and that efforts to do so were largely counter-productive. As the Establishment's fearfulness of revolution subsided with the decline of Chartism, the supposed dangers of a free press began to seem overstated. The capital-intensive development of a newspaper industry was the best insurance available, although it did not guarantee complete support for the established order.

The press was not neutered by this. Even *The Times*, despite its Establishment instincts, could not always be relied on:

HEIGHTS BEFORE SEBASTOPOL OCTOBER 25th 1854
… We could hardly believe the evidence of our senses! Surely that handful of men were not going to charge an army in position? Alas! It was but too true – their desperate valour knew no bounds and far indeed was it removed from its so called better part – discretion … At twenty-five to twelve not a British soldier, except the dead and dying, was left in front of these bloody Muscovite guns (Anon [William Russell], 1854: 7–8).

Barnes had remained in post until his death in 1841. He was succeeded by John Delane, arguably the most politically powerful newspaper editor Britain has ever seen. In 1854, Delane had dispatched William Russell, as a 'TG' – a 'Travelling Gentleman' as proto-war correspondents were then known – to cover the conflict in the Crimea between France, Britain and Turkey on the one hand and Russia on the other. This war was being fought for somewhat opaque reasons but essentially reflected the struggle of the 'Great Powers' for control of the failing Ottoman Empire and specifically suzerainty over its Christian citizens. Britain and France had carried the conflict into the Black Sea but this effort glaringly exposed the failings of the British military machine, soft after nearly four decades of peace following Waterloo.

Russell, his colleague Thomas Chenery, *The Times* correspondent in Constantinople, and Edwin Gonkin, filing for the *Daily News*, undercut the credibility of the Westminster government to the extent that a mere call for a Select Committee inquiry into the conduct of 'our forces before Sebastopol' was enough to bring it down (Knightly, 1976: 12–14). Queen Victoria wondered why *The Times* was so rude to her generals and Lord John Russell, an ex-Whig Prime Minster, wrote that: 'If England is ever to be England again, this vile tyranny of *The Times* must be cut off' (F. Williams, 1957: 81). Delane's hostility, though, was no automatic Tory response to Whig misfeasance. He could be equally hostile to the Tory interest. In 1852, for example, Benjamin Disraeli had privately sent him his election manifesto, as Delane had requested, before publication: 'I hope you will be able to back me

... but if you can't, we must take the fortunes of war witht grumbling; sensible as I am of much kindness on your part' (Disraeli, 1997 [1852]: 66). Delane repaid the compliment by calling Disraeli a 'quack doctor' and an 'inimitable illusionist' in the paper.

After the seventeenth-century Civil War, officialdom could not always expect, much less compel, support, even from the most respectable publications. Yet experience was showing that this might well matter less than had always been assumed. For centuries, it was an uncontested given that, as L'Estrange had claimed, 'the Press has made 'um mad'; but this assumption about its irresistible influence was not grounded in real evidence. The nature and extent of press power, indeed its very existence, was, and still is, not easily demonstrated in any straightforward sense. The 'vile tyranny of *The Times*' and the rest of the press was something of an illusion. The ruling class might have been sensitive to each and every attack on its prerogatives and object to having to make room in the public sphere for the press, but, essentially, it remained (and remains) in power. Delane could be rude about Disraeli but Disraeli was returned to Parliament nevertheless to become, on that occasion, Chancellor of the Exchequer. Even when the press, then being dubbed as 'the Fourth Estate of the realm',[27] did not toe the line, its power was actually less than it seemed.

Thus, although draconian legal sanctions, taxation and sureties for good behaviour simply did not achieve their ends – neither on the Establishment press nor on the radical – nevertheless the state could rest easy. After several centuries of more or less futile repressive effort, industrialization had actually produced a solution for the authorities, the best it was to get in a society with, rhetorically at least, a commitment to basic liberties. The press now needed capital to produce publications in quantities that could be sold to the urbanizing mass. The people with capital to do this could be trusted; at least, they could be trusted more than could poor printers or writers with radical agendas. The authorities could now at last safely act on Milton's advice: 'A little generous prudence, a little forbearance of one another, and some grain of charity' (Milton, 1963 [1644]: 53). This would work where repression had failed and had caused nothing but trouble; demonstrably, more trouble – in the sense of straining social cohesion – than the suppressed publications ever did. The possibility of abandoning traditional hostility became a political option; the press could be, in actual day-to-day terms, 'free'. The proof of this was now firmly embedded in the economics of newspaper publications. As the high-tide of Victorianism approached, the press became not only what it had been from the outset – a crucial engine driving the capitalist machine – but itself a capitalist enterprise.

The call for a free – that is untaxed – press had been part of the radical political agenda. The Association of Working Men to Procure a Cheap and Honest Press was formed in 1836 specifically to campaign for the repeal of the newspaper taxes. Talk of these as 'taxes on *knowledge*', as *The Times* did in 1853, was an early example of public relations genius (Strattman, 2011: 7). Newspapers positioned themselves as 'the readiest, the commonest, the chief vehicle of knowledge' (Myers and Harris, 1993: 65). With this spin, the campaign became a more broadly based Association for the Promotion of the Repeal of the Taxes on Knowledge. It was now more respectable than its predecessor, whose radical Chartist connections rendered it suspect. Moreover, *Lloyd's Weekly* and the *News of the World* had demonstrated that not only the unstamped Chartist sheets – now more or less unprosecuted for avoidance anyway – would benefit from abolition. The taxes were increasingly presented as inhibiting the full development of what could be an economically significant industry. A cheap press would emerge, following abolition, 'in the hands of men of good moral character, of respectability, and of capital' (Curran and Seaton, 2009: 20), e.g. Edward Lloyd, John Browne Bell and their peers. Newspapers had always been of value to the economy, but now they were becoming a significant industry of themselves, not just a tool of the marketplace. This last, moreover, was also increasingly important as consumerism took hold of society.

The space for advertisements created by Samuel Pecke and his fellows in the seventeenth century had become evermore significant as a source of revenue. By the nineteenth century, although books and patent medicines remained staples, a £10,000 per annum advertising spend was not unusual for a major firm – Schweppes, for instance – and, from such sources, a stamped paper could expect overall a similar sum as its advertising revenue. There had been a specialized business in supplying the provincial press with parliamentary and other metropolitan news.[28] It was natural enough for such a service to expand and for advertising copy also to be sent out for placement. In 1812, one of *The Times* printers, William Lawson, had established the first agency to deal exclusively with adverts, abandoning the wholesaling of news altogether. Advertising was also needed by the London papers, as a minimum circulation of 12,000 was necessary for a successful title to survive on cover price alone. Only *The Times* sold so many per edition, so for all the other titles advertising had become essential. By the 1830s, *The Times* was carrying around 440 adverts an edition, its nearest rival about half that.

The rising reliance on advertising brought an end to government bribery. This had by no means ceased with the fall of Walpole. John Walter I, founder *The Times*, had been quite content to sign a contract with the government of the day to print material they sent him in return for a subvention of £300 a year. The *Observer* was taking payments from the secret service to take a strong anti-radical line nearly a century after Walpole's fall; half its print run was distributed free as 'specimen copies' (F. Williams, 1957: 46, 59). The downside was that advertisers could start to assert influence over editorial matter but the papers were in a sellers' market, especially *The Times*. For example: shares in the booming railway enterprises of the 1840s were a new major source of advertising revenue. Yet, to its credit, *The Times*, set its face against the craze editorially despite benefiting from railway promoters' adverts during the height of the mania in 1845 to the tune of £6,000 a week (Smith, 1979: 121–2; Odlysko, 2010: 86–9). The threat, though, was there if advertising demand fell, leaving the press with a glut of unsold space.

Advertising's economic importance reinforced the safer nature of the heavily capitalized press. It did nothing for the radical press, stamped or unstamped. The radical papers faced a not unnatural bias on the part of advertisers, business and agitation being uneasy bedfellows, and little revenue from this source came their way (Curren and Seaton, 2003: 12, 30, 31). They had to rely on cover price alone and, instead of 'the lucrative patronage of advertisers' they could expect 'prosecutions, fines and the like etceteras' (Curren and Seaton, 2003: 12, 30, 31). Thus the heavy impost on advertisements had little effect on the radical press but was inhibiting the growth of those politically safer popular papers that were emerging to be in competition with it. In 1853, the tax on advertisements was removed.

Two years later, despite the role played by the papers in the downfall of the government over its conduct of the war in the Crimea, the same logic, suffused with liberal rhetoric, caused Parliament to abolish the stamp. After all, it had been increasingly a dead letter as a tool of repression since 1822. Anyway, Chartism was now a spent force and never since has there been so sustained an extra-parliamentary oppositional focus in British life. Certainly, no popular radical movement has enjoyed the support of the press to the extent Chartism did. The removal of the taxes was, it must be said, a radical step in comparison with the situation of the press generally in Europe and beyond. It was nonetheless safe. The new papers which appeared caused no unease to the authorities: the *Daily Telegraph*, for example, its very title proclaiming its modernity and its cover price, 1d, indicating its audience. Within a decade it had overtaken *The Times* and was claiming a circulation of 240,000 a day.

The basic principle of 'do no harm', enforced by the civil tort of libel, as well as the crimes of criminal libel, seditious libel and blasphemy, were still in place.[29] Further prohibitions were also possible should the need for control be felt by the authorities. Pornography, for example, was easily obtainable but its publishers were repeatedly brought to heel, even as the restrictions on the mainstream press were being removed. In 1857, although the campaign against 'the taxes on knowledge' had almost achieved a complete victory, the first statute specifically devoted to prohibiting pornography, the Obscene Publications Act, was passed.[30] It replaced the use of the common law on public order. The march to the removal of newspaper taxes, however, was not impeded by this and in 1861 the final tax on newsprint was abolished; the press was declared 'free'.

There was now a neat liberal narrative to hand. Control of the stage was ignored. Instead, the specifics of press freedom were trumpeted. Its liberties were declared to be the result of an:

> heroic struggle against the state. The key events of this struggle are generally said to be the abolition of the Court of the Star Chamber in 1641, the end of press licensing in 1694,[31] Fox's Libel Act, 1792 and the repeal of press taxation – the so called 'taxes on knowledge' in the period 1853 to 1861. Only with the last of these reforms, it is claimed, did the press finally become free. (Curran and Seaton, 2003: 3)

This Curran and Seaton describe as 'Whig Press History', a political myth, one that disguises the limits of the freedom achieved. As Butterfield suggests, the danger with such narratives is that 'we fly into the sky with it when in reality it needs to be brought to earth' (Butterfield, 1965 [1931]: 99). It was not merely that the press was now firmly 'in the hands of men of good moral character, of respectability, and of capital', both as advertisers and proprietors.[32] More than this, the sting of the press's oppositional potential had been blunted. The long-established popular taste for sensation was fed a product, the newspaper, which could now only be produced at a high cost in personnel and machines.

Nevertheless, all the constant threats of the King's Messengers and the magistrates; all the stresses of criminal trials; the fines and harassments; all the long hours of incarceration, or worse – these had not been for nothing. They had established a crucial right, for all that it was not quite the 'mission accomplished' claimed for it in the Whig narrative. There was general agreement – *consensu* – that in Britain and in the West the press was to be, in one fashion or another, to one degree or another, 'free'. (It did not follow, however, that other media were to be free, too – see Chapters 6, 7 and 8.)

5

Consensu: Agreed

5.1   *The King v. John Peter Zenger* (1735): Press freedom in the United States

Nowhere were the prerogatives of 'free-born Englishmen' to be more jealously guarded than in the North American settlements of the British Crown; and, within those societies, nowhere were these prerogatives, including the right of free speech, more vigorously asserted than in the colonial press. Unanimously, by general agreement – *consensu* – a free press was seen an essential element in any democratic society.

In the struggle for independence from Britain, the American newspaper played a pivotal role, one that is acknowledged in the national story and enshrined in law and practice. Prior to that struggle, in the seventeenth century, there was no hint of this. The almost total lack of overt clashes between Royalists and Parliamentarians in the North American plantations allowed absolutist censorship, maintained by both factions, to remain in place. It was as if to prove the contention that it was the conflicts of the English Civil War that were crucial to the development of printed news media. Despite the presence of printers on the *Mayflower* and the importation of the first press in 1638 (two years after Mexico City), neither in Jamestown to the south nor in Plymouth to the north did anything but the most occasional news broadsheet appear. The settlements were small enough to allow for the contents of any newsbook newly received from abroad to be readily disseminated through discussion and gossip, obviating the need for reprinting on a regular basis. Religion, a main driver of immigration, produced on that first press the English colonies' earliest publication, a psalter. There was also, exactly echoing the earliest printing done in fifteenth-century Mainz, an almanac and a printed form, not an indulgence but a 'freeman's oath', to meet secular needs (Duniway, 1906: 23).

The authorities, from Royalist Williamsburg and Baltimore to Puritan Philadelphia and Boston, did not move from an absolutist position. In fact, they sought to prevent the contagion of print from ever taking hold. As Sir William Berkeley, the Royalist governor of Virginia who, during the Interregnum, had made the colony a haven for Cavaliers, opined in 1671: 'I thank God there are no free schools nor printing and I hope we shall not have these hundred years; for learning has brought disobedience, and heresy and sects into the world, and printing has divulged them ... God keep us from both' (Wroth, 1922: 1). In 1686, James II specifically instructed the incoming Governor of New England, Sir Edmund Andros that: 'forasmuch as great inconvenience may arise by the liberty of printing within our said territory under your government you are to provide by all necessary orders that no person keep any printing-press for printing, nor that any book, pamphlet or other matters whatsoever be printed without your especial leave and license first obtained' (Duniway, 1906: 65).

Berkeley's prayer was not to be answered. In 1688, the government of Massachusetts Bay was moved to produce an official broadsheet, exactly in the style of a London newspaper, the *Present State of New-English Affairs*. It was specially designed, as its masthead stated, 'to Prevent False-Reports' on the colony's situation in the aftermath of the change of monarch in London (Pasley, 2001: 29). By 1690, there was sufficient demand for paper that a mill was established in Pennsylvania. In that year, in Boston, Benjamin Harris, a victim of the King's Messengers who had immigrated two years earlier, printed an unlicensed newspaper, *Publick Occurences, Both Forreign and Domestick*, promising to do so again on a monthly basis or 'if any Glut of Occurrences happen, oftener'. It was all that the authorities feared, retailing a false tale of incest within the French royal family, questioning the probity of the colony's alliance with certain Native American tribes and a scare story about people dying from the ague. That was just on the first of its three pages. The authorities were not amused:

> Whereas some have lately presumed to Print and Disperse a Pamphlet, Entitled, Publick Occurrences, both Forreign and Domestick: Boston, Thursday, Septemb. 25th, 1690. Without the least Privity and Countenace of Authority. As also sundry doubtful and uncertain Reports, do hereby manifest and declare their high Resentment and Disallowance of said Pamphlet, and Order that the same be Suppressed and called in. (Pasley, 2001: 29)

Harris did not try again and returned to London where, post-1695 and the abolition of the license, there was a greater measure of freedom for a newspaperman.

The fact was that a printer could not survive in the colonies without obtaining official work. There was really, outside of Boston, too little private need. Contrariwise, each colony acquired an official printer and often required more work than a single shop could meet. Even Harris undertook official printing in the four years between *Publick Occurences* and his return to London. As a result, when the first regularly published newspaper did appear, it owed more to the model of Roger L'Estrange than to Marchmont Nedham.

The *Boston News-Letter*, which began in 1704, was produced by the town's postmaster, John Campbell, who had been successfully circulating a handwritten newsletter since 1700. He saw this as part of his duties and the *Boston News-Letter*'s masthead proclaimed it as being 'Published by Authority'.

With the approval of the colonial administration, Campbell was seeking to emulate the *London Gazette* and was happy to have the entire contents of his paper vetted. The paper was, in style, an old-fashioned coranto reprinting stories gleaned from the London papers. The time-lapse was considerable, not the matter of days or weeks that had characterized continental reporting in England a century earlier, but anything from one to three months.

The *Boston News-Letter* acquired competitors in Massachusetts and similar publications appeared across the colonies but, despite some inadequacies in the licensing system, no colonial government became embroiled, as did Westminster administrations, in the struggle to contain the press. Official printing needs and the oppressive use of libel were sufficient to keep the local press in check, and the operation of the general warrant and the imposition of specific taxes were unknown. Equally, though, the momentous suspension of the Licensing Act had no effect on the colonies' patchy licensing regimes. Colonial printers thought themselves but a channel of communication. As Benjamin Franklin put it, printers were 'educated in the Belief that when Men differ in opinion both Sides ought equally to have the Advantage of being heard by the Publick' (Pasley, 2001: 28). It was possible to reprint imported opinion with a modicum of freedom, even radical opinion, such as the 'Cato' letters; local material, however, remained dangerous. Seditious libel was the real threat to the press, licensed or not.

Benjamin Franklin's elder brother James, for example, was no friend of Boston's ruling Puritan oligarchy and opened the correspondent columns of his *New-England Courant* to citizens of similar oppositional views. In 1723, the Great and General Court of the colony appointed a committee to inquire into the paper and ordered Franklin to desist personally from publishing it unless 'it be first supervised by the secretary of this province'. Initially, James sought to avoid this ban by having his young brother Ben, then aged seventeen, sign the paper as publisher; but when they fell out, he moved to the adjacent colony of Rhode Island, seeking a jurisdiction where prior constraint was less vigorously imposed. Ben betook himself to Philadelphia and, eventually, to the *Pennsylvania Gazette* (Palfrey, 1875: 410). Influenced by Joseph Addison and Richard Steele's astute, if gentle, journalistic comedy of everyday manners in the *Spectator*, Ben managed, by the wit of his writing, to produce the most popular publication in the colonies; and he did so while avoiding entanglements with the administration. In fact, he became both the Commonwealth of Pennsylvania's official printer and deputy postmaster for the colonies.

Others were less untouched. James Alexander, a New York attorney, used the *New York Weekly Journal*, which had been set up specifically as a platform for opposition, to attack the Governor, Sir William Cosby. In 1733, he placed a crude satire on Sir William in the paper, infuriating him. Alexander, though, did not bear the brunt of the Governor's displeasure; the printer, Peter Zenger, did:

> A Proclamation: Whereas by the Contrivance of some evil Disposed and Disaffected Persons, divers Journals or Printed News Papers (entitled, *The New-York Weekly Journal, containing the freshest Advices, Foreign and Domestick*) have been caused to be Printed and Published by John Peter Zenger, in many of which Journals or Printed News Papers are contained divers Scandalous, Virulent, False and Seditious Reflections, not only upon the whole Legislature, in general, and upon the most considerable persons in the most distinguished Stations in this province but also upon his Majesty's lawful and rightful Government, and just Prerogative ... Wherefore I ... have thought fit to issue this proclamation, hereby Promising a Reward of Fifty Pounds ...

Alexander represented the printer in the case of seditious libel brought against Zenger but did so in such a partisan manner that he was disbarred. Zenger languished in jail while his wife ran the paper, a not uncommon occurrence in such instances (Pasley, 2001: 31).

Eventually, the greatest colonial lawyer of his generation, the Scottish immigrant Andrew Hamilton, sometime Attorney-General of the Commonwealth of Pennsylvania, appeared on Zenger's behalf pro bono. Hamilton made exactly the argument that was to be presented some three decades later in the 'Junius' case in London, and to like effect: acquittal and the establishment of the principle that juries could hear the substance of the libel, and not merely pronounce on the fact of its publication. More than that technicality, for Hamilton, and for the jury he convinced, Zenger's cause was the 'Cause of Liberty ... That, to which Nature and the Laws of our Country have given us the Right, – the Liberty both of exposing and opposing arbitrary power ... by speaking and writing Truth' (Howell, 1816: 722).

Not for nothing had copies of the *London Journal* with 'Cato's' 'Letter No. 15' made their way across the Atlantic. There was a consensus in radical thought at home and in the colonies as to the place of free expression among the rights of 'free born English [and in this instance Scottish] men'. Here was a demand for a defence against seditious libel, truth, which was not to be established in Britain for another 108 years (see Chapter 4.5); moreover, Hamilton's general lack of deference gave an early whiff of an approaching storm:

> *Mr Hamilton*: The practice of informations for libels is a sword in the hand of a wicked king and an arrant coward to cut down and destroy the innocent ...
> *Att Gen*: Pray, Mr Hamilton, have a care what you say; don't go too far neither. I don't like those liberties.
> *Mr Hamilton*: Sure, Mr Attorney ... All men agree that we are governed by the best of kings. I cannot see the meaning of Mr Attorney's caution ... May it please your honour, I was saying, not withstanding all the duty and reverence claimed by Mr Attorney to men in authority, they are not exempt from observing the rules of common justice. (Howell, 1816: 707)

The case was indeed not merely 'the cause of a poor printer nor of New York alone' and Hamilton's rhetoric made this a self-fulfilling prophecy. A crucial connection had been made between press freedom and the general question of colonial liberty. More than that, the press was positioned as a prime agent to resist tyranny.

The role was not refused:

> Everything that is right or natural pleads for separation. The blood of the slain, the weeping voice of nature cries, 'TIS TIME TO PART' ... O! ye that love mankind! Ye that dare oppose not only the tyranny but the tyrant, stand forth! Every spot of the old world is over run with oppression. Freedom been hunted round the globe. Asia and Africa have long expelled her. Europe regards her as a stranger and England hath given her warning to depart. O! receive the fugitive, and prepare in time an asylum for mankind. (Paine, 1894b [1776]: 89)

Separation from Britain was, argued this particular 'fugitive' Thomas Paine, a matter of *Common Sense*, as he titled this pamphlet of early 1776. In the four decades since Hamilton's defence of Zenger, in Britain's North American provinces there had been forty serious riots, eighteen uprisings and six slave rebellions. Even the cautious Benjamin Franklin had been moved in 1752 to publish in his *Gazette* the famous cartoon of a snake cut into thirteen pieces, to represent the thirteen colonies, with the caption: 'Join or Die.'

The most serious issue was direct taxation. Of the specific new imposts decreed by distant Westminster, none could be better devised to act as a match to the tinderbox that Britain's American provinces had become than a stamp duty on paper. Every stamped sheet had to be imported, a direct charge impacting on the work of two of the most vociferous groups in the colonies, the lawyers and the printers (Thorpe, 1901: 49). The Stamp and 'Sugar' Acts, as the rest of the regulations came to be called, provoked the first unified response from the colonists. A continental-wide Congress appointed from nine colonies assembled, at the instigation of the Massachusetts House of Representatives, in New York. While its members, as 'natural born' Englishmen, professed their sincere devotion to the Crown 'with the warmest sentiments of affection and duty to His Majesty's Person and Government', they also insisted: 'that it is inseparably essential to the freedom of a people, and the undoubted right of Englishmen, that no taxes be imposed on them, but with their own consent, given personally, or by their representatives. The colonists were not without friends in the Westminster Parliament and the legislation was withdrawn' (Thorpe, 1901: 53, 58).

Britain's retreat, though, was merely tactical: the Crown's insistence on its right to tax continued. Nor did the colonists abandon their ever-growing sense of grievance at their subaltern status – none more so than Samuel Adams. He had been publishing in the *Independent Advertiser* since 1748 and also contributing essays to Benjamin Edes' *Boston Gazette* (Maier, 1980: 3–50;

Alexander, 2002). The Harvard-educated son of a wealthy Boston politician in the malting business, he was not himself a successful man of affairs. Adams was a tax-collector, but so incompetent was he in this role that it enhanced his political popularity. He used every available platform to advance radical, 'Patriotic', views about citizens' rights and he was well able to speak for the excluded majority of the colonists. For example, he was heard at the Boston Caucus, a debating club of the sort that had become common in the colonies in the eighteenth century; and at the democratic, but oligarchic, town meetings which were a feature of life in Massachusetts Bay.[1] Above all, though, he realized that throughout the length of the thirteen colonies – and, on horseback, some length it was – the local papers could be constituted into a network to push a political agenda.

Reprinting the contents of other published material, after all, had been the bedrock on which the colonial press rested. The network of reprinting Patriot papers Adams encouraged was to be central to the growing sense of nationhood and demands for 'independency'. To resist the imposition of import duties, metropolitan taxes and export restrictions, Adams set up a *Journal of Occurrences*. It was dedicated to distributing stories, many certainly fraudulent, of British military atrocities in Massachusetts as the authorities continued to collect money by force. He and his Patriot colleagues at last imported into the colonies an editorial model that owed more to Nedham than to L'Estrange with his newspapers printed 'by authority'. As with Nedham, so with Adams: the press was for them an agitational tool as much as it was a channel for news. It was certainly no instrument of government. Nor was Adams a bystander, a 'Mr Spectator'. He was an active political player with a prescient understanding of the importance of the press.

The print licensing system, as had happened more than once in England, faltered as the governments of the provinces were distracted by civil discord. By 1772, the Patriot news network was not only widely circulating information, true and false, about the 'occurrences'; on occasion, Adams even helped instigate such incidents – the 'Boston Tea Party', for instance. 'Sons of Liberty',[2] dressed as native Americans, threw a cargo of tea into Boston harbour in 1773 to protest a new tax imposed on importing the leaf. Adam was able to pass such stories not only to local papers, such as Isaiah Thomas's *Massachusetts Spy*, but also to John Holt's *New York Gazette and Weekly Post-Boy*. From New York, the reports were carried by the post-riders to the *Pennsylvania Chronicle*, the *Maryland Chronicle*, the *Newport Mercury* and down the line to the *Gazette of South Carolina*. By this means, it took a mere six weeks for a story, or a pamphlet, to appear in all the colonies. Not all the newspapers by any means were Patriotic, such sentiment against the mother country being seen, despite everything, as extreme. The Loyalist press, though, had a basic problem. While committed to defending the Crown, it was also naturally less eager to support the taxes, never-mind countenancing the

British audacities that were constantly being presented to the public by Patriot newsmen.

The British continued to exacerbate the situation to the public relations advantage of the Patriots. In response to the 'Tea Party', in 1774, a series of 'Intolerable' Acts designed to make an example of Massachusetts were passed. The borders of loyalist Canada were expanded southward, Catholicism was encouraged, New England town meetings were dissolved and Boston harbour was blockaded. In response, again instigated by Adams among others, the Continental Congress reassembled in Philadelphia.

Just as this Congress melded representatives of all thirteen colonial assemblies, so the first moves were made to aggregate the individual New England militias into an army of resistance. The perhaps by-now inevitable clash occurred in Lexington where, on 19 April 1775, the Minutemen, the elite element in the Massachusetts militia, faced the British 10th Regiment of Foot. The confrontation was witnessed by Isaac Thomas, the publisher of the *Massachusetts Spy*: 'the [British] commanding officer accosted the militia, in words to this effect, "Disperse, you damn'd rebels – Damn you, disperse" ... and then there seemed to be a general discharge from the whole body. Eight of our men were killed and nine wounded'.

The militia regrouped at nearby Concord and a pitched battle ensured. Echoing Samuel Pecke in the seventeenth century, Thomas ran the story, unsensationally enough, on page three in his issue of 3 May. Yet, presaging the impact of Tyas and the press corps at Peterloo half-a-century later, the consequences of the melee at Lexington and the battle at Concord were profound, not least because the report was quickly (comparatively speaking) magnified by Adam's reprinting network. Thanks to Thomas and Adams, that first shot was to be heard 'round the world'.[3]

Thus the War of Independence began with the American press attendant at its birth. A month after the *Massachusetts Spy* report, the Continental Congress, still by no means united in support of extreme Patriotic demands for independence, nevertheless voted to enhance its military response by fully combining all the provincial militias into a unified Continental Army. Now formally traitors to the Crown, they elected one of their own, a slave-owning Patriot representative from Virginia, Colonel George Washington, to have command of this force. Having held British commissions in previous French and Indian Wars, he was the most professional senior officer available to the Patriots (Alden, 1996).

In January 1776, Thomas Paine's *Common Sense* appeared, joining the 400 or so other pamphlets, Patriot or Loyalist, which had been published over the previous decades arguing for or against the colonists' positions. Tom Paine, who had worked primarily as excise-man in England, had immigrated to America, arriving in November 1774. With a letter of introduction furnished by Ben Franklin, he quickly found work as an editorial assistant on the recently established *Pennsylvania Magazine* (Wilson, 1988: 18). *Common Sense* was written a little more than a year after his arrival. No other single publication so clearly committed to independence had its impact; indeed, nothing on any subject published in the North American European settlements in the eighteenth century was as popular. It went through twenty-five editions in that first year, some 100,000 copies, far more than was needed to cover the estimated 40,000 homes that took Patriot newspapers. It can easily be imagined as reaching virtually every adult colonist in a population of two million. Before its publication, support for independence was, as Paine put it, 'a doctrine scarce and rare'. After *Common Sense*, it was a much talked about position which needed to be either refuted or acted on (Wilson, 1988: 59).

In March, General Washington drove the British out of Boston. By summer, no British forces remained in the thirteen colonies. With the help of *Common Sense*, the minority of representatives in the Continental Congress who desired 'independency', such as Samuel Adams, finally won the argument. The Congress, on 2 July 1776, resolved: 'That these United Colonies are, and of right ought to be, free and independent States.' Two days later the resolution was reinforced with an explanatory document, a 'unanimous Declaration of the thirteen united States of America'. It had been written by Thomas Jefferson, another slave-owning representative from Virginia.

Jefferson eloquently translated the philosophical theory of Locke's 1691 *On Civil Government: The Second Treatise* into powerful direct political rhetoric. He went further than Locke, though: his 'self-evident' rights substituted 'the pursuit of happiness' for Locke's more restrained 'estates'. Although himself a slave-owner, he had even wanted to charge the King with the fault of preventing the banning of the 'execrable commerce of slavery', but that was too much for the southern colonists to countenance (Guillen, 2007: 78, 115). At the time, 20 per cent of the population was enslaved and Paine's 'asylum for mankind' was to be limited to those most like the makers of the revolution – male and white, propertied and Christian. As Dr Johnson, who anyway did not believe that taxes were quite the 'tyranny' the Patriot rebels claimed, had already observed in a London pamphlet: 'How is it that we hear the loudest yelps for liberty from the drivers of negroes?' (Johnson, 1775: 89). Even the radical Paine had noted this hypocrisy. Americans, he wrote, 'complain so loudly about attempts to enslave them, while they hold so many hundred thousands in slavery' (Paine, 1894a [1775]: 5). This (considerable) stain aside, Jefferson and Locke both agreed, of course, on the self-evident primacy of the rights to 'life' and 'liberty', at least for Christian Caucasians; and that was, after all, no small matter given the circumstances of the time.

At the signing, in response to the exhortation of the Congress's elected president, John Hancock, 'We must be unanimous ... We must all hang together', the oldest representative, newspaperman Benjamin Franklin of Pennsylvania, agreed, with his usual dryness: 'We must all hang together or we shall most assuredly all hang separately' (Graydon, 1846: 131).[4] The *Declaration* was reprinted in, at the very least, twenty-nine of the colonies' thirty-five newspapers. It crossed the Atlantic in six weeks and was picked up by the *London Chronicle* and the *Daily Courant*. Throughout absolutist Europe it was banned, except in France, where the principle of support for 'the enemy of my enemy' allowed it to be published. For the autocratic French throne, though, the comfort it gave to opponents of the 'Royal Brute of Britain' was actually far outweighed by the support it provided, with its democratic and republican sentiments, for internal critics of the King of France.

These hard-fought battles over documents in Philadelphia had no effect on the British military counter-strike that was already underway through New York. In November, 1776, the augmented British forces drove Washington from the winter camp he had established on Harlem Heights in Manhattan. He retreated across the Hudson and there Paine caught up with the army. He was soon to be made secretary to one of Washington's generals, his pen being of more use than his musket. Two days before Christmas 1776, writing, according to tradition, on a drumhead by candlelight, Paine began a series of articles that were to become *The Crisis*. Washington had this first read to his troops:

> These are the times that try men's souls. The Summer soldier and the sunshine Patriot will, in this crisis, shrink from the service of their country ... Tyranny, like hell, is not easily conquered; yet we have this consolation with us, that the harder the conflict the more glorious the triumph ... What we obtain too cheap, we esteem too lightly – Tis dearness only that gives everything its value. Heaven knows how to put a proper price upon its goods; and it would be strange indeed if so celestial an article as FREEDOM should not be highly rated. (Paine, 1894c [1776]: 170).

On Christmas day, Washington, his troops' morale revived, took Trenton. The first article of *The Crisis* was printed in the *Pennsylvania Packet* on 27 December and, in the weeks thereafter, reprinted throughout the network. The war was to drag on as, in eighteenth-century fashion, the armies marched to and fro mainly across the north-eastern states until, nearly five years later, the British gave up at Yorktown in Virginia. Paine continued to write his *Crisis* pamphlets, eventually sixteen in all, until 1783.

No account of the American Revolution can ignore the press. The issue of press freedom is therefore far more central to the American struggle for national identity and basic liberties than is the parallel effort in Britain, although the pattern of repression and resistance are similar. In England, freedom of the press was a legal construct achieved by means of precedent. It received no explicit statutory protection until the Human Rights Act of 1998. In the United States of America, even before a federal constitution was agreed in 1787, many of the several states had incorporated the right of free expression into their new basic constitutional laws. Three weeks before the Declaration of Independence, George Mason's 'Declaration of Rights' was adopted by the 'by the representatives of the good people of Virginia, assembled in full and free convention'. The twelfth of the sixteen rights stated: 'That the freedom of the press is one of the great bulwarks of liberty, and can never be restrained but by despotick governments.' The right of a press free of prior constraint was written into the state constitution, the first of these to be ratified.

Not all states made such provision[5] but nine followed Virginia's lead as their constitutions were written and adopted through 1776 and the following year. The language was echoed state to state, for example, 'that the liberty/ freedom of the press be inviolably preserved'. Alternatively, a free press is 'one of the great bulwarks of liberty and therefore ought never to be restrained'; or, 'That the people have a right of/to freedom of speech and of writing and publishing their sentiments, [concerning the transactions of government] and therefore the freedom of the press ought not to be restrained.'

Despite the rhetoric, the new states were actually as open to the attractions of press control as any other authority. Tax, for example: the now independent Massachusetts Assembly imposed a newspaper tax in 1785 as if the press's role in the struggle had bought it no privilege. Samuel Adams, for whom the press had been such an aid, was a senator. The *Spy* became a monthly to avoid the duty and Isaiah Thomas cried: 'Should the liberty of the press be once destroyed, farewell the remainder of our invaluable rights and privileges' (Ingelhart, 1987: 37). The people were inclined to agree. Having learned how to stop the royal government, they were quick to protest to their republican one. The tax was withdrawn.

The newly established independent authority of the federal United States was as uncommitted to the principle of a free press as was the Commonwealth of Massachusetts. Despite the history from Zenger to the *Massachusetts Spy*, from the *Journal of Occurrences* to *Common Sense* and *The Crisis*, a free press clause was not incorporated into the Federal Constitution adopted in 1787. A conservative tendency wished to empower the central government as way of containing the more democratic instincts of the states, including their willingness to guarantee free speech. Despite the populist rhetoric of the Constitution's opening 'We, the people ...', its provisions favoured the centre over the states. James Madison, the document's prime-mover, and his fellows feared the influence of 'uncontrolled democracy' in states where un-propertied electorates could seize power, and they prevailed.

However, in the public relations campaign to obtain ratification from the states, those in favour of the proposal were forced by public opinion – especially among the un-propertied – to promise amendments remedying the omission of rights as the price of state legislative approval. The pro-central power group were known as the 'Federalists', after a series of articles they published, *The Federalist Papers*. These eighty-five pieces, which initially appeared in three papers – the *New York Packet*, the *Independent Journal* and the *Pennsylvania Packet* – were the main PR tool of their campaign. They were the work of Madison, the lawyer John Jay and, largely, Alexander Hamilton, Washington's aide-de-camp and founder of the Bank of New York.

Hamilton – no relation to Zenger's attorney – was not a man committed to creating 'an asylum for mankind'. He was more interested in sound money. In a *Federalist* article, he acknowledged that the omission of a right of a free press had been much debated but he was not impressed: 'I hold [the concept of a free press] to be impracticable' (Hamilton, Madison and Jay, 1864 [1788]: 632). He was well aware of the recent Massachusetts row about newspaper taxes and, unsurprisingly, had argued that they were legitimate, disingenuously claiming: 'We know that newspapers are taxed in Great Britain, and yet it is notorious that the press nowhere enjoys greater liberty than in that country' (Hamilton *et al.*, 1864 [1788]: 632).

The issue of a free press was but one of a number of points about rights which needed to be resolved before ratification of the Constitution was possible. The entire matter of the debate around these issues, though, perfectly illustrates the importance of a free press. The response to *The Federalist Papers* took the form of individual, largely unsigned, articles rebutting the Federalists' arguments. These scattered replies, which were to become known as *The Anti-Federalist Papers*, speak directly to Ben Franklin's vision of a press, balanced in a de facto fashion by its diversity, acting as a channel for public ideas. In the event, the Federalists got the Constitution ratified but at the cost of promising the anti-Federalists the missing Bill of Rights.

The first Congress to be elected under the ratified Constitution eventually met in 1791, and passed this 'bill' as a series of ten amendments, including, as the first of them, a right of a free press. Hamilton, though, did not lose his original point entirely. The amendments, influenced by the somewhat unnatural 'anti-Federalist' alliance of Southern slave-owning and Northern democratic opinion, were designed to contain the powers of the federal authorities. Thus the First Amendment, guaranteeing press freedom, eschewed the language of 'bulwarks' and the 'publishing' of 'sentiments' and the like. Instead, in line with the general thrust for containment, the principle of freedom of speech was expressed as a negative, a constraint on the government: 'Congress shall make no law respecting an establishment of religion, or prohibiting the free exercise thereof; or abridging the freedom of speech or of the press; or the right of the people peaceably to assemble, and to petition the Government for the redress of grievances.'

Hamilton's concern was thus accommodated. After all, his arguments against such a clause were not entirely without merit. Subsequent events were soon to indicate the limited efficacy of the First Amendment's protection, just as he had predicted.

In 1798, under the somewhat spurious threat of a war with France, a Federalist Congress passed, and President John Adams signed, 'a Sedition Act' criminalizing 'false, scandalous or malicious writing or writings against the government ... to excite against them the hatred of the good people of the United States'.[6] Given how sedition had been used by the British against the colonists, and how its removal had been among the prime objectives of revolt, this was an Orwellian move – the revolutionary 'pigs' indeed turning into 'men'. It was also clearly illegal under the First Amendment. But not for nothing had every English lawyer who immigrated to the American colonies over the previous half century carried in his baggage Blackstone's *Commentaries*. The First Amendment, they argued, only protected against prior constraint – that is, censorship. They agreed with Lord Chief Justice Mansfield in *R. v. Woodfall*, 1770; never mind that that the Crown lost that case. The government claimed that the Sedition Act, which enshrined a 'publish and be damned' approach, was no abridgement and therefore did not offend against the First Amendment.

Anti-Federalist journalists were rounded up and, with more success than was being achieved at the same time in England, ten out of twelve cases resulted in imprisonments. In 1800, Thomas Jefferson, running for president under the slogan 'Jefferson and Liberty', made the release of the journalists a plank of his platform. Upon his election they were released and the 'second American revolution' began. The offence of seditious libel, though, was revived in a new statute in 1917 as the United States entered the First World War (see Chapter 12.4).

Hamilton was right about the central importance of 'public opinion and the spirit of the people'; the Constitution, of itself, had not protected the journalists. They were freed, in effect, by the 'people' as a consequence of a democratic election. He was wrong, though, to suggest this was not aided by having statutory protection, for all that it had been abused. The law put the people in the right, should public disturbance follow any government attempt to abridge expression. In effect, statutory protection legitimated public support as, essentially, a defence of legality. Jefferson's election spoke to the value placed on the freedom of the press and the need to maintain the First Amendment. Indeed, in the survey of American opinion undertaken two centuries after the Amendment was adopted, the public held it still to be central, albeit in a dangerously pro-forma fashion (Wyatt, Neft and Badger, 1991). In fact, free expression needs both the general spirit of the people as well as statutory protection to inhibit the government's repressive instincts. Hamilton, after all, knew this: in his initial *Federalist Papers* argument he had written that the liberty of the press 'altogether' depended on 'public opinion'/'the general spirit of the people' *and* on the government. Certainly the combination of public opinion and statute in the United States worked to produce a vibrant press, one that avoided the decades of repression that the British press still had to face.

The war had taken its toll on the colonies' newspapers. Only twenty had survived, often – as had happened before in the colonies and in England – under the direction of the wives or widows of the publisher. The new political dispensation, however, allowed the press, secure from state interference and buttressed by public support, to flourish. In the United States, journalism developed far faster than in Great Britain. By 1800, there were over 150 titles, nearly 400 by 1810 and 1,200 by 1835. This growth was not without difficulties, though. The press might not have been suborned, as it often was in Britain, by the government's gold, but it was seduced by political party subventions. Hamilton, for example, had paid Noam Webster directly to start a Federalist paper in New York in 1793 immediately after the Constitution had been adopted. It was the vituperation of the party press this sort of close relationship created, especially on the anti-Federalist side, which created a context for the passing of the Alien and Sedition Act and the prosecution of anti-Federalist journalists. The support of the political parties that came to embody the pro- and anti-Federalist positions further blurred the line between paper and pamphlet and threatened any sense of the press's independence. Such a direct hold over journalism was eventually broken (or at least loosened), as was the grip of British politicians and their bribes, by the rise of an advertising-supported, more supposedly apolitical, popular press.

5.2   *R. v. Joseph Howe, Darling v. Hall, The Crown Colony of New Zealand v. Quaife* (1835–1840): A pattern

This pattern of a struggle for free expression – was more or less repeated throughout Britain's 'White Dominions'. There are early papers, 'printed by authority', dominated by official pronouncements and reprinted overseas news, months out of date. Echoing the conflicts in England and in the American colonies, printers found themselves in difficulties, but the 'spirit' of the colonists supported them, forcing a measure of real freedom. The press of other colonies used this freedom to argue the democratic case for self-government, albeit within rather than, as had happened with the thirteen American provinces, without the Empire.

In the Canadian Maritimes, for example, the first paper was established by a migrant printer from Boston in 1752, John Bushell's *Halifax Gazette*. Quebec would get its first press only after the British conquest of 1756 and its first newspaper, a bilingual *Gazette* in 1764, and that was printed by migrants from Philadelphia. As Canada remained loyalist, this press continued in colonial circumstances where controversy, or indeed much of any local politics, was eschewed. This was to change, however, following a second armed conflict between America and Great Britain in 1812. Britain lost and public opinion finally accepted the 'revolted colonies' as the independent United States. Shortly thereafter, a serious debate about the governance of Canada's provinces began. It came to occupy a central place in the news agenda (Vipond, 2000: 7–8).

As in the United States a little earlier, the papers became the creatures of party, Reform or Tory, with politician/editors using titles as platforms for their own agendas. Against a background of civil unrest and actual insurrection, in 1835, the Zenger role was played by Joseph Howe. He was arrested by the provincial government of Nova Scotia, whose police force (ironically) had been established by his father, for printing scathing attacks on the police and the magistracy in his *Novascotian* (Murray Beck, 1982: 135–41). The jury, for the first time in the loyal British North American provinces, refused to convict. In a series of constitutional reforms over the next three decades, the British, their imperialism tempered by their American experiences, lanced the boil of colonial unrest by yielding to the colonists' demands. This process culminated in the creation of a federal Canada as a dominion within the British Empire.

The key was to be the presence of a substantial Caucasian settlement of British descent, race trumping – for instance – criminality.

The First Fleet, which arrived in Botany Bay in the penal colony of New South Wales, Australia, in January 1788, carried a press for the printing of government ordinances. In 1800, another Howe, George, a convicted petty-thief and ex-London *Times* printer, whose father had been a government printer in the Caribbean, arrived and was put to work. In 1803, he produced the accurately named *Sydney Gazette and New South Wales Advertiser* reflecting, in '*Gazette*' its official role and in '*Advertiser*' its more journalistic function. It was, though, 'moral to the point of priggishness, patriotic to the point of servility, pompous in a stiff, eighteenth century fashion' (Ferguson, Foster and Green, 1936: 98). Gazettes appeared throughout the Australian settlements. As had always happened in Great Britain when formal restrictions had been relaxed, the removal of licensing in 1824 in New South Wales encouraged the appearance of oppositional titles, albeit in far smaller numbers than occurred in the mother country. Edward Smith Hall's *Monitor* was an example.

Hall was no transported convict but a Lincolnshire gentleman of educated radical opinion. His paper was conducted 'as much as possible in the style of Mr Cobbett'. He found himself in a state of war with the colony's autocratic Governor, Ralph Darling. For example, in 1827, exactly as had happened with Cobbett with a similar story in 1809, Hall's criticism of the Governor's brutal punishment of two soldiers provoked the latter into introducing two repressive bills. These sought to copy the English Six Acts' regulations on the press, reimposing licences and requiring sureties (Bonwich, 1890: 16, 30). The colony's 'Nominees Council' passed them but they were almost entirely overturned at law as being unconstitutional. The *Monitor* and a rival, the equally critical *Australian*,[7] continued to harass the Governor. Darling sued Hall for libel who was found guilty and imprisoned; but Darling remained the 'hangman of the press' in the pages of the *Australian*. To public rejoicing in the colony, Darling was recalled to Britain, in no little part because of the journalists' attacks on him. Back home, he was comforted, eventually, with a knighthood and a promotion to general. In a direct echo of the Americans half-a-century earlier, a 'Patriot' association appeared in 1835 seeking a greater measure of self-government. Hall was prominent among its members. With titles such as the *Star and Working Men's Guardian* and *John Bull*, the Australian press now smacked more of its British unstamped equivalent than of any gazette 'printed by authority' (R. Walker, 1976: 39, 45).

In the Crown colony of New Zealand, and the settlement of the New Zealand Company to its south, 'the press became a major component of the settlers' de facto political representation' (Day, 1990: 12). The 'official' phase began in 1840, with the *New Zealand Advertiser and Bay of Islands Gazette*, the colony's first paper. Dr Barzillai Quaife, its editor, got away with twenty-seven editions before he printed 'moderate suggestions for reform' on the vexed question of land rights and was hauled before the authorities (Day, 1990: 13). The Lieutenant-Governor used the repressive Darling legislation of 1827, New South Wales law being then applicable to New Zealand, to shut the paper down. The colonial administration started its own gazette and constantly frustrated any attempts to begin a more independent publication. This was easily done as it owned the colony's only press. The New Zealand Company's own paper in Wellington was often vitriolic about the Crown colony's administration to the north; but in both settlements the settlers demanded independent publications. Presses were imported and papers without 'authority' (as it were) appeared. The *Southern Cross*, for example, mounted personal attacks on the colony's governor and, when it desisted from that, argued vigorously for self-government. In Wellington, papers – the *New Zealand Spectator* and the *Cook's Strait Guardian* – were started by the settlers and managed by oversight committees they appointed (Day, 1990: 36–7). These too pushed for political reform.

From one side of the globe to the other, in the colonies being planted by 'free-born' Englishmen in the eighteenth and early nineteenth centuries, all agreed that the public sphere not only included journalism as a source of information and entertainment but also accepted and expected it to play a central role in the political life of the community. The English language press was suffused with the spirit of Nedham, Paine and Cobbett (and Crouch, Lloyd and John Browne Bell). Blackstone's writ also ran far: in the anglophone world, there was to be no prior constraint – even when the press, in conditions of industrialization, reached out to the rapidly urbanizing masses.

5.3 *New York Herald v. New York Sun* (1835–1924): Mass circulation

The newspaper had emerged in the seventeenth century as a species of chronicle, albeit one ever ready to purvey sensationalism and, on occasion, indulge in fabrication. Basically, though, the contents were determined by external factors, not imagination. Journalism was essentially reactive, responding to external events and external expressions of opinion. Overt interventions, such as Marchmont Nedham's offer of a bounty for bringing in the King, were exceptional. Samuel Adams might have set up the Boston Tea Party as a stunt to be reported but he did so as a politician, not a journalist. Original opinion, of course, ran through the early correspondents' reports and, later, in the letters to the editor; but those who conducted papers were initially restrained from editorializing directly. If fact, they sometimes resorted to inserting a fake letter as a way of expressing an opinion. Often, regular publications, the *North Briton* for instance, would be classed as newspapers but were actually more like a sequence of dated pamphlets.

Formal editorials start to appear in the later eighteenth century, one paper, the *New York Journal*, going so far as to run the column in italic – with its echo of handwriting – to distinguish it from the Roman print in which news was set. Editorials broke the basic reactive line. Such content originated not by direct reporting but by commentating on such reporting. In the United States, the Federalist's decision to publish their essays in the papers secured this bridgehead. James Gordon Bennett's introduction of the interview took the interventionism represented by the editorial to a new level (see Chapter 3). Little better illustrates the prestige gained by the American press in the struggle for independence than the freedom Gordon Bennett exploited in creating a template for the one-cent mass newspaper. He was emboldened by the esteem in which the American press was held. Crossing the police line in front of a Manhattan brothel to interview the madam, he reported that he heard an officer reply to a bystander's question, 'Why do you let that man in?' with the gratifyingly supportive answer: 'He is an editor – he is on public duty' (Gordon Bennett, 1836a: 1).

Gordon Bennett had not pioneered the one-cent, advertising-dependent paper. It was the young publisher of the one-cent *Sun*, Benjamin Day, who had first exploited this possibility. Gordon Bennett, though, can lay better claim to be a more thorough innovator. Crucially, he instituted the practice of obtaining advance money for advertisements. The two-edged nature of advertising – that it aided political independence even as it potentially threatened editorial integrity – was not yet clear. For Day and Gordon Bennett, only the advantages of this revenue stream were apparent. Day was more concerned about the appearance of Gordon Bennett's *Herald* than he had been at the arrival of other rivals. He had run a classic spoiler on the day Gordon Bennett's first edition appeared. The *Sun* claimed that Sir John Herschel, famous as the most distinguished British astronomer of his day, had spotted creatures on the moon through an enormous telescope. When unmasked, Day, in a fashion that was to become a tabloid norm, claimed the moral high ground. He was, nobly, trying to distract the public, not from buying the *Herald* of course, but from the 'bitter apples of discord' about slavery. The *Sun*, unsurprisingly, also denied that Gordon Bennett's interview with Rosina Townsend, the brothel madam, had ever taken place (Tucher, 1994: 35).

The mass circulation newspaper these one-cent New York pioneers heralded spoke to ever increasing urbanization. Technologically, the print industry made steady progress, the literate industrialized masses providing the spur – the social necessity – for speeding the presses. Steam-driven rotary machines fed by continuous rolls of paper – a format long used by the textile industry – and a constant search for mechanized typesetting were both responses to the burgeoning newspaper industry. Many thousands of copies an hour could now be printed – and sold.

The telegraph also made news a more perishable commodity than it had ever been before. The development of the modern 'pyramid structure' of news writing, whereby a report begins with the essence of a story and adds details that can be cut to fit the page, was aided by telegraphy's demand for succinctness (Mindich, 1998). Internationally, though, the use of the technology was in its infancy. It remained prohibitively expensive – if the network even existed. News of the disastrous the charge of the Light Brigade, for example, despite being sent 'By Submarine and British Telegraph', still took some twenty days to reach London in 1854. Paul Freiherr von Reuter was shortly to exploit the cable to build up a news agency. His was a new sort of company, one selling reports to papers unable to afford their own correspondents. He began by transmitting stock market information from London to subscribers in Paris using carrier-pigeons as well as the wire and he continued to do so into the 1850s (Storey, 1969: 10–11). In 1866, an operational telegraph had finally been laid across the Atlantic: the *Herald* had to be the first to exploit it. There was a war going on in Europe between Prussia and Austria and so, at vast expense – $6,500 in gold, some $90,000 today – the text of a speech by the Prussian King, Wilhelm I, was telegraphed across the Atlantic in its entirety. Sending Henry Stanley to Africa was another *Herald* 'stunt', a way of keeping in front of the competition.

The British untaxed 'free' press was subjected to similar market pressures and it is no surprise to find that James Gordon Bennett Jr had a London partner supporting Stanley's expedition. Joseph Levy had been printing the *Daily Telegraph* and had taken it over editorially in 1855 when its publisher went bankrupt. Quick to seize the opportunity finally afforded by the abolition of the newspaper stamp, he reduced the price to one penny and was soon outselling *The Times*. He also owned *The Sunday Times*. His son, Edward Levy-Lawson, and Thornton Leigh-Hunt were appointed editors and, under them, the *Daily Telegraph* modelled itself on the *New York Herald*, not just in terms of cover price but also editorially.

The proprietors, in the age of American capitalism's 'robber barons', had themselves become 'barons' of the press, legends in their own times. Gordon Bennett Jr, having outraged New York society until he was no longer welcome, retired to his yacht, *Lysistrata*, moored in the south of France, and ran the *Herald* from there. He became a byword for profligacy, his very name 'Gordon Bennett' entering the language as a British expletive expressing alarmed amazement. The untold wealth these men accumulated was mainly due to their control of multiple titles in many cities. Joseph Pulitzer and William Randolph Hearst, for example, had arrived in the New York as successful publishers of papers in St Louis and San Francisco respectively. Some made fortunes by concentrating on smaller towns, but in a large number of them spread across the country. By the 1890s, E.W. Scripps had developed thirty-four newspapers in medium-size cities in fifteen states. Eventually he owned twenty-five large papers, a wire service and a news agency. The newspaper chain is another late nineteenth-century American innovation.

In Britain, the press barons could become barons indeed. Edward Levy-Lawson, proprietor of the *Daily Telegraph*, was knighted in 1892 and created Baron Burnham in 1903. His son was appointed Viscount in 1919.[8] Alfred Harmsworth and his brother Harold, having successfully copied the sensationalist New York 'Yellow Press' with an evening paper, started the *Daily Mail* – 'a penny newspaper for one halfpenny' – in 1896. They became the Viscounts Northcliffe and Rothermere. Harmsworth's basic instruction to his *Daily Mail* staff smacks of a Yellow Paper newsroom: 'Get me a murder a day.' Interviews duly regularly appeared not only with murderers but also with the police (Kevin Williams, 2009: 54). The *Daily Mail* soon dominated the market as *The Times* had once done. Invited by the stunt-seeking Pulitzer to edit the *New York World* for its first edition of the twentieth century, Harmsworth crossed the Atlantic and reduced the paper's format for the occasion: a 'tabloid newspaper', he called it, filching a pharmaceutical company's 1884 trademark term for compressed pills. Harmsworth thought, with some justice, that compression, of story length as well paper size, would mark 'the newspaper of the twentieth century'. Half broadsheet papers, though, were far from unknown. In the 1830s, the one-cent press had used this format and the New York *Daily Graphic*, which pioneered the use of photographic halftone plates on the rotary press, had been doing so since it began publication in 1880. It adopted the smaller format because the technology would not allow for large images.

The press was now firmly a creature of entertainment – of information as entertainment. Information's value was not obviously valuable only because it was necessary to the democratic processes of society. All the press's actions – campaigns, exposés, stunts – were determined by sensationalism, often, as its traditions allowed and society tolerated, augmented by imagination. The underlying notion of sensationalism was defined in the offices of the *New York Sun*, now edited by Charles Dana. His city editor, John Bogart, summed it up thus for a tyro reporter: 'When a dog bites a man, that is not news; but when a man bites a dog, that is news' (Mott, 1962: 376).

Nevertheless, in the midst of its hysterics, the press still functioned as a guardian of the guardians. Moreover, it afforded women a rare independent platform for expression. Despite its glass ceiling, which was to persist throughout the next century, journalism was one of the first professions to admit any women as senior practitioners at all. Nellie Bly is representative of the persistent female presence in the history of the press (see Chapter 3). She was not alone. For example, the British leader writer of the 1850s, Harriet Martineau, was known as the great 'she-radical' and a celebrity in her day. There was also Lady Florence Dixie (in effect a 'Travelling Lady') who was in Zululand in 1879 and covered the war between the Zulus and the Boers, which broke out the following year, for the *Morning Post*; or Hulda Friederichs and the birth control advocate Annie Bessant, both of whom worked for W.T. Stead (Onslow, 2000; Mott, 1962). In the 1890s, Rachel Beer edited the *Sunday Times*, which she had bought from Levy-Lawson, as well as the *Observer*. This did not mean, of course, that proprietors were immune from sexism.

On 2 January 1900, Pulitzer reverted to broadsheet and Harmsworth did not reduce the size of the *Daily Mail* upon his return. He did, though, relaunch the *Daily Mirror* as a photographically 'illustrated' tabloid in 1904. It had failed in 1903 to reach its original intended female readership. Worried by rumours that Stead was thinking of starting a paper specifically for women, Harmsworth determined to strike first. The *Daily Mirror*'s editorial policy was determined by his stereotypical notions of what was of interest to women – a soft lifestyle news agenda. When women revealed this was not to their taste by ignoring the title, he barked that the experience taught him that 'women can't write and don't want to read' – a palpable nonsense, not least because of the *Daily Mail*'s notable success in attracting a female readership. Reborn as an illustrated tabloid, the halfpenny *Daily Mirror* was a success.

The *Daily Mail* was now selling 800,000 copies a day to a market which, because of geography and the rail network, covered all of England and Wales (and, in competition with Scottish titles, much of Scotland). The introduction of 'Linotype' mechanical typesetting, which finally allowed for the laborious process of hand-setting type to be done by merely sitting typing at a keyboard, brought lead-based printing to a final point of development. The Western mass circulation press was to remain, in form and content, essentially unchanged throughout the twentieth century. Technologically, the last major advances in offset-lithography, computer-aided production, remote printing via satellite and so on refined but did not transform the papers. Even as the press's dominance as a source of news declined, these technologies of production allowed, in the face of ever-greater competition from alternative media, for easier, timelier news-gathering and more targeted and wider distribution. The United States, for example, got its first national paper, *USA Today*, a possibility unexplored prior to satellite communications.

More than any technological development, as had been anticipated by the British campaign against the 'Taxes on Knowledge', the American press and the anglophone presses in the white dominions of the British Empire were now also securely 'in the hands of men of good moral character, of respectability, and of capital'. Despite this limitation on what a free press might truly be, 'the liberty of press' in these terms was an established reality. While the Whig interpretation overstated the extent of this freedom, it was certainly the case that it was no longer confined to the narrow point, 'that a man may print what he pleases without a licence' and suffer appropriately. In the English-speaking world, the battle against the licence, against the censorship of print, against specific 'regulation', had triumphed. The press had secured a measure of privilege. There was, moreover, a widespread consensus that a modern state and economy was best served by a press 'free' in terms now established for it.

5.4 *La Loi du 29 juillet 1881 sur la liberté de la presse* (1881): Press freedom in the West

It is no accident that in Lower Canada – New France – the French colonial authorities allowed no presses at all and the first one arrived in Montreal only after the British take-over (Vipond, 2000: 7). In the fifteenth and sixteenth centuries, the relationship of the authorities in England and in France to the press was more or less identical. The English revolt against the royal absolutism, however, had resulted in the King's decapitation (in 1649), whereas in France, parallel unrest in the form of a series of revolts, known as La Fronde, between 1648 and 1653 against the boy King Louis XIV was suppressed and the autocracy confirmed. Thereafter, under him, there would be no question of asserting any 'free-born' rights, at home or in the French colonies. This impacted on the respective presses. The later Stuarts could but dream of a controlled press of the sort their Tudor predecessors experienced, but the Sun King could treat his exactly as his sixteenth-century ancestors had done. Louis XIV could trumpet his victories in *occasionels* and license apolitical, sensationalist *canards* exactly as they had done. The *Chambre de syndicats* in Paris, established by Charles XIII, maintained its censorship role in ways the equivalent Company of Stationers, which anyway was less overtly a state institution, did not. The Chancellor of France, supported by a network of no less than 120 local censors, still licensed every publication, including some rude parodies of the corantos. In fact, the English seventeenth-century 'nocturnals' aped French originals such as *Nouvelles... de l'autre monde.*

The only serious challenge to this absolutist approach to printing was offered by the Dutch. Decades of upheaval, as the Netherlands provinces shook off Spanish colonial control, allowed printers to operate the least controlled presses in Europe. On these, apart from publications in their own language and Latin, they also shrewdly produced materials in other tongues more widely spoken than their own (see Chapter 4.2). Corantos were translated and smuggled into France at the same time as they were being translated into English, the first dating from 1610. A *Mercure français,*[9] written in French but printed in the Netherlands, appeared the following year. In France itself, though, the tentative exploration of further domestically produced corantos, of the sort published by London printers under James I and VI, barely occurred.

However, a start was made in the seventeenth century during the reign of Louis' father, Louis XIII (Bellanger, 1969). In 1630, Dr Théophraste Renaudot, the royal physician who was now Commissioner General of the Poor, had given substance to an idea published by the philosopher Michel de Montaigne half-a-century before. This was for a shop, Le Bureau d'Adresses et de Rencontre, designed to alleviate unemployment. Eventually, all the unemployed of Paris had to register at the Bureau. On its walls were posted notices of jobs making it a sort of labour exchange. Other advertisements for the exchange of goods could also be placed. The notices did not need to be printed but printed advertising handbills had long existed; and, in newspapers outside of France, notices and advertisements were not unknown. It was, therefore, an entirely logically step for the notices in the shop to be printed as a publication, which Renaudot began doing from time to time. Having published a digest of advertisements, it was then equally logical for him to begin publishing a digest of news.

In 1631, he began to issue, with official blessing, a small four-page weekly, the *Gazette de France*, covering the religious war then raging beyond the borders and some uncontroversial local stories. It was successful, doubling in size within the year (Smith, 1979: 26–32). The *Gazette* had two rivals, produced by Parisian printers, but they lacked Renaudot's royal connections. His paper fell firmly within the 'printed by/with authority' category, an inestimable advantage under an absolute monarch.[10] Louis XIII moved to protect Renaudot in 1635 by issuing a monopolistic licence for him alone 'to have printed and sold by those appropriate, news, gazettes and accounts of all that has happened and is happening inside and outside the Kingdom' (Smith, 1979: 29). The other papers were suppressed. Such was the efficiency of the censorship apparatus in France, the *Gazette* acquired, apart from a few parodies such as the *AntiGazette*, no further unlicensed competitors.

In 1645, Renaudot had written that the King did not bother to read the paper but that he was in touch 'almost regularly': 'Was it for me to examine the deeds of the government? My pen was only the grafting tool' (Smith, 1979: 30). Here is the justification of the licensed editor who publishes by 'authority' *tout court*. As Tobias Peucer was to put it in a doctoral dissertation on the practice of journalism, presented to the University of Leipzig in 1690, 'news should not appear in type before [being] approved by the censor'. He was especially convinced that 'the affairs of princes' should not be 'bandied about' without their prior approval (Atwood and de Beer, 2001).

Even after the circumstances of civil war are considered, the English seem imbued with a very different spirit. Marchmont Nedham, Renaudot's contemporary – although also working, *avant la lettre*, as a virtual public relations practitioner – was, nevertheless, at the same time in the more cynical journalistic business of 'taking off vizards and vailes and disguises'. Both approaches produce newspapers, but there is a fundamental difference between them. On the one hand, there is the publication of the unexamined 'deeds of the government' in a news monopoly and, on the other, there is the unmasking of those 'deeds' in a raucous marketplace of news. On this distinction the periodical press divided. As tendencies, the pen as grafting tool is separated yet from the pen as (shall one say?) chisel or demolition ball. The press's relative 'freedom' is reflected in the degree to which the 'taking off' function trumps any 'by/with authority' activity.

In seventeenth-century France, no Miltonic cries for press freedom were heard and in the eighteenth century no 'Cato', 'Junius' or Thomas Paine troubled the French throne as they did the British. France avoided the English/British press upheavals of these centuries and the French authorities did not yield the measure of freedom the British, and their colonists, obtained. Nevertheless, the idea of a free press was no English monopoly. There was, in fact, a measure of philosophical consensus as to what form press freedom might take and what could be its impact on society, whether held to be good or bad. It was a strand in a broader philosophical debate informing political thinking across Europe – the intellectual current designated the 'Enlightenment'. Philosophers increasingly questioned the legitimacy of autocracy, as they had done in England.

In France, the innocent-sounding philosophical Société de gens de lettres, credited as authors of the equally innocuously entitled *Encyclopédie, ou dictionnaire raisonné des sciences, des arts et des métiers* (from 1750–1), was an important voice for reform and modernity. Specifically on the press, in Volume XIII, Denis Diderot, translator of Locke and lead editor of the *Encyclopédie*, wrote: 'One asks if the liberty of the press is advantageous or prejudicial to a state. The reply is not difficult. It is of the greatest importance to keep this practice in all states founded on liberty.' Without free expression, a country 'must necessarily fall into stupidity, superstition and barbarism'

(Smith, 1979: 76). This was no mere radical rhetoric. Britain's emerging economic dominance and its military victories were being seen as a function of its liberal arrangements, exemplified by its uncensored press, with 'no prior constraint' its watchword. Certainly, the radical economist, the Marquis de Mirabeau, who translated the Milton's *Areopagitica* into French, believed an unlicensed press aided commerce and industry, and that Britain was the proof of that. Such debates ensured that the issue of a free press remained on the European-wide political agenda.

The essential factor conditioning press freedom was, as ever, the stability of central authority. Whenever it faltered, the press benefited. For example, during La Fronde unlicensed publications flourished. These were mainly in the form of little sheets of political verses – called, in mockery of Louis XIV's chief minister Cardinal Mazarin, *mazaridanes* – and some 4,300 of them appeared. There was even a rival newspaper to the *Gazette*, the *Courrier français*, published in the opposition's interest by Renaudot's sons. The father closed it down after a dozen issues. With the King's triumph, the *Gazette de France's* monopoly was confirmed and it was to persist for the next century and a half.

Throughout Europe, presses in an anglophone style remained rare during the eighteenth century. In 1761, the Danish parliament, exceptionally, abolished prior censorship of all but the periodical press. Denmark's King, Christian VII, a brother-in-law of George II, was a mentally challenged degenerate and no absolute monarch. His relatively liberal parliament, for the time, held sway. Similarly, in Sweden, in 1766, a proto-freedom of information Act was passed to make official documents open to the public. Its King, Adolph Fredrick, was a de facto constitutional monarch powerless against the Swedish Estates. These, though, prove the general rule. The French situation after the suppression of La Fronde was the more usual for Europe – a monopoly on news publications and an oppressive censorship regime for the rest.

European absolutism, though, had one long-standing problem: thrones needed to summon parliaments when seeking to raise taxes. The participation of the people, in however unrepresentative a fashion, was crucial to effective revenue generation; but these assemblies were also prone to make demands in return. This tendency, obviously unwelcome to the absolute monarch, had, of course, led to the English Civil War and the execution of the King. Thus, faced with pressing economic problems, in 1789, Louis XVI attempted to contain such a possibility. He gathered the nobility to address the country's financial difficulties, but they had been alienated by his previous financial misfeasance. With a radical marquis, the Marquis de Lafayette, who had fought with Washington throughout the American War of Independence, as a spokesman, this Assembly of Notables forced Louis to summon a meeting of the more representative, and likely more uncontrollable, Estates-General. It was the first to be called since 1614.

The Estates proved to be as dangerous to the royal interest as Louis had feared they would be, refusing to limit their discussions to matters financial. Louis closed down their meeting place. Retiring to the tennis court at the Palace of Versailles, they transformed themselves from a national assembly into a constitutional convention. Lafayette was elected vice president of the body and, within three days of its first meeting, moved that a declaration of rights be made. Obviously influenced by his American experience, his proposal was grounded in the provisions of the individual American state constitutions (Ungar, 2002: 223, 234). (The US federal Bill of Rights, at this point, was still a matter of contention.) Echoing their language, the 11th Article of *La Déclaration des droits de l'Homme et du Citoyen* stated: '*La libre communication des pensées et des opinions est un des droits les plus précieux de l'homme. Tout citoyen peut parler, écrire, imprimer librement, sauf à répondre l'abus de cette liberté dans les cas prévus par la loi*' ('The free communication of thought and opinions is one of the most precious of the rights of man. Every citizen can speak, write and publish freely, only to answer for an abuse of this liberty in a scheduled action at law'). It was adopted on 24 August 1789; but it was only to remain in place for just under three years.

Nevertheless, arguably: 'The press freedom that existed between 1789 and 1792 was unrivalled in history. During this short period, editors had fewer constraints than exist today: no accountability to boards of directors, shareholders or advertisers and less organizational bureaucracy. They were freed up to concentrate on their literary efforts to influence events, making a genuine impression on all levels of society' (Chapman, 2005: 17).

Already, as royal power was challenged in the summer of 1789, papers started to appear, forty by the time of the Declaration, some 500 before the right was withdrawn. Jean-Paul Marat, a leader of the extremist Jacobins and editor of *L'Ami du Peuple*, explained to his 4,000 readers how he was going about 'taking off vizards and vailes, and disguises': '*Je démasquerai les hypocrites, je dénoncerai les traîtres, j'écarterai des affaires publique les hommes avides*' ('I will unmask hypocrites, denounce traitors and banish greedy men from public life') (Gough, 1988: 211). Revolutionary journalists, such as Camille Desmoulins, stridently claimed that the press was the ultimate voice of the people with real power to denounce, absolve or condemn.

If so, this power did not last, although the complete restoration of *ancien régime*-style control would only be finally achieved by Napoleon Bonaparte. In 1792, Article VIII of a new constitution had rendered Article XI of the Declaration of 1789 a dead letter: '*Le droit de manifester sa pensée et ses opinions, soit par la voie de presse, soit de toute autre manière être interdit*' ('The right to express one's thoughts and opinions be it through the agency of the press or in any other manner is prohibited'). Already by that summer, the Paris Commune had moved to prevent the distribution of royalist papers. It was to take years of continued revolutionary violence and changing constitutional arrangements before the full force of Article VIII was felt, but when Napoleon became First Consul in 1799 total control was reasserted.

Until that time, the republican press continued to function. Overall, some 2,000 papers were to appear during the revolutionary decade 1789–99 (Chapman, 2005: 16). Their titles, François-Noël Babeuf's *Tribun du Peuple*, for example or Ève Demaillot's *Orateur plébéien*, were still calls to arms but their appearance during the Reign of Terror was merely countenanced as their right to publish had been removed. Their power to unmask, denounce and expel was, after 1792, exercised at the peril of their publishers. Desmoulins, for example, in the pages of the *Vieux Cordelier*, argued against the growing terror, and, in consequence of an inflammatory third issue of the paper, crowds gathered to demand the release of prisoners (Chapman, 2005: 21–2).

It can be noted that the paper, like many others outside France during the later decades of the century, reflected contemporary confusions as to the line between opinion and news. Like Wilkes' *No. Forty-Five*, which also caused the mob to appear (see Chapter 4.3), Desmoulins' *No. Three* was dated but it carried no datelines, no news. It was, to all intents and purposes, a dated pamphlet, one of series. The essay began reflectively, without any hint of headline, with a consideration of the essential differences between monarchical and republican governments. How that might be characterized was of little moment at the time, of course; what was really at issue was the Terror. Desmoulins argued for clemency for the Revolution's 'enemies' and the Committee of Public Safety, which had replaced the Convention and was in the de facto control of Maximilien Robespierre, had the clear authority of Article VIII to forbid this manifestation of thought and opinion. The *Vieux Cordelier*, newspaper or pamphlet, was, in effect, a nail Desmoulins' coffin. He was guillotined, 5 April 1794.

Robespierre's fall later that summer, in the revolutionary month of Thermidor, and the replacement of the Committee of Public Safety by a three-man Directory, including Napoleon, marked the turning point. The thermidorian reaction to revolutionary zeal engulfed the press. The *Gazette de France* was revived as the voice of the government and the intemperate Babeuf, for instance, was imprisoned for '*provocation à la rébellion*' – sedition. By September 1797, a stamp duty had been introduced and control of the periodical press became a police matter. Forty-four titles were closed down and their editors deported. Napoleon's coup that removed his fellows from the Directorate, on 18 Brumaire, Year VIII (9 November 1799), made him First Consul. The thermidor of the Revolution was complete. For the press, old-style repressive controls were reimposed but now with additional demands for positive propaganda. Napoleon thought that the journalist was a 'grumbler, a censurer, a giver of advice': 'Four hostile newspapers,' he claimed, 'were more to be feared than a thousand bayonets' (Ingelhart, 1995: 156). To keep them in line, he established a Political Bureau staffed by other journalists with instructions to: 'Tell the journalists that I will not judge them for the wrong which they have done, but for the lack of good which they have done.' Napoleon said, 'Newspapers say only what I wish' (Ingelhart, 1995: 156). The *Gazette de France* was really back in business: the grafting tool function was once again paramount.

Although its period of freedom was brief, French press innovations nevertheless had influence beyond France. Renaudot's activities, for example, firmly established the consanguinity of news and advertising. The Bureau was copied in London as an Office of Public Advice. The occasional printed publication of the positions vacant, goods and services it displayed became, in 1657, under Nedham's proprietorship, the *Publick Adviser*: 'Communicating unto the whole Nation the several Occasions of all persons that are in any way concerned in the matter of Buying and Selling, or in any kind of Imployment or dealings whatsoever' (Jones, 1961: 308). Advertisements on the back page had been for, say, a publisher such as Samuel Pecke, an occasional additional source of revenue; with Renaudot's model advertisements took another step forward to becoming indispensible to the West's 'free' press.

Although agency distribution of national stories began in London, cross-border news agency reporting was also a French innovation, introduced by Charles Havas who had started his agency in 1835. Eventually, as the Agence France Press, it was to become so important to the French government's conduct of foreign policy that it attracted state subsidy.

Even more significant to journalism is that the norms of modern parliamentary reporting were established at the outset of the French Revolution. In Britain at this point, covering Parliament was now concessive, largely because the Commons could not make its will to censor such reporting effective in the courts. A record of the debates of a country's highest deliberative chamber, however, was still seen as being a rather radical departure from tradition. It is no wonder, then, that in revolutionary Paris, as soon as the National Assembly began work, a *Journal de débats et décrets* appeared. The Estates-General, debating the issue of allowing such publications, determined that any democratic mission demanded this. The *Journal des débats* and a number of rival publications were seen as essential. In consequence of the importance of the reports, unlike the practices in London, accurate recording of the speeches was deemed to be critical. The publisher of the *Journal des débats*, François-Jean Baudouin, introduced a new and supposedly superior shorthand system, '*logographie*', to ensure accuracy. Nevertheless, the deputies complained these *comptes rendus* (press reports) misreported them. Apart from giving the representatives a right to edit the reports, which John Hansard was also to do in Britain, Baudouin introduced the convention of reporting responses neutrally in brackets, e.g. '[Laughter]'. Moreover, the need for *comptes rendus* ensured, as a consequence, that the French 'Fourth Estate' had a guaranteed place in which to do its work, a lobby. These innovations only slowly acquired critical legitimacy elsewhere. Even in the democratic United States Congress, it was not until 1860 that journalists achieved accreditation as a lobby. Official publication of *Hansard*, the British equivalent of *Les Comptes-rendus parlementaire*, did not begin until 1886.

Napoleon crowned himself emperor in 1804 but that brought no stability to French constitutional arrangements. After his fall, the Bourbons were restored in 1815. Fifteen years later, they lost the throne again, this time to an Orléanist cousin. Eighteen years after that, the French revolted once more, sparking a European-wide 'Year of Revolutions'. These 1848 rebellions were quickly suppressed and little permanent change was achieved, but in France a Second Republic was declared. It too fell four years later and its president, Louis Bonaparte, the first emperor's nephew, was elected 'Emperor of the French', Napoleon III. This Second Empire lasted another eighteen years until a Third Republic was established. It emerged from a further brief upheaval in Paris following a disastrous French war with the Prussians which saw the enemy at the gates of Paris.[11] In these decades, regimes, both royal and republican, imposed controls on the press. Although there were times, 1848 for example, when these were momentarily swept aside, basically one regime piled its laws on top of the others. The French press thus acquired no less than sixty-seven specific *lois*, *ordonnances*, *décrets*, *actes*, *chartes* and *Sénatus-consultes*. Prior authorization was needed to start a newspaper, which was then subjected to *l'impôt de timbre*, stamp duty, and *le dépôt de cautionment*, sureties. Newspapers were in danger of being the creature of party or worse, the victims of *amortissement*. This was a sophisticated extension of the principle of bribery, whereby the administration installed its placemen as editors of publications it covertly owned.

The history of the nineteenth-century French press can be read in two ways (Chapman, 2005: 25–6). It is either seen as the inheritor of an inalienable legacy of free expression coming from those brief years of liberty during the Revolution; or, on the contrary, it struggled to recover its ephemeral independence as it laboured under the weight of endless regulations enforced by an efficient centralizing state – Napoleon's main legacy to France. Although unquestionably hard-pressed, French journalism would seem to be better described by the former understanding.

Press developments after Napoleon well illustrate Alexander Hamilton's belief that its liberty depends on the support of the 'spirit of the people'. The thirst for news that was first met in full in the 1790s was not slaked by Napoleon's authoritarianism and satisfying it was certainly not constrained by the weaker regimes that followed his. Their efficiency was hobbled. However draconian the controls, the volatility of the public being what it was, the press could not be simply closed down – at least, not for long – or restricted to titles published 'by/with authority'. As a result, journalism flourished. Small papers, *petits journaux*, were exempted from both *l'import* and *deport*. The state's secret manoeuvrings in the *amortissement* system spoke not to the censors' strength but to their weakness. The legacy of the revolutionary press was, thus, far from forgotten. As in the anglophone lands, the French, evermore characterized by a growing, literate industrial mass, demanded papers. A general newspaper, the *Journal des débats*, for example, was outselling the London *Times* in the 1820s. An indication of the press's health, despite the regulations, was that the American steam-driven press manufacturer, Robert Hoe, made his first European sale to the *Patrie* in 1848. The press persisted, sustained by public demand, and the authorities were constrained from outright censorship.

The call for the removal of the Bourbons in 1830 had begun in the newspapers, despite another repressive law in 1828 which had been passed, exactly, in fear of revolution (Rader, 1973: 256). Whenever the state trembled, as it did in 1848, papers spouted up overnight, some 450 titles on that occasion, including echoes of 1798 such as an *Ami du peuple*. Louis Napoleon closed the presses when he became Emperor in 1852 and only allowed non-political publications to reappear. All changes of staff needed to be approved. Swingeing fines were imposed and official announcements were to be privileged; but, although all cartoons were separately vetted, he dared not reimpose overt censorship over the rest of the contents.

Being now in an industrializing capitalist state, the French press was anyway moving towards a populist news agenda. Just as British and American publishers from the 1830s onwards had realized that a sensationalist product needed no politics to sell, so in France the same conclusion was reached. The cheap, or cheaper, press was introduced by Émile de Girardin. His *Presse* sold at half the usual price and he sought to use advertisements as a regular sustaining replacement for party subventions and bribes (Chapman, 2005: 35). The first issue, 16 June 1836, promised a daily diet of '*politiques, littéraire, agricole, industriel et commercial*' news but the *Presse*'s popularity rested on innovations such as fashion coverage and fictional serials. The first tabloid appeared in February 1863, the *Petit Journal*. By June, it was selling 38,000; four months later it reached 83,000; two years after that the figure was 259,000 a day. In London, the masthead on Levy-Lawson's *Daily Telegraph* proclaimed it 'The Largest Circulation in the World' at 225,000 copies, but this was not true: the Parisian tabloid outsold it.

The French press of the Second Empire was now as safely in the hands of men of capital as was the British and, as in Britain, the controls began to be removed. The prior authorization requirement went in 1868, the stamp duty was reduced and petty interferences were removed. Among the new titles was the satirical *Figaro*. The duty was entirely abolished in 1870 as the Prussians were besieging Paris. The Second Empire collapsed. Finally, during the Third Republic, the rest of the regulations, now largely dead-letter law, were removed by an Act, *La Loi du 29 juillet 1881 sur la liberté de la presse*. Once again, just short of a hundred years after the principle of free expression was proclaimed in Article XI of the *Déclaration des droits*, a French law stated: '*L'imprimerie et la librairie sont libres*' ('Printing and publishing are free'). The London *Times* piously congratulated the French in Lockean terms: 'a better press makes exceptional laws needless' (Smith, 1979: 114). 'Better', of course, in effect meant better for business.

However, the legislation was as much haunted by the ghost of Renaudot and his grafting tool as it was by Article XI. The 1881 law still contained constraints of a kind the British had come to regard as 'very needless'. The President of the Republic, or the dead or foreign heads of state, for example, were not to be 'insulted'; nor were public officials (including priests) to be 'defamed'; nor 'public morals' outraged. Action for *delits d'opinion* – libel – of course remained in place. Were not French public addiction to debate and politics so deeply divided between left and right, royalist and republican, Catholic and anti-Catholic, this might have meant more than it did in practice. In the market place of ideas, divisive politics were everywhere. *La Loi du 29 juillet* certainly did not shut the press up.

On 13 January 1898, the novelist Émile Zola published a piece in *L'Aurore*, a radical paper edited by Georges Clemenceau, doctor, member of the Chamber of Deputies, '*le tigre*' (Bredin, 1986). The country was riven by *l'affaire Dreyfus*. In 1894, a French Army captain of Jewish descent, Alfred Dreyfus, had been wrongly convicted of treason – spying on behalf of the recently unified Germany – and sent to Devil's Island. In 1896, the real culprit had been identified, tried and acquitted. The matter became public and the press took sides. Dreyfus returned to France for a further military trial and was again convicted; but the falsity of the documentary evidence against him was exposed by a fellow officer, Major Georges Picquart. Picquart leaked the facts, including that the high command had ordered him to be silent, to the Dreyfusade press. *Figaro*, where Zola usually placed his journalism, had taken the anti-Dreyfusade side and so he went to Clemenceau with an open letter to the President of the Republic, Félix Faure.

Zola was appalled by the behaviour of the Establishment and such was his celebrity, Clemenceau produced a special edition of the paper to carry this expression of his outrage. The banner headline across all six columns, a quite recent innovation made possible by ever improving printing technology, simply read '*J'accuse … !*'. If one phrase could sum up the crucial importance of liberty of expression to a liberal society and the rule of law, this would be it: *J'accuse …*

> I accuse Lieutenant-Colonel du Paty de Clam of having been the diabolical artisan of judicial error … I accuse General Mercier … I accuse General Billot … General de Boisdeffre and General Gonse … General de Pellieux and Commandant Ravary … I accuse the three handwriting experts … I accuse the War Office … I accuse the first Court Martial … the second Court Martial … In

bringing these accusations, I am not without realizing that I expose myself in the process to articles 30 and 31 of the press law of 29 July, 1881 which punishes offences of libel. And it is quite willingly that I so expose myself ... I am waiting. Rest assured, Mister President, of my deepest respect.

Émile Zola

Clemenceau, who had come up with the headline, printed 300,000 copies.

The open letter of itself was not, of course, the end of the matter, nor, indeed, should it have been. Journalism has no right to untrammelled power. That is not what the free press means. But Zola's intervention, and the raging battle in the rest of the press, was essential to correcting a major miscarriage of justice. 'J'Accuse' is the perfect example of the press guarding the guardians. Zola, as he had anticipated, was prosecuted, convicted and he was removed from the Légion d'honneur. He fled to England but he returned to Paris, after nine months' exile, as the government fell. Picquart was court-marshalled and exiled to Tunisia and Dreyfus was sent back to Devil's Island; but, eventually, the Establishment was forced to acknowledge the truth. Dreyfus was first pardoned and then, in 1906, exonerated. Both officers were reinstated with honour and Dreyfus was himself awarded the Légion d'honneur. And, by 1906, Clemenceau, 'le tigre', was prime minister. He was to hold the office a second time as the French leader during the First World War.

Clemenceau was not the only journalist – or politician with journalistic experience – to achieve high office. Throughout the nineteenth century, the press evermore firmly embedded itself into the public sphere, including the political processes, of Western states. A bridge was built between politics and journalism in a number of countries and many politicians of all hues had journalism in their background. Prince Otto von Bismark, the architect of Germany reunification under Prussia, personally edited the *Norddeutsche Allgemeine Zeitung* in the interest of the new unified Germany of which he was the first Chancellor. The paper was thus in the old 'by authority' tradition, but that the head of the administration produced it himself was new, an acknowledgment of the growing understanding in official circles of the importance of public relations. In the midst of other obviously pressing duties, Bismark occupied the editor's chair from 1871 to 1876. This did not imply, though, any sympathy for the principle of a free press and, wearing his Chancellor's hat, he had no hesitancy in suppressing oppositional publications (Smith, 1979: 120).

The journalistic experience of Camillo Benso, the Count of Cavour, who played a Bismarkian role in the struggle for Italian unification, is rather more usual. At the outset of his political career, he used his daily *Risorgimento – Resurgence –* to argue the case first for an expanded Piedmont, then for a single state '*dall'Alpi al mar Africa*' under the aegis of the King of Piedmont. The paper, founded in 1847, just before the 'Year of Revolutions', popularized his programme and himself. It helped get him elected; but as he rose as a politician, eventually becoming Prime Minister of Piedmont, he set daily journalistic practice aside.

Both Cavour and Bismark used the apparatus of the state, its army and its alliances, to further the territorial ambitions of the rulers of their initial national bases. Far more typical than these examples of the politician as journalist is the parade of agitators, visionaries and revolutionaries who also took up their pens. Internal insurrection and revolution were their primary tools but they had a close relationship with the press, whether licensed or underground. The difference between the agitator/journalist and journalist/ agitator is hard to determine. Giuseppe Mazzini, for example, before Cavour, began a career of insurrectionist politics in the same cause, Italian unification, but for a republic not a monarchical *Regno d'Italia* (Sarti, 1997). He came closest to success in 1848 when he and Giuseppe Garibaldi proclaimed a short-lived republic in Rome. It was extinguished the following year with the help of Louis Napoleon, despite his own position having been initially secured as the result of a republican revolt. Mazzini's *modus operandi* was the secret political club, the popular movement and direct action. In exile, though, he turned to the press, starting the *Italia del Populo* (Sarti, 1997: 148–9). The press was an agitational tool to keep alive his dream of a liberal representative democracy, not just for Italy but for all Europe.

For the Hungarian Lajos Kossuth, a leader – like Mazzini – prominent in the 1848 revolts, the press played a more central role. Of modest middle-class background, he trained as a lawyer but he took up journalism as a career and came to express the nationalist aspirations of the Magyars, who were the majority within Hungary and the most self-aware ethnic group within the Habsburg Empire (Boros-Kazai, 2005: 352). He began as a latter-day 'scrivener' distributing handwritten reports of the Hungarian legislature, the Diet – handwritten because of Austrian censorship. Copies were distributed to nationalistic Hungarian nobles and made his reputation. They also earned him a three-year sentence for sedition in 1838. Upon his release, as the Habsburg Emperor Ferdinand I's autocratic grip faltered in the face of growing Magyar assertiveness, newspapers were permitted. The most important was the *Pesti Hirlap ([Buda-]Pest News)*, which Kossuth edited from its founding in 1841. Particularly admired was the brilliance of his editorials arguing for a greater measure of autonomy, a position by no means desired by all of Hungary's multi-ethnic population. Although he was elected to the Lower House of the Hungarian Diet, he 'realized the platform of the assembly could not on its own generate a sufficiently broad change in public opinion. He needed the press' (Boros-Kazai, 2005: 351). It served him well.

During the upheavals of 1848, Kossuth became Hungary's Regent-President. Shortly thereafter, a republic was declared and, facing disaster, Ferdinand yielded the Austrian throne to his young nephew, Franz-Joseph. The trial of arms between Hungary and Austria, which had been going on for a year, was brought to a conclusion when Franz-Joseph's cousin, Tsar Nicholas I, in defence of the autocracies, invaded Hungary on his behalf. The Russian Army soon extinguished Kossuth's experiment. He escaped to a peripatetic existence touring the world, conspiring with the by-then equally rootless Mazzini and eventually settling in Italy.

Seventy-nine years after the fall of the Hungarian Republic, another revolutionary brought down Nicholas' heir in a somewhat less transient upheaval. He too had appreciated the power of the press in the struggle against oppression and as a means for his own advancement: 'In our opinion, the starting-point of our activities, the first step towards creating the desired organization, or, let us say, the main thread which, if followed, would enable us steadily to develop, deepen, and extend that organization, should be the founding of an All-Russian political newspaper. A newspaper is what we most of all need'.

'Where to begin', by V.I. Lenin, appeared in the fourth issue of Искра (*Iskra, The Spark*) (Lenin, 1961 [1901]: 13). The organization was the banned Russian Social Democratic Labour Party and Lenin, its rising star, was not a journalist but a lawyer; nevertheless the well-being of *Iskra* was his first political concern after being released from Siberia and sent into foreign exile. It was printed mainly in Germany and smuggled into Russia. Lenin edited the paper, with others, for only three years but he was its most prolific contributor.

The Social Democrats split at their second Congress in 1903, held first in Brussels and, when broken up by the police, continued in London. Lenin had used the paper to help him secure the leadership of the majority, Bolshevik, faction of the organization. He abandoned *Iskra*, which in the event he did not solely control, for a series of party publications, printed as officially as any in history, 'by authority' – his own. *Iskra*, though, was at this early stage more a series of pamphlets in the tradition of the *Vieux Cordelier* than it was a newspaper. As such, it speaks to this persistent theme: as much as the press was born of mercantilism and had become a full-scale industry in the service of capital, and as much as it was a vehicle for sensation and entertainment, it was also embedded in more than one nation's revolutionary struggles.

Apart from guarding the guardians and irrespective of how these histories evolved, from the thirteen American colonies in the West in the eighteenth century to the autocracy of the Russian Empire in the East in the twentieth, for good or ill, the press has, to one degree or another, assisted the dawning of many a new political day. As Lenin's political mentor had put it, as a young journalist of twenty-four in his very first newspaper article in the *Neue Rheinische Zeitung* in 1842: 'The free press is the ubiquitous vigilant eye of a people's soul, the embodiment of a people's faith in itself, the eloquent link that connects the individual with the state and the world' (Marx, 1842).

Marx might have been a philosopher, economist, sociologist, historian and revolutionary socialist but journalism was his only conventional 'job'.[12] His early vision of it, however romantic, contains the truth which lies at the heart of the case for free expression.

In the West, at least as a matter of principle, the press had achieved the right to speak truth to power. In so doing, it answers Juvenal's ancient question, yet it often falls from this high purpose of guarding of the guardians. Nevertheless, however limited its influence over them – the authorities – actually is, journalism is still the most readily available watchdog to help monitor the powerful. Thus a Whig vision of the press as an agent of liberty is not entirely illusory, for all that it is constrained by the conservatism of the mainstream capitalist press. The exercise of press freedom in the name of truth – however few are involved and however few of those are committed to the task – is still undeniably crucial to the business of holding power accountable. The principle of guarding the guardians is not entirely forgotten even if it has been stifled to the point of suffocation lately by vicious competitiveness, corruption and moral blindness. Despite all this, journalism's high purpose can yet be asserted in evangelical terms as being: 'to comfort the afflicted and afflict the comfortable'.

The West's ability to resist challenges to the principle of free speech has always been weakened by the need to balance freedom while constraining harm. The nineteenth-century settlement that produced the mass newspaper transformed the owners of the press from being outsiders loitering at the gates of power into key stakeholders in the citadel. Just as the formal controls of the state were dissolved, victory was being compromised. The old printers' desire to avoid trouble by offering equality of access to differing opinions was closed off as the right to speak through print became evermore a function of money. Industrialization had finally put the genie released in the seventeenth century back into the bottle – more or less. It was only in safe capitalist hands that the expense of the technology needed to feed the appetite for expensively gathered content, expensively and rapidly presented, could be met. Thus, it can be argued, authority, paradoxically aided by the growth of mass readership in the nineteenth century, could finally relax about the printing press. The safe hands ensured that the mainstream press would be largely quiescent. The occasional exercise of oppositional activity by the men of capital who now owned the presses did cost authority, but it was a price worth paying. The simulacrum (as it might be) of free expression thus created was a species of social safety valve. The popular appetite for mainstream news publications effectively marginalized oppositional expression. It could be left, liberally undisturbed, to wither, unwatered by public attention. And no longer would any mob ever gather, braying defiance of authority in defence of the press.

By the mid-twentieth century, in American terms, the result was that:

> Anybody in the ten-million-dollar category is free to buy or found a paper in a great city like New York or Chicago, and anybody with around a million (plus a lot of sporting blood) is free to try it in a place of mediocre size like Worcester,

Mass. As to us, we are free to buy a paper or not, as we wish. (Liebling, 1964: 15)

Liebling's cynical assessment certainly has force. Today the figures would be at least $100,000,000 or $10,000,000 respectively. In effect: 'Freedom of the press is guaranteed only to those who own one' (Liebling, 1964: 30–31). Press freedom is a matter of balance, as much between journalisms romantic 'vigilant eye' and the thirst for profit of the 'men of property' as it is between harmful (however defined) and benign expression.

And yet ... And yet ...

In the clear light of the everyday in the West, journalism's lamp is dimmed but in darkness it still shines. As the German *blitzkrieg* engulfed the Netherlands in summer 1940, the *Nieuwsbrief van Pieter 't Hoen*[13] appeared from the underground. In the manner of a seventeenth-century newsletter, it was laboriously duplicated, although not by hand but through stencilling. Written by radical journalist Frans Goedhart, soon some 7,000 copies of each edition were being run-off. Its name was changed: *Het Parool* (the *Watchword*). As an Amsterdam afternoon paper it is, like a number of other such anti-Nazi sheets in more than one European country, published still. To defend *Het Parool* is, of course, easy. Such speaking truth to power has no moral downsides. That defence, however, cannot be mounted without also defending press freedom in general. To ensure that speaking truth to power is possible requires equally a right to offend, a right to be trivial, a right to entertain be also guaranteed – for who knows how the needed 'truth' will be expressed?

As Goedhart cut his duplicator skin in secret, across the Channel, the free press, despite the war, could still engage in frivolities. That year, for example, the *Daily Mirror*, under the headline 'WELL OF ALL THE LUCK' ran a pin-up photograph over the caption: 'On the hottest day of the year, these two girls set out for a day's work at a film studio in Denham. And found that their job was to be photographed in their undies ... And if that isn't luck on a blazing day, we'd like to know what is' (Waterhouse, 1989: 10).

However, it was not for stories like this that, in 1942, Winston Churchill threatened to ban the paper (which had long since left the Northcliffe stable and become a main organ of left-wing opinion). A front-page cartoon by Philip Zec of a shipwrecked sailor was supposed to encourage frugality in the use of petrol but was read as suggesting the man in the drawing had been endangered to increase the profits of the oil companies. The Conservative Churchill had his Labour Minister of Supply, Herbert Morrison, haul in Guy Bartholomew, the editor who perfected the British tabloid during his tenure at the *Mirror*, and hint at closure. Morrison's fellow socialist, the fiery Welsh miners' leader Aneurin Bevan, insisted on a debate in the House of Commons. 'How can we,' he asked, 'speak about liberty if the Government are doing all they can to undermine it?'[14] The consensus on a free press held and the paper was untouched.

How settled was that consensus would have seemed to be an increasingly irrelevant question both before, and certainly after, the Second World War. In the United States, where the First Amendment was – to use the old legal term – a muniment protecting the asset of free speech, there was no question of its centrality. Elsewhere it was less well fortified. Even in Britain, where the national story luxuriated in embracing the struggle for the free press (when it was remembered), the underlying right could be – and was – in increasing danger of dilution. By this new century's second decade, the excesses of press abuse threaten its privileges. Nevertheless, this history still lies at the heart of the rebuttal to any Khomeini or others who would ride roughshod over the right. It needs to be highlighted not least because, even within the West, the history, if remembered, is confused by a lack of logic and certainty in absorbing its lessons.

Moreover, nor have the freedoms the press has enjoyed ever been shared, as a logical consequence of the right, by the other modes of expression as they had developed. The role of the press about which the young Marx rhapsodized and which Bevan, in effect, defended, was firm only as to the freedom of the press. However eloquent is the lip-service paid to a general right of free expression, in actual practice the exercise of freedom by the mass media other than print has always been, and remains, far less certain. Although the principle of a free press as a social good was widely agreed and, on a more limited basis, actually established, a general media right did not follow. Tom Stoppard was correct thus far: long before Hackgate, talk of media-blind free expression was indeed a shibboleth.

6

Non Sequitur: It Doesn't Follow

6.1 *Ernst von Wolzogen v. the Censors* (1901): Censoring theatre

Freedom for the stage was a non sequitur to freedom of the press.

Even as the British articulated the principle of a free press in the first half of the eighteenth century, at exactly the same time they refined direct censorship of the stage, thus proving that no fundamental human right of free expression had actually been adopted.

Prior constraint was as well established as a control over what appeared in theatres as it was prohibited from determining what could appear in print. Any public performance had to be licensed by the Lord Chamberlain, a system imposed by Prime Minister Robert Walpole in 1737. The stage had, like the press, long been overtly censored. Under the Tudors, plays could only be publically performed 'with the allowance of the Master of the Revells' who had this duty in addition to providing court entertainment. The Revels Office functioned, as did the Company of Stationers, as a licensing authority and the Master was assisted by yeomen to enforce compliance (Dutton, 1991). Even so the Lord Mayor and the Corporation of London remained concerned at the size and heterogeneity of the crowds that assembled for these licensed entertainments – London's Globe, for example, could hold upwards of 2,000 people. To escape the Corporation's direct control, the troupes of players, who were also protected by, but subjected to, their royal or noble patrons, built their new-fangled 'stage-houses' in the 'Liberties' of Shoreditch or Southwark in London, which were outside the Corporation's jurisdiction. These were often closed nevertheless – as soon as the death toll from the recurrent plague reached forty a week 'within the Bills of Mortality' (i.e. in London).

The plague, however, was as nothing compared with the fury of the Puritans who regarded the theatre as 'a shew place of all beastly and filthy matters' (Dover Wilson, 1956 [1911]: 176); and there were eighteen of them. Women were not allowed to perform, boys taking female roles; but in courtly theatrical entertainments, masques, noblewomen did appear, often in costumes 'too light and Curtizan-like for such great ones' (Schwarz, 2000: 117). The Puritan pamphleteer William Prynne suffered the loss of his ears, perpetual imprisonment in the Tower and a £5,000 fine for calling them 'women actors, notorious whores', which was taken as meaning the Queen, Henrietta, and her ladies (Prynne, 1633). The insulting term 'actress' was coined to describe them.

In 1642, among the very earliest of the Puritans' action, two weeks after Charles I raised his standard in Nottingham, was to have Parliament close the theatres: 'it is therefore thought fit and Ordained by the Lords and Commons in the Parliament assembled, that ... publike Stage-plays shall cease and be foreborn' (Wiseman, 1998: 1). It did not work, quite. Certainly, performances before large crowds obviously stopped; and the professional companies disbanded, many to seek a living on the Continent where an established tradition of occasional visiting bands of actors became a flood of *Englische Komödiante*. Nevertheless, in 1647, the Lords had again to order local authorities to arrest people giving performances, so they must have continued in however a clandestine fashion. The Lords moved once more in 1648 and in 1649 (Wiseman, 1998: 2, 5).

Even before the Restoration, Oliver Cromwell permitted a resumption of the Lord Mayor's parades and, in 1656, Sir William D'Avenant was allowed to mount a public masque in a private hall with both men and women singers. Less than three months after he returned to the restored throne, in 1660, Charles II patented two theatres as the sole sites of spoken drama, one to be run by D'Avenant (who claimed, without evidence, to be Shakespeare's bastard son). He opened the first stage in England with a proscenium arch and introduced tickets. Thomas Killigrew, the other patentee, who was to build a Theatre Royal in Drury Lane, introduced dramatic actresses. The first role essayed was 'Desdemona', probably played by Margaret Hughes. These new indoor theatres began by seating 500 to 700 but rapidly grew. Despite the rowdiness of the pit and the gods, by charging more, they more or less avoided the worrying (to the authorities) mixing of the classes of the old Elizabethan houses. They did not avoid the threat of numbers, though. By the year of Walpole's Act, 1737, Drury Lane, having been rebuilt and expanded, could seat 3,000.

The patent system, because of pubic demand as much as anything, did not work. Private houses could be used for performances. For example, in that same year, 1737, a young Midlander of French Huguenot descent, David Garrick, began his theatrical career appearing in amateur shows at the home of Edward Cave, publisher of the *Gentleman's Magazine*. Other public spaces were permitted to stage professional performances as long as they lacked spoken words. Not only because of the recently introduced innovation of opera from Italy, this opened the door to abuse. Garrick began his ascent to stardom (he was the first person in the record to be called a 'star') with an earth-shattering naturalistic – as they thought it at the time – performance as Shakespeare's Richard III. He gave it at Goodman's Fields, an unpatented house ostensibly limited to musical entertainments.

Walpole had been widely thought to be the model for 'Mr Peachum', the master criminal in John Gay's smash hit *The Beggar's Opera* a decade earlier, and was the butt of many other theatrical satires. He finally found an occasion to bring the stage to heel with *The Golden Rump*, an anonymous scatological satire about the King. Although at the height of his power, he was not strong enough to move against the theatres on his own behalf without incurring strong opposition and ridicule; protecting the reputation of the throne was another matter. The Bill was presented in the form of a mere expansion of previous legislation on 'rogues, vagabonds, and study beggars' (who, since the sixteenth century had included players): 'An act to explain and amend so much of an act made in the 12th year of Queen Anne',[1] the 1737 Licensing Act was passed in great haste (despite Lord Chesterfield, see Chapter 4.3). It gave licensing power to the Lord Chamberlain who appointed an Examiner of Plays and unpatented theatres were closed. Although they soon reopened because of public demand, the patent system was not formally abolished until 1843. It is remembered in London's two Theatres Royal and in the same name for theatres in all the towns that acquired a patent, less an indication of patronage than a mark of control. The vetting of plays continued without hitch for the next 231 years until it collapsed under the weight of its own absurdities in 1968.

After the Licensing Act, scripts were individually licensed for performance in theatres that were licensed too. Public demand had ensured this last was not effective and unlicensed theatres proliferated, but the plays themselves were better controlled. A theatre, unlike a press, was not easily hidden and what went on in them, in the nature of the case, was very public and simple to monitor. Although the censorship had a chilling effect, a creative theatrical environment developed nonetheless. The box office – public support – was the clue to such liberty of expression as existed, in Britain as in the rest of Europe. The state, even in its most democratic form, always has a predilection to play being the guardian of society's morals, but the cost of thwarting the public appetite for theatrical entertainment in unpopularity, and even disturbance and riot, was often not worth it paying. Nevertheless, the less democratic the state, the greater official taste for – indeed, addiction to – maintaining 'morality'.

In autocratic seventeenth-century Spain much the same had occurred with the theatre as had in autocratic England. Custom-built *corrales*, echoes of the courtyards where players once performed, were built, as were the London theatres, to facilitate the collection of money as much as anything. Armed guards were employed to control the crowd (Kuritz, 1988: 179). The companies achieved financial independence and, even if hobbled, they too managed to create a national drama – Félix Lope de Vega in Madrid, for example, to match William Shakespeare in London. However, in Spain, the support of the court remained more essential than it did in England and when this flagged in next century, police interference increased. Even ad-libbing was forbidden. Spanish drama's Golden Age was over.

In Italy, the vibrant tradition of the *commedia dell'arte*, the classically determined *commedia erudita* and the new-fangled opera found aristocratic audiences as well as popular homes in Renaissance theatres closely modelled on ancient architectural plans; but the stage was also always under the watchful eye of the authorities. For example, Carlo Goldoni, who refined the ad-libbed *commedia dell'arte* in the mid-eighteenth century by composing the speeches, needed to pay careful attention not to offend. His plots could not, for example, challenge the repressive norms of behaviour imposed on respectable women in his day (Günsberg, 1997: 103). In the autocracies, even personal enthusiasm for the stage, as was the case with the Russian Empresses, Elizabeth and Catherine, offered no protection from theatrical censorship. In their Russia, it was the responsibility of the secret police. It is no wonder that the question of freedom was not at issue; after all, in these lands the press was scarcely free either.

But in those countries where greater press freedom prevailed, the stage was still fettered. The European royal courts remained important as patrons, nowhere more so than in France. The country had the same theatrical background as its rivals – the medieval tradition of the mystery play, popular and courtly amateur and professional secular drama, and the Renaissance recovery of theatre of the ancients. Despite this, in sixteenth-century Paris, riven earlier than elsewhere by the Protestant schism, only one public theatre established itself, the Confraternity of the Passion. Its monopoly, granted in 1402, had been grounded in the production of the medieval mystery plays. When religious plays were forbidden as being too divisive, its home, built in 1548 on the site of the Hôtel de Bourgogne to house over 1,500 spectators, was used by other companies. Its monopoly over the organization of public theatrical performances, however, was unaffected (Kuritz, 1988: 199–200). There was also a tradition of popular performance at the St Germaine fair but there the actors were not allowed to speak dialogue. So they resorted to monologue; and when monologue was prohibited to song; and when song was banned to mime, the audience being invited to sing the words displayed on placards. In 1595, the players won this fight and another stage was built, the Théâtre de la Foire. At this point London had eighteen theatres and Shakespeare, Marlowe and the rest.

The status-conscious French throne was to come to see a lack of internationally acclaimed drama as a disadvantage to its statecraft. International rivalries were all encompassing and included matters cultural. The Italian *commedia dell'arte* troupes were regular visitors to France, eventually establishing a permanent base in Paris. The English were also exporting their theatrical culture, especially after the theatres were closed during the Civil War and players took refuge in touring Europe. Louis XIV and his chief minister Cardinal Mazarin made the creation of a national drama a matter of state policy. Thus Corneille, Racine and Molière all wrote for the court. Louis was also passionate about dance and under his aegis the modern ballet developed. Steps were codified for the first time in the dance-company which had been founded the previous century by Catherine de Medici as Le Ballet Comique de la Reine. Similarly with the theatre: after Molière's death in 1673, the arrangements for drama were further formalized with a permanent company of actors, La Comédie-Française, vetted and engaged by a court official (J. Allen, 1983). All its work was censored. There were even official ticket collectors to ensure taxes and royalty payments were properly paid. The French Golden Age did not survive such interference any more than did the Spanish.

Of course, administrations were, by their own lights, as right to worry about the theatre as they were about the press. Words on the stage were certainly as dangerous as words on the page. For example, Marie Antoinette persuaded Louis XVI that the latest play by Pierre-Augustin Caron de Beaumarchais was too witty and wonderful not to be allowed. Against his better judgement the King agreed and *La Folle Journée, ou le Mariage de Figaro*, a frivolous sexy comedy, was performed in 1784. It was received as warmly as its predecessor, *Le Barbier de Séville*, had been a decade earlier. However, the plot, which turns on the old-fashioned feudal *Droit de seigneur*, the lord's supposed right to his serfs' daughters' maidenheads on their marriage, was scarce funny. It was far from harmless, given the tenor of the times. Applause greeted Figaro's speech, prescient in its discourtesy: 'No, Monsieur le Comte, you shall not have her ... Because you are a great lord you imagine you are a great genius! Nobility, wealth, titles and appointments, they all make you so proud'. Louis was right to have been concerned.

Thus, even when seemingly flippant, plays could be as incendiary as newspapers, as Napoleon well understood after Louis fell. Napoleon was to allow the *Comédie-Française* to run itself, but on the other hand he sought to limit the number of theatres by licence. He determined eight would be enough and what they offered – in one case, 'rope dancing' – was carefully specified. Napoleon's controls produced René Charles Guilbert de Pixérécourt, the most popular French playwright of the day. His '*mélodrames*', tragedies with happy endings designed specifically for the 'groundlings', were safe, lacking any of a Beaumarchais' critical edge. Pixérécourt's showcase was the Théâtre de la Gaîté on the Boulevard du Temple, which, after licensing was abandoned in 1830, would become the headquarters of nineteenth-century popular theatre in Paris.

Here and elsewhere, texts were the basis of prior censorship and speech therefore defined the stage. It was the prime element in the licensing system but opera, not least, made a hash of that provision. The censors were even harder pressed to control other non-spoken popular entertainments. As in Britain, popular demand, backed by the threat of public disorder if thwarted, eroded but did not remove repression. Despite this, no question of the fundamental legitimacy of regulation was raised (any more than it is today in connection with broadcasting, for instance). Anyway, the burgeoning urban population sustained a variety of public 'attractions' beyond the stage, spoken and lyric, without reference to demands for freedom. The shows to which the public flocked included everything from the circus, which first emerged in London in the 1780s as an equestrian entertainment with juggling and tumbling added, to the proto-strip club of nineteenth century, the *poses plastiques* – erotic *tableaux vivants* (Faulk, 2004: 143, 148).

In Britain, although the Lord Chamberlain's censorship powers remained in place, the licensing of theatres was removed in 1843 Theatres Act.[2] In 1852, Londoner Charles Morton built a hall next to his public house for the provision of music, permitting a formalization of the previous 'free-easy' singsongs of the inn. Public drinking had been as much subjected to attempted control as public communication in a like pattern of persistent regulation, persistently resisted. Eighteenth-century attempts, by the imposition of taxes, to control the 'gin-palaces', then proliferating, caused riots. Requiring the permission of the magistrates to sell liquor was also tried but effective regulation only began with the Beerhouse Act (1830).[3] This licensing law, and subsequent legislation which introduced licensing hours, created the culture of the English 'pub'. Publicans had already been hiring singers and specialty acts to entertain their patrons but Morton's 'Music Hall' created a contiguous social space to that of the pub, one in which music and a variety of other attractions could be more appropriately accommodated (Mayer and Richards, 1980). He still needed a licence to sell liquor but not to own a hall. Music halls, or palaces of variety, were soon being built in poor neighbourhoods, matching the architecture and opulence of 'legitimate' theatres.

Variety shows appeared elsewhere and, by the end of the century, they indeed offered wonderfully various attractions. These went beyond song and dance, comics and acrobats, magicians and trick cyclists. Performing animal acts, according to one American list of 'artistes', included not just dogs, mules and lions but also a cockatoo. There was even a man who made a living – one hopes – rapidly modelling clay on the stage (Gilbert, 1968 [1940]: 395–410). Like the popular press of the day, not much contentious political expression was involved, even in the comedian's jokes and monologues. On the other hand, although blasphemy was, of course, entirely out of the question, sex, in the context of the repressive societal norms of the time, was a little indulged. Obscenity, like blasphemy, was prohibited but what that actually meant was subject to changing standards. The right of public free expression was being calibrated – most for print, less for performances with sexual overtones, least for political opinion on the stage and not at all for blasphemy in any medium.

Old traditions, such *commedia dell'arte*, survived in England, eventually metamorphosing, via the *harlequinade*, into the (literally) much-reduced Punch and Judy puppet show. The cross-dressing of the Elizabethan *en traversti* female impersonations and the converse male-impersonating 'breeches parts' of the Restoration persisted, preserved in the entr'actes and the afterpieces that developed into the separate form of the pantomime. These, paradoxically, finished up, like Punch and Judy, as a show for children. In the United States, on the other hand, cross-dressing in burlesque, an established mode for parodying the legitimate stage, became, essentially, a new risqué form of male entertainment.

In the 1840s, the producer Michael Leavitt had began to absorb into his productions the techniques of a specifically American theatrical form, the 'blackface' minstrel show (Mayer and Richards, 1977: 159–60). These were popular from the 1840s onwards as white America amused itself watching white actors stereotyping loveable, unthreatening African American males in a show of patter, song and dance. Given there was a constant underlying fear of African American rebellion, this was one way of normalizing the essential immorality of the 'peculiar institution' of slavery.

Leavitt adapted some of the format of the 'minstrelsy' to a non-blackface variety show. This came to consist of three parts, an 'olio' – mix – of speciality acts sandwiched between a musical medley and a sketch replete with double entendres. The olio was all-male but Leavitt introduced women into other elements of the programme. Subsequently he claimed to be influenced by an English dancer, Lydia Thompson, although he was active before her arrival in the United States. She had fetched up in New York in 1868 with an all-female troupe, billed as Lydia Thompson's British Blondes. They played a burlesque retelling of a classical story, *Ixion*, with great success. Thompson's angle was to have no male actors at all. She was accomplished in 'breeches parts', costumed in tights and corset, and the blondes who played women wore the same with slit miniskirts as befitted, presumably, the ancient Greek theme. The presence of the erotic, whether due to her or to Leavitt, was to split the American variety stage between the 'men-only' presentations of burlesque, and latterly, strip-clubs and the more respectable music-hall offerings of vaudeville, a term first used in the 1880s.

Even if the British music hall and American vaudeville echoed the mass press of the day in avoiding overtly contentious political or otherwise offensive material, the sight of the lower orders 're-creating' themselves at theatrical entertainments was as concerning to the Victorian Establishment as it had been to the Elizabethan. Censorship was in place for the prior vetting of materials but the authorities also had further justification: theatres were prone to disastrous fires. Pixérécourt's Théâtre de la Gaîté was destroyed in 1835; 140 had died in Livorno in 1857; 253 in Brooklyn in 1877. A decade later, the Theatre Royal in Exeter in the United Kingdom was gutted taking

186 lives. This last caused a panic and regulations required that an expensive iron 'safety' curtain, which could be lowered to prevent backdrafts sweeping through the building, be installed. The men of capital who owned the theatres, especially the chains, were the most likely to have the financial recourses to meet this safety requirement. Thus, a not entirely unintended consequence of the safety-curtain provision was to put some 200 smaller music halls out of business and force many more to pass into chain ownership. The chains were the least likely to countenance subversive material.

The thirst of the urban population for entertainment was met by a virtual industrialization of the theatre, a process well represented by the appearance of these chains. Circuits of legitimate stages, sometimes under one management, had been a growing phenomenon since the eighteenth century (Tomalin, 1995: 28–31). In the United States, ex-circus entrepreneurs Benjamin Keith and Edward Albee, for example, took this to a far more concentrated level. They created a chain of vaudeville theatres across the United States, a significant capitalist enterprise that included a monopolistic booking system that kept the artists on the road in the most efficient fashion possible. To maximize profit, they also opened early and ran late with continuous shows suitable for the family 'double audience' of men and women (and children, too). A green-room notice proclaimed: 'If you are guilty of uttering anything sacrilegious or even suggestive you will be immediately closed and will never again be allowed in a theatre where Mr Keith is in authority'. As with the newspapers, economics were the most effective safeguard of Establishment interests. Keith's threat was serious because, as a result of mergers with rivals, it meant 100 stages in all the major cities would be closed to offending artistes (R. Allen, 1991: 188).

Nevertheless, a star with proven appeal could defy such strictures: wasp-waisted, hoyden-esque Eva Tanguay did. 'As a matter of fact,' she said, 'I am not beautiful, I can't sing, I do not know how to dance. I am not even graceful'; but she was 'box-office'. With numbers entitled 'Go as Far as You Like', she was, as she billed herself: 'The Girl Who Made Vaudeville Famous'. Keith, whom she appalled, had to put up with her for the sake of profit (Gilbert, 1968 [1940]: 328). Lesser players, though, were more cowed. Across America's cities, all of which housed at least one vaudeville theatre, only five chains operated and they formed a cartel. The artists formed a union. Already in the 1890s, the term 'show-business' was replacing 'shows' as a way of describing a sector more driven by capital than by art, never mind by free expression. By the 1890s, American vaudeville theatres, it has been estimated, were now selling a million tickets a week (R. Allen, 1980: 26–8, 36, 38).

The same factors – a history of popular theatrical forms and the pressure of the urban mass – produced the same sort of results across continental Europe (Mayer and Richards, 1980). In Paris, theatres had proliferated in Rue du Temple with a constant diet of melodramas, latterly augmented by realistic horror shows at the Théâtre de Grand Guignol. More informally, *cafés-*

spectacles, later called *cafés-chantants* and later yet *cafés-concerts*, played the role of the English music hall, although they never made the move to full theatrical facilities with fixed seating. Nor did they charge admission; the sale of food and drink remained central to their viability. The entertainment, however popular and compelling, was in effect a loss-leader. They did not spread very much beyond Paris, either (Hemmings, 2006: 199–202).

The most famous was the Folies Bergère, which opened in 1869, by which time there were well over 100 such establishments in the city. The entertainment at the Folies initially preserved elements of *commedia dell'arte* and only acquired the naked show-girls, for which it became famous in the twentieth century, after the First World War. Not that the *cafés-spectacles* lacked the erotic, some being known from their beginnings in the 1840s for the beauty of the female performers, although their lack of any dramatic talent was noted as well. The suggestive can-can was developed at the *cafés-concerts* (Dargelos, 2006: 127–8). The star of the Ambassadeurs was Yvette Guilbert. She lives 'for posterity in the posters of Toulouse-Lautrec. His one reservation was that the songs she sang were so paltry; he would have liked to hear her recite some of Baudelaire's verses' (Hemmings, 2006: 202).

If Lautrec's taste for verse was widely shared, perhaps Rodolphe Salis, an unsuccessful painter come wine-merchant who opened Le Chat Noir, the first cabaret, in Paris in 1881, was not quite as eccentric as his programme of entertainment suggests. He had writers, artists and musicians, including Erik Satie, present their work, largely for no fee. There were also complex shadow plays. Crucially, this eclectic intellectual mixture, which lacked the sexual frisson of the *cafés-concerts*, included satiric comment. The term 'cabaret' is derived from the French for a small room denoting a tavern, and dates back to the Middle Ages. It was revived by Salis to describe a place where wine, beer and food could be taken in an unabashed avant-garde bohemian atmosphere. Le Chat Noir became the rendezvous for artistic Paris, helping secure Montmartre's reputation as a centre of bohemian life. The venue did not, however, outlast Salis, closing at his death in 1897. The innovation was picked up, though; and nowhere was the cabaret to flourish more than in Germany, largely in Berlin, where Salis' emulators were to keep the satire, losing the high art but gaining the girls.

Variétés, or *Spezialitäten,* theatres first began to appear in 1871 in Berlin soon after the unification of Germany of which the city was now capital. It was closely monitored but the same *fin-de-siècle* impulses as infected the bohemians of Paris fuelled a 'Secessionist' rejection of mainstream German artistic practice. With this came the same provocative repudiation of bourgeois beliefs and behaviour. Moreover, in a country where the extreme inequalities of a rapidly industrializing society were acute, Berlin voted socialist more than did the country as whole. This also impacted on Secessionist activity across all modes of expression.

The enduring image of the German cabaret is that of *Der Blaue Engel* (1930) but that fictional establishment had more in common with a Parisian *café-concert* than with Salis' more éngagé Chat Noir. Initially, though, German cabaret was offered in a far more theatrical setting than either. When Ernst von Wolzogen opened the Kabarett Überbrettl in 1901, he was directly inspired by Salis, for all that the cabaret's venue was the more conventionally theatrical Buntes ('Motley') Theater. The mixed bill he presented of artist performance, vaudeville and drama was popular with the public despite the fact that he managed to get almost no satire past the censors who closely vetted all scripts, sketches, skits and lyrics. Unfortunately, though, it was not quite popular enough to succeed financially and by 1905 the Kabarett was closed.

Centuries before, arguing against the prohibition of women on the stage, Lope de Vega had pronounced: '*sin ellas todo es nada*' ('without women all is nothing'), a sentiment with which Wolzogen's successors enthusiastically agreed. In the words of Friedrich Hollaender, who composed the music for *Der Blaue Engel,* cabaret was 'engendered in dissolute passion, by theatre, the variety show and the political tribunal'. It was 'above all bodily art, sensual art' (Jelavich, 1996: 10, 28). And that meant the objectification of women. After the defeat of Germany in the First World War, the Weimarian cabaret, aided by a legal decision that nudity was not of itself obscene, mixed the political with the erotic more thoroughly than had ever been done anywhere. It did not, of course, survive the Nazis.

On balance, in the context of popular entertainment forms in the West, sexual expression, somewhat paradoxically perhaps, had achieved a de facto greater degree of liberty than had political comment. Artistes from Lydia Thompson to Eva Tanguay and beyond had shown that sex sells shows with, despite moral breast-beating, a lot less potential for social disruption than political criticism. The spirit of Thompson and Tanguay was containable. The evermore explicit objectification of women on the stage said nothing to the general theatrical censorship, which remained largely unquestioned. Female exploitation was less an unexpected consequence of free expression than a negative concomitant of the slow emancipation of women in the twentieth century.

6.2   *Mutual Film Corporation v. Ohio Industrial Commission* (1915): Censoring cinema

Overall, though, all performance entailed close monitoring leading some nineteenth-century entrepreneurs to dispense with actors entirely. The audience's Freudian *Schaulust* – 'scopophilia', or love of looking – ensured that shows of nothing more than scenery animated and augmented by lighting and sound effect could be profitable. The showmen needed no licence and attracted no censor. One of the most successful was the *Diorama* of Louis Daguerre. Daguerre was encouraged to explore the nascent technology of photography, eventually producing the pioneering process that bears his name, because he thought it would aid the production of his backdrops. In the event, photography, images captured on a light-sensitive flexible base exposed in a camera,[4] was eventually to be of more critical value to his rivals who were exploiting magic lantern shows (Winston, 1998).

Lanterns – projectors – date, at the latest, from the seventeenth century (Mannoni, 2000). The Danish savant, Thomas Walgensten, was noted as being in the business of demonstrating them by 1664. Before 1671, the narrative possibility of a projected sequence of slides was being explored. The earliest recorded example illustrated a Jesuit missionary expedition to China (Musser, 1990: 21). Soon itinerant lanternists were ready to put on a slide show in any available public or private space where admission could be charged or a hiring fee earned. Performances in more overtly theatrical settings, with the possibility of narrative sequences illustrating dramatic stories, date from the end of the eighteenth century. Étienne-Gaspard Robert, who took the name Robertson to acquire a more English, enlightened scientific aura, enjoyed tremendous success in Napoleonic Paris with a very elaborate lantern show. His *Fantasmagorie* (or *Phantasmagoria*), involved sound effects, including speech, as well as images, sometimes with basic animation. There were two projectors behind the screen, one handheld, for flying effects, and another mounted on rails so the image could also be made to advance on the audience. In 1822, the luminosity of such images was massively increased with the replacement of candles in the projector with lime-light.

Other optical devices were available, some designed specifically for home use. In the 1830s, the Phenakistoscope (spindle-viewer), for instance, used sequential pictures drawn on a paper-band which was slotted into the device's drum and spun. It was the first commercially produced animation toy to be widely sold but it was not the last. The principle, after all, was simple and long known, even if the reason for the drawings melding into each other to create the appearance of movement was misunderstood as 'persistence of vision'.[5] Within half a century, an arrangement was introduced for projecting such a sequence, now drawn on a gelatine strip held on either side by sprocketed leather strips. By 1892, a Théâtre Optique using the system was presenting '*Pantomimes Lumineuses*' commercially in Paris.

Replacing the drawings with photographs on such a strip was an obvious avenue to explore but the ubiquity of these drawn animations was, it would seem, a distraction. Nevertheless, the illusion of movement using sequential photographic images captured by a camera been demonstrated in February 1870 before a large audience in Philadelphia. Henry Heyl's Phasmatrope had glass-plate photographs mounted on a rotating wheel of slide holders passing through a shuttered projector. The images were of a couple dancing and an acrobat. The movement lasted for only a fleeting fraction of a second but repetitive rotations of the slide-holder allowed the illusion to last long enough to be accompanied by live music. The exercise, though, caused no stir and attracted no emulators. More interest was being shown in using photography to break movement down rather than recreate it. In 1878, Eadweard Muybridge published, in the impeccably serious pages of *Nature*, his astounding stop-motion images of a galloping horse, made with a series of cameras whose shutters were triggered by the horse's hooves. Muybridge produced a projector, the Zoopraxiscope, which duplicated Heyl's Phasmatrope but used a single disk of images rather than Heyl's rotating wheel of photographic plates (Clegg, 2007: 149).[6] He was never to adopt flexible celluloid – known since 1840 – which was being used in photography from 1879.

Each of these developments has men (always) as competitors for the honour of being first with the idea; but they are never alone.[7] As ever, such 'inventors' – like Gutenberg, really systems engineers – were responding to emerging social factors and this explains the synchronicity of their activities. The 'idea' of animating image sequences, after all, had nothing of the 'eureka' discovery about it. In the 1830s, the social determinant bringing a well-known phenomenon to market in the fresh form of a Phenakistoscope was, early consumerism apart, the growing need for bourgeois home entertainment in increasingly comfortable houses; by the 1860s, *Schaulust*-fuelled demands for popular urban mass entertainments were in full flood. By the 1890s, this demand was overwhelming the theatre industry in all its manifestations. The logic of industrialization meant that, for all the conflicting claims of 'great (male) inventors', it was the audience, buying millions of tickets a week for American vaudeville alone, that 'caused' the cinema to come into being: that, in effect, 'invented' it.

It was not that the cinema was 'waiting', as it were, for some discovery to be made by a 'great' man without which it could not exist. The camera, hand-cranked; flexible photographic film; and the projector, with a lamp (electric) capable of throwing a large image – were all to hand. As André Bazin suggests, the essential question to ask about the coming of film is simply: 'Why 1895? – the year when no less than four motion picture systems appeared more or less simultaneously?' (Bazin, 1967: 18–21). Why not earlier? The answer is that in 1895, what was different was not technological at all; it was 'show *business*', a term first noted that year – with millions of tickets sold, theatre chains, unions and so on. As these were phenomena not limited to the United States, it is no wonder that, in various countries, many are claimed as the 'inventor' of motion pictures.

Thomas Edison, perhaps stimulated by a visit from Muybridge, had already just introduced a moving photographic picture peep-show machine – no projector – the Kinetoscope. His only contribution appears to have been the idea of punching the sprockets into the film – although sprockets, flexible bands and projectors had been put together already. The rest of the apparatus is best attributed to his employee, William Laurie Dickson. Edison did not grasp the theatrical analogy and did not pursue the projection possibility. Dickson left him to create with others the projecting Eidoloscope. His partners included Thomas Arnat and Charles Jenkins whose subsequent Phanoscope introduced the stabilizing 'intermittent mechanism' in the projector's shutter system. In Berlin, the Skladanowsky brothers, Max and Emil, unveiled the Bioscope, and in Paris, the Lumière brothers, Auguste and Louis, developed the Cinématograph – a term they took from a discarded patent of 1906. Their famous screening in the Rue des Capuchines on 27 December 1895, commonly credited with being the first ticketed demonstration of the cinema, was actually the fourth time an audience had paid to see moving pictures. Edison, who now got the point, eventually bought the Arnat/Jenkins shutter for his projecting Vitascope (Winston, 1998). And this list is a by no means exhaustive roll-call of the cinema's 'inventors'.

Moving images were immediately in trouble with the censorious. Vaudeville stars and Broadway actors had been making the trek to Edison's first motion-picture studio in New Jersey to have at least a fraction of their performances captured on celluloid by W.K.L. Dickson for copying and distribution to the Kinetoscope parlours, which had quickly became the latest Victorian sensational visual attraction. Among them were John Rice and May Irvin, stars of a hit musical, *The Widow Jones*. They were filmed kissing each other, as they did nightly at the play's climax, in a close two-shot, and the cinema's capacity for 'indecency' was instantly established. That the action had occasioned no comment during the run of the play indicated that films were to be even more closely controlled than the live stage.

The Kinetoscope booths rapidly became a regular American fairground feature, akin to the 'what-the-butler-saw' devices, in which sequences of still photographs of naked women, sometimes stereoscopic, were a speciality. Given that the fair was also now the site of the most sexually permissive live theatrical displays, tented attractions such as 'hoochie-couch' dancers were quickly and profitably filmed for the Kinetoscope. Henri Joly, an associate of Charles Pathé, the first mogul to be produced by the new film industry, was charged with originating material for the Kinetoscopes Pathé had imported to Paris. French cinema begins with these early efforts of Joly with titles such as *Le Bain d'une Mondaine* (*A Society Lady's Bath*) and *Le Coucher d'une mariée* (*The Bride Retires*) (Gunning, 1986: 57).

Moving picture shows were thus either in a specialized urban space, a 'parlour'; or, less respectably, at the fairground; or, finally, as a more respectable novel vaudeville act. This last, theatrical, setting – the option first explored in Berlin – proved to be the most viable home for projected 'moving picture slides', the first single shot films. These films embraced an ever expanding range of subjects beyond the theatrical: everything from seascapes to 'phantom rides' (shots taking from the front of a moving train) to landmarks to street scenes. The subjects in the latter, shot in the morning, could be the astounded audience, looking at themselves in motion, in the evening. The rapid development of an international 'language' allowed multiple shots taken from different angles to be joined together, using a code of some complexity (for example, jumps of long-shot to close-up, fades, parallel action) to manipulate time and space. This firmly secured the 'movies' as, primarily, a narrative form. There were also shots of the news, actual events (or crude reconstructions of such events); but films were quite clearly more of a piece with dramatic performances, not the press. The ideological implications of non-fictional moving images did not figure as a potential problem of control as much as did a quickly burgeoning moral panic about sex on the screen.

It was to take the better part of a decade for the film show to become a stand-alone attraction in a custom-built theatrical space. The theatricality of the setting ensured that the same level of regulation in place for the stage would apply to the cinema. Cinema, as a new medium, demonstrated that technological advances in modes of expression would not entail any extension of the principle of free expression. For one thing, the inflammability of the nitrate film stock used by all the pioneers justified the licensing of projectionists, as well as premises, in the name of safety. In fact, less dangerous 'safety' film was patented in 1902. Serious projection booth fires were not unknown but, through the next half century, safety film was largely ignored for 35mm production, the standard film gauge for commercial exhibition. Not just the authorities but the industry itself was happier with occasional disasters justifying tight control of exhibition than with safer film and a less-controllable exhibitor environment.

Film spread with astonishing rapidity. Many nations established a production industry and, unconstrained by the limitations of language, silent cinema was a more truly international affair than it was to be after the introduction of synchronous sound. Certainly some countries dominated but the 'language' was international. Of course, national preferences were not unknown – the Russians, for example, persisted with static camera long-shot tableaux long after others were moving the camera – but the basics of the visual code were shared. Moreover, actual language in the form of whole screen inter-titles could be easily and cheaply produced for any national market. Cinemas were everywhere within the West but also across the rest of the world. Moving pictures got to the Far East and Latin America, for example, within a year of the Lumières' 1895 Grand Café film-show.

And wherever there were screens, there were censors. The British Cinematographic Act, 1909,[8] empowered the Watch Committees, ancient municipal organs which originally organised community policing and general safety, to license premises for the screening of films. They rapidly extended their remit to control opening hours (for example, not on Sunday). When this was confirmed by the court as not being ultra vires under the Act, they moved to the direct licensing of individual titles on the basis of content. The inconsistency and chaos this caused resulted in the establishment of a British Board of Film Censors (BBFC), a private industry-funded organization, to certify films for either general or limited exhibition. Although the powers of the Watch Committees remained in place, most authorities chose to abide by the decisions of the BBFC, granting cinema licences with the proviso that only BBFC approved-films could be screened. By 1937, with lingering economic depression at home and fascist hysteria and war abroad, it was possible for the chair of the BBFC, Lord Tyrrell, to claim proudly: 'there is not a single film showing in London today which deals with any of the burning questions of the day' (Dickinson and Street, 1985: 8). The cinema was free to express whatever it liked; unlike the stage, but like the press, it was not subject to prior constraint by the state. However, like the stage but unlike the press, it was in effect only allowed public expression as long as did not offend the Establishment's political predilections or society's most prudish sensitivities, as determined by Lord Tyrrell and his board. The principle of free expression did not detain them.

An exactly parallel process took place in the United States, where local government could, and did, exercise arbitrary power over screenings and some states, in clear defiance of the First Amendment, put prior censorship apparatuses in place. In response, the industry did not defend the principle of free speech but, instead, using the offices of a number of morally impeccable organizations, established a national Board of Censorship of Motion Picture Shows under their independent aegis. The Board, nevertheless, came to be characterized by the right, vociferously supported by religious fundamentalist demagoguery, as a tool of East Coast liberal opinion. A proposal for a statutory national censorship organization was debated in Congress but the political argument was overshadowed by a legal decision in 1915 arising from the State of Ohio's Industrial Commission's attempt to prevent the exhibition of a motion picture, D.W. Griffith's *The Birth of a Nation*, set in the aftermath of the American Civil War. The impulse behind the legal decision, though, can be judged as paradoxically liberal given that the film, for all its reception, then and subsequently, as a milestone in the cinema's development, is a rabid racist tract. The fraught political reception of *The Birth of a Nation*, an unashamed apologia for the slave-owning South, had occasioned racist riots and engendered a significant liberal backlash.[9] Be that as it may, the case was the first time the issue of the applicability of the right of free expression to the cinema was discussed in a legal context. The Supreme Court held that: 'The exhibition of motion pictures is a business pure and simple, organized and conducted for profit.' The movies were 'not to be regarded ... as part of the press of the country or as organs of opinion' (*Mutual Film Corporation v. Ohio Industrial Commission*, 1915). The First Amendment did not apply.

This decision dramatically highlights the inability of the law (which shall be displayed again below, more than once) to avoid being bedazzled by new technology. The irony of the *Mutual* case is that the film which occasioned it exactly encapsulates the cinema's capacity for expression, for good or ill. The broader point, though, is the clear articulation by one of the common law's highest tribunals that the right of media free expression was far from universal. New modes of expression could not expect protection and 'moral crusaders' continued to harass the industry until, following a series of off-screen scandals in the early 1920s, it imposed its own self-administered censorship system (Horowitz, 1997: 74–80). The purpose was public relations but the 'Motion Picture Production Code' that emerged with the establishment of an industry-funded censoring office under Will Hays in 1922 had teeth. General requirements as to the representation of crime, the clergy and sex were forbidden; 'Respect for the flag' and 'sedition' in effect covered the political; and, as freedom of speech did not apply, taste was free to enter the frame. Protection against offence was an objective of the Code. 'Repellent subjects' (e.g. childbirth) had to be treated with 'taste'. What had been guidelines were enforced by a certification system in 1934.

If this was the outcome in the common law lands that had struggled through centuries of conflict to establish a 'free' press, it is scarce to be wondered that, outside these borders but still within the democracies, control of cinematic expression was exercised without any question. In France, for example, after 1916, all films required a *visa* from the Interior Ministry prior to any public screening. Banning here was less driven by the sexual fixations of censorious – that was an anglophone speciality – as by political sensitivity. For example, Jean Vigo's astounding debut feature, *Zéro de conduite*, set in a boy's school, was banned in 1933 mainly because of its implicit glorification of anarchic revolution, albeit the anarchy of children. It was only finally released in 1947. Most countries established such boards for the classification, certification and, if necessary, the prohibition of films intended for public exhibition: and that was just the democracies. In authoritarian regimes, every facet of production from script to screen was monitored.

Even if the censoring process was limited to classification of finished films by the industry itself, there would appear to be a tendency for the body involved to be absorbed in some way by the state. For example, the British censor organisation, used as a substitute for local Watch Committees, was further transformed from being a private-industry organization into a full-fledged statutory censor, the British Board of Film Classification, by the Video Recordings Act, 1984.[10] This was passed, not unusually, as the result of a moral panic fanned by the tabloids into an alarum over the supposed impact of horror films, rebranded as 'video nasties'. 'Censorship', of course, is not the term used in the Act, never mind 'prior constraint'. All that is required is that the BBFC 'classifies' the materials – video-cassettes but also 'all devices capable of storing data electronically' – it vets. In effect, though, denial of classification is a form of prior censorship in all but name. It prevents the filmmaker from publishing – releasing – the work and taking the consequences, 'being damned', for so doing.

The issue is less the actual outcomes of censorship, which are determined by standards that change through time and across borders; rather, it is that the arrival of a new medium of mass communication was not an occasion to extend the right of free expression. It was barely mentioned in connection with film. Although the cinema quickly established its capacity for capturing non-theatrical – even news – images, there was no question of it being afforded the liberties of the press. On the contrary: specifically, the licensing of projectionists echoed the control levels in play in a sixteenth-century printers' guild. In general, motion pictures confirmed that, as far as media were concerned, the right of free expression in effect only applied to print: and this was to be the shape of things to come.

7

Ex Concessis: Consequentially

7.1 *'Improvement in Telegraphy'*, US Letters Patent No. 174,465 (1867): Electrifying communication, designing out freedom

The history of the theatre and film in the West reveals that limitations could be placed on the concept of free expression with impunity. For all the rhetoric of *les Droits de l'homme* and so on, as far as expression in any medium of mass communication other than print was concerned, the right's writ did not run very far. It was to become evermore obvious in the twentieth century that limitations on the right, as evidenced by the control of the stage and the screen, were not in any way reversed by the arrival of a new technology of mass communication. Given these accepted and settled precedents – *ex concessis* – it is no surprise that twentieth-century broadcasting would be regulated; indeed, would be more regulated still. Nor should questions of control and constraint about early twenty-first-century communications platforms surprise either. Technologies of communication, for all that they are often seen as a harbinger of greater freedom, are seldom any such thing. As a product of the society in which they are developed, technologies' capacity for causing social upheavals, if it has not been designed out from the beginning, is otherwise contained, if not suppressed.

Hyperbole characterizes discussion of technological change. Hyperbolic enthusiasm and technophobic distrust are agreed that contemporary communication modes have changed the social environment utterly. This has been true of the rhetoric surrounding new communication technologies throughout the twentieth century and into the twenty-first. Alternative voices to suggest that both promise and threat are overstated are seldom heard. Technicism, 'an immensely powerful and now largely orthodox view of the nature of social change', brooks no arguments: 'New technologies are discovered, by an essentially internal process of research and development, which then sets the conditions of social change and progress'; and that is that (R. Williams, 1974: 13). What, though, if this common received opinion is delusional (as Raymond Williams believed)? It could be that technology, of itself, neither bolsters free speech not does it materially undercut it. Despite the hyperbole, the underlying difficulties liberty occasions, in the matter of speech as elsewhere, remain essentially unchanged.

Technological determinism or technicism is a belief in the determining social power of technology. Society is made in technology's image. This view might be widespread, but it is in error. When it comes to communications: 'The basic assumption of technological determinism is that a new technology – a printing press or a communications satellite – 'emerges' from technical study and experiment. It then changes the society or the sector into which it has 'emerged'. 'We' adapt to it, because it is the new modern way' (R. Williams, 1989: 120; see also Chapter 9).

Raymond Williams rightly dismissed this as an inadequate explanation of our reality. For one thing, this opinion involves a cavalier view of causality. Classically, for example, this is expressed in the simplicities that see the printing press 'causing' the Reformation; or, even less convincing, the printing press 'causing' (for Marshall McLuhan, say) universal literacy – after many centuries, of course. In a theory of social change such failings of explanation are, to be charitable, debilitating. The history of communication technologies reveals few examples of new platforms being adopted as soon as they are 'invented'; or of these having the social effects subsequently claimed for them, however much technicist hyperbole says otherwise.

As touched upon in previous chapters regarding the technological history of printing and cinema, 'invention' is more often than not the result of systems engineering rather than 'eureka' moments. The elements within the system have usually been lying around for centuries before the new configuration 'emerges'. Printing from moveable type would be a case in point. Fernand Braudel offers steam, the central technology of the Industrial Revolution, as a further significant example of this. Between Vetruvius and Hero of Alexandria who described a steam-driven device (an *aeolipile*) around the time of Christ and the machines of the eighteenth century, the technology lies fallow. A pattern can be discerned which holds true into the present: idea > prototype > transformative social need > 'invention' > constraint > diffusion (Winston, 1998). For Braudel, the pattern is:

> First the accelerator, then the brake: the history of technology seems to consist of both processes, sometimes in quick succession: it propels human life onward, gradually reaches new forms of equilibrium on higher levels than in the past, only to remain there for a long time, since technology often stagnates, or advances only imperceptibly between one 'revolution' or innovation and another. (Braudel, 1981: 430)

In other words, the driver whose foot is on both the brake and the accelerator is society, not technology. Because this is the case, the 'accelerator' is actually a widespread social phenomenon, a social 'necessity'. With print, the need was primarily that of burgeoning urban culture. This is why 'inventors' of technology are like buses; they arrive in groups. The ghosts around Gutenberg are almost entirely lost to history but with later developments they crowd the scene, each demanding the accolade of 'inventor'. The cinema is not untypical in this: Dickson and Edison, Latham, Arnat and Jenkins, the Lumières, the Skladanowskys and so on (see Chapter 6.2), with never a 'eureka' moment – in the sense of discovering a previously unknown scientific factor – between them.

The interaction between the social sphere and technology is more complex than technicism allows. Technologists are not aliens working in hermetically sealed off laboratories. On the contrary, they are creatures of society just like the rest of us. Male researches produce a pill to control the fecundity of women, not men. White technologists produce film-stocks which are chemically balanced better to photograph Caucasians than people of colour (Winston, 1985). Social factors, from commercial considerations to latent prejudices and preferences, condition the research agenda. As for outcomes: 'Technics exist', wrote Lewis Mumford, 'as an element in human culture and it promises well or ill as the social groups that exploit it promise well or ill' (Mumford, 1934: 6). Social necessity is the accelerator causing any outcome of the work, the 'invention', to be widely adopted and diffused; but society also applies the brake to suppress technology's disruptive power. It does so with such regularity that it is almost possible to think of a 'law' being at work – a 'law of the suppression of radical potential'. With communications, the balance between the push of social necessity and the constraint of this 'law' leaves the Braudelian problem of liberty untouched (Winston, 1998).

So the application of electrical technology at the research and development stage, conditioned by a social need, either did not have communications in view at all only to, as it were, stumble across it as an application (e.g. computing); or, if it had it in view, did not think beyond personal communication, eschewing the possibility of broader audiences (as with telegraphy and telephony). It even, with the *wireless* variants of telegraphy and telephony, initially regarded mass access as a debilitating problem: i.e. anybody could eavesdrop. Telegraphy and telephony were seen primarily as alternatives to the post and, therefore, essentially as point-to-point private communication systems. They were not designed, 'invented', as potential mass media. In consequence, de facto insensitivity, conscious or unconscious, to public free expression is part of their technological DNA.

It was the instantaneous communication needs of the steam railway that necessitated the diffusion of electrical telegraphy. Otherwise the semaphore would do – or, for the general public, the mail. Telegraphy was, to borrow a phrase of a US senator in 1856, 'a mail operation ... a Post-office arrangement' (Oslund, 1977: 146); and, even if, as was the case in the United States, the Post Office lost out to private enterprise in its diffusion, the lack of content control certainly reflected Post Office practice. Free expression was as great as that allowed in private letters; that is, content was subjected to the general law without further media-specific constraints, unlike the public communications of the stage and the screen.

Beyond the United States, in the UK for example, telegraphy was entirely a Post Office arrangement, both in its infrastructure and in its freedom from specific censorship. The same with telephony: whether privately or publicly operated, there were no issues of content control beyond those covered by the general law. Suppressing the potential of the technology to operate on a wider than one-to-one basis meant that no specific further regulation to control expression needed to be developed. And the technology's capacity to reach out on a one-to-many basis was suppressed. It could have been differently configured.

Dedicated systems serving specific economic sectors with the mass transmission of single messages from a nodal point were developed within decades of the introduction of the telegraph. In 1856, a plan was presented to the Patent Office in Washington, DC, for 'Improvement in Telegraphy' and was awarded a patent eleven years later.[1] It envisaged a machine which automatically translated, via a typewriter mechanism, the morse code back into alphanumeric orthography. By 1871, the device had been adapted to produce a continuous printout of stock prices on a paper tape and was widely diffused in business offices. Serving these receive-only 'stock-tickers', so called because of the noise the printer made, was a central morse transmitter sending the data, simultaneously, down the wire to over 100 subscribers. Dedicated news agency wires, with tickers attached, soon followed.[2]

Even then, though, no notion emerged for a more generally available wide-area telegraphic network. The public's wires ran point-to-point between offices with no capacity – beyond reprinting in the press – for the mass distribution of telegraphed messages. The model of the post was too powerful for the possibility of a direct-to-the-home mass medium telegraphic service to be explored. Distribution from the telegraph office to the home was the business of lads on bicycles carrying alphanumeric printouts – telegrams. The very notion of anything speedier or more widely distributed was seen as rather pointless. 'We are in great haste to construct a magnetic telegraph from Maine to Texas,' wrote Henry Thoreau in 1854 as the network was being rapidly expanded, 'but Maine and Texas, it may be, have nothing to communicate' (Czitrom, 1982: 11).

Subsequently, research into a wireless form of telegraphy, which had been understood as a theoretical possibility for decades, was inhibited by exactly such cynicism. It would be able to reach multiple receivers simultaneously but with no privacy. What possible use could such an insecure mode of personal communication have? It took until 1895 for an application to emerge. The first effective wireless telegraphy proof-of-concept, as usual using readily available components, took place on board the dreadnoughts of the British and Russian imperial fleets during summer manoeuvres in 1895. So spread out were the ships that, for the first time, the vanguard was below the horizon of the rear so the flags that had served naval communication needs for centuries would no longer do. Dreadnoughts provided the supervening necessity for wireless telegraphic transmissions. Guglielmo Marconi, the physicist responsible for the Royal Navy demonstration, became wireless telegraphy's 'inventor' largely because of the effectiveness of his company's exploitation of the technology.

The telephone was a variant telegraphic device initially envisaged as an acoustic system for sending tonally distinct morse messages down a single wire. Given that a main expense for a telegraph company was the building and maintenance of long lines, profitability would obviously be massively increased if the capacity of the wires involved could be increased. Designing such a system, an 'harmonic telegraph', became a major research project, one that easily slipped into a search for an 'electric speaking telegraph' that would transmit the sound of the voice over the wire. 'Telephone' would eventually come to be used as the term for the later to distinguish it from the telegraph; but at the time the terms were interchangeable, especially in German and to a lesser extent in French and English (Rhodes, 1929: 229–30). Research into multiple morse-based signalling systems spoke of 'musical' or 'articulating telephones' while a voice system might be called a 'speaking telegraph'. While an 'harmonic telegraph' (or telephone) would be of commercial significance to the telegraph industry, the value of a 'speaking telegraph' was less obvious, It smacked somewhat of time-honoured fairground chicanery involving ventriloquism and the connection inhibited its development.

The history of the telephone, which presents the most dramatic example of simultaneous 'invention' in the record,[3] also features the failure to explore central 'unison' transmission to multiple receivers via an exchange. The supervening social necessity that brought the technology to market was modern business;[4] but it only needed private communications. Because of the postal analogy, the possibility of telephony as a mass medium was initially no more explored than telegraphy's potential in this regard had been. When telephone exchanges were built to conform with Alexander Graham Bell's vision of a network on the same lines as then modern gas and water pipes, their design specifically restricted calls so that a single transmitter could only talk to another single receiver (Fagen, 1975: 22–3; Winston, 1998: 59). More than that, since acoustic fidelity required bandwidth and providing bandwidth cost money, reducing fidelity made sound economic sense. The medium's capacity to transmit music, say, was designed out. Quality was sacrificed because the less the amount of audio information being transmitted, the greater the number of calls that could be simultaneously accommodated on the wire. The human ear/ brain allowed this ploy to work because a voice can be recognized even if only a limited range of frequencies is actually transmitted. There was, therefore, a certain futility in trying to use the telephone in a one-way 'downstream' mode to reach a mass audience.

Nevertheless, from the first years, some experiments were essayed – a live performance of *Don Pasquale*, for instance, or a news service that was offered in a number of cities (Moncel, 1879: 172). Only in Budapest, however, did telephony as mass medium show any signs of taking hold. Telefon Hírmondó (Town Crier Telephone) was established in 1893 by Tivadar Puskàs, ex-Edison engineer who had returned home. He began reading hourly news bulletins to subscribers but soon expanded content to include stock market reports, reviews, book readings, live concerts and children's programming. Telefon Hírmondó at its height employed 150 people but never gained more than 6,000 subscribers. It lasted from 1893 to 1923 (Hollins, 1984: 35). That it survived so long speaks less to the telephone's limited potential as a mass medium and more to the slowness of the realization that a wireless technology might herald not merely a variant point-to-point communication system, but a new mass medium altogether.

Wired telephony ran little danger, at least in the United States, of being 'a Post-office arrangement', i.e. a nationalized monopoly. In 1845, the Morse telegraph had initially been operated as such, a public utility run by the US Post Office. However, it was disgorged because, in its first year of operation, it made no money and exploitation of the patent was handed back to Morse (Brock, 1973: 63). Following this unfortunate start, the subsequent commercial success of telegraphy ensured that thereafter, with any other new communication system, private interests would always prevail. Attempts to mount the same case for US Post Office control of the American interest in the international sub-oceanic telegraph, which is what Senator James Bayard Jr was arguing for when, in 1856, he used the 'Post-office arrangement' phrase, were thwarted.[5] Telephony was always a private business; so was wireless telegraphy – Marconi's. As the United States entered the First World War in 1917, the AT&T telephone monopoly and the (foreign, i.e. British) Marconi wireless telegraphy stations were seized by Washington, DC, in the name of national security. However, as the telegraph itself had been in 1844, they were soon divested after the end of the war (Hilmes, 2007a: 10). The wired telephone system was handed back to AT&T and wireless telephony was privatized. A young Assistant Secretary of the Navy, Franklin Roosevelt, and the Congress created a successor company to Marconi's, the Radio Corporation of America (RCA), and handed it to the main wireless equipment manufacturers, AT&T and the United Fruit Company.[6] A measure of public ownership was also maintained. Public universities and municipalities were among the first to acquire broadcast licences; but they were soon overwhelmed by advertising supported stations (McChesney, 1990; see Chapter 7.2). The last time an argument was mounted in Congress for a new communications system being seen as a 'Post-office arrangement' was in connection with commercial exploitation of communication satellites in 1962. It was to be again dismissed (Galloway, 1977).

In Europe, on the other hand, until the late twentieth century, exactly the opposite position was taken. The European assumption was that every public communication system was indeed a 'Post-office arrangement' and, unless convincingly argued otherwise, the business of the state. Telegraphy and telephony thus came to be, largely, state enterprises in Europe but private ones in the North America. On neither side of the Atlantic (and throughout the European empires generally) was there specific consideration of these technologies as platforms for public expression. The idea that they might constitute mass media was unexamined, and there was no debate as to the dangers to free expression that state ownership of the communications infrastructure might pose. The principle that, in a free society, there should be no direct, or close, state control of the means of expression for which the press had fought was not in play when mass communication systems came online. Whether in public hands or in closely state-controlled private entities, the state was already in a central position. This was largely to be unquestioned into the present.

7.2   Samuel 'Roxy' Rothafel v. American Telephone & Telegraph (1923): American radio

By 1923, the year Telefon Hírmondó closed, wireless (voice) telephony was finally being widely diffused – as radio. This was not because it had just been 'invented'.

Wireless telephony, like wireless telegraphy, was first demonstrated with a communication to ships at sea. Eleven years after the Marconi/Popov wireless telegraph demonstration, on Christmas Eve, 1906, ships in the North Atlantic received a morse message warning them that their headphones were about to start making strange noises. Shortly thereafter music was heard and a voice wished the listeners a happy Christmas and peace on earth. The speaker, back in North America, was Roger Fessenden (Barnouw, 1969: 13). However, whereas wireless telegraphy had real purpose as nothing else would do, adding the capacity for the system to talk was quite unnecessary. Vessels in distress, to take the most pressing example, were well enough served by wireless morse transmission. Fessenden is, therefore, not recorded as being radio's 'inventor'. The technology was only slowly exploited. Its first widespread application was along the Western Front in the First World War where increased communication speed over morse messaging had some little point. But it was to take until the eve of the 1920s for it to be realized that its crippling disadvantage as a communications platform for private messages – anybody could listen – was its *raison d'être*. The supervening necessity was not to be ships or armies but the urban masses' need for entertainment, the same social pressure as had produced the cinema. Wireless telephony was actually radio.

Who would control it, on the other hand, had long been a settled question. Before it was fully formed, it was clear that radio would be distinct from the press and its privileges. For one thing, the possibility of signal interference was obvious. Wireless signals were not like telegrams and phone calls, confined to a wire. If they were not to interfere with each other, allocation of bandwidth in the radio spectrum was vital. They could not be transmitted through the 'ether' at the whims of entrepreneurs. Signal interference therefore ruled out any free-market free-for-all. It justified state intervention in allocating radio spectrum use. Anyway, radio was far too close to the military to be exploited freely. Wireless stations were licensed and allotted call-signs and wavelengths as agreed by the signatory governments at the international radio conference held in London in 1912.

It must be stressed, though, that this involved no automatic mandate for the state control of the content of wireless signals. Such interference was no more legitimate for radiotelegraphy and radiotelephony than it was in wired telegraphy and wired telephony; or, come to that, for the mail – another communication system for the most part enabled by the state. Nevertheless, as radio's broader potential as a mass medium was realized, the conditions of wireless licence-holding would be extensive enough to impose editorial as well as technical control. And there were sanctions: the licences could always be withdrawn in case of breach. This major undercutting of a fundamental element in the concept of liberty of speech was obscured by technological naivety and hyperbole as to the new medium's supposed social power. As a result, the principle of free speech for which the press had fought for centuries was breached without a fight – almost without a murmur. The theatre was censored, film was denied protected status: now, after the First World War, governments found themselves with a level of control over a technology of mass communications that they had not enjoyed since their grip on the printing press was loosened in the seventeenth century.

That there might be a problem for expression was none the less present. Lee de Forest, an 'electrician' (as pioneering engineers in the field were called), had developed the triode amplifying valve that had made Fessenden's demonstration possible. In 1909, he put the leading American women's suffragist of the day, Harriot Stanton Blatch, before a microphone to make her case. In 1910 he transmitted Enrico Caruso live from the Metropolitan Opera in New York (Hijiya, 1992: 71). The first adverts were transmitted in 1912 by Charles Herrold to publicize, aptly enough, the private training school for electricians (in the modern sense) he ran in San Francisco (Barnouw, 1969: 34–5). In May 1914, music was transmitted to ships at sea from the Marconi station in Wanamaker's New York department store (Benjamin, 2002: 102). Herrold, who seemed to have had a rather clear vision of what the medium might do, was sending regular signals but only to a small coterie of other enthusiasts using the crystal receiving sets he had sold to them (Baudino and Kittross, 1977: 67–8). Beyond these few, nobody was listening or taking much notice.

Land-based wireless telegraphy, too, was being used in the same non-point-to-point way, following the template of mass distribution – 'unison' – wired ticker-tape services. By 1915, the *New York Times* was sending out weather reports, the German Army was transmitting propaganda across the trenches and some Midwestern American universities were offering updates on agriculture market prices – all in morse and all for anybody to receive. The 'terrible beauty', born when the Irish nationalists seized the General Post Office in Dublin in revolt against British rule, Easter 1916, was announced to the world by a proclamation declaring independence, read out by Patrick Pearse to a small and somewhat bemused crowd on the steps of the building. It was also more generally distributed in Morse from the wireless telegraph station on the roof, exactly to bypass any possible British news blackout (Pine, 2002: 10). This is the prototype electrical media-message calling for revolution.

Received opinion in the world of wireless still failed to grasp that a new mass medium might be at hand in either form – Morse or voice. For one thing, while it was logical enough to exploit wireless telegraphy's lack of privacy for the sake of a sinking ship, on dry land to do so required more lateral, indeed revolutionary, thinking. With the wireless telephone, the point-to-point postal model, with its guaranteed privacy, was even harder to trump. Moreover, there was also simply no pressure to explore the alternative possibility by manufacturing an accessible receive-only apparatus, the essential key to transforming wireless telephony to radio. The record suggests that the thought of such a device occurred only to David Sarnoff. He was a young go-getting Marconi manager, who had made his reputation in 1912 when working in the New York station by ensuring news of the *Titanic*'s sinking reached the White House. Sarnoff seems to have been suggesting nothing less than a new product line – easily operated wireless telephone receivers, perhaps even with loudspeakers rather than headphones – but despite the context of the rivalry between the Marconi company and others, Lee de Forest for example, the rest is silence. Certainly there is no record of the systems engineering of any such device. The tentative transmission experiments, though, continued, only interrupted when the stations were silenced by the US government during the years, 1917–18, when the United States was at war. With the peace, the activity recommenced. E.W. Scripp's newspaper, the *Detroit Daily News*, for example, obtained an amateur wireless licence for the 8MK radio station and began reading out news stories and playing records in the summer of 1920.

It was not only that the concept of radio was not articulated. It was also that all existing potential listeners were licensed to transmit as well as receive. They were used to talking back (Salamon, 2010: 8). After one record, the 8MK voice asked: 'Did you get it?' and a chorus answered, 'It's coming in fine. We're getting everything loudly and distinctly' (Baudino and Kittross, 1977: 75). In the United States, these amateurs, 'hams', were establishing wireless telegraphy as a popular hobby. Many thousands of Morse operators in First World War armies had been trained to use wireless trans(mitter/re)ceivers and there were enough ex-signal personnel in the United States, as well as other enthusiasts, to sustain an American Radio Relay League (Hilmes, 2007a: 8). Regulation was in place, using the pre-First World War legislation which gave powers (in the Wireless Ship Act, 1910) to the Navigation Section of the Department of Commerce. These were transferred by the Radio Act, 1912,[7] to the Secretary for Commerce. Hundreds of licences for the operation of transceivers were granted and assigned wavelengths. Instead of taking up the possibilities of a central transmitter sending signals downstream to multiple receive-only devices, there was a cacophony of signals from multiple transmitters. Wireless telephony was more a social network than a new mass medium; the legislation still envisaged nothing more.

With the peace, though, an obvious particular industrial need had manifested itself immediately: what to do now with spare capacity in the new electrical industry? The manufacture of military transceivers, such as Westinghouse's SRC 70, had ceased. The comparatively small numbers of technologically sophisticated amateurs who wished to explore the world of wireless did not constitute that much of a market and, anyway, they could assemble their own devices from commercially available components. Building the set was part of the hobby but, nevertheless, most genres of what would become the medium of radio had been demonstrated – albeit often obscurely – since 1906. What was missing was a receive-only device that could be mass-produced for those who just wanted to listen to programming – not wanting or expecting to join in. This would not yet be, quite, Sarnoff's 'music box' for anybody to operate; a certain level of tuning skill would be needed as such a device was, essentially, the wartime apparatus without the transmission function. The industrial need was widespread enough to ensure that, within two years of the war ending, the conceptual breakthrough to such a receiver occurred in a number of places more or less simultaneously.

Frank Conrad, who had run the Westinghouse SRC line in Pittsburgh during the war, thought that the hams in his area might be interested in listening to records; so, using an experimental wireless licence, 8XK, he began playing them from apparatus he installed in his garage. Gramophone records, developed by Emile Berliner, one of Bell's early collaborators on the telephone, had become big business since before First World War. 'Carry Me Back to Old Virginny', recorded by Alma Gluck in 1914, was the first million-seller disc, pre-electric recording technology particularly favouring strong operatic voices. By 1919, around 100 million records a year were being pressed in the United States alone, and a much-recorded artist, an Enrico Caruso for instance, could earn millions from discs (Chanan, 1995: 30). Conrad was merely replicating pre-war demonstrations of music transmissions. A local department store lent him the records they were pushing and publicized his transmissions in the advertisements they were, of course, already placing in the local paper. Conrad did better than the *Detroit News* and others had done: listeners were really enthusiastic (Baudino and Kittross, 1977: 65). After all, although the provision of home entertainment via wireless telephony was still no more clearly seen than it had been in the years following Fessenden's initial demonstration, urban mass entertainment was evermore flourishing. Witness the success of popular theatre and its industrialization in the technology of the cinema. As post-war euphoria took hold and an appetite for entertainment blossomed, the wireless telephony demonstrations, which had been underway for more than a (admittedly interrupted) decade, were about to coalesce, at last, into radio.

Conrad's manager, Harry Davis, a Westinghouse Vice-President, was alerted to what he was doing by the ads, which not only mentioned the records but also that customized devices for listening to the transmissions – 'cat's whiskers' – were now available for sale. Finally, an electrical industry executive realized that more than a hobby for a few was in play. Despite the fact that these crystal rectifiers were difficult to tune and audible only through headphones, perhaps the public in general would nevertheless buy them in large enough numbers to make it worthwhile? Davis reopened the SRC 70 line but for the manufacturing of such domestic receiver-only devices, not transceivers. By September 1920, Conrad was regularly transmitting programmes of recorded music on behalf of the store two evenings a week (Barnouw, 1969; Aitken, 1985: 471–4). Westinghouse also increased the power of Conrad's makeshift transmitter and applied for a full licence.

There was no possible question as to the appropriateness of the government's allocative oversight of such a new development. The operation of the international agreements, the business of the US Department of Commerce, ensured that. Wireless telegraphy, even if it was only relaying music, was still of primary importance to national security and public safety. Commerce allocated Westinghouse the call sign KDKA and on 2 November, Leo H. Rosenburg, another employee of the company, read out the results of that day's election. Warren Harding had been returned as President and live news reporting joined music and the rest as a programming genre (Barnouw, 1969: 145). Despite this, content control was still not anywhere on the agenda. Radio was still not firmly established as a new mass medium: 'the primary purpose of KDKA was to encourage the sale of radio receivers' (Salamon, 2010: 8).

At exactly the same time in Canada, Marconi was responding to the same industrial need. The company owned a manufacturing plant in Montreal where it also ran station XWA, 'Experimental Wireless Apparatus', on a licence from the Canadian government. Douglas 'Darby' Coats, a wireless operator at the firm, was charged with encouraging sales by providing something to which to listen. The problem was that, as Coats recalled: 'The engineers ... ran out of breath and grew tired repeating the alphabet and saying "ninety-nine" ... Radio programmes began with the addition of music to speech at the microphone' (Vipond, 1992: 16). It was now fifteen years since Fessenden; but on both sides of the forty-ninth parallel, the initial social need was less the public appetite for home entertainment or news than it was the dictates of commerce. Westinghouse and Marconi wanted to market sets. These transmissions answered the basic question: what was the point of buying a home receive-only device – a radio or a wireless as such a thing would soon be called in Britain – without something to hear? Programming, both in Pittsburgh and Montreal, was given away free to help sell sets.

It was also the case that the commercial potential of long-distance, transoceanic telephony was still a far clearer research objective at this point than was the provision of domestic entertainment. Transoceanic wired telephony was technically not possible because of signal attenuation through the cable and wireless offered a solution. In 1916, AT&T had demonstrated that long distance wireless telephony worked by transmitting a voice across the Atlantic. After the war, firms such as Marconi were interested in using wireless to compete with the long-line telegraph cables – despite its lack of privacy – more than they were concerned about the uncharted possibilities of home entertainment; but not exclusively so. Many around the world were engaged enough in the wonders of wireless transmission to sustain research into the medium's entertainment possibilities as a secondary area of interest.

In the United States, the large firms and the other public entities that were also setting up transmitters in 1920 were obviously very different from the private hobbyists, a fact soon acknowledged in Washington. Different classes of licences were issued by the Commerce Department. Private radio transceivers were allowed an 'A' licence while organizations, from telecommunications companies to newspapers to firms to municipalities and universities, were given 'B' licences, with call signs beginning 'W' or 'K'. With their 'A' licences, the hams were prohibited from transmitting 'weather reports, market reports, music, concerts, speeches, news or similar information or entertainment'. The 'B' licence holders were not to use records. All the music they transmitted was to be live and the stations therefore incurred royalties payable to the American Society of Composers, Authors and Publishers (ASCAP), which had been collecting them for all performances, live and recorded, since 1914. The allocative function was seeping into an editorial one as well. This, though, was no deterrent to B licence applicants: KDKA, for example, was awarded the eighth such licence. In North America, transoceanic telephone research was beginning to fall into the background.

However much the allocative function was required technologically, restrictions on content were a challenge to the spirit of the First Amendment.

The constraint on state interference with speech had been predicated on the assumption that it would inhibit an individual freedom. Now, for the first time, a situation had arisen where the state might be needed to ensure freedom – the freedom of the broadcaster to give freedom to the citizen to listen to clear signals. It is radio that moves the fundamental position so that American legal theory would need, eventually, to contemplate a point where, although 'the state may be an oppressor ... it is also a source of freedom' (Fiss, 1996: 2; see also Chapter 9.4). The significance of this was unnoticed at the time. Any prior control of content implied by the licensing system was buried beneath a wash of enthusiasm from the hams, the manufacturers and commercial and public entities of various kinds.

Such was the enthusiasm that Sarnoff now got his 'music box'. Unlike his claim to have discussed the matter in 1915–6, there is no ambiguity about the memo he wrote, dated 31 January 1920, in which he outlined his ideas quite clearly:

> I have in mind a plan of development which would make radio a 'household utility' in the same sense as the piano or phonograph. The idea is to bring music into the house by wireless ... The 'Radio Music Box' can be supplied with amplifying tubes [valves] and a loudspeaking telephone, all of which can be neatly mounted in one box. The box can be placed on a table in the parlor or living room, the switch set accordingly and the transmitted music received. (Archer, 1938: 112)

He also envisaged lectures, the coverage of 'events of national importance' and baseball scores (Benjamin, 1993: 326). This was written before the widespread proliferation of programming activity of that year – all of which was to be heard through headsets.

Sarnoff remained in front of the curve conceptually, but only because he was thinking of a mass-produced electrical home entertainment device – with a loudspeaker; not because he clearly saw a new medium. On the contrary, the one flaw in his business proposition was programming. That is to say, he did not see the production of content as anything other than a subsidiary to, in fact a charge on, the manufacturing activity. Transmitting to receive-only sets would come to be called – lifting the term from an elegant eighteenth-century agricultural expression for widely scattering seed – 'broadcasting'. Broadcasting, as an activity, was not foremost in Sarnoff's mind in 1920 and he had no clear answer to the question of who was going to provide programming and how was it to be paid for. But as even the hardware – the 'music box' – was still not self-evidently a good idea, Sarnoff's reputation as a visionary can stand. When he and a colleague visited an independent engineer who had built a 'uni-control' receiver with a tuning-dial and a loudspeaker, the colleague suggested it would remove much of the pleasure involved in tuning the cat's whiskers until something could be heard. Sarnoff, though, disagreed: 'This is the radio music box of which I have dreamed' (Biting, 1977: 1017).

The programming question though would need to be answered, and quickly. With ASCAP's increasing interest in these developments and the Commerce Department's insistence on live performance, providing programming was not going to remain as cost-free as Conrad's disk-spinning was. Sarnoff's best early notion was that, by analogy with municipal bandstands, local authorities could provide the music. That might have been only a set-manufacturer's perspective but it was not unattractive to public authorities. Some municipalities had indeed obtained licences to augment their pubic services for improving and recreational purposes. For public universities, the medium seemed an ideal tool for their outreach educational mission and over 100 licences were to be awarded to them in the 1920s. These educational and cultural applications of the new medium, provided as a public good, were the first to be established and some would claim the universities especially 'were the true pioneers of US broadcasting' (McChesney, 1990: 30). By the mid-1920s, one-third of all stations were publically run.

Their funding, though, was unstable. Many pioneering universities could not maintain their commitment and a quarter of them gave up between 1925 and 1927 (McChesney, 1995: 15). Anyway, this public involvement in a communications medium butted against both the established American hostility to anything suggesting a 'Post-office arrangement' as well as emerging commercial pressure. This steadily increased as commerce evermore clearly came to be seen as the answer to the programming funding problem. Radio, obviously, had its commercial uses beyond the business of set manufacturing. Firstly, owning a station could be a useful publicity tool, with programming costs being justified on the advertising budget. For example, the *Detroit Daily News*'s amateur radio operation, having become the fully professional WWJ, was run expecting, as its manager put it, nothing more than 'good will' (Baudino and Kittross, 1977: 76). It was not alone; by the mid-1920s, stations operated by commercial organizations – many of them newspapers – to publicize their businesses were in the majority. Nevertheless, owning a station and providing regular programming was not a particularly viable option for most potential advertisers. Their products were not as suitable as a newspaper's for recycling on the radio as content – but advertising these products within and around programming was a clear second commercial possibility.

Although radio as a publicity tool was an indicator of the way forward, such use was not without criticism. The publicly run stations implicitly challenged the cultural value of advertising on the new medium. 'Should radio,' asked one astute observer in 1922, 'be used for advertising?'

> Supposing – just supposing – you are sitting down, head phones clamped to your ears, or loud-speaker distorting a trifle less than usual, enjoying a really excellent

radio concert ... All of a sudden a gruff voice or a whining voice or a nasal voice or some other kind of a voice says 'Good Morning! Have you used Hare's Soap?' ... Any one who doubts the reality, the imminence of the problem, has only to listen about him for plenty of evidence. Driblets of advertising, most of it indirect so far, to be sure, but still unmistakable, are floating through the ether every day ... More of this sort of thing may be expected. And once the avalanche gets a good start, nothing short of an Act of Congress or a repetition of Noah's excitement will suffice to stop it (Jackson, 1922: 75–6)

This was prescient. The following year, AT&T's New York station, WEAF, began to accept sponsored programming from third parties (Hilmes, 1990: 18).

That this mode of selling airtime should occur to the phone company was no accident. Just as a subscriber bought time on a phone circuit to convey personal messages, so an advertiser hired a studio to transmit public messages on the radio. The programmes were still being given away free as far as the audience was concerned. The advertiser paid the station licensee to use its 'air', as the American radio industry has it, to access the audience. AT&T's breakthrough was to charge for the programmes it provided as well as for advertising airtime. Advertisers needed no licence of their own. 'Toll Broadcasting' was born. By 1926, nearly 20 per cent of all stations had adopted the WEAF commercial model.

Older advertising media were quick to express their hostility. Here is the *New York Sun* in 1926, satirically suggesting what radio commentators were coming to: 'This, ladies and gentlemen, is the annual Yale-Harvard game being held under the auspices of the Wiggins Vegetable Soup Company, makers of fine vegetable soups ... The Yale boys have just marched on to the field, headed by the Majestic Pancake Flour Band' (Philips, 1930 [1926]: 339). Advertising – commercial speech – as expression, had lesser status as compared with editorial matter in print. American courts, for example, had long been according it less vigorous First Amendment protection than news. It was of critical importance to newspapers and periodicals but they also had their cover price as a revenue source. Advertising was also a rather minor revenue source for the theatre and cinema.

For radio, on the other hand, after public and charitable funding was reduced or withdrawn in the late 1920s and the commercial model largely swept public broadcasting aside, advertising became American broadcasters' only sources of revenue; and its tone dominated. It created a demand for airtime that could not be met by a simple expansion of outlets. At this stage, the technology operated best around the median of the medium band and only a finite number of allocations could be made to occupy this part of the spectrum. And there were already thousands of licensed hams and some hundreds of broadcast stations as well as the naval radio provision. It is no wonder that the early public broadcasters found themselves under increasing pressure as the decade progressed and their licences became evermore commercially valuable.

Despite introducing commercial sponsorship and thereby fixing the dominant style of American broadcasting, for AT&T the breakthrough brought less reward than might be expected. Essentially, the company did not understand content provision and thought, it would seem, that it was still dealing with telephony. 'The fact remains,' said A.H. Griswold, the AT&T assistant vice-president in charge of radio, in 1923, '[broadcasting]'s a telephone job, that we are telephone people, and that we can do it better than anybody else ... in one form or another, we have got to do the job' (Waldrop and Borkin, 1938: 172). This was dangerous because any such whiff of monopolistic tendencies engendered hostility in the Justice Department and among its suspicious partners in the Radio Corporation of America. There was also the unexpectedly messy business of the broadcasts themselves. That radio was a medium of expression that might have implications for the concept of free speech came as a shock to the telephone company whose 'common carrier' core activity involved no such considerations.

WEAF ran a relay – an outside broadcast – from New York's Capitol Theater, a plush cinema which offered the then usual live variety shows as well. This was hosted by the manager, impresario Samuel 'Roxy' Rothafel. The theatre was not charged for its airtime although clearly it was advertising itself, but it was nevertheless an ideal arrangement from the company's point of view. AT&T got free programming, which it could sell on to advertisers. The engineers even used the relay, initially, to test new equipment, such as a PA system with loudspeakers and microphone rather than the traditional theatrical MC's megaphone (Hilmes, 1997: 61). There was, though, a problem: content.

Rothafel's introductory monologues, 'continuities' as they would soon be called, were delivered in a direct, 'folksy' style. The company's management, however, felt this to be at odds with AT&T's not inconsiderable sense of telephone people's dignity and locution. They edited him, not, as had been the case with the earliest controversial films, because of 'obscenity'; but rather merely because of 'taste'. It was the 'tearful sentimentality and side remarks of Mr Rothafel', however much credit they gave him for pioneering a new form of presentation, that was not to corporate taste and was beyond their 'comprehension'. The company admitted: 'the musical quality of this feature, we have never questioned' (Hilmes, 1997: 62–3). Rothafel told the papers he had been censored: 'Immediately an almost unanimous protest poured in upon WEAF, the greatest expression of opinion [thus far] ever drawn from a radio audience' (Hilmes, 1997: 62–3). This public objection to an abridgement of speech came as a shock. Nevertheless, that there might be a problem with live transmissions had occurred to some, if not to AT&T. There had been contingency planning in a few studios about procedures to curb extempore inappropriate speech; for example, by employing an organist, permanently on standby during live transmissions, ready to drown out any speaker who strayed.

The press had its eighteenth-century heritage as an engine of the struggle for independence. Its infrastructure and content was specifically protected, constitutionally, from state interference. Radio had its roots in national security and safety at sea and, in the United States, it had also become commerce's shill with all the reduced protection for speech that entailed. Moreover, in clear distinction to the other media, it was a federally licensed activity. All this was also in the context of what was immediately seen as an unprecedented ability to reach into the homes of thousands. And finally, as the courts had in effect quite recently held when denying the movies strong First Amendment protection, there was no universal right of free expression. AT&T's sensitivity, for all that it was perceived as ludicrous even at the time, was a marker of how the culture of radio would develop.

Governmental management of the spectrum, because of the nature of the medium, had more obvious justification than had previously been the case for official interference with speech freedoms. The state may well have tried to control the infrastructure of the press or the stage by licensing physical machines or places of performance; but it could not do so, as was the case with radio, in the name of national security or safety. Additionally, another printing press, another theatre did not physically prevent other presses or other theatres from operating as a radio station might when its signal interfered with its neighbours on the spectrum. Courts were becoming involved in cases of conflict over such signal interference and making determinations that were, implicitly, contrary to the dispensation of the Secretary of Commerce.[8] In effect, the law was creating a species of property right over slabs (as it might be) of the incorporeal airwaves. As long as speech freedoms were not questioned, there was no other prima facie legal difficulty in transforming broadcasting licences into secure property. It was, after all, a fundamental tendency of the common law always to seek to distinguish property rights. The spectrum could be considered a natural recourse, vested in the state, like minerals, the exploitation of which could be licensed to private enterprise, which would then be secure in tenure. Faced with the challenges, though, the Commerce Secretary, Herbert Hoover, took the matter to the Attorney General in 1926 who advised that his action in assigning wavelengths was, indeed, ultra vires to the 1912 Act. Chaos ensued.

Hundreds of unlicensed stations were suddenly heard on air and many, licensed and unlicensed, began to cluster around the most effective part of the spectrum. The result was signal interference on a massive scale. Congress moved rapidly to create a Federal Radio Commission (FRC), on the model of federal trade and commerce agencies, to take matters in hand. Of course, not everybody had a right to own a broadcasting station or even to have access to a microphone. The technology, as it was understood at the time, prohibited that. The spectrum was finite and not all demands on it could be accommodated. The FRC, a temporary bureaucratic solution, came into being in March 1927 to regulate radio in the 'public interest, convenience and necessity'.[9]

Although this phrase was not glossed, the question of content was now addressed in statute for the first time. The Congress went beyond the allocative function and held that, although radio would be uncensored: 'No person within the jurisdiction of the United States shall utter any obscene, indecent, or profane language by means of radio communication.' Of these, only the first was unambiguously unprotected speech (see Chapter 11). It was felt that:

> the right of all of our people to enjoy this means of communication can be preserved only by the repudiation of the idea underlying the 1912 law that anyone who will may transmit and by the assertion in its stead of the doctrine that the right of the public to service is superior to the right of any individual to use the ether. (Goodman, 1999)

In this way: 'The public received entertainment and the right to listen, but lost the right to speak. The right to speak had become the right to listen' (Goodman, 1999). The deal was entirely acceptable because the only demand that people had was for a clear signal. Any greater issue of freedom was moot. As one journalist argued: 'If you have something to say go to an existing broadcaster and buy time' (Morecraft, 1926: 24). However, what is absolutely clear is that the traditional concept of free speech was in effect being deemed to be unsustainable in the face of the new medium. The liberty of the telephone wire – never mind of the press – was, supposedly, destroyed by the technology of the radio signal.

It is a libertarian nonsense, however, to suggest that, left to their own devices, the courts could have sorted out conflicts between the 15,111 amateur stations, 1,902 ship stations, 553 land stations for maritime use and 536 broadcasting stations then in existence in the public's, or anybody else's, interest (Goodman, 1999). Control of the infrastructure was unavoidable; but control of the content is a non sequitur to that necessity. After all: 'The censorship that followed the printing press was not entailed in Gutenberg's process' (Sola Pool, 1983: 226). Censorship had preceded print; it had no need of a new technology to justify itself. Neither did technology have anything do with censorship of the stage or film. Radio did not 'entail' censorship any more than did any other medium either. American broadcasting therefore further undercut the concept of a media-blind right of free expression. With movies, it had been a matter of denying the positive protection of the right without insisting, despite arguments from the censorious to the contrary, on further specific statutory restrictions. With radio, though, protection was not even on the agenda.

As the Rothafel incident indicated, radio was to be the occasion for extending control rather than expanding the right of free expression. Language suggesting this would be the case underlay the whole debate leading up to the passage of the 1927 Act. Hoover, for example, had said broadcasting needed be 'free of malice and unwholesomeness' – not quite the same as just avoiding the traditional 'do no harm' constraints imposed by libel, sedition, obscenity and blasphemy (Jansky, 1957: 247). The American Bar Association, arguing for the legislation, saw it as 'reducing interference, thereby securing better reception of the better programs' (Messere, 1996). 'Better', as an amorphous quality, would, in time, join 'taste' in becoming a shibboleth by which to regulate content over and above the general requirements of the law.

In 1934, the FRC was made permanent as the Federal Communications Commission (FCC) and given all telecommunications as its remit.[10] Its specific powers over radio, including issuing licences and assigning frequencies, requiring technical transmission standards and even having 'authority to require the painting and/or illumination of radio towers if and when in its judgment such towers constitute, or there is a reasonable possibility that they may constitute, a menace to air navigation'.[11] Among its range of administrative sanctions, the commission also had the power to deny licence renewal. Nevertheless, the 1934 Act, like the 1927 Act before it, was tacit about content supervision, except for the unspecified requirement that licences be operated in 'the public interest' and programming not be obscene or even 'indecent'. With this much in place, further regulation of radio's central cultural products, the programming, was scarcely a major issue before the 1970s. Nevertheless, the First Amendment's protection was undercut.

Incidents were rare but when they occurred, the FCC was not loath to threaten non-renewal of station licences. For example, a risqué remark by Mae West on a comedy show in 1937 and the broadcast of a Eugene O'Neill play with a measure of realistic language in 1938 occasioned such intimidation. Threats were to accelerate in the permissive 1960s (Semonche, 2007: 187). In 1973, KPFA-FM, Radio Pacifica's Berkeley station,[12] transmitted an obscene twelve-minute monologue by satirist George Carlin. The act, 'Seven Words You Can't Say on Television', echoed one of Lenny Bruce's notorious nightclub routines (see Conclusions). The Commission warned KPFA-FM that it might suffer administrative sanctions because of an 'indecent' broadcast. It could do this because it had judicial powers under the criminal code on obscenity.[13] Obscenity is not protected by the First Amendment but neither is it 'indecency', so Pacifica challenged the FCC. In 1978, the Supreme Court held for the Commission (FCC v. Pacifica Foundation, 1978). The 'Seven Dirty Words', as they had become known, could not be said on the radio either. There followed the usual 'creep' with the FCC finally codifying its practice in the 'Indecency Guidelines' issued in 1987. The Commission had created a specific restriction, beyond the general freedom of speech envisaged by the Constitution, on the broadcast media's right of expression. Fines for even 'indecent', 'fleeting expletives' became something of a commonplace for a generation – not least because more relaxed public standards in the matter of language were being reflected in media, guideline prohibitions or no.

Justice John Paul Stevens, for the court in *FCC v. Pacifica Foundation*, stated that: 'Of all forms of communication, it is broadcasting that has received the most limited First Amendment protection' (*FCC v. Pacifica Foundation*, 1978). This is a somewhat ahistorical observation since, exactly, there had been almost no legal examination of the radio's First Amendment rights. Such few scandals as there had been seldom reached the courts. This, however, did not mean that the American airwaves were befouled by bad language, blasphemy and seditious utterance. On the contrary: the reason why the FCC was scarcely needed to police broadcasting was the industry's enthusiastic readiness to censor itself. After all, the film industry had been told it could not rely on the First Amendment. So, instead, Hollywood had established its own system of prior censorship and this ploy had successfully quelled calls for statutory regulation of movie content. Following the Rothafel incident on the radio, it was obvious that such self-censorship was the best way for radio to avoid the blunt threat of external control by the FCC. And the most effective mechanism for self-censorship was the network.

Radio needed no network. Any single central transmitter serving an urban area could reach, simultaneously, an audience of a size unprecedented in the history of human performance culture. The logic of commercialism, however, was a further driver. As soon as the reality of programme production costs became apparent, there was pressure to increase the size of the audience and charge advertisers more for delivering larger numbers. Extra ears did not increase production costs but they could produce extra revenue. If stations shared programming, profits could be increased, even after additional signal distribution charges were met. There was a logic for networks.

AT&T determined that it would be better off both politically and financially providing the technology needed to establish a network's necessary inter-station connections – by wire – than it would by being itself a broadcaster. It therefore handed over WEAF to RCA and divested itself of its interest in that company. In so doing it protected itself against Justice's suspicion that it was seeking to control broadcasting. In 1926, RCA linked all its stations together with cables rented from AT&T, and thereby created a programming operation run by a subsidiary, the National Broadcasting Company (NBC). Sarnoff organized NBC into two networks, the Red and the Blue, and invited other owners to affiliate themselves and share the NBC schedules. Originating a schedule required no licence; one did not even need a station to do this, although sharing the programming from a licensed station – a quasi-'front' for the network – was the norm. WEAF became WNBC. Two years after NBC was created, William Paley, who had become interested in radio because his family cigar business used it for advertising, started a rival Columbia Broadcasting System (CBS), based at WCBS, also in New York. Although various attempts were made to create further networks, none managed permanently to achieve a national reach comparable to these two.

The emergence of the network, of course, did nothing to reverse radio's commercialism. On the contrary, it confirmed the sponsor's privileged position. As Bertha Brainard, NBC's first director of commercial programming, pitched it to a potential client in 1926: 'This department secures talent of known reputation and popularity, creates your program and surrounds it with announcement and atmosphere closely allied with your selling' (Hilmes, 1997: 97). The networks did produce unsponsored 'sustaining programming' 'in the public interest', normally in the form of debates or commentary on the events of the day or the occasional out-of-the-mainstream drama. The vast majority of their airtime, however, was sponsored. The programming they produced in-house was for sale; it needed sponsorship if it was to be broadcast. Broadcasters were also in the business of rebroadcasting material produced by the sponsors themselves, shows usually created by an advertising agency. Some sponsors, though, went so far as to establish in-house radio production units of their own. This is how soap powder manufacturers came to make radio dramas.

The networks, though, did more than enhance the commercial viability of radio. What might be called the 'Rothafel instinct' of WEAF's telephone men was to be further challenged by having such independent production sources. Always fearful of the FCC's possible interference, the networks created vetting procedures – 'Continuity [script] Acceptance' departments – to meet the need for control. These became evermore powerful 'Standards and Practices' operations (in NBC terminology). 'Standards' were, in effect, matters of 'taste', which turned on, primarily but not exclusively, questions of 'indecency'. Network practice responding to a potential FCC threat at the same time suggested the basis upon which the FCC could act if it so desired. Thus internal control and external threat rendered breaches of 'taste', never mind illegal speech, extremely rare. Mae West and Eugene O'Neill were the exceptions, not the rule.

After 1936, NBC's 'standards' were guarded by Janet MacRorie, another of the significant female radio pioneers. In an official photograph she sits at her desk, pencil poised over a typewritten script, the very icon of 'prior constraint'. She and her assistants were vetting ninety scripts a day and were ever vigilant for any references to 'dope fiends', 'confinement cases' or the 'neglect of the wife for other women'. After the Mae West joke – that she'd had a date with the ventriloquist dummy Charlie McCarthy and had the splinters to prove it – 'Standards' redoubled their fretting at innuendo (Semonche, 2007: 185; Hilmes, 1997: 309). They were as hostile to ad-libbing as any Spanish seventeenth-century theatrical censor had been. And it was not just sex. The aural violence of the detective show, the dominant popular dramatic genre, was suspect because it glamorized the 'colorful deeds and skills of miscreants'. All overt focus on social issues was suspect. The legacies of slavery and civil war as well as the reality of mass immigration were still lived experiences for millions in the 1920s, but radio was far from quick to tackle these topics. Broadcasters were ever fearful of the threat to their tenure of the airwaves if programming occasioned major complaints.

Cultural diversity, for example, was primarily reflected in situation comedies. These were far from being unpopular but whether they did anything for social cohesion can be doubted – even by those who uncritically believed in the power of the medium. The shows traded on stereotyping – from hillbillies, to Jews, to blacks. Radio's first nationwide sensational hit was *Amos 'n' Andy*, an aural embodiment of the patter element of the nineteenth-century minstrel show (Sokolow, 2007: 31–2). Beginning locally in Chicago in 1928, it starred two white vaudevillians, Charles Correll and Freeman Gosden, playing African Americans. Within a year it was on the NBC and one-in-three Americans was tuning in. It was the first programme to be recorded for syndication in addition to being transmitted live by the network every evening at eleven minutes past seven. But it was implicitly suffused with bigotry; even the 7.11 slot reflected a supposed African American addiction to the crap-game of that name. It was also responsible for a variant to the mode of radio advertising, the 'spot' commercial. Instead of a sponsor, identified in the name of the programme (for example, *The Champion Spark Plug Hour*), the advert was heard as a discreet interjected element. The innovation occurred with *Amos 'n' Andy* because while Pepsodent, the toothpaste firm which paid for it, was happy to be advertised in connection with such a hit, the company did not want the show to be identified too closely with them. It just wanted to trade on the supposed appositeness of white teeth and black folk. *Amos 'n' Andy* survived into the era of television (see Chapter 8.2).

Stereotyping was the price that needed to be paid for any kind of representation. When J. Walter Thompson, the agency that had been the first to seize on radio as an advertising medium, hired Louis Armstrong in 1937 for their client Fleischmann's Yeast, it was expected that in his continuities he would sound like 'Amos' or 'Andy'. Not least because he did not talk in that way, he refused and was fired in consequence. The network was no better. The previous year, it had refused to hire musicians of colour for the symphony orchestra it was founding. It was doing so for reputational management reasons as much as to provide programming. There were to be no players of colour in the NBC Symphony. The record industry was exploiting any popular black artist and jazz in general in the ghetto of 'race records', but even this ploy was eschewed by the broadcasters. As for jazz itself, its ability to offend the fastidious everywhere was reason enough to limit its exposure. The question of race could, especially, upset sensitive Southern affiliate station owners, never mind their audiences.

Politics, too, needed to avoid anything controversial, although anti-labour, pro-business programmes were apparently entirely acceptable. The role of being an essential capitalist tool as a major advertising medium meant that the networks had no hesitancy in refusing organized labour, for example, a platform in their programming. They were always ready to deny the unions the right to buy advertising time (Fones-Wolf and Godfried, 2007: 61). With war underway in Europe in 1940, Ms MacRorie, head of the now renamed 'Community Acceptance Department', was concerned about fanning pro-interventionist opinion: 'What we aim to avoid is propaganda in the guise of drama' (D. Weinstein, 2007: 105). As the NBC Vice-President for Programming, John Royle, had put it in 1933, the policy was essentially 'to give offence to nobody' (Fones-Wolf and Godfried, 2007: 63). By the later 1930s, giving no offence, even with news programming, was increasingly difficult. Reporting the Spanish Civil War, for example, could be heard as anti-Catholic. A little later, isolationists could detect a Jewish conspiracy to involve the United States in Europe's war behind reports of its progress. News production, though, was a valuable area of sponsorship. With its vast audience, this meant that if one advertiser was quick to take fright and withdraw their funding because of such perceptions – and they did – others would replace them. News was also a problem because of the hostility of the press and had been from the outset.

The press was concerned about this new and vivid rival from the beginning and the publishers had denied the broadcasters access to the agency wires, which they collectively owned. This effectively curtailed national and international reporting on the radio. Following Franklin D. Roosevelt's election and a sensational crime in 1932 – the abduction and murder of the son of celebrity aviator Charles Lindbergh – the networks established news production units despite press hostility. The American Newspaper Publishers Association (ANPA) responded by ordering its members to carry no programme listings information and the broadcasters backed off. However, all was not lost as, in an agreement signed the following year between ANPA and the networks, the broadcasters were allowed to cover exceptional stories with no threat to the listings. In the 'exceptional' decade then underway, this became an open door: the Depression, Mussolini and Hitler, Abyssinia, Spain, Manchuria, the Second World War. Radio, with increasing authority and technical resources, covered them all. The realization grew that events were so 'exceptional' that the public welcomed two news sources; indeed, that the press and the radio were not rivals but mutually supportive. This was becoming ever clearer, especially to those publishers, not a few, who also owned radio stations. However, a publisher might bask in the First Amendment's protection in print. On the air, news was subject to the Janet MacRories of Community Standards.

Mr Justice Stevens was, therefore, right to suggest radio did indeed have the least protection from the First Amendment of any of the mass media but not, primarily, because of the regulator or the courts. Rather it was the broadcasters' own self-censorship that curtailed radio's freedoms. The American situation, despite this *autocensure*, reflected as much freedom of expression as the radio was to achieve anywhere in the world. In the more statist European environment, control was more overtly exercised from the outset. There was never a question of the state's right to regulate radio, in effect content as well as infrastructure.

7.3   *The British Broadcasting Corporation v. Mr George Formby* (1937): Britain's 'third way'

In Britain, where ham radio was not so much of a factor, the problems of controlling more professional transmissions were confronted largely without that distraction (Briggs, 1985: 11). Nevertheless, the American experience of broadcasting loomed large. In 1922, a British General Post Office (GPO) official sent to investigate the US situation had reported on the useful business opportunity radio represented for the electrical industries but also the need for a single broadcaster. This last opinion was fuelled by overstating the confusions of the American airwaves, although Herbert Hoover was still assigning bandwidths at this point and interference was not the problem it was to become in 1925. Nevertheless, in London, much was made of the supposed disorder caused by having multiple signals. The GPO's views were also suffused with a certain technological naivety. It was, apparently, believed that only a single wavelength was available and that Britain was too small geographically to entertain rival broadcasters. Neither point was true. Although the median of the medium bandwidth was, given the available technology, the most effective part of the spectrum, the band could accommodate more than one viable signal; nor was covering the whole country with one signal even technologically quite possible yet. Essentially, American radio, with its multiple commercial and public local broadcasters, was being set up as a species of awful warning. 'The go-as-you-please' methods of the United States, as one official described them, were to be avoided at all costs (Briggs, 1985: 20).

Given these misapprehensions and prejudices, the idea of a single broadcaster as the only alternative to chaos took root. Yet how to put such an entity in place was not clear. A dislike of monopoly was not unknown in Britain (just as it was in the United States), so the broadcaster prima facie could not be commercial: in effect, could not be Marconi. The government's quandary was that it felt itself unable to create a private monopolist (Marconi) but it did wish to follow the United States and establish a market in programme services. A third way, one not unknown as radio established itself as a mass medium across the world, was direct state control. Although radio use was, unlike previous media, governed by international agreements and crucial to safety at sea and the military security of the nation, the British state obviously could not actually itself broadcast. It was inhibited by history from directly operating organs of mass opinion just as much as was Washington. Anyway, emulating revolutionary Radio Moscow, say, which had begun as a state organ, with a very powerful transmitter, in 1922, was scarcely attractive to a representative democracy in the hands of a Conservative government.

It took six years, from the start of broadcasting experiments in 1920, for a way to be found between, on the one hand, the Scylla of commercial ownership (whether monopoly or chaos) and, on the other, the Charybdis of state propaganda. In either case, no more than in the United States was the issue of free speech at the microphone addressed as a matter of principle. Radio was no more like the press than were the stage and the screen. Exercising the right of free speech with the new medium in a meaningful fashion was glossed as bringing 'controversy' to the airwaves and that was, simply, forbidden. At the time and subsequently, this breach of the medium's liberty was presented as no great matter: 'Only constitutional limitations – limitations, for example, on "controversial" broadcasting – prevented more from being done', as the BBC's official historian puts it (Briggs, 1995a: 7). Prohibiting 'controversy', an ambition of state censors throughout history, was not seen as any sort of flaw to the medium's social potential but merely an example of an inconsequential restriction – no great matter.

Instead, received opinion – the 'general spirit' of the British people – overwhelming admired the elegance and brilliance of the solution eventually put in place: a public non-commercial monopolist, but one formally independent of the state. This was to produce, it was to be widely held in Britain at least, the world's finest broadcaster. The settlement of 1926 was presented as a prime example of the British genius for governance, and, despite glitches, continues to be so presented (albeit less stridently in the twenty-first century). Be that as it may, the solution worked and arose so seamlessly from the country's telecommunications history that it seemed inevitable.

Telegraphy had been deemed an entirely 'Post-office arrangement' all over Europe; and while in some countries Bell had established itself as commercial telephone company, in others telephony too was a 'Post-office arrangement'. With wireless telegraphy, commercial entities such as Marconi or Telefunken were the operators, but the military importance of the technology meant they were closely supervised and licensed. The result was that, although transmission experiments were going on at the same time as in North America, the European authorities were to prove slower to license the activity on a permanent basis.

In Britain, the future of such transmissions, without any question, was seen as depending on the British General Post Office. The GPO, which had successfully asserted its control over the telegraph and the telephone, would now oversee wireless telephony as well. After all, all transmissions of whatever kind needed to be licensed by law, because of international agreements. Britain's imperial interests had led to dominance of the undersea telegraph cables – aided by a monopoly in gutta-percha insulation, which was produced only in the colony of Malaya. The value of voice communication to imperial governance could not be ignored. Nevertheless, it was no surprise that, despite this, the GPO would not be enthusiastic about the possibility of Marconi's radio within the United Kingdom. Indeed, it had been stifling the development of a telephone system to protect its wired telegraphy monopoly and appears to have regarded all new technology as a threat rather than an opportunity. This, though, is less a result of its monopolistic position than its intrinsic bureaucratic caution. It was actually unthreatened by new communications technologies because the precedent of telegraphy and telephony ensured it would have control of them, too. Rather, it was that the GPO was seized with general conservative inertia.

The picture it presented of the American situation, that the 'choice was between monopoly and confusion', had convinced public opinion (Briggs, 1985: 33). This was, however, not true: in France and Germany, for example, multiple licensed broadcasters, private and post-office controlled, were coming on stream. In the smaller nations amateurs were making the running in broadcasting 'clubs'. The GPO, though, was supported in its attitude to wireless telegraphy by the military and the fact that radio required regulation because of potential signal interference, a critical issue to safety at sea. Nevertheless, imperial necessity (primarily) did force it to issue licences to both private individuals and Marconi for scientific experimentation.

The Marconi UK parent company began duplicating the 1916 AT&T long-distance demonstration using the temporary experimental licence call-sign, GB90MZX, it obtained in 1920. Transmissions began from the company's research and development plant and wireless telegraphy station outside Chelmsford, Essex. These speech transmission experiments essentially involved increasing transmitter power and checking for range; what was transmitted was of no consequence. The object was transoceanic telephony, not entertainment. To conduct these range tests, the engineers, led by Guglielmo Marconi's personal assistant, H.J. Round, read out the names of railway stations until tedium suggested that amateur musical performances, given by other employees, might also serve for testing purposes. As with fellow employee Darby Coats and his records in Montreal later in the year, boredom was the driver.

On the other hand, in April 1920, Marconi's Dutch station, PCGG, in The Hague began transmitting live music as entertainment, not a test, to an appreciative Europe-wide audience of hams, a fact not unnoticed across the North Sea. Company policy began to change but it took a newspaper 'stunt' to make the medium's potential clear. Alfred Harmsworth, by then awarded the title Lord Northcliffe, who was a faithful disciple of American new journalism's sensationalism, paid Dame Nellie Melba, then at the height of her fame, to give an operatic recital, fifteen minutes long, at the microphone in the Chelmsford studio on 15 June 1920. The performance included 'Home Sweet Home' and an aria from *La bohème* and ended with 'God Save the King' (Baker, 1970: 185–9).

There was a massive response; the *Daily Mail*, unsurprisingly, declared that the transmission was 'wonderful'. 'Art and Science join hands and the world "listening" must have counted every minute of it precious' (Briggs, 1985: 15). The 'world' certainly heard it, with reports registering reception from all over Europe and beyond, as far as Newfoundland. Marconi, though, was still interested in wireless telephony and all the experiment suggested was other specialized uses. In the following weeks, they went back to reading material, but this time, news reports. These were specifically directed to newspaper offices around Britain and in Scandinavia – in fact, a new form of wire service was being essayed. For the GPO, though, no good could come of either of these activities, the one (singing) essentially a frivolous misuse of a crucial means of communication, and the other (news distribution) a direct threat to its own telegraphic news distribution business. Opinion within the GPO and the armed forces dismissed such misuse of a serious resource and further experimentation was therefore banned. The ten-month licence was promptly cancelled.

However, in the face of public curiosity, the GPO, although constrained by perceived security and safety needs, could not simply continue to refuse to license the activity. Faced with the hostility of the military, the alien nature of the activity (entertainment) and in the apparent grip of technical ignorance, the GPO adopted a dual approach to the problem. Music was being heard regularly from The Hague and, in February 1922, Marconi was allowed to resume broadcasting from Essex for ninety minutes a week. The company was also given a licence to operate a station in London, call sign 2LO, albeit again with restrictions. For its first six months, 2LO had an hour a day, either in the morning or the afternoon, and it was limited to transmitting only speech. Twenty-two other applications were received and all but two were told the blatant untruth that 'the ether is already full' (Briggs, 1985: 24). At the same time, as a first step towards containing the commercial monopoly problem, two of Marconi's rivals, Metropolitan-Vickers in Manchester and Westinghouse in Birmingham, were also given licences.

Serious discussions were begun on the dilemmas of having multiple companies involved. The GPO called in all the interested parties, essentially set-manufacturers who either operated or had applied for licences, to act as a committee with which it could negotiate. A sub-committee of the six biggest firms was set up and agreed with the GPO that a single company, owned by them, should be created as the programme-making entity. Despite the technical difficulties of delivering a single signal, it was agreed that it would provide content for the whole of the country. Insofar as this company was being created under the aegis of the state and would be owned by the nascent electrical industry, the pattern being followed was, if only at that level, that of the United States in 1919. The British company would be like RCA, which had also been created by government. Otherwise, all would be different. RCA became the first programming network some years after its foundation, whereas the company envisaged for Britain in 1922 would have that remit from the outset. Nor would it have a set-manufacturing arm, as RCA did, and it would have no competitors.

In creating this monopoly, the 'Broadcasting Company', the big six had some issues amongst themselves; but it was agreed that the new entity should use Marconi transmission equipment. For good or ill, the American example was 'a stimulus', as Peter Eckersley, the engineer who against the technical odds was actually to build the British national network, put it. 'If America had blundered into chaos, British broadcasting, it seemed, was now to be forced into a straight-jacket' (Briggs, 1985: 22, 27). The chaos, pre-1925, was being overstated, but the straitjacket was indeed a possibility. The British assumption that only one provider was needed to cover the whole nation was to remain more or less unquestioned for the next three decades.

The British Broadcasting Company (as it was now called) received no 'manifesto for broadcasting' from the GPO but rather a compromise, the result of a 'combination of caution and obstinacy' (Briggs, 1985: 27). Agreement was reached by October 1922; the Company was in existence by December; and the GPO finally got round to issuing it a licence in January 1923. By that time, though, the British Broadcasting Company had been on the air for over two months. John Reith, a man of strict Presbyterian instincts but who quickly became, like Sarnoff, a radio visionary, had been appointed its general manager. Neville Chamberlain, the government's Postmaster General, though, was accused of acting improperly. By creating the monopoly he was, some felt, greatly exceeding his powers under the wireless telegraphy legislation. To legitimate his action retrospectively, in 1923 his successor, Sir William Joynson-Hicks, set up a Committee of Inquiry into the company under the chairmanship of Major-General Sir Frederick Sykes, with, curiously, Reith as a member. (Curious, that is, as the object of the inquiry was the effectiveness of the organization Reith headed.)

Reith was an enthusiastic proponent of the view that a monopoly was both desirable and inevitable. His vision for the medium, however, did not see it as a new organ of free expression. On the contrary, he agreed with the Postmaster General and other opinion-makers that 'controversy' – as outlined in the company's licence – was to be avoided. Whatever else of the puritan spirit he might have shared with John Milton, he, unlike the poet, had no trouble with the 'prelatical tradition of crowding free consciences'. He told the Committee that: 'The Broadcasting Company have never, I think, broadcast anything controversial, and, of course, they[14] are taking very great care not to. Whether or not they are prevented from doing it, they obviously would not do it' (Briggs, 1985: 51). Radio, in Reith's view, was to be an educational power, a force (albeit uncontroversial) for democracy and so on – but not a platform for free expression or for even much of popular taste. In fact, Reith's vision for radio was at odds with the social necessity underpinning the thinking that had produced the application. The home delivery of entertainment, radio's *raison d'être*, was in his eyes far too limiting. It proposed, he thought, a harmful misuse of the medium. In his virtual manifesto of 1924, *Broadcast over Britain*, Reith wrote that the 'purpose and pursuit of entertainment alone' would be a 'prostitution' of 'a great scientific invention' (Reith, 1924: 17). He was not, therefore, too concerned when other parties sought to frustrate popular broadcasting.

The theatre-owners, for example, had not been considered as potential shareholders in the company, not least because they had played no part in developing the technology. They were anyway far less identifiable than the electrical companies as a coherent group. The arrival of radio initially produced little except conflict with them. They could, of course, refuse to host remote (or, in British terms, 'outside') broadcasts from their venues but they also tried especially hard to prevent any studio 'cabaret' programmes during the hours when live performances took place. In fact, they endeavoured to stop their artistes from appearing before the Broadcast Company's microphones at any time (Briggs, 1995a: 230, 314). This did not overly concern the broadcasters as they had no commitment to transmit such material. Seized with the Reithian vision of social improvement, the company was anyway far from being sympathetic to popular culture. Reith, after all, took the view: 'It is occasionally indicated to us that we are apparently setting out to give the public what we think they need – and not what they want – but few know what they need and very few what they want' (Reith, 1924: 34). Such snobbery did not go entirely unquestioned at the time, although Reith glossed it as a concern for not underestimating the intelligence of the audience. This line played well with the powers that be and was to help his ambitions for the service. The legitimate stage, in which the company was more interested, was not effectively denied it. Actors, especially theatrical stars, were not to be so controlled by the theatre-owners as were the variety artistes. The first dramatic broadcast was, of course, a scene from Shakespeare. The company was pleased to invite leading classical actors to its studios, Lewis Casson and Sibyl Thorndyke, for example, in Euripides' *Medea*. The first dramatized novel was the Rev. Charles Kingsley's *Westward Ho!* (1885).

Establishment prejudices were also served by the Broadcasting Company's music policies where giving the people what 'they need' took blatant precedent over what they wanted. Newspaper surveys in the 1920s had strongly suggested that the public had a preference for popular and dance music but the company refused to be dictated to by this. Instead, its first musical transmission was of work by Richard Wagner, played by its own symphony orchestra. A classic trio and a military band were next to be hired. In 1926, Reith took over Henry Wood's classical Promenade Concert series, a late Victorian fixture of London musical life. Probably as a result of the British Broadcasting Company (and British Broadcasting Corporation) support as much as anything, the concerts still remain a vibrant annual event. More popular fare was provided, but only with a certain unwillingness. It came from outside ensembles, often performing after the announcer had concluded regular programming by bidding the public goodnight.

This was entirely a reflection of a policy uninfluenced by outside pressure. With music, impresarios, although they fretted about the future of live concerts, were less in evidence than were the theatrical owners, producers and agents. The publishers, of course, complained about loss of sheet sales as people abandoned their living room pianos for the 'wireless'; but actually they were primarily interested in securing appropriate royalties, which the broadcasters were pleased to negotiate. The gramophone industry was positively delighted to have its products played on the wireless – which they were increasingly after the introduction of electrical recording in 1925. Enhanced record sales were very evident after exposure on the radio (Briggs, 1995a: 315–16). And as musical controversy was essentially a matter of a moral panic about jazz, it was easily dealt with: there was no 'hot' music. Moreover a certain sabbatarianism prevented even dance music on Sundays.

Controversial speech was also to be avoided. Here, too, there was to be only 'popular non-controversial matter', 'popular' being, for the most part, rather constrictively viewed. A parade of the great and the good were brought to the 2LO studios at Savoy Hill, London, to deliver lectures (known as 'talks'). Reith quickly realized the excellent public relations potential of this. These Establishment figures would be useful supporters, flattered by the company's invitation to address the microphone. They were also, almost without any exception, uncontroversial. Religious controversy was avoided by limiting programming almost exclusively to the Protestant mainstream Churches and the Catholic Church (on occasion). As for news, it did not escape the 'non-controversial' net either.

As in the United States, the press, through the mechanism of its collectively owned wire-services, could deny programming content to the broadcasters more effectively than did the theatre-owners and impresarios. This did not mean, though, no news at all but rather no news — certainly no 'new' news – before the last editions of the evening papers and the first of the morning, i.e. only between 7 p.m. and 11 p.m. The daily summary of world news then sold to the Broadcasting Company was written by, and copyrighted to, the combined wire-services (Briggs, 1995a: 121–2). Between the GPO and the newspaper barons, news on the radio – previously unpublished news even if 'uncontroversial' – was otherwise simply prohibited. This was not, the GPO told the Sykes Committee, because of any thought of controlling what news was left (Briggs, 1995a: 89, 92). It was just that 'controversy' needed to be avoided.

On occasion during the years of the British Broadcasting Company, 1923–6, the Postmaster General comported himself over the content of broadcasting much as did the Lord Chamberlain over the stage. This, though, was presented not as censorship but as a matter of 'influence' over 'undesirable' programmes. Despite the propensity of high GPO officials to be less than truthful about the radio, there is no reason to believe they were not genuinely surprised to find that the technology involved considerations of free expression. This had not occurred to them as an issue any more than it had to their opposite numbers in AT&T. For them the question was, rather, the relationship between the company and the press; and this was of a piece with the company's other relationships with the worlds of music, theatre, religion and education. Thus Joynson-Hicks, the Postmaster General – a politician, it should not be forgotten – vetoed a broadcast by the Chancellor of the Exchequer, a member of his own government, to explain the budget. Of course, a reply from the Opposition was unthinkable. He also got upset when another politician mentioned the Versailles Treaty on air without the company first seeking Foreign Office clearance (Briggs, 1995a: 326, 243–4).

For all that no comment was made as how deeply offensive the evolving situation was to British notions of free expression, some did note such restrictions would make for very dull broadcasting; but that was all. The British Establishment's failure to see radio as a new medium, even when it finally did come to realize the technology's scope, was reflected by the GPO's basically unsympathetic view of programming's potential. Chillingly, the fifth clause of the Broadcasting Company's licence required that it should provide 'a programme of broadcast matter to the reasonable satisfaction of the Postmaster General' (Briggs, 1995a: 153). This, however, had nothing to do with politics or religion, according to the subtle mandarin interpretation of the injunction by the GPO's solicitor. It was merely that his boss had the right to interfere to make sure the public got value for money; or, if that rational was unconvincing, then it was only to do with regulating potential conflicts, especially with the press. Either way, it had nothing to do with censorship. The censorship incidents were, anyway, rare and silently borne by the company; rare because of Reithian self-censorship and silently borne because Reith, from the very outset of his tenure, was playing a long and difficult game.

The arrangements of 1923 were in no way permanent even after Sir Frederick Sykes confirmed them. Reith's strategy was to exploit lingering uncertainty to secure a future for the organization, free of both the manufacturers and the GPO. The promise (and performance) of *autocensure* were crucial if this objective was to be achieved. Hence the constrained everyday production practice – the 'very great care' taken to avoid 'controversy' – and the contriteness when, inadvertently, something slipped through to enter the Postmaster General's consciousness. Anyway, Reith also had more immediate concerns. For one thing, the financial settlement was not commensurate with his ambitions for the service. The manufacturers provided monies according to the number of sets sold and operating a receiver-only set required a ten shillings receive-only licence. Radio licences had been established at the outset by the 1904 Wireless Telegraphy Act;[15] initially, of course, for transceivers. The GPO kept five shillings and passed the other half, in monthly instalments, to the Broadcasting Company.[16] The company was almost entirely free of any need to trade because the licence income was, overwhelmingly, its major source of revenue. The outcome of this reality was that its output could, and did, conform far more to Reith's high moral purposes than to any commercial driver arising from the need to help its owners sell sets. Why, logic then suggested, should it, with its Reithian claims on the cultural high-ground, be the creature of a consortium of particular commercial interests?

Any difficulty with the licence revenues was easily resolved, as far as Reith was concerned. Licence income, in his view, was at least 20 per cent short of what was required for a unified national service. The GPO levy should therefore be reduced so that licence income could meet the company's needs. Moreover, the Broadcasting Company had demonstrated by its 'care' that it was fit to provide such a service. It was performing in a way totally satisfactory to Establishment opinion, which, of course, agreed a single broadcasting company was to be preferred. Therefore, the 1923 settlement should be revisited and, in Reith's view, the company's relationship with both the GPO and the manufacturers should be reviewed. Indeed, in his view, it should be given its independence from the electrical industry.

In 1925, confirming the pattern of proceeding by inquiry that was to condition British broadcasting until Broadcasting Acts of the Thatcher era,[17] the Postmaster General established a second committee under David Lindsay, Earl of Crawford, to examine the situation. By now American radio was in the interregnum between control by the Secretary of Commerce and the Federal Radio Commission. It was, in reality, as chaotic as the British had long believed it to be. Worse, when one could hear a signal, it was increasingly likely to be suffused with the crassness of advertising. So there was no question of that avenue being explored in the UK. Advertising would not be required as long as the GPO yielded more of licence revenue. Continuing the monopoly while avoiding advertisements was also a self-evident given.

Reith went into the Crawford Committee (on which he did not sit) determined to replace the commercial company with an independent public authority, some sort of 'broadcasting commission'. The faint echoes of the inhibition on state ownership of channels of opinion were yet to be heard in the background. So, although this new entity would still require a licence from the Postmaster General, to indicate its independence of Parliament, it would be created not by stature but by royal charter. And instead of commissioners, a term which implied directly appointed public servants to operate the service, there would be directly (that is, politically) appointed governors who would independently hire the operating officers. The use of a surviving medieval absolutist instrument of government to create an organ of opinion ostensibly free of the control of a democratic assembly was not considered then, nor subsequently, as ironic. On 1 January 1927, the British Broadcasting Company became, by the same legal means of incorporation whereby a British town is transformed into a city or a public teaching institution into a university, the British Broadcasting Corporation (BBC). The licence to broadcast was for ten years.

Reith understood clearly that a central political, indeed constitutional, function of the BBC was to cement the constituent parts of the United Kingdom of Great Britain and Northern Ireland together. The broadcasting settlement was being forged as the Irish revolt of 1916 was reaching its compromised solution of an Irish, twenty-six county, 'Free State' within the Empire. This had been declared in 1922. What remained of the prior constitutional arrangement had formally become the United Kingdom of Great Britain and Northern Ireland the same year, 1927, as the Broadcasting Company metamorphosed into the BBC. Reith's vision spoke, in a fashion of no little political astuteness, to the Corporation as a unifying institution. For all that such a *rationale* has never been overly suggested, the timing is no accident. In 1924, Reith had written that the BBC's purpose was to permit the chimes of Big Ben, that aural Union Jack, to be 'heard echoing in the loneliest cottage in the land'. The BBC was among the first of the institutions of the 'new' state the radical political scientist Tom Nairn once christened 'Ukania' (Nairn, 1988).

Nothing more symbolizes this function of the BBC than the imposition of Southern Received Pronunciation (SRP), the accent of the Establishment, across the airwaves to the point where it became known as 'BBC English'. Apart from in comedy, any deviation from SRP was perceived as transgressive. A regional accent was not heard reading a news bulletin, for example, until the later 1930s, and even then it was an educated Yorkshire one. The BBC was not in the business of celebrating diversity. Its single service came to mean, thanks to the engineering genius of Peter Eckersley, a national 'Simultaneous Broadcast' programme and 'regional' broadcasting hubs; but Simultaneous Broadcast always took precedence over the outposts. Anyway, many of these, even in major centres of population with distinct cultural identities – Sheffield, for example – were merely relay stations and not equipped for origination. Frictions between the English regions, the 'national regions' (i.e. the Celtic fringe) and London tended to be always, unsurprisingly, resolved in London's favour.

The dominance of London was not the only foundational issue Crawford dealt with by its silence. There was no suggestion of taking advertisements or any problem about the fundamental right of expression. The spectre of 'uncontrolled' American radio put paid to the first and, as for the second, Crawford, in fact, spent as little time as had the Sykes Committee on debating it. Instead of general philosophical issues, the practical, essentially commercial, concerns of other interested parties were again considered – the theatrical lobby, the music publishers and the gramophone industry, the press. Educational and religious voices were also heard. The resolution of any frictions with these stakeholders, either through the processes of the Crawford inquiry or in subsequent years, was to condition the broadcasting environment in Britain in fundamental ways long into the future. The settlement, reached in 1926, was to prove its resilience in the face of infrastructural and further foundational changes, including the introduction of new audio-visual media. Although commerce and competition were to be allowed after the Second World War, 1926's most obvious legacy is the continued willingness in all quarters to accept measures of content control for broadcasting deemed otherwise inappropriate to a free society's media. Indeed, before the rise of the internet, the issue was scarcely ever addressed and is still not questioned for the older broadcasting platforms.

Crawford followed Sykes in seeking the opinion of all interested parties, most of whose positions had not altered since 1923. The theatre-owners, for example, continued their campaigns to keep the airwaves free of popular entertainment after Crawford. They were insisting on this in 1926–7 (and briefly again in 1930), but these objections eventually foundered on the rock of their own absurdity. Managements misunderstood the extent of their 'industrial' power and top-line artistes and actors, not inclined to ignore a new, national, audience as well as an additional source of income, brushed aside continued attempts at control. The players, after all, held the whip hand.

In the long term, the more significant inhibitor as far as variety was concerned came from the other side – the broadcasters. Into the late 1920s, there was no particular push for popular programming and in consequence, the attachment of the mass of its audience to the BBC, until the situation was transformed in the Second World War, was undercut by such implicit contempt. The plain fact is that of the Reithian triadic mission to 'inform, educate and entertain', during his tenure, the least was entertainment – popular entertainment. Broadcasters, by class and instinct, were unsympathetic to the popular. Even when catering to it became an obvious necessary political consequence of taking the hypothecated tax that was the licensee fee, they remained uneasy with it.

Artistes constantly offended the BBC's finely honed internal censorship apparatus by merely repeating into the microphone their stage acts or filmed performances. Greater tolerances for the content of these other media, although this had itself been censored by the Lord Chamberlain or the BBFC, were to cause problems up to the 1960s, if not beyond. In the 1930s, George Formby, for example, was an immensely popular, gauche Lancastrian performer with a speciality in comic songs. However, their mild innuendo, in 'The Window Cleaner', for example, was too much for the BBC:

Pyjamas lying side by side, ladies nighties I have spied.
I've often seen what goes inside, when I'm cleaning windows.

That Formby was, at the time of the broadcast from Birmingham, offering this in a local pantomime, a show for children, and had included it in one of his films, without causing offence was no justification for singing it into the microphone: 'The people who complain of vulgarity in broadcasting may be those who think it immoral to go to a pantomime or even to a film' was the view taken centrally (Scannell and Cardiff, 1991: 226–7). Responding to 'the people who complain' was ever more the concern of Reith's BBC than was exploiting the wider liberality of the public.

Despite the collapse of theatre-owner obstructionism, it still took the BBC a decade from the start of broadcasting to formalize the production of entertainment in a 'Radio Variety Department', initially originating three hours of programming a week. By 1935, its output was up to fifteen hours a week, but it always caused problems. In 1939, the head of 'Variety' was still complaining: 'It has been said there are only six jokes in the world, and I assure you that we cannot broadcast three of them' (Scannell and Cardiff, 1991: 227). On the other hand, the existence of the Variety Department and the dance band, which had been established post-Crawford in 1928, indicate that some sense of serving the entire licence-holding public was seen as a necessity and was being met.

But grudgingly. In drama, the popular continued to be avoided. In 1928, for example, Reith personally authorized a production unit to explore experimental avant-garde drama, 'pure radio' (Scannell and Cardiff, 1991: 135–7). Popular drama in the form of the American thriller genre had to wait until *Send for Paul Temple* in 1939. Basically, the attitude of the BBC's upper management was unrepentantly elitist. In 1930, it was perfectly acceptable for a BBC executive to opine that 'broadcasting is not and should not be democratic' (Briggs, 1995b: 242); that is to say, it should not be determined by public taste.[18] This was, though, an extreme view. The politics of the licence fee undercut snobbery and attitudes were not monolithic. The head of the Drama Department, Val Gielgud, John Gielgud's brother, more typically shared the elitism but was nevertheless concerned that the audience's preferences were neither fully understood nor readily knowable. He worried – with some justice – that the BBC's hold over the public was, as a result, less firm than it might be. At this point there was some investigation of the possibilities of audience research but, as the 1930s progressed, this became an increasingly vexatious issue.

The public were actually beginning to turn away from the BBC to commercial providers with powerful transmitters in France, the Republic of Ireland and, most significantly, Luxembourg. They were tuning out, especially on Sundays, specifically to hear popular music of all kinds (Scannell and Cardiff, 1991: 232). In fact, the commercial stations, with English-speaking disc-jockeys, more or less failed to provide anything else. The amateur radio club in the Grand Duchy of Luxembourg had begun to broadcast in 1924 but by the 1930s it had become a commercial operation (Nichols, 1983). It was the most Americanized station in Europe, advertising-supported and using, in defiance of international agreements, a long-wave transmitter three times more powerful than the BBC's strongest (5XX Daventry). Although it mainly relied on recorded music, by the mid-1930s some of Britain's most popular artists were making appearances before its microphones in London, the shows being recorded at the Scala Theatre. The European commercial stations, doing the audience research the BBC eschewed, claimed that they were reaching 60 per cent of the corporation's audience, which is plausible enough. Nothing better contradicted Reith's assertion that 'the public' did not know what they wanted than the popularity of these stations.

In 1938, the British branch of the American advertising agency that had pioneered the soaps, J. Walter Thompson, custom-built radio studios in Bush House (which were to eventually become the headquarters of the BBC World Service). The agency was soon delivering forty-four sponsored shows a week across the Channel. Reith fumed about 'this monstrous stuff from Luxembourg' and blocked the use of the continental interconnect. The Scala recordings had to be physically transported to the Continent. He also persuaded the press not to publish Luxembourg programme listings and objected to the transmitter's power in all available international fora (Scannell and Cardiff, 1991: 230–32). However, Reithian notions of broadcasting, especially on the Sabbath, undercut all these efforts. Initially, the BBC did not transmit on the Sunday before the forty-five minutes of prayer with which it began the broadcast day at 9.30 a.m. Three hours of silence followed (to allow for church attendance) and when programming resumed it avoided anything but classical music and lectures ('talks') until another church service at 8 p.m. and close-down at 11 p.m. Radio Luxembourg, on the other hand, which limited its English service to the evening during the week, broadcast dance music throughout the weekend.

Reith's austerity could not be maintained and he was forced allow some popular entertainment on Sunday. Otherwise, his response to the commercial challenge was to continue to refuse to count the audience, citing biblical authority for not doing so: 1 Chronicles 21.[19] Ignoring the research (and the consequent advertising rate cards) of one's commercial rivals was no answer.

Nor was the security of the hypothecated tax – the licence – well served either. High moral tone was one thing but, politically, taking the public's money for a service that failed, at least in part, to meet their preferences was another. Popular programming was not to be avoided. Delivering it in acceptable shows, though, was not that easy when it so went against the grain of the institution.

Nevertheless, by the mid-1930s, of 266 full-time musicians employed by the BBC, less than half were committed to the classical canon. Apart from the 119 players in the BBC Symphony Orchestra, there were now also five regional dance bands, three light orchestras and the military band. Music accounted for 65 per cent of programming and three-quarters of this was classed as 'Light' or 'Dance Music'. In BBC parlance, it was still not 'Music' because 'Music' meant, simply, classical music; indeed, it even embraced modern classical music – 'Bartok-Stravinsky type of organised musical noise' as one listener put it – which was very much an elite minority taste (Scannell and Cardiff, 1991: 216). Jazz, still, was barely tolerated: 'Hot music' was in some broadcasters' opinion only liked by 'Jews' (as also was, curiously, Arnold Schoenberg) (Scannell and Cardiff, 1991: 211). Only occasional 'swing music' concerts were allowed. A 'jam session' in 1938 threw the Controller of Programmes, Sir Cecil Graves, into a tizzy: 'A jam session? What on earth that means I don't know … Is it a new Americanism? … We must introduce some sort of supervision to prevent this sort of thing.' But then he was a man who thought that 'crooning', the *mezzo-voce* style which the technology of early electrical recording favoured, was 'a particularly odious form of singing' (Scannell and Cardiff, 1991: 191, 189). So much for Bing Crosby *et al*. Graves, a confidante of Reith, finished up as one of his successors as wartime Co-Director-General. Clearly, sensitivity to pubic taste was not a requirement for the BBC's top post.

Parallel with disdain for the popular was a strong metropolitan prejudice. It kept regional accents from the microphone except when they were being funny. Hostility was often clothed as a supposedly reasonable desire for 'quality', rather than prejudice. Gielgud certainly claimed that regional drama was substandard. On the other hand, when his department finally got round to *Send for Paul Temple*, it originated in Birmingham and was good enough to be a smash hit (Scannell and Cardiff, 1991: 378). Be that as it may, metropolitan prejudice could not be as easily maintained against music. Manchester, for example, had its Halle Orchestra, and it was therefore quite hard to condescend to it. It became something of a rival centre to London for this output, an exception that proved the rule of London's otherwise overall dominance. Eventually, Manchester was to feed the network with other material from 'Children's Hour' to documentaries.[20]

In fact, the BBC's cavalier way with the popular and the regional made it, in the 1930s, a species of awful warning to American broadcasters, just as they had been to the British in the 1920s. It was 'a middle-class institution and it sounded like one – especially in London. Its institutional voice ... was often aloof and supercilious' (Scannell and Cardiff, 1991: 176). The BBC became a stick with which, for example, American Network Standards and Practices departments could be beaten back. In the course of one row over content, NBC's Janet MacRorie was asked: 'Are we to give the radio audience what they apparently like to listen to or what we think they ought to have? The advertisers pursued the former course; the British Broadcasting Company [sic][21] the latter' (Hilmes, 1997: 126).

7.4   *The BBC v. Lord Beveridge* (1942): The limits of radio freedom

But the popular was not the most vexed difficulty the BBC faced. The worm in the bud of the arrangements determined by the Earl of Crawford lay not in the relationships with the theatre-owners or the music industries but with the press. It was here that the unstated problem of free expression and, behind it, the reality of the BBC's actual independence of the state came, as much as it ever did, to the fore.

The *Daily Telegraph*'s Viscount Burnham, distinguished from the other proprietors as publically being unafraid of the radio, represented the press on the Crawford committee. He was as concerned to define the role of the Postmaster General as he was to defend the interests of the newspaper industry. Although the case against allowing the broadcasters their own news service was again made and accepted, it was his questioning as to whether news could be banned from the airwaves at the 'mere fiat' of the Postmaster General that threw a flickering momentary light on the free expression issue (Briggs, 1995a: 153). The answers he obtained were no clearer than they had been when offered to the Sykes Committee. It took the General Strike of May 1926, two months after Crawford delivered his report recommending the creation of a corporation, to demonstrate the reality of the situation. The strike embraced the printers so no newspapers appeared and Winston Churchill, then Chancellor of the Exchequer, took upon himself the Roger L'Estrange role of publishing an official replacement, the *British Gazette*.

He also wanted, in the spirit of L'Estrange, to take over the British Broadcasting Company directly. Whatever voices were raised in opposition to this, the fact is that Reith demonstrated there was no need of such action. As he was to write to his managers after the nine-day strike was over:

> There could be no question about our supporting the Government in general, particularly since the General Strike had been declared illegal in the High Court. This being so, we were unable to permit anything which was contrary to the spirit of that judgement, and which might have prolonged or sought to justify the

strike ... The only definite complaint may be that we had no speaker from the Labour side. We asked to be allowed to do so, but the decision eventually was that since the Strike had been declared illegal this could not be allowed.

Of course, this declaration of illegality was by no means itself free of controversy and Reith's entire *apologia* was a fig leaf to cover the Company's partisanship. Reith's real reason for his self-imposed injunction on reporting the strikers' case was that he realized the threat from Churchill meant that, in effect, 'The Company existed on 8th May [a week into the strike] by sufferance'. It only maintained 'a precarious measure of independence throughout the strike' (Briggs, 1995a: 330, 347). The triumph of the previous March, when Crawford had delivered most of what Reith wanted, was put in jeopardy. Reith knew that his journalistic pusillanimity was the only way to preserve his vision for the BBC; and it worked. (The public, at least those wealthy enough to own one of the some two million licensed wirelesses in use, appreciated the BBC's effort as much as did the government. Only 176 letters of complaint were received as against the 3,696 correspondents who wrote to congratulate the company [Briggs, 1995a: 351]. In the absence of more formal audience research, such self-selecting correspondence, newspaper criticism apart, was the main method of assessing audience reception. One consequence of this was broadcasting's heightened sensitivity to the reactions of these correspondents, exceptional though they were by definition. The mass, after all, did not write in.)

For the government, the company's behaviour justified the decision to allow the corporation into being the following January. The Broadcasting Company's response to the General Strike can be considered as the defining action that secured the BBC's royal charter and licence. It was the context for the BBC's 'independence' and the basis of broadcasting's flawed 'freedom' – to the present day. Despite developments in technology, changes in the BBC governance arrangements and the post-war arrival of commercial rivals, the price of British broadcasting's freedom is the degree of compliance with authority that the company displayed in 1926. It was at a level unseen in the British press in peacetime for the previous 150 years. Reith avoided Churchill's takeover by simple dint of doing exactly what Churchill would have done had he actually seized the company. Nevertheless, Churchill's L'Estrange tendency was not entirely thwarted. Clause 19 of the licence empowered the Home Secretary, 'when in his opinion there is an emergency and it is "expedient" so to act, to send troops in to "take possession of the BBC in the name of and on behalf of His Majesty"' (Robertson and Nicol, 2008: 31–2). Moreover, the control over content was not removed as the government retained the right to prohibit any broadcast even in times of non-emergency. The only concession was that the BBC 'may' inform its public that it had been censored.

After Crawford, the ultimate control of the BBC still rested with its licensor, the Postmaster General; and the ban on 'controversy' remained in place. Reith had preserved the organization while escaping from the manufacturers. But, despite his conduct, he was not free of direct GPO – that is, political – control. The Postmaster General still had the last word on programming and the rule against 'controversy' was still in place, a millstone around broadcasting's neck. Reith, though, was no more ready to argue against this on the basis for the heroic Whig narrative of the struggle for media liberty than he had been before Sykes. The control, though, did chaff for all that no Miltonic, or even Lockean, cry for freedom was evoked. Post-Crawford, Reith, in effect, was prepared to settle for a trade. Pragmatically no doubt, this was a more effective strategy than a principled stand, for all that it might give hostages to fortune.

In 1928, Reith made clear what his action during the strike implied. To remove the constraints still in place, he made a de facto offer of *autocensure*. As Paddy Scannell and David Cardiff explain, quoting a letter of Reith's to the GPO which secured the deal, he promised that:

> There could be no expression of views contrary to the interests of the state, or on subjects likely to offend religious or moral susceptibilities. Topics would be presented with adequate safeguards for impartiality and equality of opportunity. And responsibility for this might safely be left to the broadcasters for [as Reith wrote] 'it appears from universal experience that the broadcaster himself is the most important censor of the form and extent of controversial matter, and that even where government control is so remote and loose as to be negligible, the self interest or sense of responsibility of the broadcaster requires that controversy should be prudently or tactfully introduced' (Scannell and Cardiff, 1991: 42).

The government accepted his word and the ban on broadcasting matters of political, industrial and religious controversy was lifted.

The real genius of the British in their broadcasting arrangements lay not so much in discovering the third way between commerce and propaganda but in disguising the concessionary nature of the 'independence' the BBC was granted. On the one hand, the withdrawal of the ban meant that any time complaints about broadcasting were raised in the House of Commons, the Postmaster General of the day would deny his power to intervene. On the other hand, the BBC's right of free expression was somewhat like the English right of property. With land ownership, the most that can be bought and sold is a tenancy – 'a fee simple absolute in possession' – because all land belongs to the Crown by right of the conquest of 1066. A fee simple, though, in practical terms, is identical to absolute ownership. The BBC's liberty, under the law, is equally as trouble free on a day-to-day basis as is a fee simple. Nevertheless it is also the property of the state; and the broadcaster's liberty of expression was somewhat less secure than is liberty of property possession. The fact was that Parliament could reimpose the 'controversy' ban at anytime. However, the arrangement served to create a measure of independence that appeared to be as absolute as that of any other medium. After all, there was still no right in law to publish in the UK – it too was constitutionally concessionary and was to remain so throughout the twentieth century. One could say that this constitutional failure had not, after centuries of struggle and legal fudging, prevented the emergence of one of the world's most vibrant and outspoken presses. Therefore, radio could be as untroubled. However, this to ignore a fundamental difference between broadcasting and the press: broadcasting was an activity licensed by the state. Printing had ceased to be so in the seventeenth century. On balance, the BBC's freedom was built on sand; its autonomy was 'virtual' (Briggs, 1995b: 392).

Reith's immediate objectives, though, were secured by 1928. He had already begun to negotiate a piecemeal erosion of the Broadcast Company's arrangements with the newspaper proprietors and their wire services before Crawford. The company had been given its own ticker and a measure of editorial freedom on how it used it. Other restrictions were slowly removed and in 1930, the BBC was allowed to buy full access to the all the wires. In 1934, a year before the American networks reached their crucial agreement with the newspaper industry, the BBC News Department was established (Briggs, 1985: 116–17; Briggs, 1995b: 142–5). The war would dissolve what was left of the walls of the evening news ghetto (Briggs, 1995b: 149). But there was a price to be paid. Partisanship in reporting the General Strike was not a temporary expedient. It became the template for future conduct, even in less exceptional circumstances. The news bulletins were bounded anyway by a supposed journalistic obedience to the demands of objectivity, always a guarantee that outré agenda-setting and interpretation would be avoided.

Moreover, the newsroom, following the lessons of 1926, could be 'complicit' (to use Scannell and Cardiff's word) 'with the authorities in the management of news on radio' (Scannell and Cardiff, 1991: 44). Despite pronouncements in Parliament, close relations were maintained with government that were to stand the corporation in good stead when war broke out in 1939. This, though, was done with a grace and refinement that disguised its presence and allowed the BBC to establish itself, paradoxically, as a neutral, authoritative news source. By the later 1930s the people the BBC hired even came to be secretly vetted by MI5 for security clearance, a practice that continued into the 1980s when it became generally well known within the broadcasting industry. It was not revealed to the public until the twenty-first century (Hastings, 2006). In fact, Reith's 1928 arrangement had brought censorship in general in house and the only time it did surface was when the practice of *autocensure* broke down. Yet, on the rare occasions when arguments became known, these served, again paradoxically, to enhance the impression that the majority of the output was otherwise as free from censorship as was the press. Nowhere affords more evidence of this than 'Talks', News's programming twin to which it was, from time to time, joined departmentally.

Talks was to be the most problematic area of all. For one thing, the government's lifting of the ban on controversy specifically left it in place as regards BBC editorializing. Talks, comparatively unfettered – as it were – by 'objectivity', was closer to the editorializing edge than were the bulletins. For another thing, Talks was ever prone to seek, on journalistic grounds, the controversial, if only on a 'man-bites-dog' basis. Often, the department was able to broadcast the results. The internal censorship process was somewhat leaky; the concept of free expression, conversely, strong. Hence the administration's intermittent but persistent petulant demands for 'some sort of supervision'. So the Talks Department, originally a response to the limitations imposed by the press barons on news bulletins, was the most overt arena in which the BBC pushed the envelope around controversy. In fact, the BBC was to exhibit a certain schizophrenia towards *autocensure*. Leaving aside the machinations and attitudes of its upper management, there were many within the production areas who were, because of the size and complexity of day-to-day operations, difficult to control – especially before MI5's vetting became formalized in 1937–8. They were, in modern parlance, 'creatives' with all the proclivities for disobedience that implied. Given the status of the principle of free expression and the country's liberal tradition, 'controversy' was an essential part of their DNA.

It should, therefore, be no surprise to learn that one of the earliest broadcast debates in 1923 had been on communism in which, shockingly, an avowed communist was allowed a voice. Despite the continued prohibition against 'editorializing', after Crawford, Talks nevertheless became a sort of 'liberty' within the BBC. It was a place in the schedules not quite bound by the same rules as the rest of the airwaves. Hilda Matheson became its first head (Hunter, 1994; Briggs, 1995b: 116–17). Reith, for all his conservatism, was enlightened in the matter of female employment and Matheson was one of a number of women he appointed to executive programming positions, an echo of contemporary American practice. Matheson is the model of the 'creatives' whose integrity fuelled the impression given by the output of BBC independence, but who paid the price for their efforts. She was very much a 'new woman', Oxford-educated with service in MI5 during the First World War. Reith first met her as a secretary of Lady Astor, a Conservative MP from 1919 (the first woman to serve in the House of Commons). As she 'knew everybody' Reith saw her as the perfect producer to maintain his strategy of bringing the great and the good to the microphone (Hunter, 1994: 168). She was, though, not the safe pair of hands he must have thought her. For one thing, she did not actually share Nancy Astor's politics[22] but was a social liberal who became an outspoken advocate for radio's power to enlighten public opinion through free and open debate.

Matheson was influential and effective at a technical production level. She oversaw the establishment of the news section, developed the scope of the scripted talk and created the first politics show, *The Week in Westminster*. She, and the similarly minded liberal and radical producers she gathered around her, also brought ordinary people, sometime unemployed, into the studios to tell their stories to the public. Radio documentaries, such as *Other People's Houses*, were earlier to the agenda of social problems than was John Grierson's much more celebrated documentary film unit at the GPO; and were more hard-hitting and uncompromising. 'Matheson was a woman of courage, originality and culture and she brought these qualities to broadcast talks' (Scannell and Cardiff, 1991: 33, 151). In 1931, she finally fell out with Reith over a talk in which a recording of James Joyce reading from his notorious – and banned – novel, *Ulysses*, was played. The extract was not of itself contentious, but the book was. Matheson left, handing over to her deputy Charles Siepmann, who had earned Reith's good opinions but was, unfortunately for him, no safer.

The frissons continued, not unnoticed by conservative opinion outside the confines of the BBC, as the Talks Department insisted on dealing with the unemployment crisis and other 'controversial' matters. As 1935 progressed, so too did, for the first time, the issue of the renewal of the licence and charter. The BBC, well into the post-Second World War period, was to be always sensitive in its coverage of the GPO but the renewal process was to reveal its need to adopt broader caution as regards the whole of government. This was also true when arguing, as it had to do periodically, for an always politically unpopular increase in the licence fee. A new committee of inquiry was established in 1935 under Viscount Ullswater to review the licence. However, Reith had begun worrying about this in 1933. He was still chaffing at Postmaster General control – he would have preferred a cabinet minister – and the degree of real autonomy the BBC enjoyed post the 1928 'deal' about controversy (Briggs, 1995b: 441).

With the advent of this new inquiry, Talks was sacrificed, its leadership decapitated: Siepmann was given a non-job of regional liaison and the senior producers were dispatched to the far corners of the globe. One was sent to India to establish its broadcasting system. Another, the radical Felix Green, went to be the BBC's 'representative' in New York, and he then played a role in creating the Canadian Broadcasting Corporation on BBC lines north of the forty-ninth parallel. In Siepmann's place was installed Sir Richard Maconachie whose resumé included pro-consular duties in Afghanistan. Clearly, in making this appointment, the BBC Governors had controlling the unruly natives of Talks Department more to the fore than programming experience and talent. Sir Cecil Graves, who brought the Department the news, told them that Maconachie 'is the most distinguished public servant whom I am sure you will all like' (Briggs, 1995b: 139). They did not but that was, of course, to no avail. The golden age of BBC Talks in London was over but Ullswater, which reported in 1936, having listened to a raft of complaints about the BBC's elitism, biases and other matters, nevertheless endorsed the corporation as a whole. The continuation of the licence was recommended; indeed, the report argued that it be for longer than ten years. Again, to a large extent, Reith's pusillanimity worked. And, again, the BBC was preserved intact.

Despite Maconachie, though, outside London the 'controversy' problem continued, as it had to if any reputation for addressing social realities was to be established. In Manchester, for example, from 1938 on, Olive Shapley, another woman Oxford graduate but with a lower-middle-class background, pioneered the use of a new mobile (disk) recording van to make a series of hard-hitting documentaries, with authentic local northern voices, in the tradition Matheson had established (Scannell and Cardiff, 1991: 344–50; Shapley, 1995). MI5 was, in fact, not particularly efficient. It let creatives like Shapley – whose friendship, for example, with the future Labour minister Barbara Castle they failed to spot – slip through the net (Shapley, 1995: 33; Shaw, 1999).[23] Despite the Secret Service, then, the BBC's internal control still found such mavericks in its ranks; but this did not matter. Paradoxically, the overall result of occasional censorship slippage was that the BBC's 'virtual' independence sounded real enough to the listening public.

Ullswater still did not quite give Reith all he wanted: the BBC remained within the Postmaster General's portfolio and the controversy issue was as fudged as ever. Reith, tired of the frictions within and attacks from without, quit the organization in June 1938. His tenure had revealed his genius as well as his innate social conservatism. It had also shown him to be autocratic but 'beset by doubts, fears and jealousies' (Briggs, 1995b: 396); an exceptionally tall man, he had become, as Churchill so famously was to call him, 'the Wuthering Height' (A. Boyle, 1972: 311). Reith's constant but erratic interference with programming details eroded the support of his senior colleagues on his board. He had even exhausted the patience of the BBC Governors, too. He left the BBC at the behest of the Prime Minister, Neville Chamberlain, to run Imperial Airways, supposedly because the government was seized with the assumption that he was too powerful; but he was not (A. Boyle, 1972: 289–95).

It is not the case, however, that: 'Unquestionably the BBC paid the penalty for Reith's aloof but unabashed paternalism by pulling too many punches in its staid, and often excessively cautious, approach to the unending problem of enlightening its enormous but often bewildered public' (A. Boyle, 1972: 289). Punches were certainly pulled but it can be claimed that the BBC paid no penalty because of Reith's tenure. On the contrary. Where it really mattered, in relations with government, he had actually preserved the BBC to the point where it had become too big to fail. Without Reith's pulling of punches from 1926 on, it is arguable whether the BBC's autonomy would have survived at all. The only 'penalty' the BBC paid for this was, in effect, his head. As it was, even though government over-sensitivity remained a constant, the inbuilt pusillanimity of Reith's approach secured an Establishment role for the BBC. The ongoing erosion of the audience in favour of the commercial stations, which his policies did so much to assist, was not punished. Failure to command attention from all sections of the public, though, should surely have been a cause for his removal, more substantive than the reasons that were given. His going, of course, did nothing to repair the fault lines underlying the BBC. The frictions continued as did the occasional illuminating flash revealing the limitations of BBC independence.

Reith had overseen the arrangements for a formal censorship apparatus to be put in place before he left the corporation (Briggs, 1995b: 582); but the British genius for propaganda ensured that the BBC's reputation for authoritative independent information, skilfully maintained by quietly containing controversy, continued. Partly as a result of a perceived failure of First World War public relations excesses, a very sophisticated approach was developed by the Ministry of Information as well as the BBC in the Second World War (Winston, 2011). Jacques Ellul, in his classic book on propaganda, draws a distinction between 'direct' and 'indirect' (or 'sociological') propaganda (Ellul, 1965): 'Sociological propaganda can be compared to ploughing, direct propaganda to sowing.' Direct propaganda is thus designed to impact on audiences producing action – 'direct prompting', Elul calls it (Ellul, 1965: 15). In fact, there was a certain opinion in Whitehall in the aftermath of the First World War that British efforts at direct propaganda had not worked very well. By the time of the Second World War, this lesson had been learned and the propaganda effort, leaving aside campaigns to improve diet in the face of wartime shortages and the like, tended towards the 'indirect'.

The sophistication thus engendered by indirect propaganda was effective for even the most difficult of public relations problems – turning the disaster of Dunkirk into triumph would be but the most famous example of this. Indirect propaganda was well able to play a role in sustaining the British social fabric more or less intact during the Blitz. The myth, best seen perhaps in the wartime documentaries of Humphrey Jennings, was of a nation essentially un-militaristic, un-riven by class and other social divisions, resilient, phlegmatic, liberal and tolerant; and, above all, a nation too intelligent and sophisticated to be browbeaten into action and belief. The main mechanism deployed by British indirect propaganda was always to combat the assumed cynicism of the audience by grounding its mythic messages in recognizable realities – even negative realities. This was a time-honoured technique. It was known to Shakespeare.[24]

In the Second World War, this became a willingness subtly to reference negatives, the black market for example, in the context of quiet stoicism and heroism. Like the GPO/Crown film unit, the BBC was an inheritor of this tradition, ideally placed to help maintain the social fabric in the conditions of the Blitz. Constant vigilance over the state of public morale and morals was being maintained. That reported crime, to take an instance at random, increased by 57 per cent between 1939 and 1945 was scarcely noticed at the time or since. The highest number of recorded strikes, 2,194, was registered in 1944. The BBC's role in keeping the nation calm and entertained – and, it must be said, as well informed as could be expected in wartime – bought it golden opinions at home and abroad. The BBC had, as they say, 'a good war'. Audience alienation largely became a thing of the past and a legacy of public approval was earned that was to take decades to dissipate. It has not entirely done so yet. It is, of course, absurdly to overstate the case to say that the BBC would not have survived fundamentally unchanged without Hitler. But responding to war certainly quelled welling doubts about the BBC's popularity, broadly preserving the 1926/1928 settlement.

The post-war BBC was, however, no more successful at avoiding difficulties when holding the ring between opposing political opinions than it had been in the previous decades. Take the foundational document of the post-war social settlement, Lord Beveridge's *Report of the Inter-Departmental Committee on Social Insurance and Allied Services*, which laid out the template for the Welfare State. Upon publication in December 1942, the report was a best seller. However, Beveridge himself was, through the by-now usual cavorting and deployment of spurious argument, kept from explaining it at the microphone (Briggs, 1995c: 547–56). Somehow, this was always more prone to happen with figures on the left (Beveridge was a Liberal peer). Despite this, the Conservatives came to believe, increasingly as a persistent article of faith, that – despite MI5's efforts – the BBC was a leftist conspiracy. This belief was in part grounded in a philosophical objection to public enterprise; the BBC being a creation of a Conservative administration is always forgotten. It was also sustained by constantly fretting at the liberal tendencies of the BBC's 'creatives' while ignoring the impact of the *autocensure* on the mass of the programming. For the BBC, though, the fact that both sides of the political divide complained was always held, spuriously, to indicate its objective, even-handed independence. Actually, one side had objective evidence of bias (from the 1926 strike to Beveridge) while the other was only sustained by the failures of *autocensure* to toe an acceptable, conservative line (e.g. Talks); either way, the principle of free speech was not in play.

The BBC emerged from the war as possibly second only to the monarchy in public affection. Its accommodation with the popular had been seen nowhere better than with its Forces Network, introduced in 1940. This was generally agreed to have been crucial to civilian as well as military morale. Its overseas service, directly funded by the government and operating out of the old J. Walter Thompson building, Bush House, was an immensely authoritative and effective propaganda machine.[25] Morale aside, the European resistance was sustained by the call sign, '*Ici Londres* …'. This bank of goodwill helped it survive the coming, at Conservative behest, of commercial competition. It even survived the revelations about its relationship with the secret establishment. Despite the fundamental impropriety of this for an organ of expression in a supposedly free society, the news of the MI5 man stationed in Broadcasting House made barely a ripple. However, the problems of the early 1920s as regards autonomy and controversy are still with us in the twenty-first century. The point is: for all its day-to-day liberty, broadcasting could not avail itself of the freedoms the press was now taking for granted.

By the 1960s, despite securing a central place in the nation's cultural life and affections because of its wartime role, the BBC was widely derided as an organization with all the outdated susceptibilities of an elderly maiden aunt; indeed, by then, it was often referred to as 'Auntie BBC'. Despite the Forces Network, its elitist instincts remained in place into the peace. For example, the BBC's first successful long-running radio soap opera was *Mrs Dale's Diary*, which began in 1948, about a doctor and his family in a sixteen-room mansion in south London. Nevertheless, that it was irredeemably middle-class was not good enough for Val Gielgud. It was, he felt: 'socially corrupting by its monstrous flattery of the ego of the "common man" and soul-destroying to the actors, authors and producers concerned' (Briggs, 1995c: 37). The Forces Network, which had become the Light Programme, in contrast to the word-based Home Service and the 'high-brow' Third Programme, was the corporation's bastion of popular light entertainment, but here too little had changed from the 1930s. In 1949, a 'Private & Confidential' *BBC Variety Programme Policy Guide for Writers and Producers* (informally know as 'the Green Book') prohibited:

Jokes about –
Lavatories
Effeminacy in men
Immorality of any kind

Suggestive references to –
Honeymoon couples
Chambermaids
Fig leaves

Prostitution
Ladies' underwear, e.g. winter draws on
Animal habits, e.g. rabbits
Lodgers
Commercial travellers

Extreme care should be taken in dealing with references to or jokes about –
Pre-natal influences (e.g. 'His mother was frightened by a donkey')
Marital infidelity

Good taste and decency are the obvious governing considerations. The vulgar use of such words as 'basket' must also be avoided.

Religious references
Reference to and jokes about different religions or religious
denominations are banned.

The following are also inadmissible.
Jokes about A.D. or B.C. (e.g. 'before Crosby')
Jokes or comic songs about spiritualism, christenings, religious
ceremonies of any description (e.g. weddings, funerals)
Parodies of Christmas carols
Offensive references to Jews (or any other religious sects) (Took, 1976: 86–7)[26]

George Formby would yet have been in trouble, and half the jokes in world could still not be aired on the British radio.

One reason that the BBC was saved from the unpopularity that would have been the necessary consequence of the persistence of such restrictions was the need to compete with commercial rivals. With radio these last were illegal but effective. In the early 1960s a small fleet of offshore 'pirate' unlicensed broadcasters, uninhibited by wartime memories, anchored outside the limits of territorial waters. Ship-board DJs spun discs interspersed with advertisements, updating the challenge that had been presented by continental and Irish stations to the BBC in the 1930s. Their comparative success spoke to the limitations, still, of the BBC's ability to embrace the popular. However much the BBC's playlist expanded there was always music against which it set its face. The stations were, of course, easily controlled – it was soon made an offence to place an advertisement on an unlicensed radio channel and that choked the pirates' revenue stream. The BBC revamped the post-war arrangement, in effect splitting the Light Programme. BBC Radio 1 competed directly for the young demographic, while the network was rebranded as Radio 2. The Home Service became Radio 4 and the Third Programme was now Radio 3. It had also been empowered to start local radio stations, and BBC Radio Leicester opened in 1967. Over the course of the next decades, more than fifty further local stations were set up. The advertisers responded by persuading the government to allow legitimate commercial radio and two stations began broadcasting in London in 1973. The London Broadcasting Company (LBC) and Capital Radio were the first of nineteen stations to come on air over the following thirty months. A second group of thirty-four stations were licensed between 1980 and 1984.

The BBC was only able to mount a response because the changing mores of society had eventually penetrated its upper management. By the 1960s a wind of change was blowing through the BBC's corridors allowing it, at last, to make a better fist of being popular than it had previously done in peacetime. Hugh Carleton Greene, arguably the most effective Director-General since Reith, engineered this and in the course of the decade the BBC managed to slough off the 'Auntie' epithet. Greene was aided by the lack of imagination and efficiency of the internal censoring processes. Despite the odd 'Green Book', these remained somewhat informal and could be out-manoeuvred. *Round the Horne*, for example, was a radio comedy show that ran from 1965 to 1968, starring Kenneth Horne, who had been a popular performer on the Forces Network. It featured, among others, Kenneth Williams and Hugh Paddick as two out-of-work actors, whose suggestive conversations – which managed to contravene most of the prohibitions listed above – were largely conducted in Polari, the underground slang of the gay world. BBC managers, it would seem, were none the wiser.

None of this altered broadcasting's fundamentally flawed situation as a platform for free expression. On questions of broadcasting 'standards', the censorious press was ever ready to create a scandal whenever the BBC crossed a perceived line. This sniping, much of it coming from newspaper proprietors, some of whom also now had commercial broadcasting interests, was not without effect. Also in play was the virtually unknown but ever-present right of the Home Secretary (who had succeeded the Postmaster General in this regard) to ban programmes. The power of the government so to act was successfully challenged in 1972 by Lord Hill, one of the BBC's Board of Governors most effective chairs. The Home Secretary, Reginald Maudling, had threatened an order under the powers in the licence agreement to ban a debate on the government's behaviour in Ulster, then in an early phase of the troubles. Maudling backed off when Hill threatened to make the censorship public (Robertson and Nicol, 2008: 32).

In the next decade, there was the authoritarian tendency of Thatcherism. Despite Margaret Thatcher's antipathy to 'regulation', a paradoxical willingness to allow it in the name of bourgeois sensitivities and proprieties – glossed as 'taste and decency' – informed the creation of Broadcasting Standards Commission (BSC) in 1981 in addition to the authorities already in place to regulate broadcasting. The commercial broadcasters were as caught by this as was the BBC. By the end of the century, the BSC's code was fully elaborated. Although established by statute, the BSC was mandated to exceed such strictures on expression as the common law imposed. It did so in the name of 'taste and decency', which was expressed with an ill-defined woolliness unsuitable for a quasi-legal document: for example, 'Matters of decency are based on deeper, more fundamental values and emotions' (Broadcasting Standards Commission, 1998: 16). The strictures bordered on the asinine: 'Violence takes many forms' (Broadcasting Standards Commission, 1998: 48). When glossed, these observations remained suffused with ambiguity and unstated assumptions. Take the force of 'special', 'crude', 'cruel', 'humiliate' and, particularly, 'gratuitously' in the following: 'Comedy has a special freedom but this does not give unlimited license to be crude or cruel, or to humiliate individuals or groups gratuitously' (Broadcasting Standards Commission, 1998: 15). As Sir Cecil Graves might have said, 'What on earth that means [in practice] I don't know.' The public, in essence, did not care. The millions upon millions of actual interactions with broadcasting produced, for the BSC, all of 5,000 'complaints' a year; 60 per cent of these were immediately dismissed as frivolous and half the rest were not upheld. Thus even the bloated range of prohibitions produced only around 1,000 successful cases a year. Factoring in the cost of the operation means each successful complaint cost the British taxpayer some £2,500. Special 'laws' were not only 'very needless'; they were (and are) very expensive.

The cost to the broadcasters' freedom was even greater. On 29 May 2003, the BBC's flagship radio Current Affairs (as Talks had long since become) programme, *Today*, ran a story accusing the Labour government of falsifying the evidence used to justify Britain's part in the invasion of Iraq two months earlier. Furiously, the government denounced the broadcast and named Dr David Kelly, an employee of the Ministry of Defence, as the leak. Shortly after being exposed, Kelly was found dead and the government, battered by the ongoing brouhaha occasioned by the unpopular war it had undertaken, established a committee of inquiry under Lord Hutton (Hutton, 2004). Senior officials of the BBC, including the Chair of the Governors, Gavyn Davies, and the Director-General, Greg Dyke, were called to account for the BBC's role in the affair. As a result of this inquiry, damning conclusions as to the defectiveness of the BBC's journalistic processes – controls, in effect – were drawn. Davies and Dyke resigned – more it would seem as a result of the Governors' insensitivity to free press considerations than to any further direct pressure from the government.

Be that as it may, my point is simply this: the Iraq story was also carried by the *Mail on Sunday*, written up by the same journalist who had initially broadcast it; but, before the *News of the World* affair, it was unthinkable that the proprietor and editor of the newspaper could be called to account in the same way as the BBC's leaders were. Lord Rothermere and Paul Dacre, the persons in question, were the ghosts at Hutton's feast. Davies and Dyke (arguably the most popular – with certainly the least privileged background – Director-General the BBC has ever had) fell into the fissure opened up by Reith eight decades earlier. More generally, the Kelly affair and the Hutton Inquiry speak vividly to the limitation on the media's right of free speech.

In 2008, Russell Brand, a celebrity with acting training, and Jonathan Ross, a disc jockey with a history degree from the School of Slavonic and Eastern European Studies at University College London, crudely abused on air an elderly actor, Andrew Sachs. Again, it is not the details of the incident that are of broad relevance here; but rather it is the BBC's response to its performers' crassness and boorishness. As if in answer to Sir Cecil Graves' 1930s instruction ('We must introduce some sort of supervision to prevent this sort of thing'), a whole new level of bureaucratic control was introduced. Rightly, Brand and Ross were dismissed or denied the BBC's air; but what really illustrates broadcasting's hobbled freedom is that the BSC's successor body, Ofcom (Office of Communications), saw fit to impose a fine of £150,000 for the lapse.[27] The BBC's failure to comply with its own production rules was the justification for this.

Ofcom, which has responsibility over the BBC for 'compliance', itself continues the tradition, established by the GPO in the 1920s, of obfuscating language around its censorship powers. In the UK, the word 'independent' has acquired a certain slipperiness – 'independent' television for example actually means 'commercial'. Ofcom is described on its website as the 'independent regulator and competition authority for the UK communications industries'; the term 'independent' meaning, in this instance, not a direct arm of government, although created by statute. In plainer language, though, it is nevertheless a state authority, currently with 700 or so employees, with, apart from technical management of the infrastructure and specific competition regulation, censorship powers. It announces to the public that its:

> Broadcasting Code sets standards for television and radio shows and broadcasters have to follow these rules ... These rules not only cover harm and offence, but also other areas like impartiality and accuracy, sponsorship and commercial references as well as fairness and privacy ... If we find a programme has broken these rules, then it will be found in breach of the Code and Ofcom will publish this decision. In very serious cases, we will consider further action (e.g. fining a broadcaster). (Ofcom, 2011)

This, curiously, does not amount in the official mind to censorship because: 'Ofcom does not watch or listen to programmes before they are broadcast' – but, by law, it has the procedure in place to do so if it wishes.

To cope, the broadcasters need their own compliance officers. Within the BBC, as the scandals exposed shortcomings, the response has been the imposition of enhanced internal censorship. By 2011, there was a formal Editorial Policy Unit (Room 4225, BBC White City, at the time of writing) with a staff of nineteen 'political commissars', as one witness so described them to the Communications Committee of the House of Lords. The BBC was perceived as having a 'manic compliance culture' (Preston, 2011: 41). This legacy of Reithian pusillanimity in 1920s was nowhere more vigorously required than by the British press, which assiduously maintains a somewhat antiquated sense of propriety for the BBC (but not, as Hackgate vividly reveals, for itself). The BBC continued to be attacked for its failure to comply with these restrictions. Even Lord Patten, the then-incoming Chairman of the BBC Trust (as the Board of Governors had become in the wake of Hutton), expressed the hope that expression within the BBC be not 'bound by a rather labyrinthine bureaucracy' (Brown, 2011: 1).

It is clear that radio (and then television – see Chapter 8), as compared with the press, enjoyed an ambiguous freedom. Leaving aside any question of the appropriateness of internal control, radio had no specific formal protection of its right of expression, even in the form of case law. On the contrary: the 1920s settlement is far from being old history and its consequences are with us yet. Over the decades since Reith negotiated the removal of the Postmaster General's direct control over content, the system of *autocensure* has been augmented by the creep of evermore formal internal censorship structures. Censorship has only been constrained, as Alexander Hamilton said it must be, by the 'general spirit of the people' – and then only by 'the people', usually the 'creatives' in opposition to the instincts of managers, within the broadcasting stations.

It is not the detail of the David Kelly and Brand/Ross incidents that is of concern here. It is the basic fact that there is a difference between say, Katherine Graham, as the publisher of the *Washington Post* at the time of the Watergate affair when it was exposing President Nixon, and Lord Rothermere as the proprietor of the *Daily Mail* at the time of the Kelly affair on the one hand; and William Paley, owner of CBS when it challenged the demagogic communist-baiting Senator Joe McCarthy (see Chapter 8.3), and Gavyn Davies, chairman of the BBC during the Kelly uproar. The latter two needed licences from the state while the former did not. The latter's executives – Fred Friendly at CBS and Grey Dyke at the BBC – were vulnerable in ways that their opposite numbers in print, Benjamin Bradlee of the *Post* and Paul Dacre of the *Mail*, were not. Pre-Hackgate, it was hard to imagine Dacre on the witness stand at the Hutton inquiry having to explain himself as Dyke did. Dyke's defenestration was a not-to-be-wondered-at consequence of the creep of control from the necessary allocative management of the infrastructure to tendentiously justified content regulation of the output. To say again: it is not that the broadcasters should not be held to account; it is that they should not be so held by specific content regulation beyond the general law. It is that which is 'very needless'; not the constraint of the law.

Let it not be forgotten that, to this day, the Home Secretary can ban broadcasts and the BBC licence still empowers him or her to send in the troops.

8

Et Cetera: And So On

8.1 *The Baird Television Development Co. v. Electrical Mechanical Industries Co.* (1936): 'Inventing' television

Inevitably, television would do no better than the radio in establishing a claim on free media expression, even though – unlike wireless telephony – it did not so directly involve national security and safety.[1] Technologically and organizationally, television was radio's child; and radio (as well as film) had demonstrated that the Western right of free media expression did not automatically extend to new media. Television is a mere 'etc.' in matters of free speech.

In 1884, Paul Nipkow, a German who was to have a career into the twentieth century as a railway engineer, had taken out a patent for a device that relied on the capacity of some substances to vary their resistance to electrical current according to light conditions. This exactly paralleled carbon's variable resistance when exposed to sound-wave pressure, exploitation of which phenomenon had recently enabled telephony. Nipkow's video equivalent to the telephone's mouthpiece was a camera with a spinning disk. He thought it might be useful as an '*elektrisches teleskop*'. Others were already suggesting similar electrical scanners to transform the slow proto-copying telegraph, which had been introduced soon after Morse's device, into a more viable fax machine (Garratt and Mumford, 1952: 26). Some dreamed of adding images to telephony: the videophone. None thought of a possible new medium. After all, nobody then saw either telegraphy or telephony as mass media either. Nor, as it was to turn out, was the spinning disk to be the design solution.

Mechanical scanning was to point to a false trail that investigators persisted in following into the 1930s; for example, the entrepreneur and effective self-publicist, John Logie Baird. Baird, who attended the same school as Reith, must be credited with seeing television as something new rather than an alternative to other well-established technologies. Nevertheless, he was not television's 'inventor', for all that the British still popularly consider him, quite erroneously, to be so. Although Baird saw the potential of television, his technological solution cannot be considered anything more than a prototype, and one in whose development in any case he only shared. If British national firstist *amour propre* is to be satisfied in this field, insofar as it can be, then it should celebrate Alan Campbell Swinton, a serious scientist and leading 'electrician' who had introduced Marconi to the Post Office.

In 1908 Alan Campbell Swinton envisaged what was to be the solution to the problem of transmitting images electronically. It involved no disks but, 'the employment of two beams of kathode rays (one at the transmitting and one at the receiving station) ... the moving kathode beam has only to be arranged to impinge on a sufficiently sensitive fluorescent screen, and given suitable variations in its intensity, to obtain the desired result' (Garratt and Mumford, 1952: 31).

In short – television. The viability of using cathode tubes in this way was demonstrated in Russia in 1911. By the early 1920s, the rapid diffusion of motion pictures and the slow realization of wireless telephony's potential as the mass medium of radio created an environment in which television might also flourish: not as a telescope; nor as a facsimile device (it produced no permanent copy); nor as a telephone with pictures (seeing the other person was no pressing need). Herbert Ives, AT&T's chief engineer on a 'telephonoscope' project in the late 1920s, told a visitor that he did not have 'the remotest idea whether the public want to see the fellow at the other end of the telephone line badly enough to pay a high price for the privilege' (Dinsdale, 1932: 139). A German 180-line mechanically scanned videophone system was introduced between Berlin and Nuremberg in 1937 but not to much effect. It was not until 2003 that the first widely diffused 'telephonoscope' network began to establish itself on the net – 'Sky Peer-to-Peer' or 'Skype', eighty years after a system had first been demonstrated. In the meantime, the technology was to be widely diffused as radio with pictures.

Even as radio as a home entertainment medium progressed in the 1920s, so the home delivery of movies emerged as the driver of the research into television. However, the supervening social need for home entertainment was being met by radio. Moreover, the research and development needed to bring television to market was in the hands of the radio industry, which therefore had a vested interest in containing a potential rival. Only the possibility that rivals and outsiders would take it forward kept it alive as a serious, if not pressing, lab research project Although some outsiders, Philo Farnsworth most notably, obtained crucial patents for the cathode ray tube (CRT) system, other researchers persisted with the dead-end disks. John Logie Baird, for example, compounded this distraction by offering very low definition mechanical-scanned 'televisors' for sale before 1930. Hyperbolic claims, exposed as such by demonstrations at the then popular radio 'shows', in effect added a further constraint to the radio industry's lack of enthusiasm. Nevertheless, Baird's enthusing, orchestrated by his PR advisor, caused the press to cast aspersions on the BBC's unwillingness to promote television (Briggs, 1995b: 481–5, 490–95). Years of jingoistic brouhaha, accusing the BBC of suppressing a great path-breaking British 'invention', followed, eventually forcing the GPO and the Corporation, in 1929, to allow test transmissions. Baird broadcast from 2LO outside normal radio broadcasting hours. He sold only 1,000 sets.

The great economic depression of the 1930s did not help either. Television was touted as a futuristic wonder but there was actually little appetite for it. Nevertheless, by the mid-decade, RCA and part-owned sister operations Telefunken and Electric and Musical Industries (EMI) had a fully electronic CRT system ready for market. Basically, it had been developed by Vladimir Zworykin and a team at RCA's lab in New Jersey, with input from the European partners (while the 'H' aerial was designed in Japan). By 1932, the system was viable enough for EMI to approach the BBC. The image already had 'three time as many lines per picture and twice as many pictures per second' than Baird's system (Briggs, 1995b: 527). Nevertheless, Baird did not give up. Eventually, in 1936, a run-off was arranged under the aegis of the BBC, which quickly resulted in mechanical scanning being discarded. Regular broadcasts using the RCA/EMI all-electrical system began in February 1937. Baird's reputation as television's 'inventor', though, curiously persists (Briggs, 1995b: 530–64). The same pattern of rivalry, test and victory for the electronic system also occurred in Germany. There a regular mechanical-scanned service, which had started in 1935, gave way to the same all-electric system the following year, a little in advance of the BBC.

Television was now an established technology but the public, despite responding to surveys positively, did not rush to buy (Udelson, 1982: 96). Barely 2,000 sets, for example, were sold in 1936 in London (the only area to receive BBC transmissions), despite the publicity surrounding the television coverage of the coronation of George VI in December. On the eve of the war in 1939 there were only between 20,000 and 25,000 television sets in use (Briggs, 1995b: 573). In Nazi Germany, of course, there was no possibility of domestic demand: a fear of people mocking images of the leadership in the privacy of their own homes saw to that. Instead 1,000 sets were placed in television viewing halls. Some of these sat as many as 400 people giving a maximum audience of 40,000 in a population of more than 60 million. The coverage of the Berlin Olympics did not boost demand as expected (Uricchio, 1990: 115). There were only 200 private *Fernsehapparaten* in use when the Nazis finally nerved themselves to allow derestricted sales in 1939 on the eve of war.

Television confirmed the state's allocative function. In United States, the Federal Communications Commission was acutely aware of RCA's dominance of the technology and fretted at the possibility that Sarnoff would create a monopoly of set manufacturing as well as have dominance over programme provision. It insisted, spuriously, that the RCA system, in essence identical to that being used for full-scale services in Britain and Germany, was merely 'experimental'. It would only issue temporary station-licences, which was more than enough to kill demand. An elaborate process to determine standards was put in place. That the need for it was spurious was proved when the FCC finally gave in and the RCA system, with the company now sharing its patents, was adopted. Immediately thereafter, in late 1941, the United States joined the war and nothing was done to implement the decision. The BBC had stopped transmissions at the earlier outbreak of the European war, famously in the middle of a Mickey Mouse cartoon. The Nazis, though, continued to broadcast throughout the hostilities.

After the war, in the United States, television was seen as a crucial driver of post-war economic revival: the receivers were an important consumer durable and the medium itself was now a major new advertising channel encouraging consumerism in general. A rapid expansion of the number of TV broadcasting licences began with the peace. Then, in 1948, the FCC froze the licensing of stations. The commission did not impose the 'freeze' because of the now looming possibilities of colour and the opportunity of spectrum change (from VHF to UHF). These were reasons which might have had some validity and both had been actively explored experimentally before the war. The issue was an allocative one: the newly licensed television signals were interfering with each other. However, the length of the 'freeze' – forty-three months – cannot be entirely justified on such grounds. Interference was certainly a problem; but the freeze lasted far longer than solving it required. The unstated difficulty went beyond basic frequency allocation. The FCC was concerned with content and who was to provide it – the radio networks or Hollywood? That the radio stations would receive TV licences was an unexamined given; so how could Hollywood be protected?

During the US 'freeze' an accommodation between the radio and cinema industries was achieved. In 1948, the first year the nascent American television networks operated a schedule, the programming was dominated by live transmissions from New York. In 1952, the top show was *I Love Lucy*, Lucille Ball's situation comedy, filmed in Hollywood. However, the film industry paid for its presence on the small screen because in that year the Justice Department finally broke up the monopolistic tendencies of the studios to own integrated production, distribution and exhibition arms. In the 'Paramount Decree',[2] that studio was forced to divest itself of its cinemas. The others, of course, followed. Moreover, the FCC, protecting the radio industry, refused to license the studios to transmit to theatres except on an ad hoc basis.

Radio, or better RCA, was also subject to constraint and it was forced, with the coming of television, to divest itself of its second smaller, Blue network. This became the American Broadcasting Company (ABC). The Red remained as the National Broadcasting Company (NBC). Otherwise the structure of the industry's networks was essentially determined by the AT&T tariff for use of its physical coaxial infrastructure. This stunted the growth of publicly funded television and was a barrier to other commercial entrants. No fourth network was allowed to develop in competition to NCB, CBS and ABC. Alan Dumont tried to put a group of stations together from 1946 but was squeezed out of the programming business within a decade. Various plans to force AT&T to give cheaper – or even free – access to the public television stations so they too could establish a network were also fruitlessly suggested. National Education Television (NET) had been funded by the Ford Foundation to provide a national service but initially it had to post programming material (reels of teleciné film), physically, to its affiliates from a centre in Ann Arbour.

Television posed fewer questions in Britain, either in matters of frequency allocation – without discussion, it was to be run by the BBC – or of free expression. The radio rules would automatically prevail. The BBC had emerged from the Second World War far more popular than it had been before it. In addition to the three radio networks, the television service had resumed on 7 June 1946 with an apology for the seven-year interruption and the same cartoon. The BBC faced charter renewal, and the committee under Lord Beveridge was set up to inquire into it, with some equanimity. This was not misplaced. In 1951, Beveridge confirmed the monopoly for radio and for television. Radio could not be touched, but a minority report, written by an MP, John Selwyn Lloyd, who was to become a major Conservative politician, was submitted in favour of breaking the BBC monopoly over television. As had been the case from the beginning, many commercial interests stood ready to broadcast and the Conservatives anyway distrusted state enterprises and monopolies. The BBC, although it had been born on their watch, was both.

In 1953, the Conservatives, now in power, acted on Selwyn Lloyd's report. Against dire warnings of imminent cultural collapse if advertising and brash American programming were permitted in Britain, a Television Act[3] was passed creating an Independent Television Authority ('independent' carefully avoiding the more vexatious 'commercial') to oversee a new advertising-supported service, to be known as Independent Television (ITV). Logically, in line with Tory antipathy to monopoly as well as being a sop to the BBC's prestige, the new service would be provided by a network of regional companies, none of which would be able to match the BBC in size and, therefore, in status. It began on 22 September 1955. Although the schedule was dominated by popular American imports of the sort those objecting to commercial broadcasting had warned about, their prognosis was otherwise misplaced. The BBC had too firmly established what television was in the mind of the national audience for its scheduling template and style to be simply ignored in favour of an alien American one. The companies largely came to duplicate the BBC's output and this, with the popularity of what was imported, put yet more pressure on the BBC to embrace the popular.

Commercial broadcasters live by the rate card and so audience measurement was crucial. With the coming of direct competition, it became so for the BBC as well. Reith, though, had been right to avoid it in the 1930s, and not just because his elitist policies would have been embarrassed by the revelation of the BBC's comparative unpopularity. To maintain the licence, in a competitive situation, a publicly funded broadcaster is forced to do two mutually exclusive things at the same time: provide programming deemed to be socially worthy, which the commercial rival will not and/or cannot provide, while at the same time matching the rival's popularity with identical programming. Failure to do one raises questions as to why there should be a public broadcaster, but so does managing to do the other. Commercial competition put the BBC into a cleft stick. As it tried to respond to this task, though, many advantages were gained. For one thing, it finally managed to lose the epithetic 'Auntie' as it, at last, mastered the popular.

Conversely, ITV provided breakthroughs in quality. One of the licensees, ABC Television, hired a Canadian, Sydney Newman, in 1958 and under him the first noteworthy original contemporary television drama, Alun Owens' *No Trams to Lime Street*, appeared in the *Armchair Theatre* slot: 'I said we should have an original play policy with plays that were going to be <u>about</u> the very people who owned TV sets – which is really a working-class audience.' Addressing the 'monstrous … "ego" of the "common man"', as Val Gielgud had put it, was to become television's policy. Newman went to the BBC and, taking over the Drama Department in 1963, presided over a golden age of original works (and the introduction of *Doctor Who*). ITN, the commercial network's news provider, also imported the American melding of newsreel and radio bulletin, which the BBC had failed to develop. Some broadcasting restrictions on political reporting were deliberately flouted by another commercial company, Granada, forcing them to be lifted.

Under Hugh Carleton Greene the BBC kept pace. Satire appeared as well as radical plays and even, on occasion, a female newsreader. So well did it manage to fulfil all the conflicting demands made of it, the committee of inquiry that was set up in the 1960s under Lord Pilkington confirmed its tenure yet again. Pilkington also gave the BBC colour and a second channel, in addition to local radio. This triumph, though, was something of a two-edged sword. The BBC certainly needed BBC2 if it was to provide both the popular and 'quality' TV programmes its competitive, licensed-funded position required. It had decanted, as it were, the Light and Third Programmes as well as the Home Service on to the one TV channel and the fit was uneasy. With a second channel it could more clearly compete by moving less populist offerings to the new platform. Colour on the other hand required a vast outlay for equipment against an only slowly increasing revenue stream coming from the increased cost of colour TV licences. By the 1970s, the BBC's finances were stretched, once again disadvantaging it vis-à-vis the political establishment that, ultimately, controlled its purse-strings.

8.2 *In Re: The Bobo Doll* (1958): The effects of television

In all this the content control structures of radio remained in place. Quite explicitly, for example, the BBC management, the Control Board, had already 'laid down' in January 1936, 'that all television programmes should be subject to the functional control of the broadcasting departments' (Briggs, 1995b: 557). Such fragmented oversight could not long survive; but it was the fragmentation, not the control, that was abandoned.

Television, in fact, brought new problems to strain broadcasting's internal censorship culture. As well as the visual grammar of film, the new medium also echoed the genres, scheduling structures and presentation modes of radio. Obviously, vision could make good on the promise of some of radio's most popular programming – sport, for example. Variety could now embrace wordless speciality acts. Ballet and ballroom-dancing could join music, light and classical. Television news came to embed the cinema newsreel in the sound-only bulletin with the latter now being read by a newscaster speaking to camera. This is still TV's news' dominate image, despite the long march then begun towards making pictures from around the country and the world as instantaneously available as sound reports had become (Winston, 2002). And drama would slowly emulate more and more of the production values, as well as the 'language', of the feature film as it moved from live-transmission, through 'live-on-tape' to single-camera shooting, both on film and then electronically. In all this, though, television inherited from radio its flawed claim on free expression. In fact, it exacerbated the problem. In the United States, violence and sex, always problems for Network Standards and Practices, were suddenly that much more – obviously – visible; as was race, now denied the anonymity of the radio microphone.

In 1951, an appearance on television by the singer and actor, Lena Horne, the epitome of miscegenated elegance and beauty, managed to outrage Middle America. Her décolletage (apparently unnoticed in rehearsal but rendered provocative by full lighting) offended, as did her gentle plea for religious and racial tolerance. Actually, as one outraged bigot from North Carolina pointed out, it was because: 'This Horne woman may be a good singer but if I am not misinformed [the writer was an attorney] she is a woman that married a white man and we still have a large number of states that make such a marriage a crime' (Forman, 2007: 31–2).

Leave aside the racism; décolletage was a new issue for Network Standards to fret over, one not immediately apparent when blue-pencilling a script. It needed evermore formal production codes and the like. Television aided the movement, already underway in radio's third decade as a mass medium, away from reliance on *autocensure*, informally overseen, to the internal publication of evermore prescriptive and complex formal manuals. As in Britain, these can now be within the purview of statutory state organizations, empowered to effect sanctions against broadcasters whose staffs break the rules.

In the United States of the 1950s, of course, racism could not be left aside. *Amos 'n' Andy* were still popular on the radio and transferring popular properties to the new medium was very much underway. However, Correll and Gosden, poached by CBS TV from NBC Radio in 1951, initially thought to get round the problem of the fact that they were not black by having African American actors lip-sync their voices. They had played the roles in black-face for a failed Hollywood feature in 1930 and so knew not to try that again. A modicum of sense prevailed, however, and Alvin Childress and Spencer Williams were cast with all the African American parts also played by actors of colour. Gosden and Correll had to make do with being the TV show's executive producers. Anyway, tolerance for such stereotyping, despite its persistence in the South, was being eroded, even when the actors were black. The NAACP protested and *Amos 'n' Andy* was removed from prime-time after two years, although it ran repeatedly in syndication until 1966.

By that time, television's de facto bar against non-stereotypical African Americans was crumbling. Bill Cosby, first as a stand-up comedian in 1963 and then as co-star of the spy-thriller series *I Spy* in 1965, led the way. In 1968, Diahann Carroll, another acceptably glamorous singer/actor of colour, starred as the eponymous widow in *Julia*, a situation comedy, playing a resolutely middle-class nurse. In the show, her husband – a high-status African American fighter-pilot – had been shot down and killed in Vietnam. This was the first major non-stereotypical professional role for a black woman in a prime-time series. It lasted until 1971.

Panics about sex have resulted in the explicitness of its representation on the small screen lagging behind how it appears in other media – 'taste and decency' is deemed to require no less. More covertly, avoidance of 'offence' (as 'controversy' had now become) can be said to mean that, without much obvious control or argument, political expression outside the mainstream is also eschewed. Many in the United States appear fervently to believe that (as the bumper sticker has it) 'God, Guts and Guns Made America'. Guns, in effect, sanction the violence on the screen; God, though, is thought to be somewhat intolerant of sex; and guts preclude anything smacking of liberal weak-mindedness. As a result, Network Standards and Practices were none too disturbed by violence. Their obsession was with sex and with liberalism. Sex was the more powerful source of concern; so much so that it could be used by professionals to distract attention from the nearly as fraught issue of liberalism.

For example, the original writers of *Star Trek*, Herb Solow and Robert H. Justman, frequently used the censor's focus on eroticism to slip more controversial (that is, liberal) material past them. A second series episode, 'A Private Little War', raised, in the scarcely disguised form of Captain Kirk's moral dilemma over intervening in a war on a distant planet, the vexed question of the United States' involvement in Vietnam. The US Army was reeling from the series of North Vietnamese attacks, the Tet Offensive, when the show was transmitted by NBC in February of 1968. Solow and Justman got the episode on air by sacrificing to the censors a scene they had specifically written for this purpose, which was to have Kirk and a partially dressed actress kissing each other, open-mouthed. Fighting for that drew fire from an attack on the basic situation in the script, which was what had to be protected. This was a regulatory regime, after all, in which 'Lucy' in *I Love Lucy* had not been allowed to say the word 'pregnant' (Messenger Davies and Pearson, 2007: 217).

At the same time, though, the entire edifice of sexual constraints was crumpling and the remaining censorship bastion around printed obscenity was being attacked. In Britain, in 1960, the publishers of D.H. Lawrence's *Lady Chatterley's Lover*, which had finally been published more than three decades after it was written, were sued for obscenity; but the new Obscene Publications Act of the previous year[4] allowed for artistic quality as a defence and the publishers were cleared. Not that the censorious were entirely defeated by this. In 1964, the publishers of Hubert Selby Jr's *Last Exit to Brooklyn*, which was freely published in the United States, were successfully prosecuted in Britain, only to be overturned on appeal. There were to be other incidents, the Oz trial for example (see Preface and Acknowledgements), but classic obscenity actions were falling in desuetude. *Lady Chatterley's Lover* made it to the big screen in 1981, as softcore porn, and in 1993 achieved the accolade of a BBC literary classic adaptation, the epitome of 'heritage television'.

Time lag aside, sexual or political expression easily condoned in other media remained problematic on the television screen, even though actual cases came to public attention so rarely as to become causes célèbres. They were exceptions that prove the existence of normally hidden limitations. Peter Watkins' *The War Game* (1965) was what today would be called an 'hypothetical documentary'; that is, a fiction in which the reconstructional protocols of the documentary film are deployed not to illuminate past events but to illustrate, plausibly, future ones. In the case of *The War Game*, the subject was the horror of a nuclear attack on Britain. Necessarily shocking and gruesome, it was fully approved prior to production and was subjected to only minor editing when finished. However, Hugh Carleton Greene and his Chairman, Lord Normanbrook, decided official approval needed to be sought before transmission (Briggs, 1985: 332–4). It was denied although the decision to ban was, the BBC insisted, an entirely internal one.

Dennis Potter was a new species of playwright whose highly regarded work was, more or less exclusively, for television. He was as responsible as any for probing the boundaries of 'taste and decency'. *Brimstone and Treacle* (1976) was a black, one-off drama featuring the rape of a young helpless woman in a near vegetative state following a road accident, by a young male character who was, possibly, the Devil. Sexual assault, for Potter, encapsulated the concept of the Fall and *Brimstone and Treacle* is one of a series of scripts, written at that time out of a real sense of the author's nihilism, about the nature of faith. Here, the assault brings the woman back to consciousness. This script too had been fully approved and was not only completed but its transmission slot had been fixed when, three weeks before this date and more than a year after the script was first examined, the then Director of Programmes, Alasdair Milne, banned it (Cook, 1998: 86–90, 93). The following year it was seen, without problem, on the stage in a version adapted by Potter and subsequently on the big screen, directed by Richard Loncraine and released in 1982. Eventually it was seen on the small screen in 1987. This grudging pattern of ill-applied repression was not unique. On television, there was freedom of expression but not as media generally know it.

More vexatious than either race or sex was violence, but only in connection with children. The young had been comparatively ignored by radio and anything remotely educational had been eschewed, especially in the United States, except when a matter of public relations. When Alice Keith, for example, was appointed to head a new CBS Children's Department in 1932, she soon realized that she would be given no airtime and resigned (Hilmes, 1997: 189). However, as the Depression passed, advertisers began to realize the value of the children's market. Some 10 per cent of airtime thus came to be devoted to them, mainly in the form of adventure serials.

In the 1950s, the more graphic depiction of violence that television enabled gave rise to a moral panic. Much of children's television was innocuous from this point of view, with avuncular adults offering puppets and pap; but violence suffused the popular animated cartoons that were the medium's main offering for this demographic. The contemporaneous appearance of 'horror comics' exacerbated the problem. In 1954, a US Senate subcommittee conducted hearings, which were – significantly – televised, on juvenile delinquency. The case for the supposed outbreak of youthful criminality was, it was suggested, due to comics. As Marshall McLuhan wisely noted, such was the panic that: 'the dimmest-witted convict learned to moan, "it wuz comic books done this to me"' (McLuhan, 1964: 227). However, there was more in play than just the 'naïve literary logic' (as McLuhan had it) making this casual connection. The panic was reinforced by psychological data, and it also embraced television's animated cartoons.

Perhaps one of the most influential, and certainly most persistently overtly and covertly referenced, lab-based psychological experiments of the twentieth century took place at Stanford University, California, in 1961. Albert Bandura, noted in 2002 as the most cited of living psychologists (Haggbloom, 2002: 139–52), is a behaviourist[5] who began his career by studying teenage aggression in the 1950s. A proponent of the lab-testing of concepts, he set-up a trial to test a theory of 'social learning' – the 'Bobo' doll experiment (Bandura, Ross and Ross, 1961: 575–82). It has become a 'classic'; and its finding, that children imitate aggressive behaviour, has been a central plank in justifying the case for abridging television's freedom of expression, explicitly in the area of children's programming and, implicitly, more generally. However, using the Bandura experiment as evidence to legitimate control – to impose prior constraint – is a more vexed proceeding. Despite its high-reputation and its status as widely received wisdom, the 'Bobo' doll exercise is self-evidently a most deeply flawed piece of positivist research (Bandura *et al.*, 1961). It can also be noted that contemporary ethical sensibilities to human subject research would most probably not allow approval of the exercise in the first place.[6]

Boys and girls, aged three to five, were individually placed in a room in which there was an adult. There was also a five-foot inflatable 'Bobo' doll which, weighted at its base, was of the sort designed to be punched. With one group of children, the adult 'model' was unaggressive; with the other she viciously attacked the doll with a mallet, punched and beat it and kicked it around the room, while shouting abuse at it. The child was then taken to another room wherein there were also toys – including a second Bobo doll – and invited to continue to play alone while being secretly observed. The group exposed to the violent behaviour of the model tended to replicate it, going beyond the punching that the toy was designed to encourage.

Given that behaviour – speech, even – is learned imitatively, this finding is entirely to be expected. However, as a basis for determining public policy around expression, it simply cannot be allowed to stand. The seventy-two children used in the experiment were scarcely representative of anything except an extremely privileged social group: the offspring of faculty and staff at one of the world's most prestigious universities. Bourgeois prejudice might well suggest that less privileged groups would be more likely to imitate violence but, be that as it may, the point is that an extrapolation from a specific to a general population is being made.

The children were confronted by a socially anomalous situation. Here was an adult playing, not with them and the toys, but separately with their own toys. This has to have been a highly unusual situation in a nursery or, indeed, common sense suggests, anywhere else either. Anyway, using a toy that is designed to be punched seems, to be charitable, a curious decision given that aggression is what was being tested. Had the model attacked an ordinary doll or a large teddy bear, for example – toys designed to be cherished and cuddled – that would surely have made the point with less ambiguity. The observed behaviours of the children would have been overly transgressive rather than merely an extension of the transgression the toy anyway invited.

Yet, even then, the vexed question of causality would remain. It is one thing to witness adult behaviour – very unusual deviant adult behaviour doubly anomalous given the setting where it occurred (i.e. in a nursery) – and quite another to witness it on a television screen. To assume the representation of a thing as sufficiently the thing itself as to evoke the same response is either to exhibit, as McLuhan suggested, naivety, or else it reflects a Baudrillardian postmodern sophistication. Either way, extrapolating from one to the other seems to be, shall we say, 'unsafe'. These days, received understanding of the 'Bobo' doll experiment simply avoids this problem by misquoting it altogether, claiming, to take a random example from a media studies textbook, that the children were exposed to a 'character on film behaving in an aggressive manner' (Gunter and McAleer, 1997: 107). They were not so exposed.

The test, and all those subsequently replicating it, is biased in favour of demonstrating negative imitative behaviour but, logically, positive altruistic behaviour could also be demonstrated in the lab as being learned. There is, though, no sociological or psychological research tradition looking for evidence of the impact of imitating the representation of good behaviour on television, although acts of kindness, consideration, concern and even heroism are scarce unknown.[7] When the research on the audience uncovers what might be considered a positive effect, it tends to be explained by other social factors, unlike violence, which tends to be blamed primarily on the medium. An influential British study, near-contemporaneous to the 'Bobo' doll experiment, on television and the child attributed greater ambition to children (expressed via questionnaires) who had television than was found among those who did not. This was certainly a finding of a social good, but it was explained, quite reasonably, as being largely the result of class differences, television sets then being new and expensive (Himmleweit, Oppenheim and Vince, 1958: 235–6). Despite this, when it came to violence, as usual, its findings suggested that the medium was a dominant cause (Himmleweit *et al.*, 1958: 194, 204).

By 1991, these studies, lab- or cohort-based, had been replicated a thousand times: 'most of these studies were non-experimental and predominantly used self-reported aggression, antisocial behaviour, and mood as outcome measures' (Browne and Hamilton-Giachritsis, 2005: 704). For the researchers, the possibility that they might be the victims of a sustained application of the 'it-wuz-comic-books-done-this-to-me' ploy seems to be largely unacknowledged. Instead, they have found 'a positive association between violent entertainment and [self-reported] aggressive behaviour' (Comstock and Paik, 1991). Yet a further meta-data analysis of all this work in 2005 concluded that 'empirical evidence for the notion that media violence causes crime is weak' (Savage, 2005). With children: 'there is evidence that violent imagery has short-term effects on arousal, thoughts, and emotions, increasing the likelihood of aggressive or fearful behaviour. However, the evidence is less consistent for older children and teenagers' (Browne and Hamilton-Giachritsis, 2005: 708).

The case for negative influence has been endlessly overstated and, despite the psychological and sociological research, the depiction of violence was too popular, and its effects actually too amorphous, to engender effective regulatory action. In the United States, Action for Children's Television was founded in 1968 but it took it thirty-two years to finally persuade Congress to pass legislation requiring that the broadcasters provide more educational material on television.[8] It was left to the FCC to enforce this, which it conspicuously failed to do to any great degree. As for adults, the industry, secure behind the popularity of its output, essentially took no notice of brouhahas about violence except when public relations suggested that it might be as well to be seen to be responding to the concerns. An assassination, for example, might occasion public pronouncements that violence would be eschewed in popular programming. Such resolutions have never been kept. Quinn Martin, the most consistently successful Hollywood producer of popular drama in the 1960s and 1970s, told one of his writers on *The Untouchables* (1959–63), 'I like the idea of sadism'; and his audiences agreed with him (Etter, 2003: 15). The fact is that violence sells. This has guaranteed television's freedom in this area. It trumps the panics however vociferously expressed, even as regards children.

Overall, on the question of impact, commercial broadcasters have been left in a paradoxical position. On the one hand, they strenuously defended themselves against the charge of causing violence in society; but on the other hand, they were eager to plead guilty to influencing audience consumption through the efficacy of advertising. Given that consumerism is not, basically, deviant in the West – unlike violence – this contradiction is not entirely unjustifiable. However, noxious advertising – for, say, cigarettes or alcohol – required a further twist. In effect, the industry was forced to suggest that, of course, advertisements could sell such products but that they did not sell them to excess.

The bottom line is that, despite all the psychology and sociology, the case for causality has not been made. The scientific truism that causation ('causing or producing an effect') is not the same as 'correlation' ('the mutual relation between two or more things') seems to be generally ignored, forgotten or not understood. The discussion of media effects, both popular and academic, takes little or no notice of this fundamental fact; but, in reality, at one level, society does acknowledge it. The transmission of images of massively popular, socially sanctioned violent behaviour of one degree or another remains untouched: professional footballers at work, for example, are allowed their mayhem. Although deemed to be powerful role-models for exactly the most violent-prone element in the society – young males – footballers' violence is considered, if at all, to be correlative to violence in society, not causal.

It is not a question of the impact of the image; images have impact – goods will be bought, the style of popstars will be emulated and so on. The issue is how each individual processes and uses that impact. The majority learns, as an element of its normal socialization, to distinguish between representation and reality, and to accommodate imitative action to a legally bounded and/or moral code. This guides the public in the uses and gratifications obtained from the consumption of images. It limits imitative transgressive behaviour; even among the majority of teenagers, for example, imitation has its boundaries. So to suggest that the media *causes* transgression is, it can be argued, the functional equivalent of believing it is the stirring of the leaves that causes the wind.[9] Anyway, correlation is not causation.

This is not to say that images do not 'cause' behaviour but it suggests this is limited by other factors and, moreover, grounded evidence of impact is elusive. Common sense and experience suggest that non-transgressive behaviour can be influenced by media messages: the involuntary sexual response to the erotic, the modification of consumption patterns by advertising, the imitation of a mass-entertainment role-model's style. However, responding with transgressive imitative action to, for instance, an erotic or a horror film is another matter. The mentally healthy person will not be moved into violent antisocial action by such messages. Being moved so to act is (further?) evidence of the actor's mental ill-health, social deviancy or, at its worst, psychopathy.

No sooner was the rant of the Norwegian fascist mass-murderer Anders Behring Breivik, for example, revealed as quoting Melanie Phillips, a right-wing British newspaper columnist, at length and with approval than she was being accused of inspiring or causing, in some way, his murderous spree in 2011 (Issa, 2011). But this leaves the basic correlation/causation question unanswered: namely, was the serial killer made, say, by reading de Sade? Or, by Ms Phillips of the *Daily Mail*? Or did he read de Sade or Ms Phillips because he was a serial killer? Given that everybody who reads de Sade or the *Daily Mail* does not become a practising sexual obsessive or mass murderer demonstrates that causality is not inevitable. Ms Phillips was quick to blog her defence: she did not cause Breivik to act. It was a mere correlation that he had read her. On the other hand, Breivik's casual references to some violent computer games were seen as a cause, not a correlation, resulting in some Norwegian stores, reportedly, withdrawing the titles from sale (T. Phillips, 2011).

The possibility of the potential impact of media expression on deviants, however few, is not here being denied. If a casual connection exists, it could be made the justifiable basis for a constraint on speech. The right of free expression, after all, allows for it to be limited in the name of doing no harm. In fact, this is, in classic liberal theory, the only basis upon which it can be limited. However few might be affected, it could be that the good of society requires the potential of transgressive action arising from media consumption be restricted. It could be argued that applicability of 'do no harm', as itself a principle, is absolute. It could be seen that the slightest chance of a psychopath misusing a media message is reason to restrict such expression, however harmless it is for the mass of the mentally stable. This, broadly speaking, has not been the position taken by society or at law, however. Outside of the heated debate over media influence on violent behaviour, the law has tended to ignore the issue of psychopathic or sociopathic misuse. With obscenity, for example, the test is not whether the obscene matter corrupts the susceptible but rather whether or not it has a corrupting impact on the 'average' consumer (see Chapter 11.4, 11.5).[10]

Thus, instead of a general concern about the impact of media messages, where impact is actually difficult to demonstrate, a case can be made for a more limited focus on the misuse of media messages as this could be a function of mental ill health. Here is a research agenda of surely greater potential value in terms of social risk assessment than the endless duplication of impact studies on violence and the general – especially, the general child and youth – audience. Yet, beyond the clichéd tabloid assumption of a link between the psychopath's media tastes and their violent behaviour, this is actually as little investigated as the effects of the depiction of acts of kindness: 'no firm conclusions can be drawn on the basis of the little research done in this area' (Browne and Hamilton Giachritsis, 2005: 705).

To take a most pressing example: the phenomenon of 'outbreaks' of suicide suggests a media role in causing what is known, significantly after a fictional text, as the 'Werther effect'.[11] While evidence that Goethe's novel, *Die Leiden des jungen Werthers*, actually caused copycat suicides at the time is anecdotal, more recent examples have demonstrated the possibility of 'suicide contagion' triggered by the media (Schmidtke and Häfner, 1998). In Vienna, the subway is a favoured suicide site. In a long-running study, the Viennese press was persuaded by researchers to minimize reports on suicides and a subsequent reduction was noted (Etzersdorfer and Sonneck, 1998). Conversely, significant spikes in the number of copycat incidents have been noted following media exposure of an initial incident. For example, in 2006–7, following the release of the feature documentary, *The Bridge* (directed by Eric Steel, 2006), which dealt in detail with twenty-three successful suicides from the Golden Gate Bridge in San Francisco (including images of people jumping), the number of deaths spiked (Lagos, 2007). Of course, this still does not demonstrate causation but the level of correlation, in contrast to other claims of media effects, is unusually direct. To claim cause in this instance and argue, on the basic of the harm principle, for censorship would not be out of order, for all that the press is quick to deny the connection. Suicide is the exception that proves the rule.

The 'Werther effect' phenomenon speaks to a specific and immediate causation, and it is this which is what is almost always lacking in instances of supposed direct media effects. This does not mean, of course, that common sense ought to be abandoned and only topics with externally verified evidence of consequent harm be controlled. For example, protecting the identity of children caught in media glare can be reasonably insisted on even without such 'evidence'. The regulation imposed on broadcasting, however, is largely grounded in consideration of moral imperatives (normally conditioned by class-bound assumptions) or the protection of social value (as in 'social cohesion' for example), unsupported by clear-cut evidence of media effects. The debatable results of the research tradition – the 'Bobo' doll and the questionnaires – will not serve to demonstrate media 'harm'. The 'suicide contagion' phenomenon is an exception in its specificity. The given for legitimate media constraint in a situation of true free expression is that the demonstration of harm be not refracted through the interpretations of psychologists or sociologists; never mind through the prejudices and panics of the (usually bourgeois) censorious. That is not the case and much broadcast content regulation is therefore, in terms of a right of free expression in a free society, essentially illegitimate.

8.3   *Edward R. Murrow v. Senator Joseph R. McCarthy* (1951): The limits of television freedom

Despite this, the rhetoric of a universal right of free expression is applied to broadcasting. That this disguises the reality of the situation is itself obscured. The result is a certain confusion. In British terms, this means a cultural sensitivity to free expression prevents the prior censorship of, say, a script; but then, embarrassingly, a finished programme is not transmitted, as in the above examples. Knowledge of the ban is quickly passed on to the press and, often, the offending tape or film also finds its way, samizdat-like, out of the broadcaster's hands – even before copying was made so easy by twenty-first-century technology. The underlying limitations on free expression are illuminated by such incidents. They do not, however, engender any overt assertion of Alexander Hamilton's 'general spirit' arguing the case that broadcasters should have the same measure of freedom from regulation as other media enjoy. The connection between the causes célèbres and the more generally restricted freedom of the broadcasters is not made and the case for broadcasting regulation is seldom questioned. There are three specific reasons for this – physics, intrusion and influence. Each of them can be challenged, though.

Physics: broadcasting has infrastructural limits that other mass media lack. Just as the threat of fire could be used to justify the licensing of theatres and cinemas so, with broadcasting, an equally essential need to organize the infrastructure required by the system would serve – tendentiously – as a bridgehead for the control of content. 'Tendentiously' because there was, and is, no more necessary connection between the infrastructure of an electrical mass communication system and what is transmitted via such a system, than with safety provisions of a theatrical space and what is staged there. The state does need to be involved to allocate a scarce natural resource, for example, the spectrum. Even so, that is no justification for content control. Moreover, the technology itself is not a neutral, inevitable factor arising from natural laws. On the contrary, as the above history outlines, these media, from the research-and-development agendas that produced them onwards, were in effect conditioned by a basic underlying requirement that they would be so formulated as to best enable such 'regulation'. In fact, even so-called spectrum scarcity can be questioned to a certain extent. It is a function of network design as much as it is of physics, and it always has been. The building of centralized single national networks as in Britain, or maximizing commercial opportunities as in the United States, or constructing mixed broadcasting economies as on the continent of Europe were political decisions, however much they were clothed in a language of technological inevitability. In short, the special regulation of content, unlike the allocation of bandwidth and the imposition of technical signal standards, is as needless in terms of free expression as it is with any other communication mode: that is, in the words of John Locke, 'very needless' indeed.

The other two justifications for broadcasting regulations – privacy and power – are equally flawed. The US Supreme Court summed up the privacy argument in its Pacifica judgment: 'Among the reasons for specially treating indecent broadcasting is the uniquely pervasive presence that medium of expression occupies in the lives of our people. Broadcasts extend into the privacy of the home and it is impossible completely to avoid' (*FCC v. Pacifica Foundation*, 1972; see Chapter 7.2). Yet, is this quite as self-evident as the court held? Why should the daily newspaper, thrust through the letterbox, with its ill-grounded hysterical 'splash' about some supposed threat or other on page one and its photograph of a naked young woman on page three, be deemed less intrusive than an incoming broadcast or cable or satellite signal? If the newspaper, which as its name implies is – or should be – new each morning, can be secreted, cannot domestic receivers, whose output is seldom unscheduled or unexpected, not be switched off?

And, to complete a rebuttal of the usual litany of arguments in defence of broadcasting regulation, what real evidence is there that twentieth-century media were so much more powerful than their predecessors that they needed extra control? The role of the press in the history of more than one nation suggests that media power is no new thing, unknown before the coming of the radio and television. Did not Thomas Paine speak with radical effect through thousands of copies of *Common Sense* to all engaged in politics in the revolted American colonies? In the UK, more than 12 million stamped papers a year in the late eighteenth century served the small ruling elite, located among the couple of million Britons who were literate, with no little impact; or so censorious, fearful governments endlessly thought. And what of the 'vile tyranny' of John Delane's nineteenth-century London *Times*, 'The Thunderer', destroying cabinets and upsetting Queen Victoria? While certainly Rupert Murdoch exercised great unaccountable power in the late twentieth century, so too did Hearst and Pulitzer in the nineteenth. Neither physics, nor domestic reception nor supposed influence can stand as compelling justifications for broadcasting's specific regulation.

Of course, things have changed. For one thing, the press baron of yesterday is today's media mogul – and like the Moghul, he (invariably) rules over far-flung territories. This, though, can be controlled. Murdoch, for example, operates as a broadcaster in the United States but needed to take up citizenship to do so; were Britain and Australia to demand the same of its media licence-holders, Murdoch's empire would fall. (This is not to suggest xenophobic requirements are a good thing; it is merely to point out a truth.) Power, more significantly, flows from cross-ownership, but here again the state's legitimate allocative role could prevent unhealthy concentrations from developing (see Conclusions). The rise of the international media conglomerate is no necessary consequence of technological convergence, whatever current rhetoric suggests (see Chapter 9.4). Instead, the neo-liberal state encouraged such growth. That Hackgate was a consequence of Murdoch's dominance of the British media landscape, itself the product of such a free-market media policy, cannot be denied. It was, after all, the result of legislation that deregularized media ownership, the 1990 Broadcasting Act (Goodwin, 1999). Thatcher, the free-marketeer, promised a more open environment and delivered it, essentially to Murdoch whose satellite television operation flourished. Thus was created a media conglomerate of such power as to not only abuse the accidentally newsworthy and celebrities but also to threaten the independence of politicians and the integrity of the police and other officials.

Naturally then, one response in Hackgate's aftermath was to raise the problem of media cross-ownership. Controls had been removed by Thatcherite and subsequent legislation in the name of the free market. In part, the thinking behind this was that limiting the media reach of any one managerial entity was too hard to do fairly. This same happened in the United States where there was, in essence, a straightforward limitation restricting any one company from holding more than seven AM and seven FM radio stations plus seven TV channels. This was abandoned, in response to neo-liberal pressure, for a system of assessing audience share across all platforms, a task of forbidding complexity that has never been easily accepted by the industries (see Chapter 9.4). Anyway, the FCC has been, historically, always more concerned with the quality of those who apply for licences than with what, and to whom, they broadcast when they get one. Who owns a broadcast company's shares is also of more concern than what that company transmits. This is why Murdoch, who now owns twenty-seven licensed television stations, had to become an American. But, paradoxically, who supplies programming to the licence holder is not regulated with the consequence that the networks are outside direct FCC control (although the licensed stations taking the schedule can be held responsible). Licence removals or denials of renewal are so rare as to bring the charge that obtaining one is, in fact, to gain a species of property given in perpetuity. This, whatever Reaganites think to the contrary, was not Congress' original intention (see Chapter 7.2).

Controlling ownership concentration is less intractable than neo-liberal ideology always pretends it is. It is the case that weighing readers versus viewers versus listeners versus new platform users is a doomed exercise impossible of meaningful achievement. Ownership rules based on percentage shares in any one medium are likewise fool's gold. Nevertheless, limiting ownership, however popular any discrete channel or title is, is not inconceivable except to those who think a free market is more important than free, multi-voiced speech. It is not inconceivable in a democracy that capitalists be forced to choose which medium to exploit. Concentration of capital, after all, is not ordained from above; nor is limiting dominance – monopoly and oligopoly – unknown.

Censorship – content regulation – is entirely another matter. In the name of liberty, this should be rigorously resisted unless a matter of the general law. It is in no way justified by channel scarcity or supposed impact and cannot be justified now in an age of channel abundance. Even as Thatcher unleashed Murdoch, she, no longer a libertarian but suddenly a social authoritarian, increased state interference in broadcasting content by the creation of various statutory bodies. Official programming constraints, anyway already at odds with the tradition of press liberty, were bolstered. The broadcasting authorities were made to ensure, in an evermore codified fashion, that 'standards' of 'taste and decency' were met and 'fairness' guaranteed.

The proliferation of regulatory bodies was rationalized by a comprehensive Communications Act in 2003. An Office of Communications, Ofcom, took over all their functions and today regulates non-print media of expression in the UK. Although it does have a 'fit and proper' test for broadcast licence applicants, its oversight of ownership is otherwise limited and preventing concentration – in so far as this is done – remains a function of competition law. Ofcom reflects the confusion between allocative and content control functions. Its regulatory powers embrace the material telecommunications infrastructure and it imposes, as it must, technical standards to ensure quality of signal and so on. Yet, as the licensing authority, it also, infinitely less justifiably in a 'free' society, discharges censorship functions – aka 'content regulation'. The charge of 'censorship' is denied on the technicality that the new authority lost one of its predecessor's ability to vet material prior to programming. William Blackstone's injunction against prior constraint was finally confirmed for the new media. Yet, the middle-class, curtain-twitching responsibility to monitor 'taste and decency' was still in place, albeit now this was glossed as the supposedly more objective need to counter 'harm and offence'.

In a neat ideological sleight of hand, the maintenance of broadcasting censorship became thus equated with serving the public or citizen interest and the notion of 'accepted community standards', which at this time appeared nowhere in statute law. We were, however, assured that the new framework would be 'flexible enough to recognise the differences between different services and to respond to rapid changes in technologies, services or public expectations'. This, as we shall see, would turn out to be very far from the truth (Petley, 2011: 245).

At European journalism's birth stand the two figures of Marchmont Nedham (see Chapter 4.2) and Théophraste Renaudot (see Chapter 5.4). The former's purpose was the 'taking off vizards and vailes and disguises'; the other's was to publish his King's instructions. England then, and Britain thereafter, established the press in the spirit of Nedham. What the King wanted was, exactly, what was to be ignored. The argument against benign state interference was best made in the revolted North American colonies of the British Crown. James Madison thought that speech's special protection was justified only because the state was inclined to make and enforce illegitimate judgements about its worth. Accordingly, the principle of free speech took the form of a prohibition against the enforcement of state judgments about the truth or worth of what is said, be it ever so false, tasteless, indecent or offensive – tabloidized, distrusted ... or whatever. For Madison, the notion of positive state regulation was an oxymoron, especially state interference in journalism.

The defenders of regulation exhibit cognitive dissonance when confronting the negative realities of content control. The defence requires a belief in the reality of the independence of regulatory bodies set up by statute. This done, evidence is then ignored (the lurking MI5 man at the BBC, and so on) and known history subtly reinterpreted (for example, Reith's pusillanimity is glossed as 'constrained independence') (Barnett, 2011: 37). *Death on the Rock*, an investigative documentary, produced by Thames Television in 1988, dealt with the killing of IRA members by a unit of the British Army's SAS in Gibraltar. The British government was very distressed by this exposé and, it is widely believed, the documentary was the reason for the inclusion of a 'standards and fairness' clause in the 1990 Broadcasting Act and the abolition of the authority, the Independent Broadcasting Authority (IBA), which had allowed the programme to be broadcast. Certainly, this Act, although it confirmed the general illegality of prior consent, removed any advocacy function from the IBA's successor regulators: 'the programme marked the last time that an independent regulator with real teeth would be able to exert any authority to defend journalistic integrity' (Barnett, 2011: 118).[12]

But then the legislation on broadcasting does not have the protection of speech as its purpose so much as the need to mould and contain it. This is a result of a belief in the special power of the media, fostered by thinkers such as Walter Lippmann in the 1920s and the broadcasts of Hitler in the 1930s. It can be admitted that not all objectives involved in the task of containment were totally in opposition to progressive ideas. For example, in the White Paper produced before the 2003 Act, Ofcom's 'general duties' were to include protecting 'a plurality of public expression'. But only if it was in the form of 'high quality programming'. It would also be expected to protect 'the interests of citizens' but by, nanny-like, 'maintaining accepted community standards in content, balancing freedom of speech against offensive or harmful material, and ensuring appropriate protection of fairness and privacy' (Department of Trade and Industry and Department of Culture, Media and Sport, 2000). That free expression requires, exactly, the right to offend against all of this except 'harmful material' (and, in some circumstances, privacy) is self-evidently not in view. That is why it is not the specifics of such objectives that are at issue but the appropriateness of them being circumscribed by statute in a free society in the first place. Ofcom's 'principle duty' is:

> (1) a) to further the interests of citizens in relation to communications matters; and
> b) to further the interests of consumers in relevant markets, where appropriate by promoting competition.

Of course, this could mean that the citizen's/consumer's interest are well served by a marketplace of ideas – but it does not:

> 3.2 The things which, by virtue of subsection (1), OFCOM are required to secure in the carrying out of their functions include, in particular, each of the following: ...
> e) the application, in the case of all television and radio services, of standards that provide adequate protection to members of the public from the inclusion of offensive and harmful material in such services;
> f) the application, in the case of all television and radio services, of standards that provide adequate protection to members of the public and all other persons from both:
> i) unfair treatment in programmes included in such services; and
> ii) unwarranted infringements of privacy resulting from activities

Freedom of expression, when the Act finally gets round to mentioning it, must be at an 'appropriate level'. This is ranked seventh among Ofcom's 'duties' in Part 1.3 (4):

> g) the need to secure that the application in the case of television and radio services of standards is in the manner that best guarantees an appropriate level of freedom of expression.

The 'appropriate' limiting word has moved from being applied (in the White Paper) on one side of the balance, 'the protection of fairness and privacy', to the other, 'freedom of expression'. In sum, its job is to provide 'adequate protection to members of the public from the inclusion of offensive and harmful material in such [broadcast] services'.[13]

Ofcom is separated by more than just the 282 years that have passed since John Trenchard and Thomas Gordon wrote of free speech that: 'only Check which it ought to suffer, the only Bounds which it ought to know' were that it 'does not hurt and controul the Right of another'. For broadcasters in 2003, the expression was checked and bounded, a hedged-about concession as much as a right; and Ofcom's glosses in the *Broadcasting Code* it was enjoined by the statute to draw up make this clearer yet.

The 2011 version of the *Code* (Ofcom Broadcasting Code, 2011) states that the public are to be protected from 'harmful and/or offensive material'. In this opening statement in the 'harm/offence' section is also the order that 'portrayals of factual matters must not materially mislead the audience'. The *Code* details the requirements of the Act so that the audience must also be shielded from 'offensive language, violence, sex, sexual violence, humiliation, distress, violation of human dignity, discriminatory treatment or language (for example on the grounds of age, disability, gender, race, religion, beliefs and sexual orientation)' unless 'justified by the context'. 'Context' involves consideration, among other factors, of: 'the degree of harm or offence likely to be caused by the inclusion of any particular sort of material in programmes generally or programmes of a particular description', plus eight other factors. Moreover: 'Programmes must not include material ... which, taking into account the context, condones or glamorises violent, dangerous or seriously antisocial behaviour and is likely to encourage others to copy such behaviour'. 'Demonstrations of exorcism, the occult, the paranormal, divination, or practices related to any of these that purport to be real (as opposed to entertainment) must be treated with due objectivity'. (However, suicide, the one area where there is rather strong evidence of media causation, is no more prohibited than any other: '2.5: Methods of suicide and self-harm must not be included in programmes except where they are editorially justified and are also justified by the context.')

Almost all of this goes well beyond the constraints of the common law and the impact of some sixty other pieces of legislation that impact on the media. Ofcom's rule-making is, to be charitable, not of a piece with the traditions of free expression. Nor is it, again to be charitable, a model of legislative clarity. For example, Ofcom adds to the legal requirements which affect the publication of news its own demand in Section 5.1 of its *Code*: 'News, in whatever form, must be reported with "due accuracy" and presented with "due impartiality"'. *The Broadcasting Code* glosses 'due' as follows:

> 'Due' is an important qualification to the concept of impartiality. Impartiality itself means not favouring one side over another. 'Due' means adequate or appropriate to the subject and nature of the programme. So 'due impartiality' does not mean an equal division of time has to be given to every view, or that every argument and every facet of every argument has to be represented. The approach to due impartiality may vary according to the nature of the subject, the type of programme and channel, the likely expectation of the audience as to content, and the extent to which the content and approach is signalled to the audience.

What 'due' actually means is what Ofcom, like Lewis Carroll's Humpty-Dumpty, says it means. For example, it allowed Ofcom to license Press TV, a London-based channel owned by the Iranian government and dedicated to broadcasting its propaganda. Ofcom did fine the channel £100,000 for an egregious failure to explain that an interview had been obtained from a man under duress in prison (N. Cohen, 2011: 43). On the other hand, the Commission has not got round to fining Fox, Mr Murdoch's patently partial, biased and mendacious American channel, which is allowed to rebroadcast in the UK. Other channels are banned on the ground of 'offence'. These, however, are deemed pornographic and British authorities are always eager to prevent the channel-hopping citizenry from inadvertently encountering sex; rabid political bigotry is less of a problem (Petley, 2011).

All this can be compared with the American situation. The United States, despite the loss of a 'liberal majority' in its highest court, has still 'by far the most developed' approach (Nicol, Millar and Sharland, 2009: 2).[14] Of course, here too there are aberrations but they are less pronounced than elsewhere in the West. From the Adams Sedition Act through various episodes of repression, the supposed free market in ideas has been threatened; but, however sluggardly are the corrections, the principle is still strongly defended. American law pays more than lip service to the protections afforded speech by the First Amendment. Of course, such liberalism has it price. And it does not mean that all offensive expression is permitted, nor that there is an absence of regulatory control.

In the United States, ownership aside, in licence renewal hearings, consideration as to whether or not the broadcaster is shown to 'materially mislead the audience', or any other content matter, is unthinkable. This much is settled. It is the centrality of the free press in the American national narrative which makes it so. The FCC, on which Ofcom is partly modelled, has the same charge as Ofcom as regards infrastructure, but when it comes to content regulation its hand is far less obvious. It is prohibited from censoring the stations it licenses. Only policing the federal law on obscenity, indecency and profanity is allowed. Of these, obscenity is completely unprotected and therefore a straightforward matter (apart from the difficulty of its definition and so on – see Chapter 11.4). Indecency 'as measured by contemporary community standards ... is protected by the First Amendment and cannot be banned entirely' (Federal Communications Commission, n.d.). Likewise, profanity. Both can be restricted as to time, though, to protect children. The FCC also intervenes to maintain equal time during elections. Beyond that for many decades, it insisted on the so-called 'Fairness Doctrine' requiring equal time for replies to editorials. This was held to be constitutional by the Warren Court in 1969. Broadcasters, though, continued to chaff at it as a chilling restriction of their First Amendment right until it was abandoned under Ronald Reagan as an unconstitutional restriction. It was eliminated by the FCC in

1987 on the somewhat spurious grounds that channel abundance rendered it unnecessary. The rules against personal attacks and political editorializing where left in place, though.

Much is made of this, but the Fairness Doctrine had merely mandated a limited right of reply in any specific instance. Its operation was usually experienced by the American audience as little more than a curious rider to broadcast news 'editorials'.[15] Nevertheless, the removal of the doctrine opened the door to partisanship and propaganda previously kept somewhat in check. The then FCC chairman, in defiance of the ideology that had deemed the airwaves above America to the people of America (in the preamble to the originally FCC Act in 1934), said boldly that he thought licences were a species of property. The change merely facilitated broadcasters echoing press behaviour. By comparison with Britain, all this is indeed an example of the 'light touch regulation' promised by the neo-liberal censors but not delivered.

The point is that the entire structure of special provision for the content control for broadcasting is, in John Locke's phrase, 'very needless'. The general British law – all sixty-plus statutes of it – and, for example, common law offences such as conspiracy to corrupt public morals and so on, ought to be enough. They ought to be the sole embodiment of 'generally accepted standards' (in matters of privacy, for example, or the representation of suicide or the naming of rape victims). Because the right of free expression is so foundational, regulating it outside the general law via 'independent' authorities is, of itself, suspect.

To mount this rebuttal of received opinion on the legitimacy of media regulation is not to argue for a libertarian lack of control any more than is the defence of a free printed press. It is, rather, to suggest that, if there is a right of free expression, it should apply equally to all modes of expression. This did not happen with radio and television but there was no inevitable reason why that should be so. When establishing control over the content of the new medium of radio, authority turned more to the theatre where they had continued overtly to censor expression at the pre-production stage; rather than to film where there was no formal prior constraint but a measure of licensing over the exhibition of completed work. The press, where there was neither prior constraint nor licensing, was ignored as a possible model.

In plain terms, content regulation makes broadcast freedom less a matter of right and more a concession on the part of the state, even if this wears the fig leaf of independence in the form of a statutory authority. The scope of expression (aka 'content') is determined by mandated, but tendentiously applied, interpretations of statute by the regulatory authority. The justifications for this – shibboleths as to the 'power' of broadcasting, its intrusiveness and pervasiveness – are seldom examined, much less convincingly demonstrated.

That the *Broadcasting Code* might be inappropriate for major 'platforms' of expression is never raised. Instead, the advantages of editorial 'regulation' are often insisted on. Even to consider the *Code* as any sort of real threat to liberty is to invite automatic dismissal (just as espousing republicanism for Britain did until quite recently). Nevertheless, the entire philosophy underpinning the *Code*, Ofcom and the legislation is, despite passing nods, inimical to the principles of free speech. It is not that a case for regulation's positive impact cannot be made; it is that any positives, even those not freighted with class prejudice, are outweighed by negative dangers. In times of stability the threat to liberty might be thought merely theoretical; but to believe that stability must always be with us is surely naive. Regulation, however good or bad it is thought to be, without question extends the 'only bounds' and 'controuls' speech ought to know.

On the eve of the introduction of new technologies towards the end of the twentieth century, the partial nature of the right of free speech for the media had been repeatedly demonstrated. While prior constraint over the stage was abandoned in Britain with the removal of the Lord Chamberlain as censor, Blackstone's prohibition of it has been 'badly eroded' with other non-print modes of expression (Robertson and Nicol, 2008: 25). Even with print, in Britain, injunctions are commonly used to prevent publications, normally on the grounds of breach of confidence (and this before Hackgate). With other media, content is still evaluated and prohibited albeit this is done behind the fig leaf of statutory bodies charged by law with functions (censorship) that the law denies itself (no 'prior constraint'). The British Board of Film Classification has become, de facto, one such body. It is much the same with broadcasting. Ofcom might tell the public that: 'If you would like to complain about a programme that has yet to be broadcast, you should contact the broadcaster directly' (Ofcom, 2011); but it has a statutory requirement and precedent for 'protecting' the public. And the broadcasters' compliance structures bend to its power. The Communications Act, after all, requires Ofcom to guard the public from 'offensive and harmful material'. It too is a censor with powers to impose fines and remove licences according to standards it determines and applies.

It might be thought that the BBFC and Ofcom could be challenged on the grounds that their denial of certificates and imposition of codes offend against the right of free expression guaranteed in the European Convention on Human Rights (ECHR). However, the affirmation of the right of free expression in the first sentence of Article 10.1 of the ECHR ('Everyone has the right to freedom of expression') is immediately limited by the third. This allows 'states' to limit the right by 'requiring the licensing of broadcasting, television or cinema enterprises'. The European Court of Human Rights in Strasbourg has, only on one occasion, drawn attention 'the technical or practical considerations' and the 'political concern of several States ... that broadcasting should be the preserve of the State', which led to the state limitation of broadcasting

(*Groppera AG v. Switzerland*, 1990). However, the court held that, despite the changed technological circumstances, the state's role remained legal.

The contradictions of Article 10 of the ECHR, the BBFC's certifications, Ofcom's code and the like afford Tom Stoppard's cynicism ('The "human right" of free speech is a non-starter'; see Chapters 2 and 10.1) its strongest justification. These unquestioned tools of censorship do suggest that the right of free speech is something of a mere 'shibboleth', 'a non-starter'. But beyond the usual uninterrogated justifications for regulation, there is perhaps another cause for the lack of 'general spirit' in opposing it. Despite the rare occurrences when overt control is seen to be at work, broadcasters especially and their public are seduced by a simulacrum of freedom. After all, control is seldom overtly exercised and it is all too easy to be lulled by this into complacency. Moreover, with the controls in place, the rhetoric of free expression is allowed. The space allowed for expression can be – usually is – generous. This is not to be sneered at. It needs nothing more than a measure of disagreement within the controlling political elite and broadcast journalists too can join their names to the roll-call of ardent proponents of democracy in the best eighteenth-century radical tradition of the anglophone press.

On 10.30 p.m., Tuesday, 9 March 1954, on the CBS network, Edward R. Murrow began to camera: 'Tonight, *See It Now* devotes its entire half-hour to a report on Senator Joseph R. McCarthy, told mainly in his own words and pictures.' It had been four years since McCarthy, the junior senator from Wisconsin, had made the sensational allegation that the US State Department was a nest of communist traitors, a charge that he had still to substantiate. His demagogic Red-baiting might have been fact-free but he was the public face of a deep-seated American cold-war hysteria. On the other side, this particular evening, was *See It Now*. It was the network's flagship current affairs programme and Murrow was a celebrity. His radio dispatches from London during the Blitz of 1940–41 had established his reputation, but on television his Hollywood leading-man good looks had made him the first journalist in history to be a visual 'star'. For all that, there is no question that his talent and eloquence earns him a place in journalism's pantheon.

The programme consisted of newsreel footage of the senator being rebutted live from the studio by Murrow. McCarthy's half-truths, and un-truths, were mercilessly exposed on *See it Now*. The senator, quoting Shakespeare, had accused the Secretary of the Army of being a 'Caesar'. The show concluded with Murrow to camera – it would seem without prompt cards, ad-libbing:

> We will not walk in fear, one of the other. We will not be driven by fear into an age of unreason ... The actions of the Junior Senator from Wisconsin have caused alarm and dismay amongst our allies abroad and given considerable comfort to our enemies. And whose fault is that? Not really his. He didn't create this situation of fear, he merely exploited it; and rather successfully. Cassius was right. 'The fault, dear Brutus, is not in our stars, but in ourselves.'

And then, with the payoff which he had first heard Londoners using during the dark days of the Blitz and which he had made his trademark, he closed the show: 'Good night and good luck' (Sperber, 1986: 436–9).

The CBS switchboard was jammed following the transmission and Western Union was overwhelmed with telegrams for the network, massively in support. The switchboard was still jammed nineteen hours later (Sperber, 1986: 439). The show did not bring the senator, who was already in difficulties, down. His power was finally broken not by CBS but, nine months later, when the Senate moved a vote of censure against him. Nevertheless, the intervention of *See It Now* played a role – the role of guarding the guardians – the press's most vital social function.

This does not mean, after all, that the principle of free expression applies to broadcasting, or, in general to any new media – however much the rhetoric implies that it does. Rather, the *See It Now* transmission is, in fact, an exception. Rhetorically, new media might share with print a claim on the right but, except in rare circumstances, the claim is not sustained at the same level. The West has been inconsistent in its application of a right of free expression and these exceptions obscure the history of the struggle to establish and maintain it. The inconsistencies mean that, when faced with an external challenge of a Khomeini, no simple insistence that only the demonstration of real, verifiable damage will justify the abridgement of speech is possible. Why should not the West abridge free speech to meet such demands as his when, as with media other than print, it anyway restricts expression in ways that go beyond the application of the harm principle?

9

Obita Dicta: Opinion

9.1 *Noyce v. Kilby* (1969): The coming of the digital

Technology has long cast its glamour over the West and we remain besotted; so besotted that it can be suggested new communication technologies now render all the old problems of free expression moot. But they do not.

The principle of free expression ought not to be susceptible to technical considerations as to expression's mode, but it has been. As each new medium was introduced in the twentieth century, its underlying freedom – its right to speak – was more and more circumscribed, even as, on the surface, speech was less and less restricted and inhibited. The right is not media-blind and this makes defending it more difficult than it would be if it were.

Now, in the twenty-first century, the proliferation of digitized communication platforms has engendered a hyperbolic rhetoric promising unfettered communication. It is indisputable that the claims made for the digital, presented as enabling 'technologies of freedom', further confuse the history of free speech. Such technicist enthusiasm suggests that the digital is remaking society and, concomitantly, the dilemmas caused by liberty of expression are solved. For one thing, such is the abundance of communication channels now available that they cannot be controlled. Speech, we are told, is at last truly free. This, though, can be disputed; the digital does not actually answer the problem of liberty. Questioning the claims made for new communications modes can be done, therefore, as a species of aside, in legal language: *obita dicta*.

Central to the technicist illusion is historical amnesia. It is now over eighty years since the first digital devices were built but our passion for needing to believe we live in technologically revolutionary times buries that history. A reasonable starting point would be Harry Nyquist, an AT&T engineer who, in 1928, determined the mathematics of signal sampling without which digitization cannot be done. One weekend in November 1937 George Stibitz, another telephone researcher working for Bell Laboratories, assembled, out of old relays and other readily available components, a small circuit based on Boolean logic. He did not seek a patent for this circuit, which he called K1 ('K' for the kitchen table on which he built it). The following year, A.H. Reeves, who was working at the International Telephone & Telegraph (ITT) lab in Paris, patented a digital pulse code modulation (PCM) system, using Nyquist's formulae. (PCM is a digital equivalent of amplitude or frequency modulation – AM, FM – in modulating analogue signals. One can note that, as it is a modulation system, it is not, of itself, of much significance to message content.)

This book, therefore, appears in Year 76, at the earliest, of the supposed digital 'revolution'. Despite the discombobulating technicist rhetoric, this three-quarters of a century has seen the comparatively slow, complex interaction of supervening social necessity, and the suppression and containment of the disruptive power of new technologies at steady work. Social need has conditioned design specification, which with the constraint of prior practice and the operation of patent law has worked to leech out disturbance.

The 'invention' of the computer – a calculator that alters its operations in response to the interim results of its own calculations – was a matter of visionary systems engineering requiring brilliant conceptualization rather than physical investigations. Obtaining the components, as Stibitz had illustrated, merely required a trip to the store-room. Advanced electro-mechanical business machines – which could handle everyday calculations from tabulating the census to running a payroll – ensured all parts which would be needed for a computer were being produced. The computer really required mathematical conceptualization and this was provided, for example, by Alan Turing's solution to the abstruse higher mathematical 'decidability problem' (Turing, 1936; Turing, 1937). It also needed a problem with which the calculators could not cope. This was more than supplied by a number of difficulties encountered in the Second World War – gunsights, firing tables, encryption machines; but the final supervening necessity which got the first computers built was the problems thrown up by thermonuclear research for the atom bomb. All the earliest machines were hand-built as part of the US nuclear programme and they were enormous, involving thousands and upon thousands of valves (tubes) and vast expense (Winston, 1998: 147–88).

This meant that there was little call for them. In the computer's first decade, essentially the 1950s, the suppression of its disruptive potential was grounded in a number of factors; for example, the continued profitability of advanced business calculators. International Business Machines (IBM) famously ignored the development of the computer almost completely (Winston, 1998: 196).[1] Within the nascent computing world, professional operators resisted the development of both computer languages and ergonomic input devices that would have made the machines more accessible. This, too, was a constraint on diffusion. In the longer term, though, it was the lack of any supervening necessity beyond the nuclear programme that really stunted development. Computers did calculations no other device could and were operated day-to-day by programmers mostly in their thrall. Smaller computers could not do such calculations, only simpler tasks; nevertheless, in the context of the shop-floor or the office, the increase in power, when so distributed, could have been disruptive. This impact, the promise of a baby machine, is what was constrained most. Why produce a computer adding machine? A computer typewriter? A computer game-player? Even, a small computer to control another factory machine? Yet the very first computer to operate was the 'Baby Mark 1' (as big as a desk, actually), which ran a factoring programme for fifty-two minutes at the University of Manchester on 1 December 1947. It was designed to test a peripheral memory system and, that done, it was set aside. Instead, the memory was inserted into a machine – a whole roomful of valves – which better matched the template developed for nuclear bomb computing (Lavington, 1980: 18–19, 36).

This suppressive mode was played out most vividly in computing's relationship with an emerging parallel technology – solid-state electronics. It was the technology that most facilitated the small machine but, whatever technicist understanding is to the contrary, advances in solid-state research were adopted, at best, piecemeal by the nascent computing industry. In 1977, no less a figure than Robert Noyce, a founder of Intel, put the technicist misunderstanding thus: 'It all began with the development thirty years ago of the transistor: a small, low-power amplifier that replaced the large power-hungry vacuum tube. The advent almost simultaneously of the stored program digital computer provided a large potential market for the transistor. The synergy between a new component and a new application generated an explosive growth in both' (Noyce, 1977: 30).

None of this is correct. The growth in both was not exactly explosive. There was not that much synergy between them; certainly not to the point where, without transistors, computer development would have ground to a halt. The transistor was never widely used in computers and solid-state electronics really only began to take over when Noyce and others produced cheap integrated circuits early in the 1960s. And the development of the transistor did not begin thirty years before he wrote.

He can be forgiven this last, though. Even Bell Laboratories, whence the transistor apparently burst forth in 1948, did not remember its own history. The internal Bell Labs 'Memorandum for Record', dated 27 December 1949, states: 'The history of the transistor begins with the decision to study intensively the properties of silicon and germanium. This decision was made in 1946 as a result of series of conferences intended to establish a plan for semiconductor research' (Millman, 1983: 97). In fact, Bell Labs, concerned with the possibilities of an energy-efficient, solid-state telephone exchange, had begun investigating such 'properties' more than a decade earlier. This led to a concentrated post-war effort which, after two years of hit-and-miss investigations, produced the transistor, a silicon (sand) chip that could amplify an electrical signal: a valve (tube).[2] The transistor effect was demonstrated in

1948 but it was to take such semiconductors and computers a generation to come together.

Between the first junction transistors of 1948 and a planar technique to mass produce semiconductor chips and the first integrated circuit (IC) took ten years. The only really widespread application of the transistors was in portable radios – significantly, 'trannies' in the slang – and hearing-aids. The IC was developed simultaneously by a number of researchers and, in 1969, Noyce found himself in court fighting Jack Kilby over the patent. Noyce won in the marketplace but Kilby was awarded a Nobel Prize for physics. From the IC to a microprocessor specifically designed for a calculator took a further eleven years; and it was to be another eight years before an off-the-shelf microcomputer emerged in 1977. The computer proper follows a similar trajectory. Between the paper outlining what its architecture might look like and the first large machines took some three years; from them to the first 'mini' took eighteen years and from that to the microcomputer – today's device – was thirteen years. Moreover, most of a further decade was to pass before the microcomputer became a widely diffused consumer durable. So much for 'revolution'; so much for 'synergy'. After all, the problem of redundancy persisted. What use would an office – even more, a home – microcomputer be? A control mechanism? A calculator? A typewriter? A gaming device? These functions were being met. In fact, even a computer-style game was already very much to hand.

The supervening social necessity that first brought the microprocessor into the home was the same as that which was responsible for the radio and television: entertainment. A computer student at Massachusetts Institute of Technology (MIT), Nolan Bushnell, with his peers, misused the university's huge mainframes to play a proto-computer game, *Space Wars*. On graduation, Bushnell thought to market the idea and designed *Pong*, played with a box parasitically plugged into the coaxial aerial socket of the television. By 1984, there were computer games in 15 million American homes and Bushnell sold his company, Atari, to Warner Bros for $30 million.

Pong signposted another possible pastime. As with radio after the First World War, amateur enthusiasts began to build their own minicomputers using chips bought from the semiconductor firms. The term 'micro' rather than 'mini' emerged and described the first commercially produced examples, the 'Pet' and the 'TRS-80', which were brought to market in 1977. The first shops, magazines and clubs for enthusiasts appeared, but, as with radio sixty years earlier, the device's utility was far from self-evident. Bushnell was approached by one such young enthusiast looking for capital to float a company to make micros. He declined the opportunity but Steve Jobs, and an older school-friend, Steve Wozniak, connected with an ex-Intel executive and founded Apple all the same. Technicist hyperbole was to acquire a new mytheoepic trope. Young men in their twenties – the prototypes are Bushnell, Wozniak and Jobs – were emerging from suburban garages (as it were) instantly to be transformed into millionaires by making machines whose innards were too complicated for lesser mortals to understand. Nothing like it had ever been seen before.

However, this, like much of technicist rhetoric, is largely nonsensical. Jobs, for example, represented no new phenomenon – he was an old-fashioned salesperson, a charismatic figure of great persuasive power, a certain hippie aspect notwithstanding. Apple's secret was to be exceptionally open-minded to engineering possibilities, picking up previously readily available technologies to bring hitherto unknown levels of accessibility to its products. Hence a brilliantly engineered drive to utilize the commercially available floppy-disk as a storage device; hence, ports for peripherals; hence the 'mouse' pointer-device, as used by Xerox (and, commercially, by Telefunken). The vision, shared and sold by Jobs, was a microcomputer designed so that anyone could use it. This completely reversed the cultural positioning of the machine which, because of its cold-war origins and science-fiction inflected hyperbole, had been only previously approached 'the way an ancient Greek approached an oracle' (Augarten, 1984: 253). Apples were quite other. In the first instance of what would become a Jobs' trademark, aggressively brilliant advertising, the tag was: 'Simplicity is the ultimate sophistication – Introducing Apple II. The personal computer.' Even schoolchildren could use them. Hence another advertisement with educational connotations: 'A is for Apple.' And it was with schools, as an educational tool, that it triumphed. Apple Corps proved a safe investment and, on its launch as a public company three years later in 1980, it was valued at $1.2 billion.

Wozniak liked games and the machine was good for that, too; but other uses were emerging. A word-processing programme, WordStar, had been introduced for the Altair hobbyist-kit micro in 1978, and, the following year, Apple Writer appeared for the Apple II. Apple Writer 1 was not, to be charitable, very user-friendly. For instance, it produced upper-case letters and actually to obtain upper-case one needed to highlight the already upper-case type. Nevertheless, these programmes allowed typing on a personal computer to be infinitely correctable. No typewriters, not even the then latest electrical ones with limited physical correctability, offered that.

VisiCalc, the first spreadsheet programme, was published in 1979 initially for the Apple II, then for the Pet, the TRS-80 and, Bushnell having belatedly seen the light, the Atari 800. This was arguably of greater moment than the word-processor programmes. Adding machines and the recently introduced electronic calculators had mechanized the process of drawing up spreadsheets, in part; but the task still required pen and paper. VisiCalc removed the pen, automated consequential calculations and thereby transformed the process of producing the sheets. The importance of this should not be underestimated. In the West, double-entry book-keeping had required writing from the first trace appearances of the technique in Genoese merchant account books of the early thirteenth century through the system of Fra Luca Pacioli in the fifteenth century to 1979. Without double-entry book-keeping, Western mercantilism could never have developed into capitalism. Its 'invention' was at least as crucial to Western civilization as the development of movable-type for printing or the application of steam-power to transport and manufacturing.

IBM, having played catch-up on the mainframes and declined to make minis, was yet again behind the curve. In the year of Apple's flotation, though, it woke up and acquired an operating programme from a small software company, owned by another young, highly educated entrepreneur. On leave from his studies at Harvard, Bill Gates had founded Microsoft in conjunction with Altair to develop a basic programming tool. He never returned to Harvard as the programme was a success. It was, though, being shared after the fashion of the hobbyists of the day. Gates used a newsletter to the community to suggest payment would not be out of order, easily as profound a contribution to the industry as any line of programming code he ever wrote. At the time, because of a decision of the Supreme Court, algorithms were could not be patented (*Gottschalk v. Benson*, 1972); so programmes too were widely thought to be unpatentable and were certainly considered a common good by the hobbyists. Dan Bricklin and Bob Frankston, the developers of VisiCalc, for example, never sought one.

With the Microsoft operating system, IBM finally produced a micro personal computer, marketed as the PC. As Hoover had become a term for the vacuum cleaner, so the acronym, PC, became the name for the microcomputer. Microsoft became a giant on the back of IBM. Bill Gates was to be, in more years than not, the early twenty-first century's wealthiest man.

The development of the PC can be seen as a continuation of a trajectory from the electric typewriter, the electronic calculator and the earliest computer game consoles; or it can be seen as something more. The question can be put thus: where can the line between prototype and 'invention' (in the sense of diffusible device in response to supervening social necessity) be drawn?[3] If the press, for example, is thought of as a machine capable of printing at least 1,000 pages an hour, or photography is defined as a process capable of producing infinite copies, then Gutenberg did not 'invent' the former, nor Nicéphore Niépce and Louis Daguerre the latter. By such a measure, all the early monster and later 'mini' devices are not the 'invented' computer either. They prefigure the more socially transformative machine – the PC.

This is without prejudice to a consideration of the extent to which the microcomputer is, really, a truly socially transformative device. The seductions of technicism suggest that it is. Some would hold that in the computer's wake, all nature, to quote Donna Harraway, has been 'reinvented': 'No natural or human science has been unaffected by these technical and theoretic transformations' (Harraway, 1991: 59). This, though, might not be quite the case. It could be that the PC is little more than a machine for performing a variety of everyday functions at levels of flexibility, efficiency and capacity not previously seen as being required. This is not, on its face, revolutionary, even in aggregate. Be that as it may – the evidence for revolution is dealt with below. It can be noted that, without question, even if technicist hyperbole is resisted, the impact of the PC was of a more directly felt nature than the impact of the mainframes and the minis had been. The general supervening necessity for the computer, by this account, was not thermonuclear ignition problems and other advanced scientific calculation requirements, nor even the specific demands of big business for vast computing capacity. Unlike the PC, mainframes were part of very few everyday lives in any very direct way and this limitation contained their disruptive power. Despite the threat of nuclear war and the predations of late capital aided and abetted by the early computers, the gigantism of the machines those needs produced, as Nobel argues (Nobel, 1979; Nobel, 1984), prevented them from widely disrupting social modes. The necessity which produced the diffused micro-machine was the far more universal permanent requirement for, as it were, essentially non-disruptive, better mousetraps. The computer's disruptive potential having been absorbed over four decades, this diffused social necessity could now be met: better typewriters, better ways of doing accounts, better games.

And better communications.

9.2   *Paul Baran v. AT&T* (1964): Digitizing communications

Donna Harraway continues: 'Nature is structured as a series of interlocking cybernetic systems, which are theorized as communications problems' (Harraway, 1991: 59). Thus the development of the computer leads back to communications; and, therefore, to enhanced possibilities for expression. These opportunities were to be vaunted in technicist rhetoric as a revolution in information and, in a most extreme form, proposed as a transformative moment for human interaction. Indeed, the machines were ceasing to be thought of anthropomorphically, that is: modelled on humans. Rather the contrary – humans, were considered 'mechanomorphically', echoes of the machine. Now people – 'noisy [i.e. subject to interference] narrow-band devices' – were computers: somewhat inferior computers. This was an update on an old theme. In the eighteenth century, it had been suggested that people were like clocks. In the nineteenth century they were compared to combustion engines. Sigmund Freud, and his early mentor Jean-Martin Charcot, gained insight into the workings of the brain by considering it a magnet.[4] Now, human computers, which is how Turing thought of them, were absorbed into the machine. In response, the computer's central processor was designated its 'brain'; its storage device, 'memory'; and to speak to it one needed a 'language'.

It is such cybernetic melding that was deemed, *en passant*, to render the old concerns about free speech moot.

In 1968, Joseph Licklider, and a colleague Robert Taylor, published a paper outlining exactly how a network of mainframe 'multi-access' real-time computers could be made to communicate with each other. In their vision, 'For each node [i.e. computing site] there is a small, general-purpose computer which we shall call a "message processor". The message processors of all the nodes are interconnected to form a fast store-and-forward network. The large multi-access computer at each node is connected directly to the message processor there' (Licklider and Taylor, 1968: 32). It is not to deny Licklider's reputation as a visionary to note that building such a system was already underway at the Pentagon's Advanced Research Project Agency (ARPA) when he and Taylor were writing. That was, after all, where he was working as head of computing projects, and the system was being manufactured by a defence contractor where he had also worked. Licklider's centrality to the development of the computer as a communication device cannot be denied. This description, though, was less a prophecy than a report at the time it was written in 1968.

The possibility of remote access to a computer predates its appearance. Stibitz had demonstrated the Bell Model 1 electronic calculator in 1940 using the telephone line and by the 1960s such connectivity was not unknown to mainframe operators. Moreover, as early as 1954, IBM started designing a real-time seat reservation system for American Airlines. It had come on stream, the first in the world, in 1964 with 1,200 remote terminals scattered across the United States (Augarten, 1984: 208).

But Licklider was no mere enthusiast for time-sharing computers serving multiple real-time users. He did have a vision of a network that went far beyond time-sharing interactivity. Cybernetic human/machine symbiosis suffused his rhetoric. For example, he had asked in a 1963 memo sent to the senior computer industry members who, with him, constituted an informal club they called the 'Intergalactic Computer Network', a basic question: 'Is it not desirable or even necessary for all the centres [nodes] to agree upon some language or, at least, upon some conventions for asking such questions as "What language do you speak?"' (Licklider, 1963). For Licklider and Taylor, a consequence of such (as it were) 'conversations' was the possibility of endless accessibility to information by the human user:

> investment guidance, tax counseling, selective dissemination of information in your field of specialization, announcement of cultural, sport, and entertainment events that fit your interests, etc … [There] will be dictionaries, encyclopedias, indexes, catalogues, editing programs, teaching programs, testing programs, programming systems, data bases, and – most important – communication, display, and modeling programs. All these will be – at some late date in the history of networking – systematized and coherent. (Licklider and Taylor, 1968: 39–40)

They were probably not aware of it, but a rather more sophisticated take on the possibility of massive accessibility had been outlined by Vannevar Bush, one of America's leading scientists, decades earlier.

In a (by-no-means dumbed-down) article for a popular magazine in 1945, Bush outlined a system, the 'Memex', essentially a microfilm/audio-recording device. Although he had been involved during the war in the earliest projects which had led to the first mainframes, this was not a computer. The Memex would allow for data to be accessed 'by association rather than by indexing'. Indexing alphabetically or numerically was, he thought, limiting because 'information is found (when it is) by tracing it down from subclass to subclass', and this is not the way the mind works. It operates by association: 'With one item in its grasp, it snaps instantly to the next that is suggested by the association of thoughts, in accordance with some intricate web of trails carried by the cells of the brain' (Bush, 1945: 110). The Memex would mimic this. Licklider and Taylor were, in effect, seeking the same sort of facility, but from the computer.

Computers would concentrate and interleave the concurrent, intermittent messages of many users and their programs so as to utilize wide-band transmission channels continuously and efficiently (Licklider and Taylor, 1968: 30). Again, they knew this solution would work.

In 1963, Paul Baran, a RAND Corporation researcher, had suggested that messages could be broken down into electronically viable pieces – sub-units of less than 200 bits that he called, despite them being semantically meaningless, 'messages blocks'. Donald Davies, who had worked with Turing on the first British computers, knew of Baran's work. He called the pieces 'packets', though, and this was the term to prevail (Hafner and Lyon, 1996: 64–5). Davies' objective was an exploration of what multiple computers 'talking' to each other might achieve. He sought to conduct this experiment by linking up all the computers at the UK's National Physical Laboratory. The most important immediate result was that 'packet-switching' worked. The vastly quicker processing speed of the computer allowed it to juggle multiple interactions with the vastly slow human operators. With colleagues, he gave a paper explaining their system at a seminar in Texas in 1967 (Davies, Bartlett, Scantlebury and Wilkinson, 1967). 'Our proposal,' the British explained, 'is like Baran's in its high-level network but the similarity does not extend to the manner of using the network. Baran's proposal was intended for a military communication system in the future, and carried secure speech' (Davies et al., 1967: 3).

Baran's supervening necessity was far stronger than merely advancing the frontiers of human knowledge of what networked computers might do. He had been working on a project for a digital 'survivable communications system for the air-force', the key word being 'survivable', i.e. capable of withstanding nuclear attack to avoid 'network decapitation' (P. Edwards,

2010: 143). Military uses were also in Licklider's mind; after all, he worked at the Pentagon (P. Edwards, 2010: 152). Packet-switching across a nodal store-and-forward network was crucial to 'survivability'. Linking the mainframes was as much a consequence of the cold war as the creation of the machines themselves had been in the first place. The AT&T phone company, however, thought otherwise. It insisted that it had a viable, secret system already in place and it persuaded the US Air Force to abandon the RAND project (Reed, Atta and Deichtman, 1990: 20–3). AT&T would not even give Baran its long-line network map. This would be a classic example of suppression, were not the supervening military necessity so powerful. It sustained ARPA's interest in Licklider's work and ideas.

Technicist romantics are uneasy that the survivability of the military's command and control network is the internet's initial *raison d'être*. They point to early visions of civilian potentials as a rebuttal. Baran, for example, wrote in 1964: 'Is it time now to start thinking about a new and possibly non-existent public utility, a common user digital data communication plant designed specifically for the transmission of digital data among a large set of subscribers?' (Baran, 1964: 1179). Given that his concept had been discarded in the face of AT&T hostility, clearly it was time to think again. Licklider, too, was ever ready to envision civilian possibilities. This, though, does not alter the military realities. Purely scientific or civilian purposes at this time were often a cover for military plans. Sputnik, for example, was Russia's contribution to the International Geophysical Year, 1956. It was also, de facto, a demonstration of an intercontinental ballistic missile. Licklider, in the note to the 'Intergalactic Computer Network', mused that: 'It will possibly turn out, I realize, that only on rare occasions do most or all of the computers in the overall system operate together in an integrated network' (Licklider, 1963). It seems not unreasonable to suggest that the 'rare occasions' he had in mind were nuclear attacks, rather than any 'intergalactic' event.

This is not, though, to say that the scientific cover was fraudulent. On the contrary – Sputnik, for example, was the necessary first demonstration of a manmade satellite, a technology which would indeed yield a plethora of scientific applications. It would, inter alia, enable a vast expansion of the world's transoceanic communications infrastructure. Nevertheless, the satellite was also merely an alternative to a nuclear warhead, launched by an intercontinental ballistic missile, pointing out to space rather than at a terrestrial target; similarly, the ARPA plan for a network. It too had serious implications for computing science and practical consequences for the research labs it intended to link. But it was also a demonstration of a bomb-proof, as it were, communications system. It was this – not the desire of computer scientists to see what would happened if they joined their machines together, much less theoretical, anthropomorphic explorations of the mind's 'web' – that released the not inconsiderable sums of money required to build it.

The plan was to connect fourteen nodes, situated in defence labs and defence-oriented university departments. To do so required interposing between the mainframes 'Interface Message Processors' (IMPs); in today's terminology, routers. This was primarily because the machines used incompatible languages but there was also among the mainframe community an unwillingness to sacrifice precious computing power, then still very limited, for the purpose of interconnectivity. The whole scheme would have been resisted had it not come with its own additional minicomputers. The IMPs chosen were Honeywell DDP-516s. In 1968, the first four, at $360,000 each, were acquired, in – significantly – 'ruggerdized' battlefield-proof casings. Developing the DDP-516s as routers cost ARPA a further $640,000. The IMPs were linked on leased AT&T lines. The initial exercise cost $13,000,000 in today's money: as clear a proof as any of its underlying military importance. The system worked and a Network Working Group (NWG), with input from operators at all the nodes, was established to create the translator and usage protocols.

Within two years the transcontinental spine had been built and there were forty-four nodes. Three years after that the first satellite links were established to Hawaii and Norway (P. Edwards, 2010: 141), and the system had transferred from the project-oriented ARPA (which had become Defense Advanced Research Projects Agency, DARPA) to the Pentagon's Defense Communications Agency (DCA). By 1979, only sixteen nodes were left in educational establishments. The rest were hidden in the military-industrial complex. In 1982, these were split off to form MILNET, the military network (Hardy, 1996: 7). To accommodate university computer departments not authorized as ARPANET users, the US National Science Foundation (NSF) established an alternative package-switching Computer Service Network (CSNet).

Out of the ARPANET NWG, a protocol, developed by Robert Kahn and Vinton Cerf, emerged to allow for the 'conversation' to embrace other users and networks. Commercially established subscriber networks, which had been established using the phone lines, were then connected and a super 'network of networks', soon to be christened the 'Internet', emerged. CSNet was commercialized with a tariff of different user-fees according to the range of services bought. The main cost was the long-line charges. The first private company facilitating access to this super-net was CompuServe. It was to become part of Warner Bros, servicing 3.2 million clients in 120 counties. Its biggest rival, America Online (AOL), which serviced 3.5 million users, was co-owned by the publishers Bertelsmann and Hachette. Prodigy was operated by a consortium led by CBS, involving IBM and Sears Roebuck. It attached 1.4 million users. These companies essayed a range of provision on a 'dial-up' basis, from news services, electronic mail-order shopping and electronic telegramming ('email' as it was to be), to telephone connectivity with other subscribers. In 1995, the NSF took the next logical step: it sold the basic hardware – the national spine of the internet that it had been given by the Pentagon – to three of the 'Baby Bells': Sprint, Ameritech and Pacific Bell.[5]

By this time, the introduction of a communication protocol had fulfilled the promise of Vannevar Bush's vision of a 'web'. At CERN (the acronym for Conseil Européen pour la Recherche Nucléaire, now known as the European Organization for Nuclear Research), Tim Berners-Lee created what would be introduced in 1992 as the 'World-Wide-Web'. This permitted direct 'conversations', individual PC to individual PC. These could also access dedicated electronic depositories of information along the lines envisaged by Licklider and Taylor: 'guidance … counselling … dissemination of information … announcement of … events … dictionaries … encyclopedias … indexes', etc. The 'year of the web', 1992, was the 'late date in the history of networking' they had envisaged a quarter of a century earlier. Unimaginable amounts of information of all kinds were readily available via any suitably enabled PC in, more or less, the 'systematized and coherent' fashioned they predicted (Licklider and Taylor, 1968: 40).

In addition to charges for accessing the system, now service providers accepted advertising as a further source of revenue. The military-industrial roots of the network were forgotten, its ownership by the usual telecommunication and media conglomerates was ignored and its actual costs were hidden – much as with commercial broadcasting. Instead, its entire history from ARPANET to the World Wide Web was being touted as an embodiment of a 'meritocratic, libertarian, free speech philosophy' (P. Edwards, 2010: 145): 'Remarkably this came about with no central planning, no governing body, and no overall control, other than the system for allocating the names of websites and their addresses' (Singer, 2010: 27). Actually, there is little remarkable about it.

The initial dislocation between the networked IMPs and the mainframes that stood behind them, it can be argued, is the source of such rhetoric. Making ARPANET work relied on the NWG which consisted, in the earliest stages, mainly of graduate students. Out of this interconnected little community emerged the protocols by which the machines could 'talk' to each other. Many of these are still with us. The NWG's innovations fostered an impression, entirely illusionary, that the network was somehow not deeply embedded in the military-industrial complex. Rather, its hardware and expense forgotten, increasingly it was held to be the creation of a species of spontaneous democratic process among users. Attempts to impose operating elements from above were, in effect, resisted and the illusion was that the system was 'open, meritocratic and consensus based' was confirmed (P. Edwards, 2010: 145). Obviously, countenancing this myth was useful to the camouflaging of the system's real purpose. Even when this was acknowledged, its import was downplayed: 'Originally, the Internet was a post-apocalypse command grid. And look at it now. No one really planned it this way. Its users made the Internet that way, because they had the courage to use the network to support their own values, to bend the technology to their own purposes. To serve their own liberty' (Sterling, 1993). They had, of course, actually done no such thing; but the camouflaging had worked.

The NWG, sitting in their military-industrial labs, was no band of long-haired hippy subversives seeking liberty. They were merely using the network for communications that were perfectly capable of being transmitted by other means. Yet why would the young computer post-graduates and professionals charged with collectively agreeing how to make the network work pick up the phone or type a telex when they could use the system itself? Then, as a perfectly natural consequence, why should network communications, electronic mail, be limited to computing matters? The first international email was sent in 1973. It was no call to set up barricades. Vinton Cerf, a leading figure in these developments, had been delayed getting to a conference at the University of Sussex in England because of the birth of a child. The news, transmitted via the computer network, rather than by telegram, telex or telephone, preceded him and he was greeted with applause when he arrived. Another American attendee forgot his razor and emailed back from the United States asking if it could be found (Hafner and Lyon, 1996: 185–6, 225). The NWG had not, in any meaningful way, 'seized' the infrastructure, either. This had been absorbed, as the suppression of any new technology's radical potential suggested it would be, by established interest, i.e. the telecommunication companies and the media conglomerates. Web-users' 'values', however defined, were countenanced, permitted rather than essentially guaranteed.

The capacity of the PC was such that previously discrete modes of communication could all be accommodated by it alone, modulated digitally. Technicism was further enthused by this. The internet was not only a supposed bastion of liberty; it was, supposedly, a 'converged' bastion of liberty. Convergence was transforming society's infrastructure. The world was, supposedly, in the midst of a 'digital information revolution': Al Gore, not untypically, asserts that the net 'represents the emergence of a new information ecosystem that will have a more profound impact on human civilization than did the printing press' (Krotoski, 2010: 28). Can this be doubted?

President Nicolas Sarkozy, in welcoming the internet's main players to a pre-G8 'e-summit' in 2011, said: 'Yesterday's dreams have become realities, and the universe of possibilities grows broader around us every day. In just a few years the Internet has enabled us to realize the dreams of Enlightenment philosophers, making our store of knowledge accessible to the widest possible audience. Democracy and human rights have been reinforced' (Sarkozy, 2011). Thereafter, Mark Zuckerberg of Facebook (wearing, it was noted, an unaccustomed suit and tie as befits a person admonishing the world's most prominent politicians) warned Sarkozy and the other seven heads of state not to think of controlling the net. Sarkozy, despite the rhetoric, certainly had this in mind when he set up the meeting. 'You can't isolate things you like about the internet,' Zuckerberg told them, 'and control other things you don't' (Wintour, 2011: 29). When the masters of the net speak (as they were now regularly being asked to do), the world's leaders listen. After all, the masses, certainly of the young, were with Zuckerberg and his peers. And they were, were they not, the future?

For twenty-first-century youth, social networks such as Zuckerberg's Facebook had become, even if a fad, an overwhelmingly pervasive one. Licklider and Taylor had foreseen this, although they had dispersed engineers working on common projects in mind, rather than the young: 'life will be happier for the on-line individual because the people with whom one interacts most strongly will be selected more by commonality of interests and goals than by accidents of proximity' (Licklider and Taylor, 1968: 40).

Whether the young are happier or not need not detain us. At the time of writing, vast numbers of them were certainly not being distracted by work; instead, in the collective mind of the world's potentates, they are believed to be in thrall to the technology. The statistics to support this cannot be denied. By the end of the first decade of the twenty-first century, in the UK for example, 57 per cent of mobile phone owners used 'social networking' sites, as did 62 per cent of PC owners. These are electronic personal contact services of a kind not envisaged in the 1960s. Sixty per cent of British teenagers owning smartphones 'described themselves as "highly addicted"' to social networking; 94 per cent of all British PC users sent or received emails (Halliday, 2011: 13). Digital communication via computers and other handheld micro devices of all kinds had become central to life in the developed world.

The net's top websites counted their users in millions. Fifteen years after Berners-Lee conceived the 'www' protocol, the web hosted an estimated 40 billion pages; a billion searches a day came to the search-engine Google; 100 million people watched movie clips on YouTube; 35 million shopped at Amazon; and 912,000 'visits' a day were made to Wikipedia, the online user-generated encyclopaedia (Naughton, 2006: 4–6). By 2011, half a billion people, it was said, were connected to Facebook, every thirteenth person on earth; 48 per cent of the world's eighteen to thirty-five year-olds were among them (Anon, 2011a). In 2011, within five years of its founding, Twitter, a texting service whose USP is that it can only accept messages 140 characters long, was carrying, according to Wikipedia, 300 million such sentences a day. Much was claimed for it: it 'was the first people's broadcast medium', 'an antidote to loneliness', 'transforming how we communicate' (Rushe, 2011: 35).

Scarce to be wondered, then, that the communications industry has been subjected to a tsunami of change, not least according to its spokespersons. The industries of expression – recorded music, films, broadcasting, press and publishing – insist than an uncontrolled internet is subjecting them to something akin to rape. The net is 'killing print'; audiences are fragmented; re-broadcasting 'deals' are threatened; there is 'rampant piracy'. The new technology has 'holed' all the sectors relying on the exploitation of intellectual property rights 'beneath the water'.

Yet, positively, expression itself is being transformed by the technology. The actor Stephen Fry, the best-known British embodiment of respected, independent technophilia, argues that Berners-Lee, 'created a new way of allowing communication to work … It seemed like a great new world. It seemed like a new democracy. It seemed like people coming together and spreading news, of educating … It seemed like the most fantastic, radical and extraordinary development since Gutenberg produced his Bible' (Krotoski, 2010: 28).

And yet more. John Perry Barlow, poet, sometime lyricist of the Grateful Dead and fellow at Harvard University's Berkman Center for Internet and Society, wrote a 'Declaration of the Independence of Cyberspace' in 1995:

> Governments of the Industrial World, you weary giants of flesh and steel, I come from Cyberspace, the new home of Mind. On behalf of the future, I ask you of the past to leave us alone. You are not welcome among us. You have no sovereignty where we gather … Cyberspace consists of transactions, relationships, and thought itself, arrayed like a standing wave in the web of our communications. Ours is a world that is both everywhere and nowhere, but it is not where bodies live … Your legal concepts of property, expression, identity, movement, and context do not apply to us. They are all based on matter, and there is no matter here. (Barlow, 1996)

Technicists admit no bounds to the technology's impact: 'If knowing what we know today [about neuroplasticity, the brain's ability to change in adulthood], you were to set out to invent a medium that would rewire our mental circuits as quickly and as thoroughly as possible, you would probably end up designing something that looks and works a lot like the internet' (Carr, 2010: 116).

No wonder then, that for received opinion: 'The internet, like the steam engine, is a technological breakthrough that has changed the world' (Singer, 2010: 27). 'The digital microchip is the Gothic Cathedral of our time … It will transform business, education and art. It can renew our entire culture' (Gilder, 1985: 15–16).

Or not, as the case may be.

9.3   *Authors Guild Inc., Association of American Publishers Inc. et al. v. Google, Inc.* (2008): Impact

However pervasive the rhetoric, almost all of this can be contested.

Take Nicholas Carr's contention that the internet is rewiring the brain. Neuroplasticity is certainly a reality. Brains can adapt after injury, for example;

and, in less traumatic circumstances, 'temporary synaptic rewiring happens whenever anybody learns anything' (Harris, 2011: 9). This says nothing of what occurs when an otherwise mentally stable person sits at a typewriter looking at a screen (or fingers the screen directly, while walking about). This is, after all, what any internet user actually does. 'Evidence' that the human sensorium is undergoing revolutionary change because of the technology comes from experimental psychology. Carr finds his thesis supported, for example, in the pages of the refereed *American Journal of Geriatric Psychiatry*: 'The authors studied 24 subjects (age, 55–76 years) who were neurologically normal, of whom 12 had minimal Internet search engine experience (Net Naive group) and 12 had more extensive experience (Net Savvy group). The mean age and level of education were similar in the two groups' (Small, Moody, Siddarth and Bookheimer, 2009: 116). Comparing neural activity in the two groups while browsing, the scientists concluded that: 'Internet searching may engage a greater extent of neural circuitry not activated while reading text pages but only in people without prior computer and Internet search experience': in other words, while they were learning the techniques. The psychiatrists also warned that their 'present findings must be interpreted cautiously in light of the exploratory design of this study'. However, in Carr's hands, these twenty-four elderly brains become grist to extreme technicism's hyperbolic mill.

The same hyperbolic tendency informs the debate about the supposedly deleterious effects of 'texting' on the brain. Here, as David Crystal points out, the rhetoric ignores that we have been using unorthodox orthography for years – indeed centuries. All but one of the contemporary texting modes have well-established precedents: emoticons are pictograms and rebuses are equally ancient. Post-printing initialisms, logograms ('b' for 'be', 'c' for 'see') and other contractions and non-standard spellings are also time-honoured: in print 'cos' dates from 1828, 'luv' from 1898. Our civilization has not tottered thus far when we fail to follow every jot and tittle of the lexicographer's rules and (for English) the conventions of eighteenth-century London printers. Crystal is a fan of the ludic use of language and he insists that, without prejudice to any other factors, civilization continues not to totter now because we txt. Only the punning use of unsounded letters – for example 'dn' for *de nada* – is new, btw (Crystal, 2009).

Matching such technophobias about rewired brains and destroyed orthography is the technophiliac myth of the net's uncontrollable incorporality. In 'cyberspace' (no accident that the term should be coined by science-fiction writers), 'there is', as John Perry Barlow poetically insisted, 'no matter'. This is less technicist hyperbole than straightforward obfuscation. As Armand Mattelart correctly observes, twenty-first-century life has shown that 'the supposed weightlessness of virtual communities and of the Net economy provides no protection from reality' (Mattelart, 2005: 140).

The naivety of the vision can be seen in the considerable amount of 'matter' involved in computerized communication. Each central data store run by a search engine company, for example, consumes on a constant basis enough electrical energy to power a small town. Leave aside service providers, computers and computer networking equipment manufacturers are among the largest, wealthiest corporations in the world. They produce solid things – chips, screens, wires, transmitters, metal and plastic boxes. And they create solid gross margins of profit – 40.3 per cent for the Apple Corporation in the first quarter of 2010, for example (Apple, 2010). The conditions of this manufacture are no less exploitative than are other mass production environments. One production company alone, Foxconn, employs around 1.5 million workers to make many of the world's PC brands. Far from technicism's vision of an incorporeal future, this firm and its competitors are something of a throw-back to the oppressors of the Industrial Revolution's first factories. Throughout 2010, conditions at Foxconn's Asian plants engendered an outbreak of copycat suicides which took fourteen lives and caused it to erect barbed-wire safety fences around the roofs of its factories. A Chinese investigation accused the firm of running 'labour camps' (SACOM, 2010). The 'weary giants of flesh and steel' are reinvigorated as titans of flesh and chips.

'Cyberspace', as an embodiment of incorporeal post-modernity, requires such inconvenient echoes of the past be ignored. The continuities of corporate behaviour are not limited to exploitation of the workers, though. The first 'dot. com boom' of 1995–2000 called up the 'Tulip Mania' of the Netherlands in 1634–7. Companies were being capitalized and attracting investment at levels far exceeding market norms. As the American humorist Dave Barry put it at the time: 'the more an Internet company loses the more desirable it becomes to investors. This seems like a paradox, but there's a very logical economic explanation: Internet investors have the brains of grapefruit' (Barry, 1996: 22). Put more soberly, they had the brains of gamblers. The overvalued market collapsed as the century turned. That the internet economy should be subject to normal economic fluctuations would be of little consequence had not the rhetoric claimed it would be otherwise. Business, in fact, was continuing as usual and has continued to do so. Boom follows bust follows boom, just as with the 'old' economy. Massive successes have been balanced by failures.

MySpace, the social networking site popular in the first years of the twenty-first century, with 100 million users, was sold to Rupert Murdoch for $580 million in 2002. By 2009 it was being overtaken by the even more popular Facebook. MySpace was sold on cheap in 2011: Murdoch lost $545 million. Bebo, launched in 2005, was the social site of choice for thirteen to fifteen year-olds within two years. By 2008, it had 40 million users and was sold to AOL for $850 million. Two years after that it was down to 12.5 million and AOL sold it on (Kiss, 2010: 3). Teenage fads are, exactly, 'fads' because they are grown out of as the cohort addicted to them ages; they are also likely rapidly to become 'uncool' anathemas to that original cohort's younger siblings. Fads, electronic or not, are still fads. For one social reason or another, other sites – Friendster, Geocities, Tripod – have suffered a similar fate or been absorbed by ever larger conglomerate internet companies. For all the talk of a 'new way to communicate', the old rules of the market (and of society) applied.

The internet's transformative effect on communications can anyway be questioned, and not just in terms of the performance of the companies involved. Technophiliac opinion argues implicitly that the net had rendered the Braudelian problem of liberty, at least as it applies to free expression, moot. Yet this assertion, as with the 'rewired' brain and the 'new' economy, is not necessarily the case. Contrariwise, it can be argued that the Braudelian brake is being applied as it usually is and the shock of the new technology is being absorbed. Any capacity of the digital for a radical reformulation of expression and the communications infrastructure is, all hyperbole aside, being suppressed. This is, of course, not to deny that change is underway. As ever, it is; but it is evolutionary and not revolutionary. What we are seeing, in the West in the early decades of the twenty-first century, are the processes of containment at work.

Licklider and Taylor were correctly prophetic when they wrote of the interconnected world of computers that communication functions would be transferred to the new machine: 'You will not send a letter or a telegram; you will simply identify the people whose files should be linked to yours and the parts to which they should be linked and perhaps specify a coefficient of urgency. You will seldom make a telephone call; you will ask the network to link your consoles together' (Licklider and Taylor, 1968: 38).

Clearly, this has happened and therefore to be expected is a profound impact on those providing postal and telephonic services. Yet how far is such change characteristic of the rest of communications industry, especially its entertainment-based components?

Perhaps the most pressing dramatic example of the death of old ways of business is the impact of the net as a major distribution system for recorded music. Technicism here has been reinforced by strident cries from the recording industry itself in defence of its copyrights. Peer-to-peer ('P2P') exchange of third-party copyrighted material by 'downloading' was positioned, by the technicists, as a vivid example of the end of old modes of consumption. The industry apparently concurred. That is to say, it agreed – enthusiastically – that it was threatened; but it refused to accept that this was inevitable. In a time-honoured response, it went to law. There the courts also found that considerable damage was being done, which needed to be mitigated in traditional ways. Napster, the first P2P site to achieve widespread publicity, lasted two years, 1999–2001, until it was shut down at law. It took four years to close Napster's successor Limewire, but closed it was in 2010. It had inflicted, said the Manhattan judge, 'irreparable harm' on the record companies

(*Arista Records LLC v. Lime Group LLC*, 2010). Technicism sees such events as evidence of the irresistible challenge of a hydra-headed uncontrollable new distribution system, but actually it is a mere mopping up of a containable situation. Despite downloading, and judicial opinion, the record industry is far from being irreparably harmed.

Leave aside the rising profitability of revived pre-electric modes of music delivery (i.e. live concerts – and ancillary merchandizing), a new business model has enabled paid-for downloads. These, according to UK industry statistics, rose from 17.9 per cent of the total sales in 2004 (the first year) to 95.3 per cent in 2008. The total number of transactions involved over that period also rose – from 5,771,000 to 109,769,000 (BPI, 2009: 20). The point is that the overall revenue throughout this major changeover has remained around £1 billion a year (BPI, 2008: 4). By 2009 paid-for downloads worldwide were worth some $3.7 billion, 90 per cent of which were for music, according to the main international industry body (International Federation of the Phonographic Industry) (Robinson, 2010b: 17). There can be no question that large-scale copyright infringement was (and is) taking place; and that it is illegal; and that copyright, unlike – say – blasphemy, is not a concept lingering on the statute books. It is a live constraint and, in the interest of creativity as much as corporate well-being, it is to be heeded. It is correct to suggest that we are 'in an age of plummeting CD sales' and 'rampant digital piracy' (Topping, 2011: 11). CD sales have certainly collapsed. But the impact of 'rampant' piracy is not as self-evident as the stridency of the rhetoric suggests.

There is good reason to suspect the music industry of constant overstatement (Goldacre, 2009: 16); but, whatever its actual earnings, they are still considerable. There is no reason to believe the record business is going bankrupt, certainly not because of the net. The industry, despite its rhetoric, lives and has lived with piracy for half a century. It used to be that the Recording Industry Association of America (RIAA) complained every disc its members made was illegally copied five times. RIAA was especially vocal after compact audiocassettes were introduced in the early 1960s. Nevertheless, the record industry survived. Its response was the digital compact disc which could not initially be duplicated in the home; consumers, however, were content with illegal analogue copies. The record industry still survived (Winston, 1998: 134–5). Now, consumers – a huge number of them – are content to pay for downloads. The record industry survives. It chases infringers through the courts but it still pockets around £1 billion a year (Harris, 2009: 33).

The film industry is equally strident in its hostility to the net, although the technology, because of the speed of downloading, initially posed somewhat less of an immediate threat. Nevertheless, Pirate Bay, a Swedish site, was offering a searching service allowing users to find, on a P2P basis, copyrighted materials they could then download, using the BitTorrent programme. On offer were, on occasion, features yet to be released. The Swedish court closed

Pirate Bay and the founders were sentenced to a year in prison for copyright infringement (Anderson, 2009: 20).[6] The appeal has gone to Strasbourg. The Motion Picture Association of America (MPAA) claimed that Pirate Bay was costing its members millions, which it might well have been; but what this rhetoric disguises, as with the recording industry, is that film production still earned millions despite any piracy.

From a mid-1980s low, UK box-office numbers, for example, have continued to grow despite the coming of the internet. In 2010, revenue was £998 million, up 5 per cent on the previous year (British Film Institute, 2011: 11). Worldwide, in the age of the World Wide Web, box office has increased from $4.8 billion (1992) to $10.5 billion (2010) (Box Office Mojo, 2011). As for video-recording formats, the collapse in VCR rentals has been more than made up for in DVD sales. In the UK, over the first decade of the century these more than doubled from £878 million to £2,164 million. And, even before the problems of file size and consequent downloading speeds are fully resolved, 'VoD' (video-on-demand and its variants) was already worth £100 million a year in the UK market. Moreover, to facilitate DVD commercial library distribution, the postal service – still in existence – has been utilized by companies to send discs to subscribers. Electronic theft is no doubt costing the industry millions, but it makes billions. Anticipated revenues from all sources are expected to reach $115,000 million a year by 2015, piracy or no (British Film Institute, 2011: 122).

Copyright protection might seem like a measure needed for the urgent resuscitation of nearly deceased media, when seeking it is, rather, the normal exercise of a legally protected right by healthy commercial entities. Films and records are not alone. When the soccer authorities pursue those accessing illegal satellite transmission of games they have otherwise sold to mainstream broadcasters, it is not because their revenues from such sales are actually imperilled. It is, simply, they are legally entitled to take such action and they choose to do so. Currently the English Premier League earns around £1 billion a year from sale of screen rights. Some of this money is used to hire investigators to pursue illegal downloaders. In 2008–9, 90 per cent of some 1,800 UK cases, mainly against publicans, were successfully prosecuted (Robinson, 2009: 21). The actual lost revenue involved is marginal.

Otherwise, because of advertising, broadcasting is, in general, more relaxed than are the music and film industries about new platforms. The economic effectiveness of the media, television and radio, however funded and however delivered, is measured by audience size. Obviously this is crucial for commercial channels but it becomes so for public channels too as a demonstration of their social value. Broadcasters are, of course, interested in protecting secondary and tertiary markets, but it is the attention of viewers and listeners that is being sold to third parties. Therefore, re-broadcasting cannot easily be presented as damaging. For example, theft (as it might be) of through-air broadcasters' signals by the cable television industry in the United States eventually allowed the broadcasters to increase their advertising rate cards. A cable operator was merely another viewer inviting neighbours – albeit thousands of them via a wire which they had to paid for – to watch the off-air programming the operator received. The entire cable system was built on this legal fudge (Parsons, 2008).

All additional 'platforms', as they are now designated, operate similarly. Anyway, overall audience has remained stable, despite the relative decline of the networks in the face of channel proliferation. For example, in 1991, before the net, the British watched television for just over 3.5 hours a day; in 2010, it was four hours (Broadcasters' Audience Research Board, 2011: 1). 'TV,' Ofcom official James Thickett points out, 'still has a central role in our lives', actually boosted by such technological devices as the digital video recorder (Plunkett, 2010: 6). As for radio, in 2010 some 90 per cent of the UK population was still regularly tuning in. Programme providers might rise and fall but that says nothing about overall audience size and, despite revenue fluctuations in line with the general economy, the general health of the medium.

Across all these industries, public willingness to countenance, and indeed indulge in, copyright abuse is no little to do with a sense that the creators – the writers, artists and musicians – are poorly served by the system. Cases where the companies seek hundreds of thousands of dollars compensation from one of their customers encourages many to feel that robbing them is a moral duty. A Robin Hood justification positively encourages copyright theft, although the beneficiaries of stealing from the rich in this case are not the poor artists but the poor thieves. This renders the excuse particularly infantile. The musician, writer or artist may take only cents of every dollar paid to their publishers/ producers and so on, but mass sales ensure their effort is nevertheless economically worthwhile to them. Indeed, it is the need to operate a market for their products, to ensure mass production and/or effective distribution and marketing, that ultimately protects the industries.

For example, in its heyday, MySpace boasted that a couple of million bands used the site to display their talent; but that very number mitigates public success. An economic return requires a presence in the marketplace, not merely a site in cyberspace; and that it what the industries supply. The unknown artist 'discovered' on the net, without their intervention, is largely a further figment of technicist imagining. For one thing, opinion on the net is easily manipulated. In fact, companies exist who will, for a fee, start a cyberspace hare running on a client's behalf: 'viral marketing'. This is often implicated in the social phenomenon of the 'informational cascade' (see Chapter 9.5). Of course, in cyberspace self-publishing is massively facilitated but it is also clear that nobody heeds it much without the intervention of traditional publishers of one species or another. They remain a crucial link between creator and public. Whether or not they are safe from their own managerial incompetence is, of course, another question.

Mismanagement – especially the misreading of public taste, no easy matter in the first place – can be disastrous whatever technologies are involved. The rhetoric around popular music, for example, curiously ignores any question of taste, as if assuming a fairly inelastic demand for the product. The tendency is to attribute all contemporary fluctuations to the digital challenge. However, since the seismic post-war shift that brought rock and roll to prominence in the 1950s, there has been arguably no change of similar magnitude in the mainstream 'product'. Certainly, there is a cultural distance from Elvis Presley, *Billboard*'s artist of the 1950s (via similarly garlanded musicians: the Beatles, 1960s; Elton John, 1970s; Michael Jackson, 1980s; Maria Carey, 1990s), to Eminem, half a century later in the 2000s. But that fifty-year progression can be thought to mark a smaller shift than does the change in taste seen in the single decade between Elvis Presley and Bing Crosby, the biggest recording star of the 1940s.[7] Any argument that Tin Pan Alley has lost its ear in the era of Simon Cowell is hard to make against the cacophony of technicist claims for the impact of the digital.

New platforms mean little new broadcast programme forms, either. The interactivity of dedicated shopping channels (including ones offering a simulacrum of the sale of sexual favours) is at the edge of digital screen genre innovation. (Shopping channels, like the DVD commercial lending library, need a postal service to deliver, in reality, the goods sold. Digital sex involves only virtual 'consumption'.) Otherwise cop-shows persist, aided by computer-generated graphics offering a pornography of the forensic. The news is available, still in its discrete bulletin form, but now endlessly repeated; the contents, on most days, normally changing only very slowly. Reality television brings to the observational and reflexive documentary the persistence of surveillance. In the new century's first decades, 'talent' shows enjoy a moment of prime-time dominance; but the talent-show format is scarce new and, like game shows, its cheapness ensures that the industry will exploit it if it attracts audiences. Of course, there are significant changes: the genre mix changes slowly. Westerns and variety programmes, for example, appear to have long gone the way of minstrel shows. The casual abuse of women for comedic effect is now quite rare. Positively also, there seems to be a measure of acceptance of gay characters, people of colour and a sensitivity to those with 'challenged' conditions. But none of this has much, if anything, do with the digital (except the realism of the forensic).

The persistent success of old media, however, wilts in the face of technicist/industrial hysteria. In the UK, as if the law of copyright were inadequate, Peter, Lord Mandelson introduced a Digital Economy Act[8] in 2010 allowing for the disconnection of persistent copyright offenders from having any provision of internet service – the soccer-match providing publicans, primarily. This was widely seen as draconian, largely unenforceable and arguably, given the reality of these industries, unnecessary. The statute is nothing but technicist hyperbole legalized.

Something of the same case arguing against overstating the impact of new communication modes on older forms can even be made for print. Electronic book publishing for use on specialized reading devices is gathering pace. In the summer of 2010, Amazon US announced that its e-book sales were outstripping conventional sales of hardbacks for the first time. Now a greater sale of e-books than of paperbacks is also being claimed and the common opinion is that: 'where music went first, books are set to follow' (Teather, 2010: 37). As music has not, in reality, gone anywhere (or, not very far, anyway), the publishing industry is likely not to be in too much danger either. At Amazon, e-books might well be triumphant but it can be noted that, according to official industry-wide figures, in 2010, wholesale US e-book revenues, at a healthy $250 million a year, nevertheless only represented 8 per cent of total book sales (International Digital Publishing Forum, 2011; Association of American Publishers, 2011). Forgotten in the hype is that the crucial term in play in Amazon's rhetoric is not 'e-book' but 'sales'.

It is no surprise, though, that, as with the record, film and broadcasting rights industry organizations, the UK Publishers Association (PA) has moved against peripheral exploitation of the technology by public libraries. A third of libraries were already offering e-books by 2010 and the PA was suggesting that this could develop into 'a serious threat to publishers' commercial activities' as people from far-off lands apply for local British library membership (Page and Pridd, 2010: 13). The PA began threatening 'e-book aggregators', the commercial firms providing libraries with e-book distributing potential. Nevertheless, in 2009, the PA's members sold 763 million volumes with an invoice value of just over £3,000 million (Publishers Association, 2011).

E-books are not the only electronic threat, though. Google's seemingly Napoleonic project to digitize all the world's libraries is also concerning – and not just publishers. 'So far, Google has scanned 10 million titles from libraries in America and Europe' (Skidelsky, 2009: 20). This is not quite as revolutionary as it seems at first sight. Google's plan involves the digital capture of all the world's out-of-print books. Titles out of copyright as well as being out-of-print are in the 'public domain' and, apart from the physical effort of scanning them, copying presents no immediate problems. The trouble is a third category that lies between such un-copyrighted works in the public domain and works carrying live copyright. Many of the most attractive and useful titles are out-of-print but not out of copyright, although no commercial activity attaches to them. Often the rights' holders cannot be identified and found. It is these 'orphan works' that have been causing trouble.

Google has represented this entire project, not as an attack on the principle of copyright, but rather as a public service to redistribute these 'orphaned' titles 'for the good of society'. Google's altruistic ambition, in the words of one of its executives, was to 'expand the frontiers of human knowledge' (Skidelsky, 2009: 20). Suffused with these impeccable intentions, Google began copying the 'orphans' without making any formal agreements, beyond library access, to do so.

In 2005, the Authors Guild of America and the Association of American Publishers mounted a 'class action suit'[9] against the company. Google's corporate culture would seem to be firmly anchored in the old adage that: 'it is better to ask forgiveness than permission'. In this case, the asking of forgiveness was to take many, many months of behind-the-scenes, complex (if not, in the opinion of some, incomprehensible)[10] legal wrangling. The tussle eventually produced a 385-page *Google Book Search Settlement*, which the authors' organizations and the publishers signed with Google, subject to US court approval,[11] on 28 October 2008. Google, for an initial cost of $45 million, was to have access to the 'orphans'. Each title was to cost it $60 and it would have to pay more when, and if (these titles being 'orphaned' with therefore often no obvious payee in sight), the $45 million is distributed (Authors Guild Inc., Association of American Publishers Inc., *et al.*, v. Google, Inc., 2008: 2.1[b], 19–20). This was the price of 'forgiveness'.

Others, though, still remained hostile and suspicious seeing Google's good intentions as nothing but a massive 'act of piracy'. The effort was transforming a vast amount of admittedly somewhat inaccessible but nevertheless freely available material into, potentially at least, a proprietary resource belonging to Google. Despite the company's rhetoric, there was the clear possibility that slowly but surely it would restrict access to these texts as it looked for a payback. The settlement, for example, already allowed Google to 'display advertisement on Preview Use Pages and other Online Book Pages' (Authors Guild Inc., Association of American Publishers Inc., *et al.*, v. Google, Inc., 2008: 3.14, 41); and it must not be forgotten that Google's responsibilities to its shareholders require that the company maximizes its profit. Moreover, general opinion was that, although the settlement was for 'Non-Exclusive Digitalization Rights', the de facto effect would be to grant Google a monopoly since no other organization could be expected to undertake putting a rival library of these titles online. Therefore, even without any such threats becoming actual, the agreement was being legally attacked as unsatisfactory. The Federal Department of Justice intervened before the legality of the settlement was finally determined by the court. Like many other critics, the Department of Justice 'believes the settlement raises serious legal issues and has urged the court not to approve it without changes' (Helft, 2009).

The whole business has been represented, like P2P file-sharing, as clear evidence that the new technology has destroyed the old system of copyright. However, far from the technology wrong-footing society, what has been happening is the exact reverse of technicist assumptions: social constraint is being expressed through the agency of the law – specifically the law of copyright. It is that which is determining the nature and pace of the diffusion of the technology – in this case Google's attempted exploitation of digitization's potentials. Society (using, not untypically, the law) is thus actually limiting the disruptive impact of the technology. What is being sought in this tug-of-war is a modus vivendi whereby existing economic interests can be protected against the new technology's depredations.

This is not to say the law of copyright is unproblematic or even that, in general, it is working appropriately. Far from it: copyright is in urgent need of reform – but the problems have nothing to do with technology: 'Once upon a time, three things held true. Copyrights were relatively short. You had to renew them (most people did not). You didn't get one unless you asked. Now none of those holds true and copyright can last for over 100 years. Copyright has exhausted its function yet the works remain trapped in our cultural black hole' (J. Boyle, 2009).

Copyright presents a vexatious challenge to the market, as does patent in general. The function of copyright is to ensure a viable source of income for those involved in the production and dissemination of knowledge by commoditizing intellectual property. On the one hand, creators and distributors of expression need to have their products protected so they can profit by them and live. On the other hand, the greater protection that is afforded to them the greater the long-term constraint on expression. The solution has been to limit the period of the monopoly they can enjoy. The first modern copyright law, enacted in England, claimed to be 'An Act for the Encouragement of Learning, by Vesting the Copies of Printed Books in the Authors or Purchasers of such Copies'. The *Copyright Act* of 1710[12] limited the period of the monopoly to fourteen years. Thereafter copyright lapsed. But the motivation for the act had little to do with the encouragement of learning or the rights of authors and readers. It was designed to regulate trade between publishers and booksellers. The benefit of copyright to the creators of texts was an afterthought to the English. It was, though, being developed in France as '*le Droit d'auteur*', author's rights. *Le Droit* soon crossed the Channel and eventually coalesced into a (more or less) generally agreed concept of intellectual property enshrined in the international Berne Convention for the Protection of Literary and Artistic Works, signed in 1886 and subsequently repeatedly amended. This, of course, did not in any way solve the essential problem. On the contrary: it exacerbated it by making protection universal.

The danger of copyright was well understood, as the historian and politician Lord Macaulay put it in 1841: 'It is good that authors should be remunerated; and the least exceptionable way of remunerating them is by a monopoly. Yet monopoly is an evil. For the sake of the good we must submit to the evil; but the evil ought not to last a day longer than is necessary for the purpose of securing the good' (J. Boyle, 2008: 22).

This caution has been ignored and the 'evil' of monopoly has flourished. So profitable to all parties has it proved to be that the original fourteen years has been extended again and again in jurisdiction after jurisdiction. The result is: 'because the copyright term is now so long, in many cases extending well over a century, most of twentieth-century culture is still under copyright — copyrighted but unavailable. Much of this, in other words, is lost culture. No one is reprinting the books, screening the films, or playing the songs. No one is allowed to' (J. Boyle, 2008: 9).

The lawyer James Boyle points out that some 85 per cent of all books are out-of-print within twenty-eight years of publication. Here, then, is a pressing supervening social necessity. The copyright law is in urgent need of reform. Google has latched on its imperfections as a justification for its actions but the *Book Search Settlement* case should highlight not a technologically determined revolution but, rather, a supervening social necessity – copyright reform. Reform affords Google a very sound social argument in its favour. What the situation does not do, however, is furnish evidence to the technicists that the coming of the digital is forcing a revision of the concept of copyright. The need was there anyway.

The *Book Search Settlement* argument follows the legal suppression of Napster and Pirate Bay. It also echoes all the previous historical instances where diffusion has been held up pending legal outcomes. In every one of these examples, either inside or outside the courtroom, all interested parties – those profiting from the older threatened technologies as well as rival claimants to the innovation – achieve a modus vivendi. The diffusion of telegraphy, cinema, radio, terrestrial television, satellite and cable television, and computing was subjected in every instance to delaying legal rows, cross-patenting agreements, fights around licensing and arguments about standards (Winston, 1998). The *Book Settlement* dispute is no different. That is how suppressive forces operate.

The case of the printed periodical press is significantly different from that of print publishing in general. In fact, the rhetoric fretting about its demise is far more solidly grounded than similar prognostications for all these other media. Nevertheless, however much they are exacerbated by the threat of new technology, the press's difficulties are not primarily technological in origin. Of all the established 'old' media, newspapers are currently in the most dire straits – although, even here, the straits are somewhat less dire than is popularly believed.

Certainly circulations have been shrinking but this was happening for decades prior to the arrival of the net. In this decline, arguably, broadcasting has played a greater role than the digital; but, it has been cultural factors that are the main cause. Simply, the press is returning to its pre-nineteenth-century roots: a mode of communication for the elite. The nineteenth-century newspapers' effective expansion to reach the masses is what is being rolled back most as the masses turn to other sources of news – or ignore them altogether.

Decline is everywhere. In the thirty-five years from the end of the Second World War to 1980, for example, Parisian papers were reduced from thirty-one to nine. In Germany 134 titles disappeared leaving 121; in Denmark more than two-thirds died. In the United States, most communities can now support only one paid-for title. Manhattan's fourteen twentieth-century newspapers are reduced to three. Basically, the nineteenth-century popular press has been disappearing, despite the industry's continued technical development.

The final stage of mechanization had been achieved with the 'Line-o-type' hot-metal typesetting machine of 1886. From 1889 on, photography, using rotogravure presses, became a standard feature. From 1905, as an alternative to hot-metal, complete pages of made-up images and texts were 'offset' on single rubber-sheets for printing. In the later part of the century, computing was absorbed, but slowly. In part this was because computers were no more welcome to the press than they were elsewhere. Nevertheless the Linotype machines were almost entirely replaced by them. The link between metal and print was finally widely broken by the end of the 1970s. Design became visually more flamboyant, slip editions and special sections proliferated. A combination of computing and satellite transmission, for example, allowed for multiple distant printing sites simultaneously to produce the United States' first national newspaper, *USA Today*. It was launched by the Gannett chain in 1982.

Despite all this, within the industry, the profounder impact was on the worker rather than on the product. The printers who, together with the miners and brewers, were the world's oldest organized labour force, resisted the destruction of their craft. At the *Chicago Times* as early as 1947, the International Typographical Union, the United States' oldest labour union, had struck for nearly two years against the introduction of a primitive photo-compositing process (Weiss, 2000: 107). The London *Times*, site of the country's first steam-driven presses in 1813, was closed down for nearly a year over a more advanced version of the technology in 1978. Overnight in 1986, Rupert Murdoch, echoing John Walter II in 1813 (see Chapter 4.5), moved the printing of his papers to new presses in Wapping – presses run by electricians not printers. The threat to labour was palpable; but so was the decline in advertising and circulation. The workers' skills were no protection. Murdoch's profits after the changeover rose 40 per cent but, ultimately, circulation and advertising shrinkage persisted. Between 1950 and 1970, the UK daily press lost two million sales a day, the Sundays and the locals suffering even more. After 'Wapping', the decline continued more or less unabated. Between 2007 and 2009, it shrank by 21 per cent. In the United States over these three years the decline was even more propitious: 47 per cent (Organisation for Economic Co-operation and Development, 2010: 30).

Falls elsewhere have not been quite so steep. Across most of Europe and in Mexico, Korea and Australia, for example, recent declines have been held to under 10 per cent. Despite all this, a rhetorical overstatement of the same kind as can be seen with the other media should be also avoided here. Even with newspapers, the business is still far from insignificant. Currently, in Japan, 556 copies are sold for every 1,000 of the population, the world's highest penetration. In the United States, the figure is only 160. Nevertheless, this means a total US circulation of 49 million (as opposed to Japan's 51 million) (Organisation for Economic Co-operation and Development, 2010: 33). Only eleven dailies of some 1,400 US titles have closed in recent years (Preston, 2010a: 39). Newsprint's travails can therefore also be overstated to a certain extent, but they have a greater reality than the supposed difficulties of the other 'old media'. For one, the industry has yet to unlock a widely accepted payment method for electronically delivered content.

For all that printed news is clearly hard-pressed (and has been so for rising half-a-century), for the old media as a whole the digital glass remains at least half-full. The terms of trade have changed as a consequence of the digital but the underlying social needs those modes of expression met have not. Close-up, any change looms large; distance (and some regard for the statistics) is needed for perspective. Absent technicism with its addiction to 'progress' and the faux cries of pain coming from the industries – and the information 'revolution' dwindles into (albeit significant) evolutionary change.

9.4 *Daily Herald v. Sun* (1964): Convergence

The first online newspaper, the *Palo Alto Weekly*, began in 1994 and *USA Today* erected the first pay-wall in 1998, but the more extreme predictions of digital's revolutionary impact on newspapers have not been met (Organisation for Economic Co-operation and Development, 2010: 27). 'Instead of reading what other people think is news and what other people justify as worthy of the space', the net, according to Nicolas Negroponte, could allow for personalized, customised news (Negroponte, 1996: 153). This idea came to be called 'The Daily Me' but it has yet to materialize. Negroponte misunderstood not the technology, which clearly could deliver his vision, but the totality of the press's social functions. Mass newspapers reflect the taste of their readers for titillation and entertainment but they also, crucially, in so doing retail information, establishing hegemonic agendas of social concern and interest. To ignore the press's agenda-setting role in the social sphere is, exactly, to ignore what is not, and cannot be in the nature of the case, personal.

Let us put the failure, thus far, of 'The Daily Me' into context. Such slippage from technical potential to social improbability is not uncommon in technicist prophesying. Even astute observers such as Licklider and Taylor can meld a predication grounded in an understanding of social uses with a vision that misreads social realities. For example, they correctly saw the net's ability to replace the post, telegram and telephone but took a step too far when they went on: 'You will seldom make a purely business trip, because linking consoles will be so much more efficient' (Licklider and Taylor, 1968: 38). The error here is to assume that business trips were often 'pure'; for those allowed to escape their offices, efficiency was not necessarily the overriding consideration. Business travel persists, more sensitive to economic conditions than computer capacities.[13]

As the social construction of news reflects the societal need for shared agenda and this need persists, so too will the current concept of the newspaper, however its contents are delivered, persist. Papers are certainly floundering as they seek a business model to make downloading economically viable (Preston, 2010b: 49). Nevertheless: 'The net impact of new technology [has been] modest' (Curren and Seaton, 2009: 94). Hence no 'Daily Me'. It is a condition of technicist thinking to offer predictions blind to social realities and concepts which cannot bear the weight of social significance imputed to them (e.g. the end of business travel or 'The Daily Me').

The concept of 'convergence', however it is glossed and however much it is hyperbolized, is another good example this.

At a fundamental level, convergence simply means a common modulation system for both audio and video signals. However, transducing sound and light waves into electrical impulses digitally does not so alter them so that they will no longer be perceived, separately, by the human ear and eye. Despite 'rewiring the brain' assertions from Marshall McLuhan's belief that we 'see' television differently to contemporary ideas about the supposedly deep significance of the 'pixel' and so on, the eye and the ear remain where the current level of *Homo sapiens*' evolution has left them – discrete, with separate organs able to decode sound waves between 20 and 20,000 Hz (ears) and light waves up to 50 cycles per degree (CPD) (eyes).[14] As long as modulation – whatever form it takes – remains within these parameters, the signal will be seen and heard. The radio remains a radio even if its function is within a box which also houses a television – and a calculator, a camera, a clock, a recorder, a telephone and so on. Cohabitation does not mean osmosis for any of these applications; nor does it create synaesthesia in the human receiver. The move to digital (i.e. pulse code modulation) is more like the previous changeover from amplitude to frequency modulation than the one from radio to television. Claiming greater significance for convergence at this level invites disbelief.

'Convergence', however, does not only imply a technologically naive understanding of the digital, which mistakenly sees it as some sort of '0/1' Morse code and ignores the difference between hearing and seeing. It is also used to describe the phenomenon of multimedia institutions, both public and private, with interests in what were previously discrete areas of economic activity. Again, the impact of technology in this can be disputed, such 'convergence' being far more a consequence of late capital than of science. Assuming technology is the cause of the phenomenon is little more than a cover for neo-liberal enthusiasms. It expresses a further confusing technicist trope, namely that beyond the norms of capitalism, there is a convergence of media consequent on digitization which, in effect, makes the international media conglomerate inevitable. It is asserted that technological changes are *driving* different publishing, broadcasting, filmmaking, telephony, computing, cable and satellite companies together. Rupert Murdoch and his fellows are, by this reading, a species of victim. 'Convergence' is forcing them, as it were, to media cross-ownership dominance. Actually, concentration has nothing to do with technology but has its roots in the nineteenth-century industrialization of the businesses of expression – chains of theatres as well as chains of newspapers, subsequently also reflected in film factories, cinema chains and networks of broadcasting stations. Clearly, this undercuts – destroys, even – the fundamentals of a 'marketplace of ideas', amplifying the speech of the few and silencing the majority. Such media structures have long been a dangerously distorting factor.

Regarding newspapers in the UK, for example, 60 per cent plus of weekday circulation has been controlled by no more than three entities almost constantly since the end of the Second World War. It is possible to talk of the 'fable of market democracy' at work (Curran and Seaton, 2009: 73). More than any technological development, the rise of advertising as a crucial enabler of media expression has been slowly killing off the range of opinion on offer ever since the mid-nineteenth century. For example, the *Daily Herald* had been founded in Britain by the Trade Union Congress (TUC) in 1912 in the aftermath of a printers' strike (occasioned by their general work conditions rather than any particular technological threat). The TUC was moved to get into the publishing business to balance the press barons' blanket hostility to organized labour. The *Herald*'s massive success in the 1930s, however, was not sustained after the Second World War. By then in private ownership, it was rebranded as the *Sun* but to no great effect. By 1964, it was losing £1 million a year and was sold on to Rupert Murdoch, in the process becoming a raucous, right-wing tabloid.

At the moment of the *Herald*'s collapse it had a circulation of 1.25 million, five times that of London *Times*; but this readership – characterized as male, elderly, northern, poor – was unattractive to advertisers (Curran and Seaton, 2009: 84). Cover price alone had not been enough to finance running a paper in Britain as it had not been since the era of the *News of the World*'s foundation. It was certainly not enough to do so in late twentieth century.

That the market might not fulfil the social requirement of a free press to reflect a variety of interests had caused some European states, in direct contravention of the logic behind the US First Amendment, to intervene to protect the range of – at least – mainstream political opinion and maintain a diversity of titles. Italy, France, Austria, Sweden, Finland and Norway used tax money for this purpose. More generally, special postage rates, tax breaks and the close attention of anti-monopoly authorities have been widespread. Nevertheless, despite such efforts at ensuring plurality, convergence in this sense of concentration of ownership persists. Prior to the triumph of neo-liberalism we were more alert to this problem; but, in consequence of that triumph, now only some would see a deepening difficulty (Garton Ash, 2011: 33).

Concentration is a problem but it is not a technological one. It is exacerbated by media cross-ownership; but the tendency for established media to acquire interests in new potential rivals also dates back early into the last century: to the newspapers that obtained radio licences in the United States in the 1920s. Some publishers essayed forays into film newsreel production, too. The barrier to the further development of multimedia entities was primarily not the lack media technological diversity but the understanding that plurality of ownership was a democratic necessity. Beyond the general hostility to monopoly, constraining the size of media companies was a particular requirement built in to the control of new media.

For example, before the neo-liberal assault on American broadcast regulation, the Federal Communications Commission operated a straightforward regime. It would not award any organization more than seven licences for stations operating in a given segment of the market: seven television stations, seven FM radio stations and seven AM radio stations. And, after 1975, no publishers (which included many of the pioneering radio licensees of the 1920s) were allowed a broadcasting licence in any of the top twenty markets (i.e. cities) where they also owned a newspaper. It is, of course, naive to suggest that this simple sort of regulation ensures a plurality of views. Any company owning twenty-one broadcast licences (plus perhaps a network) and as many newspapers and other print titles as it desires and, increasingly, subsidiaries operating new media such as the internet (and old, e.g. billboards) is likely to share a worldview with other companies doing likewise. Nevertheless, it is some measure of brake and, as such, it has been dismantled.[15] First the newspaper/broadcast station restriction was removed. Ownership rules were further relaxed in 2002. The result is that Clear Channel, the United States' biggest radio station owner, now has 1,200 licences – all serviced, more or less the whole time, remotely by satellite at the expense of any localism. Rupert Murdoch has twenty-seven FCC licenses, as well as a television network, cable TV, film studio, newspapers, publishers and 'next generation media properties'.[16] In Britain, it can be argued that it was deregulation under Thatcher that sowed the abuses of Hackgate. It was this that allowed Murdoch to become such an overweening power.

The rationale behind the removal of the rules was the shibboleth that 'relaxation' would increase competition, but it should come as no surprise that it has done the opposite. The removal of ownership limitations has enabled not only further concentration of ownership. It has also allowed over-powerful voices to threaten evermore overtly the speech of others. These did so already, of course, but removing licensing and other regulatory restrictions and allowing a free market across all media exacerbated the danger to democracy of dominant voices.

Faced now with a growing concentration of a few ever-larger multimedia conglomerates, the FCC, for example, has sought to contain them not by straightforward ownership restrictions but by a more complex system of audience limitation: audience share measurement. As mentioned briefly, they introduced weighted measures of the average tendency of consumers to find news across all channels, whatever the medium, however delivered, including newspapers and magazines. Sanctions for exceeding limits include fines and closure. The system proved unworkable and the news content measure was abandoned. Now a company is allowed up to 45 per cent of total audience reach, measured by the usual somewhat crude means, in any given market and nationally. Audience ratings are weighted against circulation figures and other measures. A census is taken every four years, but organizations are permitted to break the rules in terms of both local outlet ownership and national audience shares on a case-by-case basis; and they do. Moreover, between the quadrennial censuses, there are repeated rows – the FCC v. the licensees v. the audience measurement firms. The rationale is to limit power but, of course, measures in no way indicate actual influence. The irrationality of assuming that all media are equal, that all indications of use (even when weighted) are equivalent and that all data are sound is ignored. Anyway, the whole concept is fundamentally anti-democratic in that it penalizes, at least in theory, popular success. To run a dominant channel in any one medium is to invite the loss of other platforms.

Although the actual means of managing the communications infrastructure is a complex and controversial business, the liberal state does have a legitimate 'allocative' function in limiting concentration (Fiss, 1996: 26). This has nothing to do with content regulations as in, say, current Ofcom practice. That can be held to be *au fond* illegitimate and, anyway, it says nothing to the maintenance of plurality. Exercising the allocative function is by contrast both legitimate and necessary. That is to say, the state's allocative function can be legitimately exercised in a democracy at the level of ownership limitations but any other constraints are flawed. Exercise of the allocative function is least problematic where the technological infrastructure demands a measure of control (for example, broadcasting spectrum management); but it equally applies, for fundamental democratic reasons, to all platforms, irrespective of technological considerations. As Owen Fiss puts it: 'sometimes we must lower the voices of some to hear the voices of others'. Society is not, self-evidently, 'one gigantic town meeting' where opposing viewpoints, rationally expressed, contend to gain democratic approval. For Fiss, such an optimistic vision is so unrealistic as to be ultimately undemocratic exactly because the speech of one can 'silence' in some way or another the speech of others (Fiss, 1996). His desire to redress this is unimpeachable, but the problem persists – who lowers what voices and how?

Doing so on the basis of audience measurement can be said to be, in reality, impossible of performance except in an artificial and ultimately illogical, unfair fashion – better, perhaps, just to counteract convergence by limiting concentration of ownership. The owners of the platforms of expression should choose their medium. Ownership constraint can be justified because of the privileges of speech. It can be argued that this is great enough to remove the other privileges, such as those of the marketplace to acquire all that one can afford, so that those wishing to own organs of opinion need choose the medium in which to operate. Carrier functions – the wires, transmission masts, satellites, access provision of any kind – can be separated from production functions if ownership of one prohibits ownership of the other. Counter arguments as to economy of scale are essentially special pleading for conglomerate status – even for the conglomerate status of publicly funded organizations such as the BBC. Speaking truth to power, producing innovative and quality media (including innovative, quality popular media) requires integrity, talent and easy access to the public to ensure, one way or another, funding. The scale of the producing entity has little to do with this. The model of the press agency or the broadcast network allows for the dispersion of editorial and content control without a diminution of effectiveness. The consumer marketplace in any given medium might – should – be permitted to operate even if popularity creates dominant entities or, conversely, unpopularity causes demise. At worst, dominance would be limited to the one medium.

After all, democracy survived the BBC monopoly from the Licence and Charter (1927) to the Television Act (1954). The monopoly had been created, and was only preserved, by the state; and it was broken by the state, too. Others had been ready to broadcast from the outset, had they been allowed. Print news-sources have always proliferated. Social pressure has ensured more than one stage or one screen exists. Vertical integration has been resisted (as when the Hollywood studios were divested of their cinema chains by the Supreme Court in 1948). Transmission function has been split (as when an independent terrestrial television transmission company was created during the high-tide of British neo-liberalism in 1990). Satellite broadcasters do not own the satellites they use for broadcasting. The phone company, since its unhappy flirtation with US radio station ownership in 1927, has never provided content. The web presents a mosaic of owners. In the interests of democracy, a general prohibition of cross-media chaebols would not be an unprecedented example of the state's allocative function. Despite the hyperbole, there is no more a technological necessity driving a Murdoch to acquire media businesses than there is a technological reason for a Richard Branson to own cable and satellite TV channels, phone companies *and* a railway, an airline, a bank and some 395 other businesses. Concentration is certainly a problem but it is not one caused by the new technology.

In sum, then, media technology is not driving media concentration. And, this apart, the technology is, in fact, being constrained, its radical potential suppressed. It is not effecting revolutionary changes of habit, is not creating new forms of expression, is not destroying old media; or, at least, is not doing so at anything like the rates and levels being hyperbolically suggested.

9.5   *Julian Assange v. the World* (2010): The technicist illusion of freedom

This, though, is not say that new media technology requires no attention as far as freedom of expression is concerned. It is, rather, to insist that it requires no attention beyond the application of the harm principle. In fact, it poses the same problems of liberty as do the old media. That the new technology does harm certainly cannot be ignored. There is no question that the net, as presently organized, has a propensity to exacerbate the old dangers of harmful expression; nor does it, concomitantly, ensure free communication sufficient to balance and justify any enhanced capacity for damage. The net is no technology of freedom, as is becoming ever clearer. Its accessibility is no free good. Nor, for all the yelps of the masters of the internet and their technicist supporters, is there more reason to suppose that its negatives are uncontrollable than to believe in its supposed revolutionary impact. Prognostications of disaster for free expression unless the net-providers enjoy untrammelled freedom are no more convincing than are those of the newspaper proprietors resisting the application of the harm principle to their industry. That though, of itself, is no reason for special modes of control.

The internet is as much a tool of repression as of liberation. Leave aside states outside of the West, by 2011, the twenty-six governments of the world's most developed states (which include, of course, all the democracies) were making on average ninety demands a month each for information from Google. (In the East access is, simply, restricted or even withdrawn entirely, but that is not here the concern.) There are now some thirty-three organizations dedicated to specific censorship tasks. In Britain, the model has been the British Board of Film Classification. The Internet Watch Foundation is, like the BBFC, funded by the industry concerned but with some public responsibilities. It is also responsive but instead of classifying material presented to it by distributors, it reacts to alerts from the public about sites showing child pornography and abuse. Founded in 1996, because of the dominance of the companies funding it, who agree to abide by its decisions, it can block 95 per cent of UK users. In 2007, some 34,000 URLs were submitted and 3,000 'potentially illegal' sites were taken down. Its actions are unobtrusive as closed sites are marked: 'page cannot be found', not 'page has been censored' (Bland, 2008: 30). The system, of course, leaks as it is responsive rather than active, restricted by subject and by the national base. Yet it and its fellow national organizations are more limited by Hamilton's 'general spirit' than by any technical constraint.

The claims of cyber-freedom were, of course, grounded in naivety from the outset. Any nodal network has, in the nature of the case, nodes that can be controlled, however much the net is 'distributed'. Original libertarian enthusiasms have come to be balanced by the censorious dreams of previously unimaginable levels of surveillance and control. Nevermind the prevalence of pornography, hate speech or other deleterious forms of free expression – they present no new problems for all their pervasiveness and uploading can be located or, if not, material can be taken down and thus prohibited. Although this use is only being suggested outside the West (Shah, 2011: 37), any single word in any communication – site, blog, text, email – is now traceable, its use recordable and storable. 'Newspeak' embodied George Orwell's dystopian vision of the totalitarian state with omnipresent surveillance TV where a thought such as 'We hold these truths to be self evident ...' could be only expressed with the one-word 'crimethink' (Orwell, 2008 [1949]: 325). The net makes this nightmare possible – type in, say, 'liberty', 'freedom', 'Tibet', 'sex' ... whatever ... and up will pop: 'CRIMETHINK' with a knock at the door to follow.

Information revolution rhetoric has created the false impression that cyberspace was a private realm whose occupants could easily remain safe from such oversight, their privacy completely protected behind an anonymity that kept their true identities hidden. The evidence that this is far from reality has been rapidly accumulating. Identities are largely known to the providers of the services they use. Indeed, the data collection capacity of the system occasioned worries from the outset. Selling data on as a marketing tool has a blatant commercial attractiveness, but whenever the trade in it is highlighted, it is seen as a somehow illegitimate invasion of privacy. Many, including those responsible for administering data protection regimes, are ignorant of what is permissible and what is not (L. Edwards, 2009: 473). Interactions on the net are held to be a species of correspondence and as such are, to use the words in Article 8 of the ECHR, to be 'respected' as part of 'private and family life'. But, again, ever since the Supreme Court initially failed to see wiretapping as an invasion of privacy (*Olmstead v. United States*, 1928), there has been confusion about electronic 'correspondence'.

The concept of privacy is culturally determined and has an historic dynamic. Within the West, it is as much a consequence of rooms connected by corridors and domestic running water as it is the result of taboos. That is why when the Supreme Court came to rethink *Olmstead* in 1960, it still considered the physical aspect of privacy was pertinent. It was that the complainant had closed the door of his telephone kiosk that, in part, meant it was illegal for the FBI to have eavesdropped his call (*Katz v. United States*, 1967).

The rhetoric of Article 8, however, is a further reflection of the rising tide of sensitivity to each individual's feeling which, in a closed loop, can now embrace a sense of incorporeal violation. Yet the sharing of much 'private' information is, by the standards of the harm principle, comparatively harmless. With most people, retailing knowledge of consumption habits, as long as these do not of themselves embrace illegality, does no, or little, material damage. Scandals about this smack of a moral panic. Google's data-hoarding, as much as its presence in countries with repressive regimes, turned its informal 'Don't be evil' motto into a hostage to fortune, even before the company made a fortune. Facebook was embroiled in a row about its privacy policy, such as it is. By 2011, Apple was, despite the outpouring of grief occasioned by Steve Jobs' death, not immune from this negativity either: 'Forget Google – it's Apple that is turning into the Evil Empire' (Naughton, 2011: 36).

On the other hand, uploading thought and opinion can damage the 'speaker', which is improper in a democracy. 'Talk' should never endanger 'speakers'. If cyberspace is, as may well be the case, not capable of being 'private' then the danger is real. In a toxic brew of technicism and probabilistics, an English judge managed to sentence two easily found perpetrators in their twenties to four years in jail for texting invitations to join a riot to which nobody responded (Davies, 2011: 17). Sheriff Elizabeth Munro sentenced two even younger men in Dundee for three years for posting, on Facebook, notification of a 'riot in the toon'. She said this constituted 'one of the worst breaches of the peace I have ever had to deal with'. There was no rioting in Scotland (Carrell, 2011: 16). Such blatant sentencing unrestraint has seldom been seen in a crown court since the era of transportation for minor theft; but the context was the general rioting of August 2011. The sentences were also, presumably, informed by the received understanding of the power of the net. Obviously, in the mind of the Recorder of Chester, His Honour Judge Elgan Edwards, DL, and Sheriff Munro, this meant that there was a clear and present danger that the communication on Facebook would incite civil disorder. It was irrelevant that it did not. That it was, in fact, evidence of the limits of the supposed power of new media did not detain them.

In another Facebook case, under the UK Malicious Communications Act,[17] an equally easily identified man with Asperger's syndrome was jailed for eighteen weeks and ordered off the social sites for five years because of abuse of Facebook 'tribute' pages. Tributes to tragically dead teenagers had been appearing, which he had crudely mocked to the further distress of their families and friends (Morris, 2011: 9). Nothing prevents such action being taken except police and prosecution inattention and such incivility has occasioned further cases.

Moreover, internet companies can be forced to reveal the identity of subscribers to authorities of all kinds. This, though, is not to argue for anonymity. Anonymity, a creature of corporate policy rather than technology, has been a root cause of the prevalent incivility of social cyberspace. It was not supposed to be so. Amitai Etzioni, backed by the Ford Foundation, essayed using cable television to encourage communitarian participatory democracy in the late 1960s (Mattelart, 2005: 100). This was occasionally tried with two-way community-access cable TV channels, for instance in Reading, Pennsylvania (Moss, 1978). On the emerging net, the very first open forum, 'Communititree', was also set up in the 1970s by technicist communitarian utopians. It was immediately trashed, destroyed by the angry incivility of hostile users: 'the story has become almost folkloric among new-media prophets, a sort of founding myth' (Adams, 2011: 13). The failure did not, though, halt a proliferation of sites subject to such abuse. Anonymity is a crucial facilitator of social network bullying. However, harassment by such means – 'trolling' – can be illegal and anonymity need be no bar to perpetrators being identified.

Cyberspace is, indeed, a public space. In 2007, the University of Oxford proctors disciplined students they had identified as misbehaving from posts on Facebook (L. Edwards, 2009: 477). That the students were unreasonably confident that cyberspace was a private domain did not make it so. Even if the internet user seeks anonymity it is hard to find. It can be removed as easily as sites can be censored. A British local government council successfully forced Twitter in a Californian court, for example, to reveal the identity of an anonymous critic it wished to sue for defamation (Halliday and Green, 2011: 25). The anonymity of a British policeman whose candid blog, *NightJack*, on life as a working detective took the prestigious Orwell Prize for political writing in 2009, was removed by the court. Mr Justice Eady said: 'Blogging is essentially a public rather than a private activity' and Detective Constable Richard Horton had 'no reasonable expectation of privacy' (Jones and Hirsch, 2009: 3). His Honour was not even considering the possibility of hacking. Subsequently it was revealed that Horton had indeed been uncovered by illegal electronic eavesdropping by *The Times* (another Murdoch title) (Leigh, 2012a: 7), and, moreover, the paper's lawyer claimed (before the Leveson Inquiry) not to know that this was illegal (Green, 2012: 15). Much harassment and bullying, of course, anyway lacks the sophistication to attempt disguise and it is a simple matter – although not entirely without costs – to require internet service providers to yield the names of subscribers in the case of libel, harassment and bullying or invasion of privacy generally. Rhetoric claiming the contrary is increasingly threadbare.

In fact, in some jurisdictions, the search for perpetrators has been avoided in favour of denying the internet service provider common carrier protection.

Three US Google executives have been convicted of illegally invading the privacy of a minor in Italy and given six month suspended sentences *in absentia*. For two months in 2006, Google's Italian operation had failed to take down a video showing bullies abusing an autistic child, although they did so within three hours of being approached by the Italian police. The United States instantly complained about the judgment as the company protested that the prior clearance required to avoid future problems was complex, costly and so on; but here is an easy key to controlling abuse (Hooper, 2010: 1). It could be made the price of doing business, which providers such as Google would be hard-pressed to suggest they could ill-afford. Also, a process that held them liable for all anonymous communications would surely staunch the main flow of harmful posts. Newspapers, after all, have fulfilled a public right-to-know function for centuries while refusing to publish anonymous letters: or, if anonymity is legitimate, publishing but with the format 'name and address supplied'. The net could be no different.

There are lesser problems consequent on open access. High-profile sites are always subject to vandalism. Wikipedia's polders of information, the massive labour of its 'digital sharecroppers' (Finklestein, 2008: 2), are vulnerable. Although error-prone well beyond the traditional inevitability of printed mistakes, it is one of the ten most visited sites on the net and, despite shortfalls, a useful starting point for much desk research. Such integrity as it can muster is protected by volunteers guarding their own work and others. For these 'Wikipedians', the enterprise is a species of rather embattled hobby. Entries containing statistics, in particular, are a popular target for the spoilers. However, the Wikipedia Foundation is not without resource. A thousand of the Wikipedians have the power to 'revert' changes and block access to users entering deliberately misleading information. These 'administrators' (or 'admins') are prepared to undercut the site's own philosophy and act as censors. Theresa Knott, a British school teacher, is one with this power: 'The rules are whatever we say they are and we won't stick to our own rules if they are bad for Wikipedia' (Kleeman, 2007: 15). Milton in his censoring phase centuries earlier could not have put it better.

Censors, of course, are not having things their own way. It is without question more difficult to keep secrets in the age of the internet but this is, again, the result of more than just technology. For one thing, the state has a propensity to designate more and more information secret, making it that much harder to guard. Freedom of information, an outcrop of the general drift towards egalitarianism, plays a role, too.

The net facilitates exposures, but these happened on occasion before it appeared. It is forty years since Daniel Ellsberg, who worked in the heart of the military/industrial complex at the RAND Corporation, passed what came to be known as 'The Pentagon Papers' to the *New York Times*. He spent years searching for a publisher but when the *Times* eventually stepped up to the plate, Ellsberg and the paper were careful to redact the materials so that none were in fact harmed. Nor actually was the government, despite charging Ellsberg with sedition (see Chapter 11.6).

WikiLeaks was launched in 2006 as an 'untraceable and uncensorable' secure site for the publishing of secrets which would maintain the anonymity of whistleblowers, spies and informants of all kinds. It was not the first of such sites but it soon came to prominence by publishing a leaked procedures manual for Camp Delta at Guantánamo Bay and then a document detailing the kleptocratic activities of the family of Daniel arap Moi, sometime Kenyan president. It was, however, a third exposé in 2008 that secured its worldwide iconoclastic reputation and highlighted the issue of censorship on the net. WikiLeaks released a list of a Swiss bank's clients and their assets. The bank moved against the still 'shadowy' organization, obtaining an injunction from a Californian court. This ordered a local domain-name company which was carrying WikiLeaks to remove access to it – which it promptly did. Carriers' legal vulnerability had not been previously demonstrated and that providers could be attacked with such consequences shocked liberal technicist opinion. The organization using the carrier was shadowy no longer.

The driving force behind WikiLeaks was revealed as a traveller and journalist named Julian Assange. 'He's a pretty standard modern geek with a thing about dissidents,' Ben Laurie, a member of WikiLeaks' advisory board, told the *Guardian*. Assange was interested in 'deniable cryptography': 'He's quite a techie and can write code.' But, said Laurie, 'if my life were on the line, I would not be submitting to WikiLeaks' (Leigh and Franklin, 2008: 32). Assange raised the stakes in autumn 2010 not, significantly, by publishing electronically. Instead, he enlisted the *Guardian*, the *New York Times*, *Der Spiegel* and *Le Monde* to run a wide but careful selection of a large cache of US diplomatic cables he had come by. This ensured maximum publicity but, as with 'The Pentagon Papers', also involved redaction to protect vulnerable names – identifiable informants, for example.

Assange, however, was dissatisfied with this caution and, a year later, dumped the entire load, all 251,000 texts, on to the net, unredacted (Ball, 2011: 21). Flushed with cyber-freedom enthusiasms and unaware of how tarnished these were becoming, Assange was clearly unconcerned about the harm principle. The vulnerable informants were all lackeys of the American empire and he was reported as saying 'they deserved what was coming to them'. That was, in essence, his defence to harm-principle charges, but not all could agree that informing on repressive regimes and elements within them to whomever was as clearly morally reprehensible as Assange implicitly claimed. The harm was palpable; at best serious embarrassment frustrating progress as in the Middle East or, worse, real personal danger for individuals, as in Afghanistan. At least one Ethiopian journalist had to flee the country (N. Cohen, 2011: 43).

As has been repeatedly the case throughout the supposed information revolution, the incident was being heralded as clear evidence that the technology had changed the world. State privacy, like an individual's privacy, was no longer possible. However, it can be asked if the WikiLeaks were more significant than 'The Pentagon Papers' had been? Ellsberg had intended to stop the Vietnam War, but the war continued. He failed. The extent to which Assange's leaks, with no such coherent objective, impacted and damaged American foreign policy is questionable. The revelations, unfocused, were breathtakingly banal: diplomats were rude about the nations in which they served, we learned. Of course, this threw a spotlight on the limitations of mainstream media coverage of such topics as US–Pakistan relations, but the information was mainly stale and, in almost all instances, had no visible repercussions – certainly not in the State Department (Lashmar, 2011). Max Frankel, the *New York Times*' Washington bureau-chief who facilitated the publication of 'The Pentagon Papers', considered that with the Assange revelations: 'there are few facts or observations in these leaks that an American official would not confide to a respected journalist' (Frankel, 2010: 36). The notion that diplomats were less than polite and less well-informed than they would like to represent themselves as being was scarcely news. 'Loathing for Mr Assange,' wrote veteran investigative reporter Bruce Page, 'arises in horrid panic: might our politicians, faced with evidence that diplomacy and espionage as conducted are largely useless, stop paying the bills?' (Page, 2011: 24). It is just over four centuries since Sir Henry Wotton observed that a diplomat, such as himself, was '*vir bonus peregre missus ad mentiendum Respublicae causa*' ('an honest man sent to lie abroad for the good of his country') (Wotton, 1672 [1604]: xii). That he, and now she too, were continuing so to behave was scarce surprising.

The vulnerability of the network in general to surveillance is not widely understood. On the contrary, technicism has been nowhere more successful than in fostering a false belief in cyber-freedom and the safe anonymity that supposedly underpins it. In reality, it is as vulnerable as any other mode of communication, from the mail through to the telephone. The imprisoned Bradley Manning, the quickly traced 'lowly army clerk' who was charged with being Assange's treasonous source, now knows to this his cost. Assange's system was far from 'untraceable and uncensorable'.

If anything, the citizenry's danger of exposure persists with the new communication modes. Attempted legislative control of improper invasion dates back into the nineteenth century (Rahofer, 2009: 556); but a determined state, even a democracy, can and will intrude. The net's negative impact on the individual's right to be protected from intrusion into thought and opinion is considerable. Legal naivety about technology is no help. The state's enhanced technologically based capacity for surveillance, coupled with its failure clearly to conceptualize 'electronic trespass', balances any increase in the individual's freedom of expression.

Cyberspace is currently actually no more private than the street. This, though, has not been acknowledged in the restless search for proof of an information revolution. Civil disorders – for the most part tragically ineffective – against repressive regimes have become the unlikely source of stories persistently proclaiming the power of the internet. The internet's openness to invasion of privacy, however, militates against its potential as a subversive tool for undermining oppression. Nevertheless, Twitter has been hailed as the latest weapon in the revolutionary struggle.

This assertion was grounded, like other overstated claims for the technology, in the misapplication of serious scholarly analysis. In this case, it was the examination of the growth of protest in East Germany, 1989–91. The sparks (to use a Leninist metaphor) for this historical event were far from technological: the occupancy of the West German Embassy in Prague by hordes of East Germans and a weekly *Friedensgebet* (prayer for peace) for which a congregation gathered in the Nikolaikirche in Leipzig. This last spread, not because of any technology but because: 'It was commonly known that each Monday at about 6 p.m., a large number of people would come streaming out of both the Nikolai Church and other nearby churches' (Lohmann, 1994: 67). An ancient sense of sanctuary gave people a feeling of protection from their own repressive government. Then word-of-mouth created an 'informational cascade' transforming them into demonstrators as they occupied the nearby Karl Marx Platz. Political scientist Susanne Lohmann's influential account of this phenomenon applied this concept of an 'informational cascade', initially developed to describe the spread of fads and fashions (Bikhchandani, Hirshleifer and Welch, 1992), to explain how the crowd came to the square. She made no mention of media beyond the observation that the state's newspaper reports gave up minimizing the numbers attending these 'Monday Demonstrations'. Nevertheless, the idea of a web-enabled 'informational cascade' was to be readily deployed, after the development of the social networking sites in the new century, as an explanation for almost all civil disorders wherever they occurred, in whatever circumstances, irrespective of new medias' penetration levels.

It is, of course, far from impossible that Facebook, Twitter and their rivals could function in such situations. Serious investigation into the UK summer riots of 2011 highlighted police unpreparedness and inefficiencies, and pinpointed, to the distress of the government which was eager to blame 'gangs' and criminals for the disorders, widespread alienation, economic distress and distrust of authority as causes. The study also examined the role of the social media. This revealed a correlation between the geographic origination points of Twitter messages and the riot sites. Those interviewed for the study, though, knew that Twitter and Facebook were open and told the investigators that they preferred BlackBerrys, smartphones created by Research In Motion (RIM). These 'BB's were available for as little as £5 a month and they (and the investigators) believed them to be secure (Ball and Brown, 2011: 12, 14). Both were clearly unaware of how the authorities might choose to threaten RIM.[18] Anyway, informants indicated that other communications factors were also involved in the creation of the 'informational cascade': 'I just listened to the radio to find a riot. Simple as that' (Adegoke and Ball, 2011: 15).

At least one British police force also used the net during the disturbances. The *Chorley and Horley Observer* reported: 'Writing on Twitter, @sussex_police said: "Rumours of disorder in Brighton, Hastings, Eastbourne, St. Leonards and Crawley all false. Please enjoy the Sussex sunshine while it lasts!"'(Anon, 2011b). (Elsewhere sending such rumours incurred jail.)

In Lohmann's careful analysis of the realpolitik of the situation she was discussing in East Germany, the internal collapse of Soviet power and the opening of the East German borders were central, not the media. It was not word-of-mouth that 'caused' the revolt but, rather, the passing of information in a particular political situation that lead to regime change. Ignoring this, popularizers such as Clay Shirkey, 'the prime booster of the better world order being ushered in by the internet', have been quick to hype new media technology over realpolitik, especially outside the West (Appleyard, 2011: 42). The focus here, however, is the impact of new platforms within the liberal democracies.[19]

Again, overstatement is easy. The vaunted 'My.BarackObama.com' raised millions for the Obama presidential campaign in 2007–8 using new media, but it was a traditional 'well-cultivated' door-to-door operation by volunteers that turned out the vote in the crucial primaries: 'What won it was the ground game' (Bennett, 2009: 30). Without question the use of these communications systems is a most significant new factor in elections, but it doesn't wipe out the old tools of political activism. As for electronic protests in the West having an effect elsewhere, there is little evidence of efficacy. Basically, 'The technology reduces the marginal cost of protest' (Morozov, 2009: 36). The satirist Jon Stewart was far from mistaken when he wondered about Afghanistan and Iraq: 'What, we could have liberated them over the internet? Why did we send an army when we could do it the same way as we buy shoes? – by clicking'. For neo-liberal opinion particularly, the internet is a new propaganda tool of the type they have long exploited. For them, 'It's like Radio Free Europe on steroids' (Morozov, 2011: xii).

There are, of course, nevertheless clear advantages in using new media to raise public awareness and some technical advantages as well. But the fact remains: of itself, using new technology is not enough to effect political change. Those seriously intending so to do need to be more clear-sighted: 'In order for your video to make an impact, you will need to ensure that it reaches key viewers with the power to act' (Harding, 2005: 233). D2D ('direct to decision-maker') distribution of messages remains 'one of the most successful forms' of creating an informational cascade to produce a realpolitik result.

Despite such reality, the illusion of a technologically guaranteed right of expression flourishes, the claims made for it reaching something of a hyperbolic crescendo as the last century turned. Actually, the power of the digital, of itself, to render repression impotent is far more virtual than real. It is only because the processes of suppressing expression across the digital network are yet underway that this illusory technologically guaranteed freedom can be claimed. The 'technologies of freedom' are no such thing – the freedom they might bestow remains a matter of political struggle. Technology, despite hyperbolic claims to the country, has never rendered censorship impotent. Now it aids surveillance: 'Mass technology platforms and ubiquitous [surveillance] video cameras create new, networked risks to the safety and security of frontline human rights defenders (HRDs) and those they film or work with' (Padania with Gregory, Alberdingk-Thijm and Nunez, 2011: 3). Platforms for expression might increase but no greater freedom necessarily follows their introduction.

On the contrary: surveillance aside, the technologies give the demagogue the ability to speak not in one city to one crowd, nor to a mass of individuals each in their own homes, but to gatherings of thousands in hundreds of locations – millions – at once. The potential for a cyber-Hitler remains chilling. Technology does not answer the problem of liberty. It could undercut freedom even more dramatically than any Khomeini would do.

Defending against such attacks cannot rely on technological advances. This fact and all these long struggles to establish liberty of expression outlined in this defence of the right are the basis for rebuttal. These histories from Luther on must not be forgotten. Within them lies the source of the 'sacred' power and the justification of the central importance of free speech to the West.

SECTION TWO

Enlightenment – To Frustrate the Treason of the Clerks

The second prong of attack on rights encompasses a general '*trahison des clercs*' towards Western social liberalism. It rejects the legacy of the centuries of struggle to obtain a right of free expression for different media. To frustrate such 'treason', we must hear the other side – *audi alterem partem* – as 'natural justice' demands. But this can be done in short order because the *trahison* yields (in Mary Wollstonecraft's words) 'no first principle to refute'.

10

Audi Alterem Partem: Hear the Other Side

10.1   *Sir Tom Stoppard v. Heinrich Heine* (2006): In defence of free expression

The omissions and assertions of Tom Stoppard's case against the privileges of speech (see Chapter 2), are far from untypical. When, for example, he writes that the right of free expression is a 'non-starter', the starter he overlooks can be readily found by further quoting the lucid 'Cato'. John Trenchard and Thomas Gordon continued:

> This sacred Privilege [free speech] is so essential to free Government, that the Security of Property; and the Freedom of Speech, always go together; and in those wretched Countries where a Man cannot call his Tongue his own, he can scarce call any Thing else his own. Whoever would overthrow the Liberty of the Nation, must begin by subduing the Freedom of Speech; a Thing terrible to publick Traitors. ('Cato', 1721)

As mentioned, not least since he has called up Voltaire, one defends *jusqu'à la mort* Stoppard's right to dispute this contention; but simply to ignore it, baldly to cast aside the claim that without a right of free speech no other right can be guaranteed, is chilling. His argument deploys a phalanx of straw figures. To assert that free expression is the capstone right is not, as he says it is, to demand that 'it trumps the interests of the society or group' (Stoppard, 2006: 134–6). There is no 'trumping' entailed. The right does – it needs to – 'trump the interests of society' and so on, but only, it should be remembered, as far as it does not breach the harm principle. That is to say, as far as its exercise 'does not hurt and controul the Right of another' ('Cato', 1721). That the right is foundational does not mean it is without limits.

'A "human right" is, by definition, timeless', Stoppard says, only to show that, as this right was unknown to St Augustine and only became 'inalienable' and 'endowed by God' in the seventeenth century, it is no sort of right. But whence this requirement for timelessness? Inalienable rights, though, are generally as much the work of humanity as they are a reflection of divine authority. The ancient *jus naturale*/natural law was legitimated by its universality and not its divine origin. The Almighty comes into the concept as the source of these rights in later thinking; for example, the seventeenth-century Dutch jurist Grotius claimed natural law is inseparable from 'God's will' (Hunt, 2007: 117). Jefferson might have invoked the Creator as a source of his 'inalienable' rights but they were grounded at least as firmly in the man-made Magna Carta. This was deemed, by the revolted American colonists as much as any English Whig, to be the basis of the 'ancient rights and liberties of Englishmen' (Hunt, 2007: 21). Moreover, one can argue that the West's dominant political arrangement, liberal democracy, cannot survive when its laws are trumped by divine commands.

In another claim, Stoppard says that a right 'cannot adhere to some societies ... at some times'; so, again, free expression fails the test. This, though, is simply to give the intolerance of the societies where free expression is denied, or not practised, a veto over societies that deem it essential. It is not that the right is actually applied universally and at all times but that it can be potentially so applied.

Such arguments lead Stoppard up the most unfortunate moral blind alley: 'It is not impossible to imagine a group – a society – deciding collectively that censorship is desirable. On what ground can we stand and declare the decision to be deplorable?' Let us, then, imagine ourselves standing on the ground of Berlin's Operplatz on the night of 10 May 1933 and see if any reasons come to mind for insisting that the spectacle of the Nazi book-burning is not only 'deplorable' but, perhaps, something rather worse. Stoppard has forgotten Heinrich Heine: '*Dort wo man Bücher verbrennt, verbrennt man auch am Ende Menschen*' ('Where they burn books, at the end they also burn people') (Heine, 1823) – as, indeed, they did most hellishly on this occasion. Instead, Stoppard sees more acceptable and containable outcomes: 'We may say that [the collective decision to censor] is deplorable because, for example, it would lead to that society becoming moribund, or for other pragmatic reasons'. Heine's insight, which history teaches us is seemingly inevitable, on the other hand suggests an imperative for free speech that goes well beyond avoiding stagnation and mere pragmatism. Only by speaking truth to power, almost at whatever other costs, can the flames of the conflagration be doused or, better yet, prevented. Such outcomes cannot be guaranteed if any person or body is empowered, outside the processes of the law, to determine the legitimacy of such speech's 'truth'. It might take a multitude of forms and it certainly must be freely allowed to cause offence. The right of free speech has no more potent justification than this.

When, then, Tom Stoppard suggests that the right of free expression is 'a ghost ... a western liberal shibboleth', he reflects the general '*trahison des clercs*' with its dismissal of those 'ghosts' who, in the eighteenth century, espoused a belief in human rights as having the interlocking qualities of naturalness (that is, that they are inherent in all people); equality (that is, that they are the same for all people); and universality (that is, that they are applicable everywhere) (Hunt, 2007: 20–21).

10.2   *Gray et al. v. Todorov et al.* (2008): In defence of the Enlightenment

Opposition to the West's concept of freedom holds that the eighteenth-century Enlightenment's founding thinkers, who placed rights in the forefront of socio-political theory, should be seen less as advocates for individual freedoms than as hypocritical, white, Eurocentric, male chauvinist slave-owners. Moreover, they are also said to have had a vision of the future as unending progress suffused by 'reason', which history has proved to be woefully off the mark.

Some of this charge sheet, it has to be admitted, cannot be denied, at least as regards these eighteenth-century thinkers themselves. Recall Dr Johnson: 'How is it that we hear the loudest yelps for liberty from the drivers of negroes?' (Johnson, 1775: 89). Indeed, slave-owners were far from unknown among the rebellious Congressmen assembled in Philadelphia. Nor can the other elements of the ad hominem accusations – implicit or explicit chauvinism, misogyny or racism, for example – be simply dismissed. However, it is not just the often glaring hypocrisy of the men themselves that underlies these attacks on them; it is also the viability of their ideas. And it is here that the first stage of a rebuttal can be mounted. Such criticism falters as it ignores the positive consequences of Enlightenment thinking. Hypocrisy and these other failings were addressed in time and modern tolerant, democratic societies rest, however imperfectly, on Enlightenment foundations. This does not mean, though, that Enlightenment thinking does not have dangerous consequences; nor that there are not, as its critics claim, many other inherent contradictions thrown up by the thinking of the eighteenth-century *philosophes*.

Within *les Droits de l'homme* themselves, good principles can lead to bad outcomes, as John Gray, among others, has pointed out. The toleration that underpins *les Droits*, for example, is in his view 'a pre-condition of any stable *modus vivendi* among incorrigibly imperfect beings'. It is, though, 'inherently judgemental. The objects of toleration are what we judge to be evils' (Gray, 1995: 18). An enlightened, tolerant society, therefore, in the face of intolerance's 'bad manners' or worse, must be willing itself 'to be repressive'. A tolerance for faith schools might require allowing them to refuse to follow, say, a national curriculum. This requires intolerance of such institutions' refusal. If they insist on the primacy of their own agenda, by so doing they undercut the common culture, a thing which Gray, not unreasonably, holds to be a valued good. It follows that: 'The multiculturalists demand that minority cultures – however these are defined – be afforded rights and privileges denied the mainstream culture in effect delegitimatises the very idea of a common culture' (Gray, 1995: 24–5). Of course, this assumes that what is at issue is not an equivalency of demand but extra special demands by the minority. In the nature of the case these could be more a desire to redress the balance that is tilted to the majority. For Gray, though, this sort of problem means that, 'the difficulties involved in constructing a plausible theory of natural rights are formidable and in all likelihood insuperable ... the conception of natural law needed to support a theory of natural rights is incompatible with modern empiricism' (Gray, 1986: 46). As a result, liberalism, 'the political theory of the modern age', is (according to Gray) 'ill equipped to address the dilemmas of the post modern period' (Gray, 1986: 85).

In Gray's postmodern multicultural context, the problem is thus while tolerance, for example, is certainly a central Enlightenment value, it was conceived of as a defence for the individual protecting individual emancipation and autonomy. Individual emancipation and autonomy is the Enlightenment's central aspiration, which Tzvetan Todorov glosses as the necessity 'to be free from external authorities' while nevertheless being 'guided by laws, norms and rules decided by the very people to whom they are addressed' (Todorov, 2009: 49, 5). The issue of balancing the collective against the individual in the contemporary fashion, however, was alien to the thinking of those Westerners intent on formulating a then novel priority for individual rights:

> The first constituent characteristic of Enlightenment thinking consists in giving priority to what individuals decide for themselves over what is imposed upon them by an external authority ... What was rejected [in the Enlightenment] was the submission of society and individuals to precepts whose sole legitimacy came from the fact that a tradition attributed them to gods or ancestors. The lives of human beings were to be guided henceforth by a project for the future, not by an authority from the past. (Todorov, 2009: 5, 6)

Or as Kant put it: 'The maxim of thinking for yourself at all times is enlightenment' (Deligiorgi, 2005: 84). '*Sapere aude*! [Dare to know!] "Have the courage to use your own understanding", is thus the motto of the Enlightenment' (Kant, 1996 [1784]: 58).

However, as with much else in Enlightenment thinking, 'no sooner had this idea [of Jean-Jacques Rousseau's] been formulated than a distortion of it emerged' with the Marquis de Sade and the supposition that 'the only thing that counts is my pleasure' (Todorov, 2009: 47). Hence the young Marx's opinion: 'None of the so-called rights of man, therefore, go beyond egoistic man, beyond man as a member of civil society – that is, an individual withdrawn into himself, into the confines of his private interests and private caprice, and separated from the community' (Marx, 1844).

Todorov's defence of the Enlightenment turns on rebutting such distortions as necessary outcomes of the Enlightenment project. For Todorov, on this point, autonomy does not mean self-sufficiency: 'All human beings suffer from congenital insufficiency, from a sense of incompleteness that they try to fill by attaching themselves to those around them and soliciting their attachment' (Todorov, 2009: 46). The balance is achieved because, morally and economically, autonomy is needed to establish the social contract without which there can be no society (Hunt, 2007: 60). The emancipation and autonomy of the individual cannot, therefore, be absolute. That would be self-defeating; as Rousseau asserted: 'Our sweetest existence is relative and collective, and our true *self* is not entirely within us' (Rousseau, 1990 [1772–6]: 1–18).

Nor can de Sade, any more than Marx, ignore the boundaries, democratically imposed, that he/she 'do no harm'. John Stuart Mill explained the reason for such a 'harm principle' (in Joel Feinberg's phrase) was that 'the only purpose for which power can be rightfully exercised over any member of a civilized community, against his will, is to prevent harm to others' (Mill, 1998 [1859]: 14; Feinberg, 1983). Community is inseparable from self and controlling the emancipated and autonomous individual by due process is both necessary and possible. It does not require that the principles of emancipation and autonomy be abandoned because they can be subjected to abuse or because they are not absolute. After all, such notions of autonomy also lie at the heart of capitalism, another idea embraced by some Enlightenment thinkers, but capitalist abuses are not usually suggested, at least by liberals, as a reason to abandon Enlightenment rights.

The Baron de Laune, Anne-Robert-Jacques Turgot, sometime Louis XVI's comptroller-general and one of these early enthusiasts for the capitalist free-market, was convinced of the 'Successive Progress of the Human Spirit'. He believed that 'morals become gentler, the human mind becomes more enlightened, isolated nations draw nearer to one another … the whole mass of the human race … advances continually, though slowly, towards greater perfection' (Turgot, 1970 [1750]: 12). Such claims for unending progress are criticized as being not only naive, but also because they have been rendered ridiculous by history. Todorov puts Turgot's espousal of the idea down to youthful intemperance – Turgot was only twenty-three when he spoke those words – but his friend, the mathematician, the Marquis de Condorcet, had no such excuse. Condorcet, forced into hiding during the Terror, still held to this vision, writing an *Esquisse d'un tableau historique des progrès de l'esprit humain* (*Sketch for a Historical Picture of the Progress of the Human Spirit*) in 1793/4. The *philosophe*'s belief in what Todorov calls 'the mechanical march to perfection' perfectly echoes the Christian belief in the possibility of the perfectibility of human kind.

Nevertheless, the accusation against the Enlightenment as a whole for holding to an underlying crippling naivety on this point is another distortion. It is to ignore the fact that such optimism was far from being shared: 'The Enlightenment knew very well just how hard life can be. It savagely attacked the optimism that later critics attributed to it; with the exception of a few extremists, no Enlightenment thinker held progress to be inevitable' (Neiman, 2009: 134). Rousseau, for example, 'believed that all progress was inevitably paid for by regression in another area ... We can see today that Rousseau was right and that our aspiration to perfection does not imply faith in progress' (Todorov, 2009: 19–20). All the *philosophes*, however, 'decidedly rejected the claim that decline was inescapable. Conservative insistence that we're doomed to degenerate is a self-fulfilling prophecy' (Neiman, 2009: 134). Most assuredly, though, this is not *'le meilleur des mondes possible'* ('the best of all possible worlds') and all is not for the best in it. Pessimism, a belief in the inevitable failings of human nature, might logically be held to afford a stronger reason than does optimism to support the need for rights. Either way, faith in progress is not necessary to any argument in defence of human rights.

Beyond its responsibility for Sadean selfish perversity and belief in the inevitability of progress under capital, the general attack on the Enlightenment also accuses it of colonialism, totalitarianism and atheism: never mind its acceptance of patriarchy. In Todorov's view, these charges are all also grounded in 'distortions'. They are not the *necessary* consequences of Enlightenment thinking and they 'misread' its spirit: 'These distortions, and not the Enlightenment itself, were what became most often the object of rejection' (Todorov, 2009: 27).

To take these in turn:

Colonialism: Condorcet propounded the concept of *'la Mission civilisatrice'*, the 'civilizing mission' for Europeans, which was used in the later nineteenth century to justify colonialism. His idea was certainly articulated in a spirit of European superiority but, perhaps naively, not with a view that it should lead to persistent abuse and degradation. On the contrary, the very values supposedly being promulgated abroad scarcely supported abusive subjugation and the denial of rights. The evils of colonialism were no more a necessary part of the Enlightenment project than was sadism. Anyway, those evils had been manifesting themselves, in the name of Christianity, for the prior several centuries of European expansion without Condorcet's tendentious rationalization.

The Western human rights tradition is cultural specificity and its claim on universality also speaks, critics claim, to Western disdain of 'the other'. Insensitive to the realities of diversity, this concept of rights is – or could be – alien to the rest of humankind. The critique, though, can be readily overstated. Although it is the case that the concept of the rights of humanity is an embodiment of Western values, the claim of universality cannot be dismissed as a species of Western arrogance (Hunt, 2007: 20–21). Rights are not uniquely Western; and to claim that they are is itself, in effect, implicitly to suggest arrogantly that only Europeans have been concerned with 'human dignity, liberty, equality, and brotherhood'.[1] 'Modern ethics is in fact indebted to a worldwide spectrum of both secular and religious traditions' (Ishay, 2004: 4, 7). It goes without saying that equality and individuality were (are) often in abeyance – even, of course, in the West – but in, say, Hinduism, one can find five 'social assurances' and five 'virtues' or 'controls' that are echoed in the Western catalogue of basic rights.[2] And some date back millennia.

Tolerance, too, is far from being a Western monopoly. During the centuries of the Arab enlightenment, over a millennium ago, a cousin of the Caliph Abu Ja'far Abdullah al-Ma'mum, in the course of a religious dispute, could tell his opponent that he was free to: 'say whatever you please and speak your mind freely' (Ahmad, 2002). The Muslim Moghul Emperor Akbar enacted religious tolerance into law in the sixteenth century. The right to life and security has deep roots, many outside of Europe. The charge of cultural specificity against Enlightenment rights not only implicitly downgrades non-Western understanding of the basics of human well-being; it also Eurocentrically denies history. To dismiss human rights because they are supposedly a specific product of the Western culture, even in the name of multicultural sensitivity, is both ahistorical and itself Eurocentric.

Totalitarianism: a most widely received distorting syllogism accuses the Enlightenment *philosophes* of 'causing' twentieth-century totalitarianism, i.e. the Enlightenment led to the French Revolution which led to Hitler and Stalin – and Pol Pot and a number of other dreadful emulators. This charge was mounted early. The British objected to the theoretical basis of the French Revolution, opposing it, for example in Edmund Burke's thinking which so outraged Mary Wollstonecraft, with their own supposed pragmatism. With 'mole-eyed' vision and in 'tones of lofty disdain', as Kant described them, Burke denounced *les philosophes*: 'What is the use of discussing a man's abstract right to food or to medicine? The question is upon the method of procuring and administering them. In this deliberation I shall always advise to call in the aid of the farmer and the physician, rather than the professor' (Burke, 1790: 89). This, for Kant, was merely 'On the old saw: that may be right in theory, but it won't work practice' (as he entitled the pamphlet he wrote, in part, to rebut – albeit not by name – Burke) (Kant, 1970 [1793]: 63). Mary Wollstonecraft, confronting Edmund Burke, wrote, more forcefully, that she would 'glow with indignation when I attempt, methodically to unravel your slavish paradoxes, in which I can find no first principle to refute' (Wollstonecraft, 1999 [1791]: 7).

Yet Burke's prescience in predicting a bloody disaster – the Reign of Terror was not to begin in earnest until some years after he wrote – seemed to prove, incontrovertibly, the correctness of his scepticism. It was forgotten, except by his critics also writing before the blood-letting, that the Revolution's causes were 'the wretched condition of man, under the monarchical and hereditary systems of Government, dragged from his home by one power, or driven by another, and impoverished by taxes more than by enemies', as Thomas Paine put it at the time (Paine, 1792: 1). Instead, received critical opinion agreed with Burke and held that: 'it was philosophers who were chiefly responsible for propagating the concepts of toleration, equality, democracy, republicanism, individual freedom, and the liberty of expression in the press, the batch of ideas identified as the principle cause of the near overthrow of authority, tradition, faith and privilege. Hence, philosophers specifically had caused the revolution' (Jonathan Israel, quoted in Neiman, 2009: 147). Which in turn produced the Terror.

That terror was an inevitable consequence of any revolution based on a demand for human rights quickly became a given: 'The Revolution began with the Declaration of the Rights of Man which is why it ended in blood' (Bonald, 1823). This, though, is syllogistically fallacious, the Terror not being in anyway necessary to Revolution whether it was caused by *les philosophes* or not. The Stalinist claim to Enlightenment understanding, for instance, through knowledge of all the sciences (including the 'science' of history), similarly lived alongside a 'terror', an abnegation of individual autonomy, which was, in fact, a de facto rejection of the central values of emancipation (Todorov, 2009: 36).

The attack, coming from both right and left political thinking, accuses the Enlightenment of being the general root of totalitarianism. It is 'an extreme form of Western thought – reason that hopes to master the universe' and this 'allegiance to reason made the Enlightenment totalitarian. All agreed that reason is instrumental, calculating, domineering, and condemned to futility' (Neiman, 2009: 190). Such a plenitude of power for reason, though, was never claimed, even by the *philosophes* who came nearest to making it supreme. In fact, all-determining reason, especially as the clue to human happiness, was denied as a desirable by Kant and satirized by Voltaire (Neiman, 2009: 189–93). As with colonialism, so with the Terror and totalitarianism: it is a species of Orwellian 'newspeak', by critics, to so reverse the Enlightenment's 'spirit' as to claim it as a template for totalitarians. In fact, their actions blatantly subvert the protections that the central Enlightenment concept of individual human rights is designed to afford.

Atheism: the Enlightenment's 'enthronement' of 'man's reason' means, the religious claim, an end of morality because, without divinity, morality is impossible; and this is why the Terror is always but a step away. Men without God are quick to destroy each other, it is believed; but the history of persecution in the name of faith, without any other contrary arguments, itself gives the lie to this assertion. However, this debate is an irrelevance. The *philosophes* were, without question, as critical of religious practices as their heretical Christian forebears had been for the better part of the past millennium. The demand of emancipation required nothing less. Certainly, illumined by the ever-growing light of eighteenth-century science, some of the *philosophes* were animated by more than a deistic anti-clericalism, and modern atheism was born under their wing. Yet, the principles of autonomy equally demanded that individual faith also be protected as of right. Thus: 'Nothing was said ... about religious experience per se, or about the idea of transcendence, or about any of the various moral doctrines propounded by particular religions. The criticism was aimed at the structure of society not the content of belief' (Todorov, 2009: 6).

A last count on the charge-sheet against the Enlightenment is that *les philosophes* failed to contemplate *les Droits de la femme et la Citoyenne*. Indeed, Rousseau, who coined the phrase '*les Droits de l'homme*', was an enthusiast for patriarchy and woman's 'place' in the natural order: 'In any feminist Chamber of Horrors, Jean-Jacques Rousseau would occupy a prominent place ... Rousseau did not ignore women: he deliberately excluded them from public life' (Canovan, 1987: 78). Kant managed to undercut the universality of the concept of individual autonomy by suggesting the citizenry be either active or passive. Women, of course, were 'passive' as the first requirement of the active citizen was that the person be an 'adult male' (Kant, 1970 [1785]). The Enlightenment's justification of the patriarchy, though, is more a sin of omission than commission. The *philosophes* did not invent it, after all. As Mary Wollstonecraft, writing *A Vindication of the Rights of Woman* in revolutionary Paris, asserted: 'Let not men ... in the pride of power, use the same arguments that tyrannic kings and venal ministers have used and fallaciously assert that women ought to be subjected because she has always been so' (Wollstonecraft, 1992 [1792]: 133). It is, indeed, a serious flaw that the *philosophes* did not rise above the fundamental misogyny of their forefathers; but the sin is an inherited one. The same is true of slavery.

As in all the other Enlightenment sins, the supposed negative impact of liberal eighteenth-century thought relies on its positive effects being ignored or forgotten. In this case, as Neiman, points out, Enlightenment logic ensured that the first steps towards women's equality in the West were taken under its aegis: 'If you granted rights to Protestants, you had no reason to deny them to Jews; if you granted them to Jews, you had no reason to deny them to free blacks; if to free blacks, could slavery continue? Once slavery fell, a few souls even proposed that equal rights applied to women as well' (Neiman, 2009: 292).

Indeed, some did so suggest: 'Condorcet argued that boys and girls should be given the same course in the same place by the same professors, whether they were men or women, and he held that women should not be barred from any career' (Todorov, 2009: 113). By the next century, the drive for female emancipation had become a liberal and radical given. 'Whatever has been said or written,' argued J.S. Mill, '... of the ennobling influence of free government ... is every particle as true of women as of men' (Mill, 1998 [1861]: 577). It must of course be admitted, as Todorov does, that women were well behind in the parade – in France, for instance, equality for Jewish males was instituted in 1789; slavery was abolished in 1848; and women's suffrage, finally, ninety-six years after that, arrived in 1944. Nevertheless, despite the achievement of this last during the Vichy regime, it had been, in essence, an Enlightenment parade.

By 1944, though, such a move could be easily seen as the twitching of Enlightenment's corpse. Theodor Adorno and Max Horkheimer, writing in the midst of the Second World War, pessimistically (if understandably) saw 'the self-destruction of the Enlightenment' as being underway. A 'universally apparent' reversal of its values threatened their '*petitio principii*', namely, 'that social freedom is inseparable from enlightened thought' (Adorno and Horkheimer, 1997 [1944]: xiii). For them the Enlightenment was under literal physical attack; for us, the battle rages in the marketplace of ideas (a space very much the Enlightenment's creation).

The contemporary rhetorical attack on the Enlightenment, of which intellectual hostility to Salman Rushdie can be seen as a clear example, is generally to be rebutted – once the unavoidable embarrassment of Jefferson's slaves and the fact that *les Droits* were *de l'homme* are acknowledged – as being mistakenly grounded. Hostility arises from assumptions about the failures of the Enlightenment as commonly caricatured as the achieved triumph of reason; but the Enlightenment is not this caricature. It is actually an unfinished process of emancipation, correctly beset by the inevitable doubts arising exactly from the limits of reason (Garnham, 2000: 8). 'The task is not the conservation of the past but rather the redemption of past hope' (Pecora, 1992: 164). In fact: 'The Enlightenment did not realise its own ideals – but that's what ideals are all about' (Neiman, 2009: 135–6). That is no reason to abandon the project; certainly not in the face of such attacks as these. The treason must be frustrated. As Wollstonecraft put it to Burke: 'The birthright of man, to give you, Sir, a short definition of this disputed right, is such a degree of liberty, civil and religious as is compatible with the liberty of every other individual with whom he is united in a social company, and the continued existence of that compact' (Wollstonecraft, 1999 [1791]: 7).

With that we rebut the internal intellectual Western attack on free expression by, as it were, kicking a stone – as Doctor Johnson did, in reality, when confronting sophistry he did not like.

SECTION THREE

Law – To Correct the Abuses of Hackgate

Beyond the shadow of the *fatwa* and the uncertainties of the *clercs* lies the threat of control and regulation occasioned by abuses of media power. None claim the privilege of speech for such abuse but containing it suggests levels of constraint above the general law, exactly the 'very needless' sanctions against which John Locke warned. The general law should be all. This is not to claim that the law is perfect, perfectly applied. Rather it is that, however imperfect it might be, it is, properly, the guarantor of rights, including the right of free expression.

11

Rationes Decidendi: The Reasons for Decision

11.1 *Sir Paul Stephenson et al. v. Alan Rusbridger and Paul Johnson* (2010–11): Guarding the guardians

It is not an unthinkable conjecture to suppose that Sir Paul Stephenson, the then Metropolitan Police Commissioner, was unfamiliar with the name of Sir Roger L'Estrange, Charles II's Surveyor of the Press (see Chapter 4.2). Indeed, it is unlikely that Assistant Commissioner John Yates and Dick Fedorcio, Sir Paul's Director of Public Affairs, have much knowledge of late seventeenth-century press history either. Had this been otherwise, their private visits to the editor of the *Guardian*, Alan Rusbridger, and his deputy, Paul Johnson, on 10 December 2009 (by Stephenson and Fedorcio) and 19 February 2010 (by Yates) might have struck them as somewhat improper. On each occasion they castigated the editors for stories they had run which suggested that the Metropolitan Police had been failing to investigate possible criminal behaviour by employees of News International. As it transpired, it would seem that they had. At the time, the journalists steadfastly stood their ground and Stephenson, Yates and Fedorcio, after the ramifications of the *News of the World*'s abuses finally engulfed them, vacated theirs (Leigh, 2012c: 14).

One could not wish for a more dramatic example of free speech as the capstone right guaranteeing all others. Hackgate and other crimes and misdemeanours are of no interest to the Braudelian problem of liberty as such illegalities wipe out any privilege – all spurious claims that the abusive journalistic actions involved were necessary to free expression notwithstanding. Simply, those charged with enforcing the law – the police, the Director of Public Prosecutions, the Data Protection Commissioner *et al.* – should have done so. The matter is straightforward. From the standpoint of essential liberties, the scandal is notable only because the *Guardian*'s role, as – indeed – guardian of the guards, is a perfect illustration of why free expression is so vital.

The price, though, for this classic display of the press's most essential function is a public discussion contemplating controls previously long thought unacceptable – statutory regulators for the press, accreditation and registration for journalists, and fines for misfeasance outside of legal prohibitions. Much of this, of course, is in place for newer media – but a case could be made for how improper that already was (see Chapter 8). Post-Hackgate, sentiment was all for expanding such interferences, not contracting them. Arguments, already barely heard, that regulation was the proper business of the courts only, and not of 'very needless' regulators and extra regulations, withered in Hackgate's wake. The deficiencies of the law and its officers matched the misfeasance of the press. It could not be trusted to sort either the mess or itself out. Paradoxically, the very power that had exposed the corruption therefore threatened a possible final 'regulatory' outcome that would undercut its doing the same in the future.

Nevertheless, the right of free expression is grounded in legal contexts and any response to the abuses of media power must be located there, too. The nature as well as the content of 'speech', the 'harm' it can cause and the casual relationship between speech and harm can, and have been, differently defined, both popularly and at law. Western legal decisions are conditioned by the application of those concepts – they are their *rationes decidendi*. These, though, address a multiplicity of circumstances and vary not only between but within jurisdictions through time. This dynamic has resulted in levels of legal subtlety that can often leave general understanding bemused. Yet, there is a coherence to be explicated, even in the midst of the law's complexities, contradictions and uncertainties.

11.2 *National Socialist Party of America v. Village of Skokie* (1977): Gesture as speech

Consider first the nature of the 'speech' for which the privileges of freedom are demanded by the right.

Especially in the United States, judicial action has moved to expand the notion of 'speech' beyond its dictionary meaning. The constitutional phrase, 'the freedom of speech', has been glossed to embrace 'an act of expression', namely, 'any act that is intended by its agent to communicate to one or more persons some proposition or attitude':

> In addition to many acts of speech and publication, [act of expression] includes displays of symbols, failures to display them, demonstrations, many musical performances, and some bombings, assassinations, and self-immolations. In order for any act to be classified as an act of expression it is sufficient that it be linked with some proposition or attitude which it is intended to convey. (Scanlon, 1972: 206)

St Paul's distinction between 'word and deed' has been blurred.[1]

Following wartime regulation that required that the flag be saluted, a rash of Jehovah's Witnesses, whose faith prohibited them obeying this, were prosecuted. In finding for them, the US Supreme Court had then, for impeccable constitutional reasons, stepped out on the road that was to lead to expressive acts being considered as speech. The justices held that saluting (or refusing to salute) was cognate with 'speech'. Therefore, the Supreme Court declared that the requirement to salute was unconstitutional being, exactly, a law 'abridging the freedom of speech' and thus prohibited by the First Amendment. Justice Robert Jackson:

> If there is any fixed star in our constitutional constellation, it is that no official, high or petty, can prescribe what shall be orthodox in politics, nationalism, religion, or other matters of opinion or force citizens to confess by word or act their faith therein. If there are any circumstances which permit an exception, they do not now occur to us. (*West Virginia State Board of Education v. Barnette*, 1943)

Cloaked by the same rhetoric, the Supreme Court would eventually go further. Not only need the flag be un-saluted; it could be burned. Justice William Brennan saw this also as expression: 'If there is a bedrock principle underlying the First Amendment, it is that the government may not prohibit the expression of an idea simply because society finds the idea itself offensive or disagreeable' (*Texas v. Johnson*, 1989). By this time, despite some cases that went the other way, the court's view was settled: 'government has no power to restrict expression because of its message, its ideas, its subject matter, or its content'.

The high-spot of Frank Collins' leadership of the putative Übermenschen who joined his minuscule National Socialist Party of America came when he proposed to march his coterie of followers in full authentic SS uniforms, Swastika armbands prominently displayed, through the 40 per cent Jewish suburban township of Skokie, Chicago. The locals, of whom a significant number were Holocaust survivors, protested to the town's council. Ordinances against 'hate speech' were hastily passed and the march was banned. Collins, supported – to the distress of much liberal American opinion – by the American Civil Liberties Union (ACLU), argued successfully that his First Amendment right was being abridged. The Supreme Court agreed that the proposed silent march, which involved no planned distribution of printed materials, was 'symbolic speech' of a political nature and as such was protected by the First Amendment. Collins was allowed his demonstration (*National Socialist Party of America v. Village of Skokie*, 1977; *Collins v. Smith*, 1978).[2]

There is a distinction in American law between 'symbolic political speech' and, as Feinberg puts it, 'symbolic abusive acts' (Feinberg, 1985: 92). A city ordinance to prohibit cross-burning has been held to be unconstitutional because it was discriminatory in that it specified the class of persons it was intended to protect (i.e. African Americans). A divided Court stated that even otherwise prohibited speech (in this case, hate speech in the form of cross-burning) cannot be discriminated against on the basis of content alone (*R.A.V. v. City of St Paul*, 1992). A similar state law was subsequently declared to be constitutional (*Virginia v. Black*, 2003). The same action – cross-burning – was described as a 'virulent form of intimidation', weighted by history as a threat and by experience as a precursor to violence, but the law had no discriminatory reference to a specific group of victims to be protected. The Court also drew a distinction between a 'true threat', e.g. burning a cross on an individual's lawn, and the protected nature of the same action when done in other circumstances. At a Ku Klux Klan rally, burning crosses were fully protected as a 'potent symbol of shared group identity', an example of 'core political speech'. Collins' proposed prancing about in Skokie would have been of a piece with this.

Despite the distress the decision to allow the march caused (and the negative impact its support for the neo-Nazis had on the ACLU), the logic leading to the protection of the act itself – the marching – was unimpeachable. Indeed, the basic blurring of the line between deed and word has been entirely reasonable throughout and it is the contrary decisions, which on occasion have denied protection, that smack of illogicality. For example, the court in 1968, at the height of the country's imbroglio in Vietnam, held that burning a draft-card was not a form of protected expression (*United States v. O'Brien*, 1968). It did so by 'distinguishing' its previous decisions protecting expressive acts. David Paul O'Brien lost on the technicality that the offence was not the expressive burning of the card but the failure to carry it as required by an amendment of the Selective Service Act. It was this ordinance that, in 1965 in the midst of rising hostility to the war, had made non-possession an offence of which all draft-card burners were guilty.[3] The burners, it was held, could still publically express their hostility but not in the form of destroying the card. The First Amendment was therefore deemed not to be at issue.

Elsewhere in the West, without the stimulus of the First Amendment, there has been less vigorous legal exploration of the range of expression, but 'symbolic speech' is protected. For one thing, the European Convention of Human Rights, unlike the First Amendment, speaks not of 'speech' but of 'expression' thus reducing the need for a gloss: 'Everyone has the right to freedom of expression' (European Convention of Human Rights, 1950 [1948]).[4] Therefore: 'Expression includes words both spoken and written, the display or dissemination of pictures or images, and also certain forms of conduct (for example, a peaceful march or demonstration, the purpose of which is to communicate a political message) ... even ... light music' (Nicol *et al.*, 2009: 17). The protection of non-verbal expressive acts, though, is less settled in Europe than in the United States. It has not come clearly before the European Court of Human Rights (ECrtHR) in Strasbourg, although Article 10.1 is thought 'likely to extend to symbolic speech or expressive conduct such as flag burning' (Nicol *et al.*, 2009: 17). Certainly, this is the case in England and Wales where a case of defacing the Stars and Stripes has been heard and the action has been protected (*Percy v. DPP*, 2002).

In Europe generally a distinction is drawn between political, commercial and artistic expression, with the first attracting the most powerful protection. The European Court, sensitive to the differences in moral and religious norms across the Continent, has tended to give states greater scope for determining their own standards of acceptable artistic expression, verbal and non-verbal. In consequence, in the UK, and in the north of Europe generally, this flexibility – a 'margin of appreciation' as it is termed – offers greater protection to artistic expression than in more southern states (Nicol *et al.*, 2009: 29).

The Supreme Court in Washington, too, has been 'distinguishing' its view of non-verbal expression. It is now less liberal than once it was and the test in *United States v. O'Brien* – that the act prohibited is a means of expression and banning it does not ban expression itself – has been used, for example, to roll back the protection of nude public dancing as 'speech' (*Barnes v. Glen Theatre, Inc.*, 1991). The Court, though, did not deny the possibility of non-verbal expression in general, nor was nude dancing specifically refused protection. In the words of Justice David Souter: 'Although such performance dancing is inherently expressive, nudity per se is not'. Therefore, using the test in *United States v. O'Brien*, the First Amendment's protection was deemed to be 'marginal'.

The Supreme Court might well be no longer as infused with liberal opinion as it was from 1960s to the 1990s under Chief Justice Earl Warren and to a lesser extent during the more divided era under the tenure of his conservative successor, Warren Burger.[5] Yet, although now markedly conservative and despite such judgments as *Barnes v. Glen Theatre, Inc.*, it does still recognize that the principle of free speech is not to be limited to words alone. For the purposes of acquiring US constitutional or European charter right protection, expressive deeds are considered as words; albeit perhaps these days in the United States a little more marginally than they once were.

11.3   *Chaplinsky v. State of New Hampshire* (1942): Speech as deed

The obverse of this expansion, or blurring, is that words, spoken or written, can be considered deeds; but, in this case, the result has been by no means necessarily liberating. Although there is little evidence that the rationale – the *ratio decidendi* – of the Supreme Court's free speech cases has been informed by general philosophical rather than specific legal concerns, there is a parallel with some post-Second World War philosophical thinking. The blurring of word and expressive deed echoes, for example, the phenomenological assertion of Maurice Merleau-Ponty that the spoken word is itself 'gesture' (Merleau-Ponty, 1964: 43–4). J.L. Austin's pragmatic concept of the 'performative speech act' is also of a piece: for example, 'I name this ship XXX', and it is thus so named (Austin, 1962: 6).

Yet if words can have a positive effect, then they can also be negative.[6]

When we claim to have been injured by language, what kind of claim do we make? We ascribe an agency to language, a power to injure, and position ourselves as the objects of its injurious trajectory. We claim that language acts, and acts against us. (Butler, 1997: 1)

The old distinction between word and deed suggests that such language cannot be, in common sense terms, a deed; at least, a deed such as a physical blow. It is holding that it can that suggests such a modern melding of the two might have a chilling effect on free speech. Although it was pleased to see deeds as words, the court therefore became cautious when invited to see words as expressive deeds. The reason for this was a concern over the most salient precedent that had treated words in this way: this had, exactly, judged the words in question as being of themselves assaultive, without any further consideration.

Weeks before the United States joined the Second World War in 1941, Walter Chaplinsky, another Jehovah's Witness, was arrested in the small town of Rochester, New Hampshire. He had called the Town Marshal 'a God-damned racketeer' and 'a damned Fascist' (*Chaplinsky v. New Hampshire*, 1942). (He denied the 'God-damned' but otherwise admitted that these were his words.) He had been 'preaching' his belief that all organized religion was a 'racket', a view not held by the large crowd he attracted and, it would seem, had infuriated. They attacked him physically. It was Chaplinsky, though, who was arrested by a police officer. The Town Marshal he insulted was encountered on their way to the station. Chaplinsky was found guilty because of a New Hampshire law, untested for its constitutionality, that forbad using 'any offensive, derisive or annoying word to anyone who is lawfully in any street or public place ... or to call him by an offensive or derisive name'.[7]

In upholding the decision, the Supreme Court ignored the basic constitutional question raised by the state law. Instead, it chose to articulate a general principle restricting First Amendment rights, holding that the very words 'assaulted' the Town Marshall. Justice Frank Murphy, for the court, said:

There are certain well-defined and narrowly limited classes of speech the prevention and punishment of which have never been thought to raise any Constitutional problem. These include the lewd and obscene, the profane, the libelous, and the insulting or 'fighting' words – those which by their very utterance inflict injury or tend to incite an immediate breach of the peace are not afforded constitutional protection. (*Chaplinsky v. New Hampshire*, 1942)

Even allowing for the fact that in late 1941 calling an American official a fascist had a force it perhaps lacks today, this cannot be considered entirely sound. Justice Murphy sought to position 'fighting words' with obscene, profane (blasphemous) and libellous (defamatory) expression, all of which are denied protection and prohibited. Without question these are categories of unprotected speech but insisting that 'fighting words' or 'assaultive speech' was of a piece with them is somewhat problematic (Herbeck, 2003).

The common law has always needed intentional deeds as well as words for an assault action to lie. In England, on a day in 1669, one Turberville was having an argument, it would seem heated, with a man named Savage. At one point, Turberville reached for his sword, saying, as he half withdrew it, 'Were it not for assize-time, I would not take such language from you'; 'assize time' being when the royal judges were in town and public order was, apparently, expected to be better kept than usual. Savage, true to his name, attacked Turberville, putting out his eye. His defence to Turberville's action for assault was provocation: Turberville, in going for his sword, in effect used 'fighting words' and so justified Savage's response. 'The question was, If that were an assault — The Court agreed that it was not; for the declaration of the plaintiff was, that he would not assault him, the Judges being in town; and *the intention* as well as *the act* makes an assault — In the principal case the plaintiff had judgment' (*Turberville v. Savage*, 1669).

First Amendment protection does indeed not apply to all and any public expression, as Justice Murphy observed. Apart from obscenity, blasphemy and defamation, words containing a direct threat of violence are not protected. However, in Chaplinsky's case, twentieth-century levels of public order meant that it was, arguably, the equivalent of 'assize time'. He did not say, for example, 'I will kill you', or 'Town Marshals deserve to die'. Cries of 'Fascist' or 'racketeer' (even 'God-damned racketeer'), even in 1941, are scarce of a piece with such direct threats. On its face, Chaplinsky's language was 'highly implausible' as an example of 'fighting words'. To refuse them protection withdraws so large a class of utterances as to threaten the right (Feinberg, 1985: 231; J. Weinstein, 2010a: 53). Moreover 'fighting words', provocations, are not the same as threatening words but the unprotected nature of these last was not at issue. This has not been questioned. For example, in *Watts v. United States* (*Watts v. United States*, 1969), the constitutionality of a 1917 statute prohibiting 'knowingly and wilfully [making] any threat to take the life of or to inflict bodily harm upon the President of the United States'[8] was confirmed.

In general, the degree to which the content of the various types of unprotected expression stands alone, as it were, differs. With defamation, as with the *Chaplinsky* court's view of 'fighting words', an infinity of expressions, given a specific context, can be held to be defamatory; but this is not true of obscenity or blasphemy. The range of expression in them is, obviously, by comparison limited. Concomitantly, the need to demonstrate damage on an actual person is reduced; the consideration of the content itself – the expression 'on its face' – is sufficient. Slander or libel and threats always require a victim, whereas obscenity and blasphemy do not need a personally harmed individual to be successfully prosecuted. Unprotected expression is therefore more self-evident, less dependent on context, than is defamatory or threatening utterance. Moreover, while Justice Murphy's view of what categories of speech were 'well-defined' as unprotected might have been reasonable in 1941, that is scarcely still the case today with any of these categories.

To take, then, these categories in turn.

11.4   *United States v. One Book Called 'Ulysses'* (1933): Obscenity

Although the obscene has a conventional meaning as characterizing certain 'impolite' words, images and actions, the law has been primarily concerned with material judged, on a balance of probabilities, likely to produce 'certain kinds of offended states of mind in observers'; and, more specifically in the United States, because it is intended to provoke an erotic response (Feinberg, 1985: 97–8). In English law, the Victorian definition of obscenity was 'whether the tendency of the matter charged with obscenity is to deprave and corrupt those whose minds are open to such immoral influences and into whose hands such a publication might fall' (*R. v. Hicklin*, 1868). This, since it assumes a class of suggestible persons of little moral fibre and further assesses the probability of the obscenity falling into their hands, also fudges the question of actual victim. This is of great significance to the right of free speech. The right's 'only Check', 'the only Bounds which it ought to know', is that 'by it' no other person is hurt or controlled ('Cato', 1721). Protection of speech should be removed only 'to prevent harm to others'. The limitation thus classically expressed – the harm principle – did not stretch to embracing the intention to harm. Much less did it, as the *Hicklin* test required, prohibit merely having a possible consequence of harming. The test did not even involve an examination of the mind of the perpetrator, their *mens rea*, to establish guilt. The law was prepared to assume intent. As Justice Oliver Wendell Holmes, Jr, put it: 'the word "intent" as vaguely used in ordinary legal discussion means no more than knowledge at the time of the act that the consequences said to be intended will ensue' (*Abrams v. U.S.*, 1919).

Not only was the perpetrator's motivation assumed; so too was the effect of the obscene expression. The law was to dispense with testimony from witnesses attesting that they had been, in fact, been corrupted. 'These [obscene] words, simply as words, have an inherent capacity to offend and shock, and in some cases even to fill with dread and horror' (Feinberg, 1985: 190): so much so that it now needs no person to come forward as being so offended, shocked, filled with dread or horrified. The tendency is sufficient. The casual relationship between expression and effect becomes hypothetical rather than actual.

Content alone, therefore, is what is under consideration – in obscenity, this is the depictions or descriptions of sexual acts using specific, but changing, levels of explicitness of image and/or language. Such determinations are, in Feinberg's term, 'judgemental' as to the depravity and corruption the matter could possibly cause. The victim is conjectural and the material's corrupting potential is, in essence, a question of opinion: the simple depiction of nudity or even of sexual congress (or deviant sexuality involving adults) will not do to prove its presence. 'The riddles of obscenity' have long been a matter of contentious opinion causing judges 'collective despair' (Feinberg, 1985: 185, 175). As Justice Potter Stewart put it of 'hard core pornography': 'I know it when I see it.' In this case (*Jacobellis v. Ohio*, 1964), the matter in question was Louis Malle's prize-winning 1958 film, *Les Amants*, and the court knew it did not, in fact, see obscenity. Victorian certainties had been replaced by twentieth-century confusions.

In 1933, the prosecution of James Joyce's *Ulysses* in the United States led to the first major breach of the test in *Hicklin*. Attention needed to be paid, the court determined, to the extent of the objectionable matter. The *Hicklin* test had been blind to this: even the smallest amount of obscenity would contaminate, as it were, the whole. In the United States after 1933, it was the 'dominate theme' of the work, not just the explicit material, which had to be considered. In the case of *Ulysses* the work overall, despite passages that were still deemed obscene by the *Hicklin* standard, was a literary masterpiece deserving of protection (*United States v. One Book Called 'Ulysses'*, 1933).

The *Hicklin* test was 'retired' in the United States twenty-three years later by Justice Brennan (*Roth v. United States*, 1957). Brennan now suggested that the 'suggestible person' test was as unreasonable as was the refusal to consider the extent of the obscene passages within the material. *Hicklin* also assumed obscenity was of an unchanging nature unaffected by alterations in social attitudes. To correct these failings he proposed a new test: 'whether to the average person, applying contemporary community standards, the dominant theme of the material taken as a whole appeals to a prurient [lewd or lustful] interest'. Brennan also reaffirmed that obscenity, if proved, would not have protection but his definition of it – that it be 'utterly without redeeming social importance' – has proved difficult to determine, especially in the context of 'contemporary community standards'.

These last have come to be interpreted, by the more conservative Supreme Court of Warren Burger, as *local* – not the arguably possibly more liberal 'national' – contemporary community standards. Although it is as hard as ever to establish, a lack of 'serious literary, artistic, political, or scientific value' is now enough to demonstrate the absence of 'redeeming social importance'. And the 'average person' is deemed to be present for the purposes of the obscenity test even when the materials (for example, sado-masochistic publications, which might be supposed to disgust an average person rather than titillate) are targeted at specific groups which would not be corrupted by them (*Miller v. California*, 1973: *Paris Adult Theatre I v. Slaton*, 1973). This still leaves areas of uncertainty. The Burger Court was after, in his words, '"hard core" sexual conduct', namely, 'patently offensive representations or descriptions of ultimate sexual acts, normal or perverted, actual or simulated ... masturbation, excretory functions, and lewd exhibitions of genitals'. Such commendable explicitness, however, did not exclude such depictions in works of literary merit, and so on, which did not offend local community standards or incite prurience in the opinion of the average person. The result is that what actually constitutes obscene expression in the United States continues to cause 'a good deal of confusion' (Feinberg, 1985: 173).

Much the same uncertainty exists elsewhere. An official British government inquiry into obscenity and film censorship in 1979, which was not acted upon, characterized the legal situation as being 'a mess'. This is no mere matter of untidiness as certainty is a central requirement of the rule of law. Confusion delegitimizes it. So crucial is it that Justice Louis Brandeis could once go so far as to hold: 'it is more important that the applicable rule of law be settled than that it be settled right' (*Burnet v. Coronado Oil & Gas Co.*, 1932). Although in any mature legal system there will be provision for flexibility, certainty 'reigned supreme, if not unchallenged, since the birth of jurisprudence as a science ... As law exists for security, confidence and freedom, it must be invested with as much certainty and uniformity as can be provided by the wavering structures of human institutions' (Wade, 1941: 188, 199). By this measure the English law of obscenity, which relies on some twenty statutes as well as the common law precedents dating back to *Hicklin*, is deficient (Nicol *et al.*, 2009: 141).

The 1959 Obscene Publications Act[9] defined an obscene article as one whose: 'effects ... if taken as a whole, such as to tend to deprave and corrupt persons who are likely, having regard to all relevant circumstances, to read, see or hear the matter contained or embodied in it'. In all but very rare situations where a printer can claim ignorance, the Act does not otherwise consider the intention of the originators of the publication; but neither does it require an actual individual to attest to effects. It is the probability of the impact which the court will assess. Nevertheless, the Act, eventually, has 'worked to secure almost total freedom for the written word in Britain'. On the other hand, because of the connection in certain works between sex and drugs, it has also been wide enough to prohibit materials encouraging drug use (Robertson and Nicol, 2008: 204, 197, 215; Nicol *et al.*, 2009: 141). Cases involving sexual expression, though, are still possible. It took some time for 'the revolutionary implications of the legislation' to be become fully apparent. For one thing, the jailing of corrupt Metropolitan police in the Vice Squad in 1977 for turning the 1959 Act 'into a vast protection racket' inhibited prosecutions for some time (Cox, Shirley and Short, 1977: 158).

Other statutes remained in force (Robertson and Nicol, 2008: 196). For example, the law dealing with 'indecency', which can be applied to permit actions for de facto obscenity, was unchanged. While obscenity is corrupting, indecency is analogous to nuisance: 'an outrage to public susceptibilities … generally confined to maintaining decorum in public places' (Robertson and Nicol, 2008: 238–9). Indecency is not necessarily involved in matters of expression, nor is it limited to sexual activity; but it can be both.

Despite the abolition of theatrical censorship in 1968, Mary Whitehouse (who in the nineteenth century would have been described as a leading member of the 'purity' lobby) brought a private prosecution under Section 13, the Sexual Offences Act (1956), for indecency on the stage. Whitehouse was upset that the Attorney General declined to prosecute the National Theatre in 1981 for homosexual indecency in Howard Brenton's *The Romans in Britain*, a play which she did not personally attend. The case collapsed when her witness to this outrage could not be sure, when giving his evidence, whether or not he saw one actor approach another with his erect penis in hand or with thumb 'adroitly rising from a fist clenched over his organ' (Robertson and Nicol, 1993: 145).

The right of expression conferred in Article 10.1 of the ECHR, alone among the rights protected by the Convention, also involves 'duties and responsibilities'. Expression, according to Article 10.2, 'may be subject to such formalities, conditions, restrictions or penalties as are prescribed by law and are necessary in a democratic society, in the interests of', in the case of obscenity, 'the protection of health or morals' (European Convention of Human Rights, 1950 [1948]). Each state has a different concept of 'the health and morals' it wishes to protect and this is accommodated in the ECrtHR in Strasbourg by allowing a measure of national judicial independence – a 'margin of appreciation'. The result has been the source of much confusion. Strasbourg is as capable as Washington of voicing general ringing rhetoric: 'Freedom of expression constitutes one of the essential foundations of a democratic society, one of the basic conditions for its progress and for the development of every man' (*Handyside v. UK*, 1979–80). Such an impeccable liberal position is, however, 'tarnished' by the application of the margin of appreciation test; for example, in this very case (Robertson and Nicol, 2008: 193).

Richard Handyside was the publisher of *The Little Red Schoolbook*, a subversive and anarchic text written by two Danish school-teachers. It had appeared in the early 1970s in a number of European languages. Handyside published the English translation in 1971. There were twenty-six pages of frank information on sex from masturbation to abortion, nearly as many on drugs and the work was clearly targeted at children. It can also be noted that the very name – with its echo of the title of Mao Tse-tung's collected quotations – and the sections on 'work' and 'the system' were equally disturbing to the bench. Despite the language of the ECHR, the European Court supported the guilty verdict against Handyside, giving the UK a margin of appreciation because of the 1959 Obscene Publications Act. In Britain's 'democratic society', it was 'necessary' to censor *The Little Red Schoolbook*. On the other hand, one can argue that, after the liberation of the 1960s, this was clearly not so great a matter as it had once been. Handyside was fined a paltry £50 plus £110 costs. (It is, perhaps, in such incidents as this that a justification of Stoppard's view of freedom of speech as a shibboleth can be found. It is surely not wrong, when considering the language of the Strasbourg Court in contrast to its decision, to conclude that talk is cheap and the concept of free speech indeed a shibboleth (see Chapters 2, 10.1).)

Since 2000, the ECHR has been incorporated into English and Scottish law by the Human Rights Act (HRA).[10] The margin of appreciation test applied by the European Court means that the right in Article 10 will not automatically protect expression deemed to transgress English legal limits. To take an example of indecency rather than obscenity: an anti-abortion activist, Veronica Connolly, who sent disturbing photographs of aborted foetuses to pharmacists, was guilty of an offence, not under the obscenity law but under another of the proliferating control statutes, the Malicious Communications Act, 1988.[11] As with *Handyside*, the European judges used the margin of appreciation test to accept the judgment against her because, in the UK, this activist's technique was deemed to be excessive and within the prohibition described in the Act. Moreover, the ruling did not prohibit Connolly from expressing her anti-abortion opinions by other means (*Connolly v. DPP*, 2007).[12] And to go beyond indecency, it is also illegal in the UK to use the electronic network for 'the purpose of causing annoyance, inconvenience or needless anxiety' (see Chapters 9.5, 12.2).

Obscenity and indecency laws in Europe have been thus complicated by the margin of appreciation test. Its use has been most limited in cases concerned with political expression and the court is therefore most consistent in protecting this across the Continent, irrespective of national standards. No constraints on such communications, obviously, can readily be considered 'necessary in a democratic society'. Conversely, with artistic expression, the necessity of constraint is thought to be more easily demonstrated. Thus any issue of 'morals' – including questions of obscenity, indecency and other matters of offensive expression such as blasphemy – is more to the fore (Nicol *et al.*, 2009: 32). European judicial thinking considers that:

> obscene and blasphemous speech usually occur in the artistic rather than the political, or the commercial fields. The Court has consistently granted States a substantial margin of appreciation in this regard, first, because the expression

in question (unlike political speech) is not considered of central importance, and secondly, because the Court is peculiarly deferential to state regulation of expression where the protection of morals is in issue. (Nichol *et al.*, 2009: 140)

The result is that the application of the margin of appreciation test has worked to allow less liberal states to restrict artistic expression – but, even here, not consistently. Thus, while the banning of the depiction of bestiality at an art exhibition in Switzerland did not violate the exercise of the right in Article 10.1, given Switzerland's margin of appreciation, such an action might not be so elsewhere (*Müller and others v. Switzerland*, 1988). In Austria, by contrast, twenty years later, a painting depicting various public figures, including Mother Teresa, in orgiastic sexual congress was protected by Article 10.1 (*Vereinigung Bildender Künstler v. Austria*, 2008). 'The Court's use of margin of appreciation has been described as "illustrat[ing] a disappointing lack of clarity"' (Nicol *et al.*, 2009: 29). This, though, is somewhat of a piece with the underlying logic of the American local standards test.[13]

If obscenity can render the concept of free speech so uncertain, how much greater is the potential of 'fighting words' to do so? The principle that constraint should only be applied in limited circumstances is fundamentally threatened, should expression, on its face, be deemed to be of an unprotected class of 'deeds'. In *Chaplinsky*, the Supreme Court simply asserted that the words were assaultive of themselves. Even requiring more provocative and challenging expression than the insults actually at issue in *Chaplinsky* would nevertheless still be very chilling. Blasphemy, the second class of Justice Murphy's unprotected expressions, is much the same as obscenity. It too is of elusive character, less easy to define than it seems to be at first glance; albeit, like obscenity, it is likely to be more bounded than are 'fighting words'. Blasphemy is as problematic as obscenity as an analogy for removing protection from 'fighting words'

11.5   *Gay News Ltd and Lemon v. United Kingdom* (1982): Blasphemy

By the end of the Second World War, blasphemy seemed to be a spent force. Lord Denning, then in the English Court of Appeal, remarked in a speech: 'The reason for the law was because it was thought that a denial of Christianity was liable to shake the fabric of society ... There is no such danger to society now and the offence of blasphemy is a dead letter.'[14] Nevertheless, blasphemy cannot be dismissed as an essentially religious concept of little interest to a secular society. In terms of the challenge to the West illustrated by the Rushdie affair, although there was also a measure of supposed obscenity in *The Satanic*

Verses, it was the confusions surrounding blasphemy which played the central role.

In response to the rise of secularism, blasphemy has been severely subject to changing legal interpretations but it shares much with obscenity. At the time Denning spoke and, indeed, for just under half-a-century longer, straightforward prosecutions for blasphemy in England and Wales, although rare, were possible. Harm to the victim, being the divine, perforce cannot be in question. Like obscenity, though, no actually harmed, or even shocked or horrified, bystander need be involved either. The determination of the offence – in jurisdictions that allow for its prosecution – relies on judging the content of the expression alone. This is, again, to illuminate the danger that these categories of expression present as analogy when considering other less obviously bounded classes of speech, for example, threatening or 'fighting words' and defamation. Blasphemy also illustrates the difficulties involved in removing a constraint on speech once it has become established, however much the circumstances which led to its introduction change.

'Blasphemy means speaking ill of sacred matters ... it affronts the priestly caste, the deep-seated beliefs of worshippers, and the basic values that a community shares' (Levy, 1995: 1). In the West it means that speaking ill of sacred Christian matters and, even then, not all such matters – and not all Christians – are equally protected. Indeed, there was the specific offence of heresy, which is, exactly, a practice of religion – as it might be Christianity – that offends the orthodoxy. Heresy offers a direct challenge to the arrangements of the orthodox but heretics can be polite about the other distinct faiths.[15] Blasphemers, exactly, are not. They attack the reputation of God as it is conceived of by the majority of the faithful and, although – obviously – the Almighty's own view of such offensiveness cannot be known, this upsets them. It also potentially offends the Charter right in Article 17 of the ECHR, which guarantees all the other rights, including freedom for religious beliefs in Article 9.

Blasphemous ill-speaking becomes a matter for the law when it threatens, actually or potentially, social cohesion, i.e. when it actually or potentially provokes a disturbance. This is especially so if the state has adopted an official, established religion. Legally, in England in the seventeenth-century, blasphemy, as a non-capital offence, replaced heresy, and the death penalty for profane utterance was abolished. The offence, though, was as much to deny that the Anglican Church possessed a monopoly of Christian truth as it was to attack Christianity itself. Non-conformity of any kind in such a situation can be, and was, subjected to a variety of disabilities including the suppression of the right to speak, especially if so doing in any way was thought to discomfort the faithful majority.

It should be noted that has little to do with a right to profess a faith as guaranteed, for example, by Article 9 of the ECHR. Blasphemy assumes a further right, that a faith cannot be attacked by third parties, thereby abridging yet another right, that of free expression in Article 10. This last claim of right, though, is of a different order. As Jefferson put it in the clear light of eighteenth-century rationalism: 'it does me no injury for my neighbour to say there are twenty gods, or no gods. It neither picks my pocket nor breaks my leg' (Jefferson, 1904 [1784]). The right in Article 9 (reinforced by 10) is to allow the 'neighbour' to believe and say what they like. Blasphemy says nothing to Article 9 but rather constrains Article 10.

The United States can lay some claim to have among the most religiously inclined populations in the West. Nevertheless, already in a nineteenth-century America heedful of Jefferson's liberalism, 'the frequency of blasphemy prosecutions barely exceeded the number of boojums sighted on the high seas' (Levy, 1995: 506). American courts took the view that:

> from the standpoint of freedom of speech and the press, it is enough to point out that the state has no legitimate interest in protecting any or all religions from views distasteful to them which is sufficient to justify prior restraints upon the expression of those views. It is not the business of government in our nation to suppress real or imagined attacks upon a particular religious doctrine, whether they appear in publications, speeches, or motion pictures. (*Joseph Burstyn, Inc. v. Wilson*, 1952)

Although many state codes contained (and some still do contain) blasphemy as an offence, this freedom became as deeply embedded, as is the right of free expression in general.

Against their better judgement (and the thrust of their Puritan convictions), many of the founding settlers and their heirs grudgingly came to accept religious freedom as a principle. After all, they were largely religious enthusiasts who were themselves 'blasphemous' victims of persecution by the mainstream European Churches. As the eighteenth century progressed and the variety of colonial beliefs proliferated, no single religion or sect would be established in the American states, despite the fervour of their faiths. The last attempt to do so was abandoned in 1833. The federal government never tried, adopting instead Jefferson's 'wall of separation between church and state'. In the Act he wrote in 1786 guaranteeing religious tolerance in Virginia, he argued that: 'to restrain the profession or propagation of principles on supposition of their ill tendency is a dangerous falacy [sic], which at once destroys all religious liberty' (Jefferson, 1785/6).[16]

The 'grudges', as it were, continue to be reflected in a number of long-standing conflicts. These include repeated rows over the teaching of evolution (declared by the Supreme Court in the 1960s to be constitutionally protected); or the public displays of religious insignia (declared not to be protected but still producing cases for the Supreme Court to hear). Such matters reflect the tension between Jeffersonian rationalism and the founding fathers' exclusionist faiths. In a nod to the latter, US banknotes declare 'In God we trust' and American children every school morning swear allegiance to 'one nation under God'; but it is the Jeffersonian view that renders blasphemy, in effect, unactionable at law in the United States.

Established state religions tend towards a different view. In England, Christianity was held to be, in the words of the Lord Chief Justice Matthew Hale, 'parcel of the laws of England' (*R. v. Taylor*, 1676). By the nineteenth century it was judged most often to be cognate with obscenity. If Christianity, of any variety now, was attacked and 'the decencies of controversy observed' (as Coleridge, a successor of Hale, put it in 1883), it was not a blasphemous libel and therefore protected (*R. v. Ramsey and Foote*, 1883). The last case of the statutory offence of blasphemy to be subjected to Coleridge's 'decency test' was heard in 1921. An atheist provocateur, John Gott, who had three previous convictions for blasphemy, published a pamphlet in which Christ was characterized as a circus clown because he rode into Jerusalem on two donkeys at the same time.[17] Gott was again prosecuted. Without evidence, the trial judge averred that any Christian might have 'the instinct to thrash' Gott, for the prevention of which he committed the man to the maximum sentence of nine months hard labour (*R. v Gott*, 1922). Even at the time, characterizing Gott as 'dangerous' without any evidence of the impact of the danger he presented, and judging his expression to be some species of irresistible provocation, was seen as harsh and excessive. Gott, who had already been ailing, died in the year after his release, aged fifty-six (Levy, 1995: 501–2).

The rational deployed in Gott's trial was analogous to the *ratio decidendi* across the Atlantic twenty years later in *Chaplinsky*: never mind the disrespect to Christ, the complained-of expression was such as possibly to provoke disorder. The 'fighting words' doctrine in *Chaplinsky* has been called the 'heckler's charter' for exactly this reason. It allows 'hostile audiences [or the threat of hostile audiences] to cause the abridgement of speech'. If applied, it 'would make the audiences the ultimate judges of constitutional rights' (Herbeck, 2003: 52). And this without any actual disturbance occurring; even without any audience being present. The offence – blasphemy or assaultive words – occurred in both *Gott* and *Chaplinsky* without disorderly hecklers. That a thrashing *might* happen caused the court to imprison Gott. The only actual witnessed responses to him that were registered were cries of 'shame' and 'disgusting', scarcely evidence of social disorder. The Town Marshal merely locked Chaplinsky up; those who actually assaulted Chaplinsky were not present when the officer was insulted. They had not been arrested. Compare *The Satanic Verses*: here were exactly 'hostile audiences' intent on making themselves 'the ultimate judges of constitutional rights' by, if necessary (in their view), breaking the law. They too were not arrested. The appearance of an actual 'heckler', however, scarcely makes the offence friendlier to the right in Article 10 – the right to impart 'information and ideas'.

In the UK, after the Second World War, opinion would seem to have settled that blasphemy would no longer be prosecuted. Eventually, in 1967, the statutory offence was repealed, although the common law offence was not abolished at the same time. Blasphemy was not therefore so dead that its corpse could not still twitch. In 1976, before her failures to prosecute the National Theatre (1981) and the Independent Broadcasting Authority (1984), Mary Whitehouse felt that her faith had been so abused by a poem in *Gay News* that she needed to prosecute the publication, necessarily privately, using the common law (*R. v. Lemon*, 1979; *Whitehouse v. Lemon*, 1979; *Gay News Ltd and Lemon v. United Kingdom*, 1982). The words that so distressed her were in a poem graphically fantasizing about a homosexual liaison between a centurion and the dead Christ. As this was a proceeding in blasphemy, not obscenity, there was no issue of assessing the material's capacity to deprave and corrupt its targeted audience; or indeed its capacity to do so with an average reader; or its artistic merit or otherwise. Moreover, no question of intent was admitted either. Lord Scarman, the then exceptional law lord who actually consistently supported a right of free expression (Robertson and Nicol, 2008: vii), nevertheless, in an 'imaginative opinion' (Levy, 1995: 548), wrote that blasphemy: 'belongs to a group of criminal offences designed to safeguard the internal tranquillity of the kingdom. In an increasingly plural society such as that of modern Britain it is necessary now not only to respect differing religious beliefs ... but to protect them from scrutiny, vilification, ridicule and contempt' (*R. v. Lemon*, 1979). (One more instance, then, to support Stoppard's view of the right of expression as a shibboleth.)

In the aftermath, the poem was widely disseminated, without further action. It did not, however, mark a revival of blasphemy per se: 'Attacks on Christianity, no matter how devastating, will not be blasphemous unless expressed in an outrageously indecent or scurrilous manner' (Robertson and Nicol, 2008: 252). A book suggesting Christianity was the creation of a drugged, mushroom-addicted ancient sect was published without consequence, as were a number of other such texts. Trouble, though, always lurked. In an extreme case of art following life, Monty Python's satire on the messianic delusions of ancient Judeans, *Life of Brian*, caused protests and demonstrations in the United States when it was released in 1979. Rabbi Abraham Hecht, president of the Rabbinical Alliance of America, told *Variety*: 'Never have we come across such a foul, disgusting, blasphemous film before' (Sellers, 2003). One can surely be forgiven for thinking he might in reality have been another fervid Python creation, not least because he seemed unfamiliar with the limited Jewish concept of blasphemy.[18]

Mary Whitehouse, triumphant over *Gay News*, continued her attempts to hold various authorities to the grindstone of suppression. To the IBA (whom she had sued in 1984 for failure to ban a programme) and the Attorney General, she added the British Board of Film Censors. She sued them for failing to refuse the film a licence. Her case was rejected, and three times as many UK cinemas as originally planned showed the film. The protestors had, John Cleese joked, 'actually made me rich ... I feel we should send them a crate of champagne'.[19] Although locally refused a certificate by a number of councils, it broke box office records. Eventually, after seventeen years, even Swansea, a hold-out council, licensed the film, causing the late Eric Idle to say: 'What a shame, is nothing sacred?' (Sellers, 2003).

In 1985, a commission again called for abolition of the common law offence but nothing was done and blasphemy still refused to die. In 1989, *Visions of Ecstasy*, a film directed by Nigel Wingrove containing scenes in which St Teresa of Ávila fantasizes an erotic heterosexual relationship with the dead Christ, was, unlike *Life of Brian*, denied a certificate by the BBFC. Chilled perhaps by the Whitehouse attack on it, the authority did so on the grounds that the film infringed the still existing common law of blasphemy. Wingrove sued and lost. The case went to the European Court. Shibboleth well to the fore, the judges ruled 14: 2 that the BBFC's action offended against Article 10; but they nevertheless allowed a margin of appreciation and denied Wingrove and his film the protection of the Article (*Wingrove v. UK*, 1997). 'The [Strasbourg] Court shows a reluctance to become involved with standard-setting in the area of sexual or religious morality. A case containing both sex and religion was probably particularly difficult in that respect' (Stone, 2008: 397). One of the two dissenting judges in the case, though, also held that all prior constraint is illegal under Article 10. This has never been accepted by his brethren (Nicol *et al.*, 2009: 34).

Another decade was to pass but, finally, in 2008 the English common law offence was abolished. Adherents, even to the Church of England, now have to be strong enough in their faith to withstand 'affronts' to their belief without the protection of the law, unless the facts permit a case under the 1990s Public Order Acts. The Torbay Council in Devon responded to the abolition by allowing a screening of the *Life of Brian*, thirty-nine years after its release (Saville, 2008). There were no riots.

Elsewhere, blasphemy is also in desuetude. The last prosecution in Norway was in 1912, in Australia in 1919, in New Zealand in 1922, in Denmark (when it was used to curb local Nazi anti-Semitism) in 1938; yet, in many countries, it remains in place as blasphemy proper or as a prohibition against religious insults or as both. And it is live; even, on occasion, in the West. In the last twenty years there have been cases in Germany and Finland, although the offence each time has also involved other elements such as causing or threatening to cause a disturbance (*à la Chaplinsky*) or falling within the vexed category of 'hate speech' (see Chapters 11.2, 12.3). Punishment for casual public blasphemous utterance proper is still found in Malta. In 2008, 621 people were prosecuted and, in the first three months of 2009, a further 162 (Anon, 2009). The Strasbourg Court allowed Catholic Austria a margin of

286 A RIGHT TO OFFEND

appreciation in banning a club-screening of a film because it was thought to be blasphemous (*Otto-Preminger-Institut v. Austria*, 1994). This judgment, which has not been distinguished, reflects the court's 'main free speech failing, namely its refusal to protect works of literary and artistic merit' on a European-wide basis (Robertson and Nicol, 2008: 66).

In fact, it has gone further in sustaining, at least on a national basis, blasphemy. In a majority decision in *IA v. Turkey*, the court, the chair of the bench being a Turkish judge, ruled that in a Muslim country a margin of appreciation would allow an insult to the faith in a novel (such as *The Satanic Verses*) to justify censorship (*IA v. Turkey*, 2005). The basis of the decision, its *ratio decidendi*, was an unambiguous misreading of Article 9 of the ECHR. This gives a person the right to hold beliefs and practise a faith but the court misunderstood this to mean third parties were prohibited from commenting on such belief and practices thereby creating a presumption of a 'defamation-of-religion' offence. Despite this extension, rarely anywhere in the world is blasphemy still considered a capital offence.[20]

There is a sense in which blasphemy has become a measure of religious commitment on the part of those who argue for its continued presence. For example, the sometime Puritan Commonwealth of Massachusetts, in 1977 refused to remove it from state law where it had been since colonial days in deference to those who would censor artistic expression. Law is always uncertain, but it is extremely improbable that a conviction in that state would be upheld by the Supreme Court, however conservative it were to become. Blasphemy seems to be clung to as the last vestige of a complex system of spiritual jurisprudence that once governed much of Western life. Even where there can be no chance of a prosecution, as in Massachusetts, it thus remains, symbolically, on the statute book.

On the other hand, blasphemy shows how potent even a dying constraint can be on expression. Anyway, the extent to which it is dead in any society grappling with the sensitivities of a multi-faith population can be disputed. It is not any longer simple a matter of abolishing an offence relating only to Christianity because many think, in the name of social cohesion, a better solution would be its extension to other faiths. From such a viewpoint, it is not unreasonable to ask if there should not be a more universal withdrawal of protection of speech so that blasphemy, broadly defined, can embrace all religions.

The ECHR itself avoids the problem because it protects the right to profess whatever an individual claims to be a religion; it involves no consideration of the viability of such a claim and therefore requires no definitions. The cases that have been heard have been largely concerned with seeking to impose a religion or restrain its expression: for example, displaying a crucifix (*Lautsi and others v. Italy*, 2011) or wearing a *hijab* (*Leyla Şahin v. Turkey*, 2005). In these decisions touching on religion, the court has tended to apply a margin of appreciation to local laws and standards. Despite *IA v. Turkey*, it has usually avoided considering a right to be protected from religious insult, i.e. blasphemy, and, by so doing, has also evaded the difficulties of defining religion (for example, *Universelles Leben e.V. v. Germany*, 1996).

What is religion? Arguably, it is not even like the 'mess' of obscenity, for who, in reality, knows one when they see it? In the aftermath of the Rushdie affair, Keith Ward, an Anglican cleric and a former professor of the philosophy of religion at the University of London, considering the possibility of extending blasphemy to all faiths, said: 'I am supposed to tell you what religion is, but I have failed' (Levy, 1995: 566). For example: that the concept of a God be present would exclude Buddhism; but if one included Buddhism, how could one exclude, say, Scientology?[21] This uncertainty has not prevented ongoing attempts to introduce an all-embracing offence of blasphemy at various levels from national law to international charter.

The Dutch proposed expanding blasphemy to embrace all faiths in 2008 but gave up in 2009 because a statute to prevent religious insults was too difficult to draft.[22] Such attempts, though, are not unknown. The Irish, in a defamation law in 2009, attempted it:

> a person publishes or utters blasphemous matter if (a) he or she publishes or utters matter that is grossly abusive or insulting in relation to matters held sacred by any religion, thereby causing outrage among a substantial number of the adherents of that religion, and (b) he or she intends, by the publication or utterance of the matter concerned, to cause such outrage.[23]

No sooner enacted, this provoked strenuous moves for its abolition and the following year the government was forced to promise a referendum on this.[24]

As a result of the initiative proposed by the United Nations Alliance of Civilizations (UNAOC),[25] 'a High-level Group of experts was formed by former Secretary-General Kofi Annan to explore the roots of polarization between societies and cultures today, and to recommend a practical programme of action to address this issue' (United Nations Alliance of Civilizations, n.d.). Given that the establishment of a UN forum ranks in many Western newsrooms as a nadir of newsworthiness, this event was not much noticed. However, on 25 February 2006, in the midst of 'the day of rage' violence following the publication of the Danish cartoons, the nascent committee was holding a second preparatory meeting in Doha, Qatar. The hosts of the meeting – Qatar, Spain and Turkey – together with representatives of the Organization of the Islamic Conference, the Arab League and the UN as well as (surprisingly) the European Union, took the opportunity to suggest that the UN Universal Declaration of Human Rights (UDHR) be amended to include respect for religious figures as a human right.

How the proposed addendum might mesh with the UNAOC's mission statement, that its programme of action be practical, was not immediately apparent. Given that this suggestion was a reaction to mayhem caused by people simply declaring themselves affronted, there would be presumably no objection to others similarly declaring any opinion as being essential – sacred – to their inner being and therefore protected. Why would not Nazis declare their adoration of the Führer to be religious in nature and therefore protected, justifying any physical attack they chose to make on those who said Hitler was a murderous megalomaniac? Were this revision to be in place, one could presumably be censored for suggesting that the science-fiction writer L. Ron Hubbard had cynically determined that, given the religiosity of the United States, a sure way to make a fortune was to invent a religion; and that the religion of Scientology, which he duly invented, was exactly such a cynical route to wealth. Censorship under the proposed UDHR revision would be all the more probable, not least because in 1993, in a curious about-face after years of refusal, the US Internal Revenue Service suddenly awarded Hubbard's 'Church' religious and charitable status (Frantz, 1997). That the story of the origins of the 'Church' was true, and admitted by Hubbard himself, would presumably not protect any who retailed it (Miller, 1987: 133).[26] Or would it be the case that the constraint on the right of free expression would deal only with old religions? And if so, how old? Would one be prohibited from publishing the view that Joseph Smith, Jr was a fraud and that no angel ever revealed to him any golden plates containing the *Book of Mormon*? Or is 180 years enough to earn the sensitivities of Mr Smith, Jr's followers protection under the revised right?

Specificity does not solve this problem as it readily produces discrimination, as with the English law of blasphemy's concern only with Christianity. In 2010, for (a necessarily non-Western) example, the Indonesian High Court confirmed the constitutionality of a blasphemy law which prohibits the 'distortion' or 'misrepresentation' of the country's five recognized faiths: Islam, Christianity, Buddhism, Hinduism and Confucianism. Never mind Scientologists and Mormons – or Sikhs, Jews and Jains, among many, many others – who are unprotected and, indeed, threatened by the law.

A reform of the UDHR, however worthy its intention and although it has nothing more than the status of a UN General Assembly resolution, cannot but be considered potentially extremely unfortunate. In the slow debate engendered by the original suggestion, UDHR revision was lost but a planned international blasphemy law was discussed. The argument in the UN was divisive; the Muslim states were largely in favour of a universal constraint of expression to protect religion but the West (including an awoken EU, with Ireland now in a second-thought phase on the matter) was against. The effort would appear to have stalled, albeit not entirely. In the ECrtHR, the decision in *IA v. Turkey* has yet to be distinguished. On the other hand, in March 2011: 'the United Nations Human Rights Council rebuffed a drive for an international blasphemy law, instead adopting a resolution against religious intolerance that excluded the infamous "defamation-of-religions" language of prior years' (United States Committee on International Religious Freedom, 2011: 1).

The moves by that section of the British Muslim community who had been most incensed by *The Satanic Verses* to argue for an extension of the law of blasphemy to embrace Islam were then not only a matter of strategy. Certainly, the ploy was grievously flawed legally in that it ignored the general desuetude of the offence of blasphemy in England and Wales and its specificity as offering protection for Christianity alone; but, equally, the protestors did have encouragement in thinking the idea might conceivably work. As a result of the Rushdie uproar, there were many non-Muslims who felt an offence that prohibited anti-religious expression of any kind was to be welcomed in the name of social cohesion. The effort, still then fitfully underway, to abolish blasphemy was, from this viewpoint, to move in completely the wrong direction. Instead, it should be reformed to make it protect all religions. Take Lord Scarman's language embracing 'differing religions' in the *Gay News* case. His liberal motivation was, as in the Netherlands and Ireland, the worthwhile protection of minority religious communities. His suggestion that there should not even be 'scrutiny' of religion, however, well illustrates the opinion that prior to the Human Rights Act: 'The English judiciary, subject to certain notable exceptions, consistently failed to give sufficient regard to the freedom of expression' (Nicol *et al.*, 2009: 32).

Liberals exhibit a certain schizophrenia here. On the one hand, they are properly eager to protect minorities but take little note of the consequences of so doing. Hence left-wing attacks on Rushdie. On the other hand, when addressing the free speech issue, they 'too often behave like Chicken Little, giving the impression that one case of suppression means the sky is falling and Shakespeare will be next' (Levy, 1995: 576). However, if the capstone importance of free expression is acknowledged, not even the protection of minorities can be bought at its expense. Their protection ultimately cannot be sustained if the right is undercut. There is, then, good reason to emulate Chicken Little. In a culture where the interpretation of precedents and their possible reapplication in cognate circumstances is a basic fact, 'one case of suppression' easily leads to another. And discarding law and precedent once established, never mind 'distinguishing' cases, is nowhere any easier than it has proved to be throughout the many decades it took to remove blasphemy in England and Wales – insofar as total abolition has been achieved, even now. It is, therefore, no species of liberal over-sensitivity always to defend the perimeter of free expression on all fronts as, for example, the American newspaper industry is prone to do.

The language of Lord Scarman, the placatory statements of some politicians or the sentiments of *bien pensants*[27] and many others offered support, in the name of social cohesion, for a faith-blind (as it were) blasphemy law. However, any revival, much less extension, of blasphemy, threatens to chill free speech. It is the nature of the offence itself that has always made it threatening to free speech. As Jefferson warned: 'the civil magistrate ... will make his opinions the rule of judgment, and approve or condemn the sentiments of others only as they shall square with or differ from his own' (Jefferson, 1785/6). 'Speaking ill of sacred matters', like uttering 'fighting words', is too prone to encourage the courts in a 'Humpty Dumpty tendency': 'When I say a word [in this case 'religion'], it means just what I choose it to mean − neither more nor less' (Carroll, 1865).

11.6   *Attorney-General (United Kingdom) v. Heinemann Publishers Australia Pty Ltd* (1988): Sedition

In *Chaplinsky*, Justice Murphy did not mention seditious expression in his list of unprotected areas of speech, but he could have. Despite the First Amendment, a specific statute, the Sedition Act of 1798 (see Chapter 5.1), had made seditious libel a criminal offence in the United States, just as it had been since the Star Chamber created the crime in England in the seventeenth century (see Chapters 4.2 and 4.3). However, in the United States, no sooner was it passed than it was challenged. Jefferson pledged its removal during his successful run for the presidency in 1800. Nevertheless, it was revived during the First World War as an adjunct to the Espionage Act.[28] Over a thousand cases were heard, largely against anti-war, left-wing pacifists. As was to be the case with *Chaplinsky*, the words at issue were often hard to see as carrying the weight attributed to them. For example, how 'disloyal, profane, scurrilous or abusive' (as the Sedition Act required)[29] was it, in a supposedly free country, to say: 'No government which is for the profiteers can also be for the people, and I am for the people while the government is for the profiteers'? Yet this sentiment, published in 1918 on the letters' page of the *Kansas City Star*, earned Rose Pastor Stokes, a prominent radical, a sentence of ten years imprisonment (Anon, 1918: 1).[30]

The twentieth-century Sedition Act might have been as clearly in breach of the First Amendment as that of 1798, but neither yielded a case for the Supreme Court to pronounce on their constitutionality. From 1918 on, the court avoided examining sedition's implications for the First Amendment. It initially held, in the words of Justice Oliver Wendell Holmes, Jr, that: 'When a nation is at war many things that might be said in time of peace are such a hindrance to its effort that their utterance will not be endured' (*Schenck v. United States*, 1919). At issue was a pamphlet arguing for conscripts to resist the draft. However, as the 1920s progressed, less focused expression was treated as being as unprotected as was this piece of direct advocacy. The

International Workers of the World, an anarcho-socialist general trade union that had been founded in Chicago in 1905, was particularly targeted with sedition offences in the 1920s. It was the main tool used to combat the 'Red Scare' of the 1930s. Together with the repressive 'Smith Act' (1940),[31] which prohibited the advocacy of the overthrow of the government, it bolstered the 'Red Menace' hysteria of the 1950s.

However, as with blasphemy, the blatant contradiction between the crime of sedition and the right of free speech slowly led to an inevitable conclusion. By the 1960s, despite no direct pronouncement, sedition had been so reduced in scope that Justice William Douglas could say, in a case of a speech advocating (exactly) resisting the draft: 'The Alien and Sedition Laws constituted one of our sorriest chapters; and I had thought we had done with them forever ... Suppression of speech as an effective police measure is an old, old device, outlawed by our Constitution' (*Watts v. United States*, 1969). The specifics of this case – a threat to shoot the president – caused further difficulties (see Chapter 11.3); but Watts' words, unlike those of Chaplinsky, were seen by the court as hyperbolic and the threat they contained was deemed unreal.[32] But then, of course, the war in question was Vietnam, and hostility to it was not, as with the World Wars, limited to a minority.

In 1971, with Vietnam still continuing, the *New York Times* printed a secret dossier, leaked by Daniel Ellsberg, outlining the United States' 'duplicitous path to an unwinnable war in Vietnam' (Frankel, 2010: 35). The Attorney-General had sought an injunction to prevent publication of what soon became known as 'The Pentagon Papers' on the grounds of national security (see Chapter 9.5). The Court reaffirmed Douglas' opinion and denied the government: 'Any system of prior constraint comes to this Court bearing a heavy presumption against its constitutional validity' (*New York Times Co. v. United States*, 1971). Mr Justice Potter Stewart argued:

> We are asked, quite simply, to prevent the publication ... of material that the Executive Branch insists should not, in the national interest, be published. I am convinced that the Executive is correct with respect to some of the documents involved. But I cannot say that disclosure of any of them will surely result in direct, immediate, and irreparable damage to our Nation or its people.

There was no clear and present danger.

Despite this, the American state has never given up on the prosecution of sedition and arrests are yet possible as it is, *pace* the liberality of these judgments, recognized in the United States Code:[33]

> Whoever knowingly and willfully communicates, furnishes, transmits, or otherwise makes available to an unauthorized person, or publishes, or uses in any manner prejudicial to the safety or interest of the United States or for the benefit of any foreign government to the detriment of the United States any

classified information ... shall be fined under this title or imprisoned not more than ten years, or both.[34]

And in such cases, the First Amendment will not be at issue. In 1985, Samuel Morison, a government security analyst, passed classified photographs of Soviet naval vessels to a British publication, the authoritative *Jane's Fighting Ships*. His motivation, he claimed, was to alert the American public to the threat, but, not least because he was actually working for *Jane's* on the side, he was imprisoned. His offence was straightforwardly espionage and the theft of government property. Free speech was held to be irrelevant to the case. However, bolstered by this and similar successes, William Casey, President Reagan's CIA director, called in the publisher of the *Washington Post*, Ben Bradlee, to warn him off another story because, if it were published, Casey:

> would recommend that the paper be prosecuted under the 'intelligence statute'. According to Administration officials, Casey apparently has in mind Section 798 of Title 18 of the U.S. Code. Passed into law in 1951, the so-called COMINT statute makes it illegal for anyone to disclose classified information about U.S. ciphers, code breaking and other communications intelligence. Though Section 798 specifically forbids the publication of secrets, it has never before been invoked against newspapers or magazines. (Kelly, Constable and Halevy, 1986)

The *Post* published anyway.

None of this is to deny that state security is obviously a quite proper and urgent concern. It is, however, also concerning to those who would defend the right of free speech. Seditious libel is of a piece with obscenity, blasphemy and Murphy's 'fighting words' doctrine. Like those, it is an offence determined on its face. Expression speaks for itself. It needs no context, intention is deduced from content and its effects need not be demonstrated. States, typically addicted to secrecy, have always been especially convinced that information is power with the chilling concomitant view that it should not be shared with the citizenry at large. And the state, with the certainty of Carroll's Humpty Dumpty, knows that its security is threatened when it says it is. The damage – and here again it need only be potential – is also what the state says it is or could be. In fact, the nature of the damage might itself be a state secret. And, finally, the offence is judged by the state. This last obviously raises a further problem not necessarily present with obscenity, blasphemy or 'fighting words'. Seditious libel, by its very nature, makes a state the judge in its own cause, and the result is often more Kafka than Carroll.

In the twenty-first century, the United States, engaged in a 'war' against a host of perceived 'terrorist' dangers, finds itself constantly becoming evermore a 'security state'. This is quite understandable. What the liberal Senator Daniel Moynihan characterized as a 'culture of secrecy' feeds on civil tensions and foreign uncertainties and challenges (Moynihan, 1999: 155). The WikiLeaks revelations merely exposed the US government's obsessive desire to keep information to itself but, as Frankel observed: 'Governments must finally acknowledge that secrets shared with millions of "cleared" officials, including lowly army clerks are not secret. They must decide that the random stamping of millions of papers and computer files each year does not a security system make' (Frankel, 2010: 32). Bradley Manning, the lowly army clerk who was Assange's informant, is on trial for sedition as this is being written.

Like the US and other Western democracies, Her Majesty's Government has also found it hard to distinguish damage from embarrassment. In practice, because 'the day-to-day running of the British government is infected with an ethos of secrecy', it is peculiarly pone to being embarrassed (Feldman, 1993: 633). Secrecy is the British Establishment's fail-safe setting. It pervades all aspects of governance from the insensitivity of the bench to free expression rights to the political culture of obfuscation, chillingly characterized by Tony Blair in his memoirs as 'sensible government'. With an illuminating passion, he there revealed that what he most regrets having done as Prime Minister is not lead the country into the Iraq War and so on. Rather, it is to have passed a Freedom of Information Act. Upon reflection, falling for the liberal argument, Blair feels, reduced him to the level of a 'nincompoop' (Blair, 2010: 516).[35] To have these sentiments thus set down by a supposedly democratic political leader (and a lawyer by training) is at best surprising, at worst seriously alarming.

The UK's 'official secrets' were first protected by statute in 1911. This Official Secrets Act (OSA), passed 'in great haste, was the subject of sustained criticism over many years' (Lord Bingham, *R. v. Shayler*, 2007). However, the official impulse to suppress information was no new thing and resisting it has been merely another front in Western authorities' long war on liberty. Officialdom finds it difficult to restrain its demands for constraining expression. In a democratic society, this means restrictive laws, such as the 1911 Act, tend to be overdrawn. In consequence, as a right of free expression also exists, the courts have found that the OSA's 'excessive scope had proved an obstacle to its effective enforcement'. Although this was acknowledged by a committee of inquiry (Departmental Committee on Section 2 of the Official Secrets Act 1911, Oliver Franks, Baron Franks, 1972) in 1971, the new reformed OSA of 1989, scarcely undercut the culture of secrecy. Sections 1.1 and 4 specifically excluded a defence of public interest, the most obvious legal shield for 'unhelpful' investigative journalism. Even after the Human Rights Act, the protection of Article 10 can be denied if suppression is 'in the interests of national security, territorial integrity or public safety' (European Convention of Human Rights (1950 [1948]), Article 10.2). The OSA does need to be within, as the Charter put it, the legal 'conditions, restrictions or penalties necessary in a democratic society'; but it is – having been duly enacted exactly to protect the interests of national security, and so on – 'necessary'. With or without the Human Rights Act, the OSA has created, over a century, a more restrictive atmosphere than prevails in the United States. The cost, though, can well be 'embarrassment'.

Like 'The Pentagon Papers' or WikiLeaks, the official response to *Spycatcher* was hysterical and embarrassing. Written by a disaffected retired MI5 assistant director, Peter Wright, it revealed many of the department's past covert operations and bumbling inefficiencies, clearly matters of public interest. The Thatcher government took a different view and was able to prevent UK publication because of the standard confidentiality clause in Wright's contract of employment, reinforced by the OSA. It was held by the Court of Appeal that the recipient of information was constrained from repeating it if it was reasonable to suppose it was confidential. There was, in effect, a 'duty of confidence' in play. Peter Wright certainly had such a duty vis-à-vis the government, but any publication using material from him that was in breach was equally in breach. A public right to know did not enter into the matter (*Attorney-General v Guardian Newspapers Ltd (No 2)*, 1990). Nevertheless, a third of the national press refused to desist from running the story and ignored injunctions so to do, risking contempt of court proceedings. 'The furor,' *Time Magazine* reported, only slightly perhaps over-egging the pudding, 'underscores the conflict between Britain's shaky tradition of press rights and stolid tradition of government secrecy' (Zuckerman, Hofheinz and Mehta, 1987). The European Court eventually held that the injunctions offended against Article 10 (*Observer & Guardian v. UK*, 1991).

Publication was proposed in Australia, which Her Majesty's Government also attempted to prevent. The Australian court was 'robust' in rejecting official claims by the British Attorney-General as to the security threat the book posed (Feldman, 1993: 665). The judge decided that British government's embarrassment was more at issue and refused the injunction (*Attorney-General [United Kingdom] v. Heinemann Publishers Australia Pty Ltd*, 1987). The book was published; and it was also published in the United States. Copies were brought into Britain. The row made it a bestseller and the continued attempts of the government and the English courts to prevent its distribution made a fool of the law.

The twenty-first century has been characterized by an 'avalanche' of, at best partially redundant, anti-'terror' laws, many of which could impact on freedom of speech (Robertson and Nicol, 2008: 660). Following the model of panicked legislation established by the original OSA in 1911, these could well be overdrawn. The Terrorism Act, 2006, for example seeks to prohibit incitement to terrorism but its justification for this as a measure to protect British national security is blurred as it applies to intentions directed against states and persons abroad. (This is not its only problem; see Chapter 12.4.) It will not be likely soon removed, though, whatever its failings as legislation. It should not be forgotten that the Star Chamber's offence of sedition had already long ceased to be much use to authority. Thanks to the hostility of juries, it was already falling into desuetude, for the control of the press at least, in the nineteenth century (see Chapter 4.5). It was finally abolished (with blasphemy) only in 2008.

All these offences dampen speech and all share the same limited need to demonstrate, in contrast to, say, defamation, damage to an actual person or persons. Unprotected expression, under the headings of obscenity, blasphemy and seditious libel, did not need any victims. To one degree or another, these offences sought to support the general maintenance of, as it were, 'the tranquillity of the kingdom' or 'the fabric of society'. 'Social cohesion' is how we would have it today: the victim is society at large. The law, in effect, had long turned obscene, blasphemous and seditious words into deeds, the semantics and/or semiotics of which it was prepared to judge more or less in isolation. The response to unprotected speech seemed to be: 'I know it when I see it.'

11.7   *Hammond v. DPP* [2004]: The limits of protected speech

Although determination of what is obscenity, blasphemy and sedition is hard, with 'fighting words' it is yet harder. Assaultive words need not be bound by sex, faith or state secrets; they are far more dependent on intention and context. In short, to return to the linguistic philosophers, judgment of assaultive speech's harm requires a consideration of 'the total situation in which the utterance is issued', as J.L. Austin put it (Austin, 1962: 52; Butler, 1997: 3).

In the decades after the Second World War, the doctrine of 'fighting words' in *Chaplinsky* was 'distinguished' in a number of cases, i.e. in effect it became so limited as to be whittled away. The Supreme Court not only eschewed the development of a doctrine of 'fighting words'; it actually moved in the other direction. It came to deny itself, in the changed social circumstances of the 1960s, any examination of the utterance on its face by adopting a doctrine of 'content neutrality'. Whether spoken or written, speech, unless obscene or seditious, broadly defined, could not be abridged on its face. (Blasphemy had anyway fallen by the wayside.) By the early 1970s, the court had come to hold, in the words of Justice Thurgood Marshall, that, 'above all else, the First Amendment means that government has no power to restrict expression because of its message, its ideas, its subject matter or its content' (*Police Department of City of Chicago v. Mosley*, 1972). This applies to writing as much as it does to speech or symbolic non-verbal gesture. A jacket emblazoned with the legend, 'Fuck the draft', although worn to a court appearance, did not constitute a disturbance of the peace and was protected as 'speech'. Justice John Marshall Harvey: 'For, while the particular four-letter word being litigated here is perhaps more distasteful than most others of its genre, it is nevertheless true that one man's vulgarity is another's lyric' (*Cohen v. California*, 1971). Public utterance, of itself, cannot be assaultive in American law.

Although less well established in Europe, a rhetoric not unlike that of the Supreme Court can be found in free expression cases (Nicol *et al.*, 2009: 4, 8, 19). For example, Lord Reid said that 'vigorous and it may be distasteful or unmannerly speech or behaviour is permitted' (*Brutus v. Cozens*, 1973). Lord Justice Sedley, a quarter of a century later, held that: 'Free speech includes not only the inoffensive but the irritating, the contentious, the eccentric, the heretical, the unwelcome and the provocative ... From the condemnation of Socrates to the persecution of modern writer and journalists our world has seen too many examples of the state control of unofficial ideas ... Freedom to speak only inoffensively is not worth having' (*Redmond-Bate v. DPP*, 1999).

However, these opinions are qualified, there often being a certain gap between the bench's rhetorical support of the principle and what in practice it might mean. Although Lord Reid thought, 'it would be going much too far to prohibit all speech or conduct likely to occasion a breach of the peace', he nevertheless required that such speech or conduct be subjected to three 'limits': 'It must not be threatening. It must not be abusive. It must not be insulting.' As to the definition of these terms: 'They are all limits easily recognisable by the ordinary man. Free speech is not impaired by ruling them out.' The ordinary man, though, stands ever ready to morph into Humpty-Dumpty. Which is to say: he will know the words to be threatening, abusive or insulting when he says they are.

For Sedley, 'the irritating, the contentious' and so on is protected but with the proviso that 'it does not tend to provoke violence'. Free speech becomes a question of public order. He upheld Ms Redmond-Bate's right to preach, *à la* Chaplinsky, on the steps of Wakefield Cathedral; but then her language was merely a generalized doomed-laden evangelical attack on the immorality of the times. Some of the crowd were upset by her performance, but three heckling lads were moved on by a policeman without further disturbance. He nevertheless – wrongly in Sedley's view – arrested Redmond-Bate. Police error of this type was also corrected in the case of the teenager threatened with a charge under the Public Order Act (1986)[36] for carrying a sign deemed to be insulting to Scientology by calling it a 'dangerous cult' (even though at least one of which terms is perhaps merely factual). The City of London Chief Superintendent who defended the arrest of the fifteen-year-old thought, apparently, that there was, at law, a right for 'sections of the community' (i.e. Scientologists) 'not to be alarmed' (J. Weinstein, 2010a: 40). The zealousness of the police in this instance has been attributed to the 'Church' of Scientology's reported provision of film premiere tickets and other invitations to numbers of officers; it was not shared by the Crown Prosecution Service and the boy was not prosecuted (J. Weinstein, 2010a: 40).

On the other hand, the hecklers, actual or potential, would have seemed to have had their way in suppressing speech in some other cases involving 'sections of the community' – i.e. groups. A poster, placed in the window of a private home in Shropshire, showed the World Trade Center in flames with the words 'Islam out of Britain' and 'Protect British People' superimposed. Mark Norwood, a local organizer of the fascist British National Party, whose work this was, was charged under the Public Order Act. In finding him guilty, the divisional court equated intentionally insulting expression with unprotected unreasonable behaviour (*Norwood v. DPP*, 2003). In *Hammond v. DPP* (*Hammond v. DPP*, 2004), another evangelical with a sign equating immorality with lesbianism and homosexuality, and demanding they cease forthwith, did provoke overt attacks on himself. Harry Hammond, being the more effective provocateur on the street, was less fortunate than Redmond-Bate in the court. He too was arrested under the Public Order Act and his 'speech' was deemed by the court unreasonable and therefore unprotected.

It was implied that Hammond was, with his placard, interfering with the rights of others; but such a rationale for his guilt is hard to understand. Moreover, the problem with the vagueness of 'fighting words' returns: 'in modern pluralistic societies there are few matters worth debating that somebody will not elicit a viewpoint that someone will find offensive, shocking or disturbing' (J. Weinstein, 2010a: 33). Any supposed general right 'not to be insulted' is potentially extremely chilling – as the events in the Rushdie affair so dramatically illustrate. It too easily leads to 'a strategy of overprotection' (J. Weinstein, 2010a: 52). It was exactly to avoid this danger that, in the United States, the Supreme Court backed-off from making 'fighting words' into a full-scale category of unprotected speech. British speakers can, for the moment, be rude about Scientology but not about Islam. One can attack immorality but not homosexuality.

Some groups are protected by specific legislation that is framed both within and beyond the issue of free speech. Persons of a certain age, gender, sexual orientation, disability, ethnicity or religion can be legally defined as a group – but then not all, and not in every circumstance. For some of the groups so defined, the workplace is more a more protected site than is the public square. For others protection covers both. A subset of general anti-discrimination law deals with speech. In all instances, the question of detriment is central, but it is most contentious with speech. The impact of discriminatory pay, for example, is far easier to determine than is the impact of discriminatory oratory, or a placard or printed article. The right of free speech means that, as a general rule, the population at large (including members of some of these groups when not in environments of especial detrimental threat) is not protected at all.

There is an obvious explanation for this. The anti-discrimination laws and the public order decisions represent a response to a reality, namely, recorded incidents of crimes engendered against an individual because of nothing other than their membership of a group.[37] Expression, then, however far removed in time and place from effect, is deemed to be the cause, and the harm principle justifies curtailing it.

It is the tenuousness of such connections that turns protection into overprotection and moves the right of free expression towards being 'not worth having'. It cannot be avoided but uttering negatives or objectionable lies about groups is inextricably intertwined with positive speaking of 'inconvenient truths'. Effects ought to be considered and, in the absence of a clear, demonstrated detrimental outcome, the right of free expression ought to prevail. The hard cases – the fascist and the homophobe, for example – need to be protected. Otherwise, silencing them can be described as (or, as coming close to) 'core breaches' of the right to participate in the democratic process by speaking (J. Weinstein, 2010a: 32, 50). The bigots stand with their placards and their rants just within the perimeter, which must be guarded so that equally supposedly offensive utterances – those of the whistle-blower and the hypercritical observer, for example – can also be guaranteed a hearing.

Despite the *Hammond* case and the opinion of the City of London police, 'there is no general right in the UK to recover damages for insulting ideas expressed in public discourse' (J. Weinstein, 2010a: 34). There is, though, beyond and before any specific legislation to protect some identified groups, a good measure of such a right if the damaging speech is directed at an individual – defamation.

11.8   *Reynolds v. Times Newspapers Ltd* [1999]: Defamation

Defamation, slander and libel, can constitute, within the harm principle, an easily justified restriction on speech. If doing no harm is the only legitimate such restriction, then treating harmful speech as a tort presents no challenge to democratic principle; it poses no threat to free expression. The problem is that the tort is easily expanded so that it becomes available as a remedy for lesser self-attested harms – offence, upset, distress; and therein lies the danger. Defamation's history reveals that slander and especially libel have been used less justifiably to control, or attempt to control, unwelcome expression generally.

The contemporary civil tort considers the truth or falsity of the words, the possibility of malicious intention and the presence, in some form, of measurable damage. A reputation must be there to be damaged and so a basic defence of truth is available to the speaker (although once it was not, see Chapter 4.3). Not only individuals have damageable reputations, other entities such as corporations do, too, and so can bring actions for defamation. (Defamation of legally protected groups is dealt with below – see Chapter 12.3.) The burden is on the speaker to prove the veracity of what has been said.

By the nineteenth century, untrue speech was unprotected in England and Wales if the words being complained about 'tended' to bring a person into 'hatred, ridicule or contempt' (*Parmiter v. Coupland*, 1840). In the still socially conservative, class-bound society of the early twentieth century, the test in the *Parmiter* case was, in effect, expanded by Lord Aitken. He held, in 1936, that actionable defamation occurred when expression merely 'lowered a person ... in the estimation of right thinking members of society' (*Sim v. Strech*, 1936). Intention is irrelevant.

This is true of libel. It basically protects the individual, not any amorphous group (*Knuppfer v. London Express Newspapers*, 1944). It requires that a remark be written and then made known – published – to a third party. The distinction from slander is that the words should be in more permanent form, although live words in the theatre or being broadcast are considered libellous, not slanderous. There is a further crucial, historically determined but today illogical 'distinction between libel and slander on the basis that damage would be presumed in libel, but the plaintiff would have to prove special damage before slander would lie' (Street, 1959: 289).[38] As with obscenity, so with libel: publication is the offence. In direct contradiction to any doctrine of content neutrality, libel is therefore determined on its face with no assessment of actual consequences. Libel can, of course, redress real damage but the lack of a requirement always to do so directly undercuts the harm principle again. It weakens 'the only Check which [free speech] ought to suffer, the only Bounds which it ought to know'. Rationalization has been proposed but, thus far, to no avail (Stone, 2008: 439). Defamation is not – as is, say, obscenity – substantively a matter of contention; yet it is also something of a 'mess'. With defamation as in other areas of unprotected speech, the problem is not that harmful expression is prohibited but, rather, that determining the nature and impact of the harm is so worryingly subjective.

Libel has come: 'to call for a metaphysical evaluation of dignity ... Damage to reputation is a concept that has no equivalent in money or money's worth [with the result that] those who throw sticks and stones that break bones can be better off in law than those who project hurtful words that leave no permanent mark' (Robertson and Nicol, 2008: 96, 180, 178).

Worse: in the UK, libel does not attract legal aid and is therefore a remedy whose availability is limited to the moneyed class. Little better illustrates the continued truth of the nineteenth-century aphorism of Lord Justice Matthews that: 'In England justice is open to all, like the Ritz'. As often as not it serves only to salve the *amour propre* of the wealthy and, in doing so, it especially hobbles the press. Additionally, the ongoing weak commitment from the English bench to the actual business of free expression (as opposed to its rhetoric) has fuelled the propensity of English juries to award far from 'metaphysical' libel damages. All this has made London the 'libel capital of the world'; so much so that President Obama signed an Act to make foreign (i.e. British) libel judgments unenforceable in the United States.[39]

It is not the case that the press is as unfettered and out of control as the lurid evidence given to the Leveson Inquiry suggests. That unacceptable behaviour occurred because of the misuse of power and a series of failures to use the legal and political constraints available should not disguise the fact that the law can be hostile, especially in defamation. For a supposedly free society, the situation verges on the absurd. John Cleese, for example, was portrayed in an article in the *London Evening Standard* in 2003 as having flopped in a US television sitcom in which he had appeared; an indication of his failing career. The statement was both true because the show had indeed flopped and untrue because he had been praised by the American critics. There was no evidence that his career was particularly in decline and he brought no witnesses or documents to show that the article, however unflattering, had materially damaged him in any way. Here was no harassment, no 'door-stopping', no phone-hacking. There was no evidence of any kind of damage beyond Cleese's hurt feelings. The judge, Mr Justice Eady, who over that decade was to become somewhat notorious as a scourge of media free expression, held that: 'I doubt in the light of the evidence, despite [Cleese's] own apprehensions, that his well-established reputation here and elsewhere will have been significantly damaged, if at all.' Nevertheless Eady thought that there was a problem: Cleese was upset. This was, he held 'damaging'; but, it can be noted, it was, as with the feelings of the protesters against *The Satanic Verses*, in essence self-attested damage. Eady nevertheless considered it real enough to rule that: 'On the facts of this case, it seems to me the major element in assessing compensation has to be the impact upon Mr Cleese's feelings', and in consequence awarded him £13,500. The newspaper incurred a further £120,000 in costs (Byrne, 2003).

This is no laughing matter. Corporations as well as celebrities can sue their critics for libel and need to present no evidence that their enterprise has suffered one iota – or, in the most notorious instance of this, one unsold hamburger (*Steel and Morris v. UK*, 2005). Helen Steel and David Morris, penniless activists, after distributing leaflets hostile to the McDonald's fast-food chain outside one of its stores, were pursued through the UK courts for libel in the longest case on record, 313 days. Other restaurants in Britain, the United States and Australia have also sued critics and won. In McDonald's case, too, the honour of its hamburgers was vindicated and it was awarded £60,000 in damages. Given the economic status of their libellers, this money was never collected. On appeal to Strasbourg the whole affair was judged to be so weighted against them – not least because Steel and Morris were, as is always the case with defamation, denied legal aid – as to offend against Article 6 of the ECHR, the right to a fair trial.

It is because the English law of libel inhibits expression on the grounds of untruth without requiring proof of damage that it begins to destroy the principle of free expression. In the restaurant cases, 'untruth' becomes glossed instead as a lack of 'fair comment'. All criticism, a clearly socially valuable function of the press, is thereby theoretically threatened. The even more democratically vital role of investigative reporting also comes within its purview, for libel does not just protect the finer feelings of celebrities and the integrity of hamburger makers. What journalistic exposés have been prevented or curtailed by this cannot, of course, be known. Witness, though, the protracted struggle through almost the whole decade of the 1970s to tell the British public that the Distillers Company had marketed a drug to pregnant women, Thalidomide, which produced seriously deformed babies (*Sunday Times v. UK*, 1979). The paper was prevented from running the story in 1973 and it took six years before the European Court determined that this restraint was offensive to the right under Article 10 of the ECHR. It is not to be wondered that American courts, despite the shared common law tradition, have taken to refusing to acknowledge English libel judgments at all.

This balances (but does not, of course, excuse) the illegalities, misfeasances and immorality of the British press exposed by Leveson. It is to say, though, that it is not the case that the press is entirely uncontrolled. Even over the most protected areas, there are question marks.

An absolute, unqualified – if very specific – privilege of speech exists as a clause in the only written part of the English Constitution – the Bill of Rights, 1688. Article 9 states, 'That the freedom of speech and debate or proceedings in Parliament ought not to be impeached or questioned in any court or place out of Parliament'.[40] Members of Parliament cannot be sued for defamation, even if inspired by malice; and since the case of John Wilkes and Brass Crosby in 1771 (see Chapters 4.3 and 4.4), neither can those who report their speeches and debates.[41] Lord Denning reaffirmed this in 1973: 'Whatever comments are made in Parliament, they can be repeated in the newspapers without any fear of an action for liable or proceedings for contempt of court' (*Attorney-General v Times Newspapers Ltd*, 1973). This parliamentary privilege applies however an MP comes by the information, even if privately from a journalist. After the matter is raised in Parliament, it can be reported, whether or not an injunction otherwise prohibiting this is in place (*R. v. Z*, 1997; Evans, 2011: 12). The truth about a number of high-level spies, for example, was revealed in this way. Yet, as is not unusual in Britain, the right is confirmed essentially by omission: no attorney-general has mounted a case to challenge Denning's opinion. Others, though, have been, and continue to be, less inhibited.

In 2009, Carter-Ruck, a UK legal firm specializing in libel, moved to close the parliamentary privilege loophole (as the firm saw it) on behalf of Trafigura, a corporate client. The matter involved an injunction, a prior constraint on publication clearly offensive to William Blackstone's principle but nevertheless well-established in law. Media-hostile judges were increasingly happy to use injunctions in all cases, political and not, against a press which, it must be admitted, was respecting ever fewer bounds. Prurience apart, inexorably falling circulations were a main cause of this. Injunctions were justified, when straight denial of the doctrine of 'no prior constraint' was not advanced, with assumptions as to the supposed destructive power of modern media (a power of which libel anyway did not require actual demonstration).

Evermore sensitive to complaints about the media, judges elaborated a further level of constraint by developing the so-called 'super-injunction' which forbad any media mention of its very existence. The super-injunction moves the English law from the realm of Blackstone to the alien country of Kafka. However, the ploy of hiding behind parliamentary privilege blunts this judicial tool of repression. The bench could not claim that injunctions overrode parliamentary privilege or its extension to parliamentary reporting. Nevertheless, the point on super-injunctions' ability to hobble the reporting of Parliament being untested was again to be tried. After 238 years, lawyers, blatantly disregarding this de facto consequence of the *Brass* case, tried to prevent the *Guardian* reporting a parliamentary question. It came as a shock that super-injunctions might mean that 'debates or proceedings in Parliament' were not as privileged as had been thought for the past three centuries (Anon, 2009).

The attempt was, in the words *Guardian* editor Alan Rusbridger, 'a fiasco' (Rusbridger, 2009). Trafigura, a 'comfortably anonymous trading company' was being sued for poisoning many thousands of people by dumping toxic waste in Côte d'Ivoire, but obtained a super-injunction preventing any mention of this – the poisoning and the injunction – in the British media. The legal plan, he explained in a rare signed article:

> began to unravel rather rapidly ... when it transpired that an MP, Paul Farrelly, had tabled a question about the injunction ... in parliament. That was bad enough, what with the nuisance of 300-odd years of precedent affirming the right of the press to report whatever MPs say or do. There was a tiresomely teasing story on the Guardian front page. And then there was Twitter ... I tapped: 'Now Guardian prevented from reporting parliament for unreportable reasons. Did John Wilkes live in vain?' Twitter's detractors are used to sneering that nothing of value can be said in 140 characters. My 104 characters did just fine ... Trafigura threw in the towel. (Rusbridger, 2009)

It is reasonable to suggest that the decision might easily have gone the other way and the right to report on Parliament, essential to a representative democracy, would have been seriously undercut. Pessimists could argue, nevermind this outcome, that the ad hoc arrangements for covering Parliament are an inadequate protection of the basic human right of free expression. Optimists, on the other hand, can counter that the arrangements represent a British genius at solving conflicts with ambiguous solutions, a consequence of the Bill of Rights and, latterly, the HRA/ECHR. The very defeat of an overly smart move by lawyers that were too clever by half proved the underlying strength of the settlement achieved in the 1770s. The Bill of Rights remained inviolate.[42] Well, nearly inviolate.

After a protracted debate that ran from 1964 to 1983, television cameras were allowed into Westminster. The rules then established specific restrictions on footage of proceedings being used 'in comedy shows or other light entertainment such as political satire' (O'Farrell, 2011: 27). Leave aside the question of political satire's 'lightness' and note that, in the summer of 2011, the use of such material in an American TV satire programme normally seen in Britain got it banned. It turns out that the freedom to speak of or debate the doings of Parliament without being 'impeached or questioned in any court or place out of Parliament' does not embrace, it would seem, Jon Stewart's *The Daily Show* or the like. This echoes Nazi reasons for their suspicion of home TVs – fears that the leadership might be privately mocked.

One can admire Rusbridger's lightness of tone and applaud his paper's victory, and one can smirk at the antics of MPs seeking official-issue fig leaves to protect their reputations. The fact remains: these incidents, like the Cleese and 'McLibel' cases, are no jokes. Injunctions, super or not, speak to an underlying legal coolness towards media in the UK; as, in fact, does the limited nature of absolute privilege. An attack on long-settled law might be laughably dismissed as the work of solicitors 'as bold as brass'; but, more sinisterly, it is also a mark of fragility – more worrying than ever in the light of 'Hackgate'. These incidents too much support Hamilton's cynical belief that constitutional guarantees of speech, of themselves, are not worth the parchment upon which they are written. It should be remembered that here, being tested, probed and in the case of a television show, ignored, is one of the few English constitutional rights actually to be written down. The Bill of Rights, limited as it is, turns out to be somewhat less of a muniment than, say, the First Amendment.

None of this is to deny that parliamentary privilege poses a problem for the application of the harm principle. After all, if injunctions are bypassed in this way, the rule of law suffers; a judgment is being held in blatant contempt. With the Trafigura incident, there was good reason for this as the matter was of clear political interest; but, in May 2011, the ploy was used to draw attention to super-injunctions themselves in a situation far from such a weighty issue. The story concerned a footballer's sexual promiscuity, the sort of item that had been interesting the press since it began in the seventeenth century; but, in the environment of declining circulations, it was reaching unprecedented heights as the twentieth century drew to a close. His name was revealed to the House and, within minutes, it was being repeated in news broadcasts. The naming had little purpose except, quite deliberately, to flaunt the super-injunction that had been obtained. Coincidentally, just days earlier, a judicial report on the use of injunctions had again raised the possibility that parliamentary privilege might not always be absolute and the media might still be held in contempt in just such circumstances.

The rule of law also has as an absolute that none can be above the law. Egregious use of parliamentary privilege flaunts the judicial intention to put MPs and those who report them exactly in such a position. The answer, though, is for the Attorney-General to bring any offending MPs before the House's own Standards and Privileges Committee, not to threaten parliamentary privilege by pursuing them in the courts. Internal proceedings of this kind had been undertaken in 1977 when MPs deliberately chose to reveal the names of secret service operatives in a case involving a journalistic exposure of what the authorities claimed were official secrets. It is by no means clear, though, that a hearing before the Standards and Privileges Committee is confirmed as a course of action when mere scandal-fodder is involved. With this doubt comes the possibility that privilege once breached over trivia will then be breached further, seriously to undermine the public right to know.

This is no mere matter of obscure constitutional law, nor is its prime significance that it vividly illustrates the confused legal thickets surrounding the capstone right of speech. What is of consequence is that arguments around parliamentary privilege highlight how fragile is the right of free expression in practice; how open to attack; how much dependent on Hamilton's 'spirit of the people' (although the extent to which 'the people' know or care about such a business is moot). There is no clear definition in play as to what the public interest is either in matters of privilege or more generally, as with the *New of the World* scandal. For example, the Press Complaints Commission's *Editors' Code of Practice* allows the 'public interest' to cover material that is 'already in the public domain, or will become so'. This obviously cannot be a self-fulfilling prophecy nor can it be a comment on the eventual publication of all official documents after thirty years and so on; but it does allow for ethical wriggle-space. No difference has been established between what the public is interested by (the reporting of which can be constrained with no threat to free speech) and what the public has an interest – a title – in knowing (i.e. that which must, in a democracy, be made public). 'Interest' as an expression of curiosity should not be as privileged – or, indeed, privileged at all – as 'interest' as an expression of entitlement.

On the eve of the HRA coming into force, the London *Times* published a claim that, when Taoiseach (Prime Minister) of Ireland, Albert Reynolds, had misled the Dáil. After considering a range of factors, the UK House of Lords deemed the article was of serious public interest (i.e. that which the public has a title in knowing) and the paper had pursued the story professionally. This is to say that it met the requirements of 'responsible journalism', especially that it was published without malice (*Reynolds v Times Newspapers Ltd*, 1999). 'Without freedom of expression by the media, freedom of expression would be a hollow concept', reaffirmed Lord Nicholls, in the usual rhetorical manner of the liberal wing of the English bench. He went on: 'The Press discharges vital functions as a bloodhound as well as a watchdog. The Court should be slow to conclude that a publication was not in the public interest and that, therefore, the public had a right to know, especially when the information is in the field of political discussion.'

This time, however, the rhetoric sat well with the court's decision. The concept of a 'public right to know' draws a reasonable line between entirely private libel and libel involving non-personal matters of clear public importance: as in this case, the political.

The public interest would seem to imply that if the matter attracting attention was serious, as in *Reynolds*, then the public did have a legitimate right to know. Seeking to draw a distinction between the trivial and titillating (i.e. interested by) on the one hand and the serious and weighty (i.e. having an interest in) on the other is indeed complex; but, without a clearer understanding of the distinction, press freedom, and free speech generally, is threatened. Information which speaks to the operation of the public sphere – communication truly 'necessary in a democratic society' – is the interest that must be protected: that is, it is the second meaning of 'interest', that which implies entitlement, which is crucial.

The distinction drawn between what interests the public as a matter of curiosity and what the public has an interest in knowing as a matter 'necessary in a democratic society' must assume, which is not currently the case, that the judiciary does not limit this to political discourse. Necessary communication must embrace the human need for information and stimulation of all kinds. The law has no difficulty in recognizing the factors that might be involved. A public interest test could be developed that depended on an assessment of the closeness of the activity being reported or represented in the media and the *persona* of the people concerned. *Persona* has both a private and a public aspect: so, is the media's focus on their public role or their private being? The more public a person, the more restricted his or her private *persona*. Attention should be paid to domain, which can also be private or public or private with public access. What can be reported or represented depends on where it occurs. Similarly, socially determined levels of deviancy should be considered. Activities with are deviant in public are not so in private. Other activities, though, are absolutely deviant, such as crimes. From such considerations could emerge a public interest test that takes account of the need for necessary communication in a democratic society which the public has an interest in knowing. Such a right to know includes the legitimate public thirst for gossip and tittle-tattle.

Such a closer definition of the public right to know would chill, if not halt, the pursuit of celebrity, which caused such problems in the *News of the World* scandal; but what would be lost is not actually crucial to the public interest. The distinction would allow for the clear application of the general law, for example on harassment. No public interest defence would be possible unless the claim of a right to know relates to the public sphere. A test could be elaborated that determined whether or not the information actually or potentially impacted on the public so that without knowing of it they could actually, or potentially, be disadvantaged in some way. This could begin with a consideration of the original essential element that leads to the concept of public interest – the oversight of public officers performing acceptably. Judges, for example, hold office as long as they 'behave well', essentially 'when in their places doing their duties'. The public is entitled to know of such matters because that knowledge is 'necessary' in a democracy'. Three-in-a-bed romps, that time-honoured marker of what interests the public, could not be justified as necessary by this measure; but so be it. However, if the romper were, not a footballer or actor, but a politician or a moralist (or a judge) given to arbitrating public behaviour, the right would be in place. As it is, without a clear distinction, media misfeasance has flourished and the press's necessary investigative power is threatened.

The *Reynolds* case updates the nineteenth-century defence of qualified privilege – whereby, for instance, masters were entitled to be rude about their servants – but this was subjected to strict interpretation.[43] Subsequent to *Reynolds*, over the next years, the privilege was also narrowly to be construed. In effect, it was something of 'a false dawn for media freedom' (Robertson and Nicol, 2008: 160). To be considered 'responsible journalism', judges required the ten criteria outlined in *Reynolds* all be met, for example, cross-checked facts, the determination of source reliability and the publication of the claimant's explanation of the matter. Failure to jump these 'hurdles' – if, for example, a claimant refused to talk – removed the privilege (Nicol *et al.*, 2009: 100). The press was put in a cleft stick. Publish without informing and the risk of being 'damned' increased; inform and the risk of being injuncted loomed.

It was not until 2007, in *Jameel v. Wall Street Journal Europe Sprl*, that this approach was seen as being, as Lord Hoffman put it, 'against the spirit of *Reynolds*'. *The Journal* had erroneously claimed that the plaintiff (a Saudi Arabian and CEO of the Abdul Latif Jameel Group) was being monitored as a possible funder of terrorism, an untruth. (Note, the plaintiff had no presence in the UK beyond his reputation and the newspaper is published across Europe, including in the UK, but incorporated in Belgium. London, however, not Brussels, is the 'libel capital of the world'.) Qualified privilege was not only upheld but, as has long been the case with obscenity, the entire article was considered, not just the words that had led to the complaint. Most significantly, the requirement – a virtual veto – that the claimant's case be printed as rebuttal or corrective in the original article was removed as being necessary evidence of responsible journalism.

Reynolds and *Jameel* are of a piece with some other decisions of the European Court in Strasbourg that acknowledge the critical importance of the press; although there, too, it is dealt with in far from absolute terms. After all, in Article 10, the 'freedom to hold opinions and to receive and impart information and ideas' is immediately constrained, in its second paragraph, by a string of 'formalities, conditions, restrictions or penalties as are prescribed by law and are necessary in a democratic society'. Moreover: 'The exercise of these freedoms, since it carries with it duties and responsibilities' also works to weaken the overall right.

The impact of these limitations is further enhanced by the use of margins of appreciation to avoid intervening in restrictive national law. In *Handyside*, the Strasbourg Court rhetorically affirmed that freedom of expression was 'fundamental' to democracy (see Chapter 11.4). Moreover, this applied not only to '"information and ideas" that are favourably received or regarded as inoffensive but also to those that offend, shock or disturb the state or any sector of the population' (*Handyside v. UK*, 1979–80). The European bench, however, is as capable as the English of displaying cognitive dissonance so this rhetoric in practice meant little. Because of the willingness of the court to invoke a margin of appreciation in all cases involving non-political speech, Richard Handyside's fine was not set aside nor his right of expression restored.

Certainly states have tried, beyond what they can demand contractually, to use 'duties and responsibilities' to limit the range of expression permitted to officials such as judges or army personnel (Nicol *et al.*, 2009: 33). On the other hand, in the words of Lord Justice Sedley, 'a central purpose of the European Convention on Human Rights has been to set close limits to such an assumed power' (*Redmond-Bate v. DPP*, 1999). Article 10, despite occasional examples of rhetorical gap, usually works in this way. For example, the right to receive, as well as impart, information has meant that a (Irish) government's attempt to prevent dissemination of information (about abortion) was illegal. There is even a certain overt tendency in some European judgments towards American-style content neutrality over political expression (Nicol *et al.*, 2009: 19).

Given that 'duties and responsibilities' are involved, the court tends to rely on local self-administered codes of journalistic practice to determine 'professionalism'.[44] Strasbourg's normal granting of a margin of appreciation in non-political free expression cases is markedly less when the speech is political. This is, self-evidently, because such speech is more central to the needs of 'a democratic society' than is title-tattle about personal behaviour. Political speech falls within the second 'entitlement' meaning of interest. Although contentious political speech can easily overlap with obscenity, generally its presence in a case will reduce the chances that the court will allow a margin of appreciation.

Peter Lingens, a Viennese magazine publisher, wrote an article in which he called the Austrian Chancellor an immoral, undignified opportunist. The country's criminal code required proof, none of which could supplied, this being merely Lingens' opinion. The Strasbourg Court nevertheless refused

Austria a margin of appreciation (in contrast to that granted to Austria in a matter of obscenity, see Chapter 11.4). The court held:

> Whilst the Press must not overstep the bounds set, inter alia, for the 'protection of the reputation of others', it is nevertheless incumbent on it to impart information and ideas on political issues just as on those in other areas of public interest. Not only does the Press have the task of imparting such information and ideas: the public also has a right to receive them. (*Lingens v. Austria*, 1986)[45]

That is, it has an entitlement, an interest.

This doctrine has been repeated to overturn a judgment against a journalist who had published allegations of police brutality (*Thorgeirson v. Iceland*, 1992); and against a Basque member of the Spanish Cortes Generales who claimed in an article that the Madrid government was supporting attacks on Basque militants (*Castells v. Spain*, 1992). The ECrtHR also has considered overall output – a series of articles, for instance – rather than particular offending passages (*Bladet Tromsø and Stensaas v. Norway*, 2000). In *Castells*, the court insisted that: 'Freedom of the Press affords the public one of the best means of discovering and forming an opinion on the ideas and attitudes of their political leaders ... it thus enables everyone to participate in the free political debate which is at the core of the concept of a democratic society.' This includes protecting the airing of otherwise reprehensible views if this is done in the course of responsible reporting. In the interest of open debate, for example, television interviewers cannot be accused of aiding and abetting even the possibly illegal racist views of an interviewee (*Jersild v. Denmark*, 1995) (for hate speech, see Chapters 11.2, 12.3).

The Court does not always resist applying the margin of appreciation rule to produce an outcome that goes against the overall tendency of these decisions. It did not do so, for example, in the case of a journalist who attacked a judge in Austria. That article was 'not in keeping with the rules of journalistic ethics' and the Austrian verdict was allowed to stand (*Prager and Oberschlick v. Austria*, 1996). Basically, though, the decisions of the ECrtHR in Strasbourg on expression have been more consistently in its favour than have those of the English courts, certainly prior to the HRA.

It is no surprise that neither UK nor European law more generally can match the scope of privilege as a defence to defamation afforded by the American courts.

On 29 March 1960, the *New York Times* ran an advertisement, paid for by a liberal pressure group, to raise money for the civil rights campaign. 'Heed Their Rising Voices' was the headline and the violent suppression of student protest in Alabama was the focus. L.B. Sullivan, the elected Public Safety Commissioner of Montgomery who had responsibility for the city's police, sued on the grounds that a number of the facts in the advertisement's text were wrong. In sum, these constituted a libel against his force and, although he was not mentioned specifically, against him. He had suffered no loss, although an ex-employee did testify that he would not want to employ a man whose police department had behaved in the ways claimed. The 'errors' at half a century's distance seem, to use a word appropriate to this Southern context, 'picayune'. However, the trial jury and the Alabama Supreme Court agreed that the *Times* had published falsehoods and had displayed malice, the nub of Sullivan's case. It was malicious, the Alabama Supreme Court held, for the paper not to have checked its own 'morgue' (cuttings library), and for apologizing to the Governor of Alabama, but not to Sullivan. The asked-for $500,000 was awarded, such punitive damages then being in vogue as a way for the Southern states to attempt to control the liberal press.

The federal Supreme Court did not agree. In a refinement of doctrine, it determined that it expected, in cases where public officials had been libelled with inaccuracies, evidence that these arose out of actual malice: i.e. 'publishing a statement either knowing it to be false or in reckless disregard of its falsity', not merely forgetting to check something. Otherwise, the need for public accountability and debate was paramount. Sullivan's claim of malice was defective; his claim that he was clearly implicated, although he was not mentioned by name, was also defective. There was no malice and no mention; therefore, there was no libel. Justice Brennan: 'The judgment of the Supreme Court of Alabama is reversed and the case is remanded to that court for further proceedings not inconsistent with this judgment' (*New York Times Co. v. Sullivan*, 1964). Sullivan did not get his half million but America got a new test for libel. The revolutionary implication for defamation was that, with public figures, it was not a question of untruth but of untruth maliciously retailed. The philosopher Alexander Meiklejohn, then ninety-two, hailed the decision as 'an occasion for dancing in the streets' (Lewis, 1991: 154).

Of course, despite the heroic role of the press in the American national myth, the court has been known to limit speech, especially if coming from the left. The lamentable history of the legal persecution of the Workers of the World trade union in the 1920s and the McCarthy pursuit of 'Communists' in the early 1950s are egregious examples of this failure (see Chapter 8.3). As with many other Western countries, it has also moved to protect the state on other shaky grounds. Overall, however, as *Sullivan* illustrates, the situation in the United States is exceptional. Within the spectrum of sensitivity to the right of expression in the West, the United States stands at one pole.

Surprisingly far towards the other end stands the UK – despite the shared common law and the 'Whig' narrative of its press's role in the struggle for English liberty. The traditional English judicial position on speech, never mind the rhetoric, was, until very recently, better exemplified by the hostility of a Justice Eady than by any liberal judge. The press was fearful enough, then, to argue that the protection of its rights be specifically reinforced by the HRA when that statute incorporated the ECHR into British law in 1998.[46] It worried, not without reason, that although Article 10 of the ECHR would give a direct statutory right of expression for the first time, other Articles would be seized on by the bench to, in effect, reduce its freedom. That it was in the throes of abusing the freedoms it has does not alter the main point – free expression is far from being an immovable, inviolate right, especially when it is conflict with other rights: privacy, most obviously.

12

Causa Sine Qua Non: The Indispensible Cause

12.1 *Campbell v. MGN Ltd* [2004]: Privacy

As the debate on the incorporation of the ECHR into British law was underway in late 1990s, the press was much exercised to preserve untrammelled what were to be revealed, at the Leveson Inquiry, as its abuses of power. The objections to the ECHR are suffused, both by the press and in much of the political class, by an atavistic hostility to 'Europe'. This entity is shorthanded, in British newspapering, to 'Brussels', supposedly a suppurating source of endless, largely absurdly petty, meddlings in the life of (as it were) 'free-born Englishmen'. Forgotten was that the ECHR had been drafted by English lawyers in the late 1940s better to reflect the common law than any Napoleonic or other European code. The lawyers, after all, were speaking for the winning side in the Second World War and were attempting formally to guarantee the rights that had been so conspicuously and murderously abused by the losers. Moreover, it has nothing to do with the European Union (aka 'Brussels') but is based on the UN Declaration, belongs to the larger European Council (which includes Turkey) and is housed in Strasbourg. Nor was it remembered that it was the Convention right in Article 10 that had won the press, in the European Court, the freedom denied it in the UK to tell the truth about, for example, the Distillers Company and Thalidomide. Ignored was the fact that the UK Human Rights Act (HRA), for the first time since the Bill of Rights, would enshrine a right to publish in statute – and that more generally than just reporting Parliament.

The industry was more concerned about Article 8: '8.1. Everyone has the right to respect for his private and family life, his home and his correspondence.'

For the British press, especially the tabloids, a disrespectful approach to the family life of any remotely newsworthy person was deemed essential to popularity and, therefore, to its economic well-being. The public interest had to be what interested the public at whatever cost to those whom the tabloids spotlighted. If the HRA brought a statutory right to publish via clause 12.4 and the Convention right in Article 10, it also let in this previously unknown restriction via the Convention right in Article 8. This was, in reality, much overstated as the expanding culture of illegitimate activities reported to

Leveson revealed; but the newspaper industry was as hysterical about privacy as was the recording industry about unpaid downloads.

Under the common law, privacy had been a joke:

> A much discussed point is whether the law of torts recognises a 'right to privacy'. There may be circumstances where invasions of privacy will not constitute defamation or any other tort ... For example, the jilted lover who makes his former sweetheart a present of a bathing costume which dissolves in chlorinated water ... the newspaper reporters who, regrettably, sometimes stop at no invasion of privacy in order to 'get a story'. No English decision has yet recognised that infringement of privacy is a tort unless it comes within one of the existing heads of liability. (Street, 1959: 411)

In the half-century since this textbook comment was written, 'getting a story' had become an increasingly amoral, if not actually criminal activity.

In the beginning, Queen Victoria and Prince Albert were not amused when an enterprising printer, Strange, sought to publish copies of the drawings they had made of their family life for their own satisfaction. Wishing to distribute these innocuous images privately to friends, the Prince had sent them to Strange for impressions to be made. The printer thought to exhibit a set of copies he kept and announced his intention so to do in a catalogue. The court held that a breach of confidence had occurred, adding that the incident was 'a sordid spying into the privacy of domestic life' (*Prince Albert v. Strange*, 1849).[1]

Despite this reference to 'privacy', until the HRA breach of confidence (a contractual matter) rather than invasion of privacy (potentially a tort) remained the only remedy for intrusion of personal privacy at English common law. Actual material, physical invasion of private property was well understood – trespass; and the edge of trespass, harassment of individuals (including persistent harassment, 'stalking') had also been criminalized.[2] Intimidation, too, was a crime but as it requires a proof of intention, *mens rea*, the press has a basis for defending itself. However, post-Hackgate, this could be harder to do. There was a combination of factors at work that meant these laws, anyway, had little impact on journalism. Official inaction – possibly influenced by fear of press hostility and improper relationships with journalists – coupled with the press's obfuscating insistence that the public interest did indeed mean whatever they said interested the public became the basis for abuse. Anyway, the immaterial invasion of privacy was hard to conceptualize and always had been since the Supreme Court failed to contain phone-hacking in the 1920s.

The use of contract as a substitute, with the possibility of breaches of confidence, required an agreement, actual or implied, with terms, written, verbal or assumed. This was of little use to those whose privacy had been invaded by the press except in exceptional circumstances. For example, the gym-owner who took unauthorized photographs of Princess Diana exercising on his premises breached an implied term of his agreement with her (Anon, 1993). It was, he told the press on the day that the *Daily Mirror* 'splashed' the images, an irresistible 'legal scam' to make money. This, though, had not worked for Strange and, a century-and-a-half later, it still did not work. A settlement, based on breach of confidence, was obtained.[3] That she was in the image, a basis for considering privacy, mattered not to the common law. Similarly with Albert. That he too was in the pictures did not matter. Moreover, the necessity of a contractual basis, one way or another, for such actions was giving way to the concept of a general 'duty of confidence' growing from the *Spycatcher* affair (see Chapter 11.6). Should any matter, reasonably understood to be private, fall into unauthorized hands, a duty exists not to publish it. It no longer required, as it did with Peter Wright and *Spycatcher*, an original constraint; in that case, Wright's contract of employment. For example, after the introduction of data protection legislation, although this too proved to be less effective as a control on the press than it might have been, at least in theory any information covered by its provision is confidential and repeating it is a breach.

In the United States, the situation was different and a right to privacy had been more seriously considered at law.

In 1890, two brilliant Boston lawyers, Samuel Warren and Louis Brandeis, in what is regularly referred to as one of the most influential law journal articles ever written, had postulated 'a right to privacy', cognate to defamation (Warren and Brandeis, 1890). That it was based on the spurious premise that a tort to protect this actually already existed in the common law and needed merely to be uncovered only increases the essay's mythological status. Although a 'right to be left alone' had been articulated two years previously, again in an academic legal context (Cooley, 1888: 29), Warren and Brandeis' revolutionary proposal was occasioned independently by a quite specific and limited objective. The lawyers wished to afford Nob Hill grandees a ground of legal action to curtail their appearances in the society pages of the Boston press:

> The press is overstepping in every direction the obvious bounds of propriety and of decency. Gossip is no longer the resource of the idle and of the vicious, but has become a trade, which is pursued with industry as well as effrontery ... Each crop of unseemly gossip, thus harvested, becomes the seed of more, and, in direct proportion to its circulation, results in a lowering of social standards and of morality. Even gossip apparently harmless, when widely and persistently circulated, is potent for evil. (Warren and Brandeis, 1890: 197)

They added, somewhat piously, a prophylactic against misuse of the tort by suggesting that remedies would include an 'injunction, in perhaps a very limited class of cases' (Warren and Brandeis, 1890: 220). This last is, perhaps, to say that they were not looking for business and that they acknowledged the potential for abuse.

Caveats aside, not only was the proposal offensive to free speech and legally tendentious as a tort, it was also undercut by the ambiguous nature of celebrity. It was one thing to develop a concept of 'inviolate personality' for the *haut bourgeoisie*, although that, of itself, was somewhat dubious – a project smacking rather too much of 'elitist Republican mugwumpery' as some put it (Gains, 1991: 283).[4] Yet if grandees were one thing, what about those whose well-being depended on having a public persona? Actors and all other show-business personalities, for example? It was nearly 300 years since the Shakespearean clown William Kempe had so successfully trialled the modern concept of celebrity,[5] but the intervening centuries had brought little respectability. Certainly in the late nineteenth and early twentieth centuries, show-business celebrities were, in conservative opinion, mostly not respectable enough to be able to claim violations of their reputation. Moreover, as they lived by publicity, claiming to be harmed by it smacked of hypocrisy. Protecting them was clearly not so pressing. In the long run, though, it was the *déclassé* show-business types whose problems were to be of greater significance. Gossip about professional (as it were) celebrities was not so much a 'potent' for evil as it was a wealth generator both for the gossiped-about as well as the gossipers of the press. It is this complicity that was to lower the British press's inhibitions about the harassment of celebrities a century later.

Within years of the Warren/Brandeis article the first cases for privacy were being brought: but the right, outside of show business, was being strictly limited. In a case where a well-known inventor's widow endeavoured to prevent the publication of an unauthorized biography of her deceased husband, the judge held: 'It would be a remarkable exception to the liberty of the press if the lives of great inventors could not be given to the public without their own consent while living, or the approval of their family when dead' (*Corliss v. Walker*, 1894).

The possibility of using privacy instead of libel was dismissed by the New York court in 1908 (*Moser v. Press Pub. Co.*, 1908). A child prodigy, who deliberately shunned publicity his entire adult life, was rediscovered for a 'Where are they now?' article in the *New Yorker*. He sued for invasion of privacy but the court said: 'Regrettably or not, the misfortunes and frailties of neighbours and "public figures" are subjects of considerable interest and discussion to the rest of the population' (*Sidis v. F-R Publishing Corp*, 1940).

The Warren and Brandeis article might be famous but that it was as influential as has been claimed can be doubted.

However, in 1960 another article refined it, breaking the tort down – intrusion (which, at its extreme, becomes trespass and harassment), publicizing private facts (e.g. medical records), false light (as when the news camera catches an innocent bystander at a crime scene) and commercial appropriation (as when one's unauthorized image appears in an advertisement) (Prosser, 1960). Actions began to be mounted but when a case of defamation involving primarily the privacy issue finally reached the Supreme Court in 1967, the principle in *Sullivan* was applied. The article would need to be published knowing it to be untruthful or with a reckless disregard for the truth and malice (*Time Inc. v. Hill*, 1967). James Hill and his family, having been the victims in a notorious hostage-taking crime in 1953, were famous and as there had been no journalistic malice in the reporting, he lost. In *Gertz v. Welch* (*Gertz v. Welch*, 1974), Elmer Gertz, an ordinary attorney not deemed to be in the public eye, had been called a communist in a publication of the fascist John Birch Society. The court held that, as had been established in *Hill*, if the famous needed to show malice, the ordinary citizen needed to show, if not malice, then misfeasance of some kind on the defamer's part. Otherwise, such invasions of privacy would become too threatening to free speech.

On the other hand, the courts were more sympathetic where commercial exploitation was involved (Gaines, 1991). This was where the Warren and Brandeis initiative took hold, insofar as it can be said to have done so. 'Commercial speech' had anyway always attracted weaker First Amendment protection and, by the 1950s, the American courts had articulated 'a right to publicity' to ensure celebrities protected what had become important sources of revenue for them. In *Haelan Laboratories, Inc. v. Topps Chewing Gum, Inc.* (*Haelan Laboratories, Inc. v. Topps Chewing Gum, Inc.*, 1953), the right of baseball players to control their images – in this instance on the collectable cards in chewing-gum packs – was firmly acknowledged. They would need recompense: trade, contracts (actual or implied) and recompense – all were in play – as much as privacy. Three decades after *Haelan*, in 1985, a 'right of publicity' came to be enshrined in the Californian 'Celebrity Rights Act' (Gaines, 1991: 200–1), and many states followed suit.[6] This principle also applied to ordinary persons whose images were used commercially without their authorization. Specific releases, however informal, need to be obtained. This applies most obviously to advertisements but releases are also needed by broadcasters. Fictional and non-fictional programmes, e.g. documentaries, are not exempt. The degree to which subjects give informed consent when confronted by the media has been, thus far, more of a moral than a legal question (Winston, 2000: 84–6). The news, though, is unaffected by this. It was in *Moser* (*Moser v. Press Pub. Co.*, 1908) that the New York court had held news, for all that it was an industry, was not 'trade'. A person whose image, lawfully acquired (for instance, because it was taken in a public place), appeared in a newspaper or a news broadcast need not have given a release but could not look for recompense.

Needless to say, British law has not elaborated legal remedies in this area. In fact, the English common law would have little truck with privacy at all. A century after the Warren and Brandeis paper, even as press intrusion was increasing, the UK Court of Appeal was still simply asserting: 'It is well known that in English law there is no right of privacy' (*Kaye v. Robertson*, 1991). Nevermind ancient lights (not even unwanted aerial photography was an invasion of privacy) (*Bernstein of Leigh v. Skyviews & General Ltd*, 1977); never mind *Strange*. It would need legislative action, an Act of Parliament. Parliament declined but in 1997 it passed the Protection from Harassment Act; and in 1998, it passed the HRA, which by incorporating the ECHR brought directly into UK law the right of privacy in Article 8. Despite this, judges, on occasion, would still opine that Parliament should legislate on privacy and some held that breach of confidence would still apply in, at least, interim hearings such as 'kiss-and-tell' injunction proceedings (*A v. B & C*, 2002). It was not until 2005 (*Campbell v. MGN Ltd*, 2004) that a divided House of Lords overtly balanced, for the first time, Article 8 against Article 10.

The model, Naomi Campbell, had previously denied drug-taking but the *Daily Mirror*'s front-page 'splash' of 1 February 2001 ran a photograph of her, taken in the street, leaving a Narcotics Anonymous building. The headline, 'I am a drug addict', was reinforced with the caption: 'Therapy: Naomi outside meeting'. This 'exclusive' ran to three pages but was essentially supportive, praising her for grappling with addiction. Subsequent to her quickly commencing proceedings, still on the grounds of breach of confidence – not privacy – the *Mirror*'s tone abruptly changed. The Law Lords heard how the paper hit back with a series of hostile articles, the burden of which was, as one of these put it: 'If Naomi Campbell wants to live like a nun, let her join a nunnery. If she wants the excitement of a show business life, she must accept what comes with it' (*Campbell v. MGN Ltd*, 2004). Clearly Piers Morgan, the paper's then editor, was a strong believer in the old American newspaper adage: 'never pick a fight with people who buy their ink by the barrel'.[7] Hackgate revealed the extent to which he was not alone in this.

Campbell's case rested on a breach of the 'duty of confidence', which generally constrains the retailing of information known to be, or reasonably supposed to be, confidential, i.e. information about her drug problem. There was no need for any further contractual relationship between her and the paper. Some of the judges, however, were uneasy that this termed details of everyday life 'confidential' when the word 'private' would so much more accurately describe them. This minority therefore proposed treating the matter as an issue of invasion of privacy under Article 8:

> In this country, unlike the United States of America,[8] there is no over-arching, all-embracing cause of action for 'invasion of privacy' ... But protection of various aspects of privacy is a fast developing area of the law, here and in some other common law jurisdictions. In this country development of the law has been spurred by enactment of the Human Rights Act 1998. (*Campbell v. MGN Ltd*, 2004)

The majority, on the other hand, considered that the confidential information in this case was in the nature of a medical record, exactly the sort of data the law was most concerned to protect. For them, Article 10 did not prevail and even the photograph was unprotected, despite being taken in a public place, because the building Campbell was seen leaving belonged to Narcotics Anonymous. The *Mirror* had breached the duty of confidence it owed her. Privacy was no more primary than it had been in *Strange*. The only aspect of the decision to support free speech was the finding that the prohibition of the street photograph was quite specific. It did not mean that more innocuous images would be similarly unprotected. As Lady Hale, although voting with the majority, put it in her speech, this did not mean anything like a blanket prohibition:

> If this had been, and had been presented as, a picture of Naomi Campbell going about her business in a public street, there could have been no complaint. She makes a substantial part of her living out of being photographed looking stunning in designer clothing. Readers will obviously be interested to see how she looks if and when she pops out to the shops for a bottle of milk. (*Campbell v. MGN Ltd*, 2004)

Despite Article 8 and *Campbell*, the status of a tort of privacy remains unsettled. It was still being avoided by actions for breach of confidentiality even as the *News of the World* scandal erupted. For example, Michael Douglas and Catherine Zeta-Jones, film stars, sold exclusive rights to photographs of their wedding to *OK* magazine (*Douglas and another and others v Hello! Limited and others*, 2007). Its rival, *Hello!*, obtained unauthorized pictures and published them as a 'spoiler'. This clearly breached the Douglas' confidentiality as the wedding was not in a public place and it was irrelevant that they had chosen to allow others to publish images. Moreover, the House of Lords held, *OK*'s agreement with them gave it also a right of 'commercial confidentiality' against *Hello!* Commerce was at least as much in play as was privacy and free speech; but those in the press who fretted about the introduction of restrictive privacy protection 'by the back door' had further cause for alarm.

Even more directly worrying have been developments in Europe.

With Campbell the issue had been her drug dependency, and, although this can be disputed as being critical to a public need to know, the story was at some level a matter of newsworthy deviancy. With Prinzessin Caroline von Hannover, a Grimaldi, heir to throne of Monaco, there was no such frisson. The photographs at issue were all taken and published in the 1990s when she was between marriages and were largely of her, in public, engaging in activities far less problematic than attending Narcotics Anonymous. All appeared in German magazines: a tête-à-tête dinner with an actor, canoeing with her children, horse-riding, skiing, shopping in Paris. Some were of her tripping up on the beach at Monte Carlo in the company of another man – Prinz Ernst

August von Hannover – who was to become her third husband. Compared with the indignities foisted by the press upon the English branch of the family into which she was to marry, this might be thought minimal.

Nevertheless, she sued; but her repeated attempts to stop the coverage failed in the German courts. An implied distinction was drawn not only between public and private places, deviant and un-deviant actions, and the public and private aspects as with any individual: a further subdivision of this last rebalanced, as it were, public and private aspects of a persona so that the greater an individual's celebrity the more limited their privacy.

In Germany, Caroline, as something of a major celebrity, had to tolerate being photographed in public places, even when going about what would be, for lesser mortals, private activities. She could not expect that sites of public resort be, as it were, privatized when she entered them. Without question, such attention as Caroline attracted is wearing; but it is, many may think, a small price to pay for a life of unimaginable privilege and comfort.[9] (Without prejudice to the distinction between interest as curiosity and interest as entitlement, the rhetoric of the British press along such lines, although it is used to justify unacceptable levels of persistence and intrusion, is nevertheless not entirely without merit.)

The European Court, however, took another view (*Von Hannover v. Germany*, 2005). It could find no evidence of public interest in the life of Princess Caroline – nevermind that she was the glamorous daughter of a famous film star destined for a crown (albeit a small one) and could produce a file of cuttings. The German test of Caroline being in the public eye was, the court held, too vague to justify intrusion. The Americans, as in other areas, knew celebrity 'when they saw it'; for Strasbourg this proved too hard a task. Instead, the court had absorbed a Council of Europe doctrine of 'positive obligations', which requires states to ensure that Convention rights are honoured.

As regard the right in Article 8 this was held to mean that: 'It it is incumbent on states to ensure that the right of persons under their jurisdiction to their image is respected by third parties, including journalists' (Akandji-Kombe, 2007: 39). Positive obligation renders the right in Article 8, by this reading, blind to status. Thus Germany was at fault for not protecting Caroline:

> the Court ... considers that the decisive factor in balancing the protection of private life against freedom of expression should lie in the contribution that the published photos and articles make to a debate of general interest. It is clear in the instant case that they made no such contribution, since the applicant exercises no official function and the photos and articles related exclusively to details of her private life.

As Caroline had, in their judgment, no 'official function' in Monégasque politics (an absurd view of the heir to the throne in constitutional monarchy), she could be of no 'general interest' to her subjects-to-be in Monaco or anybody else. This offers an extreme restriction on the second meaning of interest. To believe it is to adopt the reasoning of those royalists who claim the state would totter if a republic were declared but, at the same time, insist a crown has no power whatsoever in a representative democracy and so should not be of any concern. It is to deny that those citizens who, in effect, pay her wages have any interest (claim or stake) that entitles them to know what she does with their money.

Anyway, without consideration of status, except on this very narrow – and indeed arbitrarily – limited basis, the court was prepared to reject a positive obligation under Article 10 to ensure a right to impart and receive information. It was, in effect, suggesting that the only information Europeans are entitled to receive and impart as being necessary in a democratic society are expressions of mainstream politics.

British courts have no reason to be totally bound by the judgments of Strasbourg as the HRA merely states that cognisance of the decisions of that court be taken – just as cognisance is taken of national precedents. In conflicts between the European Court and the British Supreme Court, the British precedent takes precedence (*Kay and others and another (FC) (Appellants) v. London Borough of Lambeth and others (Respondents)*, 2006). This does not mean 'distinguishing' a British case from Europe can be guaranteed. A superior court might take another view. J.K. Rowling, who was to give evidence to Leveson, sought to prevent the publication of a photograph, taken unobtrusively, of her eighteen-month-old son, herself and her husband, Dr Neil Murray, on an Edinburgh street. Through his parents, the baby sued. The court held that this was exactly the circumstance envisaged in *Campbell* of a protected image – 'popping out for a bottle of milk'. Unlike being caught in the compromising situation of leaving a drug rehabilitation centre, here the family was merely walking along: 'The law does not allow the claimant's parents to carve out a press-free zone for their children in respect of absolutely everything they do'. The judge robustly rejected *Von Hannover*: 'Even after that case, there remains I believe, an area of routine activity which when conducted in public places carries no guarantee of privacy' (*Murray v. Express Newspapers Ltd and Big Pictures (UK) Ltd*, 2007).

The Court of Appeal agreed that the judge of the first instance was right to hold, following Lady Hale, that *Campbell* could trump *Von Hannover*. It was thus possible that, as he suggested, situations might arise to allow for everyday images of celebrities, even after *Von Hannover*. Nevertheless, his finding was reversed: his reasoning (and Lady Hale's) might apply to a famous adult but it does not follow that it applies to such a celebrity's child; even if, as was the case in this instance, there was no question of harassment. As in Germany, the court held that the question of privacy depended on a number of factors: 'attributes of the claimant, the nature of the activity in which the claimant was engaged, the place at which it was happening, the nature and purpose of the intrusion, the absence of consent and whether it was known or could be inferred' (*Murray v. Express Newspapers Ltd and Big Pictures [UK] Ltd*, 2007). Curiosity alone is not enough to pass a 'public interest' test.

It was easy, prior to Hackgate, to dismiss these cases as involving 'a lying and petulant model, a minor Euro-royal and two Hollywood luvvies' (Robertson and Nicol, 2008: 271). And a baby. It is a measure of the damage the press has inflicted on itself that it is no longer possible, in all conscience, to do so. Nevertheless, for all that they are difficult to justify as crucial to free speech (especially the last), seismic consequences for free expression can easily ensue from such incidents. In the absence of a clear definition of the public interest, *Campbell* (press-free zones), *Von Hannover* (press-free zones and quotidian activities), *Douglas* (consequential restrictive rights on publication) and *Murray* (protection of celebrities' children) all threaten free speech in general. Given the web of improper influences now revealed as being essential to these and other more egregious examples of abuses involving ordinary members of the public, the press has a serious case to answer.

The Milly Dowler incident and the other instances of press intervention into criminal investigations (see Chapter 3), as well these celebrity cases, illustrate the propensity of the press, noted by Warren and Brandeis over a century ago, to overstep 'in every direction the obvious bounds of propriety and of decency'. This has grown ever greater in ways they would be horrified to see. Press shamelessness and insensitivity might have a history as long as it does, it might be as inexorably a part of journalism as it clearly is; but this does not justify misfeasance and illegality. Neither, though, do these abuses remove or reduce the need for a free press – on the contrary – but this could be Hackgate's legacy. A right of free expression which only allows for unexceptional bland communications is not worth having, and will, almost certainly, not be capable of speaking truth to power when the need arises. Although the chance of the serious exposé cannot be ensured but with the possibility also of tittle-tattle, a clear understanding of both the public interest and the harm principle could rebut the internal challenge to free speech. In Britain, however, events of 2011 made this almost impossible. The press was facing its most serious threat for generations.

In the rest of Europe too, there is in practice a somewhat less committed understanding of free speech than the rhetoric suggests: for example, *Von Hannover*. Speech is constrained in the Convention by 'duties and responsibilities' and by restrictions deemed 'necessary in a democratic society'; and, in the court by the margin of appreciation test. There is also the question of history. In the twentieth century, speech became so blood-soaked that measures of control seem to be as much an inevitable consequence as is the rhetorical lauding of free expression as a democratic essential.

The answer to these failings of commitment in the judiciary, however, is not the imposition of further authority but reform – of substance and of attitude. It is not impossible to imagine a bench and a body of law within the Western tradition doing this. After all, something of the sort exists the United States. Unsurprisingly, at the start of the twenty-first century, the broadest protections for expression in play, and therefore the freest jurisdictions, were in North America.[10] The effectiveness, or otherwise, of the specific regulation of expression in the West in general is not what is at issue. There is an unavoidable basic illegitimacy to special laws and media-specific codes. This stands irrespective of the failings of general law. It follows that the problem of Hackgate, then, is not to be solved by the imposition of an Ofcom. Ofcom, of itself, undercuts the right of free expression, whatever lip-service is paid in passing to the spirit of Article 10 of the ECHR.

A press regulator, 'Ofpress' or a 'Surveyor of the Imprimery' (the title used by England's last such official in the seventeenth century), does not answer the problems posed by the confused state of privacy law. The *News of the World* scandal highlights the dilemmas arising from a lack of a clear definition of the public interest as well as the limitations, within the plethora of laws affecting the press, of effective constraints on harassment or protections of data and so on. Often it has not been that the law is lacking but that it has not been applied. Moreover, the curious unwillingness of Parliament to legislate on privacy is now revealed as possibly being the result of fear of an over-powerful, unscrupulous and economically rather desperate press.

Privacy and the public interest, though, are not the only problems. It is also the case that the elision (to use Ofcom's terms) of 'harm' with 'offence' is another major source of difficulty. Certainly free expression can only be maintained in a civilized society with some method of constraining the harm it can do. Yet the concept of harm is easily expanded to the point where it undercuts the right so much as to render it meaningless. 'Harm' or 'control' (never mind 'hurt', 'injury', 'abuse' or 'offence') are no more readily defined than is the public interest. The greater the indeterminacy of the meaning of these words, the more free speech is threatened. It is the expanding concept of harm which also lies at the heart of the *News of the World* scandal. The immorality and illegality of hacking aside, the question of exactly what damage was done and to whom remains central. It is not only the questionable legitimacy of the censor and the inappropriateness of a regulatory regime controlling content in a democracy; it is also that, in such circles, the deeper danger lies in confusing these terms. Nothing so blatantly reflects insensitivity to the right of free expression than does rising sensitivity to hurts, harms and offence. Answering the internal Western challenge to the right is complicated by nothing so much as the repeated glib elision – 'harmful and/or offensive'.

12.2   *Hustler Magazine, Inc. v. Falwell* (1988): The 'Offence Principle'

'Harm' once normally meant, in J.S. Mill's phrase, 'perceptible hurt', 'hurt' being its synonym (Mill, 1998 [1859]: 48). This is comparatively easy to discern: 'a knock, blow, or stroke causing a wound or damage'; and 'control' was also understood in a physical sense. And the result, 'damage', was a measurable 'loss or detriment effecting estate, conditions, or circumstances' (*Oxford English Dictionary*). Anything less 'neither picks my pocket nor does it break my leg'. It is when harm expands any distance beyond such easily determined material consequences that the right of free expression becomes potentially evermore threatened. This happens when the law distinguishes injury from damage and assumes that the former can occur without the latter, which it does in tort – *injuria sine damno*.

In English, by the seventeenth century, 'offence' had distanced itself somewhat in meaning from the term 'harm', by acquiring a connotation involving emotional 'feeling' (*Oxford English Dictionary*). However, increasingly of late, the concept of harm in the West has also been expanding and it too has been moving towards embracing hurt feelings; in effect, *injuria sine damno*. The change is of a piece with the otherwise welcome decline of deference and the rise of liberal social attitudes sensitive to the interior life of individuals. A growing sympathy for others, for non-human animal others even, has been a necessary precursor to the development of the concept of individual rights. Over the past 200 years and more, empathy and sympathy in particular increasingly determined the relationships of individuals in the social sphere. *Pace* de Sade, empathy and sympathy are necessary concomitants of Enlightenment individual autonomy.

In medicine, for example, this trajectory is nowhere more dramatically illustrated than in a growing – albeit still perhaps too limited – understanding of mental health. The ancient 'distempers', conditions from 'melancholy' to 'fits', were medicalized in the eighteenth century. Thereafter: 'it became increasingly fashionable to interpret a broad range of everyday, non-lethal complains ... as signs of *bona fide* illness' (Dowbiggin, 2011: 11). Thus acknowledged, mental health could conceivably be damaged by external causes analogous to physical injury.

Sympathy for animals is another symptom of this basic attitudinal change. They were held, on occasion, capable of committing crimes and standing trial for them and were denied souls. By 1781, though, Restif de La Brettone, for instance, could note the closeness of orang-utans to men more empathetically (Lamb, 2009: 112). In the children's writer Dorothy Kilner's popular book of 1783, *The Life and Perambulations of a Mouse*, a boy is ordered by his father to desist from torturing the poor animal: 'I promise you the smallest creature can feel as acutely as you. I never knew a man that was cruel to animals and compassionate towards his fellow creatures' (Lamb, 2009: 70–71). The mouse here was no Aesopian human in animal form but an actual creature; one in no way an unthinking machine as René Descartes, say, would have had it in the previous century. Shortly, of course, Paris was to drown in a sea of blood during the Terror. Sentimentality to animals was not necessarily intrinsic to the era's rising scientific impulse, either. The old uncaring attitudes persisted. In the early nineteenth century, Sir Joseph Banks was still able to sneer about a Royal Society meeting which descended into uproar when the lecturer severed the nerves of a live rabbit: 'the nonsense of the meeting on this occasion overpowered the sense' (Lamb, 2009: 109).

Despite such old-fashioned disdain about sympathy, empathy and other 'enthusiasms' and Madame Guillotine (itself, after all, a 'simple mechanism' to limit pain),[11] sensitivity prevailed. In the name of 'humanity', bull-baiting, for example, was prohibited in Britain in 1802 (Lamb, 2009: 109). A journey had begun which now reaches a point where the maximal protection of every individual's physical and mental well-being is considered a reasonable social aim. The control – the elimination – of the all the risks and hazards of everyday life has become an apparently viable objective for the West. By the twenty-first century, for example, even the basic fact of soldiering – that one's life is at increased risk in service – could be widely questioned as being in some way improper, especially if deaths occurred during conflicts deemed to be of marginal legitimacy. It was as if the concept of 'duty' only applied in individually determined 'appropriate' (as it might be) circumstances. As regards electronic communications, the British government's sensitivity could now abridge electronic communication which intended or caused 'annoyance, inconvenience or needless anxiety' (see Chapter 11.4); or it could embrace an instruction to broadcasters that the 'special needs of people with disabilities and of the elderly, of those on low income and of persons living in rural areas' be catered for (White Paper, December 2000, quoted in Robertson and Nicol, 2008: 868).

The rise of such sensitivity cannot but be celebrated, yet expanding the concept of legal harm, a consequence of its ever more enlarging scope, needs also to be addressed. There is a line to be drawn from Miss Kilner's mouse through the pervious unthinkable idea of animal rights to psychotherapy and institutional codified requirements of civility; but also joined is John Cleese's sensitivity to opinion in the newspapers and *The Satanic Verses* mob justifying their action because of the 'harm' the book has caused them. Thomas Jefferson therefore speaks in the old-fashioned tones of the *ancien régime* when he limits actionable damage to his purse or his physical well-being. States of mind can now be 'harmed', and by words alone, although this, necessarily, involves no robbed pocket or broken leg. Being annoyed, inconvenienced or made (unnecessarily) anxious will, in some circumstances, do.

Attempts, arising out of rising sensitivity, to expand the harm principle to embrace an offence principle should be resisted in the name of free expression. On the contrary, the range of harms arising from the impact of speech that the law will address should be returned to older limitations. Basically, self-attested hurts should not be remediable at law. This requires a revised understanding of the nature of the relationship between expression and the harm it is said to cause. Causation is often confused with correlation and the threat to expression is then increased as proven connections are not always necessarily present. The acceptance of self-attested harm, the potential of the expression to cause harm and the lack of any demonstration of harm caused all inhibit freedom. Moreover, the nature of the impact of expression, despite the faith of advertisers and the labour of social scientists, remains elusive. The more diffuse the claimed impact, the more tenuous the connection between expression and harm, and the less legitimate are attempts to abridge it. Attempts to enforce civility, for example, through restricting speech are largely – but very poorly – justified by assumptions in this regard.

Actionable harms have expanded to include the possibility of recognizing unverifiable mental distress: that is, a range of distress, essentially self-reported, which deals with mental states outside the classifications of psychiatric illness. It is now possible for liberal opinion to see that there is some basis for, say, the protests of *The Satanic Verses* book-burners. Given the Western commitment to sympathy and empathy, why would the burners, insisting that they had been 'harmed', not believe that they had a species of 'right' on their side and that their cry for redress was legitimate? The 'harm' they had suffered might have been incorporeal but it was real enough to them. With a concomitant growing understanding of mental distress, why should this harm not be acknowledged? It is suggested that this is especially needed in the context of increasingly heterogeneous populations. In the context of modern Western attitudes, including the Enlightenment value of tolerance, the demand is not unreasonable. Why should speech enjoy a privilege of causing, in any circumstances, distress?

Some legal scholars have taken just such a stand and have overtly attacked the overall Enlightenment settlement. These, as it might be, 'treasonous legal clerks' argue that, not least because of changing perceptions of harm as well as the pervasiveness of contemporary communications, expression's privilege is indeed too easily abused. The protection being offered to speech, particularly by the Supreme Court in the United States, is, in their view, too wide, too indiscriminate.

In 1985, with the right-wing in political ascendency in the United States and the Supreme Court even on this issue somewhat less liberally inclined than it had been, the philosopher Joel Feinberg asked: 'are any human experiences that are harmless in themselves yet so unpleasant that we can rightly demand legal protection from them even at a cost of other persons' liberty?' (Feinberg,

1985: 10). Although himself liberal, Feinberg felt there were and that, when it came to speech, the court had set the bar of 'harm' too high. He asked that the tort of nuisance be considered as an analogy. This might not require too great a step. After all, the law classes some aspects of the consequences of free expression as a nuisance already.

In the English law, indecency 'is a public nuisance, an unnecessary affront to people's sense of priority' (Robertson and Nicol, 2008: 238–90). It differs from obscenity because it involves 'unlooked for confrontations with unseemly displays', rather than the consideration of the corruptive potential of expressive materials. It is a nuisance because it involves offence, just as, for example, the persistence of harmful emission from one property to another – chemicals, smoke, smell, noise – does. This is what Feinberg had in mind as the basis of an analogy. For him it is no accident to talk of some expression as 'smut' or 'filth' (Feinberg, 1985: 33).

In the United States, determining the illegality of such nuisances involves consideration of usefulness, intention, incompatible use (for example, raucous all night parties), the nature of the neighbourhood, the numbers affected, the ease with which the nuisance can be avoided (for example, by closing the window) and so on. However:

> Social philosophers very rarely argue about the role of law in the control of noise, dust, smoke, barking dogs, obstructed roads and the like. They prefer instead to enter the ancient controversies about the role of law in the control of shocking or unsettling indecencies, obscene utterances, pornography, blasphemy, nudity and similar affronts to sensibilities. But the offended and otherwise unpleasant states caused by these more interesting activities are objectionable for roughly the same kind of reasons as the evils combated by nuisance laws ... They are indeed nuisances in a perfectly ordinary sense. (Feinberg, 1985: 10)

Is, then, the analogy, if more widely applied than just with indecency, chilling of free speech?

Feinberg suggests extending the Millian harm principle so that protection is removed from offensive, as well as harmful, speech: 'It is always a good reason in support of penal legislation that it is probably necessary to prevent *serious* offence to persons other than the actor and would probably be an effective means to that end if enacted' (Feinberg, 1985: xiii, emphasis added). Glossing 'offence' as 'serious offence' acknowledges that there is a problem with his 'offence principle' from the outset: 'People take offence – perfectly genuine offence – at many socially useful or even necessary activities from commercial advertising to inane chatter' (Feinberg, 1985: 25). Nor would he, for example, protect the bigot from feelings of disgust at seeing an interracial couple.

Feinberg knows, as he himself quotes, that: 'The law doesn't concern itself with trifles or seek to remedy all the petty annoyances and disturbances of everyday life' (Prosser, 1955: 557). This formulation, though, dates from decades earlier. English law in the 1950s, for example, similarly reflected a more robust society. With defamation, 'harm' still meant, in effect, a picked pocket or a broken leg, as it were: 'The primary purpose of the law of defamation is not to protect against nervous shock, or nervous shock resulting from the apprehension of the effects of the defamatory matter being published to third persons' (Street, 1959: 411). Street offered a further amusing hypothetical case to illustrate his point: elderly spinsters exposed by an impish neighbouring farmer to witnessing a bull servicing his herd in a field adjacent to their property, for example, would have no cause of action (Street, 1959: 296). But times change and sensitivity has been gaining evermore ground and the 'offence principle' speaks to this.

Feinberg would therefore withdraw protection from offending expression, but not all expression that offends; the difference, that it be 'serious', being determined not only by liberal bourgeois sentiment but by analogy with the nuisance tort. 'Serious offence' would need to be established by virtue of duration, intention, situation and so on, just as with any other nuisance. 'Serious offence' suggests that the principle is grounded on speech-act assumptions – a word or an expression works, and works directly. And the law, in also assuming this, should consider the total speech act situation, as J.L. Austin suggests. Feinberg offers no less than thirty-one scenarios (for example, the couple on a crowded bus whose sexual congress 'eventually climaxes in coitus, somewhat acrobatically performed as required by the crowded circumstances') to illustrate six varieties of 'offended state' (Feinberg, 1985: 12).[12] These are elaborated across an entire volume of a four-volume work. Nevertheless, the fact remains: he was in danger of rejecting the paradox that free expression can only be said to exist exactly if its potential to offend, even 'seriously' offend, is protected. Beyond the United States, de facto cognisance of the offence principle has already led, for example in the UK, to specific statutory language prohibiting, without any qualifying as to seriousness, communication causing 'annoyance' or 'inconvenience', and only allow it to cause 'anxiety' when that is 'necessary'. This is a long way from 'nuisance' and it is a distance that the American Supreme Court has refused to travel. For the justices in Washington, as with 'fighting' words, so with 'serious offence': removing protection jeopardizes the right.

Under the title 'Jerry Falwell talks about his first time', an item, announced as a fiction, in the pornographic magazine *Hustler* included a portrait photograph of the Fundamentalist preacher Jerry Falwell and text of an 'interview' in which he supposedly revealed his sexual initiation was with his mother. The Supreme Court acknowledged that the admitted intention was to cause a public figure offence. However, if free expression is to be a proven right, there was a right to so offend: 'The appeal of the political cartoon or caricature is often based on exploitation of unfortunate physical traits or politically embarrassing events – an exploitation often calculated to injure the feelings of the subject of the portrayal' (*Hustler Magazine, Inc. v. Falwell*, 1988). Had this not been the opinion of the court, all American television satire from *Saturday Night Live* through to *The Daily Show with Jon Stewart* might well have been jeopardized.

Although this is specific to the satire of public figures, nevertheless, the Supreme Court, despite its liberal majority being long retired, persists in holding to the broad position (in *R.A.V.* and other cases) that speech in general cannot be discriminated against (see Chapter 11.2). Its doctrine of content neutrality abandons the very idea of controlling expression on its face. This has been termed an 'excessive liberal position' (Schauer, 1982b: 5); and it has to be admitted, such legal logic (and Enlightenment philosophy) has a price. In its practical consequences, content neutrality seems often as nothing so much as a licence to attack the fabric of society, rending social cohesion. Anxieties, for some outside the bench on the right, range from fretting about nude public dancing and so on, abuse of religion or general attacks on authority. For others, on the left, concerns focus on the marching neo-Nazis, *The Satanic Verses* and such like, and a general tolerance for the intolerant. All such expression causes 'serious' offence to one party or another.

'Excessive' liberalism or not, restricting offence also carries a high cost. To recognize offence means dealing with feelings – which are actually unknowable to others – and this is potentially very constraining. To say we understand the feelings of, say, *The Satanic Verses* protestors and judge the offence caused to have been genuinely felt is one thing; then to allow an action to remedy this hurt is quite another. It abridges the writer's speech and offends in turn, perhaps deeply, all who would support him. Once the protestors' hurt would have been seen as one of life's hardships, a distressing consequence of the human condition. Expression might cause offence (from nuisance, through distress, to 'annoyance, inconvenience or needless anxiety') but could not be offered remedy on that basis alone. Further, such interior 'harm' might provoke protest or other overt recognizable responses, but, causally, that perceptible outcome would be a crucial step away from the original expression. The will of the protestor, who is not an automaton, interposes itself. Adopting an offence principle excises that link in this chain. Neither of these considerations – the possibility of offence nor its outcomes in action – supports the right of free expression: the hurt remains imperceptible, the harm is always self-attested and the chilling effect on speech is still unbounded.

Nevertheless, as we have seen in many contexts, the possibility of addressing offence is being explored. There are existing remedies for the individual, from libel to malicious electronic communication, which do not require externally verifiable damage. Privacy, not being trespass or harassment, is also in major part a matter of self-attested distress. Other actions lie for offences against society in general which too require no evidence of actual harm – obscenity, for example. Cognisance of individual feelings is therefore already being taken. The possibility of doing so also underpins recent specific legislation, widespread in the West except in the United States, which seeks to protect the feelings of identifiable groups in society. The right's weasel dismissal of this effort as 'political correctness' (which is usually held in such circles, with the regularity of an Homeric kenning, to have 'gone mad') need not detain us.[13] This unbaked response – like the broader jejune no-nothingism that seeks to dismiss all 'yuman rights' (Littlejohn, 2008: 15) – ignores that the impulse to control speech on this ground is driven by a sense of social inequality and the need to maintain social cohesion.

Such an objective cannot be treated with contempt. Nevertheless, worthiness does not mean the threat posed to speech is dissolved. It is too easy, as the case of the City of London police's (unexpected) sensitivity to the feelings of Scientologists, indiscriminately to declare groups to be protected (see Chapter 11.7). Demonizing 'political correctness' is despicable, but it is short-sighted not to acknowledge that protecting individuals and groups against offence does challenge free speech. In essence, it forces the question as to, exactly, what classes of utterance, if any, might be legitimately prohibited as being 'seriously offensive' so that speech does no 'harm'.

12.3   *Doe v. University of Michigan* (1989): From 'civility' to 'hate'

Speech that provokes individual distress or socially disruptive reaction has become an obvious candidate for some measure of control and censorship. Yet, expanding harm to this extent means the variety, range and indeterminacy of expression actually, or held potentially, to have this effect threatens the right. In the name of social cohesion, it is 'civility' – considered as the constraint of harassment – which must now be maintained. This is an even broader limitation on speech than controlling 'serious' offence through the use of the tort of nuisance, as Feinberg originally suggested.

In April 1989, following incidents of written racial abuse appearing on a blackboard and in a flyer, the University of Michigan introduced a code of conduct to control unacceptable expression. A 'substantial number' of higher educational institutions had done likewise (J. Cohen, 1993: 207). At Michigan after the code was adopted, in short order, students were disciplined for suggesting ethnic minorities found a course difficult; for reading a homophobic limerick in the course of a discussion; for reporting on psychologically counselling gays as a 'cure' (*Doe v. University of Michigan*, 1989). In the *University of Michigan* case, and repeatedly with other codes and local ordinances, the 'excessively' liberal Supreme Court held the restrictions were too broad and vague not to have a chilling effect on expression. The harm being addressed was not firmly enough demonstrated to justify abridging speech. As with 'fighting words', the range of expression is amorphous, being so subject to the particular circumstances of the utterance – the totality of the speech situation. And its uncertainties are made more so because, like the other species of expression being judged on their face, it can require no actual demonstration of harm but only an assessment of its harmful potential. (Indeed, assessing even its potential can be vexed; see Chapter 12.4.)

Incivility of expression is implicitly considered by these codes to cause offence, with or without nuisance and harassment being considered. It lies, in effect, on the offence continuum at one end of which is 'hate speech'. Hate speech also involves suppressing speech 'that violates civility norms' (Post, 2011: 136). Both hate speech and the civility codes are subsumed by the concept of 'serious' offence, if not entirely by Feinberg's notions of how it might be applied. Instead of dismissively glossing the prohibition of incivility as 'political correctness', incivility has become a species of hate. This gloss is a public relations masterstroke akin, to take another progressive example, to the transformation of the imposts on newspapers into 'taxes on knowledge' in nineteenth century Britain (see Chapter 4.5). And just as 'knowledge', as an implied unqualified social good, is not quite what the newspapers provided, so 'hate', as an implied social evil, is perhaps not a totally reasonable description of the range of expression in view. (It could be suggested, perhaps, that within this overstatement lies the basis of political correctness's supposed 'madness'.)

Hate speech has one advantage over incivility: it is more easily recognized. It is the most obvious and least contentious aspect of harm's expanding compass. Ignoring the volition of the provoked, it 'is any expression with a potential to incite damaging action against any individual or group on the basis of race, nationality, religion, gender or sexual orientation'. Nevertheless, it is still not quite so inherently evil as to always cause 'harm'. As Robert Post puts it: 'Hatred in its proper place would seem socially desirable' (Post, 2011: 124). Such socially sanctioned hatred might, for democrats, include a hatred of tyrants, for example. Writing some six years before the assassination of Abraham Lincoln, J.S. Mill addressed the specific issue of the promulgation of tyrannicide, a doctrine (if 'it deserves that title') the illegality of which he suggested was of some ambiguity. Mill allowed that tyrannicide could be 'an act of exulted virtue' and therefore speech encouraging it could be equally praiseworthy (Mill, 1998 [1859]: 21). Leaving aside so extreme a circumstance of speech-act, in more everyday situations, prohibiting 'hate speech' is a laudable attempt to enforce, for the sake of public order and social cohesion, a measure of civility on society.

However easily hate speech is indentified, though, the uncertainties of 'incivility' are far from being left behind by categorizing it as 'hate'. Many ambiguities remain with the categories 'protected' from hate – races overlap with religions; religions or national identities are unrecognized as such; and many groups are not in the primary list – perhaps the disabled and certainly the obese, for example. Still, despite the somewhat arbitrary nature of the application of the concept, hate speech is, most obviously, that expression which most directly threatens society's diversity. As a liberal principle it is as easy to agree to prohibit hate speech as it is to defend free speech – as long as the potential cognitive dissonance of doing both simultaneously is ignored.

Consider the difficulties of the American Civil Liberties Union (ACLU).

In the United States, the meshing of civility and hate speech well reflected the long-term efforts of particular representative groups dedicated to the protection of oppressed and abused minorities. These had been established in the early twentieth century, notably, the National Association for the Advancement of Colored People (NAACP, founded 1909) and the American Jewish Congress (1918). The ACLU also dates from this era. It was founded in 1917, initially as an anti-war movement against American involvement in the First World War and it became a champion of the persecuted left in the 1920s. Its defence of free speech, however, has found it more than once in opposition to liberal opinion, wherein usually it could expect to find its allies and supporters. Long before *National Socialist Party of America v. Village of Skokie* in 1977 (see Chapter 11.2), it was defending the speech rights of the racist Ku Klux Klan and the anti-Semitic car manufacturer, Henry Ford (S. Walker, 1994).

Its logic, though, is, to a large extent, shared by the Supreme Court. Formal codifications as well as local ordinances – dealing with civility and/or hatred, remain unconstitutional: 'The United States is perhaps unique among the developed world in that under law hate speech *regulation* is incompatible with free speech' (Schauer, 2005).

> There appears to be a strong international consensus that the principles of freedom of expression are either overridden or irrelevant when what is being expressed is racial, ethnic or religious hatred. In contrast to this international consensus that various forms of hate speech need to be prohibited by law and that such prohibition creates no or few free speech issues, the United States remains steadfastly committed to the opposite view... In much of the developed world, one uses racial epithets at one's legal peril, one displays Nazi regalia and the other trappings of ethnic hatred at significant legal risk and one urges discrimination against religious minorities under threat of fine or imprisonment, but in the United States, all such speech remains constitutionally protected. (Schauer, 2005)

Certainly, the European Court of Human Rights has indeed been quicker than the Supreme Court to muzzle expression on these bases, usually by allowing national margins of appreciation.[14] 'The European Court of Human Rights (ECrtHR) has accepted that certain forms of extreme speech are protected by Article 10 [but] the degree of protection for speech is extremely limited' (Hare, 2010: 73). Article 17 of the ECHR prohibits the denial of any of the Charter rights, and this includes the advocacy of such denial to any individual or group. Clearly this withdraws any protection from hate speech, strictly understood. It is felt that this can be done because, in essence, what constitutes hate speech is 'known' when it is heard. In this sense it is a good deal less ambiguous than incivility of 'offence' generally. The question of which groups are protected from hate speech might be an issue; but, as to its content, it is rather predictable. It is actually far less variegated than incivility in expression; or than fighting words; or, indeed than obscenity, which is constantly being redefined in the light of community standards. Hate speech, as befits the bigoted intelligences that use it, has only the most limited range of expression and has exhibited a terrifying consistency down the ages.

In psychology, the role of the 'other' is deemed a necessary concomitant of the establishment of an individual's personality. In European culture, without such a Lacanian 'other', individual or group, against which to define themselves, some appear to find difficulty maintaining an identity. The role of this 'other' has been played by many social groups but few have – like, for example, the Romany and the Jews – functioned in this way on a continental scale over centuries. Arguable among the most persistent strands – if not the most persistent stand – of extremely prejudicial speech of this kind in the West are the rabid outpourings of the anti-Semite.

The case for the evil influence of speech seems nowhere more easily made than here. Luther's 1543 tract, *Von den Jüden und jren Lügen* (*On the Jews and their Lies*) (Luther 1971 [1543]), with its seven-point answer to the Jewish question, reads as the action plan for *Die Endlösung*, the Nazi's final solution four centuries later – although they went further than he did.[15] Luther thought to let the Jews live, albeit without schools, synagogues, texts and rabbis, in barns and sheds as agricultural slaves. It was a Nazi innovation to determine that the Jews could not live at all. How, then, can Luther's tract and all the bile, in every form of expression, that appeared between it and the Holocaust not be implicated in mass murder? How can even the protection of speech denying that atrocity ever be justified?

In 1994, a case came before the German Constitutional Court, arising from the banning by the Munich authorities of a meeting to discuss how the Allies started the Second World War. This had been planned by the marginal Nationaldemokratische Partei Deutschlands but as the star speaker was the notorious Holocaust denier David Irving, discussion (as it were) of this topic was also in prospect. The judgment upholding the ban led to the adoption of a revision of the criminal code, s. 130 (3) (Grimm, 2010b). This criminalizes, 'publically or at a meeting', the approval, denial or marginalization of 'an act' of a specific kind (defined elsewhere in the code) committed 'under the rule of National Socialism': in other words, although not in so many words, Holocaust denial. The court reasoned:

The historical fact itself that human beings were singled out according to the criteria of the so-called 'Nuremberg Laws' and were robbed of their individuality for the purposes of extermination puts Jews living in the Federal Republic into a special personal relationship vis-à-vis their fellow citizens ... Whoever seeks to deny these events denies, vis-à-vis each individual, the personal worth due to each [Jewish person] ... for the person concerned this means continuing discrimination against the group to which he belongs and, as part of the group, against himself. (Grimm, 2010b: 557–8)

But Germany's historical experience means that there is an equally deep commitment to maintaining democracy and the free speech that is seen as fundamental to it. Article 5 of the German Basic Law guarantees freedom of opinion, albeit this is conditioned by history, too. Article 21 bans parties and Article 18 prohibits speech recommending the overthrow of democracy. The conflict is solved by the application of a legal theory of balance.

Since the late nineteenth century, German administrative law has developed a principle of 'proportionality' (Grimm, 2010a: 12–14). This allows for a balance to be struck between contending objectives, as for instance between freedom of speech and the other rights. It does not therefore mean that even anti-democratic speech is necessarily unprotected. The court will ask what loss is entailed for each right if the other prevails. Is the damage to German Jewry assessed as likely to be greater than the damage to free speech? (Grimm, 2010b: 560). In this case it was and subsequently Holocaust denial was written into statute. Such an approach is widespread, even if it is not so described. Holocaust denial is widely seen as offending against Article 17 of the ECHR which prohibits attacks on any or all of the other Convention rights. The negation of clear historical fact – i.e. the Holocaust – is a species of group libel and is enough to remove the protection of ECHR Article 10 (Nicol *et al.*, 2009: 40). When Norwood (see Chapter 11.7), who had been found guilty under the UK Public Order Act for displaying Islamophobic posters, reached the European Court, the same finding applied: on balance, Article 17 trumps 10. In France, identical logic was used to deny protection to a defence of collaboration with the Nazi occupation, thereby indirectly denying the evil of the Holocaust and the French collaborators' part in it (*Lehideux and Isorni v. France*, 1998). In the United States, despite the doctrine of content neutrality, no less than eight separate tests have been distinguished in Supreme Court judgments, which together amount to the same sensitivities 'proportionality' addresses elsewhere.

A main object of preventative legislation, such as that directed against Holocaust denial, is deterrence. As the Marquess of Halifax (1633–95) explained: 'Men are not hang'd for stealing Horses but that Horses may not be stolen' (Savile, 1912 [1750]). Holocaust denial is now on the statute books of fourteen countries and one thing is clear – such legislation does not deter the deniers (Whine, 2010). By Lord Halifax's measure, the denial laws

– though backed by Article 17 of the ECHR – are none too efficient. Even those most concerned with the establishment of this limitation of speech admit that 'the fact that there are repeated offenders' demonstrates that deniers in 'a hostile legal environment have not stopped publishing denial material nor making public statements ... To defeat denial, more effective than laws alone is education' (Whine, 2010: 555–6). The Supreme Court would agree with this, at least in principle. Justice Brandeis, in *Whitney v. California*, stated that the 'evil' of speech has to be averted 'by the processes of education, the remedy to be applied is more speech, not enforced silence' (*Whitney v. California*, 1927, see Chapter 12.4).

Consideration of the failure of the denial legislation to halt the deniers could easily lead to a species of 'null-effects hypothesis'[16] – that hate speech laws are ineffective in the broader sense of removing or restricting prejudice from society. On the one hand, it could be held that the United States is a society riven by hatred and bigotry, burdened by its slave-owning history, and that this reality is self-evidently not helped, or is even exacerbated, by its insistence on free speech. On the other hand, a question may be put: is hatred and bigotry worse in the United States than elsewhere? Neutral measures are slippery (and certainly 'attitude surveys' constitute at best 'soft' facts) but take the existence of avowedly bigoted political parties. Those erstwhile twentieth-century bastions of tolerance, the Netherlands and Denmark, for example, now harbour in their parliaments parties for whom Islamophobia is the *raison d'être*. The Dutch party, although excluded from government, dictates its fate; and Denmark's immigration laws are now Europe's toughest. These states have anti-'hate speech' statutes. It is easy to explain this in terms of modern communication systems which render all national borders too porous to make such legislation effective (see Chapter 9.5). Be that as it may, the point here is that, the extreme US liberal legal position notwithstanding, the United States is, by such objective measures, no more bigoted than are these other states. It is also, of course, certainly no less bigoted. Moreover, the United States does have an advantage: in seeking to avoid breaching the principle of free speech, it limits – at least in theory – the danger to the right of expression which all those states with anti-'hate-speech' laws accommodate.

Dealing – or failing to deal – with the bigots is, though, not the main problem. A decision that they should be 'hanged' (as it were) is straightforward, whether it works or not. The problem is distinguishing them from other speakers. Not all would agree that there is no difference between, say, Irving and Rushdie; or between Hitler and Ezra Pound. Not only the speech of provocateurs but also that of the thoughtless (seized with, to use Pound's phrase, 'suburban prejudice') (Beck, 1968: 29) can be snared by civility codes and hate-speech legislation. Leave aside whether or not speakers are intentionally hurtful or casually rude, this complication suggests that at least four further intertwined issues are involved: damage, reaction, constraint and causality. That is, firstly:

what is the nature and range of the damage, actual or potential, to the targets of incivility, including the consequences of hate speech? The second question is: what are the potential reactions for which the civility codes and hate-speech legislation are a prophylactic? Thirdly, what are the consequences, if any, of abridging speech to avoid damage and reaction? And finally, what evidence is there for making the connection between incivility of expression or hate speech and the reactions provoked, consequences actual or feared?

Firstly, then, 'damage'. For example, how exactly is Holocaust denial discriminatory? To say, as much legislation does, that it is a clear denial of history cannot of itself be actionable. Where would that stop? Am I liable if I say there was no Russian Revolution in 1917? No Terror in France from autumn 1793 to the following summer? The Spanish Armada never sailed, and so on? Holocaust denial might well amount to a sort of insulting group libel, but how is it discriminatory beyond that? Put more generally, what does incivility of expression/hate speech of itself mean as discrimination?

Experience suggests that, whatever it means, the plight of the people targeted constitutes an obvious case to limit those forms of speech which, in sum, seek to deny their humanity (i.e. Article 17 of the ECHR). The overt results of discrimination – from genocide to 'Paki-bashing', from seats at the back of the bus to membership bars, from bullies in the playground to the bigotry of sports crowds – demand no less. And, on balance, such outrages outweigh any right of expression (i.e. Article 10). Horses, after all, are stolen whether the thieves are hanged or not. Permitting theft is not an option. Why should permitting bigoted expression be an exception?

What, however, if the expression did not cause the damage but merely reflects it? Reverse the terms on anti-Semitism, for example, and ask: what would the effect on the Jews of Europe have been of a dominant philo-Semitic, instead of anti-Semitic, strand in expression? How different would the history of European Jewry have been had Luther not written *Von den Jüden*? What if he had stuck to his first position, outlined two decades earlier, in *Daß Jesus ein Geborner Jude Sei* (*That Jesus was born a Jew*)? 'If I had been a Jew and had seen such dolts and blockheads govern and teach the Christian faith, I would sooner have become a hog than a Christian. They have dealt with the Jews as if they were dogs rather than human beings; they have done little else than deride them and seize their property' (Luther, 1962 [1523]).

Would this have prevented the appearance of the Nazi tabloid *Der Stürmer* in 1923, the year of that pamphlet's 400th anniversary? Would European history have not been stained by anti-Semitism? The damage to Jewry might have been exacerbated by speech but it was surely caused by other deeper factors. Cauterizing the speech does nothing to excise the cancer, the plight of the 'other' in society.

This caveat as to damage applies yet more firmly when considering supposed effects far less cataclysmically evil than genocide. We are, properly, concerned with each individually targeted person's feelings, whether or not externally verifiable harm can be seen. This expansion of harm's compass is a welcome advance as our sensitivity to the targets of hostile expression has grown; but a reality remains. Expression does not pick pockets, it does not break legs, unless the target is disturbed: suicidal, for example. It is yet the case – for the mentally stable majority, anyway – that: 'sticks and stones may break bones, but words will never hurt me'. Once the law agreed more consistently with this adage than it does now, and it did not consider mental states caused by expression. It regarded the possibility as trivial. Speech was bound by the harm principle more narrowly conceived than it is currently.

So, secondly, reaction. The codes and laws are directed at speakers, but the damage to society is caused not only *to* the targets of expression but *by* the target's reaction and the reaction of those who stand with them. This, though, is a matter for the general law. However, so heinous is such provocation now considered that the target's response, on occasion, can be given a latitude it would otherwise have not earned. Thus are created most unfortunate precedents, albeit for good liberal reasons. The Sikh death-threats in Birmingham and the official lack of response – in fact, de facto support – would be a case in point (see Chapter 1).

To say speech has been socially divisive – not potentially so, but actually – is to comment on the target's or the heckler's action as much as on the speaker's expression. This, though, is no basis upon which to abridge speech. The target's reaction should not be condoned. Provocation, at law, is limited as a defence, proportionality a necessary given. Society's sensitivity to each individual's sensitivities might well, and welcomely, have grown; but it is still the case that the rule of law should be used to ensure that any reactions provoked by expression be proportionate. This is, prima facie, better than banning speech. However upset you are, you cannot go round disturbing the peace and burning books or the homes of publishers; you cannot kill, or threaten the lives of, writers and artists because you do not like what they say – however wounded, hurt or abused you say you are. You cannot transfer the threat to social cohesion arising from your actions back to the words you say provoked you. Otherwise, never mind Article 17, it is the 'heckler's charter' which trumps the right.

Avoiding the constraint of speech, the third point, despite the damage that it does, should still be the prime objective. However, common sense (as it were) insists this cannot be so. Arguments against constraining the constraint are, it is felt, foolhardy. For example, when considering Rushdie, Richard Webster wrote: 'In the rational utopia … words would not wound, insults would not hurt, and abuse, however obscene, would provoke neither anger nor violence. But in the real political world which we all perforce inhabit, words *do* wound, insults *do* hurt, and abuse – especially extreme and obscene abuse – *does* provoke both anger and violence' (Webster, 1990: 129). As ever, though, common sense needs be queried. This rhetoric still does not address the consequential dangers of constraint.

Prohibiting expression, as Webster and many others suggest, is hard to do in the 'real political world'. For one thing, as ever, the very terms used here for the class of speech to be banned – 'extreme' 'obscene', 'abuse' – defy clear definition. Webster, in effect, proposes to make matters worse – to heap Pelion on Ossa – with restrictive confusions. The sentiment behind this rhetoric is admirable but, in practice, responding to it remains extremely vexed. Given the significance of the capstone right of free expression, the position, although seductively grounded, has deleterious consequences. As Trenchard and Gordon corrected asserted as 'Cato': 'Whoever would overthrow the liberty of a nation, must begin by subduing the freedom of speech' ('Cato', 1721). Even though control is proposed in the name of containing hatreds, it still must be resisted. It threatens to bring in the very censorship which *bien-pensant* opinion otherwise would wish to avoid.

Such an observation, though, risks further attack from those who think along Webster's lines. For the intellectuals prepared to attack the right, any restriction of free expression, especially in the name of hate speech, can be defended and any limitation is thought capable of being effectively contained. For those who would defend the right, on the other hand, any limitation runs the danger of creating precedents and therefore constitutes a threat. Hate speech melds with serious offence which morphs into incivility of expression which then undercuts the freedom to transmit and receive ideas. This is dismissed by the clerks treasonous to this aspect of the West's Enlightenment ideology as a '"falling dominos argument," or the "foot-in-the-door argument," or the empirical (or political) "slippery slope argument"' (Feinberg, 1985: 92).

It is all well and good to dismiss the possibility of 'creep' in these terms; but behaving like Chicken Little is not unreasonable. In the 'real political world which we all perforce inhabit', any constraining legal decision, especially in the common law tradition, does constitute a precedent which must be considered thereafter. Think of the ever-widening scope of hypothetical consequences. Constraint becomes arbitrary: 'If we were truly serious about prohibiting speech that might cause actual racial or ethnic or national violence, we would proscribe … all manner of cinema, novels and popular entertainment' (Post, 2011: 136). It is true that we are actually inconsistent about these restrictions, guided more by politics than evidence; but we could easily become more chillingly consistent (as the persistent attempts to resuscitate blasphemy demonstrate). A Miltonic 'crowding' of 'free consciences' is ever in view.

And finally, causality – i.e. the nature of the causality linking the 'harm', however defined, and the damage it causes, however defined – is also a matter of dispute. To argue that it is dangerous to restrict speech, including hate speech, is not to make a libertarian point denying any and all constraint exactly because expression *does* have a potential for inflicting harm. Clearly, for the good of society, unprotected speech must be a possibility. What is protected, as Alexander Meiklejohn put it in defence of the First Amendment, is 'the freedom of speech', not freedom to speak, i.e. to say anything in any situation (Meiklejohn, 1961: 255). As Justice Holmes argued: 'The most stringent protection of free speech would not protect a man falsely shouting fire in a theater and causing a panic' (*Schenck v. United States*, 1919). The problem is that, in the irrational, dystopian 'real political world', indisputable connections – e.g. 'fire' (falsely cried) leads to panic (e.g. broken legs in the rush to leave) – can seldom be found; and the right of free speech, whatever the rhetoric says to the contrary, suffers. Causality becomes a matter of assessment, prediction and prejudice, and a question of probabilistics. At law, too often, it needs no evidence of actual effect.

Increasing the harms remediable at law to embrace actions grounded in offence threaten free expression. Instead, the range of harms arising from the impact of speech that the law will address should be returned to older limitations. Self-attested hurts should not be remediable at law. This requires a revised understanding of the nature of the relationship between expression and the harm it is said to cause. Causation is often confused with correlation and this threat to expression is increased because causation is anyway not limited to proved connections. The acceptance of self-attested harm, the potential of the expression to cause harm and the lack of any demonstration of harm caused all inhibit freedom. The truth is that we do not have any very clear evidence as to the effects of expression beyond a common sense assumption that it can have effects, sometimes negative. However, its essentially unsafe nature suggests that causality should not always so readily be assumed to justify abridging speech. Certainly, evidence that speech impacts directly on the underlying causes of incivility and bigotry is deficient.

12.4   *Schenck v. United States* (1919): Proof of damage

'There is no doubt that speech which conveys messages of extreme abhorrence may be causally related to harmful effects, like violence or discrimination. But in most cases speech merely has a tendency to cause these harmful effects' (Post, 2011: 134). 'Tendency', however, is enough for most people and, since *Hicklin*, their legal systems, too. Without actual verifiable harm, it nevertheless allows for speech's potential impact to be determined and made the basis of the judgment. The test in *Hicklin* was to find that the '*tendency* of the matter charged with obscenity is to deprave and corrupt', limiting sexual representation as much as possible being an area of particular interest to the British law (*R. v. Hicklin*, 1868; emphasis added). The author of an obscenity automatically, as it were, exhibited what the law calls 'constructive intent' –

the *mens rea* needed for the offence. In more general terms, such an approach has come to mean that, as Justice Holmes explained, 'intent' means 'knowledge at the time of the act that the consequences said to be intended will ensue' (*Abrams v. United States*, 1919). This is why Turberville did not threaten Strange whatever the action he made with his sword (*Turberville v. Savage*, 1669; see Chapter 11.3). Holmes qualified his definition by adding that this is 'vaguely' what intent meant. Expression could be the 'indirect causation' of harm. The need for evidence of actual corruption, offence, damage or suchlike occurring was thus removed.

Effects can be hypothetical. Add in to this the growth of sensitivity and estimations, especially since the truth about interior states of mind anyway cannot be known, become the norm. All this removes free speech protection in many situations without evidence of any specific effect on any actual person. In runs counter to J.S. Mill's opinion that the prohibition of speech ought to be limited and was legitimate only in certain cases when it constituted an overt incitement – i.e. a speech act intended to provoke the hearer into action – and an 'overt' act has followed. It would then be possible to establish, or not, a probable connection 'between the act and the instigation' (Mill, 1998 [1859]: 21, note). We are some distance from that because we think the 'probable connection' can be taken as read. We think we know it is always there.

Received understanding underlying all legal bans and codified restrictions holds that expression – all expression – does have direct effects, even if these cannot be specifically indentified. For example, the descriptor words in the British legislation for the harms to be prohibited were altered from the subjective (a cynic might say, blatantly middle-class) 'taste and decency' to the new standards of 'harm and offence'. A justification was that the latter were more objective (Millwood Hargrave and Livingstone, 2009: 27). Objectivity, though, is not really in play. The justification is flawed from the outset because, essentially unproblematically, the melded words 'harm' and 'offence' assume media's power. This has caused universal Establishment worry from the outset: 'it is the Press that has made 'um Mad', opined Sir Roger L'Estrange, the Restoration Licenser of the Press, 'and the Press must set 'um Right again' (Goldie, 2008). Setting them right again (or trying to do so) is what, for example, the entire advertising industry does.

When actual reaction to information, in the form of market response to advertisements, is left behind, assessing impact becomes a far less easily determined matter. A daily flow of 'evidence' apparently supports Sir Roger's general view of media power to the point where the connection between expression and its effects is, more or less, unquestioned. Representations of violence, for example, are always assumed to encourage, if not cause, violence in society.[17] This assumption suffuses production codes where sociological research is often now referenced to justify repression (Millwood Hargrave and Livingstone, 2009).[18] However, despite nearly a century of sociological investigation into the media, this will not serve the regulators' turn. The conclusions of positivist media-effects researchers, another group of treasonous clerks, are persistently inconclusive and contentious. Whatever they carefully (or otherwise) find, the results, when popularly received, illustrate a seemingly irresistible tendency to confuse correlation with causation. And this is true whatever the type of expression is said to represent or encourage: hatred, offence, incivility or even permitted, but frowned-upon, behaviours such as smoking.[19] The wonder is that the best (or, perhaps, only) example of proven causation – copycat suicides (the 'Werther effect', see Chapter 8.2) – has produced no bans. The failure to distinguish correlation from causation muddles the surface, i.e. utterance, with the underlying structure: in the case of hate speech, for example, this would be the social position of the 'other'.

Most dangerously, the cavalier discarding of causality's usual boundaries, actual or potential, has been particularly used to chill political speech. Objectionable political speech – 'subversive advocacy' – is speech harmful to the state yet it is deemed necessary in a democracy (Rawls, 1996: 341). The best illustration of this is the United States, and its history of the repression of political speech is the blemish on its claim to a consistent superior protection of expression. On the one hand, little better illustrates the vibrancy of the American Enlightenment tradition into the twentieth century than the rhetoric of the liberal wing of the Supreme Court when considering the First Amendment's impact political debate; but on the other, little more vividly illuminates the dangers of fudging the harm principle.

In 1919, Justice Holmes, glossing *Hicklin*'s 'bad tendency', argued in *Schenk* that: 'The question in every case is whether the words used are used in such circumstances and are of such a nature as to create a clear and present danger that they will bring about the substantive evils that the United States Congress has a right to prevent. It is a question of proximity and degree' (*Schenk v. United States*, 1919). But this statement, for all its anthologized status as an expression of the United States' fundamental commitment to liberty, meant in practice less than it seemed. If each and every possible consequence, even the most unlikely, can be considered, then 'clear and present danger' and the questions of 'proximity and degree' can mean little. The situation famously summed up by Holmes at another point in the *Schenk* judgment, the prohibition of a false cry of fire in a crowded theatre, is far from view.

During the First World War, Charles Schenk, secretary of the Socialist Party of America, produced a pamphlet advocating draft resistance in contravention of the then existing Federal Espionage Act passed as the United States entered the First World War in 1917. This had been amended the following year to incorporate a revived Sedition Act.[20] Prohibited were: 'any disloyal, profane, scurrilous, or abusive language about the form of government of the United States, or the Constitution of the United States, [etc.] or any language intended to bring [any of the above] into contempt, scorn, contumely, or disrepute'.

And Holmes, Brandeis and the rest of the Supreme Court unanimously judged that this was indeed what Schenk had done and intended to do. Whether or not any draftee actually acted on his advice and resisted was not at issue. The possibility that one might was enough of a clear and present danger to convict Schenk. After all, the First World War was underway and was sufficiently proximate and sufficiently grave to render his 'speech' unprotected. A 'clear and present danger' should only exist in a time of what Rawls describes as an 'emergency' (Rawls, 1996: 345, 354). This was such a time. Self-evidently, for a state, war was the most obvious of emergencies. Hence Holmes' view in this case that it was possible for free utterances to be abridged legally 'so long as men fight, and that no Court could regard them as protected by any constitutional right' (*Schenk v. United States*, 1919). The other liberal justice, Brandeis, concurred.

That year, Harvard law professor Zechariah Chafee, Jr, writing in the *Harvard Law Review*, disputed this contention. He was not impressed with his friend Holmes' 'falsely crying "fire"' analogy:

> How about the man who gets up in a theatre between the acts and informs the audience honestly but perhaps mistakenly that the fire exits are too few or locked. He is a much closer parallel to Schenk ... The zealous, in times of excitement like war ... realize that all condemnation of the war or of conscription may conceivably lead to active resistance or insubordination. Is it not better to kill the serpent in the egg. All writings that have a tendency to hinder the war must be suppressed. Such has always been the arguments of the opponents of free speech. (Chaffee, 1919: 944, 949)

Chafee complained that Holmes was more concerned as to the question of the Espionage Act's constitutionality than its impact: 'it is regrettable that Justice Holmes did nothing to emphasize the social interest behind free speech and show the need of balancing even in war time ... His liberalism seems held in abeyance by his belief in the relativity of values' (Chafee, 1919: 968–9). Chafee shared the piece with Holmes prior to publication.

Six months after *Schenk*, and days after the Chafee article appeared, Holmes delivered a judgment in another 'Sedition Act' case, *Abrams v. United States*. Here the defendant and others had produced two pamphlets protesting American intervention against the Red Army in Russia; but this time, Holmes (and Brandeis) dissented:

> I wholly disagree with the argument of the Government that the First Amendment left the common law as to seditious libel in force. History seems to me against the notion. I had conceived that the United States through many years had shown its repentance for the Sedition Act of 1798 by repaying fines that it imposed. Only the emergency that makes it immediately dangerous to leave the correction of evil counsels to time warrants making any exception to the sweeping command, 'Congress shall make no law abridging the freedom of speech.' Of course I am speaking only of expressions of opinion and exhortations, which were all that

were uttered here, but I regret that I cannot put into more impressive words my belief that in their conviction upon this indictment the defendants were deprived of their rights under the Constitution of the United States. (*Abrams v. United States*, 1919)

His words were not impressive enough. Abrams and his comrades' twenty-year sentences were confirmed.

Nor did Chafee's intervention prevent the two liberal justices from further displaying cognitive dissonance in First Amendment cases. Ringing endorsements of the principle did not mean that particular circumstances could not undercut the right. Eight years after the 1919 cases, Justice Brandeis wrote that: 'The right of free speech, the right to teach, and the right of assembly are, of course, fundamental rights ... These may not be denied or abridged' (*Whitney v. California*, 1927). Referring to the founding fathers of the constitution, he said:

> To courageous, self-reliant men, with confidence in the power of free and fearless reasoning applied through the processes of popular government, no danger flowing from speech can be deemed clear and present unless the incidence of the evil apprehended is so imminent that it may befall before there is opportunity for full discussion. If there be time to expose through discussion the falsehood and fallacies, to avert the evil by the processes of education, the remedy to be applied is more speech, not enforced silence. Only an emergency can justify repression. Such must be the rule if authority is to be reconciled with freedom. (*Whitney v. California*, 1927)

Yet this again did not mean the 'speech' at issue in *Whitney* was not, in fact, dangerously 'evil' and that an 'emergency' was in train, giving no opportunity for 'more speech'.

Although it had taken eight years to reach the Supreme Court, the events in *Whitney* occurred in the immediate post-war period. Anita Whitney had been convicted under the Californian Criminal Syndicalism Act of organizing, and participating in, the Communist Labor Party of California, which was held to advocate the violent overthrow of the government. Evidence was produced to this effect, much, though, coming from another movement, the syndicalist Industrial Workers of the World (IWW aka the 'Wobblies'). Such details did not detain the court. Nor were they much concerned with the fact that Whitney was only a temporary member of the party. As with Holmes (with Brandeis concurring) in *Schenk*, so with Brandeis (Holmes concurring) in *Whitney*.

Citing Holmes in *Schenk*, Brandeis held: 'although the rights of free speech and assembly are fundamental, they are not, in their nature, absolute'. The California Syndicalism Act,[21] section 4, stated that it was a necessary law for 'the *immediate* preservation of the public peace and safety' (emphasis added). California was alarmed that 'at the present time, large numbers of persons are going from place to place in this state advocating, teaching and practicing criminal syndicalism': that is, they were part of radical unions, or parties, communists – whatever. This was the time of the first American 'Red Scare' in the wake of the Russian Revolution. Revolution was perhaps contagious and domestic revolution was therefore threatened, at least rhetorically, by these 'large numbers of persons'. The 'substantive evil' was communism, which the state of California knew when it saw it. The spilt blood of the Tsar and his family, after all, was still warm; and, worse, the means of production in Russia had been seized. No time, then, for 'more speech'. Whitney was guilty as charged. That she was a prominent socialite, a wealthy lawyer's daughter whose relatives included Supreme Court justices and the millionaire who had backed the first transatlantic telegraph cable, cannot have helped her case either. Temporary party member or not, she was a class traitor. What greater evidence of the penetration of dangerous alien political thought could one ask for? Communists were another 'other'. And on a technicality, despite the rhetoric, Brandeis and Holmes agreed her sentence.

Articulating communist/socialist ideology in the first half of the twentieth century in the United States exposed a speaker to as much 'legal peril', 'risk' and 'threat' as hate speech utterance did towards the end of the century in the rest of West. In fact, more. Congress made the advocacy of the overthrow of the government a crime with the 1940 Smith Act.[22] Despite the Second World War alliance with the Soviet Union, the Act's constitutionality was confirmed by the Supreme Court in 1951 as the Senator Joseph McCarthy-induced Red Scare was gathering pace. Clear and present danger remained in place allowing hypothetical outcomes, however unlikely and tenuously connected to expression, to prohibit radical speech.

In *Dennis v. United States* (*Dennis v. United States*, 1951), the justices considered causality directly. Was a communist revolution a clear and present enough danger to warrant the removal of First Amendment protection from those who advocated it? Did the 'gravity of the "evil"', even when 'discounted by its improbability', justify abridging free speech 'to avoid the danger'? Yes, said a majority of the court. In fact, Eugene Dennis, the general secretary of the Communist Party USA, was guilty even though no evidence of planned insurrection or even talk of it was called. As with Anita Whitney, being a communist was offence enough. The country, after all, was at war – the 'cold war'. The Soviet Union, now armed with nuclear weapons, was the enemy. Dennis was guilty.

However, the book of fine rhetorical statements in defence of the right of free speech and the First Amendment, so comforting to liberals, acquired another ringing endorsement. Justice Hugo Black:

These petitioners were not charged with an attempt to overthrow the Government. They were not charged with overt acts of any kind designed to overthrow the Government. They were not even charged with saying anything or writing anything designed to overthrow the Government. The charge was that they agreed to assemble and to talk and publish certain ideas at a later date ... No matter how it is worded, this is a virulent form of prior censorship of speech and press, which I believe the First Amendment forbids. I would hold §3 of the Smith Act authorizing this prior restraint unconstitutional on its face and as applied ... I cannot agree that the First Amendment permits us to sustain laws suppressing freedom of speech and press on the basis of Congress' or our own notions of mere 'reasonableness'. Such a doctrine waters down the First Amendment so that it amounts to little more than an admonition to Congress. (*Dennis v. United States*, 1951)

Black followed Holmes in *Abrams*, not Brandeis in *Whitney*. He did not argue his way back to support the majority decision. He dissented, as did Justice William O. Douglas. He added: 'There is hope, however, that in calmer times, when present pressures, passions and fears subside, this or some later Court will restore the First Amendment liberties to the high preferred place where they belong in a free society'.

In *Yates v. United States* six years later, although the cold war was still afoot, Black had his chance. Fourteen Californians were convicted simply of being members of the Communist Party and Black insisted that the evidence upon which their conviction rested was: 'comparatively insignificant. Guilt or innocence may turn on what Marx or Engels or someone else wrote or advocated as much as a hundred years or more ago ... When the propriety of obnoxious or unfamiliar views about government is in reality made the crucial issue ... prejudice makes conviction inevitable except in the rarest circumstances' (*Yates v. United States*, 1957). This time, finally, the brethren agreed with him. The conviction was reversed and the Smith Act was, in effect, dead.

In 1969, the common-sense implications of Holmes' 'clear and present danger' test were finally redefined to mean political speech was protected, irrespective of overt or constructive intent without reference indirect causation. A more restricted Millian level of probability was admitted by the liberal Warren Court to be the basis of the test: 'the constitutional guarantees of free speech and free press do not permit a state to forbid or proscribe the advocacy of the use of force or of law violation except where such advocacy is directed to inciting or producing imminent lawless action and is likely to incite or produce such action' (*Brandenburg v. Ohio*, 1969).

Some might think it unfortunate that the speech which occasioned this opinion was that of a Ku Klux Klansman.

In 1964, Clarence Brandenburg, TV repair shop-owner in Hamilton County in rural Ohio, invited a local TV station, WLWT-TV to a meeting. Eleven hooded and robed men and Brandenburg burned a cross and he spewed forth the usual tired racist rhetoric. On the Fourth of July, he intended to march on

Washington and thereby stop the President, the Congress and the Supreme Court 'suppressing the white Caucasian race'. The Ohio Criminal Syndicalism Statute,[23] which was passed – as was California's – at the height of the first Red Scare in 1919, forbade such talk and Brandenburg was convicted. Represented by the American Civil Liberties Union (an organization he detested), he appealed, eventually to the Supreme Court (Kissing, 2001: 15). For Brandenburg's conviction to be safe, there had to be, Justice Abe Fortis held for the court, this 'imminent lawless action'; but there was none. Although it was not unknown for such gatherings to produce extreme violence, on this occasion nothing had ensued nor was any disturbance in view. There was no proof of any damaging outcome, however possible and indeed probable it might previously have been thought to be. Moreover, Justices Douglas and Black, as the most liberal members of Earl Warren's liberal bench, insisted that the reference to 'no law' in the First Amendment meant what it said, i.e. 'Congress [and the State of Ohio] shall make no law abridging the freedom of speech'. It had taken fifty years from *Schenk* to secure this point and for clear and present danger to also mean what common sense suggested it did.

Since 1969, on the basis if *Brandenburg*, American speakers have been free to express themselves as they will free from 'legal peril' or 'significant legal risk' and without 'threat of fine or imprisonment'. One can even say one is a communist. Content neutrality coupled with a more restricted Millian view of causality have produced a markedly different environment for vexatious expression than exists elsewhere in the West.

Although in Britain there is a general tendency in matters of libel and hate speech to incline more towards the United States than Europe, a restricted view of causality along American lines does not necessarily follow. Hence the extreme version of the sort of blindness found in the *Hicklin* test when, in 2011, the 'instigators' of 'a riot to which no one turned up' were jailed (see Chapter 9.5). In general, that summer, the judiciary, rather like the Manchester Yeoman Cavalry at Peterloo, 'lost all control of temper' in sentencing actual rioters. Here, though, the convicted were merely ineffective provocateurs. Their sentences vividly spoke to the suppression of speech that a failure to limit the notion of causality entails. It is disregard of the realities of connectivity that sustains incivility and hate speech legislation. It is not so much that the law fails to contain the damage caused by speech; it is that there is, in reality, no damage to contain – only a 'tendency' to damage of which the law, anyway, needs little evidence beyond its own prejudices (however liberal or otherwise).

These were given full reign, in the first decade of the twenty-first century, because there was another war going on – the 'War Against Terror'. As with the First World War, a plethora of hasty statutes appeared; although the more general one, the Terrorism Act (2000), was fundamentally the latest iteration of a line of legislation, which because of unrest in Northern Ireland, dated back to the 1930s. Terrorism is defined as: 'the use or threat of action …

designed to influence the government or to intimidate the public or a section of the public ... for the purpose of advancing a political, religious or ideological cause' (Terrorism Act, 2000: [1], [1]). This purpose, 'involves serious violence against a person'; or 'serious damage to property'; or it 'endangers a person's life'; or it produces 'a serious risk to the health or safety of the public' or it attacks electronic communications (Terrorism Act, 2000: [1], [2]).[24] The government can designate terrorist organizations and proscribe them. Often, though, these might be oppositional groups to foreign regimes and the terrorist designation has as much to do the realpolitik of British foreign policy as with 'the preservation of peace and the maintenance of order', which is the Act's announced purpose.

Although the Act spoke of the promotion or encouragement of terrorism, following the London bombings of July 2005, further legislation was passed specifically targeted at expression in sympathy with terrorism, as previously defined. Following the 'tendency' logic of the Obscene Publications Act, now prohibited was any 'statement that is likely to be understood by some or all of the members of the public to whom it is published as a direct or indirect encouragement or other inducement to them to the commission, preparation or instigation of acts of terrorism or Convention [i.e. ECHR] offences' (Terrorism Act, 2006: [1], [1]). This includes 'every statement which ... glorifies the commission or preparation (whether in the past, or future or generally)' of terrorism as previously defined (Terrorism Act, 2006 [1], [3]). A defence shall be that the views were not those of the speaker (i.e. journalists reporting such opinions were protected). The 'glorification' must be intended although a 'reckless' communication could amount to unwarranted dissemination.

So to the established and chilling ambiguities of 'fighting words', 'serious offence', 'due' and the rest is now added 'glorification'. It is clear that the framers of this Act were ignorant of Mill's defence of tyrannicide and those who argue for it. In terms of their legislation, strictly construed, now prohibited would be an expression of admiration for that other Schenk, Claus Schenk, Graf von Stauffenberg, who endeavoured to blow up Hitler in the terrorist 'July Plot' of 1944.[25] As Robertson and Nicol point out: 'one person's terrorist is another's "freedom fighter". Blue plaques adorn the London homes of Karl Marx and those who plotted the overthrow of tyranny by forces of arms – Mazzini, Sun Yat Sen, Kropotkin' (Robertson and Nicol, 2008: 660). A case was brought under the Act against a Libyan plotting in London against Colonel Gaddafi, but that was in 2007, some years before the RAF's bombing campaign against the Colonel (*R. v. F.*, 2007). Such absurdities, though, are not the main point. It is that the legislation is grounded in an assumption about both the power and the legitimacy of the state to control expression.

At an even more fundamental level, it speaks to a further assumption about the power of the expression it wishes to control and the connectivity of that speech with the actions it wishes to prevent in the name of 'the preservation of peace and the maintenance of order'. This all turns on the question of causality. All too glib is the assumption that expression's effects are so direct that censoring it will cauterize the supposed harms it causes. Specifically, at law, the question of causality has been rendered moot by the removal of the need for verifiable hurt and, if necessary witnesses to attest to it. Treasonous legal clerks, within and without the courts, argue for limitations on speech on the basis of this faulty vision of causality.

For example, the distinguished academic First Amendment lawyer, Frederick Schauer noted a new 'attention to the underlying premises of the principle of freedom of speech' in the Reaganite 1980s, querying why 'we [Americans] want to protect speech not because it causes no harm, but *despite* the harm it may cause' (Schauer, 1983: 1,284, 1,295). The answer he gives is, of course, because of the constitutional mandate in the First Amendment: 'Speech is special by stipulation'; but, Schauer adds, 'now the stipulation may seem a bit odd' (Schauer, 1983: 1,298). The purpose of free speech, he argues, is, in essence, grounded in the Enlightenment concept that each individual must be allowed to express their personhood. So, for him, the question can be illuminated thus: 'I would imagine, for example, that many motorcyclists ... feel that they can better express their personhood at eighty miles an hour than at fifty-five [the usual US speed limit]. Are they responsible for the harms they negligently cause when riding at eighty? I hope so. Are newspapers responsible for negligently causing harms of the same magnitude? No' (Schauer, 1983: 1,299).

Leave aside the assumption that the mental distress or even the possible physical harms caused by media exposure (such as provoked attacks, financial damage) is meaningfully the equivalent of being hit by a motorcycle at 80 miles an hour: Schauer here falls into the Sadean trap to create the straw-man of unbridled individualism, which was, and is, nowhere intended.

But what is even more worrying is that, like many, Schauer does not consider the issue of speech as a guarantor of other rights. For him the problem is simply that:

> speech often causes a balance of utilitarian harms over goods graver than those caused by actions, and so is often more justifiably suppressed on grounds of utilitarian advantage. So it is a puzzle that the state's burden of justification for the restriction of speech is much greater than its burden of justification for the restriction of other (less harmful) activities. (Richards, 1988: 324)

This argument cannot be categorized as coming from either the right or the left. It is not, after all, only conservative opinion that is constantly, it would seem, perturbed at the logical outcomes of a commitment to free expression. The American courts, by insisting on it to a degree unmatched elsewhere, also failed rising liberal sensitivities, equally concerned that speech is too privileged.

For Owen Fiss, that the government should make 'no law' might well now be counter-productive. For example, the very democratic process itself has been distorted by a lack of control over campaign spending in the United States: money, via the media, 'buys' speech (Fiss, 1996: 14). In this way money has constrained the Fourteenth Amendment's guarantee of equality, by in effect silencing the many who cannot avail themselves of the right of free speech under the First Amendment. Liberty undercuts equality and only the state can now correct this:

> The debates of the past were premised on the view that the state was the natural enemy of freedom. It was the state that was trying to silence the individual speaker, and it was the state that had to be curbed. There is much wisdom in this view, but it represents only a half truth. Surely, the state may be an oppressor, but it may also be the source of freedom. (Fiss, 1996: 9)

Schauer concurs:

> Controlling government by insisting on freedom of speech is no longer the main problem. In the eighteenth century, there was a need to correct the state's predilection to repress all criticism because it feared it could not survive it, but government's capacity for survival is no longer at issue. Any such considerations cannot be used to justify putting speech's privilege beyond question. (Schauer, 1982a: 12)

In Europe, there is anyway a liberal willingness, greater than in the United States, to judge and to legislate against perceived harms. In essence, what is being questioned here from all sides is, in effect, the capstone importance of a right of free expression.

The rebuttal to such attacks is, firstly, Madison's on secular speech and Jefferson's parallel argument on religious expression. Whatever the problems caused, the state cannot be trusted to correct them without acting on its own prejudices and without establishing precedents for further action. At the level of infrastructure – ownership of the system, provision of service, technical standards – the point is taken and the state must operate. However, despite the validity of Fiss' point about liberty's power to silence voices as much as it enables them, the state must have nothing to do with expression at the level of content. The matter of controlling 'harm' because of expression is quite other. Once the state is admitted into controlling content specifically, the right is at risk. A second argument, that free expression is the insurance for all other rights, make this unacceptable.

For Mill, expression is essential for the discovery of truth in the marketplace of ideas: 'there ought to exist the fullest liberty of professing and discussing, as a matter of ethical conviction, any doctrine, however immoral it may be considered; however much it exceeds the limits of social embarrassment ... It is only by the collision of adverse opinion that the truth will out' (Mill, 1998 [1859]: 20).

For the philosopher Alexander Meiklejohn, it is a necessary corollary of universal suffrage in a representative democracy (Meiklejohn, 1961: 27). It is, in the words of Lord Styne in the English Court of Appeal, the 'lifeblood of democracy' (*R. v. Secretary of State for the Home Department ex parte Simms*, 2000). Of free speech, (in *Procunier v. Martine*, 1974), Justice Thurgood Marshall of the US Supreme Court said, 'it serves not only the needs of the polity but also those of the human spirit – a spirit that demands self-expression'. It is thus correct that the default position should be that expression's harms (albeit well-defined and within well-established limits) be countenanced because of these positives. Lose the right of free speech and lose, or at best endanger, all the rest: 'The constitutional law of free speech tends to be protective even of speech causing much harm and little ostensible good because such protection offsets the political evil of pervasive intolerance' (Richards, 1988: 325).

Of course, subtle legal *clercs* are aware of the dangers involved in their questioning the right; and these are addressed. The Millian rhetoric as to expression's crucial role in democracy is heard, but is rejected. Characterized as seeing society as nothing but a university seminar room in which rational arguments contend, such a vision is dismissed – it's too 'Ivory Tower' to be viable. And today's media, as the prime 'guardians' who guard the political process, are now themselves overwhelmingly in the hands of conglomerates. They are as much a problem for freedom as the state. Murdoch's 'soaraway' empire is a case in point. More is at stake in today's real, multicultural, mass-media, technologized society, imply critics such as Schauer and Fiss, than the pursuit of 'truth'. The main anxiety is no longer the compatibility of government with freedom; rather, it is a concern for the physical and mental well-being of each individual citizen.

The problem is that the law has scarcely kept up with this or any other aspect of the problems of free expression. It nevertheless remains the best, indeed the only, basis upon which the internal criticism of the right can be resisted, however much its inconsistencies, incoherence and uncertainty of operation are debilitating. It can and should be made to work, and the internal critical voices can be stilled were this to happen.

12.5   *Sir Ian Trethowan v. Tom Mangold* (1981): Dangers of regulation

Media freedom should be guaranteed by the law, just as control of the media's capacity for harm should also be a matter for the law and the law alone. This is not to deny that media law is in anything but a parlous state, worse in some places than others, but everywhere subject to inconsistencies and uncertainties; nor that its eighteenth-century roots make it too much focused on constraint of government when today the greater threat to freedom comes at least as much from concentration of ownership and over-sensitivity to 'harm'. After all, as an entity, 'media law' is itself a most recent creation, arguably 'invented' by Geoffrey Robertson and Andrew Nicol in their *Media Law* of 1984. Therein was first assembled a motley collection of cases and statutes all of which dealt with one aspect of media or another. It is a scarcely coherent body of law. Moreover, some of the sixty-plus other pieces of legislation affecting free expression in the UK were ill-considered, hurried responses to perceived dangers and moral panics.[26] Nevertheless, it remains the case that: 'The one and only proposition which is both absolute and undeniable in media law', as Geoffrey Robertson and Andrew Nicol aver, 'is that thought is free' (Robertson and Nicol, 2008: xix).

However, when 'emitted' thought becomes 'subject to interceptions by a network of laws designed to jam and distort it in the interests of States or corporations or other persons or entities whom the thought disquietens' (Robertson and Nicol, 2008: xix). For the law to act as the defender of the right of free expression, apart from the support of 'the general spirit of the people' its focus needs to be: 'not so much on the message (which may be false, or horrible, or both) but on the messenger, the human being with an absolute right to think and hence (we infer) a presumptive right to put the information or the opinion into the public domain' (Robertson and Nicol, 2008: xx).

After all, none of the reasons as to why free speech is necessary in a democracy have been removed for all the questions – legitimate as to ownership, less so as to content – raised by the legal, and other, philosophers.

And free speech is fragile and easily undercut, often for very good reasons. Take ethics. Lord Leveson's inquiry, for example, is to make 'recommendations for a more effective policy and regulation that supports the integrity and freedom of the press while encouraging the highest ethical standards'. In such a context, 'ethical' becomes a weasel word. If not firmly attached to the harm principle, itself carefully constrained by a strict notion of what constitutes injury, ethics can be nothing but a cover for restricting expression. To all intents and purposes, it imposes censorship. Broadcasting, as is suggested above (see Chapters 7.4 and 8.3), has been subjected to this exactly via such an 'ethical' requirement, glossed as 'balance', 'fairness' and so on. But this control is widely considered to be a very strong positive:

> Why, in the UK and most other developed countries, is television still seen in the twenty-first century as a vital conduit of serious, accurate journalism? … Why is television news implicitly believed while most newspapers – especially the tabloids – are despised? How is it that, when asked to rate different kinds of journalists for trustworthiness, over half of the UK population feel they can

trust TV journalists (nearly two-thirds for the BBC) compared to 43 per cent for broadsheet newspaper journalists, and a shocking 15 per cent for tabloid journalists .... The answer to these questions ... lies in external regulation and, ultimately, statutory interference. (Barnett, 2011: 22)

It might undoubtedly be the case that broadcast news is seen as 'serious', is 'believed', is held to be more 'trustworthy' than are the papers; but why is this assumed to be such a good? Credibility and trustworthiness, after all, are as much the ambitions of the propagandist as they are objectives of any truth-speaker. Is not broadcast news' trustworthiness merely a measure of ideological effectiveness?

Within a healthy democracy the reception of news requires that it be treated with scepticism. Authority drew the teeth of the radical press in the nineteenth century by allowing capitalists to exploit a thirst for sensation at the expense of dangerous political expression. In the twentieth century, authority drew the teeth even more effectively from the new media by the sleight of hand that disguised news produced under conditions of censorship – nevermind the mealy-mouthed wordplay about content control and so on – as trustworthy 'serious, accurate journalism'. It might be those things (quite a lot of the time) but it is also too limited in the range of opinions it conveys, too constrained in its agenda-setting; and if it were not, let it not be forgotten that, in Britain, the Home Secretary could send in the troops. To suggest a parallel regime to produce a press along the same lines is unthinkable and has been since the British Broadcasting Company's initial performance in the General Strike. Anyway, is not scepticism a healthy thing, very 'necessary in a democratic society'?

Even if a root and branch objection to regulation except directly at law is rejected, the worm in the bud of regulation remains that authority must be benign. As Barnett puts it:

If governments are prepared to provide the statutory framework and regulators are prepared to implement the rules of that framework with toughness and consistency, television journalism can indeed educate, illuminate and stimulate. It is not a comfortable lesson for those who distrust the principle of political interference, and in particular the motives of those who seek to impose rules on a free media. (Barnett, 2011: 23)

This is a most enormous 'if'. Without faith in authority, as Barnett admits, regulation would be 'disastrous': 'There is no question that, in the hands of the unscrupulous, the incompetent, the autocratic or the power-hungry, political constraints on the media can be potentially disastrous' (Barnett, 2011: 23). The irony is that Barnett's account of such improper interferences in British broadcasting as are known, for all that he carefully attempts to exculpate the regulators on each occasion, is quite the best available. It proffers all the evidence needed to rebut his own argument.

Evidence of censorship takes decades to appear. For example, in 1981, the Director-General of the BBC, Sir Ian Trethowan, allowed MI5 to re-edit a pioneering exposé of its work, made by Tom Mangold for *Panorama* (a most trusted programme); 50 per cent of it was removed, a fact revealed by the release of papers from the National Archive under the thirty-year rule (Corera, 2011). Proponents of regulation are quick to argue that 'that was then' and to assert that such an incident would not happen today. Presumably, in thirty years when evidence of today's tampering is made clear, their heirs and successors will be saying much the same. Anyway, it is not the *causes célèbres* that matter but the overall chilling effect of regulation and the compliance culture.

And let it not be forgotten: who, after all, was responsible for Hackgate? The regulated broadcast news or the untrustworthy press?

> Talk, at very elevated levels, to the great and the good at the BBC and they will admit that the corporation could not have done the hacking story for itself, could not have followed every allegation of the way, and could not have investigated it as prober of the first resort. Why not? Because of the statutory thing. Because of the rules on 'impartiality', on fairness and balance. (Preston, 2011: 50)

Even Lord Patten, the chair of the BBC Trust, acknowledged as much when he pointed out that, because of regulations, the BBC could not have 'pursued the hacking story at News International as remorselessly as the *Guardian* campaign did' (Greenslade, 2011). The same applies to all who have to comply with the Ofcom Broadcasting Code. It is another tragedy of Hackgate that it so draws attention away from the broadcasters' fraught constitutional situation. Broadcasting regulation is (to borrow a phrase from Tom Paine) 'in plain terms a very paltry rascally original' to use as a template for cleaning up the law's 'mess' (Paine, 1772).

This is not, of course, to say that the law is without blemish. In the face of modern mass communications, it is indeed seriously deficient, and one in most urgent need of attention. Worse: prior to the HRA, judges – especially in their fondness for injunctions (see Chapter 11.8) – 'were knee-jerk suppressors of any information, however newsworthy, that might discomfort the security services or the government or the royal family or Mrs Mary Whitehouse' (Robertson and Nicol, 2008: vi). The bench was never entirely comfortable with Blackstone's prohibition of 'prior constraint', except perhaps in matters of libel, and were generally happy if any offending speech was, in some measure, an oxymoronic (as it might be) 'polite offensiveness'. To revisit Lord Reid's triad: speech which is unthreatening, non-abusive and non-insulting shall be that expression which is protected. With the English law a certain persistent dissonance can be noticed between rhetoric and practice.

For the law to operate effectively this all needs correction.

Reasons to resist expanding the harm principle to embrace an offence principle should be grounded in a consideration of the nature of the harm supposedly caused by expression. Causation should be more firmly established as grounds for the constraint of speech. Injury without damage and the self-attestation of harm should be closely regarded. A proper public interest test is crucial. A law of privacy, for example, could then follow with no dampening effect on free speech. Equally, were the position to be adopted that ownership of a platform of expression was so privileged that it abridged free-market rights to acquire other platforms, the problem of over-mighty media speakers – the cross-owning media moguls – would be solved. Their power to suborn would be reduced and the law's writ could run properly to protect as much as to 'controul' expression. As it is, the right to speak is more fragile than is usually supposed and the law, which is its best guarantor, is ailing and unequal to the task of defence.

Conclusions

Did you know that Eleanor Roosevelt gave Lou Gehrig the clap? [laughter]
What'd he say? Jesus, does he have to get that low for laughs? What's the
point? That's really bad taste ...
The point ... the point is the suppression of words.

Lenny Bruce (American album, 1961)

On 7 October 2006 Anna Stepanovna Politkovskaya, journalist, was
murdered by as yet unidentified assassins as she was returning home to her
flat in Moscow. Her fearless reporting of the Russian attack on Chechnya had
earned her the enmity of President Vladimir Putin. It is, of course, completely
unacceptable to suggest there is any connection between her murder and his
being offended by her. Putin's press-conference statement lamented her killing
as a blow to Russian democracy, though, also remembered, with regret, was
exactly the offensive quality of her journalism. The unmasked face of soft-
spoken, hostile power he presented menacingly dramatizes what this book
has been about. In the documentary on her life, *A Bitter Taste of Freedom*,
Poltikovskaya's friend, filmmaker Marina Goldovskaya, catches her on the
phone in what is rare footage of the press actually in the process of speaking
truth to power. Politkovskaya is on to a corrupt policeman, naming him to his
superiors, detailing his crimes, demanding explanations. Such behaviour, such
offensiveness, such exercise of her 'birthright' (as Mary Wollstonecraft has it)
are what, it cannot be doubted, cost her life.

On 4 October 1961, the comedian Lenny Bruce, after performing at San
Francisco's Jazz Workshop, was arrested for the first time on an obscenity
charge. In the course of his act, he used the word 'cocksucker' as part of a joke.
He concluded with what he called a 'big drum solo':

> 'To' is a preposition. 'Come' is a verb, the verb intransitive. 'To come.' 'To come.'
> I've heard these two words my whole adult life ... 'Did you come good? Did you
> come good? Did you come good? Did you come good?' ... Now if anyone in this
> room or the world finds those two words decadent, obscene, amoral, asexual –
> the words 'to come' really make you feel uncomfortable. If you think I'm rank
> for saying it to you ... you probably can't come ...

And then you're of no use. (Lenny Bruce, *American* album, 1961)

On this first occasion, he beat the rap but he was to be increasingly hounded
by the police. He recorded his gigs not only for release as LPs (whence these
quotations) but also for subsequent use in the trials that he knew would

follow. Five years after that first arrest, he was dead of a drug overdose in his Los Angeles home.

There is no blue water between Lenny Bruce's live hysterical foul-mouthed rants, confronting, with increasing hysteria, American hypocrisies, and Anna Politkovskaya tearing at the 'vizards and vailes and disguises' of Putin's state. The offence a Politkovskaya causes a Putin no more gives him (or whomever) the right to silence her voice than do the curtain-twitching perceptions of the various police departments that pursued Bruce legitimate their attempts to silence him. Nor does *The Satanic Verses*' affront (however real or imaginary that might have been) to the sensibilities of the Imam Ruhollah al-Musavi al-Khomeini – let him invoke the name of 'Him, the Highest' as much as he likes – give him the right to put Rushdie to silence either. The treasonous Western clerks are more modest in their demands but they too are uncommitted to the principle and would emasculate it. That they do so in the name of tolerance, for the cause of social cohesion or out of sensitivity to the feelings of others does not reduce the danger to speech in any way. Rupert Murdoch and his competitors and minions, too, are complicit in that their attempts to corrupt a society in the name of their desire for profit undercut our ability to defend the right. The ties that bind Bruce to Politkovskaya also tie Khomeini, the clerks and, in effect, those who abuse the right for no or little good cause to the forces of repression. The threats they variously pose should – simply – be vigorously and unambiguously resisted. The right to free speech and the right within it to offend, because without it we have no free speech, must be maintained. At whatever cost.

This, though, is not to defend the status quo. Far from it. In the course of this argument, I have made the following suggestions:

- special regulations for expression beyond the general law are 'very needless';
- existing legislation should be refined, coalesced and applied;
- ready access to law should be a necessary concomitant of the right of free expression;
- the right of free expression should be media blind;
- a public interest test which distinguishes curiosity from entitlement should be developed;
- the harm principle should be strictly defined to exclude self-attested harm or damage;
- remedy for injury without damage should be exceptional;
- causation should be distinguished from correlation and actual evidence of it, rather than the possibility of it, should become the normal basis for determining remedy and constraining speech;

- content regulation and control of the media system's infrastructures should be distinguished and the former abandoned (in favour of the law proper);
- the state should exercise its legitimate allocative function to limit media ownership.

All this (or something similar) must be done because, as 'Junius' put it, in different circumstances but in response to identical societal needs: 'Let it be impressed upon your mind, let it be instilled into your children, that the liberty of the press is the palladium of all civil, political, and religious rights' ('Junius', 1978 [1769]). *'La libre communication des pensées et des opinions est un des droits les plus précieux de l'homme'* ('The free communication of thoughts and of opinions is one of the most precious rights of man'). We can readily admit that, since *The Declaration of the Rights of Man and of the Citizen* was written in 1789 after the French Revolution, this requires an amendment and a clarification: *de l'homme* should be *de l'humanité* but history has shown that *le droit* in question is not *un des droits les plus précieux* but *le droit plus précieu*. Otherwise: *stet* – let it stand.

Lincoln, UK
November 2009–April 2012

Notes

Chapter 1 The Shadow of the *Fatwa*

1 Farah has been forced to work in exile by his government but because of his critical political position, not his supposed 'apostasy'.

2 There is even a story, too pat to be readily accepted, that Khomeini had received a digest of the book after its London publication the previous year and was reported to have said: 'The world has always been full of lunatics who have talked nonsense. It is not worth replying to this sort of thing. Do not take it seriously' (Moin, 1999: 283). This anecdote however is fleshed out by Andrew Anthony: 'a delegation of mullahs from the Holy city of Qum read a section of the book to Khomeini, including a part featuring a mad mullah in exile, which was an obvious caricature of Khomeini' (Anthony, 2009: 6).

3 He died, aged eighty, in 1995.

4 It follows that I am not here concerned with censorship and repression per se.

5 Political and public distress soon had the production restored; but the chill remains.

6 His equating at the time of *The Satanic Verses* to the Holocaust can be seen as evidence of the overheated moment rather than his usual insightful, and indeed, brave views.

Chapter 2 The Treason of the Clerks

1 Usually rendered, as in this instance by Stoppard, as: 'I disagree with what you say but I will defend to the death your right to say it.' Voltaire did not say it, the aphorism being coined in the early twentieth century as a summation of his views on expression. An earlier attribution has *'Je déteste ce que vous écrivez, mais je donnerai ma vie pour que vous puissiez continuer à écrire'* ('I detest what you write, but I would give my life to make it possible for you to continue to write'). In 1963, this was claimed to be a sentence in a letter of Voltaire's written on 6 February 1770 to l'Abbé Le Riche, but it is not in fact in that text (Boller and George, 1989: 124–5).

Chapter 3 The Abuses of 'Hackgate'

1 Actually, the possibility of the phone being hacked had been raised by Tom Watson, MP, during a parliamentary select committee cross-examination of the acting Deputy Commissioner John Yates of Scotland Yard on 24 March 2011. The possibility was again raised in the pages of the *New Statesman* the following month by the actor Hugh Grant, who was taking an increasing prominent role as the voice of the tabloids 'victims' (Bernstein, 2011: 51).

2 'Who guards the guards?' has become a tag to justify journalism's highest social purposes but its original formulation, Juvenal's *'Quis custodiet ipsos custodes?'* was concerned not with politics but with straying wives and daughters and the impossibility of locking them up to enforce morality. The guards could not be trusted any more than the women and themselves needed watching: hence

journalism. In this context, the tag suggests a fundamental role for the press and justification for a right of free expression.

3 The origins of the term are disputed, but most likely it relates to a cartoon strip. The cartoon character, 'The Yellow Kid', was the creation of Richard Outcault and first published in the *World* in 1894. Two years later Hearst poached the popular Outcault from Pulitzer, but Pulitzer hired another artist, George Luks, to continue to draw the strip. The inevitable legal battle resulted in both papers being allowed to carry 'Yellow Kid' cartoons, becoming, therefore, the 'Yellow Papers', giving rise to 'Yellow Journalism' and the 'Yellow Press'.

4 The latest figures from the Press Complaints Commission (the Press Council's successor) are less accessible than they have been previously. In 2008, for example, there were 4,698 complaints or which 1,420 were adjudicated, the rest being deemed frivolous; 71.4 per cent were over accuracy, 8.8 per cent privacy, 6.9 per cent intrusion into grief and 3.4 per cent over harassment (Press Complaints Commission, 2009). That is: there were some 897 complaints in the areas raised by Hackgate many – if not three-quarters – of which were deemed unfounded by the self-regulator (Press Complaints Commission, 2009).

5 An even truer successor to the original *Mecurius Fumigosus* than the *News of the World*, the *Sport* ceased publication in 2011.

6 Supposedly, Claude Cockburn's winning entry to a private competition within the *Times* newsroom, when he worked there as a sub-editor in the 1930s, for the most boring headline imaginable. 'Chile' is sometimes given as an alternative to 'Peru' but Cockburn was a writer sensitive enough to prefer 'roo' to 'lay' (or, in the 1930s, 'lee'). Anyway, 'Peru' is a letter shorter.

7 Speaking personally, I, as the dean of a state journalism college, was never able to extend hospitality, even a lunch-time soup and a sandwich, to the editor of my local paper, a small title in a major newspaper group, for fear compromising his ability to report on the university, the biggest enterprise in his circulation area.

8 Actually, she claimed ten.

9 Protection from Harassment Act 1997 c. 40.

10 Serious Organised Crime and Police Act 2005 c. 15.

Part Two   Defence

1 Actual court cases are covered in sections 4.1, 4.3, 4.4, 4.5, 5.1, 5.4, 6.2, 7.1, 9.1, 9.3, 11.2, 11.3, 11. 4, 11.5, 11.6, 11.7, 11.8, 12.1, 12.2, 12.3 and 12.4.

Chapter 4   *Actiones*: Cases

1 Their rhetoric persists into the present. For example, the late 1960s Californian cult leader Charles Manson, whatever might have overtly influenced his murderous thinking, certainly inadvertently echoed the amorality of later adepts of the Free Spirit.

2 For example, surviving contracts dated 1444–6 mention, in connection with a silversmith of Prague, Procopius Waldvogel, then working in Avignon, the art of artificial writing ('*ars artificialiter scribendi*') and the existence of Latin and Hebrew letters in various metals. No examples survive (Febvre and Martin, 1977: 52).

3 He also produced *italic* in the style of the cursive script in use in the Papal Chancery.

4　The title was withdrawn by the Pope when Henry broke with Rome but was re-established by Parliament. His descendants carry it to this day.

5　The word 'gazette' had been in use for a century or more and derives from dangerously republican Venice. Although it became a term for public news publications in many European languages, including English, gazette was also being used to denote the private newsletter well into the seventeenth century.

6　Centuries later, companies can still be quick to seek legal prohibition against the publication of merely embarrassing as well as commercially damaging information in the name of commercial confidentiality – as if there was such a thing as corporate sensibility to be protected, as against a more legitimate need to prevent overt disadvantage (see Chapter 11.8).

7　Butter might be the model for Cymbal, the head of the *Staple*, in Jonson's *The Staple of News*.

8　An Act for Preventing Abuses in Printing Seditious, Treasonable, and Unlicensed Books and Pamphlets, and for Regulating of Printing and Printing Presses (the 'Licensing Act') (1662) 13 & 14 Car. II, c. 33.

9　It is now online: http://www.london-gazette.co.uk.

10　12 Anne, stat. 2 c. 23.

11　Defoe, who wrote for Mist, was also employed by the government to spy on him and moderate his output if at all possible.

12　Libel Act (1792), 32 Geo. III, c. 60.

13　Libel Act (1843), 6 & 7 Victoria, c. 96.

14　Libel remains as a civil action; sedition and obscenity are also still crimes.

15　Martin points out that Johnson's memory was flawed as by that date he was living in Castle Street, not Exeter Street (Martin, 2008: 205).

16　Cave not only employed Johnson. He also gave Johnson's companion from Lichfield, young David Garrick, who had accompanied him to London in 1737, his first opportunity to act (see Chapter 6.1).

17　Some would trace the sayings 'bold as brass' and 'brass neck' to this incident and Cosby's forename.

18　The probation against writing is still in force for members of the general public.

19　Dowell gives the yield for 1749, the first year available, as £16,450, about three times what Robert Walpole would have spent per annum in the 1730s on bribing the press (Dowell, 1884: 341).

20　Now renamed Milton Street, it had been the site of the profession since the 1630s.

21　Using the National Archives calculator: http://www.nationalarchives.gov.uk/currency/results.asp#mid [accessed 5 November 2010].

22　Pepys used one and, indeed, tachygraphy had been employed by the ancients.

23　Blasphemous and Seditious Libels Act (or Criminal Libel Act), 60 Geo. III & 1 Geo. IV, c. 8.

24　Newspaper and Stamp Duties Act, 60 Geo. III & 1 Geo. IV, c. 9.

25　Sunday newspapers, in defiance of the ban on Sunday trade, started in the 1779 with Mrs E. Johnson's *British Gazette and Sunday Monitor*.

26　Thereby starting a tradition: in 1986, faced with hostility from the printers and journalist to new print technology, Walter's successor as proprietor, Rupert Murdoch, sacked his entire striking workforce and moved his main national titles overnight to a plant at Wapping manned by electricians.

27　Thomas Carlyle, in a lecture given in 1840, was quoting Burke: 'Burke said there were Three Estates in Parliament; but, in the Reporters' Gallery yonder, there sat a Fourth Estate more important far than they all' (Carlyle, 1859 [1840]: 147).

28 Charles Havas, also an advertising agent, began an exactly similar business in Paris in 1835.

29 These crimes were to persist as offences until 2010.

30 The Obscene Publications Act (1857), 20 & 21 Vict., c. 83.

31 The Act lapsed in 1694 but Clarke's intervention and, perhaps, Locke's comments as well, quoted above, date from the following year.

32 This last must, of course, be glossed: the proprietors were certainly men of capital and their respectability became a self-fulfilling prophecy as these 'press barons' were soon ennobled as real barons – or lords. As to their moral character, little need be said.

Chapter 5 *Consensu*: Agreed

1 These were a hangover, like the well-armed local militias, of the pioneering settlements in the seventeenth century.

2 A phrase first used to describe the American colonists during the debates to repeal the Stamp and 'Sugar' Acts in the House of Commons in 1765 (Thorpe, 1901: 48).

3 Ralph Waldo Emerson, *The Concord Hymn* (1837):
By the rude bridge that arched the flood,
Their flag to April's breeze unfurled,
Here once the embattled farmers stood,
And fired the shot heard round the world.

4 Attribution is, as ever, disputed. Representative John Penn of North Carolina is also credited with the joke; or it was made the following year by his brother Richard Franklin. Both had been governors of Pennsylvania (Graydon, 1846: 131).

5 Delaware, for instance. On the other hand, it did have a rare clause expressly forbidding slavery.

6 July 14, 1798, c. 73, 1 Stat. 59: 65 USC section LXXIV (1798).

7 It ceased publication in 1848 but the title was revived by Rupert Murdoch for the country's first national newspaper in 1964.

8 The family sold their interest in the *Daily Telegraph* in 1928 but remained on the board until 1986. They no longer use Levy in the family name.

9 The title was revived for a nineteenth-century literary review.

10 It was to survive, latterly as a journal no more official than any other and always in the Bourbonist interest, until 1915.

11 It was the speech of the Prussian king, Wilhelm I, in the course of this war that Gordon Bennett had telegraphed across the Atlantic (see Chapter 5.3).

12 Marx was editor of the paper by October 1842 and fell foul of the censors the following January. It was closed down. He was to start others but the only regular paid employment he ever enjoyed was as a foreign correspondent of Horace Greeley's *New York Tribune*. This came about because in 1848 he had met Charles Dana, then covering the 'Year of Revolutions' for that paper, in Cologne. Dana hired him in 1851 (Wheen, 2005: xvii).

13 Peter the Chicken: named after a central eighteenth-century figure in the history of the Dutch press. By 1944, after the name change to *Het Parool*, it was properly (but secretly) printed with a run of 60,000. Its editor, Frans Goedhart, was arrested by the Nazis twice but escaped each time. Four of his fellow editors were executed or died in the camps. Two escaped to England (Warmbrunn, 1963: 238–9).

14 The government had banned two communist papers, the *Daily Worker* and the news-sheet, the *Week*, in January 1941, Stalin then being in alliance with Hitler and the papers therefore echoing, in the tradition that Lenin had early established, the Moscow party line. This clearly raised the issue of sedition and, in wartime, justified the decision. The irony was that the *Week* had been noted by Joseph Goebbels in the 1930s as a main source of anti-Nazi news in Britain. Its editor and publisher, Claude Cockburn, was proud to be top of Goebbels list of people to round-up when the successful invasion of Britain was complete (Cockburn, 1967).

Chapter 6   *Non Sequitur*: It Doesn't Follow

1   12 Anne, stat. 2, c. 23.
2   6 & 7 Vict., c. 68.
3   1830 11 Geo. 4 and 1 Will. 4., c. 64.
4   *Camera* = room in Latin. A dark room, *camera obscura*, with a small aperture in one wall was known, via earlier Arab sources, to Renaissance savants. The hole, if small enough, would cause an image to appear on the wall. The room shrunk until it became by the seventeenth century a box – *camera obscura portabilis*. It also acquired a lens with a shutter mechanism behind it. Researchers (e.g. Daguerre), from the mid-eighteenth to the early nineteenth century, eventually perfected methods of capturing and fixing the images of these *camera*s, i.e. photography.
5   It is actually caused by a limitation of the eye/brain, a 'critical fusion factor'.
6   The Zoopraxographical Hall Muybridge opened as a showcase for his lectures at the 'World's Columbian Exhibition' in Chicago in 1892 has been claimed as 'without doubt, the first ever commercial movie theatre' (Clegg, 2007: 226). The assertion does little but illustrate the perils of over-enthusiastic 'firstism'. It was neither the first, nor was any moving image, a split second of which he could undoubtedly produce on his wheel of images, unambiguously photographic.
7   For example, Simon von Stampfer was working at the same time as Joseph Plateau, the 'inventor' of the Phenakistoscope and his term for the device, the Stroboscope, was to prevail over Plateau's even archer pseudo-Greek coining. Similarly, Louis Ducos du Hauron, a major figure in the history of colour photography, outlined a sequencing projector system before Heyl and along much the same lines, although he probably never built it. From 1879, John Carbutt was offering celluloid-based plates from his Dry Plate Works but George Eastman, a competitor, perfected the manufacture of celluloid 'film'. Dr Étienne-Jules Marey, a rather more respectable scientific figure than Muybridge, created a *fusil photographic* (photographic rifle) with which he stunningly caught birds in flight; but all a bird's progressive movement was reproduced within the frame of a single image.
8   9 Edw. VII, c. 30.
9   The incident was also of significance for the National Association for the Advancement of Colored People (NAACP), founded in 1909 in reaction to continued lynchings. It was a main agent organizing opposition to *The Birth of a Nation*, a campaign which increased the NAACP's visibility in the northern cities.
10 c. 39, 1984.

Chapter 7   *EX CONCESSIS*: Consequentially

1   Improvement in Telegraphs Patent No. 14917, 20 May 1867.

2 The reprinting of journalistic telegrams had preceded this to become a feature of the press (see Chapter 5.3). Before the Morse telegraph, a young Paul Reuter, who was living in Göttingen in the 1830s, had been impressed by the early dynamic telegraph physicists at the university there had built (Storey, 1969: 4). He established his news agency with carrier pigeons but was quick also to use telegrams as the network spread. Pigeons, and the semaphore, were main factors suppressing the electric telegraph's research and development throughout the first decades of the nineteenth century.

3 Alexander Graham Bell and Elisha Gray both presented plans for acoustic devices on 14 February 1876 at the Washington Patent Office (Prescott, 1972: 453). Each was entitled by the patent law of the time to be informed of the other but, although Bell was told of Gray's work, Gray was not informed about Bell. It would seem that Bell's first successful telephone device, however, owed more to Gray's scheme than to his own thinking (Winston, 1998: 41).

4 The limited company, an Anglo-American legal creation of the 1860s designed to accommodate entrepreneurialism after the first phase railway boom, played the railway's role as the supervening social necessity for the telephone. It had caused the stock-ticker (1871), the calculator (1875), the typewriter (1878) and the safety passenger elevator (1885) to be diffused in their modern form – and its needs produced increasingly tall skyscraper offices in which all these devices were housed.

5 'It is,' he went on, 'for the transmission of intelligence … therefore legitimately within the powers of government,' namely the constitutional power of the federal government, 'to establish Post-offices and Post Roads' (Oslund, 1977: 146). Even so, his case was rejected.

6 It held some radio patents because it used the technology to communicate with its Latin American plantations.

7 Public Law 264 (S 6412), 1912.

8 *Hoover v. Intercity Radio Co.*, 286 Fed. 1003 (Appeals D.C., 1923); and *United States v. Zenith Radio Corp.*, 12 F. 2d 614 (N.D. 111, 1926).

9 Radio Act 1972 Title 47 USC.

10 The Communications Act (1934), 47 U.S.C., section 151 *et seq.*

11 The Communications Act (1934), 47 U.S.C., Title III Section 303 @ 'q'.

12 Radio Pacifica, founded in 1949, operates five advert-free community 'listener-sponsored' stations and has some 150 affiliates.

13 47 U.S.C., section 1416.

14 'They', of course, really means him.

15 4 Ed. 7, ch. 24.

16 This use of the licence fee was not unique. In Germany, broadcasting was similarly funded.

17 Broadcasting Act 1980, c. 64; British Telecommunications Act 1981, c. 68.

18 Although limited to matters of taste rather than an overt statement of political attitude, the opinion is nevertheless rather sinister given the context of the time. What such a view, carried to its logical end, could in effect mean was shortly to be dramatically illustrated on the Continent by the Reichs-Rundfunk-Gesellschaft (RRG). The RRG had been created in 1932 from the locally based stations that had come on stream – in part commercially funded, in part licence-fee supported – in the Weimar Republic in the 1920s. On the RRG, though, advertising was banned. It was to be funded exactly on the same basis as the BBC. The Nazis, when they came to power the following year, ordered the manufacturers to

produce a cheap receiver – the Volksempfänger – which they further subsidized. They were convinced of the importance of government control of new media – radio (and film) – to their fascist project. Radio, for Goebbels, was 'the eighth great power' (Goebbels, 1938: 197).

19 21: 1: 'And Satan stood up against Israel, and provoked David to number Israel …'; 21: 7: 'And God was displeased with this thing; therefore he smote Israel.'

20 In 2011, the BBC began a seismic move of much of its production, 2,300 posts and five departments, from London to a massive new broadcasting centre in Manchester at Salford Quays.

21 It was, however, already a corporation by the time of this remark.

22 Lady Astor, as the mistress of Cliveden House, went ever further to right as the 1930s progressed until she and her set were Hitler's most prominent English supporters.

23 In 1939 Olive Shapley married the Northern Region programme director John Salt and was forced, by BBC policy which forbade the employment of couples, to resign. She became a freelance and was, after the war, the third presenter of the newly established 'Woman's Hour'. The radical theatre producer, Joan Littlewood, worked with Shapley in Manchester in the 1930s.

24 The great patriotic paean given by Shakespeare to Henry V on the eve of Agincourt is preceded by a scene in which the King, in disguise, visits his soldiers to bring them, as he says, 'a little touch of Harry in the night'. These common men, with utter candour, realistically reveal – in everyday prose, not poetry – a lot less enthusiasm for the coming battle than has the King. Of the King, one cockney soldier tells the unrecognized Henry: 'He may show what outward courage he will; but I believe, as cold a night as 'tis, he could wish himself in Thames up to the neck; and so I would he were, and I by him, at all adventures, so we were quit here' (*Henry V*, Act Four, Sc 1).

25 It should not surprise that the BBC World Service was subject to direct political pressure and, indeed, in time of war, this could be justified as necessary. All Bush House applicants were also vetted by MI5. The BBC's triumph, though, was that, as with the domestic services, this control was so well hidden that the reputation of the service for independent and reliability as a news source was not impunged. For example, the Portuguese Service was subject, via the Foreign Office, to constant pressure from the dictator António de Oliveira Salazar to which it, on occasion, was forced to submit. Opponents of the Lisbon regime were kept from the London microphone and questions of democracy avoided. Nevertheless, the Portuguese, unaware of this, trusted it more than any other source (Ribiero, 2011: 428–46).

26 Judaism was not, therefore, considered a religion. Rather it is a 'sect', which falls outside the general prohibition against offending 'different religions and religious denominations'. As a species of casual cultural anti-Semitism it would probably be best to attribute this taxonomy to ignorance and stupidity, not unfamiliar characteristics in a censor.

27 This fine over a matter of taste should be distinguished from other repeated fines that Ofcom levied during the same period for various misfeasances deceiving the public over game shows (see Sweney, 2008). The series began with a particularly egregious case involved in fixing a supposed competition to name a pet dog on a popular children's programme, 'making a child complicit in the deception'. This cost the BBC a £50,000 Ofcom fine and the programme editor his job. The BBC Trust said it expected 'management to learn from these breaches' (Anon, 2007b: 8;

Sweney, 2008); although a cynic might think it a little late in life to acquire such basic rudiments of honesty. On the other hand, Ofcom's power to deal with fraud in this way begs the question as to why the general law was not used in these cases instead (see Chapter 12).

Chapter 8 *Et Cetera*: And So On

1 At least not so overtly. Television did eventually play some comparative role in weapon telemetry but this application was subsequent to its development, not part of its research-and-development agenda.

2 *United States v. Paramount Pictures, Inc.*, 334 US 131 (1948).

3 Television Act, 2 & 3 Eliz. 2, c. 55 (1954).

4 Obscene Publications Act, 7 & 8 Eliz. 2, c. 66 (1959).

5 Or neo-behaviourist, although he denies both descriptions, despite publishing work on behaviour modification (Cherry, n.d.).

6 I am grateful to Ian Baguley for this observation.

7 I am grateful to Graham Murdoch for this observation.

8 The Children's Television Act, 1990, 47 U.S.C. sections 303a–303b, 393a, 394 (Supp. III 1991).

9 This observation is that of Guy Cumberbatch.

10 This test has been extended in English law on one occasion to material inciting violence but in the special circumstances that the matter was directed at children; cards depicting violent action included in bubble-gum packets (*DPP v. A&BC Chewing Gum Ltd*, 1968). Significantly the case was the first in which expert psychological opinion was admitted by the court on the grounds that assessing impact on children might be beyond the expertise of a jury. The precedent, however, has not been followed (Stone, 2008: 411). The case is thus the exception that proves the general rule that such putative connections between expression and imitative violence will not be interrogated.

11 *Die Leiden des jungen Werthers* (*The Sorrows of Young Werther*) by Johann Wolfgang von Goethe (1774) is the template for the theme of unrequited love in the *Sturm und Drang*/Romantic period. The eponymous Werther, in love with an unattainable married woman, shoots himself. He leaves a lengthy 'note': 'They are loaded – the clock strikes twelve. I say amen.' 'The Werther Effect' was coined to describe contagion by David Phillips (D. Phillips, 1974).

12 The present state of historical knowledge confidently asserts that it is a myth to believe that the film cost Thames its licence in the first round of renewals after the 1990 Act. Julian Petley makes the further point (by private communication) that the 'deregulation' of commercial television in this Act was also species of 'economic censorship' because the licensees were allowed to substitute more popular and profitable programming for current affairs. There was no need to control programming overtly when it was being limited to the politically inoffensive effectively by 'market forces'. It was, after all, the ploy that allowed for the removal of the newspaper taxes in the nineteenth century.

13 Communications Act, 2003: 2e, c. 21.

14 Iceland has been attempting since 2010 to establish itself as a digital haven guaranteeing freedom and anonymity, which is yet to come to fruition as legislators in the Althing grapple, as others have been doing for some centuries, with the problems of harm, national interests and so on (Tran, 2010).

15 A representative of the station would pop up at the bulletin's end and announce some normally uncontroversial mainstream opinion as the station's policy. He (usually) would then invite those who disagreed to have their minute on air. This was declared a restriction of the broadcasters' free speech by the Reaganite FCC in 1985 following a station's refusal to give an anti-nuclear power group its minute to rebut the broadcaster's pro-nuclear position. The FCC chair, Mark Fowler, pontificated that: 'The perception of broadcasters as community trustees should be replaced by a view of broadcasters as marketplace participants.' The Reaganite Supreme Court concurrently agreed that the doctrine was not mandated by statute (*Telecommunications Research & Action Center (TRAC) v. FCC*). In 1989, the DC District Court accepted the FCC's view (*Meredith Corp. v. FCC,* 1989). Attempts by the Democratic Congress to reinstate the policy were vetoed by Reagan and George Bush Sr.

Chapter 9   *Obita Dicta*: Opinion

1 Although its head, Thomas Watson, never said that he thought there would only ever be five computers in the world, the opinion is often attributed to him.
2 Silicon, from the First World War onwards, had been used as a diode – non-amplifying – in some brands of the cat's-whisker radio transceivers and receivers. The research and development was to build an amplifying triode.
3 The supervening social necessity being the crucial determinant excludes the possibility of the criterion being merely whether or not prototypes work (Winston, 1998).
4 See, for example, Metterie's anti-Cartesian *L'Homme machine*: '*le corps humain est une horloge*' (Metterie, 1748: 93) or for Freud and magnetism, see Pérez-Rincón, 2011.
5 The original AT&T was broken up by the Justice Department in 1984.
6 A political party of the same name appeared in Sweden in 2006. In 2011, its German manifestation, Piratenpartei Deutschland, it took 15 per cent of the vote in the Berlin city-state elections to win one seat (Pridd, 2011: 31; Cadwalladr, 2012: 32).
7 Cosby's 1941 version of Irving Berlin's 'White Christmas' remains, the *Guinness Book of Records* insists, the best-selling recorded performance of all time at 50 million copies sold.
8 Eliz. II, c. 24.
9 A 'class action suit' is an American legal device that allows for persons to be involved in a court action even though they are not present or have not been identified or are even aware of their involvement. This 'virtual representation' allows a plaintiff (in this case the collective organizations representing authors and publishers) to sue (in this case for violation of copyright) a third party (in this case Google) on behalf of all their members and all others in the class of 'authors' and 'publishers' even though these others are not necessarily known.
10 There are, for instance, no less than 160 specialized definitions of the terms (many coined specifically), running to seventeen pages of text in the *Book Settlement Agreement* (Authors Guild Inc., Association of American Publishers Inc., *et al.*, v. Google, Inc., 2008: 2–19).
11 This is needed because the class action was a suit against Google in court. The court therefore has to satisfy itself that the parties have resolved matters satisfactorily.

12 8 Anne, c. 19.

13 The same slippage can be seen with other possible social effects, endlessly reinforced by a tendency to manipulate statistics. As with business travel, so with shopping. Britain by 2010 had the largest e-commerce market in the world, yet it is still only 7.5 per cent of retail, according to official figures (Robinson, 2010a: 35) – and why should this surprise? After all, the 'gothic cathedral' of our civilization is surely more the shopping mall than the internet site. Embedded social norms, such as shopping, do not simply disappear in the face of the digital.

14 This level of definition ('super hi-vision') will produce images at the limit of visual acuity. To reach this limit with electronic scanning requires, in terms of the digital, a picture 8,000 pixels by 4,000 pixels (sixteen times current hi-definition). In terms of the old analogue TV signal, this would be about 4,000 lines. That is what, in nature, we see; so looking at the screen will be, in theory, exactly like looking through a window.

15 Starting with the Telecommunications Act, P.L. No. 104–104, 110 Stat. 56 (1996).

16 All he had to do to acquire the TV stations, apart from supplying the money, was renounce his Australian citizenship. As mentioned, the FCC still requires citizenship from its licensees.

17 Eliz. II, c. 21, 2003.

18 This has not happened in the West, but the Saudis threatened to close the provider down in 2011 unless a router was placed in its territory (Al-Shihri, 2010: 38; Wray, 2010: 25).

19 It can be noted that even outside the West technological impact is easily overstated. The 2010–12 upheavals across the Middle East, heralded as 'Twitter revolutions', owed less to Western technology than was claimed by the technicists. Technology's apparent importance was a 'trick of the light' (Appleyard, 2011: 42). Informed opinion knew that, 'The changes in Tunisia and Egypt were not driven by technology. These were revolutions driven by people' (Fisher, 2011: 150). The very idea that 'the revolution will be twittered' was a hare started by an American blogger about the 2010 disturbances in Iran. At the time less than 1,000 Iranian people were connected to the site (Morozov, 2011: 1).

Chapter 10 *Audi Alterem Partem*: Hear the Other Side

1 As one of the drafters of the UN 1948 Declaration characterized the essential 'pillars' supporting all basic rights.

2 'Freedom from violence (*Ahimsa*), freedom from want (*Asteya*), freedom from exploitation (*Aparigraha*), freedom from early death and disease (*Armritatva and Arogya'*)' as well as 'absence of intolerance (*Akrodha*), compassion (*Bhutadaya, Adroha*), knowledge (*Jnana, Vidya*), freedom of conscience and freedom from fear, frustration and despair (*Pravrtti, Abhaya, Dhrti*)' (Ishay, 2004: 20).

Chapter 11 *Rationes Decidendi*: The Reasons for Decision

1 'And whatsoever ye do in word or deed, do all in the name of the Lord Jesus, giving thanks to God and the Father by him', Letter to the Colossians, 3: 17.

2 In the event, though, the march did not take place. In a deal, the city of Chicago allowed Collins to hold a rally in a park, which it had previously forbidden him to do. His career as fascist leader was curtailed shortly thereafter when his father was revealed to be a Jew named Cohen.

3 Pub.L. 90–40, 62 Stat. 604, as amended 50 U.S.C. section 462 (1965).

4 The full text of Article 10:

   Freedom of expression

   1 Everyone has the right to freedom of expression. This right shall include freedom to hold opinions and to receive and impart information and ideas without interference by public authority and regardless of frontiers. This article shall not prevent States from requiring the licensing of broadcasting, television or cinema enterprises.

   2 The exercise of these freedoms, since it carries with it duties and responsibilities, may be subject to such formalities, conditions, restrictions or penalties as are prescribed by law and are necessary in a democratic society, in the interests of national security, territorial integrity or public safety, for the prevention of disorder or crime, for the protection of health or morals, for the protection of the reputation or rights of others, for preventing the disclosure of information received in confidence, or for maintaining the authority and impartiality of the judiciary.

5 Souter was the liberal William Brennan's replacement, an indication of the Court's changing political tendency over recent decades.

6 Needless to say, the law has never been inhibited by the further philosophical observation that prohibited words needed to be repeated if objected too, so that their offensiveness can be examined: 'the claim we make is a further instance of language, one which seeks to arrest the force of the prior instance. Thus, we exercise the force of language even as we seek to counter its force, caught up in a bind that no act of censorship can undo' (Butler, 1997: 1). Indeed, one can add, if expression is to be prosecuted in an open legal system, it likely will be retailed.

7 New Hampshire Public Laws, ch. 378, para. 2.

8 1917, c. 64, 39, Stat. 919.

9 7 & 8 Eliz. 2, c. 66.

10 1998, c. 42.

11 Eliz. II, ch. 27.

12 See also the American rationale, in part, in *United States v. O'Brien* (see Chapter 11.2).

13 All of the above discussion of obscenity is without prejudice to the matter of the exploitation of people in the production of pornography. The use of coercion for such a purpose has nothing to do with the right of free expression; it is a separate matter from the question of obscene publication. Exploitation is potentially a criminal offence and is so automatically, as it were, in all circumstances if minors are involved. It is not of a piece with the actual, potential or supposed corruptive impact on an individual consumer of the material, or on society in general. This is not in any way to downgrade the concerns of those who view adult participation in the production of pornography as sufficiently damaging to warrant its banning.

14 The speech was quoted at a General Assembly of Unitarian and Free Christian Churches in Edinburgh in 1988 as having been made in 1949. It was thereafter reprinted in a report by the House of Lords' Religious Offences in England and Wales Committee (Religious Offences in England and Wales Committee, 2003).

15 A third time-honoured offence, apostasy, is the personal renunciation of a particular system of belief and this clearly is to be protected by the concept of free expression in Article 10 of the ECHR.

16 This was not the first state law. In 1777, the New York Assembly meeting in Kingston, NY, passed an act that all religious practices 'shall forever hereafter be allowed within this state for all mankind'.

17 'And the disciples went, and did as Jesus commanded them. And brought the ass, and the colt, and put on them their clothes, and they set him thereon' (Matthew 21: 6–7).

18 It only applies to directly 'cursing God', according to Chief Rabbi Lord Jacobovits (Levy, 1995: 565); and it carries the death penalty according to Leviticus 24: 16.

19 Perhaps this might have been done to help Mrs Whitehouse celebrate her CBE in 1980. Nothing better illustrates the tolerance of the British than the evaluation of her career since her death in 2001. She was not only honoured as a person of worth but she also became a 'character', described in the *Dictionary of National Biography* as being 'of serious intent' and 'an influence for good at a crucial stage in the development both of the BBC and of ITV'. No, she was not. She was an unenlightened demagogue out of touch with the society upon which she sought to impose her will. There was nothing amusing or quaint about her.

20 And where it is, Pakistan for example, capital sentences have not been carried out. Those accused in Pakistan, however, are often murdered extra-judicially (Schackle, 2011: 36).

21 Ward also reached the conclusion that, for Christians, 'it was profoundly *irreligious* to take offence when offence is offered' (Levy, 1995: 565–7; italics in original). After all, the Christian injunction was to turn the other cheek and, moreover, was not Jesus' death, according to the Gospels at least, the direct result of his perceived blasphemy towards his original faith.

22 Utterances against Christianity remain prohibited although there has been no recent action on this.

23 Irish Defamation Act, No. 31 of 2009: Article 36: 2.

24 Unsurprisingly, given Ireland's economic crisis, this had yet to happen at the time of writing.

25 The AOC was established within the UN by Spain and Turkey following the Madrid bombings of 2005.

26 In the UK, a boy carrying a sign: 'Scientology is not a religion, it is a dangerous cult' was arrested under the Public Order Act, 1986 (see Chapter 11.7).

27 Even the ambition of the Prince of Wales indirectly supports this view. He said in 1994: 'I personally would rather see [the title '*Fidei Defensor*'] as Defender of Faith, not "The Faith"'. 'Defender of the Faith' was bestowed by Parliament on Henry VIII. It was originally awarded by the Pope but Henry's subsequent behaviour caused it to be revoked. This did not hinder its continued use by the English monarch. In 2008, the Prince indeed announced he would like to take the title 'Defender of Faith' should the occasion present itself and Parliament, in whose gift it now is, agreed (Pierce, 2008).

28 1917, 40 Stat. 217.

29 Sedition Act, 1918, 40 Stat. 553.

30 She was released in 1921.

31 The Alien Registration Act, 1940, 54 Stat. 670. This was held to be constitutional by the court in 1951 (*Dennis v. United States*, 1951).

32 Were he to be inducted and given a rifle, he told a small crowd: 'the first man I want to get in my sights is L.B.J.' (Lyndon Baines Johnson, the President).

33 18 U.S.C. section 792 *et seq*.

34 18 U.S.C. section 798: 'Disclosure of classified information', clarifies 'classified information' as matter:

'(1), concerning the nature, preparation, or use of any code, cipher, or cryptographic system of the United States or any foreign government; or

(2), concerning the design, construction, use, maintenance, or repair of any device, apparatus, or appliance used or prepared or planned for use by the United States or any foreign government for cryptographic or communication intelligence purposes; or

(3), concerning the communication intelligence activities of the United States or any foreign government; or

(4), obtained by the processes of communication intelligence from the communications of any foreign government, knowing the same to have been obtained by such processes'.

35 'Freedom of Information. Three harmless words. I look at those words as I write them, and feel like shaking my head till it drops off my shoulders. You idiot. You naive, foolish, irresponsible nincompoop. There is really no description of stupidity, no matter how vivid, that is adequate. I quake at the imbecility of it. Once I appreciated the full enormity of the blunder, I used to say – more than a little unfairly – to any civil servant who would listen: Where was Sir Humphrey when I needed him? We had legislated in the first throes of power. How could you, knowing what you know have allowed us to do such a thing so utterly undermining of sensible government?' Conceivably, in his mind, the 'sensible government' that took Britain to war in Iraq (for example) would not have been as 'undermined' as it was if he had not succumbed to the liberal impulse that led to the passing of the Freedom of Information Act.

36 Eliz. 2, c. 64.

37 In the English public order cases, the disturbance did not necessarily involve the group being attacked.

38 In the United States there is in slander a distinction between general and special damages, the former being awarded for distress, the later for externally proved damaged. It can be an automatic offence if certain classes of remark are proved, for example, saying that a person, in the hearing of others, is incompetent at work or (falsely) has a criminal record, an immoral lifestyle, a sexually transmitted disease and so on.

39 PL 111–233, 2010: Securing the Protection of our Enduring and Established Constitutional Heritage (SPEECH) Act.

40 1 Will. & Mary, Sess. 2, c. 2.

41 Absolute privilege also involves court proceedings and the contemporaneous reporting of them; and lawyer-client communication.

42 It would appear so. For instance, in 2011, John Hemming, MP, revealed in a parliamentary question that Sir Fred Goodwin, the ex-head of the Royal Bank of Scotland which was at the centre of the economic meltdown, had obtained a super-injunction 'preventing him being identified as a banker'. The law's silence confirmed that both Mr Hemming, and the reporting of his intervention, were protected by privilege (Hirsch, 2011: 17). It would be perhaps wrong to see in Sir Fred's move a rare example of banking being acknowledged as an unworthy occupation.

43 There is also a qualified privilege available as a defence to defamation. Needless to say, this is scarcely of unambiguous utility.

44 In Britain, by contrast, the Press Complaints Commission's *Editors' Code of Practice* lacks, as does the PCC itself, the measure of credibility some other European codes enjoy (Press Complaints Commission, 2011).

45 The question of insults to the head of state, or the state itself (as opposed, in democracies at least, to its politicians) falls under the issue of *lèse majesté*.

46 The UK Human Rights Act glosses the ECHR in favour of the press at 12.4: 'The court must have particular regard to the importance of the Convention right to freedom of expression ... where the proceedings relate to material which the respondent claims, or which appears to the court to be, journalistic, literary or artistic material'.

Chapter 12 *Causa Sine Qua Non*: The Indispensible Cause

1 An action for breach of copyright was clearly a possibility in Prince Albert's case – or would have been had not the scarce respectable role of 'artist' not been an unthinkable one for a member of the royal family. Copyright, anyway, has little or nothing to do with privacy.

2 The Protection from Harassment Act, Eliz. 2, c. 40 (1997), is primarily a civil workplace measure but there is also provision in the 1986 Public Order Act prohibiting harassment as a crime.

3 Robertson and Nicol give a rather more dramatic explanation of this incident suggesting that the Princess balked from pursuing the matter because her own indiscretions about her marriage would be used against her in court; and, indeed, paid the gym-owner, 'a vast sum of money to pretend he had lost the case' (Robertson and Nicol, 2008: 267). Either way, the possibility of an action for breach of confidence remains.

4 This opinion highlights the surprising connection of Brandeis' name to the article. A lawyer of stunning intellectual capacity, he was to make his name defending radical causes and became, after a very contentious confirmation hearing, one of the Supreme Court's most consistently liberal justices. There is some question as to his actual involvement in writing the article.

5 By dancing from London to Norwich in the winter of 1603. He was the original 'nine days wonder' (Winston, 2005: 182–3).

6 California Civil Code, section 990(a); current version: California Civil Code, section 3344.1(a). Such statutes even protect the deceased but they have limits. This Californian law did not, for example, prevent the Franklin mint from marketing unauthorized memorabilia of Princess Diana. It cost her memorial fund millions of dollars in legal fees to discover that California recognizes the law of the deceased's country before applying its own code; and her memory was not so protected in Britain (*Cairns LVO JP MBE v. Franklin Mint Company*, 2002).

7 Morgan had to leave his post in disgrace in 2004 because he had scandalously 'splashed' faked photos of British soldiers abusing Iraqi prisoners. He is currently a broadcast 'celebrity'.

8 Although true of some state codes (for example, California), it is not quite the case with federal law. The Fourth Amendment to the Constitution guarantees 'the right of the people to be secure in their persons, houses, papers, and effects, against unreasonable searches and seizures'. There is no mention of privacy or the publication of details obtained without physical intrusion per se.

9 I obtained, for me, a most moving insight into celebrity privacy from this other side (as it were) at the celebration of the life of English theatre critic, Sheridan Morley, in the Gielgud Theatre in London, following his death in February 2007. Among the tributes was one from a fellow critic, John Lahr, who had known Morley since nursery school in Manhattan. They had attended this together in the late 1940s because both their fathers, leading internationally known character actors, were starring on Broadway at the time (Lahr Sr is best known as the

Cowardly Lion in *The Wizard of Oz*.) Lahr remarked, poignantly, that you soon knew, as a child of such a famous person, that however much they loved you, you never wholly possessed their attention. They had to be shared with their public.

10 As with the American Constitution, the Canadian Charter of Rights gives the right to freedom of expression as a 'fundamental', although, like Article 10.2 of the ECHR, this comes with the proviso that the right be exercised within 'such reasonable limits prescribed by law as can be demonstrably justified in a free and democratic society' Nicol *et al.*, 2009: 2).

11 Perhaps this concern for the welfare for its victims is why the machine is, in French, a feminine noun?

12 It is a curiosity of this literature that illustrative cases, invented to make a jurisprudential point, tend always to be amusingly ludicrous.

13 The term is originally from the left; a phrase, often used ironically, arising from the imposition of rigidities of Marxist-Leninist democratic centralism on the party faithful.

14 Because of culturally determined national differences, Britain remains somewhat more unwilling to curtail hate speech than is the case elsewhere in Europe. In this British law is closer to the American. On the other hand, as Robertson and Nicol point out, Britain is likely to be far more concerned with obscenity than are its near neighbours (Robertson and Nicol, 2008: 64).

15 Luther's was the first solution to the Jewish question. In full he suggested: (1) Jewish synagogues and schools to be burned to the ground, and the remnants buried out of sight; (2) houses owned by Jews to be likewise razed, and the owners made to live in agricultural outbuildings; (3) their religious writings to be taken away; (4) rabbis to be forbidden to preach, and to be executed if they do; (5) safe conduct on the roads to be abolished for Jews; (6) usury to be prohibited, and all silver and gold to be removed and 'put aside for safekeeping'; and (7) the Jewish population to be put to work as agricultural slave labour (Luther, 1971 [1543]).

16 In 1950s and 1960s media sociology, the hypothesis was, in essence, that media effects, since they cannot be demonstrated, cannot exist. Since denying effects simply because they cannot be proved according to the standards of social science is absurd, the hypothesis was subsequently abandoned by some in favour of 'uses and gratification' theory. This looked at how people actually use the media rather than investigating how the media used them (as it were). The term, 'null effect', in the physical sciences was coined before the Second World War. It relates to the lack of demonstrable relationships in the course of experimentation.

17 Again, consider the reverse: nobody researches the impact of acts of kindness, toleration, politeness and so on portrayed in the media.

18 This despite the fact that the number of actual complaints, although on occasion a scandal can engender some thousands, remains minuscule on an everyday basis as a percentage of audience/media interactions (see Chapter 3).

19 For example, researchers at the School of Public Health at the Imperial College of Science wanted tax credits withdrawn from the British film industry. This was because feature films (and they had looked at 600 recent ones made between 2003 and 2009) showed people smoking – a thing (like suicide) to be avoided according to the World Health Organization. Nevermind that the Tobacco Manufacturers' Association's monitoring of consumption trends, agreed by the UK Office of National Statistics, suggested a decline in sales from 73.8 billion taxed and untaxed cigarettes sold to 48.5 billion during these years. Handrolled tobacco use had admittedly increased but not to the point where it affected the steady

downward rate of lung cancer (Doward, 2011: 15; Cancer Research UK, 2012; Tobacco Manufacturers' Association, 2011). And the UK Film Council production figures for the films reveal the 'researchers' anyway only watched two-thirds of the 931 British releases in these years. The 'researchers' might as well have found that smoking in feature films discouraged tobacco consumption. At least they would have had some statistical evidence with which to confuse the issue.

20 Pub.L. 65–24, 40 Stat. 217, 1917; amended by the Sedition Act (40 Stat. 553), 1918.

21 Statutes, 1919, c. 188.

22 18 USC, section 2385.

23 Ohio Rev. Code Ann. section 2923.13.

24 c. 11.

25 Hasty legislation, responding to moral panics, often exhibits similar overdrawn prohibitions, e.g. the Dangerous Dogs Act, 1991, c. 65, never mind the Official Secrets Act.

26 Section 2 of the original Official Secrets Act, for example, was passed in a flurry of hysteria about German spies on the eve of the First World War, did not require any demonstration of damage and applied to all government departments. This took seventy-eight years to reform. (It is still the case that a public interest defence is not available to a charge under sections 4 and 5 of the current legislation.) The Children and Young Persons (Harmful Publications) Act responded to the mid-1950s hysteria about comic books. In the early 1980s, Mrs Whitehouse panicked about 'video nasties' and the consequence was the 1984 Video Recording Act. The Racial and Religious Hatred Act in 2006 stemmed from the Blair government's attempt to appease minority opinion in the light of the Rushdie affair and its protracted aftermath.

References

A v. B & C [2002] EWCA Civ 337.

Abrams v. United States, 250 U.S. 616 (1919).

Adams, Tim (2011), 'The angry brigade', *Observer*, 'New Review', 24 July.

Addison, Joseph and Steel, Richard (1836 [1710/11]), *Spectator*, 1 March 1710, London: Isaac, Tuckey & Co.

Adegoke, Yemisi and Ball, James (2011), 'I just listened to the radio to find a riot. Simple as that', *Guardian*, 8 December.

Adorno, Theodor and Horkheimer, Max (1997 [1944]), *Dialectics of the Enlightenment*, trans. John Cumming, London: Verso.

Attorney-General (United Kingdom) v. Heinemann Publishers Australia Pty Ltd (1987) 8NSWLR 341.

Ahmad, Imad-ad-Dean (2002), 'The rise and fall of Islamic science: the calendar as a case study', *Minaret of Freedom Institute*, http://www.minaret.org/ifrane.pdf [accessed 25 October 2011].

Aitchison, Jean (2007), *The Word-Weavers: Newshounds and Wordsmiths*, Cambridge: Cambridge University Press.

Aitken, Hugh (1985), *The Continuous Waves: Technology and American Radio, 1900–1932*, Princeton, NJ: Princeton University Press.

Akandji-Kombe, Jean-François (2007), 'Positive obligations under the European Convention on Human Rights: A guide to the implementation of the European Convention on Human Rights', *Human Rights*, 44: 7.

Alden, John (1996), *George Washington: A Biography*, Baton Rouge, LA: Louisiana State University Press.

Alexander, John (2002), *Samuel Adams: America's Revolutionary Politician*, Lanham, MD: Rowman & Littlefield.

Allen, John (1983), *A History of the Theatre In Europe*, London: Heinemann.

Allen, Robert (1980), *Vaudeville and Film 1895-1915: A Study in Media Interaction*, New York, NY: Arno Press.

Allen, Robert (1991), *Horrible Prettiness: Burlesque and American Culture*, Chapel Hill, NC: University of North Carolina Press.

Al-Shihri, Abdullah (2010), 'BlackBerry users told: text away, so long as we can spy on messages', *Independent on Sunday*, 8 August.

Anderson, Kevin (2009), 'Pirate Bay sunk by court order', *Guardian*, 26 August.

Andrews, Alexander (1859), *A History of British Journalism Vol. I*, London: Richard Bentley.

Anon (Joseph Addison) (1712), *Spectator*, no. 445, 1 August.

Anon (J. & E. Kimber) (1737), 'Journal of the proceedings and debates in the last session of Parliament', *London Magazine*, 14 August.

Anon (1819), 'Abstract of Foreign and Domestic Intelligence', *European Magazine and London Review*, 76, August.

Anon (William Russell) (1854), 'HEIGHTS BEFORE SEBASTOPOL OCTOBER 25th 1854', *The Times*, 14 November.

Anon (1885), *New York World*, 16 March.

Anon (1918), 'Mrs. Rose P. Stokes Convicted of Disloyalty; Illegal to Impair National Morale, Says Judge', *New York Times*, 25 May.

Anon (1993), 'Gym owner defends Princess pictures: Bryce Taylor says 98 per cent of people would also have tried his "legal scam" to make money', *Independent*, 17 November [accessed 2 September, 2011].

Anon (2006a), 'Threats from Hindu Extremists Lead to London Art Show Being Cancelled', *National Secular Society*, http://www.secularism.org.uk/threatsfromhinduextremistsleadto.html [accessed 21 October 2010].

Anon (2006b), 'Fury as Berlin Opera cancels performance', *Der Spiegel*, 26 September, http://www.spiegel.de/international/0,1518,439393,00.html [accessed 1 August 2010].

Anon (2007a), 'Nobody Turns Up for Rushdie Protest', *Bolton Telegraph,* 23 July, http://www.theboltonnews.co.uk/archive/2007/07/23/Blackburn+%28blackburn%29/1565023.No_one_turns_up_for_Rushdie_protest [accessed 19 May 2010].

Anon (2007b), 'BBC regrets unprecedented Ofcom fine over *Blue* Peter', *Prospero*, September.

Anon (2009), 'How the Trafigura story unfolded', *Guardian*, 13 October http://www.guardian.co.uk/world/2009/oct/13/how-trafigura-story-unfolded?INTCMP=SRCH [accessed 1 April 2012].

Anon (2011a), 'Facebook statistics, stats and facts for 2011', *digitalbuzz*, 18 January, http://www.digitalbuzzblog.com/facebook-statistics-stats-facts-2011/ [accessed 31 October 2011].

Anon (2011b), 'London riots: Sussex Police dismiss rumours of disorder in Crawley', *Crawley and Horley Observer*, 9 August, http://www.crawleyobserver.co.uk/news/local/london_riots_sussex_police_dismiss_rumours_of_disorder_in_crawley_1_2947102 [accessed 12 December 2011].

Anon (2011c), 'L'incendie à "Charlie Hebdo" soulève un raz de marée d'indignations', *Le Parisien,* 2 November, http://www.leparisien.fr/faits-divers/l-incendie-a-charlie-hebdo-souleve-un-raz-de-maree-d-indignations-02-11-2011-1698074.php [accessed 3 November 2011].

Anthony, Andrew (2009), 'How one book ignited a culture war', *Observer*, 'Review', 11 January.

Apple (2010), 'Apple Reports First Quarter Results', *Apple*, 25 January 2010, http://www.apple.com/pr/library/2010/01/25Apple-Reports-First-Quarter-Results.html [accessed 12 November 2011].

Appleyard, Bryan (2011), 'A trick of the light', *New Statesman*, 20 January.

Archer, G. (1938), *History of Radio to 1926*, New York, NY: American Historical Society.

Arista Records LLC v. Lime Group LLC, 715 F. Supp. 2d 481 (2010).

Association of American Publishers (2011), *Association of American Publishers*, http://www.publishers.org [accessed 21 November 2011].

Attorney-General v Guardian Newspapers Ltd (No 2) [1990] 1 AC 109, 281.

Attorney-General v Times Newspapers Ltd [1973] 3 All ER 54.

Atwood, Roy and de Beer, Arnold (2001), 'The roots of academic news research: Tobias Peucer's *De relationibus novellis* (1690)', *Journalism Studies*, 2.4. November.

Augarten, S. (1984), *Bit by Bit: An Illustrated History of Computers*, New York, NY: Ticknor and Fields.

Austin, J.L (1962), *How to Do Things with Words*, Cambridge, MA: University of Harvard Press.

Authors Guild Inc., Association of American Publishers Inc., *et al.*, v. Google, Inc., *Book Settlement Agreement* (28 October 2008), Case No. 05 CV 8136-JES. http://books.google.com/googlebooks/agreement [accessed 29 September 2009].

Baker, W.J. (1970), *History of the Marconi Company 1874–1965*, London: Methuen.

Ball, James (2011), 'Wikileaks risks exposing secret sources after publishing unredacted cables', *Guardian*, 3 September.

Ball, James and Brown, Symeon (2011), 'Cheap, secure and efficient: the gadget of choice for rioters', *Guardian*, 8 December.

Bandura, Albert, Ross, Dorothea, and Ross, Sheila A (1961), 'Transmission of aggression through imitation of aggressive models', *Journal of Abnormal and Social Psychology*, 63.

Baran, P. (1964), 'On distributed communications networks', *IEEE Transactions on Communications Systems*, 1 March.

Barker, Revel (2012), 'I call myself a reporter', *Gentlemen Ranters*, http://www.gentlemenranters.com/ [accessed 1 December 2011].

Barlow, John Perry (1996), 'Declaration of the Independence of Cyberspace', Davos, Switzerland, 8 February, https://projects.eff.org/~barlow/Declaration-Final.html [accessed 31 October, 2011].

Barnes v. Glen Theatre, Inc., 501 U.S. 560 (1991).

Barnett, Steven (2011), *The Rise and Fall of Television Journalism*, London: Bloomsbury Academic.

Barnouw, Erik (1969), *A Tower in Babel*, New York, NY: Oxford University Press.

Baron, Sabrina (2001), 'The guises of dissemination in early seventeenth century England: News in manuscript and print', in Brendan Dooley and Sabrina Baron (eds), *The Politics of Information in Early Modern Europe*, London: Routledge.

Barry, Dave (1996), *Dave Barry in Cyberspace*, New York, NY: Crown.

Baruma, Ian (2006), *Murder in Amsterdam: The Death of Theo van Gogh and the Limits of Tolerance*, Harmondsworth: Penguin.

Baudino, Joseph and Kittross, John (1977), 'Broadcasting's oldest stations: an examination of four claimants', *Journal of Broadcasting*, 21: 1, Winter.

Bazin, André (1967), *What Is Cinema? Vol. 1*, Berkeley, CA: University of California Press.

BBC (1991), '1991: On this day', *BBC*, http://news.bbc.co.uk/onthisday/hi/dates/stories/november/18/newsid_2520000/2520055.stm [accessed 19 August 2010].

Beck, Michael (1968), 'A conversation between Ezra Pound and Allen Ginsberg', *Everygreen Review*, 55, June.

Bellanger, C. (1969), *Histoire General de la Presse Française*, Paris: Press Universitaires de France.

Benjamin, L. (1993), 'In search of the Sarnoff "Music Box" Memo: Separating myth from reality', *Journal* of *Broadcasting and Electronic Media*, 37: 3.

Benjamin, L. (2002), 'In search of the Sarnoff "Radio Music Box" memo: Nally's reply', *Journal of Radio and Audio Media*, 9: 1, May.

Bennett, Mark (2009), 'Bring home the revolution'. *New Statesman*, 23 March 2009.

Bernstein, Jon (2011), '"I felt like a conspiracy theorist"', *New Statesman*, 26 September.

Bernstein of Leigh v. Skyviews & General Ltd [1978] 1 QB 479.

Bikhchandani, Sushil, Hirshleifer, David and Welch, Ivo (1992), 'A Theory of Fads, Fashion, Custom, and Cultural Change in Informational Cascades', *Journal of Political Economy*, 100: 5, October.

Biting, R.C. (1977), 'Creating an industry', in G. Shiers (ed.), *Technical Development of Television*, New York, NY: Arno.

Blackstone, William (1979 [1769]), *Commentaries on the Laws of England: A Facsimile of the First Edition of 1765–1769, Vol. 4*, Chicago, IL: University of Chicago Press.

Black, Jeremy (2001), *The English Press 1621–1861*, Stroud: Sutton.

Bladet Tromsø and Stensaas v. Norway (2000) 29 EHHR 125.

Blagden, Cyprian (1960), *The Stationers' Company: A History, 1403–1959*, Cambridge, MA: Harvard University Press.

Blair, Tony (2010), *A Journey*, London: Hutchinson.

Bland, Archie (2008), 'What does censoring Wikipedia tell us about the way the internet is policed?', *Independent*, 9 December.

Bland, Archie (2010), 'South Park censored after death threats from Islamists', *Independent*, 23 April.

Boller, Paul and George, John (1989), *They Never Said It*, New York, NY: Barnes and Noble.

Bonald, Le Vicompte de (1823), *Législation Primitive*, Paris: Le Clère.

Boros-Kazai, András (2005), 'Hungary', in Richard Frucht, *Eastern Europe: An Introduction to the People, Lands, and Culture. Vol. 1*, Santa Barbara, CA: ABC-Clio.

Bonwich, James (1890), *The Early Struggle of the Australian Press*, London: Gordon & Gooch.

Box Office Mojo (2011), 'Yearly Box Office', *Box Office Mojo*, http://boxofficemojo.com/yearly/?view2=domestic&view=releasedate&p=.htm [accessed 4 November 2011].

Boyce, George, Curran, James and Wingate, Pauline (eds) (1978), *Newspaper History from the 17th Century to the Present Day*, London: Constable.

Boyle, Andrew (1972), *Only the Wind Will Listen: Reith of the BBC*, London: Hutchinson.

Boyle, James (2008), *The Public Domain: Enclosing the Commons of the Mind*, New Haven, CT: Yale.

Boyle, James (2009), 'A copyright black hole swallows our culture', *Financial Times*, 6 September, http//www.thepublicdomain.org/2009/09/06/google-books-and-the-escape-from-the-black-hole [accessed 29 September 2009].

BPI (British Recorded Music Industry) (2008), *Statistical Handbook*, London: BPI.

BPI (British Recorded Music Industry) (2009), *Statistical Handbook*, London: BPI.

Brandenburg v. Ohio, 395 U.S. 444 (1969).

Braudel, F. (1981), *Civilisation and Capitalism 15th–18th Century Volume I: The Structures of Everyday Life, The Limits of the Possible*, New York, NY: Harper & Row.

Braudel, F. (1995), *A History of Civilizations*, trans. Richard Mayne, New York, NY: Penguin.

Bredin, Jean-Denis (1986), *The Affair: The Case of Alfred Dreyfus*, New York, NY: George Braziller.

Briggs, Asa (1985), *The BBC: The First Fifty Years*, Oxford: Oxford University Press.

Briggs, Asa (1995a), *The History of Broadcasting in the United Kingdom: The Birth of Broadcasting 1896–1927*, Oxford: Oxford University Press.

Briggs, Asa (1995b), *The History of Broadcasting in the United Kingdom: The Golden Age of Wireless 1927–1939*, Oxford: Oxford University Press.

Briggs, Asa (1995c), *The History of Broadcasting in the United Kingdom: The War of Words 1939-1945*, Oxford: Oxford University Press.

British Film Institute (2011), *BFI Statistical Year Book 2011*, London: British Film Institute.

Broadcasters' Audience Research Board (2011), *Trends in Television Viewing 2010*, London: Broadcasters' Audience Research Board.

Broadcasting Standards Commission (1998), *Code on Standards*, London: BSC.

Brock, W.R. (1973), *Conflict and Transformation: The United States 1844–1877*, Harmondsworth: Penguin.

Brown, Maggie (2011), 'Has the BBC become too afraid to take risks?', *Guardian*, 'Media', 25 April.

Browne, Kevin and Hamilton-Giachritsis, Catherine (2005), 'The influence of violent media on children and adolescents: a public-health approach', *Lancet*, 365: 19, February.

Brutus v. Cozens [1973] AC 854, 867.

Bunglawala, Inayat (2007), 'I was wrong about Salman', *Guardian*, 20 June.

Burnet v. Coronado Oil & Gas Co., 285 U.S. 393 (1932).

Burke, Edmund (1790), *Reflections on the Revolution in France*, London: J. Dodsley.

Bush, V. (1945), 'As we may think', *Atlantic Monthly*, July.

Butler, Judith (1997), *Excitable Speech: A Politics of the Performative*, New York, NY: Routledge.

Butterfield, Herbert (1965 [1931]), *The Whig Interpretation of History*, London: Norton.

Byrne, Ciar (2003), 'Cleese "vindicated" by libel victory', *Guardian*, 'Media', 6 February, http://www.guardian.co.uk/media/2003/feb/06/pressandpublishing2?INTCMP=SRCH [accessed 31 August 2011].

Cadwalladr, Carole (2012), 'The Swedish radical leading fight over web freedoms', *Observer*, 22 January.

Cairns LVO JP MBE v. Franklin Mint Company, 292 F.3d 1139 (2002).

Calcutt, David (1993), *Review of Press Self-regulation*, Cmnd 2131, London: Stationery Office.

Campbell, Duncan (2007), 'Reid cites Life of Brian over Rushdie award', *Guardian*, 21 June.

Campbell v. MGN Ltd [2004] UKHL 22.

Cancer Research UK (2012), 'Smoking – statistics', *Cancer Research UK*, http://info.cancerresearchuk.org/cancerstats/types/lung/smoking [accessed 28 August 2011].

Canovan, Margaret (1987), 'Rousseau's two concepts of citizenship', in Ellen Kennedy and Susan Mendus (eds), *Women in Western Political Philosophy*, Brighton: Wheatsheaf Books.

Carlyle, Thomas (1859 [1840]), *On Heroes, Hero-worship, and the Heroic in History: Six Lectures: Reported*, London: Wiley & Halsted.

Carr, Nicholas (2010), *The Shallows: What the Internet is Doping to Our Brains*, New York, NY: W.W. Norton.

Carrell, Severin (2011), 'Pair jailed for trying to start a riot in Dundee via Facebook', *Guardian*, 13 December.

Carroll, Lewis (1865), *Alice's Adventure in Wonderland*, London: Macmillan.

Castells v. Spain (1992) 14 EHRR 445.

'Cato' (1721), 'Letter No. 15', *London Journal*, 4 February.

Chafee, Zechariah (1919), 'Freedom of speech in war-time', *Harvard Law Review*, 33: 1, November.

Chaplinsky v. New Hampshire, 315 U.S. 568 (1942).

Chapman, Jane (2005), *Comparative Media History*, Cambridge: Polity.

Chanan, Michael (1995), *Repeated Takes: A Short History of Recording and its Effects on Music*, London: Verso.

Cherry, Kenda (n.d.), 'Albert Bandura biography', *About.com*, http://psychology.about.com/od/profilesofmajorthinkers/p/bio_bandura.htm [accessed 31 March 2012)

Chesterfield, Earl of (Philip Stanhope) (1737), 'Journal of the proceedings and debates in the last session of Parliament', *London Magazine*, 14 August.

Clegg, Brian (2007), *The Man Who Stopped Time: The Illuminating Story of Eadweard Muybridge: Pioneer Photographer, Father of the Motion Picture, Murderer*, Washington, DC: Joseph Henry Press.

Cobbett, William (1809), *Weekly Political Register*, XV: 26, 1 July.

Cobbett, William, Howell, Thomas Baily and Howell, Thomas Jones (eds) (1811), *Cobbett's A Complete Collection of State Trials for High Treason Volume XXV*, London: Longman, Hurst, Rees, Orme and Brown.

Cockburn, Claude (1967), *I, Claude*, Harmondsworth: Penguin.

Cohen, Joshua (1993), 'Freedom of Expression', *Philosophy and Public Affairs*, 22: 3, Summer.

Cohen, Nick (2011), 'The betrayal and treachery of Julian Assange', *Observer*, 18 September.

Cohen v. California, 403 U.S. 15 (1971)

Coke, Edward (2003), 'The Case de Libellis Famosis', *The Selected Writings and Speeches of Sir Edward Coke. Vol. 1*, ed. Steve Sheppard, Indianapolis, IN: Liberty Fund, Chapter 125a, http://oll.libertyfund.org/title/911/106331 [accessed from on 26 November 2010].

Collet, Collet Dobson (1899), *A History of the Taxes on Knowledge*, London: T.F. Unwin.

Collins v. Smith, 447 F. Supp 676 (N.D. III 1978), aff'd, 578 F.2d 1197 (7th Cir. 1978).

Comstock G. and Paik, H. (1991), *Television and the American Child*, San Diego, CA: Academic Press.

Connolly v. DPP [2007] EWHC 237.

Cook, John (1998), *Dennis Potter: A Life on Screen*, Manchester: Manchester University Press.

Cooley, Thomas (1888), *A Treatise on the Law of Torts*, Chicago. IL: Callaghan.

Convention for the Protection of Human Rights and Fundamental Freedoms, Rome, 1950 [1948] (aka *European Convention on Human Rights*), in *European Issues: European Convention on Human Rights Collected Texts*, Strasbourg: Council of Europe Press, 1995.

Corera, Gordon (2011), 'Secret service pressed BBC to censor Panorama – papers', *BBC*, http://www.bbc.co.uk/news/uk-16358075 [accessed 25 February 2012].

Corliss v. Walker, 64 Fed. Rep. 280 (1894).

Coughlin, Con (2009), *Khomeini's Ghost: Iran since 1979*, London: Pan.

Cox, Barry, Shirley, John and Short, Martin (1977), *The Fall of Scotland Yard*, Harmondsworth: Penguin.

Cranfield, G.A. (1978), *The Press and Society; From Caxton to Northcliffe*, London: Longman.

Crouch, John (1654–5), *Mecurius Fumigosus*, http://www.lancs.ac.uk/fass/projects/newsbooks/fumig.htm [accessed 24 October 2010].

Crystal, David (2009), *Txtin: the Gr8 Db8*, Oxford: Oxford University Press.

Curran, Charles and Seaton, Jean (2003), *Power without Responsibility* (6th edition), London: Routledge.

Curran, Charles and Seaton, Jean (2009), *Power without Responsibility* (7th edition), London: Routledge.

Czitrom, D.J. (1982), *Media and the American Mind*, Chapel Hill, NC: University of North Carolina Press.

Dargelos, Betrand (2006), 'Cabaret (France)', in Jack Blocker, David Fahey and Ian R. Tyrrell (eds), *Alcohol and Temperance in Modern History*, Santa Barbara, CA: ABC-Clio.

Davies, Caroline (2011), 'Rioters' appeal hearings to start next week', *Guardian*, 22 September.

Davies, D. W., Bartlett, K.A., Scantlebury, R.A. and Wilkinson, P.T. (1967), 'A digital communication network for computers giving rapid response at remote terminals', ACM Symposium on Operating System Principles, Gatlinburg, Tennessee, 1–4 October, http://dl.acm.org/citation.cfm?id=811669 [accessed 29 October 2011].

Day, Patrick (1990), *The Making of the New Zealand Press: 1840–1880*, Wellington: Victoria University Press.

Deligiorgi, Katrina (2005), *Kant and the Culture of the Enlightenment*, New York, NY: State University of New York Press.

Dennis v. United States, 341 U.S. 494 (1951).

Department of Trade and Industry and Department of Culture, Media and Sport (2000), *A New Future for Communications*, Cm 5010, London: The Stationery Office.

Departmental Committee on Section 2 of the Official Secrets Act 1911, Oliver Franks, Baron Franks (1972), *Departmental Committee on Section 2 of the Official Secrets Act 1911, chairman Lord Franks. Vol.1, Report of the Committee*, London: HMSO.

Dickinson, Margaret and Street, Sarah (1985), *Cinema and the State: The Film Industry and the British Government 1927–1984*, London: BFI.

Dinsdale, A.A. (1932), 'Television in America today', in G. Shiers (ed.), *Technical Development of Television*, New York, NY: Arno.

Disraeli, Benjamin (1997 [1852]), *Benjamin Disraeli, Letters 1852–1856*, Toronto: University of Toronto Press.

Doe v. University of Michigan, 721 F. Supp. 852 (E.D. Mich. 1989).

Douglas and another and others v Hello! Limited and others [2007] UKHL 21.

Dover Wilson, John (1956 [1911]), *Life in Shakespeare's England*, Cambridge: Cambridge University Press.

Doward, Jamie (2011), 'Films that "encourage smoking" claim £338m in UK tax credits', *Observer*, 28 August.

Doward, Jamie (2012), 'Murdoch faces fresh crisis as key Sun staff arrested', *Observer*, 12 February.

Doward, James and Townsend, Mark (2008), 'Firebomb attack on book publisher', *Observer*, 28 September.

Dowbiggin, Ian (2011), *The Quest for Mental Health: A Tale of Science, Medicine, Scandal and Sorrow, and Mass Society*, New York, NY: Cambridge University Press.

Dowell, Stephen (1884), *A History of Taxation and Taxes in England*, London: Longmans, Green.

Duniway, Clyde (1906), *The Development of the Freedom of the Press in Massachusetts*, New York, NY: Franklin.

Dutton, Richard (1991), *Mastering the Revels: The Regulation and Censorship of English Renaissance Drama*, Basingstoke: Palgrave Macmillan.

Dworkin, Ronald (2010), 'Foreword', in Ivan Hare and James Weinstein (eds), *Extreme Speech and Democracy*, Oxford: Oxford University Press.

Earle, John (1811 [1628]), *Microcosmography*, London: White & Cochrane.

Edwards, Lilian (2009), 'Privacy and data protection on line: the laws don't work?', Lilian Edwards and Charlotte Waelde (eds) (2009), *Law and the Internet*, Oxford: Hart.

Edwards, Lilian and Waelde, Charlotte (eds) (2009), *Law and the Internet*, Oxford: Hart.

Edwards, Paul (2010), 'Some say the internet should never have happened', in Neuman, W. Russell (ed.), *Media, Technology and Society: Theories of Media Evolution*, Ann Arbor, MI: University of Michigan Press.

Eisenstein, Elizabeth (1983), *The Printing Revolution in Early Modern Europe*, Cambridge: Cambridge University Press.

Eliot, Simon and Rose, Jonathan (eds) (2009), *A Companion to the History of The Book*, Oxford: Wiley-Blackwell.

Ellul, Jacques (1965), *Propaganda: The Formation of Men's Attitudes*, trans. Konrad Kellen and Jean Lerner, New York, NY: Vintage.

Etter, Jonathan (2003), *Quinn Martin, Producer*, Jefferson, NC: McFarland.

Etzersdorfer, Elmar and Sonneck, Gernot (1998), 'Preventing suicide by mass media report: the Viennese experience 1980–1986', *Archives of Suicide Research*, 4: 67–7.

European Convention of Human Rights (1950 [1948]), *Convention for the Protection of Human Rights and Fundamental Freedoms*, Rome: European Convention of Human Rights.

European Convention on Human Rights (1995), *European Issues: European Convention on Human Rights Collected Texts*, Strasbourg: Council of Europe Press.

Evans, Rob (2011), 'How the Guardian was gagged from revealing tax secrets', *Guardian*, 19 February.

Fagen, M.D. (ed.) (1975), *History of Engineering and Science in the Bell System: The Early Years 1875–1925*, New York, NY: Bell Laboratories.

Faulk, Barry (2004), *Music Hall and Modernity: The Late Victorian Discovery of Popular Culture*, Athens, OH: University of Ohio Press.

FCC v. Pacifica Foundation, 438 U.S. 726 (1978).

Febvre, Lucien and Martin, Henri-Jean (1977), *The Coming of the Book: The Impact of Printing 1480–1800*, London: Verso.

Federal Communications Commission (n.d.), 'Obscenity, indecency and profanity guide', *Federal Communications Commission*, http://www.fcc.gov/guides/obscenity-indecency-and-profanity [accessed 7 September 2011].

Feinberg, Joel (1983), *Harm to Others: The Moral Limits of the Criminal Law I*, New York, NY: Oxford University Press.

Feinberg, Joel (1985), *Offense to Others: The Moral Limits of the Criminal Law II*, New York, NY: Oxford University Press.

Feldman, David (1993), *Civil Liberties and Human Rights in England and Wales*. Oxford: Oxford University Press.

Ferguson, J.A., Foster, A.G. and Green, H.M. (1936), *The Howes and Their Press*, Sydney: Sunnybrook Press.

Finklestein, Seth (2008) 'You say you've never considered the politics of search engines', *Guardian*, 24 January.

Fish, Stanley (2008), 'Crying Censorship', *Opinionator: Exclusive Online Commentary from The Times*, 24 August, http://opinionator.blogs.nytimes.com/2008/08/24/crying-censorship [accessed 22 June 2011].

Fisher, Alan (2011), 'The "Arab Spring", social media and Al-Jazeera', in John Mair and Richard Keeble (eds), *Journalism: Dead or Alive?*, Bury St. Edmunds: Abramis.

Fisher, Trevor (1995), *Scandal: The Sexual Politics of Late Victorian Britain*, Stroud: Sutton.

Fiss, Owen (1996), *The Irony of Free Speech*, Cambridge, MA: Harvard University Press.

Fones-Wolf, Elizabeth and Godfried, Nathan (2007), 'Regulating class conflict: NBC's relationship with business and organized labour', in Michelle Hilmes (ed.), *NBC: America's Network*, Berkeley, CA: University of California Press.

Forman, Murray (2007), 'Employment and blue pencils, NBC, race, and representation', in Michelle Hilmes (ed.), *NBC: America's Network*, Berkeley, CA: University of California Press.

Forsyth, Neil (2009), *John Milton: A Biography*, Oxford: Lion Hudson.

Frank, Joseph (1961), *The Beginnings of the English Newspaper 1620–1660*, Cambridge, MA: Harvard University Press.

Frankel, Max (2010), 'Shared with millions, it is not secret', *Guardian*, 1 December.

Franklin, Benjamin (1731), 'An apology for printers', *Pennsylvania Gazette*, 10 June.

Frantz, Douglas (1997), 'The shadowy story behind Scientology's tax-exempt status', *New York Times*, 9 March, http://www.cs.cmu.edu/~dst/Cowen/essays/nytimes.html [accessed 10 September 2011].

Gaines, Jane (1991), *Contested Cultures*, Chapel Hill, NC: University of North Carolina Press.

Galloway, John (1977), 'Domestic economic issues', in J.N. Pelton and M. Snow (eds), *Economic and Policy Problems in Satellite Communications*, New York, NY: Praeger.

Garner, Peter (1996), *John Wilkes: A Friend to Liberty*, Oxford: Oxford University Press.

Garnham, Nicholas (2000), *Emancipation, the Media and Modernity*, Oxford: Oxford University Press.

Garratt, G.R.M. and Mumford, A.H. (1952), 'The history of television', *Proceedings of the Institution of Electrical Engineers*, 99, Part IIIA.

Garton Ash, Timothy (2011), 'The internet nourished Norway's killer, but censorship would be folly', *Guardian*, 29 July.

Gay News Ltd and Lemon v. United Kingdom, 5 EHRR 123 (1982), App. No. 8710/79 .

Gertz v. Robert Welch, Inc., 418 U.S. 323 (1974).

Gilbert, Douglas (1968 [1940]), *American Vaudeville: Its Life and Times*, New York, NY: Dover.

Gilder, George (1985), *Life after Television*, Nashville, TN: Whittle Books.

Gilliat-Ray, Sophie (2010), *Muslims in Britain: An Introduction*, Cambridge: Cambridge University Press.

Glanville, Jo (2008), 'Respect for religion now makes censorship the norm', *Guardian*, 30 March.

Goebbels, Joseph (1938), 'Der Rundfunk als achte Großmacht', *Signale der neuen Zeit. 25 ausgewählte Reden von Dr Joseph Goebbels*, Munich: Zentralverlag der NSDAP, http://www.calvin.edu/academic/cas/gpa/goeb56.htm [accessed 25 April 2011].

Goldacre, Ben (2009), 'Illegal downloads and dodgy figures', *Guardian*, 6 June.

Goldie, Mark (ed.) (1997), *Locke: Political Essays*, Cambridge: Cambridge University Press.

Goldie, Mark (2008), 'Roger L'Estrange's *Obsevator*', in Anne Dunan-Page and Beth Lynch (eds), *Roger L'Estrange and the Making of Restoration Culture*, Aldershot: Ashgate.

Goodman, Mark (1999), 'The Radio Act of 1927 as a product of Progressivism', *Media History Monographs*, 2: 2, http://www.scripps.ohiou.edu/mediahistory/mhmjour2-2.htm [accessed 1 March 2011].

Goodwin, Peter (1999), *Television under the Tories: Broadcasting Policy 1979–1997*, London: British Film Institute.

Gordon Bennett, James (1836a), *New York Herald*, 11 April.

Gordon Bennett, James (1836b), *New York Herald*, 16 April.

Gottschalk v. Benson, 409 U.S. 63 (1972).

Gough, Hugh (1988), *The Newspaper Press in the French Revolution*, London: Routledge

Gray, John (1986), *Liberalism*, Buckingham: Open University Press.

Gray, John (1995), *Enlightenment's Wake: Politics and Culture at the Close of the Modern Age*, London, Routledge.

Graydon, Arthur (1846), *Memoirs of His Own Time*, Philadelphia, PA: Lindsay & Blackiston.

Green, David Allen (2012), 'Lessons from Leveson', *New Statesman*, 2 April.

Greenslade, Roy (2004), *Press Gang: How Newspapers Make Profits from Propaganda*, London: Pan.

Greenslade, Roy (2011), 'Patten of the BBC backs press self-regulation', *Guardian: Greenslade Blog*, http://www.guardian.co.uk/media/greenslade/2011/nov/13/lord-patten-editors [accessed 31 November 2011].

Gregory, Sam, Caldwell, Gillian, Avni, Ronit and Harding, Thomas (2005), *Video for Change: A Guide for Advocacy and Activism*, London: Pluto Press.

Grimm, Dieter (2010a), 'Freedom of Speech in a Globalized World', in Ivan Hare and James Weinstein (eds), *Extreme Speech and Democracy*, Oxford: Oxford University Press.

Grimm, Dieter (2010b), 'The Holocaust denial decision of the Federal Constitutional Court of Germany', in Ivan Hare and James Weinstein (eds), *Extreme Speech and Democracy*, Oxford: Oxford University Press.

Groppera Radio AG v Switzerland, 28 March 1990, Application No. 10890/84.

Guillen, Matthew (2007), *Reading America: Text as a Cultural Force*, Washington, DC: Academica.

Gunning, Tom (1986), 'The cinema of attractions: early film, its spectator and the avant-garde', *Wide Angle*, 8: 3–4, Fall.

Günsberg, Maggie (1997), *Gender and the Italian Stage: From the Renaissance to the Present Day*, Cambridge: Cambridge University Press.

Gunter, Barrie and McAleer, Jill (1997), *Children and Television*, London: Routledge.

Haelan Laboratories, Inc. v. Topps Chewing Gum, Inc., 202 F.2d 866 (1953).

Hafner, K. and Lyon, M. (1996), *Where Wizards Stay Up Late: The Origins of the Internet*, New York, NY: Simon & Schuster.

Haggbloom, S.J. (2002), 'The 100 most eminent psychologists of the 20th century', *Review of General Psychology*, 6: 2: 139–52.

Halliday, Josh (2011), 'Ofcom report: Smartphone sales up as 60% of teenage users confess to being highly addicted', *Guardian*, 4 August.

Halliday, Josh and Green, Nigel (2011), 'Council lawsuit forces Twitter to reveal user's detail', *Guardian*, 30 May.

Hamilton, Alexander, Madison, James and Jay, John (1864 [1788]) 'Certain general and miscellaneous objections to the constitution considered and answered', *The Federalist*, ed. John Hamilton, Philadelphia: J.B. Lippincott.

Hammond v. DPP [2004] EWHC 69 (Admin).

Hansard (1994), 'Terrorism', HC Deb 21 January 1994, vol. 235, cc906-15W, http://hansard.millbanksystems.com/written_answers/1994/jan/21/terrorism [accessed 29 July 2010].

Handyside v. UK (1979–80) 1 EHRR 737.

Harding, Thomas (2005), 'Strategic distribution: reaching keys audiences in innovative ways', in Sam Gregory, Gillian Caldwell, Ronit Avni and Thomas Harding (2005), *Video for Change: A Guide for Advocacy and Activism*, London: Pluto Press.

Hardy, H. (1996), 'The history of the net', MA Thesis, Grand Valley State University, Michigan, umcc.umich.edu/pub/seraphim/doc/nethist8.text.

Hare, Ivan (2010), 'Extreme speech under international and regional human rights standards', in Ivan Hare and James Weinstein (eds), *Extreme Speech and Democracy*, Oxford: Oxford University Press.

Hare, Ivan and Weinstein, James (eds) (2010), *Extreme Speech and Democracy*, Oxford: Oxford University Press.

Harraway, Donna (1991), *Simians, Cyborgs and Women*, New York, NY: Routledge.

Harris, John (2009), 'The pirates thrive on a scrap with the analogue crowd', *Guardian*, 27 August.

Harris, John (2011), 'How the Net is altering your mind', *Guardian*, G2, 20 August.

Harris, Michael and Lee, Alan (eds) (1986), *The Press in English Society from the Seventeenth to the Nineteenth Centuries*, Rutherford, NJ: Fairleigh Dickinson University Press.

Hassaballa, Hesham (2010), 'What would Prophet Muhammad do?', *Chicago Tribune*, 26 April, http://newsblogs.chicagotribune.com/religion_theseeker/2010/04/hesham-hassaballa-author-of-the-blog-god-faith-and-a-pen----i-must-admit-i-was-offended-i-was-really-bothered-by-t.html [accessed 1 August 2011].

Hastings, Chris (2006), 'Revealed: how the BBC used MI5 to vet thousands of staff', *Daily Telegraph*, 2 July, http://www.telegraph.co.uk/news/uknews/1522875/Revealed-how-the-BBC-used-MI5-to-vet-thousands-of-staff.html [accessed 3 May 2011].

Hazlett, William (2009 [1821]) 'Mrs Siddons', *Examiner*, 16 June, reprinted in William Hazlett, *Dramatic Essays Selected (from a View of the English Stage)*, ed. William Archer and Robert Lowe, Whitefish, MT: Kessinger Publishing.

Heawood, Jonathan (2009), 'Let's cheer the demise of criminal libel', *Guardian*, 27 October, http://www.guardian.co.uk/commentisfree/libertycentral/2009/oct/27/criminal-libel-free-speech [accessed 30 October 2010].

Heine, Heinrich (1823), *Tragödien, Nebst Einem Lyrischen Intermezzo*, Berlin: Ferdinand Dümmler.

Helft, Miguel (2009), 'Google working to revise digital books settlement', *New York Times*, 20 September, http://www.nytimes.com/2009/09/21/technology/internet/21google.html [accessed 30 September 2009]

Hemmings, Frederick (2006), *Theatre and State in France, 1760–1905*, Cambridge: Cambridge University Press.

Herbeck, Dale (2003), 'Chaplinsky v. New Hampshire', in Richard Parker (ed.), *Free Speech on Trial: Communication Perspectives on Landmark Supreme Court Decisions*, Tuscaloosa, AL: University of Alabama Press.

Hijiya, James (1992), *Lee de Forest and the Fatherhood of Radio*, Cranbury, NJ: Associated University Presses.

Hilmes, Michelle (1990), *Hollywood and Broadcasting*, Urbana, IL: University of Illinois Press.

Hilmes, Michelle (1997), *Radio Voices: American Broadcasting 1922–1952*, Minneapolis, MN: University of Minnesota Press.

Hilmes, Michelle (ed.) (2007a), *NBC: America's Network*, Berkeley, CA: University of California Press.

Hilmes, Michelle (2007b), 'NBC and the network idea: defining the "American System"', in Michelle Hilmes (ed.), *NBC: America's Network*, Berkeley, CA: University of California Press.

Himmelweit, H.T., Oppenheim, A.N. and Vince, P. (1958), *Television and the Child: An Empirical Study of the Effect of Television on the Young*, Oxford: Oxford University Press.

Hirsch, Afua (2011), 'Fred Goodwin gets superinjunction to stop him being called a banker', *Guardian*, 10 March.

Hobbes, Thomas (2002 [1651]), *The Leviathan: On Man*, London: Penguin.

Hollins, T. (1984), *Beyond Broadcasting: Into the Cable Age*, London: BFI.

Holt, Francis (1816), *The Law of Libel*, London: Butterworth.

Hooper, John (2010), 'US anger as Italian court finds Google bosses guilty', *Guardian*, 25 February.

Horowitz, David (1997), *Beyond Left and Right: Insurgency and the Establishment*, Champagne-Urbana, IL: University of Illinois Press.

Howell, T.B. (1816), *State Trials, Vol. XVII*, London: Longman, Hurst, Rees, Orme and Brown.

Hunt, Lynn (2007), *Inventing Human Rights*, New York, NY: W.W. Norton.

Hunter, Fred (1994), 'Hilda Matheson and the BBC 1926–1940', in Sybil Oldfield, (ed.), *This Working Day World: Women's Lives and Cultures in Britain, 1914–45*, London: Taylor & Francis.

Hustler Magazine, Inc. v. Falwell, 485 U.S. 46 (1988).

Hutton, Lord (2004), *Report of the Inquiry into the Circumstances Surrounding the Death of Dr David Kelly C.M.G.*, HC 247, London: The Stationery Office.

IA v. Turkey (2005) 45 EHRR 30.

Ingelhart, Louis (1987), *Press Freedoms: A Descriptive Calendar of Concepts, Interpretations, Events*, Westport, CT: Greenwood.

International Digital Publishing Forum (2011), *International Digital Publishing Forum*, http://idpf.org/about-us/industry-statistics [accessed 21 November 2011].

Ishay, Micheline (2004), *The History of Human Rights: From Ancient Times to the Globalization Era*, Berkeley, CA: University of California Press.

Issa, Nada (2011), 'Daily Mail writer Melanie Phillips hits back at "crude smears" after she is referenced by Norway killer', *Wire (The Press Gazette)*, 26 July, http://blogs.pressgazette.co.uk/wire/8049 [accessed 8 August 2011].

Ivimey, Joseph (1833), *John Milton: His Life and Times, Religious and Political Opinions*, London: Effingham Wilson.

Jackson, Joseph (1922), 'Should radio be used for advertising', *Radio Broadcast*, November 1922.

Jacobellis v. Ohio, 378 U.S. 184 (1964).

Jacobs, Jason (2005), 'Sidney Newman', *Encyclopaedia of Television Vol. 3*, Chicago, IL: Fitzroy Dearborn.

Jameel v. Wall Street Journal Europe Sprl [2007] UKHL 44, 1 AC 359.

James, T.B. and Simons, John (eds) (1989), *The Poems of Laurence Minot*, Exeter: University of Exeter Press.

Jansky, C.M. (1957), 'The contribution of Herbert Hoover to broadcasting', *Journal of Broadcasting*, 3.

Jebb, Richard (ed.) (1918), *Milton: Areopagitica*, Cambridge: Cambridge University Press.

Jefferson, Thomas (1787 [1782]), *Notes on the State of Virginia*, London: John Stockdale.

Jefferson, Thomas (1904 [1784]), *Notes on the State of Virginia*, in Thomas Jefferson, *The Works of Thomas Jefferson, Vol. 4*, New York, NY: Putnam and Sons.

Jefferson, Thomas (1785/6), *An Act for Establishing Religious Freedom*, *The Religious Freedom Page*, http://religiousfreedom.lib.virginia.edu/sacred/vaact.html [accessed 2 August 2011].

Jefferson, Thomas (1950), *The Papers of Thomas Jefferson Vol. 2*, ed. Julian Boyd, Princeton: Princeton University Press.

Jelavich, Peter (1996), *Berlin Cabaret*, Cambridge, MA: Harvard.

Jensen, De Lamar (1973), *Confrontation at Worms: Martin Luther and the Diet of Worms*. Provo, UT: Brigham Young University Press.

Jersild v. Denmark (1995) 19 EHRR 1.

Johnson, Samuel (1775), *Taxation No Tyranny: Answer to the Resolutions and Address of the American Congress*, London: T. Cadell.

Jones, Richard (1961), *Ancients and Moderns: A Study of the Rise of the Scientific Movement in Seventeenth-Century England*, Gloucester, MA: Peter Smith.

Jones, Sam and Hirsch, Afua (2009), ''Ello 'ello 'ello. Blogging detective unmasked', *Guardian*, 16 June.

Jonson, Ben (1625), *The Staple of News*, *Holloway Pages*, http://hollowaypages.com/jonson1692news.htm [accessed 13 March 2012].

Joseph Burstyn, Inc. v. Wilson, 343 U.S. 495 (1952).

'Junius' (1978), *Letters*, ed. John Cannon, Oxford: Oxford University Press.

Kant, Emmanuel (1970 [1785]), *Grundlegung zur Metaphysik der Sitten (Groundwork of the Metaphysics of Morals)*, in Emmanuel Kant, *Kant: Political Writing*, ed. H.R. Reiss, Cambridge: Cambridge University Press.

Kant, Emmanuel (1970 [1793]), *Über den Gemeinspruch: Das mag in der Theorie richtig sein, taugt aber nicht für die Praxis (On the Old Saw: That May be Right in Theory, but It Won't Work in Practice)*, in Emmanuel Kant, *Kant: Political Writing*, ed. H.R. Reiss (ed.), Cambridge: Cambridge University Press.

Kant, Emmanuel (1996 [1784]), *Beantwortung der Frage: Was ist Aufklärung? (An Answer to the Question: What is the Enlightenment?)*, in James Schmidt (ed.), *Eighteenth-Century Answers and Twentieth Century Questions*, Berkeley, CA: University of California Press.

Katz v. United States, 389 U.S. 347 (1967).

Kay and others and another (FC) (Appellants) v. London Borough of Lambeth and others (Respondents) [2006], UKHL 10.

Kaye v. Robertson [1991] FSR 62.

Kelly, James, Constable, Anne and Halevy, David (1986), 'Press: shifting the attack on leaks' *Time*, 19 May, http://www.time.com/time/magazine/article/0,9171,961418,00.html#ixzz1UM6uo2Rh [accessed 7 August 2011].

Kelly, Ruth (2007), 'Time for a British version of Islam', *New Statesman*, 9 April.

Kennedy, Ellen and Mendus, Susan (eds) (1987), *Women in Western Political Philosophy*, Brighton: Wheatsheaf.

King, Peter (Lord King) (1829), *The Life of John Locke: With Extracts from His Correspondence, Journals and Common-Place Books*, London: Henry Colburn.

Kiss, Jemima (2010), 'From teen favourite to web graveyard, Bebo faces closure as members log off', *Guardian*, 8 April.

Kissing, Steve (2001), 'Brandenburg v. Ohio', *Cincinnati Magazine*, August.

Klausen, Jytte (2009), *The Cartoons that Shook the World*, New Haven, CT: Yale University Press.

Kleeman, Jenny (2007), 'WIKIWARS', *Observer*, 25 March.

Knightly, Philip (1976), *The First Casualty*, New York, NY: Harcourt, Brace, Jovanovitch.

Knuppfer v. London Express Newspapers Ltd [1944] AC 116.

Krotoski, Aleks (2010), 'Democratic, but dangerous too: how the web changed our world', *Observer*, 24 January.

Kuritz, Paul (1988), *The Making of Theatre History*, Englewood, NJ: Prentice Hall.

Lagos, Maria (2007), 'Fatal jumps from bridge rise sharply', *San Francisco Chronicle*, 18 January, http://articles.sfgate.com/2007-01-18/news/17227643_1_bridge-suicides-golden-gate-bridge-bridge-officials [accessed 20 December 2011] .

Lamb, Jonathon (2009), *The Evolution of Sympathy in the Long Eighteenth Century*, London: Pickering & Chatto.

Lambert, Malcolm (1998), *The Cathars*, Oxford: Blackwell.

Lashmar, Paul (2011), in John Mair and Richard Keeble (eds), *Journalism: Dead or Alive?*, Bury St. Edmunds: Abramis.

Lasky, Melvin (2000), *The Language of Journalism: Vol. 1 Newspaper Culture*, New Brunswick, NJ: Transaction.

Lautsi and others v. Italy App no 30814/06 (ECHR, 18 March 2011).

Lavington, S. (1980), *Early British Computers*, Manchester: Manchester University Press.

Law, Graham (2000), *Serializing Fiction in the Victorian Press*, Houndsmill, NY: Palgrave.

Lehideux and Isorni v. France (1998) 5 BHRC 540.

Leigh, David (2012a), 'Times reporter hacked into police blogger's email to reveal identity', *Guardian*, 18 January.

Leigh, David (2012b), 'Police files expose NOW interference and harassment in Milly Dowler case', *Guardian*, 24 January.

Leigh, David (2012c), 'Yard chief ate with Wallis just after bid to halt Guardian story', *Guardian*, 6 March.

Leigh, David and Franklin, Jonathan (2008), 'Whistle while you work', *Guardian*, 23 February.

Lenin, V.I. (1961 [1901]) 'Where to begin', *Iskra*, 4, reprinted in V.I. Lenin, *Lenin Collected Works, Volume 5*, Moscow: Foreign Languages Publishing House.

Levy, Leonard (1995), *Blasphemy: Verbal Offence against the Sacred*, Chapel Hill, NC: University of North Carolina Press.

Lewis, Anthony (1991), *Make No Law*, New York, NY: Random House.

Leyla Şahin v. Turkey (2005) Application no. 44774/98, EHRR 2.

Licklider, J.C.R. (1960), 'Man-Computer Symbiosis', *IRE Transactions on Human Factors in Electronics*, 1, March.

Licklider, J.C.R. (1963), 'Topics for discussion at the forthcoming meeting', 23 April, Washington, DC: ARPA, http://www.packet.cc/files/memo.html [accessed 28 October 2011].

Licklider, J.C.R and Taylor, Robert (1968), 'The computer as a communications device', *Science and Technology*, April.

Liebling, A.J. (1964), *The Press*, New York, NY: Pantheon.

Lingens v. Austria (1986) 8 EHRR 407.

Littlejohn, Richard (2008), 'Why haven't the Left Got Georgia on their Minds', *Daily Mail*, 19 August.

Lohmann, Susanne (1994), 'Dynamics of informational cascades: the Monday Demonstrations in Leipzig, East Germany, 1989–1991', *World Politics*, 47.

Luther, Martin (1962 [1523]), *That Jesus Christ was Born a Jew*, in Martin Luther, *Luther's Works*, trans. Walter I. Brandt, Philadelphia, PA: Fortress Press.

Luther, Martin (1971 [1543]), *On the Jews and Their Lies*, trans. Martin H. Bertram, Philadelphia, PA: Fortress Press.

Maier, Pauline (1980), *The Old Revolutionaries: Political Lives in the Age of Samuel Adams*, New York, NY: Norton.

Maclay, Kathleen (1989) 'Bookstores selling "Verses" firebombed', *Modesto Bee*, 1 March.

Malik, Amin (2005), *Muslim Narrative and the Discourse of English*, Albany, NY: State University of New York Press.

Malik, Kenan (2009), *From Fatwa to Jihad: The Rushdie Affair and its Legacy*, London: Atlantic.

Mannoni, Laurent (2000), *The Great Art of Light and Shadow*, Exeter: University of Exeter Press.

Manzoor, Sarfraz (2007), 'Funny Old World', *Guardian*, 'G2', 6 April.

Martin, Peter (2008), *Samuel Johnson: A Biography*, London: Weidenfeld and Nicolson.

Marx, Karl (1842), 'The freedom of the press', *Neue Rheinische Zeitung*, 135, Supplement, 15 May, http://www.marxists.org/archive/marx/works/1842/free-press/ch01.htm [accessed 27 September 2010].

Marx, Karl (1844), 'Zur Judenfrage' ('On the Jewish Question'), *Deutsch-Französische Jahrbücher*, February, http://www.marxists.org/archive/marx/works/1844/jewish-question [accessed 27 September 2010].

Mattelart, Armand (2005), *The Information Society*, trans. Susan Taponier and James Cohen, London: Sage.

Mayer, David and Richards, Kenneth (eds) (1977), *Western Popular Theatre*, London: Methuen.

Mazrui, Ali (1990), 'Satanic verses or a satanic novel? Moral dilemmas of the Rushdie affair', *Third World Quarterly*, 12: 1.

Mazrui, Ali (1992), 'Mapping Islam in Farah's *Maps*', in Feroza Jussawala and Reed Way Daenbrock (eds), *The Marabout and the Muse: New Approaches to Islam in African Literature*, Jackson, MS: University of Mississippi University Press.

McCarthy, Justin (1901), *A History of Our Times*, London: Chatto & Windus.

McChesney, R. (1990), 'The battle for the US airways, 1928–1935', *Journal of Communication*, 40: 4, Autumn.

McChesney, R. (1995), *Telecommunications, Mass Media, and Democracy: The Battle for the Control of US Broadcasting, 1928–1935*, New York, NY: Oxford University Press.

McDowell, Paula (1998), *The Women of Grub Street: Press, Politics, and Gender in the London Literary Marketplace 1678–1730*, Oxford: Oxford University Press 1998.

McLuhan, Marshall (1964), *Understanding Media: The Extensions of Man*, New York, NY: McGraw Hill.

McLuhan, Marshall (1967), *The Medium is the Massage*, New York, NY: Random House.

McVeigh, Tracy (2010), 'Assassin shot in cartoonist's home has al-Qaida terror links', *Observer*, 3 January.

Meiklejohn, Alexander (1961), 'The First Amendment is an absolute', *Supreme Court Review*.

Meredith Corp. v. FCC, 809 F.2d 863 (D.C. Cir. 1987).

Merleau-Ponty, Maurice (1964), *Signs*, trans. Richard McCleary, Chicago, IL: Northwestern University Press.

Messenger Davies, Máire and Pearson, Roberta (2007), 'The little programme that could', in Michelle Hilmes (ed.), *NBC: America's Network*, Berkeley, CA: University of California Press.

Messere, Fritz (1996), *Documents of the Federal Radio Commission*, http://www.oswego.edu/~messere/FRCdavis.html [accessed 1 March, 2011].

Metropolis, N., Howlett, J. and Rota, G.-C. (eds) (1980), *A History of Computing in the Twentieth Century*, New York, NY: Academic Press.

Metterie, Julien Offray de la (1748), *L'Homme Machine*, Leiden: Elie Luzac, Fils.

Mill, John Stuart (1998 [1859]), *On Liberty* in *John Stuart Mill on Liberty and Other Essays*, ed. John Gray, Oxford: Oxford University Press.

Mill, John Stuart (1998 [1861]), *The Subjection of Women* in *John Stuart Mill on Liberty and Other Essays*, ed. John Gray, Oxford: Oxford University Press.

Miller, Russell (1987), *Bare-faced Messiah, The True Story of L. Ron Hubbard*, New York, NY: Henry Holt & Co.

Miller v. California, 413 U.S. 15 (1973).

Millman, S. (ed.) (1983), *A History of Engineering and Science in the Bell System – Physical Sciences (1925–1980)*, New York, NY: Bell Laboratories.

Millwood Hargrave, Andrea and Livingstone, Sonia (2009), *Harm and Offence in Media Content: A Review of the Literature*, London: Intellect.

Milton, John (1963 [1644], *Areopagitica and Of Education*, London: Macmillan.

Mindich, David (1998), *Just the Facts*, New York, NY: New York University Press.

Moin, Baqer (1999), *Khomeini: Life of the Ayatollah*, London: I.B.Tauris.

Monbiot, George (2009), *Guardian*, 5 February.

Moncel, Le Compte du (1879), *The Telephone, the Microphone and the Phonograph*, New York, NY: Harper & Brothers.

Monod, Paul (1993), *Jacobinism and the English People, 1688–1788*, Cambridge: Cambridge University Press.

Morecraft, J.H. (1926), 'The march of radio', *Radio Broadcast*, May.

Morozov, Evgeny (2009), 'How dictators watch us on the web', *Prospect*, December.

Morozov, Evgeny (2011), *The Net Delusion: How Not to Liberate the World*, London: Allen Lane.

Morris, Steve (2011), 'Man jailed for mocking teenagers' deaths online', *Guardian*, 14 September.

Moser v. Press Pub. Co., 109 N.Y.S. 963 (1908).

Moss, Mitchell (1978), *Two-Way Cable Television: An Evaluation of Community Uses in Reading, Pennsylvania*, New York, NY: New York University Alternative Media Center.

Mott, Frank Luther (1962), *History of American Journalism*, New York, NY: Macmillan.

Moynihan, Daniel (1999), *Secrecy: The American Experience*, New Haven, CT: Yale University Press.

Muir, Hugh (2009), 'Diary', *Guardian*, 13 February.

Müller and others v. Switzerland (1988) 13 EHRR 212.

Mumford, Lewis (1934), *Technics and Civilization*, New York, NY: Harcourt.

Murray Beck, James (1982), *Joseph Howe: Conservative Reformer 1803–1848*, Montreal: McGill University Press.

Murray v. Express Newspapers Ltd and Big Pictures (UK) Ltd [2007] EWHC 1908.

Musser, Charles (1990), *The Emergence of Cinema*, New York, NY: Charles Scribner's Sons.

Mutual Film Corporation v. Ohio Industrial Commission, 236 U.S. 230 (1915).

Myers, Robin and Harris, Michael (1993), *Serials and Their Readers, 1620–1914*, Winchester: Oak Knoll Press.

Nairn, Tom (1988), *The Enchanted Glass: Britain and its Monarchy*, London: Radius.

Nasaw, David (2000), *The Chief: The Life of William Randolph Hearst*, New York, NY: Houghton Mifflin.

National Socialist Party of America v. the Village of Skokie, 432 U.S. 43 (1977).

Naughton, John (2006), 'Websites that changed the world', *Observer*, 13 August.

Naughton, John (2011), 'Forget Google – it's Apple that is turning into the Evil Empire', *Observer*, 6 March.

Nedham, Marchmont (1645), *Mecurius Britannicus*, 92, 28 July–4 August.

Negroponte, Nicholas (1996), *Being Digital*, New York, NY: Vintage.

Neiman, Susan (2009), *Moral Clarity: A Guide for Grown-up Idealists*, London: Bodley Head.

New York Times Co. v. Sullivan, 376 U.S. 254 (1964).

New York Times Co. v. United States, 403 U.S. 713 (1971).

Nichols, Richard (1983), *Radio Luxembourg: The Station of the Stars*, London: Comet.

Nicol, Andrew, Millar, Gavin and Sharland, Andrew (2009), *Media Law and Human Rights*, Oxford: Oxford University Press.

Nobel, David (1979), *America by Design: Science, Technology and the Rise of Corporate Capitalism*, New York, NY: Knopf.

Nobel, David (1984), *Forces of Production*, New York, NY: Knopf.

Norwood v. DPP [2003] EWCH 1564 [Admin].

Noyce, R.N. (1977), 'Microelectronics', *Scientific American*, 237, 3 September.

Oates, J.C.T. (1951), 'The *Trewe Encountre*: a pamphlet on Flodden Field', Cambridge: Cambridge Bibliographic Society.

Observer & Guardian v. UK [1991] 14 EHRR 153.

Odlysko, Andrew (2010), 'Collective hallucinations and inefficient markets: the British railway mania of the 1840s', *Digital Technology Center, University of Minnesota*, http://www.dtc.umn.edu/~odlyzko/doc/hallucinations.pdf [accessed 13 March 2012].

O'Farrell, John (2011), 'Not poke fun at Parliament? That's a laugh', *Observer*, 31 July.

Ofcom (2011), *Ofcom*, http://consumers.ofcom.org.uk/2011/04/how-to-complain-about-television-radio-or-on-demand-services [accessed 28 August 2011].

Ofcom Broadcasting Code (2011), *Ofcom*, http://stakeholders.ofcom.org.uk/broadcasting/broadcast-codes/broadcast-code/harmoffence [accessed 28 August 2011].

Olmstead v. United States, 277 U.S. 438 (1928).

Onslow, Barbara (2000), *Women and the Press in Nineteenth Century Britain*, London: Palgrave.

Organisation for Economic Co-operation and Development (2010), *News in the Internet Age: New Trends in News Publishing*, Paris: Organisation for Economic Co-operation and Development, http://dx.doi.org/10.1787/9789264088702-en [accessed 16 December 2011].

Orwell, George (2008 [1948]), *Animal Farm*, London: Penguin.

Oslund, J. (1977), 'Open shores to open skies', in J.N. Pelton and M. Snow (eds), *Economic and Policy Problems in Satellite Communications.*, New York, NY: Praeger.

Otto-Preminger-Institut v. Austria (1994) 19 EHRR 34.

Padania, Sameer with Gregory, Sam, Alberdingk-Thijm, Yvette and Nunez, Bryan (2011), *Cameras Everywhere: A Report and Recommendations on Addressing Key Challenges and Opportunities in the Near Future of Human Rights, Video and Technology*, New York, NY: Witness.

Page, Benedict and Pridd, Helen (2010), 'Access denied: libraries face a virtual lockout over new ebook restrictions', *Guardian*, 26 October.

Page, Bruce (2011), 'Diplomatic baggage', *British Journalism Review*, 22: 1.

Paine, Thomas (1792), *The Rights of Man: Being an Answer to Mr Burke's Attack on the French Revolution*, London: J. Parsons.

Paine, Thomas (1894a [1775]), 'On African slavery', in Thomas Paine, *The Writings of Thomas Paine*, London: G.P. Putnam's Sons.

Paine, Thomas (1894b [1776]) 'Common sense', in Thomas Paine, *The Writings of Thomas Paine*, London: G.P. Putnam's Sons.

Paine, Thomas (1894c [1776]), 'The crisis', in Thomas Paine, *The Writings of Thomas Paine*, London: G.P. Putnam's Sons.

Palfrey, John (1875), *History of New England, Volume 2*, Boston, MA: Little, Brown.

Paris Adult Theatre I v. Slaton, 413 U.S. 49 (1973).

Parmiter v. Coupland (1840) 6 M & W 105.

Parsons, Patrick (2008), *Blue Skies: A History of Cable Television*, Philadelphia, PA: Temple University Press.

Pasley, James (2001), *The Tyranny of Printers: Newspaper Politics in the Early American Republic*, Charlottesville, VA: University of Virginia Press.

Pecora, Vincent (1992), 'Habermas, the Enlightenment and anti-Semitism', in Saul Friedländer (ed.), *Probing the Limits of Representation: Nazism and the 'Final Solution'*, Cambridge, MA: Harvard University Press.

Pepys, Samuel (1659–60), *The Diary of Samuel Pepys*, 9 January, http://www.pepysdiary.com/archive/1660/01 [accessed 24 October 2010].

Percy v. DPP [2002] Crim LR 735.

Pérez-Rincón, Héctor (2011), 'Pierre Janet, Sigmund Freud and Charcot's psychological and psychiatric legacy', in Julien Bogousslavsky (ed.), *Following Charcot: A Forgotten History of Neurology and Psychiatry*, Basel: Karger.

Petley, Julian (2009), *Censorship: A Beginner's Guide*, Oxford: One World.

Petley, Julian (2011), 'Doublethink: "Deregulation, censure and "adult sex" on television', in Peter Bramham and Stephen Wagg (eds), *The New Politics of Leisure and Pleasure*, London: Palgrave.

Philips, H.I. (1930 [1926]) 'What are radio reports coming to', in Arthur Goldsmith and Austin Lescarboura, *This Thing Called Broadcasting: A Simple Tale of an Idea, an Experiment, a Mighty Industry, a Daily Habit, and a Basic Influence in Our Modern Civilization*, New York, NY: H. Holt.

Phillips, David (1974), 'The influence of suggestion on suicides: substantial and theoretical applications of the Werther Effect', *American Sociological Review*, 39, June.

Phillips, Tom (2011c), 'Norway stores pull violent video games including Call of Duty', *Metro*, 2 August, http://www.metro.co.uk/tech/games/871121-norway-stores-pull-violent-video-games-including-call-of-duty-after-massacre#ixzz1URrbTVSq [accessed 8 August 2011].

Pierce, Andrew (2008), 'Prince Charles to be known as Defender of Faith', *Daily Telegraph*, 13 November, http://www.telegraph.co.uk/news/uknews/theroyalfamily/3454271/Prince-Charles-to-be-known-as-Defender-of-Faith.html [accessed 13 March 2011].

Pine, Richard (2002), *2NT and the Origins of Irish Radio*, Dublin: Four Courts Press.

Pipes, Daniel (2003), *The Rushdie Affair: The Novel, the Ayatollah, and the West*, New Brunswick, NJ: Transaction Press.

Plunkett, James (2010), 'Long live TV – time spent in front of the box grows despite the internet', *Guardian*, 19 August.

Police Department of City of Chicago v. Mosley, 408 U.S. 92, 95 (1972).

Poole, Elizabeth (2002), *Reporting Islam: Media Representation of British Muslims*, London: I.B. Tauris.

Post, Robert (2011), 'Hate Speech', in Ivan Hare and James Weinstein (eds), *Extreme Speech and Democracy*, Oxford: Oxford University Press.

Prager and Oberschlick v. Austria (1996) 21 EHRR 1.

Prescott, G.B. (1972), *Bell's Electric Speaking Telephone*, New York, NY: Arno.

Press Complaints Commission (2009), *Annual Report, UK Parliament Website*, http://www.publications.parliament.uk/pa/cm200910/cmselect/cmcumeds/362/36209.htm [accessed 12 January 2012].

Press Complaints Commission (2011), *Editors' Code of Practice, Press Complaints Commission*, http://www.pcc.org.uk/cop/practice.html [accessed 13 March 2012].

Preston, Peter (2010a), 'Print beats the doomsayers final deadline', *Observer*, 8 August.

Preston, Peter (2010b), 'We thought the web was killing print. But it isn't', *Observer*, 17 September.

Preston, Peter (2011), 'You can't deliver quality if you cut the BBC's best', *Observer*, 19 June.

Pridd, Helen (2011), 'Pirate on the ship of state: the new breed of parties out to change European politics', *Guardian*, 29 October.

Prince Albert v. Strange (1849), 2 DeGex & Sm. 652, 694.

Procunier v. Martine, 416 U.S. 472 (1974).

Prosser, William (1955), *Handbook on the Law of Torts*, St Pauls, MI: West Publishing.

Prosser, William (1960), 'Privacy', *California Law Review*, 48: 385, August.

Prynne, William (1633), *Histrio-mastix: The Players Scourge, or, Actors Tragœdie*, London: Michael Sparkes.

Publishers Association (2010), *The UK Book Publishing Industry in Statistics 2009*, London: Publishers Association, http://www.publishers.org.uk [accessed 13 March 2012].

Putnam, G.H. (2003 [1906]), *Censorship of the Church of Rome and Its Influence upon the Production and Distribution of Literature Vol. 2*, Whitefish, MT: Kessinger.

R. v. Chief Metropolitan Magistrate, ex parte Chaudhury [1991], QB 429, [1991] All ER 306.

R. v. F. [2007] 2 All ER 193.

R. v. Gay News Ltd [1979] 143 JPJ 323.

R. v. Gott [1922] 16 Cr. App. R. 87.

R. v. Hicklin (1868) LR 3 QB 360.

R. v. Independent Broadcasting Authority ex parte Whitehouse (1984), *The Times*, 14 April.

R. v. Lemon [1979] AC 617, 664.

R. v. Ramsey and Foote (1883) 15 Cox CC 213.

R. v. Secretary of State for the Home Department ex parte Simms [2000] 2 AC 115.

R. v. Shayler [2002] UK HL11, [2003] 1 AC 247.

R. v. Taylor (1676), 3 Keble 607 and 1 Ventris 293.

R. v. Tutchin (1704) Holt's Rep. 424. St. Trial, vol. 5.

R. v. Woodfall (1770) 5 Burr. 2667.

R. v. Z. [2005] UKHL 35.

Rader, Daniel (1973), *The Journalists and the July Revolution in France: The Role of the Political Press in the Overthrow of the Bourbon Restoration 1827–1830*, The Hague: Nijhoff.

Rahofer, Judith (2009), 'Privacy and surveillance', in Lilian Edwards and Charlotte Waelde (2009), *Law and the Internet*, Oxford: Hart.

R.A.V. v. City of St Paul, 505 U.S. 377 (1992).

Rawls, John (1993), *Political Liberalism*, New York, NY: Columbia University Press.

Raymond, Joad (2005), *The Invention of the Newspaper: English Newsbooks, 1641–1649*, Oxford: Oxford University Press.

Redmond-Bate v. DPP 163 JP 789, [1999] Crim LR 998, [1999] 7 BHRC 375.

Reed, Sidney, Van Atta, Richard and Deichtman, Seymour (1990), *DARPA Technical Accomplishments: An Historical Review of Selected DARPA Projects Vol. 1*, Arlington, VA: Institute for Defense Analysis.

Reith, John (1924), *Broadcast over Britain*, London: Hodder & Stoughton.

Reynolds v Times Newspapers Ltd [1999], 4 All ER 609.

Rhodes, F.L. (1929), *Beginnings of Telephony*, New York, NY: Harper & Brothers.

Ribiero, Nelson (2011), *BBC Broadcasts to Portugal in World War Two*, Lampeter: Edwin Mellen Press.

Richards, David (1988), 'Toleration and free speech', *Philosophy and Public Affairs*, 17: 4, Autumn.

Robertson, Geoffrey and Nicol, Andrew (1993), *Media Law*, 3rd edition, Harmondsworth: Penguin.

Robertson, Geoffrey and Nicol, Andrew (2008), *Media Law*, 5th edition, Harmondsworth: Penguin.

Robinson, James (2009), 'Football chiefs clamp down on web pirates' *Observer*, 20 September.

Robinson, James (2010a), 'Britain logs on to a world-beating £100bn internet economy', *Guardian*, 28 October.

Robinson, James (2010b), 'Three quarters of music tracks "downloaded illegally"', *Guardian*, 17 December.

Robinson, James and O'Carroll, Lisa (2011), 'Data watchdog was not "afraid of newspapers", Leveson inquiry told', *Guardian*, 10 December.

Robinson, James and Sabbagh, Dan (2011), 'Lawyers raised questions over editors' activities, Leveson told', *Guardian*, 6 December.

Robinson, James, O'Carroll, Lisa and Halliday, Josh (2011), 'Sienna Miller and J.K. Rowling tell Leveson inquiry of tabloid "siege"', *Guardian*, 24 November, http://www.guardian.co.uk/media/2011/nov/24/sienna-miller-jk-rowling-leveson [accessed 15 December 2011].

Roth v. United States, 354 U.S. 476, 77 S. Ct. 1304, 1 L. Ed. 2d 1498 (1957).

Rousseau, J.J. (1990 [1772–6]) 'Dialogues', in J.J. Rousseau, *The Collected Writings of Rousseau*, Hanover, NH, and London: University of New England Press.

Royal Commission on the Press (1949), *Royal Commission on the Press 1947–49, Report*, Cmnd 7770, London: HMSO.

Royal Commission on the Press (1962), *Royal Commission on the Press 1961–62, Report*, Cmnd 1811, London: HMSO.

Royal Commission on the Press (1976), *The National Newspaper Industry, Interim Report*, Cmnd 6433, London: HMSO.

Royal Commission on the Press (1977), *The National Newspaper Industry, Final Report*, Cmnd 6810-1, London: HMSO.

Rusbridger, Alan (2009), 'The Trafigura fiasco tears up the textbook: a mix of old media and the Twittersphere blew away conventional efforts to buy silence', *Guardian*, 14 October, http://www.guardian.co.uk/commentisfree/libertycentral/2009/oct/14/trafigura-fiasco-tears-up-textbook [accessed 3 September 2011].

Rushdie, Salman (1988), *The Satanic Verses*, London: Viking.

Rushe, Dominic (2011), 'Twitter is five years old. How big can it grow?', *Observer*, 13 February.

Ruthven, Malise (2002), *A Fury for God: The Islamist Attack on America*, London: Granta.

Ruthven, Malise (2006), *Islam in the World*, London: Granta.

SACOM (Students and Scholars against Corporate Misbehaviour) (2010), 'Foxconn factories are labour camps', *South China Morning Post*, 11 October, http://engb.facebook.com/note.php?note_id=156848724349172&comments&ref=mf [accessed 1 November 2011].

Said, Edward (1997), *Covering Islam: How the Media and the Experts Determine How We See the Rest of World*, London: Vintage.

Said, Edward (2003 [1978]), *Orientalism*, Harmondsworth: Penguin.

Salamon, Ed (2010), *Pittsburgh's Golden Years of Radio*, Charleston, SC: Arcadia.

Sardar, Ziauddin (2008), 'Fatwa against terrorism', *New Statesman*, 19 June, http://www.newstatesman.com/religion/2008/06/terrorism-fatwa-india-islam [accessed 2 August 2010].

Sarkozy, Nicolas (2011), 'The internet: accelerating growth', *The e→G8 Forum*, Paris, 24–5 May, http://www.eg8forum.com/en/e-g8 [accessed 28 November 2011].

Sarti, Roland (1997), *Mazzini: A Life for the Religion of Politics*, Westport, CT: Praeger.

Savage, J. (2005), 'Does viewing violent media really cause criminal violence? A methodological review', *Aggression and Violent Behaviours*, 10: 1, November–December.

Savile, George (1912 [1750]) 'Of Punishment', in *Political, Moral and Miscellaneous Thoughts and Reflections*, in George Savile, *Complete Works*, Oxford: Clarendon Press.

Saville, Richard (2008), 'Monty Python's The Life Of Brian film ban lifted after 28 years', *Daily Telegraph*, 24 September. http://www.telegraph.co.uk/news/3073308/Monty-Pythons-The-Life-Of-Brian-film-ban-lifted-after-28-years.html [accessed 3 August 2011).

Scanlon, Thomas (1972), 'A Theory of Freedom of Expression', *Philosophy and Public Affairs*, 1: 2, Winter.

Scannell, Paddy and Cardiff, David (1991), *A Social History of Broadcasting Vol. 1 1922–1939: Serving the Nation*, Oxford: Blackwell.

Schackle, Samira (2011), 'Extreme injustice', *New Statesman*, 8 August.

Schauer, Frederick (1982a), *Free Speech: A Philosophical Inquiry*, Cambridge: Cambridge University Press

Schauer, Frederick (1982b), 'An essay on constitutional language', *UCLA Law Review*, 29.

Schauer, Frederick (1983), 'Must speech be special', *Northwestern University Law Review*, 78.

Schauer, Frederick (2005), 'The exceptional First Amendment', *KSG Faculty Working Paper Series*, Cambridge, MA: John F. Kennedy School of Government, Harvard University, doi:10.2139/ssrn.668543, http://ssrn.com/abstract=668543 or doi:10.2139/ssrn.668543 [accessed 15 September, 2011].

Schenck v. United States, 249 U.S. 47 (1919).

Schmidtke, A. and Häfner, H. (1998), 'The Werther effect after television films: new evidence for an old hypothesis', *Psychological Medicine*, 18: 3.

Schwarz, Kathryn (2000), *Tough Love: Amazon Encounters in the English Renaissance*, Durham, NC: Duke University Press.

Select Committee on Religious Offences in England and Wales (2003), 'Appendix II', *Religious Offences in England and Wales – First Report, Vol.II*, London: House of Lords.

Sellers, Robert (2003), 'Wealease Bwian', *Guardian*, 28 March, http://www.guardian.co.uk/culture/2003/mar/28/artsfeatures1 [accessed 1 April 2012].

Semonche, John (2007), *Censoring Sex: A Historical Journey through American Media*, Lantham, MD: Rowman & Littlefield.

Shaaber, M.A. (1966 [1929]), *Some Forerunners of the Newspaper in England*, London: Frank Cass & Co.

Shah, Saheed (2011), 'Butt out! Rude words banned from Pakistani text messages', *Guardian*, 18 November.

Shapley, Olive (1995), *Broadcasting a Life: The Autobiography of Olive Shapley*, London: Scarlett Press.

Shaw, Allan (1999), 'Obituary: Olive Shapley', *Independent*, 20 March, http://www.independent.co.uk/arts-entertainment/obituary-olive-shapley-1081732.html [accessed 3 May 2011].

Sherrard, Owen (1971 [1930]), *A Life of John Wilkes*, Freeport, NY: Libraries Press.

Sidis v. F-R Publishing Co., 311 U.S. 711, 61 S. Ct. 393, 85 L. Ed. 462 (1940).

Sim v. Strech [1936] All ER 1237 (HL).

Singer, Peter (2010), 'The promise of the web', *Guardian*, 5 April.

Sjølie, Marie Louise (2010), '"I'm not a particularly brave man"', *Guardian*, 'G2', 5 January.

Skidelsky, William (2009), 'Google's plan for world's online library: philanthropy or act of piracy?', *Observer*, 30 August.

Small, Gary, Moody, Teena D., Siddarth, Prabha and Bookheimer, Susan (2009), 'Your brain on Google: patterns of cerebral activation during internet searching', *American Journal of Geriatric Psychiatry*, 17: 2, February.

Smith, Anthony (1979), *The Newspaper; An International History*, London: Thames & Hudson.

Society of Professional Journalists (1996–2011), 'Code of Ethics', *Society of Professional Journalists*, http://www.spj.org/ethicscode.asp [accessed 7 September 2011].

Sokolow, Michael (2007), 'Always in friendly competition: NBC and CBS in the first decade of national broadcasting', in Michelle Hilmes (ed.), *NBC: America's Network*, Berkeley, CA: University of California Press.

Sola Pool, Ithiel de (1983), *Technologies of Freedom*, Cambridge, MA: Harvard University Press.

Sperber, Ann (1986), *Murrow: His Life and Times*, New York, NY: Knopf.

Stead, W.T. (1885a), 'Notice to our readers: a frank warning', *Pall Mall Gazette*, 4 July.

Stead, W.T. (1885b), 'The Maiden Tribute of Modern Babylon I: the report of our Secret Commission', *Pall Mall Gazette*, 6 July.

Steel and Morris v. UK (2005) 41 EHRR 22.

Steinberg, Samuel (1955), *500 Years of Printing*, Harmondsworth: Penguin.

Sterling, Bruce (1993), 'Literary freeway – not for commercial use, Speech to National Academy of Science Convocation on Technology and Education, 10 May', *Computer Underground Digest*, 5: 54.

Sterngold, James (1998), 'Censorship in the Age of Anything Goes; for artistic freedom, it's not the worst of times', *New York Times*, 20 September, http://www.nytimes.com/1998/09/20/arts/censorship-age-anything-goes-for-artistic-freedom-it-s-not-worst-times.html?pagewanted=all [accessed 14 June 2010].

Stone, Richard (2008), *Civil Liberties and Human Rights*, Oxford: Oxford University Press.

Stoppard, Tom (2006), 'Playing the trump card', *Index on Censorship*, 35: 1, February.

Storey, Graham (1969), *Reuters; The Story of a Century of News-gathering*, New York, NY: Greenwood Press.

Stratmann, Linda (2011), *Cruel Deeds and Dreadful Calamities: The Illustrated Police News 1864–1938*, London: British Library.

Street, Harry (1959), *The Law of Torts*, London: Butterworth.

Sunday Times v. UK (1979) 2 EHRR 245.

Sutherland, James (2004), *The Restoration Newspaper and Its Development*, Cambridge: Cambridge University Press.

Swedberg, Richard (2005), *The Max Weber Dictionary: Key Words and Central Concepts*, Stanford, CA: Stanford University Press.

Sweney, Mark (2008), 'BBC fined £95,000 over Dermot O'Leary and Tony Blackburn phone-ins', *Guardian*, 18 December, http://www.guardian.co.uk/media/2008/dec/18/bbc-fined-for-oleary-and-blackburn-phone-ins?INTCMP=ILCNETTXT3487 [accessed 2 May 2011].

Swift, Jonathan (1948 [1712]), 'Letter LI, London, Aug. 7. 1712', *Journal to Stella Vol. 1*, ed. Harold Williams, Oxford: Oxford University Press.

Teather, David (2010), 'Digital books? Just another page in the history of publishing', *Guardian*, 30 July.

Telecommunications Research and Action Center (TRAC) v. FCC, 801 F.2d 501 (1986).

Texas v. Johnson, 491 U.S. 397 (1989).

Thompson, Dorothy (1986), *The Chartists: Popular Politics in the Industrial Revolution*, Farnham: Ashgate.

Thorgeirson v. Iceland (1992) 14 EHRR 843.

Thorpe, Francis (1901), *The Constitutional History of the United States, 1765–1895, Volume 1*. Chicago Callaghan.

Time, Inc. v. Hill, 385 U.S. 374 (1967).

Tobacco Manufacturers' Association (2011), 'UK Cigarette Consumption', *Tobacco Manufacturers' Association*, http://www.the-tma.org.uk/tma-publications-research/facts-figures/uk-cigarette-consumption [accessed 6 April 2012].

Todorov, Tzvetan (2009), *In Defence of the Enlightenment*, trans. Gila Walker, London: Atlantic.

Tomalin, Claire (1995), *Mrs Jordan Profession: The Story of a Great Actress and a Future King*, Harmondsworth: Penguin.

Took, Barry (1976), *Laughter in the Air*, London: Robson Books.

Topping, Alexandra (2011), 'Jarvis Cocker backs independents in battle of the music labels', *Guardian*, 1 July.

Tran, Mark (2010) 'Iceland plans future as global haven for freedom of speech', *Guardian*, 12 February, http://www.guardian.co.uk/world/2010/feb/12/iceland-haven-freedom-speech-wikileaks [accessed 31 March 2011].

Tripathi, Salil (2009), 'Get up, stand up', *New Statesman*, 27 April.

Trofimov, Yaroslav (2007), *The Siege of Makkah: The Forgotten Uprising*, London: Allen Lane, Penguin Press.

Tucher, Andie (1994), *Froth and Scum: Truth, Beauty, Goodness and the Ax Murder in America's First Mass Medium*, Chapel Hill, NC: University of North Carolina Press.

Turberville v. Savage (1669) 6 Mod. 149.

Turgot, Anne-Robert-Jacques (1970 [1750]), *Tableaux philosophique des progrès successifs de l'esprit humain*, Paris: Calman-Levy.

Turing, Alan (1936), 'On computable numbers with an application to the *Entscheidungsproblem*', *Proceedings of the London Mathematical Society*, 42, November.

Turing, Alan (1937), 'On computable numbers – with an application to the *Entscheidungsproblem*. A correction', *Proceedings of the London Mathematical Society*, 43.

Udelson, J.H. (1982), *The Great Television Race*, Tuscaloosa, AL: University of Alabama Press.

Ungar, Harlow (2002), *Lafayette*, Hoboken, NJ: Wiley.

United Nations Alliance of Civilizations (n.d.), *United Nations Alliance of Civilizations*, http://www.unaoc.org/about/history [accessed 1 April 2012].

United States Commission on International Religious Freedom (2011), *Report*, Washington, DC: United States Commission on International Religious Freedom.

United States v. O'Brien, 391 U.S. 367, 369–70 (1968).

United States v. One Book Called 'Ulysses', 5 F. Supp. 182 (S.D.N.Y. 1933), aff'd 72 F.2d 705 (2d Cir. 1934).

Universelles Leben e.V. v. Germany App no 29745/96 (ECHR, 1996).

Uricchio, W. (1990) 'Introduction to the history of German television, 1935–1944', *Historical Journal of Film, Radio and Television*, 10: 2.

Vereinigung Bildender Künstler v. Austria App no 68354/01 (ECHR, 25 January 2007).

Vipond, Mary (1992), *Listening In: The First Decade of Broadcasting in Canada 1922–1932*, Montreal: McGill University Press.

Vipond, Mary (2000), *The Mass Media in Canada*, Toronto: James Lorimer and Co.

Virginia v. Black, 538 U.S. 343 (2003).

Von Hannover v. Germany (2005) 40 EHRR 1.

Wade, H.W.R (1941), 'The concept of legal certainty: a preliminary skirmish', *Modern Law Review*, 4:3.

Waldrop, F.C. and Borkin, J. (1938), *Television: A Struggle for Power*, New York, NY: William Morrow.

Walker, Robin (1976), *The Newspaper Press in New South Wales, 1803–1920*, Sydney: Sydney University Press.

Walker, Sam (1994), *Hate Speech: The History of an American Controversy*, Lincoln, NE: University of Nebraska Press.

Warmbrunn, Werner (1963), *The Dutch under German Occupation, 1940–1945*, Stanford, CA: Stanford University Press.

Warren, Samuel and Brandeis, Louis (1890), 'A right to privacy', *Harvard Law Review*, 4: 5, December.

Waterhouse, Keith (1989), *On Newspapering*, Harmondsworth: Penguin.

Watts v. United States, 394 U.S. 705 (1969).

Webster, Richard (1990), *A Brief History of Blasphemy*, Southwold: Orwell Press.

Weiberger, Eliot (2000), 'Anonymous sources: a talk on translators and translation', *Encuentros*, 39, November, http://www.iadb.org/exr/cultural/documents/encuentros/39.pdf [accessed 19 May 2010].

Weinstein, David (2007), 'Why Sarnoff slept: NBC and the Holocaust', in Michelle Hilmes (ed.), *NBC: America's Network*, Berkeley, CA: University of California Press.

Weinstein, James (2010a), 'Extreme speech, public order and democracy', in Ivan Hare and James Weinstein (eds), *Extreme Speech and Democracy*, Oxford: Oxford University Press.

Weinstein, James (2010b), 'An overview of American free speech doctrine', in Ivan Hare and James Weinstein (eds), *Extreme Speech and Democracy*, Oxford: Oxford University Press.

Weiss, Heidi (2000), '1947', in Adrienne Drell (ed.), *20th Century Chicago: 100 Years, 100 Voices*, Chicago: Chicago Sun Times.

West Virginia State Board of Education v. Barnette, 319 U.S. 624 (1943).

Wheen, Francis (2008), 'Introduction', in Karl Marx, *Dispatches for the New York Tribune: Selected Journalism of Karl Marx*, ed. James Ledbetter, Harmondsworth: Penguin.

Whine, Michael (2010), 'Expanding Holocaust denial and legislation against it', in Ivan Hare and James Weinstein (eds), *Extreme Speech and Democracy*, Oxford: Oxford University Press.

White, Michael (2012), 'Giggling, sniggering and wriggling: express pawns avoid the P-word', *Guardian*, 13 January.

Whitehouse v. Lemon [1979] 2 WLR 281.

Whitney v. California, 274 U.S. 357, 375–76, 377 (1927).

Wilkes, John (2009 [1763]), *The North Britain No. 45*, in Guy Lee (2009), *Leading Documents of English History Together with Illustrative Material from*

Contemporary Writers and a Bibliography of Sources, Ann Arbour, MI: University of Michigan Library.

Williams, Francis (1957), *Dangerous Estate: The Anatomy of Newspapers*, London: Longman Greene.

Williams, Keith (1977), *The English Newspaper*, London: Springwood Books.

Williams, Kevin (2009), *Get Me a Murder a Day*, London: Bloomsbury Academic.

Williams, Raymond (1974), *Television: Technology and Cultural Form*, London: Fontana.

Williams, Raymond (1989), *The Politics of Modernism*, London and New York, NY: Verso.

Wilson, David (1988), *Paine and Cobbett: The Transatlantic Connection*, Montreal: McGill-Queens University Press.

Wingrove v. UK (1997) 24 EHRR 1.

Winston, Brian (1985), 'A whole technology of dyeing: a note on ideology and the apparatus of the chromatic moving image', *Daedalus*, 114: 4, Fall.

Winston, Brian (1995), *Technologies of Seeing: Photography, Film, Television*, London: British Film Institute.

Winston, Brian (1998), *Media Technology and Society: From the Telegraph to the Internet*, London: Routledge.

Winston, Brian (2000), *Lies, Damn Lies and Documentaries*, London: British Film Institute.

Winston, Brian (2002), 'Towards tabloidization?: Glasgow revisited 1975–2001', *Journalism Studies*, 13:1.

Winston, Brian (2005), *Messages: Free Expression Media and the West from Gutenberg to Google*, London: Routledge.

Winston, Brian (2011), '"The Last Refuge of a Scoundrel": Propaganda in eine Kulture, die Propaganda abelhnt', in Rainer Rother and Judith Prolasky (eds), *Die Kamera als Waffe: Propagandabilder des Zweiten Weltkrieges*, Munich: Text + Kritik (Richard Boorberg Verlag).

Wintour, Patrick (2011), 'Don't try to regulate web. Zuckerberg and other internet pioneers warn leaders', *Guardian*, 27 May.

Wiseman, Susan (1998), *Drama and Politics in the English Civil War*, Cambridge: Cambridge University Press.

Wollstonecraft, Mary (1992 [1792]), *A Vindication of the Rights of Woman*, Harmondsworth: Penguin.

Wollstonecraft, Mary (1999 [1791]), *A Vindication of the Rights of Men*, Cambridge: Cambridge University Press.

Wolff, Robert Paul, Moore, Barrington and Marcuse, Herbert (1969), *A Critique of Pure Tolerance*, Boston: Beacon Press.

Wotton, Henry (1672 [1604]), *Reliquiae Wottoniana*, London: Marriott, Tyton,

Wray, Richard, (2010), 'How RIM created the Blackberry and the secure network it relies on', *Guardian*, 3 August.

Wroth, Lawrence (1922), *A History of Printing in Colonial Maryland, 1686–1776*, Baltimore, MD: Typothetae.

Wyatt, Robert, Neft, David, Badger, David P. (1991), *Free Expression and the American Public*, Murfreesboro, TN: Middle State University.

Yates v. United States, 354 U.S. 298 (1957).

Young, Noel (2011), 'What if Milly had been found alive', *British Journalism Review*, 24: 4, December.

Zuckerman, Laurence, Hofheinz, Paul and Mehta, Naushad (1987), 'Press: how not to silence a spy', *Time*, 17 August, http://www.time.com/time/magazine/article/0,9171,965233-2,00.html [accessed 9 August 2011].

Index